WAR WITHOUT FRONTS

A historian and political scientist, Bernd Greiner is a professor at the University of Hamburg and directs the research programme on the theory and history of violence at the Hamburg Institute of Social Research.

BERND GREINER

War Without Fronts

The USA in Vietnam

TRANSLATED FROM THE GERMAN BY
Anne Wyburd with Victoria Fern

Published by Vintage 2010

2 4 6 8 10 9 7 5 3 1

Copyright © Hamburger Edition 2007, 2009
English translation copyright © Anne Wyburd 2009

Bernd Greiner has asserted his right under the Copyright, Designs
and Patents Act 1988 to be identified as the author of this work

Anne Wyburd has asserted her right under the Copyright, Designs
and Patents Act 1988 to be identified as the translator of this work

First published in Germany in 2007 as
Krieg ohne Fronten: Die USA in Vietnam by Hamburger Edition

First published in Great Britain in 2009 by
The Bodley Head

Vintage
Random House, 20 Vauxhall Bridge Road,
London SW1V 2SA

www.vintage-books.co.uk

Addresses for companies within The Random House Group Limited
can be found at: www.randomhouse.co.uk/offices.htm

The Random House Group Limited Reg. No. 954009

A CIP catalogue record for this book
is available from the British Library

ISBN 9780099532590

The Random House Group Limited supports The Forest
Stewardship Council (FSC), the leading international forest
certification organisation. All our titles that are printed on
Greenpeace approved FSC certified paper carry the FSC logo.
Our paper procurement policy can be found at:
www.rbooks.co.uk/environment

Mixed Sources
Product group from well-managed
forests and other controlled sources
www.fsc.org Cert no. TT-COC-2139
© 1996 Forest Stewardship Council

Printed and bound in Great Britain by
CPI Cox & Wyman, Reading, RG1 8EX

For Bettina Greiner

The translation of this work was funded by *Geisteswissenschaften International* – Translation Funding for Humanities and Social Sciences from Germany, a joint initiative of the Fritz Thyssen Foundation, the German Federal Foreign Office and the German Publishers & Booksellers Association

Contents

List of Maps

The War in Vietnam

Introduction

If we learn to accept this, there is nothing we will not accept.
    Jonathan Schell[1]

CBS viewers had probably been waiting for news of Apollo 12 and the return of American heroes from the second moon landing. And then it came: Walter Cronkite, the doyen of television journalists and according to various opinion polls the 'most trustworthy man in America', announced on 20 November 1969 that the evening news was possibly 'not fit for a juvenile audience'. What followed was a slow camera movement over a series of colour photographs taken by an Army photographer in My Lai (4), showing a group of peasants shot dead on a field track: old people, women, children and babies, victims of C Company Task Force Barker, which on the morning of 16 March 1968 had attacked several villages in the Son My district and within a few hours had massacred 500 civilians.[2]

Four days later CBS broadcast on the Walter Cronkite Show an interview which Mike Wallace had conducted with one of the perpetrators, Paul Meadlo:

MEADLO: 'I fired them on automatic, so you can't – you just spray the area on them and so you can't know how many you killed, 'cause they were going fast. I might have killed ten or fifteen of them.'
WALLACE: 'Men, women, and children?'

M: 'Men, women, and children.'

W: 'And babies?'

M: 'And babies ... And so we started shooting them, and somebody told us to switch to single shot so that we could save our ammo. So we switched to single shot, and fired a few more rounds.' ...

W: 'Why did you do it?'

M: 'Why did I do it? Because I felt like I was ordered to do it, and it seemed like that, at the time I felt like I was doing the right thing, because like I said I lost buddies ... So after I done it, I felt good, but later on that day it was gettin' to me.'

W: 'You're married?'

M: 'Right.'

W: 'Children.'

M: 'Two.'

W: 'How old?'

M: 'The boy is two and a half, and the little girl is a year and a half.'

W: 'Obviously, the question comes to mind – the father of two little kids like that – how can he shoot babies?'

M: 'I didn't have the little girl. I just had the little boy at the time.'

W: 'Uh-huh. How do you shoot babies?'

M: 'I don't know. It's just one of them things.'

W: 'How many people would you imagine were killed that day?'

M: 'I'd say about 370.' ...

W: 'You yourself were responsible for how many of them?' ...

M: 'I couldn't say – Just too many.' ...

W: 'And nothing went through your mind or heart –'

M: 'Many a times – many a times –'

W: 'While you were doing it?'

M: 'Not while I was doing it. It just seemed like it was the natural thing to do at the time. I don't know. It just – I was getting relieved from what I'd seen earlier over there.'

W: 'What do you mean?'

M: 'Well, I was getting – like the – my buddies getting killed or wounded or – we weren't getting no satisfaction from it, so what it really was, it was just mostly revenge.'[3]

Up to this point the American media had ignored the lives and deaths of Vietnamese civilians. Apart from a few exceptions that could be counted on the fingers of both hands,[4] the civilians who had been killed by bombs or massacred by ground troops played no part in press, radio or television coverage – they were simply invisible. 'We missed the big one. We surely did,' Neil Sheehan from the *New York Times* observed self-critically, looking back at his year-long coverage.[5] Whether it was the tradition of war journalism, which made heroes of the American soldiers, that decided the issue or whether there was a feeling of obligation to follow the line, promoted in February 1962 by the Departments of State and Defense, that reports of casualties amongst the Vietnamese civilian population 'are clearly inimical to the national interest'[6] is an open question.[7]

'The policy is what they [the officers] say it is,' maintained the *Washington Post* in mid August 1965 in an article entitled 'Civilized Warfare', which dealt with the operations of the Marine Corps and led to a comparison with the practices of the German armed forces in the Second World War. 'Americans have no stomach for [it] . . . Thank goodness the Marines are not engaged in that kind of barbarism . . . The American military is well aware of the importance of protecting and safeguarding civilians whenever possible.'[8] The reason for this tribute to the 'humane, compassionate and gallant American Fighting Man' was a Morley Safer film broadcast by CBS on 5 August 1965, which had shown the Marines burning down a village. The dissident Safer was treated the same way as other journalists who deviated from the firmly held policies of the mainstream. When, for example, shortly before Christmas 1966 Harrison E. Salisbury reported in the *New York Times* on the havoc wreaked by US bombers in North Vietnam, the relevant head of department accused him of irresponsible bias towards Hanoi and countered with several articles justifying Washington's policies.[9] Even in the wake of the Tet Offensive of January 1968, when the fighting entered its bloodiest phase and acts of terror against civilians increased rapidly, the human cost of the war was mentioned only in passing in the press, and on television virtually not at all.[10]

Instead, most of the media maintained the position they had championed from the start: that in Vietnam an outpost of the Free World would and must be defended – as could be seen from an analysis of thirty-nine daily newspapers carried out in February 1968, of which not a single one argued for a withdrawal from Vietnam.[11] Their criticism, which grew ever louder after Tet, was therefore directed not so much at the aims of the war, but rather at their implementation by the Johnson administration, which was perceived as inadequate. In other words, it was about disappointed expectations of victory, false promises of a speedy end to the fighting and the impression that personal sacrifices had been made in vain.[12] Because the suffering of others was of no interest, the transcripts of the 'Russell Tribunal', which took place in Stockholm in 1967 and provided proof of a military strategy that regularly contravened international laws of warfare, were generally ignored; as was the memorandum 'In the Name of America', which was presented shortly afterwards: a 420-page documentation of atrocities and war crimes in Vietnam, published by the organisation 'Clergymen and Laymen Concerned' and drawn up by twenty-nine Protestant, Catholic and Jewish clerics. 'The energies of liberals and conservatives alike were devoted to discrediting its evidence,' said the lawyer Richard Falk of this press boycott.[13] As Clarence R. Wyatt asserted at the time, Vietnam was 'in journalistic terms the most covered but least understood war in American history'.[14]

No attention was given even to the My Lai (4) massacre for a year and a half. In principle the accredited journalists in South Vietnam might easily have done so. Soldiers from various units circulated the story for months; Radio Hanoi repeatedly broadcast corroboratory reports; some reporters admitted later to having known about it.[15] However, the majority of war reporters had, according to Peter Braestrup of the *Washington Post*, 'subscribed to herd journalism'. They corroborated each other in the expectation that in the wake of Tet the war would be decided in the towns and lost sight of the rest of the country in their short-sighted rivalry for the most impressive 'Saigon Stories'. 'Competition between NBC and CBS seemed at times a contest over who could shout the same words more loudly . . . It was "news", but not information.'[16] Those few reporters who did not chase after feel-good stories nor were after rapid success to further their careers, but instead accompanied fighting troops on sorties, nonetheless did not remain critically detached from the objects of their coverage – partly because they marvelled at the courage and endurance of the soldiers, partly because they needed them for protection and partly because they feared for their own accreditation in the case of critical coverage.[17] But those who fell into the trap of closing ranks subjected themselves inevitably to self-censorship, according to Neil Sheehan,[18] regardless of any interest which their editors at home had in political patronage and how they made use of it.

It took an outsider, the thirty-one-year-old Seymour M. Hersh, to force the journalistic fraternity into action. After an apprenticeship at City News Bureau and a regional paper in his hometown of Chicago, in 1965 he became Pentagon correspondent for Associated Press and made a name for himself with articles on biological and chemical warfare. In 1968 Hersh took on the job of press spokesman for Eugene McCarthy, who ran for presidential candidate as a 'peace senator', but gave that up again shortly afterwards due to differences of political opinion. Convinced that he would have more problems than opportunities as an investigative reporter for the established papers, Hersh opted for freelance journalism – and in autumn 1969 this judgement was borne out in an unexpected manner.

At the beginning of September the public information office at Fort Benning had announced that one Lieutenant Calley was to be charged over the death of an 'unknown number of civilians' in My Lai (4). The newsflash was printed by Associated Press, the *Washington Post*, the *New York Times*, the *Los Angeles Times* and countless other national newspapers. But none of the editors commissioned further investigations – to the astonishment of the military, which had feared a vigorous inquiry.[19] Hersh himself only learnt of the imminent military tribunal in October 1969 from a lawyer friend and from another contact in the Pentagon. 'This Calley is just a madman, Sy, just a madman! He just went around killing all those people. Little babies! There's no story in that. He's just pathetic and should be locked up in an institution.' Even a Congress employee advised him against investigating the supposed psychopath. 'By this time I knew I had a story,' remembers Hersh.[20]

Furnished with $2,000 for travel expenses from the 'Fund for Investigative Journalism' – one of the foundations established by Sears-Roebuck heir Philip Stern – Hersh flew 30,000 kilometres in three weeks when making his initial inquiries, spoke for hours with William Calley and his barrister and in mid November 1969 came up with an article that correctly described the fundamentals of the My Lai (4) massacre. 'I believed that kid [Calley] at My Lai and I know these guys are telling me the truth. There's just no formula for sources.'[21] Yet he was turned away everywhere. *Look* showed no interest and *Life* did not want to take the risk, although the editors had already been told about My Lai (4) by the former GI Ronald Ridenhour. Hersh received a negative reply from the *New York Times* and was brushed off by one editor as a 'peddler'. 'It was in effect part of the snobbery of the paper, as if it fancied itself above the fray, distant from events. Its reporters were not supposed to scurry around in dark alleys looking for corruption and injustice,' says its longstanding reporter David Halberstam.[22]

Hersh reached his goal only in a roundabout way via the previously insignificant Dispatch News Service. Its director presented the article to the public with a white lie: by getting the undecided and hesitant editors of fifty newspapers to believe that the competition might have already bitten and was on the point of pocketing single-handedly the credit for the scandal story. The rest virtually happened by itself. On 13 May 1969 thirty-six newspapers printed Hersh's first article about My Lai (4); the *New York Times* and the *Washington Post* followed suit; the foreign press and the British government took up the subject. On 20 November Hersh published a second article, with the deliberately provocative headline 'It Was Like A Nazi Thing', and on the same day the shots taken by the Army photographer Ronald Haeberle in My Lai (4) appeared in the *Cleveland Plain Dealer* – the same photos which CBS presented in that day's evening news to an audience of millions.

Seymour Hersh is rightly given the credit for single-handedly bringing to light one of the most frightful massacres that ever took place in Vietnam. Yet the repercussions of his initiative are still generally underestimated, for in the end the scandal spread far beyond the My Lai (4) story. The fact that historians today are in the position to describe events on the killing fields of Vietnam and thereby to present the profile of an asymmetrical war without front lines is due to a collection of source material which was only compiled under the impact of the public discussion provoked by Hersh – material which no one working individually could ever have discovered and which might well have been too much even for research groups to put together. From the beginning of 1970 the Department of Defense had these reports compiled, in a bureaucratic panic attack, in order to weather a public controversy, through which it was apparently no longer able to steer its way with the usual means of political damage limitation.

To begin with, the leading media reacted to the initial shellshock with questions which for the majority of the public were just as disturbing as the pictures from Vietnam. 'My Lai is a token of the violence that hovers beneath the surface of American life: where else, and in what ways will it next erupt?' commented *Time*. Did the military strategy pursued in Vietnam encourage the mass murder of civilians? To what extent can society be held responsible for the behaviour of its soldiers? 'They were Everymen, decent in their daily lives.' Was the population of the United States morally insensitive? Was violence as American as the Stars and Stripes? 'When the Kerner Commission[23] suggested that America was a racist nation, the U.S. public reacted with "Who, me?" protests of innocence. But there is a dark underside to American history.' Was the mental mobilisation of the Cold War, during which people lived in a permanent state of tension, now exacting its price? 'How much injustice and corruption distort the reality of democracy that the U.S. offers to the world? The answers are debatable; the questions are not.'[24] Regardless of whether or not the self-image America had cultivated since its foundation – that of a 'redeemer nation' chosen by God to fight for salvation – was a delusion,[25] and no matter how many 'My Lais' there had actually been, the country stood at a crossroads. As Jonathan Schell wrote in the *New Yorker* in mid December 1969: 'If we learn to accept this, there is nothing we will not accept.'[26]

In addition, prominent politicians, amongst them a notable number of conservatives as well as community activists, demanded a say in the My Lai inquiry. Instead of the official military prosecutor, a so-called 'Blue Ribbon Panel' – a non-partisan commission, independent of government and bureaucracy – should be convened and commissioned, not just to look into the background to the massacre, but also to investigate the question of whether the military strategy followed in Vietnam was compatible with the letter and the spirit of international laws governing warfare. Since the end of November 1969, Senators John Stennis and Margaret Chase Smith, former Vice President Hubert Humphrey and a group of former employees of the State Department, together with thirty-four well-known practising and academic lawyers, had expressed themselves along the same lines.[27]

From today's perspective this might seem an obvious demand. Yet the White House under Richard Nixon sensed a general attack on the competence of the Executive. General Alexander Haig, deputy to

National Security Adviser Henry Kissinger, said, 'I can think of nothing worse than assembling a group of high-level civilians to look into the ethics of conducting military operations . . . Military discipline [and] the effectiveness of our military [would be] seriously damaged.'[28] Kissinger himself rejected the suggestion on other grounds: 'I suspect it [the Blue Ribbon Commission] would tend to prolong public interest in the incident which has, hopefully, already passed its peak.' On the other hand he drew attention to the unpredictability of the situation and told President Nixon,

There is one dangerous trend which may build that would reverse my judgement on this matter, however. This is the possibility that other Vietnam veterans will publicize additional atrocities in an effort to achieve personal notoriety or because this incident has created real or imagined recollections of similar incidents. Should the situation develop over the coming weeks in which a series of additional accusations appear then I believe you will be forced to resort to a commission of the type proposed.[29]

What Kissinger had feared did indeed occur: scarcely had the first newspaper articles about My Lai (4) appeared than former members of the unit based there[30] as well as dozens of other GIs went public and produced evidence of crimes that they wanted to be understood as the rule rather than the exception in Vietnam.[31] The 'National Committee for a Citizens' Commission of Inquiry on United States War Crimes in Vietnam' – CCI for short – was the hub for collecting and disseminating this evidence. Set up in December 1969 by anti-war activists and well-known intellectuals in reaction to the news over My Lai (4),[32] the CCI and its coordinator Jeremy Rifkin held public hearings for Vietnam veterans across the United States, and with the help of their evidence lobbied Congress to establish independent inquiries or to set up an international tribunal under the patronage of the United Nations. At the CCI's invitation 200 former Vietnam servicemen reported over the course of the following months on their experiences in different units and in all parts of Vietnam.[33]

Nevertheless the biggest stir was created neither by the CCI nor by initiatives like the closely linked 'Concerned Officers Movement'[34] but by 'Vietnam Veterans Against the War', an association of several thousand servicemen formerly based in Vietnam, which was brought into being in 1967.[35] At the end of January 1971 it held the historic 'Winter Soldiers' hearing in Detroit. (The name referred to the troops loyal to George Washington who, in their camp at Valley Forge in 1776, had not allowed themselves to be scared off by either the superior numbers of British troops or the impact of a hard winter.) In the course of three days 150 witnesses described what they had seen or had themselves done in Vietnam. They reported on rapes, on the random murder of civilians, on water and electric torture, on the custom of ripping out the gold teeth of slaughtered enemies, cutting off their heads and limbs or other mutilation; they claimed that captured Viet Cong were used as mine dogs or thrown from flying helicopters, that surplus ammunition was used for target practice on peasants in the fields or in settlements; they spoke of a scorched-earth policy reminiscent of the practices of Genghis Khan or, to be more precise, the premeditated annihilation of all means of livelihood – and repeatedly of the mass execution of bystanders. 'On this bloody canvas,' wrote *Life* correspondents, 'the massacre at My Lai emerges not as an isolated aberration but as an extension of all that had gone before and was going on at the time, different in only two respects: the large number of civilians killed, and the fact that men were caught and brought to trial.'[36]

Admittedly the Winter Soldiers were suspected of pursuing sensationalism by questionable means. Because most of the witnesses refused to name the perpetrators, instead placing prime responsibility on the political and military leadership, some critics cast doubt on the fundamental credibility of their statements. It also happened that a handful of participants testified under false names.[37] And finally, on one interview tape a prominent Winter Soldier, Mark Lane, had recorded a number of GIs who had either not been stationed in Vietnam or served in different units from the ones they claimed to have been in.[38] On the other hand, the organisers of the Detroit hearing could point to the predominant number of trustworthy witnesses and, with the legal adviser Ramsey Clark (formerly attorney general under Lyndon B. Johnson) and their spokesman John F. Kerry, summon up representatives who cut an impressive figure on any stage. In mid April 1971, when Kerry brought the results of the various hearings before the Senate Committee for International Affairs, he was met with spontaneous applause from the chairman J. William Fulbright and the five other members present. According to one Army observer, 'Mr Kerry's intensity prompted the Chairman to urge him not to lose confidence in the political system because of the "errors in judgement" of some of those within the system . . . The Committee members were sympathetic to Mr Kerry's views; Senator Pell opined that the witness would become one of his "colleagues" in the Senate.'[39] From that point of view, the Winter Soldiers, like all other veterans who were willing to testify, represented an incalculable hidden risk. And the Army had to steel itself as far as possible against a multitude of possible revelations – particularly since President Nixon did not want to commission an independent board of inquiry and therefore gave the management of the crisis to the Pentagon alone.

On 11 December 1969 Secretary of Defense Melvin Laird called on the minister responsible for each branch of the armed forces to put together all the accusations of atrocities and war crimes which had been made publicly and in the press, to initiate relevant inquiries and to report regularly and in full on the state of the investigations.[40] To this end the Army set up a working group solely dedicated to this task – the Vietnam War Crimes Working Group (VWCWG), initially a political early-warning device and, at the end of its four-year activity, the Pentagon's institutional memory for all war-crime matters. Based on media reports and the publications of veteran organisations, the members of VWCWG drew up monthly – and sometimes weekly – 'talking papers' to offer briefing for statements to the press and for background discussions with politicians and journalists – with occasional tips on how to shake the credibility of critics, in particular of former officers. Moreover, all the investigations carried out or still pending between 1970 and 1974 were documented in the form of 'central files' and 'war crimes allegations case files'. By using the records of the Criminal Investigation Division of the Army and the Judge Advocate General's office, there was thus created the most extensive archive about American war crimes in Vietnam, comprising about 10,000 pages in which – excluding the massacre of My Lai (4) – 246 cases and accusations against several hundred suspects are documented.[41]

After a twenty-year waiting period, the records of the Vietnam War Crimes Working Group were handed over to the National Archives in

College Park, Maryland in 1994. Strangely enough, historians have up to now hardly made any use of this archive, which can only be described as a gold mine.[42] This is the first book published anywhere in the world which uses this material to reconstruct both the daily grind of war in Vietnam and the political and legal handling of war crimes.[43] The present worry is that in the foreseeable future interested parties will only have restricted access to the sources. The mania for secrecy of the George W. Bush administration did not stop even at documents released long ago. When, in the aftermath of the new Balkan wars in 2000, a debate was started over sexual violence in wartime and whether it should be punished under international or military law,[44] many records of rape during the Vietnam war were conspicuously blocked or 'reclassified' without further explanation. Since 2004 it has only been possible to view parts of the remaining files of the VWCWG, on the pretext of data protection. This is particularly directed at the interrogation reports prepared by various investigating authorities of the armed forces, in which not just the name but also the social security number of the suspected perpetrators were routinely noted. It remains to be seen whether the archives administration provides the means and the staff to black out the incriminating information and eventually make unhindered access possible again. There is also a legal argument as to whether under the Freedom of Information Act access to the full records really can be denied in such cases.

Unrestrictedly available, however, are the records of the Peers Commission, an Army investigating committee set up shortly before the establishment of the Vietnam War Crimes Working Group, which similarly owes its existence to the impact of the My Lai (4) scandal. Its remit was originally only to clarify the internal cover-up of the massacre, but the chairman of the commission, General William R. Peers, won his demand for a detailed reconstruction of the event. Apart from My Lai (4) and Task Force Barker, which was responsible for the massacre, on Peers's instructions several dozen researchers assembled extensive dossiers on the type, extent and dynamics of excessive violence in Vietnam, on the history of the units involved, their composition, training and battle experience, as well as on the thinking of the officer corps – to name just a few aspects of their investigations. The records, which fill over a hundred archive boxes and are an essential resource for any historical approach to the war, I have analysed system-atically for the present task. In March and April 1970 Peers handed in his four-volume final report to the Defense Department: an annotated summary of the material and 500 pieces of written evidence, together with statements given by over 400 witnesses to the Army's Criminal Investigation Division and the investigators appointed by Peers himself. These four volumes, which became universally accessible in 1975 and were published in shortened form in 1979,[45] are an integral part of all relevant accounts of the My Lai (4) massacre.[46] However, historians have up to now ignored the complete documentation of the Peers Commission.

Based on the records of the Vietnam War Crimes Working Group and the Peers Commission, as well as a multitude of corresponding sources, this study focuses on a hitherto neglected perspective on the Vietnam War. The vast majority of the accounts published in the past forty years are studies devoted to the writing of political history and therefore concerned with administrative decision-making processes, diplomatic manoeuvring and the global strategic framework of the Cold War.[47] Or, influenced by the so-called 'cultural turn' in international history, they address the cultural and psychological side of events, ranging from memories of the war and its aesthetic presentation and 'coding' in the media, literature and film, to those traumatised by war, returning veterans or protagonists on the home front. One could argue that in general the war is written about without being actually described as such.[48] In contrast this book attempts to decode the often repeated claim that in Vietnam 'there was more of it' and to inquire into the conditions and manifestations of a violence that can be neither described nor comprehended with the customary rhetoric about brutality common to all wars.

'There was more of it in Vietnam.' At the heart of this book are the wartime atrocities and war crimes committed by the ground troops. To be more precise, acts of violence which were carried out in close proximity to the victims and in the full knowledge of their identity. We are talking of attacks on the physical inviolability of non-combatants or those no longer involved in fighting – torture, rape, murder and mutilation. The victims are not tormented, abused or murdered from an anonymous distance, are not harmed by aerial weapons and bombs but move in sight of the perpetrators and frequently come face to face with them. The international laws governing warfare – from the Hague Convention on the conduct of land warfare to the various Geneva Conventions – address primarily, though not exclusively, this type of violence. It can neither be brushed off as 'collateral damage' nor excused as the unintentional price of operations, nor is it aimed at the troops, logistics or material resources of the enemy. This is violence committed outside the theatres of war and beyond the hostilities, where the perpetrators do not fight like soldiers but slaughter like cowardly marauders. Because they do not accept any front lines, they regularly, if not systematically, extend the area of operations to the civilian population and shrink as little from attacks on individuals as from group massacres.

In an analysis of this unlimited violence, situational circumstances deserve particular attention: factors which cannot be understood by referring to strategic planning, goal-driven intentions or deliberate calculations. It goes without saying that the conduct of a war reflects the doctrinal and operational premises conceived by military leaders and endorsed by politicians. For this reason it is crucial that the roles of the masters of war in the White House and the generals in the Pentagon should be considered in as much depth as the behaviour of the officers who were in tactical command in the field and who put strategic policy into effect at operational level. On the other hand, wars follow a logic of their own, a dynamic dictated by chance, unpredictability and chaos. This truism has been borne out empirically in all armed conflicts since early history – a theory spelt out, effectively as ever, by Clausewitz. His dictum on the 'frictions of war' can be applied especially to asymmetrical conflicts, in which the combatants fight not only with fundamentally different means but also with a diametrically opposed understanding of warfare. In addition, if a war like that in Vietnam is conducted over a wide area by small groups which act for days or weeks on their own initiative and consequently often without any control, further opportunities for the exercise of excessive violence arise. This is not to imply that the increased chances to commit deeds of violence were inevitably seized; it is more a question of specific 'windows of opportunity', in which such deeds were decided and acted upon. In short, in analysing these deeds and decisions it is more appropriate to look at contingent factors rather than to assume what might be expected or indeed what might be regarded as logical behaviour.

It is impossible to gauge accurately the extent of excess violence in Vietnam or the numbers of servicemen stationed there who were involved directly or indirectly. Efforts have been repeatedly made to estimate the number of victims and culprits. Guenter Lewy draws an analogy with criminal statistics from the late 1960s, according to which the US police were only informed about half of the violent crimes which were actually committed in the United States. He implies that, in similar vein, the figure for crimes committed in Vietnam could be twice as high as the number of criminal investigations undertaken by the military.[49] However much this comparison might appeal, it loses all validity in the face of one banal fact: in the case of Vietnam we lack reference data. Nowhere in the American military were accounts kept of submitted findings, pending investigations, or ongoing or completed military trials, so no analogies with the civilian crime rate can be drawn. Other authors refer to surveys of soldiers and point out that between ten and twelve per cent of those questioned acknowledged their culpability and thirty-three per cent had supposedly witnessed specific offences.[50] How this data was gathered, however, and whether it is representative, even if only approximately, is not discussed. Any attempt to search military reports for evidence would be completely pointless. Quite apart from the fact that culprits did not report of their own free will, no one was responsible for the scrutiny of action and after-action reports. They were without exception drawn up in the certainty that striking contradictions and inconsistencies would not come to light – not even subsequent deliberate falsification or destruction of files. To give just one example, countless references in the official archives of the units responsible for My Lai (4) should have given rise to suspicion – but no records indicate that the obvious questions had been asked, let alone examined for validity.

In addition, a number of factors restrict the reach and usefulness of the available sources. Firstly, the Vietnam War Crimes Working Group and the Peers Commission concentrated exclusively on cases which had already been scrutinised by the appropriate military authorities. It is as difficult to answer conclusively why, out of hundreds of allegations, 244 were selected for the opening of the judicial inquiry, as it is to ask on what grounds only a scant half of those who were allegedly involved were brought before a court of law. Secondly, the vast majority of the reports focus on two of the four war zones – on the I Corps Tactical Zone in the north of South Vietnam and on the IV Corps Tactical Zone in the south. This leads undoubtedly to a corresponding narrowing of perception. On the other hand, these areas were key strategic zones in the war: in the northern provinces there were supply lines, deployment areas and political strongholds for the Viet Cong; in the provinces near the capital Saigon the fighting was over a symbolic presence and the claim of both sides to be in control. Third and last, the records relevant for our purposes cover only four of the ten war years – the period from summer 1967, when the heaviest battles in the I and IV Corps Tactical Zones began, to the withdrawal of American combat troops, which was already in full swing in spring 1971.

No further information can be expected to come out of Vietnam itself. Even the interviewing of actual witnesses there comes up against tightly defined political restrictions. As was made clear to journalists who recently tried to obtain reports of recollections of well-known events such as My Lai (4), this examination of the past has no place in the present – out of consideration for the real or supposed sensitivity of Vietnam's trading partner, the United States. In a society in which approximately sixty-five per cent of the population was born in the last years of the war or shortly after it ended, it will in any case soon be pointless to search for people with reliable first-hand memories of these events. Little is known about the type or extent of written records. Whether they will ever be made available for historical research freely and without prior amendment or censorship is a legitimate concern, for looking into the escalating violence of this war would in the final analysis involve addressing the atrocities meted out to their own people – in other words, attacks that can be ascribed probably in equal measure to the South Vietnamese Army on the one side and to the guerrillas and the North Vietnamese armed forces on the other.[51]

Regardless of how much data and factual evidence may come to light in the future, these will only be isolated examples, revealing in detail but unsuitable for drawing conclusions on the whole. Yet leaving aside these unavoidable limitations, the following picture can be pieced together for the most heavily contested regions of the I and IV Corps Tactical Zones between summer 1967 and spring 1971.

- Seven massacres were officially confirmed by the American side. My Lai (4) and My Khe (4) claimed the largest number of murder victims with 420 and 90 respectively, and in five other places altogether about 100 civilians were executed – occasionally all those who had remained behind in their villages. These cases are comprehensively described in the following pages.

- Two further massacres were reported by soldiers who had taken part in them. North of Duc Pho in Quang Ngai Province (I Corps Tactical Zone), members of D Company, 19th Engineer Battalion, 18th Engineer Brigade (Separate) took revenge on local peasants for a mine victim and murdered fourteen people in summer of 1968.[52] The neighbouring province, Binh Dinh (II Corps Tactical Zone), was allegedly the stage for a further mass murder on 20 July 1969. Soldiers of A Company, 1st Battalion, 503rd Infantry Regiment, 173rd Airborne Brigade (Separate) claimed that their platoon had stormed the village of Chau Truc, burned it down and murdered twenty-five people.[53] The investigations initiated in both cases were discontinued because of contradictory witness statements.

- Tiger Force, a special unit set up for patrols, murdered hundreds, possibly over a thousand, peasants in the space of a few weeks. Because its practices were only investigated years later, it was no longer possible to reconstruct accurately the date and location of the incidents. The fact that no more exact information about the number of dead can be given is also due to the unit's practice of blowing up cellars and bunkers full of terrified villagers with grenades.

- An unknown number of massacres were the work of gunship crews who attacked civilians at low altitude and in the full knowledge of their identity. One can only speculate as to the number of casualties. Some observers estimated that they may have been in the low thousands.

- In the case of large-scale operations, which lasted between a few days and several weeks, an unknown number of non-combatants were killed – at a conservative estimate thought to be between 5,000 and 7,000 in the course of Operation Speedy Express alone, as described in Chapter 7. Excluding the deaths from artillery and air attacks, the total number of victims may have reached tens of thousands.

- It is not at all clear how many POWs were murdered nor how common was the incidence of other violent crimes such as torture and rape. It is certain, however, that a striking number of veterans described violent acts of that kind as daily practice or 'Standing Operating Procedure'.
- Most of the accusations made by the Communist side will probably remain unsolved. According to the 'Information Bureau of the Provisional Revolutionary Government of South Vietnam' (PRG), between April 1968 and the end of 1970 – that is, after My Lai (4) – American ground troops are said to have repeatedly committed mass murder and killed about 6,500 civilians in the course of twenty-one operations either on their own or alongside their allies. With regard to Operation Speedy Express and the massacre of Son Thang, the figures were probably accurate. In three further cases American investigators had well-founded initial suspicions, but the inquiries were shelved after a short time due to a lack of public response. Three of the massacres detected on the American side were not mentioned at all on the PRG list. No further accusations can be either verified or refuted.

'I want no prisoners. The more you kill and burn, the more it will please me. Make the interior of Sama a howling wilderness.'[54] With these orders Brigadier Jacob Smith sent American troops on their way against resisting Filipinos in 1899. Records indicate that similar orders were given in King Philip's War and in the battle against the natives of New England in the early days of settlement, or at the time of the French and Indian War in the mid eighteenth century, when settler militia and soldiers loyal to the British Crown fell back on the guerrilla tactics of the Indian tribes, who were intermittently allies but at times cooperated with the French. Seen like this, Vietnam was a case of déjà-vu – a return to the scenario of an asymmetrical war. The principles and conduct of asymmetrical wars are discussed in Chapters 1 ('Masters of War') and 2 ('Generals'), in particular the key feature of such confrontations: that the adversaries in the end make use of symmetrical means and that both sides try to force the issue by using terrorism against all who are suspected of collaboration with the enemy.[55] Yet Vietnam was more than an example of the immutable expansion of the battle zone into civilian areas. Here one can study how the imperatives of the global Cold War overlaid a regional conflict and released a particular dynamic owing to the circumstances of the time. Hence Brigadier Smith's successors did not just represent his spirit in a different guise.

In this context two problems require independent discussion: why did the US Army conduct the guerrilla war in Vietnam with a strategy designed for conventional war, thus opening the way for additional radicalisation? And why did the political leadership itself see no exit options, even when it became aware that its policies were doomed to failure? The oft-quoted references to ignorance, self-deception and wishful thinking are inadequate explanations for either the conduct of the military or the politicians. It makes no sense to talk of 'drifting' into war or of fatal misperceptions. On the contrary, here were elites who had access to clear evaluations of the situation and many alternative courses of action. With the support of the bureaucratic machine at their disposal, they might have been able to strike out on another course – without political damage or other danger to their own careers. Where does this inflexibility come from, this reluctance and ultimately this incapacity for self-correction – in short, this policy of being unable to stop?

The answers, which are outlined in Chapters 1 and 2, point towards an interpretation of American foreign and military policy during the Cold War and therefore go beyond the subject of Vietnam. They start with the ideological twins of the Cold War – the domino theory and the picture of Communism as a monolithic block – go into the connection between 'imperial presidency' and political self-blockade and introduce the 'institutional crisis' of the US Army – an Army which for a long time found no place in its doctrine for the concept of a 'small war' overshadowed by nuclear weapons, and which saw Vietnam as an opportunity to enhance both its prestige and its institutional weight in competition with the other branches of the armed forces. Above all else, as Barbara Tuchman put it, it is a question of the way in which a policy that focused on political and personal credibility was applied under Cold War conditions and in the end fell into a self-made credibility trap.[56]

The implementation of overall political and military policy depends to a great extent on the behaviour of those involved at the middle level: those officers who are responsible for leading the troops, for planning, implementation and especially control of military operations. Here we need to focus on the 'kings in the field', as the brigade, battalion and company commanders in the US Army were called – an allusion to their traditionally wide discretionary powers and corresponding tendency towards autonomous, if not autocratic, decisions. In former wars their special position had never been perceived as a problem; in Vietnam it soon proved to be a burden. On the one hand, because of the crying need for non-commissioned officers men were brought in who could not match up to the requisite criteria either by training or character and in other circumstances would scarcely have been promoted from the bottom ranks. On the other hand, a disproportionate number of officers at captain, major and lieutenant-colonel level were sent out to Vietnam for one reason: to solve a lack of promotion opportunities in an officer corps which had been overblown since the mid 1950s. Thus a large number of the unqualified were joined by a no less sizeable group of the uninterested, who saw their grotesquely short six-month term primarily from the viewpoint of individual career management. The disparaging talk of the 'Vietnam Only Army' or the 'Shake and Bake Army' reflects this staffing policy and its serious consequences.

Officers and non-commissioned officers contributed greatly to the escalation of violence against non-combatants. Silent tolerance towards the perpetrators played as much of a role as active backing, complicity or collaboration. Apart from the well-documented relevant case studies, Chapter 3 ('Officers') also discusses the causes of leadership breakdown. I will argue that the roots of this evil lay not so much in poor preparation or inadequate contact with the troops. Officers were criticised with good reason: they were not necessarily unable to contain excessive violence but rather, they had no problem with it. This is already obvious from their understanding of the 'Rules of Engagement'. These rules were certainly open to interpretation and, if in doubt, made it possible to put the imperative of 'military necessity' before the principle that civilians should be protected. But the fact that in practice all loopholes were exploited and regulations dealing with exceptions became binding rules reflects an endemic contempt for international military law. The particular circumstances had another repercussion: it seems the decision to give the troops a free hand and to tolerate their overstepping the limits was also considered a means to calm the rage and need for revenge of overtaxed GIs. Above all, many commanding officers were personally committed to a strategy of aggressive war unfettered by scruples. Because their success was measured in a 'body count' balance sheet and future promotion depended on a positive assessment in Vietnam, in the end it did not matter by what ways and means the desired 'kill ratios' were reached. Seen like this, it is not so much a question of 'leadership breakdown', as persistently putting into practice a specific concept of leadership.

Long after the end of the war the role and conduct of the officer corps in Vietnam continued to cause concern. The Pentagon had to battle not only with criticism from opponents of the war but also with unaccustomed protest from its own ranks. Many younger officers resigned their commissions, claiming that they had never served in an Army with acceptable professional standards, while others demanded a fundamental revision of officer training, committed to international military law. Even on the eve of 'Desert Storm', the 1991 war against Saddam Hussein, there were echoes of the Vietnam experience. 'No My Lais in this division. You hear me?' two divisional commanders told their officers in a pre-deployment briefing.[57] Certainly countless reforms in training and operational doctrine were discussed and in part implemented in the 1970s.[58] Yet with a few exceptions,[59] no contemporary research into the subject has been undertaken, either with regard to the US armed forces or those officers from the Third World who were and are still trained in counter-insurgency by American personnel. The present study cannot make good this deficiency. An important element is still missing in the discussion of the historical context of the Vietnam war and consequently in the debate about the self-image and mindset of those leaders to whom America entrusts its current and future wars.

The analysis of the role of the various players reaches its conclusion with Chapter 4 ('Warriors'), which deals with those soldiers for whom killing another human being and the risk of being killed themselves were a daily experience. These 'grunts' differed from the 'front pigs' of earlier wars in several ways. Firstly, their number in the US armed forces was lower than ever before. Only ten per cent of all GIs stationed in Vietnam were posted to combat units and employed in pursuing guerrillas, combing through settlement areas, destroying infrastructure useful to the enemy or fighting regular units of the North Vietnamese

Army. Secondly, as far as background, socialisation, education and training were concerned, they had less in common than any of their predecessors with the ideal of the 'citizen soldier'. It was not a representative cross-section of young Americans who bore the brunt of the war, but the youngest and poorest in society. Thirdly, the grunts broke a taboo that had been carefully fostered over many wars: they testified to their experiences of violence, in contributions to political forums, in 'oral history' – conversations with journalists, psychologists and historians – in statements to Army commissions of inquiry or before military tribunals, and lastly in autobiographical accounts ranging from the traditional soldier's novel to ambitious literary fiction and poetry.

It is by no means obvious that these accounts deserve special consideration in a history of violence during the war, for soldiers returning home as losers, wanting to rid themselves of the stigma of defeat, will first of all seek to justify themselves to third parties. Even the Winter Soldiers with their shocking reports of war atrocities wanted to be seen as reluctant murderers and ultimately as victims of a military apparatus which had brainwashed them, dehumanised them and denied them any possibility of choice. 'You can see this sadistic state of mind that my government put me into . . . Don't ever let your government do this to you. Okay – that's me. I'm holding a dead body – smiling.'[60] – 'They had to completely re-socialize us, which they were very effective at doing.'[61] – 'The executions are secondary because the executions are created by the policy that is, I believe, a conscious policy within the military.'[62] Soldiers reported on crimes to make it clear that they themselves were not basically criminals but patriots, fighting for America's true values, dedicated to those virtues that Thomas Paine had firstly identified in the original Winter Soldiers: 'These are the times that try men's souls. The summer soldier and the sunshine patriot will, in this crisis, shrink from the service of their country; but he that stands it now, deserves the love and thanks of man and woman.'[63]

Regardless of this bid for recognition, one decisive dimension of these soldiers' testimonies should not be overlooked: they equally reflect the need to come to terms with a heavy burden and to transfer traumatic memories into topics for public self-therapy.[64] In this sense their reflections on Vietnam can also be read as attempts to make sense of the violence they committed or witnessed and to construct a portrait of a war that damaged the self-image of everyone involved – because anyone, at any time, could turn into a culprit. These soldiers debate with themselves about the violence in an attempt to reach a retrospective understanding that goes beyond any resentful bid for approval.

The essential outcome of these studies lies in the answer to striking yet rarely asked questions: how it was that the radical changes in behaviour of the soldiers in Vietnam took only a few weeks or months to accomplish and why the explanations derived from other wars – that this was primarily proof of intense battle stress or similar problems accumulating over long periods – in this case were meaningless. 'Disposable soldier' and 'instant death' – these are the terms around which the grunts' memories revolve. Regardless of whether they wanted to prove their masculinity and affirm their warrior status or to fulfil an unpleasant duty and come home as quickly as possible – all expectations and hopes were abruptly reduced to nothing in the jungle and the rice paddies. The enemy was either beyond reach or dictated the time and place of combat, superior weaponry yielded no advantage, they suffered casualties without being able to inflict significant loss on the other side, the front line was everywhere and nowhere and death threatened them all out of the blue and at any time in the shape of mines, booby-traps or snipers. 'Do something physical': GIs used this exhortation to turn violence against the defenceless into a mandate – an assertion of power by other means and a sign of soldierly presence on imaginary killing fields. However, this kind of self-affirmation needed to be constantly repeated because soldiers fighting in the jungle had no control over either the invisible front lines or their own fears. They remained first and last disposable soldiers, threatened by instant death.

In short, the premises of the American conduct of the war in Vietnam were, at the lowest level, a process of self-justification to use violence, the body-count mania in the middle ranks of leadership and the fighting for political credibility and military prestige on the part of the commanders-in-chief in Washington and Saigon. Understanding in what circumstances and how these factors came into effect must take the form of an independent examination, which also needs to take into account the strategy and tactics of the Viet Cong and the North Vietnamese Army. These questions therefore stand at the heart of a chronology of the history of violence in Vietnam spread over Chapters 5 to 7: '1967', '16 March 1968' and '1968–1971'. From the areas of I and IV Corps Tactical Zones – those combat areas in which both sides were battling for a decisive outcome of the war – three different operations are examined, together with their origins and consequences, and three units typical of the ground war are portrayed: a reconnaissance patrol of about four dozen men called Tiger Force, a special unit of company strength known as Task Force Barker, and a larger unit, 9th Infantry Division, made up of several brigades. The study of these examples illustrates how wide the influence 'from above' stretched and what power to determine what happened came 'from below'.

Operation Speedy Express, carried out by troops of 9th Infantry Division in the Mekong Delta between November 1968 and April 1969, has so far not featured in historical accounts – even though it was probably the biggest and indisputably the bloodiest 'pacification operation' of the entire war. Based on the sources of the Vietnam War Crimes Working Group, the Peers Commission and various files of correspondence, this book reconstructs, for the first time, the political background and military planning and examines the implementation of an operation that left nearly 11,000 dead but in which only about 700 weapons were captured. Contemporary US Army evaluations confirmed that civilians made up at least half the dead but justified this by referring to the supposedly compelling military necessity of the operation. This refers to the directive issued by the Military Assistance Command, Vietnam (MACV) to exploit the dramatic losses suffered by the Viet Cong during the Tet Offensive and to give backing to the South Vietnamese Army in the projected 'Vietnamisation' of the war.

The orders given to Task Force Barker had also been prepared under the impact of the Tet Offensive and as a sign of an 'intensified pacification': in Quang Ngai Province, a traditional Viet Cong stronghold, the intention was to wipe out the 48th Local Force Battalion of guerrillas and eliminate the political leadership of the insurgents. However, the murder, pillage and rape during the operation on 16 March 1968 cannot be explained as part of the strategic plan and can only to a limited extent be attributed to the influence of troop leaders. The differing behaviour of the platoons of C and B Company, stationed in different places, points to this conclusion, confirmed by an examination of the course of the massacre in My Lai (4) which inquires into the preconditions under which the massacre began, when it reached its peak, whether the method of killing stemmed from detached calculation or raging fury, at what point and above all why the perpetrators stopped, who took no part and how many actively revolted against the slaughter. In general such questions can only be answered unsatisfactorily due to a lack of source material. The minute reconstruction of the events of My Lai (4) on the part of the Criminal Investigation Division of the Army and the Peers Commission, however, allows one to draw empirically well-substantiated inferences – conclusions which look beyond the specific incident and can be discussed as fundamental contributions towards our understanding of escalating violence in wartime.

At first glance the Tiger Force special unit, which raged through Quang Ngai and Quang Tin Provinces in 1967 like a death squad, falls outside the parameters: we know of no other unit which murdered in that way for so long and virtually on its own account. Stationed for weeks on its own in the Song Ve Valley and in the mountainous jungle near the demarcation line on the 17th Parallel, the patrol spared nothing and no one – neither peasants working in their fields nor the old people, women or children they found when ambushing villages at night. On the other hand, it must be remembered that the war in Vietnam was conducted in many places by small groups which, like Tiger Force, did not feel themselves bound to any official operational directives but followed their own Rules of Engagement outside any control. From the example of Tiger Force it is possible to observe why small units in particular tended towards excessive violence and how indeed this use of violence became normal practice for those serving in them. That violence can enhance one's distinction and reputation and secure or promote one's position in the group hierarchy is as evident as the pleasure, delight and fun of killing – attributes experienced and regarded by the perpetrators of violence as proof of their freedom of action. This also shows that mere habit or peer pressure created by ringleaders cannot be held responsible exclusively, or possibly not even primarily, for the coherence of a small group. This is not to say that nobody protested, or deviated from the general behaviour. A handful of GIs from Tiger Force reported on the incidents to their superiors but no action was taken by the military command. Anyone wanting to sever the bond between the civilian population and the Viet Cong could not do so without using the dead to give a message to the living: that they all had to reckon with everything, because some were capable of anything.

Chapter 8 ('Judges') discusses the possibilities and limitations of a prosecution of war crimes. As far as the legal norms were concerned the necessary preconditions were given in the Uniform Code of Military Justice (UCMJ). The norms of international laws of warfare applied without limitation in all aspects and following the Nuremberg and Tokyo trials, the principles of *'respondeat superior'* and *'mens rea'* had been adopted – clauses by which superiors could be brought to account for the behaviour of their subordinates without, on the other hand, granting the subordinates the possibility of citing the orders of their superiors as their defence for illegal actions. What needs to be explained is why only a fraction of suspected offenders had to answer to military courts and how in a large proportion of cases military law was diluted to the point of being unrecognisable. Without doubt many proceedings failed at an early stage because sufficient evidence to stand up in a court of law could not be collected. In addition, Army prosecutors together with officials and high-ranking politicians sometimes hindered investigations or successfully lobbied behind the scenes for them to be terminated. However, the significance of conspiracy and inadequate evidence should not be overstated; in fact, prosecutions under the laws of war could be impeded using features of military legal process – and certainly by referring to the Uniform Code of Military Justice, according to which the corps commanders in whose formations the incriminating acts had been committed had to decide how to deal with the results of the investigations. Whether they spared suspects or imposed purely administrative punishments, whether they arranged for further examination of evidence or did not even consider a court martial, lay solely in their discretion. Last but not least, they could at any time amend judgments or quash them completely. The fact that the convening authorities used these opportunities to the full is at the heart of the problem: an erosion of the culture of military law by legal process.

Since the mid nineteenth century the American public had been repeatedly confronted with the punishment of war crimes. When in

1862 the Dakota started an uprising of the Sioux under their chief Little Crow in southern Minnesota and possibly murdered up to 1,000 settlers in the course of one week, 306 of the perpetrators were initially sentenced to be hanged; 36 were then executed in December 1862 after the sentences had been reviewed and proof of individual responsibility established without doubt.[65] Following the Sand Creek Massacre of 500 Cheyenne and Arapaho at the end of November 1864 an inquiry was opened into the conduct of the officer responsible, Colonel John M. Chivington of the Colorado Militia. In 1902, Brigadier General Jacob Smith was discharged as a result of the massacre in the Philippines. Yet there was no lasting outrage.[66] On the contrary: the Second World War – regarded as a 'good war' – in the course of which nearly 300 American soldiers were sentenced by courts martial and executed, immunised the public against the conduct of their troops – despite the fact that most of the sentences had been given for rape and murder. Reports about those crimes in high-circulation newspapers and magazines died away without trace or were dismissed with the words, 'War is War'.[67]

The Army photographer Ronald Haeberle, who had been present at My Lai (4), also experienced this lack of interest. He had shown his pictures of the massacre in a slide show about Vietnam on several occasions in Cleveland, Ohio to a total of 600 people – once each at an Optimist and a Kiwanis Club, twice to members of Jaycee clubs, to a group of teachers, a church youth group and pupils at a high school.[68] With a few exceptions, most of the audience felt they had been manipulated and made Haeberle the target for their criticism. '"Why would American GIs do this, especially to old men, women, and children?" A couple thought that it had been done in Hollywood, that it was made up. They just didn't want to believe it.'[69]

Even the horror at the pictures shown on CBS television and confirmed as authentic proved to be a fleeting instant of being frozen with shock. In the weeks and months following, the White House, the Pentagon and newspaper editors were literally showered with expressions of solidarity with the murderers of My Lai (4) – with hundreds of thousands of letters and petitions from all parts of the country, drawn up by writers from all sections of the population and of all shades of political opinion. To my knowledge, no other historian has ever examined this material and presented an analysis of it.[70] This is one of the reasons why these texts are discussed in detail in my Conclusion. Drawing on over 900 documents, I shall assess the political and moral standpoint of the protestors, and from their collective reactions I shall draw conclusions about the relationship between the military and society in the United States.

At this point at the latest the boundaries between contemporary history and the diagnosis of our own times become blurred. The fan mail sent to William Calley and others raises the question of the political will and institutional potential for self-correction within American society; also of whether Richard Rorty is right in his observation that since the 1960s the argument over competing political and social concepts has been increasingly displaced by the politics of emotion[71] – politics which for the purpose of strengthening national solidarity, require a state of emergency on different 'fronts', and ultimately cannot do without war.[72] But that would be – and is – the subject for another book.

1

Masters of War

> If I had lost Vietnam, there would be Robert Kennedy out in
> front leading the fight against me, telling everyone that I had
> betrayed John Kennedy's commitment to South Vietnam . . . That
> I was a coward. An unmanly man. A man without a spine. Oh, I
> could see it coming all right. Every night when I fell asleep I
> would see myself tied to the ground in the middle of a long,
> open space. In the distance I could hear the voices of thousands
> of people. They were all shouting at me and running toward me:
> 'Coward! Traitor! Weakling!'
>   Lyndon B. Johnson[1]

> What we're really doing in Vietnam is killing the cause of 'wars
> of liberation'. It's a testing ground – like Germany in Spain. It's
> an example to Central America and other guerrilla prone areas.
>   Bernard B. Fall[2]

It was the longest 'hot' war of the Cold War period – and a war with
the most appalling record in all history: at no other time and in no
other place were so many weapons of destruction deployed as in
Vietnam. Between 1966 and 1968 the war planes of the United States
and its allies dropped 2,865,808 tons of bombs on Vietnam, Laos and
Cambodia – at least 800,000 tons more than in all theatres of the whole
Second World War combined. After two years of aerial warfare –

between August 1964 and December 1966 – 860,000 tons of bombs had already landed on the northern part of the country alone. By 1975 the US armed forces had exploded seven million tons of bombs and artillery grenades in North and South Vietnam. This number, too, is well in excess of the fire-power deployed by the United States in the course of the Second World War. A country of 330,000 square kilo-metres, somewhat smaller than Germany, was left at the end of the war with twenty-six million bomb craters.[3]

'There was more of it in Vietnam.' This catchphrase of the Amer-ican soldiers not only describes the extent of the war in the air; it also refers to the fact that this war in South-East Asia was a strange amalgam of all the kinds of armed conflicts we have known in modern times. The fighting in the jungle and the rice paddies bore features of the colonial wars fought since the sixteenth century on the periphery of the imperial world – fought out on perpetually changing, invisible fronts and often over unexpectedly long periods. At the same time one finds the history of guerrilla warfare reflected in Vietnam. Its original setting can be found in the middle of the eighteenth century, when the British used scattered, irregular troops to destroy the supply lines or the forts of French or Indian enemies. As the Vietnam War progressed the North Vietnamese Army and the Viet Cong developed this combination of regular and irregular troops to perfection. On the other hand the Viet Cong also assumed the role of guerrillas fighting on their own account with unconventional strate-gies and unhampered by an orderly official military command – a role which had been played since the Spanish underground resistance against Napoleon. The siege of Khe Sanh, which lasted for months, or the battle at 'Ap Bia Mountain' in the A Shau valley, where in May 1969 American and North Vietnamese troops conducted a pointless slaughter for a strategically worthless hilltop, find a parallel in the trench warfare of the First World War. The GIs called that engagement 'Hamburger Hill' – an unconscious play on the so-called 'mincer' at Verdun. Last but not least the Vietnam war was conducted over wide areas in the main as total war, as the distinction between combatants and non-combatants was in part intentionally ignored, in part blurred as a consequence of military action.

The price of the war was correspondingly high. 'There was more of it in Vietnam' indicates that any attempt to formulate a concrete image is destined to fail – particularly concerning the number of civilians killed. The horrors only emerge sketchily and in the sort of statistics which conceal more than they reveal. One customary method of appraisal – to assess the probable number of dead by counting the number treated in hospital – is proved in this case to be naïve. Many of the villages subject to widespread bombardment or drawn into other battle zones were beyond the range of medical help. In such hamlets and villages a nameless death was rampant – not to mention the countless settlements not shown on any map and literally wiped off the face of the earth without a trace. Besides, daily life in the medical centres, as often described, shows that using hospital statistics is pointless. Poorly equipped, chronically short of staff and confronted with the task of bringing order to a chaotic situation, they were anything but places where reliable paperwork could be compiled. In addition, one must take into account that at least a third of the enemy soldiers recorded as dead were actually civilians who had been reclassified in the reports of engagements as bearing arms, in order to improve the success rate.

If we accept the lowest assessment, between 1965 and the end of 1974 627,000 civilians died in North and South Vietnam as a consequence of hostilities on both sides; well over eighty per cent of them lived in the south of the country. The North Vietnamese Army and the Viet Cong – minus the civilians recorded incorrectly among the dead – lost 444,000 men, the United States just over 56,000 and their allies about 226,000, so that about 726,000 soldiers may be assumed killed. Put together, the number of all the war dead would therefore come to 1,353,000. Other writers consider these figures greatly underestimated: they talk of a million Vietnamese soldiers killed, over two million Vietnamese dead and over four million wounded – in a land which at the time had between thirty-five and forty million inhabitants. It is idle to try to choose between these calculations; the truth lies somewhere in between. At any rate the proportion of civilians among the war victims is exorbitant – somewhere between forty-six and sixty-six per cent. Any average used exceeds the presumed forty-two per cent of civilian dead for the Second World War. Consequently, alongside Korea, Vietnam had the highest death toll of all the 'hot wars' waged during the Cold War.[4]

THE DYNAMICS OF ASYMMETRICAL WARFARE

What caused this excessive violence? What conditions combined to trigger such a development? And how did the various factors affect each other? To address these questions it is useful to look back at the discussions going on since the middle of the 1970s about 'asymmetrical' wars – wars in which opponents have different-quality armaments, differently trained troops and a fundamentally different understanding of warfare. On the face of it, there would therefore be one strong and one weak side, but historical study reveals time and again that material superiority is not necessarily a blessing in such wars. It may indeed be more of a curse. No matter whether one takes examples from classical, medieval or modern times wars fought on asymmetrical terms follow their own logic. They are not subject to the dictates of economy or technology and suspend any mathematical calculation of manpower or efficiency. Much more decisive is the way in which each side handles the time factor – and the fact that they make apposite use of that resource. The side which appears to be weak has no interest in ending the war swiftly. On the contrary, time is its strongest ally. So long as it does not lose, it has won. 'We don't need to win military victories,' said a former colonel in the North Vietnamese Army, 'we only need to hit them until they give up and get out.'[5] On the other hand, if the ostensibly strong side is not to lose, it is condemned to winning. The longer the war lasts, the worse are its chances of winning and the more vulnerable does its position become. In such a scenario, however, there thrives the readiness for excessive violence, through which the weak side can delay a decision and thus gain time, while the strong side makes the mistake of using violence to force a decision and thus recoup lost time. In other words, there is a direct connection between asymmetry and unfettered violence.[6]

The difference in equipment and armaments in the Vietnam War could hardly have been greater. The United States put a fully mechanised army into the field, while the guerrillas often used bicycles to transport their military equipment through the thickets of the Ho Chi Minh Trail. The air space belonged to American helicopters, fighter-bombers and B-52s, which were capable of carrying atomic warheads, and off the coast US aircraft carriers were anchored – weapons systems which could not be fought off with Kalashnikovs, obsolete anti-aircraft guns or patrol boats. Many such examples can be cited at will but they all illustrate the same point: that the weak side only survives if it does not enter into the kind of warfare for which the strong side is well prepared and in which it can operate more effectively. Under asymmetrical conditions risking open battles or entering into a race for the same kind of military equipment would mean certain defeat for the weak side. It cannot even count on having a second chance.[7]

A guerrilla has only one resort: to employ invisible and indirect means. This requires far-reaching support from non-combatants, merging with the civilian population and demanding their protection. To swim like the fish in the water – to quote Mao's famous dictum – your ears must be open to the needs, fears and wishes of the underprivileged and they must recognise that you represent their interests. But guerrillas can never count on such acceptance: it is only 'borrowed strength'. Fighting an opponent with vastly superior firepower on one's own territory means reckoning with wholesale destruction. While wars that enter into everyone's daily life can weld people together, they can equally make them rebel, as countless examples show – and of course the more the longer the war lasts. In every case the success of the weak side depends on civilians being permanently prepared for any sacrifice or suffering. No one can forecast when they will come to the end of their endurance and unreasonable demands will trigger resignation, recalcitrance or even open antagonism. It is this unknown risk factor in the background which breeds in the weak side the temptation to repress or even terrorise. The situation will determine the choice of method, but the objective is not in doubt – since the guerrilla's very survival is at stake. Only with constant mobilisation of non-combatants can the material deficit of the armed troops be kept within limits or even equalised. The price of this equalisation is therefore to carry the battle to the civilians – both mentally and physically.

There is no doubt that the Viet Cong were accepted as the 'people's representatives' in many places and over long periods of the war. In the northern provinces of Quang Ngai, Quang Tin and Quang Nam, for instance, 30,000 political and military cadres controlled the plains at the beginning of the 1960s. The influence of the Saigon government was restricted to a few towns; everywhere else local authorities, schools, health and the distribution of economic surpluses were in Communist hands. 'With the Viet Cong there isn't any distinction,' said an Army report on the situation in Quang Ngai at the beginning of 1967. 'The Viet Cong *are* the people.'[8] In those regions a generation grew up not knowing anything different. For them land reform and social security were no promises for the future; they existed here and now. At the least they had shared in rejecting foreign domination or outside intervention, virulently in the nineteenth century and militarily since the 1930s. This equally deep-rooted opposition to the Japanese, the French or the Americans remained the most important resource of the Viet Cong and it seems entirely appropriate to speak of a wartime 'emotional force of production'. On the other hand, important areas of social life remained closed to Communist influence even outside the towns. The permanent presence of tax collectors certainly did not recommend them unreservedly to farmers working for meagre returns. It can be assumed in the absence of empirical counter-evidence that the majority of the rural population wanted nothing to do with politics and valued their traditional way of life above any ideology. First to come under suspicion for their philosophy of life were the Catholics and the Buddhists – a significant section of society, not only because of their large numbers but also because they formed the elite of intellectuals and journalists, and shared with them a fundamentally different understanding of popular representation.[9]

These actual or imagined 'unreliables' felt the extension of the battle zone physically. When they did not respond to calls for self-criticism or when re-education programmes did not bear fruit, the Viet Cong 'propaganda teams' at work in individual villages did not baulk at sending recalcitrant people into military service or forced labour, nor to bringing them before a 'People's Court' for sentencing and subsequent public execution. A 'security service' estimated at 25,000 kept records of hostile civil functionaries – village elders, officials, policemen, social workers, prison warders, teachers and journalists – from which hit lists for murder or abduction squads were drawn up. It is hard to estimate how many people fell victim to the commandos; probably about 37,000 people were murdered and around 58,000 abducted between 1957 and 1972, apart from a large number never accounted for. 'The struggles must be daring and violent. By no means, should they be led in the form of legal petitions or requests. Struggles of all kinds must be conducted with high determination and violence,'[10] according to a dossier dated 25 February 1968. It seems that only twenty per cent of victims were in government or police service – a hardly surprising fact, since the call 'to completely annihilate puppet government agents'[11] left the way open for the terrorism to go off the rails. 'We attacked on too large a front,' admitted General Giap with hindsight, 'and, seeing enemies everywhere, resorted to terror, which became far too widespread . . . Worse still, torture came to be regarded as normal practice.'[12] When in February 1968 12,000 soldiers of the North Vietnamese Army and the Viet Cong held the town of Huê for 26 days, about 3,000 civilians on their blacklists were massacred and the same number abducted – 'hooligan lackeys' in the words of Radio Hanoi.[13] There are good grounds for assuming that refugee camps or villages suspected of collaborating with the enemy were repeatedly shot up – whether as a punishment or in order to prove that the Americans and South Vietnamese could not substantiate their claim to protect them, is an open question. Hundreds, if not thousands, paid for this with their lives.[14]

The strong side also inclines towards carrying the war to the civilians. The history of European colonial wars in Asia and Africa since the late nineteenth century and not least in the Philippines at the turn of the twentieth century offer a regularly repeating pattern. As soon as the enemy is supported and sheltered by the population, the 'soft targets' come into sight. Cutting off the guerrillas' retreat and denying them their sources of material reinforcements was to hit them in their most vulnerable spot. Now thousands were forcibly resettled at a distance in 'strategic hamlets' surrounded with barbed-wire and sealed off by the militia to prevent communication with the insurgents; now cattle were confiscated or crops destroyed; now whole swathes of countryside together with their settlements were turned into dead zones – also to warn and threaten the inhabitants. Anyone supporting the enemy had to realise that he was putting his own life on the line and had an utterly unscrupulous power to reckon with. A strategy with ground rules like this included murder and massacre and when necessary would be translated into actions which literally had no bounds, and excluded no object in the natural or social environment. There is no doubt that such wars were waged without regard for any rules or conventions of warfare. But because lowering the threshold of inhibitions was seen as imperative and therefore legitimate, even the *ius in bello* lost its effectiveness.[15]

The American conduct of the war in Vietnam seamlessly carried on in this succession. On foreign soil, against the backdrop of an impenetrable landscape – woods, mountains and marshes – the troops encountered a population they regarded as no less threatening: peasants, who did not welcome their protectors with open arms, who neither warned them about ambushes nor told them of the whereabouts of booby-traps; young men and old women whom they suspected of turning into guerrillas at night after their day's work in the fields. It did not matter where the boundary lay between reality and imagination; the determining factor was the suspicion of hostility and the military methods it engendered. Quite apart from the victims of air raids, the fate of the civilian population offers a horrendous scenario: ten million were forced to flee through the policy of resettlement; no one knows how many lost their crops for years to come through attacks with Agent Orange and other herbicides or had their health and that of their unborn children ruined through poisoned food; thousands died in armed attacks on their villages; there were dozens of massacres; a programme known as Operation Phoenix, aimed at rooting out the leadership cadres of the Viet Cong, cost the lives of 20,000–40,000 people between mid 1968 and mid 1971 – in nine out of ten cases the identity of the murder victims was unknown and they were retrospectively listed as 'functionary'. Though much of this may sound familiar when put in a historical context, what was new was the ruthlessness with which those well-known practices were employed: 'There was more of it in Vietnam.'

We shall return later to these events in more detail. It is sufficient here to indicate the fundamental dynamics: however different their interests and motives may be, the opponents in asymmetrical wars end up by using symmetrical methods: deliberate, calculated acts of terror against unarmed people, their lives and their whole world. This is not to allege unavoidable necessity; however, in view of the centuries-old score sheet it was irrefutably a regularly recurring process. Trying to beat guerrillas at their own game does not only involve expanding the battle zone; the war against 'soft targets' also implies a brutalised military strategy – so long as the strong side sees no other methods of overcoming its own weakness and as soon as the weak side is convinced that only in this way can it strengthen its precarious power base.

From the point of view of the Viet Cong the escalation of the struggle promised an important pay-off for other reasons as well. They reckoned that the more the fear and terror spread, the more swiftly would the moral resources of their opponent be exhausted – an opponent of whom General Vo Nguyen Giap, Hanoi's supreme commander, said that 'he does not possess . . . the psychological and political means to fight a long drawn-out war.'[16] Statements like this were made in the knowledge that the guerrillas had an insuperable advantage: their superior geographical knowledge enabled them to operate like ghosts. Assault parties vanished as quickly as they had emerged, at places and times of their own choosing – invisible, unpredictable and therefore in control of events. Yet in attacks on 'soft targets' such as reinforcement and communication routes, weapons depots or troop quarters were not enough; more important was to cause any front line to disintegrate. The enemy must not feel safe anywhere, have no line of retreat and no assembly-point where he could gather and regroup. 'Considering the positions of friend and foe, it is found that our daring and surprise attacks transform the enemy from strong to weak and our forces from small to large.'[17] So every rice paddy, every dyke, tree or bush must be assumed to be a danger to life, and a densely woven net of booby-traps was laid over the whole country, in the expectation that the customary battle-zone stress would become the enemy's constant companion wherever he went.

So ran the logic of the politics of terrorism which permanently employs dramatic effects to achieve its objectives. Pinpricks were not enough on their own to shake the mindset and morale of the enemy troops; the GIs were to receive a double message: that their superior weapons were useless in the jungle and – more importantly – that they could not count on being captured but were facing an enemy who did not take prisoners. The Viet Minh had sent the same message to the French in the 1950s and reports from the 1960s which confirm this are too numerous to be overlooked. American soldiers who were ambushed and separated from their units, were tortured and mutilated, their disfigured bodies put on view in prominent places – flayed, slit open, with limbs or sexual organs cut off.

The US military command had good reason for not spreading such news, for apart from the morale of the troops, such atrocities were aimed at the home front as well – in the hope of finding the weak point which since the killing of US troops by local warlords in the 1990s has been known as the 'Mogadishu effect'. This means involving the moral resources of American civilian society, its reluctance to make large sacrifices in small wars and its inclination to plead for withdrawal rather than find itself humiliated in the eyes of the world by appearing to be ineffectual. 'The American rear was vulnerable,' explained Colonel Bui Tin. 'Every day our leadership would listen to world news over the radio at 9 a.m. to follow the growth of the American antiwar movement . . . The conscience of America was part of its war-making capability, and we were turning that power in our favor. America lost because of its democracy; through dissent and protest it lost the ability to mobilize a will to win.'[18] Thus terror can become a means of communication and no amount of manpower can really compensate for its efficacy. Of course it would be an exaggeration to narrow down the guerrillas' war strategy to this calculation, but disregarding psychological demoralisation would mean overlooking an essential part of the asymmetrical war in Vietnam.[19]

Any method is normally effective when attacking the moral weak points of the strong side. Whether this conclusion was drawn from studying colonial wars in general or the experiences in the war against the French is an open question. In any case it seemed legitimate to the guerrillas in Vietnam to draw civilians directly into the military line of fire – whether as human shields or as provocation for an enemy unsure of his objectives and already feeling the strain. Anyone familiar with the history of the war since the 1950s will repeatedly come across examples to support this contention. Bernard B. Fall reported the case of Highway One, which runs along the coast of the South China Sea and where the Viet Minh turned dozens of small villages into a fortification system with ditches and underground passages thirty kilometres long and hundreds of metres deep, covering an area that was difficult to assess. This defined the civilian environment as a battle line. And only when the enemy could distinguish between their defensive shelters and a purely military installation were non-combatants not drawn into the fighting. The guerrillas happily accepted that they would not make this distinction, thereby deliberately and even intentionally risking the lives of non-participants. This practice is confirmed in a statement by a Vietnamese political functionary in a US Army study: 'The Party has been guided by the principle that it is better to kill ten innocent people than to let one enemy escape.'[20]

The Viet Cong also emphasized this principle in the 1960s. They repeatedly sent troops into settlements close to well-worn military routes, from which they opened fire on US convoys – in spite of or because they knew that those attacked would resort to their own brand of terror and would return even light fire with a heavy-calibre air attack. Or they occupied villages with the intention of inciting American troops into storming these 'soft targets'. The price the civilians paid was of no account; the importance was the price to be extorted from the enemy: the fact that he was gradually renouncing his claim to represent a morally superior cause, was exposed in the eyes of the people he had come to Vietnam to protect, and not least discredited in world opinion. A psychological war radicalised in this way was one of the guerrillas' most effective weapons.[21]

Yet credibility and legitimisation are rare commodities for the strong side and they lie at the very core of its war calculations – the time factor. Long before the US involvement in Vietnam, colonial powers waging war on the periphery had constantly found their parliaments cutting budgets in an attempt to bring to a premature end any war which had become unpopular. The British had to wrestle with this during the American War of Independence as did the French troops in South-East Asia in the 1950s. Since national survival was never an issue for the strong side, high investment without recognisable gain could not be defended indefinitely. 'Get out or win' was therefore the slogan of the silent majority in the United States in the late 1960s. In such circumstances masters of war are greatly tempted to take the bull by the horns. In other words, the greater the moral and political pressure, the stronger seems the tendency to bring the situation to a head through a military strike. Increasing troop numbers is not an option on grounds of cost and acceptability. Basically the fight against time can only be won, if at all, by maximising material strength. The choices are defined in two slogans: 'spend shells, not men' and 'set-piece battle' – one being to increase fire-power, the other to force the opponents into a conventional, decisive major engagement.

The Communist side could in fact respond by mobilising resources which by definition make the image of a weak side an unsustainable metaphor. The United States was dealing with an armed force capable of making exorbitant sacrifices. At the climax of the war at the end of 1967 it relied on a force of about 200,000 combat troops, half divided into units of company strength at least and half into small, platoon-sized groups which, unlike the larger groups, only operated locally. Including supply and administration units the maximum manpower reached 240,000. In the period from 1964 to 1975, however, about 444,000 soldiers of the Viet Cong and the North Vietnamese Army lost their lives on the battlefield.[22] In other words, the Communist side lost a complete Army twice over, thereby sacrificing in armed personnel twice as large a percentage of their pre-war population as did Japan in the Second World War and twelve times as large as the Chinese and North Koreans during the Korean War.[23] If the US Army had paid the equivalent death toll, a million American soldiers would not have returned home, instead of 50,000. It is historically rare, if not unique, for one party to a war to be ready and willing to pay such a price. Several factors had obviously combined here: the indomitable will to throw off the yoke of foreign determination and colonialism, the motivation derived from successfully fighting the Japanese and the French, and the unsurpassed ruthlessness of the political and military leadership. 'Every minute,' said General Giap, 'hundreds of thousands of people die all over the world. The life or death of thousands of human beings, even if they are compatriots, represent really very little.'[24]

Yet a special circumstance in world politics was a decisive factor: the solidarity effect of the Cold War. At no point were the South Vietnamese guerrillas left to their own devices; they could rely on massive support from North Vietnam in men and materials. Of the over 100,000 soldiers fighting in the large troop formations, at the end of 1967 more than half came from the North – well trained soldiers in the tradition of a force which, under the title of Viet Minh, had faced and beaten the French in the early 1950s, partly in open battle. General Giap, who was already supreme commander at the time, therefore regarded guerrilla war only as a preliminary: 'When we shall have reached the third stage . . . mobile warfare will become the principal activity, positional warfare and guerrilla warfare will become secondary.'[25] From 1952 on the means to do this came from the Soviet Union and the People's Republic of China, who together provided almost 400,000 'military advisers', supplied heavy equipment such as trucks, artillery and anti-aircraft guns, and shored up North Vietnam economically with substantial funds. This aid was not altruistic, nor was it only for the sake of the dignity and independence of a former colony. Moscow and Peking wanted to see the strength and sustainability of the socialist model confirmed in Vietnam. Defeating the United States would then be seen as a beacon – a message to insurgents far beyond the frontiers of Vietnam. But anyone who wages a symbolic war, defining it as a global struggle for ultimate values, is the most reliable of all partners. In addition he is open to blackmail, for he can only escape from the solidarity trap he has set himself at the cost of substantial loss of face. It was precisely the political susceptibility of its allies which made North Vietnam strong.[26]

Simultaneously this represents the greatest weakness of the so-called strong side. There was no question of the United States marching into North Vietnam to wipe out the military power base of the guerrillas. There was too great a risk of escalating the war close to the Chinese frontier, and the interests of the third atomic power, the Soviet Union, were too unclear. Under the given conditions, and in view of the fact that the resources of legitimacy and time were fast running out, the range of military options shrank to one only: as a first priority to attack the economic centres and infrastructure of the North with a widespread bombing campaign, in addition to the supply lines for men and materials. We know that Presidents Lyndon B. Johnson and Richard Nixon went down this road – and copied the guerrillas' terror tactics. Although the methods used were on a far heavier scale, the US strategy was based on the same ideological prerequisite: to bring the enemy to his knees through spreading fear and terror and above all acting unpredictably. It is no coincidence that the relevant operational plans of the US Air Force were composed in the style and language of torturers. There was talk of 'fast/full squeeze', 'thresholds of pain' to be discovered and passed, of 'the hot-cold treatment', and again and again of reaching a 'breaking-point' in the enemy's social structure, which would bring the war to a speedy end.[27] In the event the attack was aimed at civilian centres and therefore borrowed from the strategy of total war. Anyone trying to compensate for his weaknesses by such means carries the logic of the asymmetrical war to its apogee and closes the circle of a dynamic designed by both sides to brutalise.

POLITICAL DECISION-MAKING

Why did the US political and military decision-makers fall into this trap? Why did they risk a war which could only end in fiasco and would cost countless lives? What understanding of politics, what world view was at the root of these decisions? And above all, what made them so stubborn and persistent – reluctant to change course and finally incapable of stopping?

There were plenty of warnings. Opinion leaders in Congress such as Mike Mansfield, Richard Russell and J. William Fulbright spoke out in the early days against the war and in favour of a timely withdrawal. Allies such as Charles de Gaulle and neutral negotiators like the UN Secretary General U Thant repeated their points and called for a 'neutrality model' for Vietnam. Many openly sceptical or negative memoranda came from the CIA and other secret services. McGeorge Bundy, national security adviser to Kennedy and Johnson, commented in June 1965 on the demand for an increase in the number of troops with the words: 'My first reaction is that this program is rash to the point of folly.'[28] Edward Lansdale, who years before had successfully coordinated the campaign against the rebels in the Philippines, wrote in *Foreign Affairs* at the end of 1964 that revolutionary élan is always and everywhere superior to sheer firepower.[29] His military disciple in Vietnam, John Paul Vann, forecast the failure of an overstretched US Army: either the South Vietnamese wage their war themselves or 'We'd end up shooting at everything – men, women, kids, and the buffalos.'[30] Defense Secretary Robert McNamara also knew the price of the war: 'The VC/NVA [Viet Cong/North Vietnamese Army] apparently lose only about one-sixth as many weapons as people,' he stressed in a letter to Lyndon Johnson of November 1966, 'suggesting the possibility that many of the killed are unarmed porters or bystanders.'[31] Clark Clifford, who replaced McNamara as secretary of defense in 1968, said: 'I can't see anything but catastrophe for our nation in this area.'[32] The critics had their most reliable and sharp-tongued spokesman in Under Secretary of State George F. Ball. Ball had been branded as a Cassandra in Kennedy's day. Johnson had heard his remonstrations so often that he must have known them by heart: 'No one can assure you that we can beat the Viet Cong or even force them to the conference table on our terms no matter how many hundred thousand white foreign [US] troops we deploy. No one has demonstrated that a white ground force of whatever size can win a guerrilla war.'[33]

One could easily fill a book with these and similar statements. They boiled down to the same conclusion: from Harry Truman to Richard Nixon every president was faced with sustained criticism from within the inner circle of power, articulated by men whom they valued polit-ically and to whose judgement they attached great weight. The longer the war lasted, the louder were the objections and the more second- and third-rank sceptics joined in. Daniel Ellsberg even believes that at the end of 1967 there was a greater readiness for complete withdrawal among conservative officers than among the public. Be that as it may, the warnings were taken to heart. Every president conceded in his own way that any hopes for a short war were delusions, that the risk of failure in Vietnam was substantially greater than the prospects of success, and that the price threatened to exceed by far the returns – in foreign policy, in military terms and even more in domestic policy. In other words, the Communists or a coalition with Communist partic-ipation taking over the government was being delayed but could not eventually be prevented. Presidents Truman and Eisenhower foretold the failure of the French in their breakaway colony – and by the end were financing about eighty per cent of the French war chest. Kennedy compared his situation with that of an alcoholic: 'It's like a drink. After the initial input the effects wear off and you have to take another one.'[34] Nevertheless he gave 10,000 new military advisers their marching orders, thereby opening wide the door to sending in ground troops – anticipating a pattern of decision-making which was to become a trade-mark to Lyndon B. Johnson. Looking back, Nixon confirmed several times that he knew he should and could have ended the war at the beginning of 1969. His answer: 'We had to see it through.'[35]

The history of the American masters of war in Vietnam is therefore the history of men who persuaded themselves and their entourage in the teeth of all the evidence that they had the solution. They were politicians who did not fail to appreciate the obvious but lacked the will to draw the appropriate conclusions. The well-worn image of 'drifting into war' and of presidents who were ignorant, misinformed or deliberately misled must be corrected; equally so the image of a president who only takes the next step because he anticipates it resulting in an ultimate breakthrough. From Truman to Nixon, they had all sunk into a 'quagmire', but their decisions were not due to tragic misunderstandings nor based on a naïve tendency towards optimism and certainly not engineered by whispering intriguers around them. There is little sign of them wandering around in the 'fog of war', as McNamara retrospectively asserted.[36] Instead realism overlaid with gloomy expectations was the dominant feature. Ignorance, as Barbara Tuchman rightly assumed before the relevant archives were opened, was not an overriding factor. On the contrary, it is difficult to refute Ellsberg's thesis that events would still have taken the same course if even more pessimistic prognoses and even more unvarnished assessments of the situation had come into play. The alternatives were available, the decision-makers knew about them and could have spoken out in their favour with the support of a substantial part of the political elite. To understand the Vietnam War from the American point of view involves understanding why five presidents for twenty-five years based their agenda on one and the same mantra: 'We had to see it through.'[37]

The search for an explanation usually starts with the twin philosophies of the Cold War – the domino theory and the image of monolithic Communism. Because its edifice was deemed to be unshakably cohesive, it even seemed plausible to believe that the 'loss' of one strategic domino piece could trigger an unstoppable sequence of events which in the worst-case scenario would end in fighting for freedom on the coast of California. Since the Chinese Revolution in 1949 such scenarios – particularly the image of Asia on the brink of collapse – occupied the political imagination right across all camps and among both the elites and the general electorate. Since the late 1940s everyone knew what a furore the extreme right could unleash if they adopted the rhetoric of 'Vital Regions'. The debate at that time over the 'Loss of China' had not only brought Senator McCarthy to prominence but had also given every president a clear warning: anyone laying themselves open to the accusation of being 'soft' on the Communists ran the risk of losing the support of the conservative leadership in Congress and with it the majority required for the legislative process. Accordingly the political classes showed signs of being irritated and strangely insecure, as though they had to be prepared to be overrun by populist machinations at any time. It is hardly an exaggeration to talk of the

McCarthy right secretly dominating the political argument. At any rate we are dealing with a constant which left its stamp on the Cold War epoch in America.

The political decision-making in favour of a war of attrition in Vietnam will be discussed here as an expression of those changes which the political system of the United States had undergone in the aftermath of the Second World War. Since the appearance of Arthur Schlesinger's book *Imperial Presidency*, which became a catchphrase, the power of the executive has been critically examined. Some detect a shift of the political centre of gravity in favour of the military and secret service bureaucracies, others even talk of a 'dictatorship' of the national security elites. But above all it is the expansion, even the overstretching, of presidential authority which is discussed. With the National Security Act of 1947 the existing delicate balance in the power structure was shifted permanently in favour of the executive and to the detriment of the legislature and the judiciary. Of course this new adjustment in the rules governing the political framework is only one side of the problem; there is also the normative premise of the National Security Act – a perception of national security focusing solely on the military. This maxim is extended in the context of 'permanent preparedness'. The state of emergency is not regarded as the exception to the rule, but regulates politics. Against a background of totalitarian challenges this broad concept could be read as an unwritten constitutional amendment. Doing justice to the primacy of the military from now on defined the 'ethos of the executive' and the self-image of the occupant of the White House. To that extent the 'imperial presidency' goes hand in hand with the claim to be able or to have to put the usages of parliamentary control and political accountability out of action in the name of 'national security'. According to Schlesinger, protagonists adopting this logic tend to authorise themselves. An equally apt description would be self-immunisation against criticism: both imply damaging those mechanisms which in democratic constitutions are designed for self-correction.[38]

References to the domino theory, monolithic Communism, imperial presidency and 'managing the state of emergency' point to the heart of political decision-making over Vietnam. Truman believed it would have been political suicide to overlook Ho Chi Minh's contacts with Moscow and grant Hanoi's 1946 request for economic aid. As a lesser evil, according to State Secretary Dean Acheson, the United States let the French draw them into siding with them in a hopeless enterprise as quid pro quo for France's help against the Communist steamroller in Europe.[39] Kennedy also suspected the Republicans of wanting to instigate a new 'Loss of China' debate at any moment and to topple him by accusing him of appeasement, particularly after Nikita Khrushchev had described national wars of liberation as vehicles for the spreading of Communism and had pompously stated his support for these 'just wars'. Kennedy countered with the simple image of Vietnam as 'cornerstone of the free world in South-east Asia', 'the keystone of the arch' or alternatively, 'the finger in the dyke'.[40] Johnson as usual expressed himself forcefully: the loss of China and the rise of McCarthy were 'Chickenshit compared with what might happen if we lost Vietnam'.[41] Even Nixon was overtaken by the populist spirits which he himself had been courting in the 1950s. In the 1972 electoral campaign the spectre of McCarthy met him in the person of George Wallace, who applied McCarthy's words about 'peace with victory' in Korea to Vietnam and won one primary after another until an assassin's bullet chained him to a wheelchair. Not least because of this, what General Maxwell Taylor had preached to his predecessors was law to Nixon: 'If we leave Vietnam with our tail between our legs, the consequences of this defeat in the rest of Asia, Africa, and Latin America would be disastrous.'[42]

Finally and conclusively Vietnam also turned on the dilemmas of national security policy. Since Eisenhower's 'New Look' the United States had built up a military force that was unsuitable for warfare. Atomic weapons were political weapons in the sense of deterrence; if this political objective failed to work, annihilating the opponent was as guaranteed as was obliterating oneself. For this reason Kennedy and McNamara discarded the option of pre-emptive nuclear strikes – against serious opposition from some parts of the military elite. Even though he rejected their objections, Kennedy was in agreement with the military leadership on one point: if the strongest of all weapons were not to lead to disabling military strength, lesser means must be given a chance. Devaluing a 'major war' therefore involved evaluating 'minor wars' more highly. This explains the obsession with fighting insurgency and 'Special Forces' in the early 1960s. By mid May 1961 Kennedy's advisers had already put together the foregoing discussions in a National

Security Action Memorandum. Kennedy approved the submission, classified as NSAM No. 52, and instructed Defense Secretary McNamara to make significant increases in the capacity of the anti-guerrilla troops in both men and materials. In a public speech the president said:

We are opposed around the world by a monolithic and ruthless conspiracy that relies primarily on covert means for expanding its sphere of influence – on infiltration instead of invasion, on subversion instead of elections, on intimidation instead of free choice, on guerrillas by night instead of armies by day. It is a system which has conscripted vast human and material resources into the building of a tightly knit, highly efficient machine . . . We intent to profit from this lesson. We intend to re-examine and re-orient our forces of all kinds . . . We intend to intensify our efforts for a struggle in many ways more difficult than war.[43]

Thus Vietnam became a laboratory for the 'war of the future'. 'We have a problem,' said Kennedy, 'in trying to make our power credible, and Vietnam looks like the place.'[44] Vietnam became a place of symbolic self-assurance and a means of sending an unequivocal message to the atomic powers of the Soviet Union and the People's Republic of China: America was very good at respecting frontiers while opening up new opportunities for its armies.[45]

It is said that nonetheless Kennedy harboured doubts about Vietnam and wanted to withdraw the military advisers by the end of 1963. On the other hand he seems to have linked this option to the condition of a quick victory over the guerrillas.[46] How it would eventually have turned out, had Kennedy survived assassination, no one will ever know. His successor Johnson either could not or would not even consider anything of the kind. Far from questioning the purely military credo of national security, he acted as though driven on by the security elites: 'Just let me get elected and then you can have your war.'[47] We know that Johnson, like Nixon after him, managed to stand his ground over the years – although there was no light at the end of the tunnel; although he went behind Congress's back over and over again; and although he deceived the public over the size of the armed forces and the tasks they faced. Their terms of office give empirical proof of the theory of self-aggrandisement and the loss of checks and balances – not least in the light of those admissions which Robert Komer, the presidential envoy in charge of pacification programmes from 1966 to 1968, set down in writing on behalf of many of his colleagues, who did not act on their views: 'When the president of the United States says he wants you to do something, you just don't say no to him. When he says you're the one who's got to do this, the one he wants, you've got to do it, no matter how hopeless it is.'[48]

It is against this background that Barbara Tuchman detects a 'cognitive discord' and intellectual self-blockade. 'When objective evidence disproves strongly held beliefs, what occurs . . . is not rejection of the beliefs but rigidifying, accompanied by attempts to rationalize the disproof.'[49] It is debatable how far this observation is valid in general, but it does certainly apply to American policy in Vietnam. For in the end a further factor came into play, which worked like a catalyst on the inclination to act against one's better judgement: this is the motive for action to be found in the annals of all great powers – credibility.

Firstly, all American presidents since the Second World War slipped into the role of imperial or hegemonic wielders of power. In this capacity they defined 'credibility' as the most important psychological resource of power – keeping your word, not losing face and above all presenting yourself as someone who is unequivocally even-handed towards friend and foe alike. It follows that a world power could only survive if there was no suspicion of it hesitating to use the instruments at its disposal – political, economic, psychological or military. Credibility is therefore based on a simple but all-embracing premise: the tools of power become insignia of power only when they are accompanied by a constantly proven will to maintain and develop them. In this context, however, America's political classes cultivated a kind of inferiority complex. Countless debates reveal an underlying anxiety about not being taken seriously as a newcomer to the club of great powers. The sense was that America had not had enough opportunity to prove its credibility and therefore found itself faced with hostile scepticism on the part of the international community – particularly as the patent volatility it displayed after the First World War with the rejection of the League of Nations' Charter could be taken as proof of a deep-rooted tradition which would therefore be hard to change. Such an insecure self-image is wholly compatible with its familiar display of omnipotence: the two mutually determine and strengthen each other. On this soil a domino theory interwoven with panic thrives as copiously as does the temptation to feel compelled to refute the real or imaginary doubts of third parties at every possible opportunity. Thus Johnson saw the tragic death of his predecessor as sufficient grounds for the war in Vietnam. He had to demonstrate that America's resolve was not at all affected by the events in Dallas. 'The [Chinese will] think . . . we've lost heart. So they'll think we're yellow and we don't mean what we say. The fellas in the Kremlin . . . they'll be wondering just how far they can go . . . By God, I want them [American generals] to get off their butts and get out in those jungles and whip hell out of some Communists.'[50] Nixon argued along the same lines: 'We must regain the respect for our military or we will end up with a country and a world which is unsafe'.[51]

In this context Vietnam's geographical position was irrelevant – a territory with no raw materials worth mentioning, marginal as a market and geo-strategically unimportant. Nixon said: 'Vietnam was important not for itself but because of what it demonstrated in terms of support for our friends and allies and in terms of showing our will to our enemies.'[52] What mattered was the symbolism of action – to appear in Asia, as in the key region of Europe, with a determination which would send the same signal to friend and foe: that the United States stood by its obligations and, moreover, did not abandon anyone who found themselves in turmoil like South Vietnam. And that even in difficult times isolationism no longer presented a temptation. According to Nixon: 'We're not going to lose this war – "we", the United States . . . Under no circumstances can I, with all the things I believe, fail to use the total power of this office . . . to see that the United States does not lose. I put it quite bluntly. Now, I'm being quite precise. South Vietnam may lose, but the United States cannot lose.'[53]

Secondly, under Cold War conditions credibility thus defined acquired an exaggerated amount of significance. As Johnson put it: 'Because, [if you] show a little weakness, and if those sons of bitches [the Soviets] think you're weak, they're like a country dog – you stand still, they'll chew you to death, if you run, they'll eat your ass out.'[54] According to Barbara Tuchman, it occasionally even looked as though America was fighting simply and solely for its credibility. The American journalist and political adviser Leslie Gelb correctly stated that in the Cold War in general, and Vietnam in particular, there was no question of a military victory in the classical sense of conquering, securing and controlling new territory. It was more a question of a psychological war of attrition with the objective at best of exhausting the willpower and strength of the other side, at worst of harnessing it by incessantly wearing it down.[55] An invasion of North Vietnam was consequently never seriously debated. But at all events the North had to fail in the eyes of the whole world in its attempt to aggravate and win a guerrilla war in the South. The United States wanted its status as a power which guaranteed against subversion and insurgency to go down in history – in the form of an agreement on Vietnam in which the opposing side would sign a renunciation of political power. In this scenario credibility would lie with the one who, possessing more staying power and perseverance, drove the enemy to breaking-point. More precisely, the one who reached the point at which the enemy acknowledged the inadequacy of his military means and laid down his political weapons as well. To draw the short straw in the race for this tipping-point in a country like Vietnam would in the American perspective have turned upside down all the parameters of its policies as a world power. What could not be allowed to happen must not happen. 'I refuse to believe that a little fourth-rate power like North Vietnam does not have a breaking-point,' said Henry Kissinger in the summer of 1969.[56]

When Barbara Tuchman states that the struggle for credibility in the Cold War was blown up to the point of auto-hypnosis,[57] she puts her finger on a third characteristic of American policy in Vietnam: how a policy rooted in credibility robs itself of its options one by one and finally falls into a credibility trap of its own making. Since Truman, every president escalated the engagement in Vietnam and thus the pressure to reach the designated targets. The borderline between committing oneself and tying oneself down was crossed on the day when the word 'vital' was heard for the first time. This word fundamentally changed the standards by which policies were measured. Anyone investing symbolic capital and prestige to this extent must fulfil his promise at whatever price for the sake of his political reputation. He is condemned to succeed and from then on has 'to see it through' – including making decisions against his better judgement and ignoring the reality. In this context the much derided saying that Berlin was being defended in Saigon hits the nail on the head. As Leslie Gelb writes: 'Words were making Vietnam into a showcase – an Asian Berlin.'[58]

Accordingly the intellectual and political horizon started to narrow in the 1950s. Kennedy succumbed to it in his own way – hesitating, wrestling with himself and finally deluding himself that he could find an indirect escape route through escalation. His decisions in this regard have been amply set out and commented on. They range from raising the number of military advisers to 11,000, through secret commando operations in the North to attacks with defoliation agents and napalm. Most momentous of all was of course indirectly supporting the coup against the dictator Ngo Dinh Diem at the beginning of November 1963. With it Washington was not only taking sides in the power games of Saigon domestic politics: from now on maintaining American prestige also depended on the success or failure of a clique of feuding colonels. Ironing out their incompetence was only possible at the cost of intensified US involvement. Just because Kennedy had burned most of his bridges, his brother Robert and his advisers Theodore Sorensen and William Bundy voiced serious doubts about the possibility of de-escalation. The point is that the new rulers in Saigon knew that their partner had tied himself down and used blackmail in the way they played their cards until the ceasefire settlement was ratified in January 1973. 'In a dependent relationship,' remarked Barbara Tuchman, 'the protégé can always control the protector by threatening to collapse.'[59] The saying about the tail wagging the dog could also apply here.

In Johnson's and Nixon's day the credibility trap finally snapped shut. The monotonous rhetoric of those years proclaims it: withdrawal stands for defeat, defeat for humiliation, humiliation for national catastrophe and therefore for the end of America as a world power. The political vocabulary was reduced to a fund of carefully graded semantics and sounded like a cracked gramophone record: 'Vietnam: 70% – To avoid a humiliating U.S. defeat,' said Deputy Defense Secretary John McNaughton in March 1965.[60] 'America wins the wars it started. Always keep that in mind,' exhorted Johnson in 1967.[61] 'What was at stake now,' argued Nixon in the autumn of 1969, 'is . . . the survival of the U.S. as a world power . . . If we were defeated in Vietnam, the U.S. people would never stand firm elsewhere.'[62] 'The manner in which we end the war . . . is crucial both for America's global position and for the fabric of our society,' argued Henry Kissinger in the autumn of 1967 and on countless other occasions.[63]

The longer the war lasted and the gloomier the prospects of success, the more strongly did a fourth dimension enter the 'politics of credibility': the personal credibility of the masters of war in the White House. Johnson and Nixon repeatedly made it clear that on no account did they want to be the first president to lose a war – and indeed in such a way as to imply that they placed their own standing on a level with the aura of the United States as a world power. Undoubtedly idiosyncrasies played an important part in this – the combination of personal characteristics, preferences and inclinations. Simultaneously, beyond these individual features an experience common to all protagonists seems to have entered into the equation: the world view of the 'GI generation', which had experienced the Second World War as America's 'finest hour' and wanted to continue the success story of those years as part of a grand patriotic narrative. Not to take up this challenge meant renouncing the responsibilities of their office – all the less excusably when the 'imperial presidency' had put into their hands historically unprecedented means and opportunities. Here lies the nucleus of the much-quoted 'victory culture' or the show of manliness and toughness typical of the 1960s. It basically implies a heroic understanding of politics and the assumption that the future of their country depended on two things: on the periodic assertion of the will to stand firm in crises and wars, and on the politicians who through charismatic leadership in exceptional situations give this will its profile. In other words: in and with Vietnam American presidents also conducted their personal cold war.[64]

For Nixon the Vietnam War was the real touchstone of his personal work and life. Kennedy and Johnson had failed over Vietnam; he, the outsider from rural California, would give the country back its pride and dignity and earn in real life both the 'Profile in Courage' which JFK had only pontificated about in books and immortal renown as a president 'of character and steel'.[65] The atmosphere in the White House in the late 1960s and early 1970s has been passed down to posterity on thousands of tape recordings. They show Nixon regularly working himself up into a virtually uncontrollable state of hysteria, roaring, banging on the table, cursing and swearing and conjuring up imaginary maps of bombing targets. 'Just, just, just cream the fuckers.'[66] – 'Don't worry, we're not gonna go out whimpering. We're gonna blast the goddamn hell out of them.'[67] Doubts and uncertainty are banished with ritual incantations: 'To hell with it! We're gonna win. We've got to. *I've got to*. We've got some cards to play . . . and we're gonna play 'em as tough as hell.'[68] He regarded himself as harder than anyone before him had dared to be and was carried along by the certainty that he could fulfil the longing for strength and the wish for victory of the silent majority. 'I'm the one man in this country who can do it, Bob,' he said to his adviser Harry Robbins 'Bob' Haldeman.[69]

Nixon had a name for this investment of 'personal capital'. 'I call it the Madman Theory, Bob,' he told Haldeman, explaining in depth how one could make political capital by insinuating that one was mad. 'I want the North Vietnamese to believe I've reached the point where I might do anything to stop the war. We'll just slip the word to them that, "for God's sake, you know Nixon is obsessed about Communism. We can't restrain him when he's angry – and he has his hand on the nuclear button" – and Ho Chi Minh himself will be in Paris in two days begging for peace.'[70] Again and again Nixon explained how one could play politics with irrationality. In his eyes it offered an escape route from the political dilemma of the atomic age: any state which refused to create a threatening façade in the pursuit of its own interests for fear of atomic self-annihilation, condemned itself in the long term to political impotence. It would only be capable of action if third parties could at no point be sure of it acting in a restrained or rational manner. Anyone with a reputation for losing all sense of proportion and running excessive risks at moments of doubt would be taken seriously. In other words: he no longer scares himself but returns to the essence of politics – deterring other people. With anecdotes from the Korean War Nixon illustrated how the fear of unpredictability and irrational decisions do actually pay off. Eisenhower had been able to force a ceasefire just by threatening that otherwise he would attack the North with atomic weapons. Whether this was true or – more probably – an invention, does not matter in this context. The crucial factor is the self-image of a president who tries to make political capital out of a cult of madness and believes he has a mission to remind a society which had forgotten about the nature of power of the usefulness of this strategy.[71]

It was with Nixon at the latest that the consequences of a policy rooted in demonstrating credibility became clear: falling into the trap of being unable to stop. Nixon knew that the chances of a solution satisfactory to him were diminishing day by day. He only won the 1968 election by promising a speedy withdrawal of ground troops, and at

the Paris negotiations in the autumn of 1970 he had to accept the
North Vietnamese troops remaining in the South as a basis for a truce.
This negated the principle of both sides withdrawing their troops,
which for years had been non-negotiable. It was an illusion that the
South Vietnamese Army would nevertheless be able to hold their positions. Less than half of their 16,000 crack troops had returned from
the incursion into Laos between December 1970 and March 1971 –
which was regarded as a 'test of toughness'. But by means of his
'madman' policy Nixon was determined to give the Saigon government
a 'decent interval' through a bombing campaign. Even if its downfall
was inevitable, it should not happen immediately after the withdrawal
of all US troops, but at the earliest after the election in November 1972
and best of all after the end of Nixon's second term of office in January
1977. Only by drawing out the war for years could the impression be
avoided that the United States had abandoned an ally and was principally responsible for its downfall. And only in this way could the
personal prestige of the president as a skilful crisis manager and a
great master of war be ostensibly ensured.[72]

The civilians in North Vietnam paid the price. They were the
sufferers in a war which was waged solely in the air after the withdrawal
of the ground troops. To inflict painful wounds on the unbeatable
enemy and to extort from him the highest possible price for his delayed
triumph was Nixon's strategy, documented on tape in 1971 and 1972.
'We're gonna take out the dikes, we're gonna take out the power
plants, we're gonna take out Haiphong,' exclaimed Nixon on 2 June
1971, drumming on the table with his fists.[73] 'We're gonna level that
goddamn country . . . It's no idle threat . . . Right now there's not a
goddamn thing to lose. Nothin' to lose . . . We're gonna hit 'em, bomb
the livin' bejesus out of 'em.'[74] This was music in Kissinger's ears. 'Mr
President, I will enthusiastically support that, and I think it's the right
thing to do.'[75] This major air attack against industrial centres and military infrastructure in the North was named Operation Linebacker and
began on 8 May 1972. It is hard to assess the extent of the destruction.
In any case, as it lasted over six months and expended a bomb load
of 155,000 tons, it was the most massive attack in the history of aerial
warfare. After 14 December 1972 the hour of the 'madman' struck
again, because Nixon wanted to demonstrate to the Saigon government
the credibility of the American guarantees of help after the withdrawal

of American ground troops. In the course of Operation Linebacker II, better known as the 'Christmas Bombardment', about 3,500 sorties were flown with the explicit intention of demoralising the civilian population in Hanoi and Haiphong. Only twelve per cent of the attacks hit military targets. Thanks to the mass evacuation in the spring of 1972 after Linebacker I, only 2,200 died and 1,600 people were wounded in Hanoi.[76]

2

Generals

> We were going to a foreign country where our only superiority
> was our weaponry . . . The other side had absolute political
> superiority, which allowed them to keep coming and to keep
> recruiting. Essentially, we were fighting the birthrate of a nation.
>   David Halberstam[1]

Richard Nixon's terror bombing reflects the military strategy
employed throughout in Vietnam. One could even call it 'tonnage
ideology' – therefore the idea that optimum success and maximum
use of firepower were one and the same thing. 'The solution in
Vietnam is more bombs, more shells, more napalm . . . till the other
side cracks and gives up . . . We are going to stomp them to death.'[2]
Similar statements – in this case by William DePuy, Head of Operations for the US forces in Vietnam – are legion. They can be regarded
as consistently continuing and carrying to excess that 'strategy of
attrition' which had been popular with the American military since
the War of Independence. It would also be justifiable to talk about
loss of 'institutional memory', since the experiences gained in various
guerrilla wars, from the French and Indian War in the mid eighteenth
century to the fighting against insurgents in Latin America in the
1930s, seemed to have been obliterated without trace. At any rate, a
principle of total warfare – 'shock and awe' – was transferred to the
scene of a minor war, the intention being to force an adversary to

his knees through a combination of unpredictable action and un-expected means of destruction.[3]

The strategy of attrition practised in Vietnam became known as 'search and destroy'. At first glance this is hardly a surprising descrip-tion, as that is precisely what is expected of armed forces everywhere and at all times: to seek out the enemy and annihilate him. As already shown, in asymmetrical wars this includes destroying the enemy's escape routes and militarily useful infrastructure – eliminating his supply depots, destroying the harvest and resettling large sections of the population. The American war-planners reacted to the special circumstances in Vietnam by extending this in a specific way; because for political reasons US ground troops could not march into North Vietnam, the objective was to lure as many North Vietnamese soldiers as possible to the South and to annihilate them there, until the comrades-in-arms of the guerrillas were bled dry. Unlike earlier wars of attrition, it was not a question of conquering, defending and holding strategically important territory. Instead the model of the 'vacuum trap' was adopted: an area was occupied, cleared out, occupied once more and again cleared out by one's own troops, over and over again and always in the hope that the enemy would follow up with fresh troops which would fall under massive fire from American units. Since mid 1966 more than ninety per cent of the battalions equipped for action were used in search-and-destroy attacks. In principle, repeatedly combing through the same territory, luring, striking and immediately retiring were copied from the Viet Cong's own hit-and-run tactics. In the Pentagon they used the even better metaphor of the meat grinder. 'We'll just go on bleeding them,' said William Westmoreland, supreme commander in Vietnam from 1965 to early 1968, 'until Hanoi wakes up to the fact that they have bled their country to the point of national disaster for generations. Then they will have to reassess their position.'[4] In the words of David Halberstam, quoted above, 'search and destroy' was directed against a nation's birth rate.

As a result the number of enemy dead became the main yardstick of military success. Gaining territory, establishing strategically import-ant strongholds or inhabited areas, the value of materials seized or the number of prisoners taken were of no interest. What mattered was the body count. In 1967 the leadership still believed they would imminently reach the cross-over point, when North Vietnam would no longer be in a position to match its losses with newly recruited soldiers. Whatever expectations went into these calculations, in the light of cost alone they were unrealistic. According to an internal assessment, the United States had to spend $185,000 just to kill one single guerrilla.[5] To reach the cross-over point would have presumed the killing of 250,000 Vietnamese warriors every year and for this purpose at least to double the number of US troops stationed in Indochina – that is, to a total of one million. Nevertheless the war of attrition was not abandoned. On the contrary, its architects ordered even more materiel and even more fire-power to be brought in. Sometimes they sent out groups of soldiers as bait to provoke attacks, which were immediately countered with high-calibre deployment of fighter-planes and artillery. Sometimes they massively increased the pressure on each individual unit to improve its 'killing quota' – thereby implicitly accepting that those who became their victims in the south of the country were precisely those whom they had come to protect: the peasants in the densely populated regions between the demarcation line on the 17th Parallel and the Mekong Delta.[6]

MILITARY DECISION-MAKING

The alternative to 'pumping out blood' was already discussed at the beginning of the war. It was based on the consideration that the strong side in an asymmetrical scenario cannot compensate for its weaknesses through the use of superior military technology. This in no way implied renouncing military intervention. The essential condition was to contain the guerrillas and publicly prove the hopelessness of their situation. A decisive factor was of course self-restraint in the choice of weaponry. Anyone who declared the peasants' environment a battle zone, they argued, had forfeited from the outset his prospects of success. Instead, a catalogue of 'civic action' measures was proposed: economic aid, development of material and social infrastructure and not least land reform, which would offer the exploited peasants long-term prospects and immunise them against the promises of the social revolutionaries. Whatever was proposed in detail, it narrowed down to a radical re-definition of military duties. American soldiers in Vietnam had to be at the same time development workers in uniform

– 'pacification workers', living among the local population and participating in the implementation of reform projects – as well as performing their duties as defenders. Above all, however, one thing was required: readiness to abandon an offensive strategy aimed at short-term success in favour of the defensive strategy of taking a long view – investing in time and giving oneself plenty of time.

Arguments along these lines took place between members of the State Department, the Agency for International Development and the CIA, together with leading generals of the Marine Corps like Victor Krulak, Wallace Greene Jr. and Lewis W. Walt and the long-serving commander of the Marines, Admiral Ulysses S. Grant Sharp. It is open to debate whether the leadership team of the Marines could therefore be described, in the words of Neil Sheehan, the *New York Times* Vietnam correspondent, as a 'school for pacification strategy', especially in the light of Sharp's passionate advocacy of a widespread bombing campaign against North Vietnam. What is certain, however, is that they were concerned with putting their ideas into practice in the shape of the Combined Action Platoons (CAPs), which were first set up in August 1965, intended as a model of 'pacification units'. A CAP consisted on average of fifty-three men, one-third Marines and two-thirds soldiers from the so-called 'Popular Forces', or locally recruited units. They were stationed for a lengthy period in a village, where their day-to-day duties of supporting the inhabitants were combined with spying out enemy posts and installing extensive 'security perimeters', in order to curtail the radius of enemy operations – in short, to keep the 'fish' (guerrillas) away from their 'water' (social environment). Moreover, the CAPs were to send a symbolic signal to the South Vietnamese comrades, who were trained by the Americans but not under their command in their joint operations, and also to the rural population, which could thereby count on the US Marines actually risking their lives for them.[7]

All kinds of criticisms can be levelled against the model of the CAPs: that they took the experiences of the successful counter-insurgency operations in the Philippines in the 1950s as a yardstick without considering the completely different circumstances in Vietnam, and also that in this case they clung to the much-scorned idea that one could direct social processes from above and counter the strength of indigenous nationalism with Western concepts of modernisation. Or that they wanted to swim 'like fish in water' themselves, so conveying that they were naïvely copying Communist strategies. In this present context, however, there are other matters of significance: firstly, that the unsuitability of the attrition strategy was discussed and secondly, that the relevant criticism of the theory and practice of search and destroy was not imposed on the political and military elites from without; it came from the inner circle of decision-makers and was voiced by people who were not against the Vietnam War in principle, but wanted to conduct it in fundamentally different ways. From this point of view the inherent weaknesses of the counter-proposal are of secondary importance; what is decisive is how the objections were dealt with.

The administrative and political resistance could hardly have been more forceful. We have a record of an instruction issued to his staff by George S. Patton III, the commanding general of the 11th Armored Cavalry Regiment, 'that a ratio of ten per cent pacification and ninety per cent killing was just about right'.[8] In this he was reflecting the views of most of the officers stationed in Vietnam. Others chose still more drastic terms, even when addressing their superiors: 'I'll be damned if I permit the United States Army, its institutions, its doctrine, and its traditions to be destroyed just to win this lousy war.'[9] A factual basis was not important to the critics of pacification and accordingly there was no question of discussion, but rather a barrage of emotionally charged verdicts. Presumably behind them lurked a sense of the politically explosive force of the subject. Taking the alternative seriously would in fact have meant convincing the Saigon government to adopt a process of economic reform and also demanding the overhaul of an inefficient, if not actually corrupt, South Vietnamese Army. Institutional considerations may also have played a part – for example, the idea of training soldiers to exercise a high degree of autonomy in order to perform their duties, which would make it difficult to incorporate them into the traditional hierarchical structure. General Westmoreland was not at all prepared to go that far. He applied purely operative reasons and in so doing gave his officers a clear message: anyone supporting the Combined Action Platoons was obstructing the delivery of a rapid victory with little outlay and need no longer contemplate a career in the American armed forces.[10]

Policies of combating rebellion, pacification and counter-insurgency were dead in the water before they had even begun. By the end of 1967 seventy-nine CAPs had been set up under the command of I

Corps, at least 4,000 men strong and operating between the provinces of Quang Tri and Quang Ngai in an area which, with 17,000 guerrillas and 34,000 North Vietnamese soldiers, ranked among the enemy strongholds. At the climax of the war there was a maximum of two per cent American Marines serving in the CAPs.[11] But it was not just the numbers ratio which militated against their successfully mastering their duties; instead of elite troops, only those for whom the Marines had no other use were assigned to the CAPs. 'We were hardly the combat-tested ambassadors-in-green described in books and official accounts,' commented one of the participants. 'I believe we never could have found sufficient numbers of Marines with the intelligence, sensitivity, and tolerance to make Combined Action work on a large scale.'[12] A look at the war chest confirms this finding. In the budget year 1968 fourteen billion US dollars were expended on operations within the framework of the war of attrition; 850 million dollars were earmarked for civil aid projects including the pacification programmes. On the other hand, the consequences of this policy were converted into an argument against the CAPs – that is, that the losses of these poorly trained and inadequately manned units were well in excess of the average of the rest of the Marine Corps.[13]

The concept of pacification did indeed continue to belong in the political vocabulary of the time but it was a dishonest misnomer. When Lyndon Johnson appointed Robert Komer as Special Assistant for Pacification in summer 1966 and a few months later handed over to him the management of a new department called Civil Operations and Revolutionary Development Support (CORDS), he had decided on a man who principally defined his remit from a military viewpoint: 'We are grinding the enemy down by sheer weight and mass.'[14] In Operation Phoenix Komer demonstrated that these and other similar remarks were not empty words. Phoenix was rightly regarded as the most graphic example of how the model of pacification had rid itself of its political and social foundations and turned into a policy characterised by repression, torture and murder.

The Phoenix programme in particular illustrates one important cause of the militarily blinkered outlook of the elites charged with decision-making. To them insurgency movements were principally conspiracies by a radical minority on the borderline between politics and criminality rather than representative of a national or social idea.

One could even call it a variation on the concept of 'monolithic Communism'. 'The VCI [Viet Cong Infrastructure],' so ran a memorandum from the American Supreme Command in Vietnam at the end of December 1969, '. . . might be better understood as the secret, war-making and supporting Mafia in South Vietnamese society.'[15] Decapitating this 'mafia' – estimated at 75,000 men – had been one of the tasks of various 'Counter Terror Teams' of the South Vietnamese Army and Secret Police since the early 1960s. Directed by members of the CIA, about 3,500 men were divided into small groups and tore through villages like death squads, arresting, abducting and murdering Viet Cong civilian functionaries – or rather, anyone they thought might be one. Their motto was: 'Recruit them; if you can't recruit them, defect them . . .; if you can't defect them, capture them; if you can't capture them, kill them.'[16] It did indeed immediately become clear that these raids had nothing whatever to do with fighting the Viet Cong. The attacks were not usually directed against groups or people identified by name; by far the majority of the suspects – at an estimate, over eighty per cent – were captured for ransom and released again within six months. Apart from spreading fear and terror and enriching several brigands in the ranks of the South Vietnamese provincial potentates, Phoenix had been pointless, but nevertheless the American military and secret services let 'anti-terrorism' have its head. When it did not succeed in putting the 'mafia' behind bars, it clung to the hope of at least being able to extort militarily relevant information from those it had captured.[17] Just because of this, the Phoenix programme was stepped up in 1968. From 1 July of that year it was formally handed over to the South Vietnamese Government and William Colby of the CIA and Robert Komer of CORDS, following a directive from the White House, pressed for a monthly 'neutralisation' of 3,000 members of the Viet Cong infrastructure and an intensification of reliance on US Army advisers and operational personnel.[18]

We still know comparatively little about the training and day-to-day work of the American anti-terrorism experts because the available sources cannot be adequately checked for reliability. One report comes from Lieutenant Francis Reitemeyer, who had undergone several months of training at the US Army Intelligence School in Fort Holabird, Maryland in 1968, and as a result of his experiences there applied to resign his commission. In the course of the legal dispute, Reitemeyer's lawyer gave a civil court in Maryland a comprehensive account of his client's position. Apparently Reitemeyer was put in charge of eight Chinese mercenaries. In order to achieve the monthly 'kill quota' of fifty Viet Cong or their sympathisers, he was apparently urged by his instructors to use any form of torture whatever and instructed with examples from Vietnam. The stories told of prisoners beheaded after interrogation, of corpses whose limbs had been severed and eyes put out in order to intimidate others and of suspects blown out of a waterway with hand grenades. According to Reitemeyer, one of his superiors said, 'It was actually a lot of fun, to watch the bodies of the Cong soldiers fly into the air like fish.'[19]

As has been said, the reliability of this report cannot be vouched for, but Reitemeyer's was not the only one. Reconnaissance officers stationed in Vietnam in 1968 described their experiences in similarly dramatic terms: 'We had no way of determining the background of these sources, nor their motivation for providing American units with information . . . Our paid sources could easily have been either provocateurs or opportunists with a score to settle . . . In effect, a huge dragnet was cast out in our area of operations and whatever looked good in the catch, regardless of evidence, was classified as VCI.'[20] But that was not the end of the arbitrary acts of terror. In many cases information extorted in this way was passed on to military command posts, where it was incorporated into the planning of operations by artillery units and Air Force fighter squadrons. 'I could submit a report to the First Marine Division and within an hour get a B-52 strike destroying an entire grid square [one square kilometre] on a map, and we did that.'[21] Using B-52 bombers against suspected hideouts of Viet Cong functionaries – this too was the result of politically-driven pressure to win the war of attrition as quickly as possible. No one knows whether Phoenix is therefore also responsible for dozens of My Lais, as the historian Douglas Valentine maintains. In any case there are grounds for assuming that the total given of those killed as a result of Phoenix, which varies between 20,000 and 40,000, is far too conservative an estimate.[22]

'In single-mindedly attempting to achieve the destruction of the VC/NVA forces . . . ,' according to a Strategic Objectives Plan of the US Supreme Command in early 1969, 'we have failed to do what was urgently required: steadily provide genuine security to increasingly large numbers of people.'[23] This and a quantity of other memoranda leave no doubt that the military leadership was aware that a war was being waged against the civilian population which as a result would lead to political defeat. Their reluctance or inability to change course seems therefore all the more puzzling. Why were the critics on a hiding to nothing from the start? How is it that the initiatives for political pacification never got beyond their paltry beginnings? And why was there no serious debate about exit options – about terms and conditions for a timely and orderly withdrawal? What were the origins of the American military machine's inability to move and its doctrinaire and operational inflexibility?[24]

From the debate on this question, which has been conducted since the early 1970s, three aspects emerge, worth noting for their own sakes and especially because of the dynamics of their interaction. There is the indication that past successes can become detrimental to preparedness for future innovation. Then the massive mobilisation during the Cold War seems to have resulted in unexpected collateral damage at home, in that it actually plunged the Army – that traditional nucleus of the armed forces – into crisis. And thirdly one must ask whether responsibility for a good part of the malaise does not lie with the political leadership – or more precisely, with four administrations which had fallen into their own traps and so were no longer in a position as civilians to control or correct the military.

If there is one constant in the history of modern armies, or indeed of all armies at any time, it is this: the planning of future wars is based on battle strategies from the past, particularly when experience with them has been good. And there is no alternative to the maxim of bringing an engagement to an end as swiftly as possible and with minimum losses on one's own side. Perhaps the obsession with firepower and attrition is by tradition particularly marked in the American forces; at any rate, the way in which the First World War was discussed internally in the 1920s and 1930s leads one to this conclusion: democracies, it was said at that time, do not tolerate long wars, the readiness for sacrifice is quickly exhausted and can only be resuscitated once war arrives on one's own doorstep – a scenario which of course the United States had been spared. In other words, if you spend the sparse resource of time recklessly, you defeat yourself. After the Second World War this lesson turned into a doctrinaire traditionalism and Andrew

Krepinevich, like other military historians, speaks of an 'iron concept', set in stone like the Ten Commandments.[25]

'We cannot lose.' Behind this mantra from the 1950s and 1960s lies a conviction of the unfailing effect and universal practicability of the strategy of attrition practised in the Second World War. Neil Sheehan and Loren Baritz speak of the 'disease of victory', meaning an arrogance on or beyond the edge of self-delusion and nurtured by power and success.[26] Barbara Tuchman was reminded of an 'illusion of omnipotence, cousin to the Popes' illusion of invulnerability.'[27] Whatever one may think of the fascination with technological superiority – which undoubtedly exists – and the knowledge of absolutely inexhaustible wealth, success and power, these have always been bad counsellors for rethinking military strategy outside the customary parameters. That even a negligibly armed enemy, confined to the ground and operating without an air force, may be successful, was deemed a passing pinprick and answered with the customary: 'More of the same'. A colonel in the Americal Division outlined the prevailing attitude in Vietnam like this: 'You fight as you were taught in World War II and Korea; you fight the enemy offensively, using all support weapons available to you and using them properly.'[28] The ideas on 'small wars', formulated in the 1960s by the civilian bosses in the Pentagon under Robert McNamara, were not suited to opening up this limited horizon. On the contrary, McNamara's insistence on the body count, together with the concept of a mathematically calculable breaking-point of the enemy, presented the usual delusion of feasibility in the unusual form of business management statistics.

The institutional crisis in the US Army consolidated the dogma of a war of attrition in its own way. We are still far from seeing a satisfactory inventory of this crisis, but Dennis Showalter gives us its starting-point and most important characteristics: 'The American Army . . . since its modern birth in 1940 had been operating under emergency conditions, with its institutional clock set at five minutes to midnight.'[29] One of the most astonishing achievements in military history is how the skeleton force which existed at the beginning of the Second World War was fit for war within a few months, and by 1943 even able to go into action on two fronts. Ironically, its greatest success led the Army once again into stormy weather, for the triumph in 1945 fell to what was its bitterest rival in the wrangle over financial resources: the Air

Force was the symbol of nuclear supremacy and Eisenhower's future strategy – strikingly named the 'New Look' – was tailored to its wishes and needs. The Army was not starving as a result, but it came second in the pecking order for allocation of materiel. If deterrence were to fail and it came to 'massive retaliation', long-range bombers and intercontinental missiles were the guarantors of survival. In an emergency the Army was little more than the clean-up squad at the bottom of the heap, and moreover, once Kennedy was in the White House, there was even anxiety about using it in 'small wars'. The upgrading of the Special Forces and other specialist units for counter-insurgency was received by many people within the Army as a declaration of war. As a result its prestige as an institution and the self-image of its members were at stake.

Also, and in this precise context, the 'institutional clock' was set at five to twelve, as Dennis Showalter puts it. In principle it is possible for such pressure to become the pretext for a general systematic shake-up. Yet the US Army paid tribute to its traditionalism, declaring that revitalising the old system was the way out of its legitimacy crisis. This does not mean that it became the driving force behind the decision to go to war, but it certainly used for its purposes the famous Kennedy saying: 'Vietnam is the place.' It was the place to prove that a strategy based on maximum fire-power was indispensable even in small wars – particularly when a regular army was sitting immediately behind the demarcation line of the 17th Parallel, supposedly waiting for the order to launch a major conventional attack on the South. Vietnam was the place where the Army would not be subjected to wrangling with the Air Force about institutional responsibilities and prerogatives, for even the latter had an interest in testing its new technology, particularly the fighter-jets developed for a 'major war', which flew over ninety per cent of all sorties in South-East Asia. And Vietnam was the place to give a generation of conventionally trained officers the opportunity of proving themselves and eventually gaining promotion. From their ranks came the massive resistance to an alternative pacification strategy; they tended to reprimand commanders who questioned the dogma of a war of attrition. Rarely did individual ambition and the prospect of an institutional comeback coincide so closely and together they neutralised all the experiences gathered in the operational field about the ineffectiveness of fire-power and attrition.[30]

As a consequence, the impetus to correct doctrinaire traditionalism would have had to come from the political leadership. There was no lack of the necessary insight, but every administration retorted by pointing to the political calendar: there was too little time for experimentation. And anyone – such as supporters of the pacification strategy – suggesting any time-consuming course of action was dismissed out of hand. This happened to the head of the Marine Corps when he argued with Robert McNamara and to countless others. The defense secretary only needed two words to nip every discussion in the bud: 'Too slow.'[31] This verdict is not surprising; in the Cold War time counted as symbolic capital and a precariously sparse resource. Permanently in place for large-scale events, the confrontation of the two major blocs was particularly intolerant of any impression of indecisiveness on a small scale. The aura of any strong power would have been lastingly damaged if it let itself be drawn into years of unresolved struggle with a weak one; and anyone who, like the American political classes, was reckoning on a number of small wars in the future, was wise not to try the patience of its public too far. In McNamara's words, 'The greatest contribution Vietnam is making . . . is developing an ability in the United States to fight a limited war, to go to war without arousing the public ire . . . because this is the kind of war we'll likely be facing for the next fifty years.'[32]

The story of wartime presidents can therefore be told as a hopeless race against time. On the one side they left no stone unturned in their attempts to gain time. They did this through constantly reiterating electoral promises not to escalate the war any further or to end it in short order, or through temporarily calming the home front by making concessions to their principal middle-classes supporters – as for instance Johnson's refusal to call up the Reserves, his stubborn insistence on only a one-year term of service for those sent to Vietnam and not least the decision to favour students with a generous exemption from military service. However, time so gained was immediately squandered, for in the light of *realpolitik* the electoral promises quickly turned out to be deception, lies and betrayal – in Johnson's case in spring 1965, when he sent the first ground troops to Vietnam a few months after being elected; in Nixon's case when he extended the bombing campaign to include Cambodia only weeks after moving into the White House. But lies make for political vulnerability. Even if they bring no scandal in their wake, they gnaw away secretly at confidence in the watertight quality of the adopted course and therefore lead to forcing the timetable on the basis of a premature decision. Just because time seemed to be running away from them, the presidents regularly involved themselves in changing military strategy. Johnson did so because he believed he could reach his goal more swiftly through a phased escalation of the bombing campaign in the North, and Nixon because he wanted to reach the same goal by means of random terror bombing. The masters of war in the White House did many things which annoyed the military, who were protective of their autonomy. Only one thing did they refrain from: a veto against the attrition strategy. Obviously the hope of repeating past triumphs was stronger than all the current evidence.[33]

The most apt definition of the reluctance to change course in Vietnam came from political scientists Leslie Gelb and Richard K. Betts: 'The system worked.' Faulty perceptions and their cumulative impetus were less the problem than was the interplay of historical experiences, hegemonic self-images, personal idiosyncrasies and bureaucratic interests. The Vietnam policy was defined not by deviation from the norm, but by keeping to well-rehearsed rules in a situation which they had no experience in mastering. Defined by the poles of credibility on the political side and attrition on the military side, a programme could be maintained which in one way was designed as a war of long duration and in another resistant to any consideration of exit options.[34]

IN THE LINE OF FIRE: CIVILIANS IN THE WAR OF ATTRITION

The war in Vietnam had its own peculiar features at different times and in different places. Events in the Central Highlands were different from those in the Mekong Delta; the fighting in the provinces south of the 17th Parallel between Quang Tri and Quang Ngai raged more fiercely than in the middle of the country between Kontum and Lam Dong; after January 1968 the towns were also more affected, while parallel with the house-to-house fighting, the number of battles in open country increased. Soldiers' experience of the warfare differed according to their type of weaponry or where they were posted. Many belonged to units which just patrolled endlessly without making contact with the enemy, while others were under fire for weeks or months on end, and the large majority of the troops – members of supply, administration and logistics teams – were never anywhere near the 'shooting war'. It was the same for the Vietnamese. Whether a peasant's fields lay in I Corps Tactical Zone or III Corps Tactical Zone often made a vital difference. In the former he was incessantly exposed to American air and infantry attacks and to harassment by the Viet Cong, while in the latter he would at least periodically enjoy a more peaceful life. If in the Central Highlands there were still withdrawal areas, in the 'Iron Triangle' northwest of Saigon and beyond the Cambodian frontier there was nothing of the kind, in view of almost ceaseless aerial warfare.

In spite of and aside from such variations, this war had its own trademark – a constant radicalisation of violence and above all the spread of the battle zones to include civilians. In the next chapters the necessary details will be given; at this point we are looking at a typology of overstepping limits – for instance, of the 'overkill' in attacks and the 'political cleansing' of rural settlements. The price in both cases was predominantly paid by non-combatants.

'When you must use these tactics, I know we are losing the war.' With these words from a South Vietnamese confidant the American diplomat Charles Sweet concluded an angry letter to Ambassador Ellsworth Bunker.[35] The cause of his grievance was a major attack by 3rd Brigade of 9th Infantry Division, which was operating in conjunction with South Vietnamese soldiers of 5th Ranger Group in the neighbourhood of Saigon in May 1968. South of the Kinh Doi canal and in the area around Phu Tho Hoa they were engaged in blocking off a 3,000-strong force of Viet Cong and the North Vietnamese Army from access to the eastern outskirts of Saigon. When after six days the fighting had died down, more than 10,000 houses in an area of 470,000 square metres lay in ruins, 500 civilians had lost their lives and thousands had been badly wounded. An inquiry initiated by the US Supreme Command on account of Sweet's complaint confirmed that the inhabitants of Phu Tho Hoa had good reason to be resentful. The devastation was mostly wreaked by American troops who had deployed excessive firepower and had also given the teams of helicopter gunships a free hand. 'Ground commanders,' it continued, 'appear to consider gunships in the same light as their organic weapons and control procedures tend to become excessively informal . . . it appears that a tendency to permit over-kill prevailed.'[36]

Reports of uncontrolled or 'unobserved fire' are part of the regular repertoire of the Vietnam forces, from ordinary soldiers to four-star generals. 'In the Delta, the villages were very small, like a mound in a swamp,' explained an Air Force captain. 'There were no names for some of them . . . the U.S. Air Force had spotters looking for muzzle flashes, and if that flash came from that dot, they'd wipe out the village. It was that simple.'[37] At the end of 1965 the *New York Times* reporter Neil Sheehan had already reported artillery attacks on five fishing villages, in the course of which about 600 civilians were killed.[38] Obviously a practice already in use in the Korean War became a habit in Vietnam: 'close air support' meant calling up air and artillery support on the slightest pretext and even responding to sniper fire with attacks by fighter-bombers. There are also cases on record in which commanders just pretended to detect enemy movement and then made sure that whole villages were destroyed from the air.[39] 'That's our Search and Destroy. If there wasn't an enemy out there, we made it be the enemy'[40] – whether out of revenge, frustration or pure greed for battle statistics to help one's reputation. Whatever the pretext may have been, in view of the quantity of individual stories and official Army dossiers it does not seem exaggerated to speak of a confirmed pattern of warfare on the part of the Americans in all theatres in Vietnam.[41]

Ground-based weapons made their contribution to the overkill in the form of 'reconnaissance by fire', 'harassment-and-interdiction fire' and 'pre-assault strikes'. In every case it was a matter of forcing an invisible enemy out of hiding with blanket fire, of keeping the Viet Cong on the move or of laying down an impenetrable 'wall of fire' between their own troops and the enemy. Different weapons were used, from tear gas through small-calibre 'mini-guns' with 4,000 shots a minute to eight-inch shells which obliterated all life within a radius of seventy-five metres. These varied according to whether the troops were shooting on suspicion or aiming at a previously identified enemy position. The assault leaders were committed to ordering civilians to leave the areas in question in advance, provided the operational situation and the demand for speed allowed. In such cases they were permitted to carry out surprise strikes, even in the immediate vicinity of settlements, with maximum material force and 'humanitarian reasons notwithstanding', as it said in the after-action report on such an assault.[42] No region was safe from this kind of attack and everywhere the peasants had to be aware that there were assault commanders who wasted no time bothering about their lives: 'Tough shit. They know we're operating in this area, they can hear us, and they ought to be in their bunkers. I'm not taking any unnecessary chances with my men.'[43]

At the end of a tour of inspection in 1967 Army Chief of Staff Harold K. Johnson voiced his horror at these practices. So far as he could see, over ninety per cent of artillery bombardments had had nothing to do with the actual ground fighting. In nine out of ten cases they were aimed at alleged, therefore not positively identified, targets or raked general areas with precautionary fire[44] – as for instance in Quang Ngai Province, where 52,000 people living near Duc Pho had to live with 'harassment and interdiction fire' night after night during summer 1967.[45] A study undertaken as a consequence by the Defense Department confirmed Johnson's assumptions and its findings about the Air Force were even worse: only four per cent of their combat sorties were to support ground troops heavily involved in the fighting. In other words, in general these were so-called 'unobserved missions' – attacks with missiles and bombs on unspecified objects and with no quantifiable effects. In most cases the choice of target was based on out-of-date information or, in the absence of any valid intelligence, enemy troop movements were simply calculated by map references.[46] 'In the last decade,' wrote John Paul Vann, recalling his term of service with the Army and with CORDS,

I have walked through hundreds of hamlets that have been destroyed in the course of a battle, the majority as the result of the heavier friendly fires . . . Indeed, it has not been unusual to have a hamlet destroyed and find absolutely no evidence of damage to the enemy. I recall in May 1969 the destruction and burning by air strike of 900 houses in a hamlet in Chau Doc Province without evidence of a single enemy being killed.[47]

If at all, damage to civilian targets was recorded in 'friendly fire' statistics or 'accident case files' from which certainly no more than the tip of the iceberg can be extracted.[48] On the one hand, they were not collated until January 1968 and on the other, it can be assumed that an unconfirmed number of injured parties did not lodge any complaint. It was definitely known that in each of the three-month periods from October 1968 to March 1969 there had been a hundred incidents with about 500 victims in all, so that over a year one can assume that there were about 400 'incidents' with 2,000 killed or wounded. In any case these figures do not include any information about devastation by Air Force 'friendly fire'.[49] More enlightening than this sort of number game, therefore, are the memoranda circulating among the command staff which contain complaints about an unacceptable accumulation of cases. One undated report, probably written in late 1969 and addressed to the Deputy Chief of Staff of the US Army Vietnam states:

Death or injury among civilians which . . . is caused by ground delivered small arms and machine gun fire, tank guns, grenades, flares, mines and other devices is not automatically investigated nor is a determination made and recorded as to whether or not Rules of Engagement and other applicable regulations were adhered to. This leads to the conclusion that an incident of the type alleged to have occurred at My Lai could actually occur and not be recorded anywhere in the Army system. It appears that there is a definite problem, but since experience data are not available, there is no way of determining its magnitude.[50]

So investigations into 'friendly fire' damage are of very limited value and there is no point in trying to quantify them, but they do yield information about the background to misdirected fire and particularly about the conduct of the participating troops and their officers. There were doubtless tragic complications in one case or another – from defective ammunition to commonplace errors in transmitting or evaluating data. Sometimes the execution and control of attacks lay in the hands of unqualified personnel – there is mention of those in charge having no idea of the destructive power of their weapons or of the guidelines for their use, or of GIs who could neither read a map nor calculate the trajectory of a shot.[51] And lastly, procedures governing clearance for artillery fire were deliberately ignored. That also applies to South Vietnamese provincial administrators, who on paper had to authorise each attack by the US Army and Air Force – and in so doing attached less importance to protecting civilians than to the objective of bombing the peasants out of their support for the guerrillas.[52] However different the individual pretexts may have been, the one basic thing they have in common keeps emerging: the disinterest and indifference of the troop commanders directly responsible. Having committed themselves to the maxims of attrition strategy, they accepted the victims of friendly fire as regrettable but equally unavoidable collateral damage.[53]

Licence to destroy and annihilate on a large-scale applied unrestrictedly in the so-called 'Free Fire Zones'. Set by the South Vietnamese authorities – either the civil administration or the commanders of an Army corps or a division[54] – the US forces operated within them as though in areas outside the law: 'Prior to entrance into the area we as soldiers were told all that was left in the area after civilian evacuation were Viet Cong and thus fair game.'[55] Virtually all recollections of the war contain such a statement or something similar, simultaneously referring to the fact that anyone who did not want to be evacuated had forfeited the right to protection, since in the Free Fire Zones the distinction between combatant and non-combatant was, a priori, lifted. 'If these people want to stay there and support the Communists, then they can expect to be bombed,' said an adviser to 25th Infantry Division.[56] As a result even populated areas were identified as Free Fire Zones, the suspicion of active or passive support for the Viet Cong being grounds enough. 'Because of the nature of the war,' so ran an internal comment on the guidelines for attacks,

there was a definite need to cut down the freedom of movement enjoyed by the enemy who took full advantage of the opportunity to blend with the civilian population by day and to fight by night . . . The program [the selection of Free Fire Zones] was designed to bring and keep under fire areas in which there were known enemy formations, facilities, and infiltration routes, with a random pattern of fire . . . If the Viet Cong decided to fight from a hamlet, civilian casualties and the destruction of homes and property were certain to follow. [57]

In the words of James A. May, the senior American adviser in Quang Ngai province: 'The V.C. use villages as protection, the way a gangster uses a hostage. So in the process of getting at Charlie [Viet Cong] it's inevitable that the village gets it . . . There isn't any way to get them but level the villages they are located in.'[58]

In other words, the standard official talk about Free Fire Zones as evacuated areas is a defensive lie[59] and besides reveals a view of the war which had nothing to do with the Vietnamese peasants' everyday lives. In the eyes of their inhabitants, villages were much more than places to live or cultivate; they were revered as shrines, the natural world around them was the home of the spirits they prayed to and the graves of their ancestors were symbols of death and reincarnation. Leaving these places was unthinkable except in dire emergency and thus many, who had given in to pressure from the US military and let themselves be resettled in refugee camps or fortified defensive villages, availed themselves of every opportunity to return home, also because the reception camps were appallingly overcrowded or provided undignified living conditions. Flouting tradition and individual dignity, the American troops used loud-speaker vehicles and dropped millions of leaflets from the air, expecting the illiterate to understand the warnings or peasants who lived by the rhythm of nature to observe the curfew which divided the day into free and forbidden time zones. Essentially these leaflets fulfilled only one purpose: to give their own soldiers the feeling that when in doubt they had in fact killed the right people: 'Dear Citizens: . . . The U.S. Marines will not hesitate to destroy immediately, any village or hamlet harbouring the Vietcong . . . The choice is yours . . . Attention Villagers: . . . You can protect your homes by cooperating with the G.V.N. [Government of Vietnam] and the Allied Forces.'[60]

In the end the inevitable happened. As soon as a commander believed that warning villagers in advance might endanger the success of an assault, no more leaflets were dropped. As soon as ground troops saw anything suspicious in closed military areas, they shot indiscriminately at anything which moved, without seeing or identifying it and regardless of the consequences. According to a study by the US Senate, 300,000 people were killed in the Free Fire Zones between 1965 and the end of 1968, but it is too late now to establish whether this was actually the case.[61] There are plenty of records of reports from soldiers, identical in their narrative pattern, in which they speak of dozens of victims,[62] and also internal investigations which only vary in the frankness of the language. Someone said about shooting up a village, in the course of which twenty-one villagers were killed and a further twenty-one wounded: 'The Deputy Senior Advisor . . . stated that he and the Province Chief agreed that personnel from friendly villages had no right to be in the areas in question and that if they were, they were paying or helping the VC in killing American citizens.'[63] And the report about an attack by A Company, 2nd Battalion, 60th Infantry Regiment, 25th Infantry Division, in the course of which ten peasants returning home fell into a GI ambush and were shot dead without warning, states: 'The incident meets the criteria of a "firing accident" . . . which occurs in the course of military operations . . . in unauthorized areas.'[64]

There was another side to the strategy of attrition and destruction of enemy resources besides overkill through superior weapon technology: 'political cleansing', or the 'anti-Maoist principle'. To strand the guerrillas – the fish which swam in water – the hinterland had to be made unusable. This policy was never declared officially or established in the form of military directives. In practice, however, three goals were pursued with rigorous determination: resettling peasants, burning down villages and destroying the harvest. By creating 'dead zones' it seemed certain that the peasants did not return to enemy-controlled regions but began a new life under the supervision of the Saigon government. And perhaps the fighting morale of the guerrillas was undermined by permanently separating families, as the US military were sometimes heard to say. As a result, many units regarded their scorched-earth policy as Standing Operating Procedure – a job to be done without further question.[65]

In this the US forces were carrying on a project initiated by the South Vietnamese dictator Ngo Dinh Diem in the late 1950s, in which more than four million people were forcibly resettled in the space of a few years in some 3,000 fortified sites called 'agrovilles' or strategic hamlets.[66] Yet even such numbers pale beside the Americans' radical actions. After removing the inhabitants, one of those responsible told journalist Jonathan Schell, 'we are going to destroy everything in the Iron Triangle. Make it into a flat field. The V.C. can no longer hide there.'[67] This was Operation Cedar Falls in the Iron Triangle fifty kilometres north of Saigon. What Schell observed in the village of Ben Suc in January 1967 was typical of the entire operation: first pioneers came in with bulldozers, tore down the houses and set them on fire. Then the Air Force pulverised the rubble with heavy bombs in the hope of collapsing the guerrilla's tunnels which they assumed lay underneath. Cedar Falls had countless predecessors and successors, such as Operation Masher/Whitewing or Operation Russell Beach/ Bold Mariner, just to mention the best known. The last-named took place from January to July 1969 in Quang Ngai Province – in a region in which US troops and their allies had already destroyed seventy per cent of the villages and all occupied houses by the end of 1967.[68]

There is still no inventory of the damage inflicted on Vietnam as a whole, though here and there specific data can provide some idea of its extent. For instance, 600,000 people could have been fed each year with the crops which had been made unusable by attacks with herbicides,[69] and millions were without the necessities of life, especially those who had been deliberately uprooted, driven out and deported and were euphemistically called 'refugees'. Between 1964 and 1969 3.5 million South Vietnamese – twenty per cent of the population – spent all or a part of their lives in flight. In Quang Ngai Province this proportion was at times over forty per cent. It is uncertain how many returned home and when; all we know is that most of them had to languish in camps for more than two years – in temporary huts behind barbed wire, in indescribable sanitary conditions and without adequate food or clothing. These and other examples ultimately illustrate one and the same thing: that in the particularly heavily fought-over regions of the Central Highlands and the northern provinces of South Vietnam, the United States' war policies resulted in the ruin of rural life.[70]

There is no sign that the US military had developed any feeling for the human costs of this war. On the contrary, high numbers of refugees were interpreted as a successful weakening of the Viet Cong[71] and besides, it was assumed that the Vietnamese, like all Asiatics, had no links with time and place and could therefore live anywhere. 'Also, these mud houses with thatched roofs can be built up overnight'[72] – a statement repeatedly quoted by various media correspondents which was also proof of the home-made malaise: that the American military were exacerbating the very problem which they had come to Vietnam to solve.

The resulting increased support for the guerrillas and the accusation that the population was 'ungrateful' brought a further element of the anti-Maoist strategy into play: the hunt for suspects and the systematic and widespread combing through of operational targets. Prisoners of war – that is, peripatetic guerrilla fighters – were rarely taken. In the first place, actual or presumed Viet Cong supporters were to be sought out and the suspects interrogated or detained. Depending on the size of the area in question and the troops available, the raids were carried out in different ways. Sometimes only those carrying arms or under suspicion for other reasons were detained; sometimes everyone possible was rounded up – including old people, women and children – and taken to so-called 'interrogation centres' for questioning. One American officer involved said: 'We know they're Charlie – maybe saboteurs, collaborators, and like that . . . These here are hard-core V.C. You can tell just by lookin' at 'em.'[73] In principle every commander had a free hand to act as he wished with no need to give reasons for detaining people before trial, as they were interchangeable at will. 'In Duc Pho,' reported a military policeman from the Americal Division, 'where the 11th Brigade base camp was located, we could arrest and detain at will any Vietnamese civilian we desired.'[74] Journalists report on suspects in handcuffs with sacks over their heads being jammed into transport planes, flown out to the nearest camp and ill-treated or humiliated on the way. Deterring those who remained behind was obviously just as important as the expectation of getting valuable information from the detainees.[75]

According to US Army statistics, about 220,000 people were in allied custody between the beginning of 1966 and the end of October 1970, for barely half of whom American troops were responsible. There was also an unknown number of people tracked down by the Saigon police and secret services, assumed to be tens of thousands if not more, the South Vietnamese authorities being responsible for screening them. On what criteria this screening was based is as obscure today as it was then, and whether the data passed on to the Americans bore any relation to the truth seems no less questionable. Allowing for these reservations, the following picture emerges about the 220,000 who were officially arrested: about thirteen per cent were classed as prisoners-of-war and put in camps set up for them; about sixty per cent, or 132,000, were classed as 'innocent civilians' and released after a brief examination;[76] the remaining 56,000, or twenty-seven per cent of those arrested, fell into the category of 'civilian defendants', supposedly spies, saboteurs, collaborators or terrorists. There were probably hundreds of enemy soldiers among them, prisoners to whom no one wanted to give the special protection of POW status prescribed by the Geneva Convention.[77] It is hard to say who the large majority of 'civilian defendants' actually were. 'Actually it is a convenient designation for anyone about whom the interrogation teams cannot make up their minds,' wrote Orville Schell after weeks of research in Quang Ngai Province.[78]

As a rule 'civilian defendants' found themselves in the torture cells of the despotic Saigon authorities, distributed among four national and thirty-seven provincial prisons. That 200,000 people were incarcerated in them was a lie put out by Hanoi.[79] The American estimate of 41,000 detainees in summer 1970, including many ordinary criminals, seem more realistic. The conditions in the prisons first came to light when two US congressmen, Augustus F. Hawkins and William R. Anderson, went public. They had visited the largest establishment of Con Son housing 10,000 inmates, on an island 140 miles south-east of Saigon, and established that a quarter of them were being held without trial or verdict. Many spent weeks in isolation, many were kept in minute 'tiger cages' like animals and others lay in chains in their cells, eating rice dishes mixed with sand and stones or dried fish which was normally used for plant manure.[80] When American doctors, accompanied by military advisers, inspected Con Son in September and November 1970, they found 1,500 prisoners in chains and 109 of the 110 examined showed symptoms of paralysis in their lower extremities. In every case these were the results of forced immobility but probably also symptoms of other methods of torture. All in all, everything points to the South Vietamese having systematically used torture for years, not only in their POW camps but also in civilian prisons.[82]

'American officials, diplomats and congressmen are guilty of trying to cover up an intolerable situation,' wrote the *Washington Star* on 8 July 1970 about Hawkins's and Anderson's report.[83] High-ranking US officers had repeatedly voiced their concerns internally about the detention policies of the South Vietnamese in general and criticised their treatment of prisoners-of-war in particular as breaching international rules of warfare.[84] In accordance with the Geneva Convention and its clause which laid down that a power waging war bore responsibility for prisoners handed over to a third party, the American authorities in Saigon would have had an obligation to intervene, but neither the US Supreme Command nor the embassy showed any interest. 'It is felt that some deficiencies noted by the ICRC [International Committee of the Red Cross] result from the unrealistic application of occidental standards to those of the Orient, and of the Vietnamese people in particular,' ran a memorandum from the Joint Chiefs of Staff in October 1970 concerning the conditions in the Phu Quoc POW camp,[85] and a US diplomat said in July 1970 about the situation in civilian prisons: 'Possibly by Asian standards the prisons aren't that bad.'[86]

Torture was also one of the commonplace practices of the US Army. In 1968 and 1969 representatives of the International Red Cross had paid sixty visits to US-run transit detainee facilities and collecting points, where suspects were interrogated before being handed over to the Vietnamese authorities. Their summary read that in all the camps civilians and prisoners-of-war were ill-treated and wounds could be diagnosed as the result of beatings, burnings and electric shocks.[87] When veterans returning to the United States repeatedly made similar accusations public, it strengthened the suspicion of countless units using torture. The finger was particularly pointed at 173rd Airborne Brigade (Separate), 101st Airborne Division, 9th, 23rd and 25th Infantry Divisions, 1st and 3rd Marine Divisions, 11th Armored Cavalry Regiment and other troops from 1st Cavalry Division, as well as various sections of the Special Forces. The map showing their positions demonstrated that no region of South Vietnam was excluded and the accusations covered a period of several years. They included electric and water torture, sexual humiliation, beatings, mutilations, locking suspects in rooms with pythons, spraying them with liquids which attracted mosquitoes, dehydrating them or locking them in small barbed-wire cages,[88] not to mention the frequently reported 'half chopper ride' or 'airborne interrogation', which involved making suspects talk by seizing one or more from among them at random and throwing them out of helicopters when in flight.[89]

The accusations against 173rd Airborne Brigade (Separate) were investigated with relatively intensive effort and vigour, not least because a high-ranking officer, Lieutenant Colonel Anthony B. Herbert, had gone public with some dramatic details in September 1970: 'The noise, the crying and screaming and the scene was unbelievable for a US Army installation.'[90] After sixteen months and interviews conducted with 333 witnesses worldwide, the charges were established in all essential points: in the territory of Landing Zone English in Binh Dinh

Province men and women were regularly tortured by South Vietnamese and American interrogation specialists over a period of eighteen months, from March 1968 to October 1969. The torturers kicked and beat them with sticks, they urinated on their victims' bodies, put hoods over their heads and drenched the cloth with water until the victim was about to suffocate, they bound suspects to metal chairs, fixed electric wires to their fingers, earlobes or genitalia and sent electric shocks through their bodies with field telephones specially prepared for the purposes. On the US side at least twenty-three military policemen of 173rd Airborne Brigade were involved. These violent interrogations were repeatedly attended by GIs who recommended them as an 'entertainment programme', And, according to a telegram from the commander of the brigade to the supreme commander of the US forces in the Pacific and Vietnam: 'Several US soldiers were observed smoking marihuana at one of the sessions.'[91]

These and comparable incidents were known to the military leadership long before the report on investigations into 173rd Airborne Brigade (Separate). In the office of the Army Chief of Staff there were several memoranda circulating at the beginning of 1968 which drew attention to 'damage to the image' of the armed forces: 'The incidents authoritatively alleged show a cruel, sophisticated, calculated torture for information and make pious hypocritical arguments of statements about our treatment of POWs by the President . . .'[92] For his part, Chief of Staff Harold K. Johnson remarked that American prisoners in the hands of the Viet Cong seemed to have been better treated than vice versa and that this conclusion could at least be drawn from the photographs of torture which became known at the end of 1967 and the beginning of 1968: 'The unconcern portrayed by those photographed . . . lead the viewer to the conclusion that the individuals depicted felt no sense of shame or wrong, did not expect disapproval of their military superiors, and felt entirely secure in being permanently recorded in the performance of acceptable acts before the camera.'[93]

In June 1968 the deputy commander of the US Army (Vietnam), Lieutenant General Bruce Palmer, told the Army Chief of Staff that most of these offences were committed immediately after arrest or during evacuation – and certainly with the knowledge and approval of officers who were obviously concerned with obtaining as quickly as possible such information on enemy strength and positions which would otherwise be worthless.[94] It was also clear that torture was being used equally on both soldiers and civilians accused of collaborating. In the light of similar accusations against soldiers of 5th Special Force Group (Airborne), Brigadier General Edward Bautz asserted in a fact sheet that torture was regarded as a military necessity and was part of the daily routine everywhere in Vietnam: 'It seems there are altogether too many who feel the rules of treatment for PW are simply pap to assuage old women' – meaning primarily instructors returning from Vietnam, who intimidated soldiers with their expert knowledge and portrayed torture as crucial. Those responsible in the present case and in many others had no interest in explaining anything and sent their victims hastily back to their villages in the expectation of being able to buy their silence with money and other gifts. Then again, according to Bautz, many officers were not intent on observing the rules of warfare but only the outward appearance of correct behaviour. 'What would be the result of world-wide knowledge of the facts as they stand today?'[95] Only as a result of the public debate over the My Lai (4) massacre did the Army come to realise that Field Manual 30-15 – permitting the instigation of fear as a method of interrogation – contravened the Geneva Convention and should therefore be amended.[96]

'It doesn't matter what you do to them . . . The trouble is, no one sees the Vietnamese as people.' – 'we don't understand what they're thinking. When we got here, we landed on a different planet. In Germany and Japan, I guess there was a thread of contact, but even when a Vietnamese guy speaks perfect English I don't know what the hell he's talking about.'[97] Many of their colleagues would have endorsed these remarks by two GIs from Texas and California, for they shared this distrust of the Vietnamese as a whole and primarily of those they had to deal with in action. In the practice of combing through suspected regions it was shown that the rigorously defined barrier between 'us' and 'them' can lead to blurring another kind of dividing line – that is, the borderline between being prepared to use force and making it a practice and between atrocities and war crimes.

Alongside torture, indiscriminately aiming fire at civilians was another feature of this war. Even trying to reconstruct a partially realistic overall picture seems impossible in view of the incomplete records. Yet it is established that, as a former military adviser wrote in the *New*

York Times, 'military officers and civilian officials at the highest levels constantly registered complaints of indiscriminate rocket fire from . . . observation planes and "joy rides" by helicopter pilots that finished up as massacres of peasants'.[98] From internal investigations by the Army it emerged that, between January and October 1969 in a single district of Binh Long Province called Chon Thanh, there were fourteen proven cases of helicopter crews of 1st Cavalry Division, 1st Infantry Division and 12th Aviation Group shooting up foresters, peasants working in the fields and whole villages, killing about thirty people. The crews had dishonestly obtained permission to fire by deliberately deceiving the command posts[99] – a practice which had clearly been in use for years, according to one of the pilots stationed there in 1967:

He claimed that one helicopter would radio for permission to shoot, while one accompanying it at lower altitude would immediately commence firing. If no clearance was given, no one would mention the kill, otherwise, a body count would be claimed. He next described how helicopters of his unit, equipped with sirens, would fly over people in rice paddies. When the people ran, they were fired upon because they appeared to be taking evasive action.[100]

Some pilots were so appalled by their air gunners' actions that they put notices on the backs of their seats: 'Unlawful to fire from this aircraft.'[101]

There was a particular slang for acts of terror from the air: 'joy rides', 'squirrel-hunting', 'hunter-killer teams' or 'MAM', standing for 'military-age male' and the practice of looking out for anyone who seemed to be of weapon-bearing age. 'Well, he walked real proud,' said one pilot about a victim who found himself in the wrong place at the wrong time, 'with a kind of bounce in his gait, like a soldier, instead of just shuffling along, like the farmers do.'[102] Officially such attacks were called 'people snatcher operations',[103] a term which many crews understood as a licence to lasso peasants and fly around with them until they lost their hold and fell to the ground or their necks broke. 'That happened more often than you can imagine,' maintained Seymour M. Hersh during a television interview in 1971. 'The classic killer in Vietnam is the helicopter man who just goes around and shoots anybody . . . And that isn't hyperbole . . . You know, in terms of numbers, the massacres committed by helicopters certainly outweigh the massacres committed by men like Calley.'[104]

Such wide-ranging accusations can hardly be verified and are difficult to refute. No journalist has ever got beyond initial, incriminating, research, while the competent authorities revealed a patent lack of interest in getting to the bottom of them, in spite of serious indications of hundreds of people having been killed.[105] Here are six examples from files which are incomplete and have subsequently been partially censored:[106]

- A helicopter crew of 3rd Brigade, 25th Infantry Division was accused of having shot dead sixty-nine 'suspects' in June 1967. Although the examiner from the Criminal Investigation Division gave little credence to disclaimers from Brigade Commander James G. Shanahan, further investigations were called off.[107]

- In June or July 1967, according to the sworn statement of a gunner involved, a helicopter of Dragon Platoon, 334th Armed Helicopter Company, 145th Aviation Group attacked nine unarmed people to the west of Duc Hoa (III Corps Tactical Zone). 'If they stood still, they were supposedly friendly. If they ran, [I] had permission to shoot them.'[108] Thirteen unarmed people are thought to have been killed. Due to contradictory evidence the Criminal Investigation Division closed the file with the comment 'unfounded'.

- At the beginning of August 1967 B Troop, 1st Squadron, 9th Cavalry Regiment of 1st Cavalry Division is said to have murdered thirty-three civilians near Duc Pho. In spite of reliable leads, after a superficial examination the Criminal Investigation Division filed the case away as 'unsubstantiated'.[109]

- It was alleged that on the Sung Chau river to the north of Nha Trang (II Corps Tactical Zone) on 28 November 1967 helicopter gunships of Joker Platoon, 48th Aviation Company, 1st Aviation Brigade (Provisional) fired on a hundred sampans and killed an unknown number of people who had already shown they were refugees by waving South Vietnamese flags. One witness informed the White House about it in May 1970 but, after three members of the unit made a deposition that they knew nothing of the incident, no further efforts were made to investigate.[110]

- At the end of January or beginning of February 1968, according to three GIs, six Cobra helicopters of D Troop, 1st Squadron, 10th Cavalry Regiment, 4th Infantry Division attacked the village of Thanh An near Pleiku (II Corps Tactical Zone) and mowed down 300 Montagnards, indigenous inhabitants of the Central Highlands. Whether they had previously been shot at from the village, took unarmed men for Viet Cong troops or for whatever other reason was not clear from the statements.[111] The examinations by the Military Assistance Command Vietnam (MACV) were carried out very sluggishly and were soon concluded, with the lapidary remark that the accused units 'had a "big" fight that day and apparently did an excellent job . . . The matter appears to be another case of "memory stimulation" by the My Lai investigation.'[112]

- In May and August 1969 airmen of 2nd Squadron, 8th Cavalry Regiment, 1st Cavalry Division were said to have executed about thirty Viet Cong and North Vietnamese Army prisoners. The files were closed in March 1971 with the comment 'Not sufficient to prove or disprove.'[113]

Because of the increase of attacks in the Mekong Delta, several rice dealers went to the Ministry of Economic Affairs in Saigon in March 1968 to complain about drastically reduced trade, due to the terror attacks by helicopters. Robert Komer, the deputy director of CORDS responsible for such complaints, sent on the transcript of the meeting to the civil adviser of IV Corps Tactical Zone with the words: 'I don't know if Westy [William Westmoreland] talked with you about attached, or whether practice is widespread if true. But I'm inclined to agree with author.'[114] It seems that Komer's intervention at least led to a more detailed monitoring of helicopter attacks in this region. Little more is known about it, except that at the end of 1970 military tribunal proceedings were prepared against eight crew members from 335th Aviation Company, 1st Aviation Brigade (Provisional). In the previous months they had attacked villages, peasants in the fields or traders in boats on several occasions. On the basis of an intervention by the general commanding the Separate Troops, USAV, the proceedings were quashed from the outset.[115]

Target shooting at civilians was a widespread practice among infantrymen, too, even in No Fire Zones or Controlled Fire Zones. Whether in interviews, memoirs or public statements it is striking how often they mention terrorising peasants in the fields, fishermen, traders on rivers in their junks and sampans, women collecting firewood or children hunting for treasure on rubbish heaps in the neighbourhood of military bases by using them as targets. 'When we kill a pregnant woman, we count it as two V.C. – one soldier and one cadet.'[116] Some of them even described these 'mad minutes' as 'Standing Operating Procedure', as though it were part of everyday military practice to test out weapons or dump surplus ammunition by loosing off at random all over the place: 'A mad minute – everybody gets in line, everybody in the company, and you play Machine Gun Murphy . . . and you just pepper the countryside. Usually you do this about six o'clock at night because you get colors off the tracers.'[117] To the question why their unit in June 1969 shot up some huts in which obviously only women and children were living, two GIs of C Company, 2nd Battalion, 39th Infantry Regiment, 1st Brigade, 9th Infantry Division replied under oath: 'I guess to see if I could hit it.'[118] – 'The CO came up to me . . . and he told me to put a couple more rounds in the hootch "to see if you can shut those gooks up".'[119]

Many of the corroborating reports refer to small groups like platoons or squads, patrolling on their own, far away from larger units, for long periods of time, but even more often they indicate that such procedure when mounting raids on villages was all in the day's work. Anyone who fled in fear of the advancing troops had forfeited his life. 'Shot while trying to escape' was the standard formula in the operational reports. The risk was just as great for those who took refuge in underground bunkers. Because shelters could not be immediately distinguished from enemy tunnel systems, many GIs took no risk and blew up anything suspicious, sight unseen. Even those stoical people who remained in their houses could not be sure of their safety. Whether out of fear or lust for murder, or as a result of a tragic oversight, many people died in a hail of bullets from the invading soldiers. 'They're all VC or at least helping them – same difference. You can't convert them, only kill them. Don't lose any sleep over those dead children – they grow up to be commies too . . . This is a war and we have to stop the commies any way we can, using whatever we've got.'[120] This recollection published in 1967 comes closest to the dubious purpose of the raids: they were situations ripe for slaughter.

Jonathan Schell is of course right when he warns against unreliable generalisations and refers to the unnamed examples of all those who even when under stress retained their respect for the lives of others. This is no exculpation, but rather an incentive to track down the causes for the excessive use of force.[121] No war in history is free from such excess, especially in a colonial or post-colonial setting, when fighting takes place on the territory of an alien, peripheral culture and adversaries confront each other in an asymmetrical scenario. Yet something more had to happen to turn the Vietnam War into the bloodiest 'hot war' since 1945: firstly, Washington's refusal, born of the spirit of the Cold War, to draw conclusions from seeing that something was unattainable; secondly, settling on a war strategy which was bound to result in self-brutalisation of the armed forces and an invitation to commit war crimes. 'Victory was a high body-count,' explains the writer Philip Caputo, 'defeat a low kill-ratio, war a matter of arithmetic. The pressure on unit commanders . . . was intense, and they in turn communicated it to their troops. This led to such practices as counting civilians as Viet Cong. "If it's dead and Vietnamese, it's VC," was a rule of thumb in the bush.'[122] Caputo, stationed as a Marine in Vietnam, does not attempt to use this as an excuse for the contempt his comrades felt for the cheapness of life. He says the same thing as Jonathan Schell, only the other way round – and like those soldiers who wrote in their diaries: 'They wouldn't believe it back home.'[123] In this context the journalist Peter Arnett found the most apt description in a quote from a major in the US Air Force: 'It became necessary to destroy the town [Ben Tre] to save it.'[124]

3

Officers

> The soldier, be he friend or foe, is charged with the protection of
> the weak and unarmed. It is the very essence and reason of his
> being. When he violates this sacred trust he not only profanes his
> entire cult but threatens the very fabric of international society.
>   Douglas MacArthur[1]

> It is apparent that the Army's procedures for the prevention,
> detection, and punishment of war crimes have failed abysmally.
>   Telford Taylor[2]

'Reports available to this headquarters suggest an attitude of disaffec-
tion toward the Vietnamese may be developing among our personnel
. . . Sufficient evidence is available to require firm and immediate
command action through the medium of troop indoctrination to arrest
the growth of a potentially dangerous development during the incipient
stage . . . Comments such as "the only good village is a burned village",
are indicative of the trend.'[3] During his four years serving in Saigon
William Westmoreland, supreme commander of the US forces in
Vietnam, sent at least a dozen similar letters of warning and complaint
to the commanders of all units. They concerned in equal measure the
ill-treatment of prisoners of war and the ruthless deployment of firepower in populated areas. Above all, however, he criticised behaviour
towards civilians. 'People more than terrain are the objectives in this

war and we will not and cannot be callous about these people.'[4] Between October 1967 and February 1968 alone Westmoreland wrote on this subject six times – in circulars, New Year's messages or when addressing meetings of commanders. There was no need to read between the lines to understand the message: without drastically improved leadership of the troops the war will end in disaster. 'We realize we have a great problem.'[5]

This also influenced how the Supreme Command drew up its directives for planning and implementing military operations – the so-called 'Rules of Engagement'. For example, in MACV 525-3 we read that 'The circumstances described above call for the exercise of restraint not normally required of soldiers on the battlefield . . . Commanders will conduct continuing programs to emphasize both the short and long range importance of minimizing non-combatant casualties'[6] – and indeed not only during basic training but also in the course of the usual briefing of troops directly before deployment. In other words, anyone engaging in an asymmetrical war without clear fronts must have at his disposal a pool of senior officers who combine military skill with political expertise and who also weigh up the consequences of their actions from a moral and ethical standpoint; who do not therefore authorise bombarding the area around a sniper with indiscriminate fire or burning down a village because of some scattered Viet Cong. In his final report on My Lai William Peers wrote: 'Directives and regulations, no matter how well prepared and intended, are only pieces of paper unless they are enforced aggressively and firmly throughout the chain of command.'[7]

'Before we become executioners . . . it is better to go home.'[8] Behind this warning in August 1965 from the commander of the US Army, 1st Aviation Brigade (Provisional), lies an unspoken rule of thumb also maintained by military sociologists and historians beyond Vietnam: troops who do not feel any permanent commitment to the norms of warfare tend to be dominated by violent ringleaders – by bullies who quickly enforce the ruthlessness of a minority as normal behaviour accepted by the majority. In these circumstances, the younger and less experienced the unit, the greater the probability of it being transformed into a marauding rabble.[9] Whether and with what consequences they take the downward path does not therefore only depend on the wording of an order, but primarily on how orders are communicated, what practices are tolerated and whether sanctions are actually enforced by imposing penalties. This leads on to the question of the professional self-awareness, standing and authority of the officers in the field. Without overemphasising their role and responsibility, one can assert that superiors with the power of command define the limits of what is permissible, obligatory or forbidden. They set the climate of command.

THE 'VIETNAM ONLY ARMY'

In view of the public discussion over the My Lai (4) massacre, the Army War College commissioned in 1970 a wide-ranging study of the 'moral and ethical climate in the US Army'. Group interviews with 250 officers were carried out between April and June and a further 450 answered individual questionnaires. According to information from the project leaders, those questioned comprised a representative selection of officers at seven military academies, together with a group of the leadership elite, earmarked for middle and senior ranks within the next ten years. They were to provide information on the one hand about the fundamental expectations placed on commanders and on the other about the realities of everyday life in the Army. Without exception the results were graded as 'surprising' and in parts as 'shocking'. In fact a large majority of those interviewed gave a devastating verdict. They regarded the Army as an institution which promoted self-interest, incompetence and dishonesty to the point of corruption, and which nipped in the bud any attempt at internal reform – inevitably producing a type of leader characterised as a 'perfunctory figure'. This was 'the ambitious, transitory commander, who is marginally skilled in the complexities of his duties, engulfed in producing statistical results, fearful of personal failure, too busy to talk with or listen to his subordinates, and determined to submit acceptably optimistic reports that reflect faultless completion of a variety of tasks at the expense of the sweat and frustration of his subordinates.'[10] The fact that falsified activity and deployment reports were as widespread as the unwillingness to stop such practices provoked the harshest criticism, which turned into cynical contempt for the pre-deployment preparation and execution of operations, and therefore for the countless cases in which greed for rapid and well-publicised success led to gambling with unnecessary risks and even their own soldiers' lives. Regardless of how many examples were given, the ultimate picture was of an erosion of professional and ethical standards which called for 'fundamental and revolutionary changes' rather than for cautious reform.[11]

These results became a political issue, because high-ranking officers promptly went public with similar complaints. These included Colonel David H. Hackworth, who with seventy-eight action medals was the most decorated US Army infantry soldier of the twentieth century;[12] Edward L. King, a lieutenant colonel distinguished by the President's Order of Merit after twenty years of service; Anthony Herbert, a lieutenant colonel respected in both Korea and Vietnam as a brilliant strategist; and significantly, General Bruce Palmer Jr., who after service in Vietnam had been promoted to Acting Chief of Staff of the Army. In books, newspaper articles and interviews they ignored their caste's vow of silence, which until then had been accepted without question. The Army, as they claimed unanimously, is no longer led by soldiers who see the business of war as their vocation, but by managers who hope to be appointed to a better paid job in the shortest possible time – '"Get on the team" bootlickers, . . . unthinking, subservient yes-men' (King)[13] and 'ambitious prince[s]' (Hackworth),[14] who see commanding a troop as a necessary evil in their climb up the promotion ladder. According to King, however, the result of such a scenario is a vicious circle: anyone showing no interest in leading his soldiers invites indiscipline and in order to counter this must do everything to ensure that the effects of corrupted troop morale do not rebound onto him. Therefore immaculate deployment reports and personnel files do not reflect the reality at the front but the professional fears of their author working in the hinterland: 'The whole Army structure is pervaded with fear of reprisals that stifles any whisper of dissent.'[15]

At first glance a shadow of suspicion falls over these accusations. Were they by any chance created by disappointed losers – men who had themselves accepted the rules of the game in the Vietnam War for years and now wanted to steal away from personal responsibility by talking about the effects of anonymous structures; men who were taking their revenge for promotions missed? In the case of Anthony Herbert these questions reverberated for years – also because he cultivated both the self-righteous air of the strategist misjudged by everyone and the myth of lost victories.[16] Or did others wish themselves back in the era when officers were still 'gladiators' and cultivated the scenario of heroic manliness in the wake of Theodore Roosevelt? This patina certainly lies over the utterances of David H. Hackworth, who left no doubt as to his political ulterior motives: first and foremost in his judgement, reforming the Army was to protect battle-tried professionals against the criticism of unqualified amateurs. 'Return the Army to its mission of soldiering . . . Tell Congress to stop interfering in the Army's internal affairs and provide it assurance that the Army will police itself.'[17] Was this then just a cheap excuse for denouncing the civilian control over the armed forces? The fact that Hackworth's and Herbert's criticisms are reflected in countless recollections by ordinary soldiers does not remove all doubt; veterans themselves tend to write their own stories as histories of their superiors' failures.

In order to answer these questions, one would need to be given a comparative history of the fighting units deployed in Vietnam over a period of ten years – or at least a micro-historical comparison of two divisions with different reputations. One obvious choice would be the 1st Infantry Division ('The Big Red One'), whose commander William E. DePuy reputedly ruled with a rod of iron and knew how to check infringements by his units. As Harry G. Summers said of his time under DePuy, 'If an artillery round landed within a hundred yards of a shrine or temple, the battalion commander could count on being relieved . . . What I'm trying to get across is that the command climate in that unit was what protected it from these kinds of atrocities.'[18] In contrast, the 9th Infantry Division had a reputation for unbridled ruthlessness. Thus a comparative examination of both might provide a more penetrating overall picture. The same applies to a comparison of the 173rd Airborne Brigade (Separate) and any unit of the Marines, who traditionally cultivated the self-image of a disciplined body. However, such comparisons have not so far been produced and it is doubtful if they ever could be written – on the basis of divisional files which contain painstaking entries about supposedly stolen bags of rice or the number of chickens requisitioned, but where little is to be found about the 'command climate', apart from stereotypical records of successes.

Nonetheless, it may be said that the war in Vietnam is in large part about the unwillingness or inability of the middle and lower levels of command to comply with the requirements of the rules of warfare. This is the net result of investigations by military sociologists and contemporary historians, and General William Peers drew this conclusion at the end of his expert report; this is what historians mean when they use the term 'comprehensive leadership breakdown'.

The reasons for this failure extend far beyond Vietnam. The Pentagon planners, committed to the 'worst case' scenarios of the Cold War, wanted to be prepared at all times for a major war against the Warsaw Pact. To this end the strength of the officer corps was also drastically increased but above all it was a question of committing the leadership elite on a long-term basis and making provision against their premature return to civilian life. In fact, the chances of promotion in the US Army were better than ever before, but there remained one bureaucratic hurdle: anyone wanting to rise to middle-ranking officer level, or especially to the top, needed more than good references from the military academies. Experience in commanding troops had to be proved by those seeking leadership roles in battalions, brigades, divisions or the Pentagon administration. In principle applicants could have met this requirement at any US Army base around the world, but command under battle conditions carried much more weight and promised advantages over the competition. However, after the US withdrawal from Korea there were too few hot wars involving Americans in which the necessary battle experience could have been acquired. Vietnam was the place where the interests of both sides coincided: the Chiefs of Staff were able to disperse the queue for promotion which had built up over the years and ambitious candidates were presented with the opportunity for a premature career leap. Soon there were more applicants for Vietnam than positions available. According to an internal memorandum, 'Officers have been scrambling around to get the jobs that lead to the quickest promotion without regard for the effect this will have on his unit or what he is best suited for.'[19] In more than 1,500 cases the Pentagon even turned down applications to retire, pointing out that lieutenant colonels, majors and captains had to complete a 'Vietnam tour' before they were released.[20] They were called 'ticket punchers' – soldiers on a tour of duty who had bought a ticket to South-East Asia but were trying to arrive at a completely different place.

The results are well known. Countless soldiers in Vietnam were entrusted to young officers who up till then had never led a unit. The need to compensate for such a handicap – especially in an emergency – is a large but not insuperable challenge; the same thing had happened to the civilian soldiers in the Second World War and the Korean War, who were torn from their regular jobs at a day's notice. However, in Vietnam even the willing ones were not given a chance. In order to avoid disappointing the large numbers of applicants, the Pentagon decided on an unprecedented rotation policy, limiting command of fighting troops to six months. There were some exceptions: in the 1st Marine Division, 1st Battalion of 7th Regiment was led by three commanders in the space of five months.[21] The observation made by military sociologists such as Morris Janowitz since the early 1950s, namely that armies which are technologically advanced anyhow tend to overvalue knowledge of management and technology to the detriment of military leadership skills, was carried to excess in Vietnam.[22] Scarcely had commanders collected their first jungle experiences than they were moved again – relieved by successors who paid for their own inexperience while repeating well-known mistakes. Others wanted at all costs to avoid such an embarrassment, for the sake of an unblemished personal file. They preferred to work to rule and, as a brigadier general from the 1st Marine Division recorded in his final report, attended to administrative tasks in air-conditioned offices far away from the fighting zone.[23]

The White House ultimately steered a fundamentally misdirected policy into the ground. Johnson wanted to have his cake and eat it. In other words, the decision in favour of escalation had been evident since spring 1965 but the public were not to learn of the expense needed to fight a 'fourth-class opponent'. Vietnam was depicted as a tiresome police action, a routine deployment that required no further justification in the form of an official declaration of war, and therefore calling up the Reserves and sections of the National Guard was out of the question. Johnson repeatedly refused the military's demands for this – even at the cost of slimming down the US armed forces in strategic focal points like Europe. Mobilising the reservists would have signalled an admission of a national state of emergency and would inevitably have intensified the controversy over the aim and purpose of the war. But above all it would have raised the question of the staying power of a society which, despite all its heroic rhetoric, expressed outspoken aversion to making personal sacrifices or to investing much time in going to war. To spare the psychological and moral resources of civilian society Johnson was prepared to put to the test the resilience of the leadership resources of the military in terms of personnel.

It is an open question whether, in view of the increasing numbers of troops being dispatched, the enormous pool of officers and non-commissioned officers standing by in the Reserves and the National Guard would have been sufficient to meet the increased need for officers at lower and middle levels, and whether indeed they would have done more justice to their remit than the 'ticket-punchers' did. What is certain is that remedies which had been reliable up to then had no more effect either, once protesting students had started targeting the ROTC programme in the universities and in many places had put a stop to the recruitment of young officers from the next generation of graduates. Improvisation and stopgap solutions were all that was left within the framework of the presidential agenda.

One solution was to take refuge in drastically curtailing the training programme and enhancing the status of officer candidate schools, which compared poorly with traditional military academies. Although they were known for their poor-quality instruction, they awarded commissions to half of all officers newly appointed in 1967. In that year alone more fledgling lieutenants were granted the OCS than in the entire previous decade.[24] If the qualifications of these commissioned officers left something to be desired, the professionalism of the non-commissioned officers became an object of open condemnation. 'Shake and bake' was the name given to the courses which an average of 13,000 non-commissioned officers passed through annually at the end of the 1960s – in the rank of corporal, sergeant, staff sergeant and sergeant major, mostly to be sent to Vietnam. Undoubtedly one cannot make a judgement on individuals by lumping them all together and ignoring any distinctions between them. All the more remarkable is the self-critical view of the group of these officers in a contemporary assessment to be found in the personnel department of the Army Chief of Staff. It talks of officers who under normal circumstances never could or should have reached this rank and, in addition, of a negligent disregard of written selection and assessment criteria. 'Our present officer personnel records system too often discourages or prohibits filing information concerning deficiencies and shortcomings in an officer's character or professional performance. This results in some instances of officers of questionable suitability being considered for sensitive positions of authority and responsibility because of a lack of information.'[25] From this perspective the comment of one colonel on the My Lai (4) case conceals more than just one grain of truth: 'We have at least two or three thousand more Calleys in the Army just waiting for the next calamity.'[26]

On the other hand, a questionable promotion policy additionally emphasised the deficiencies in training. At the end of the 1960s, officers could be promoted to first lieutenant after twelve months' service and to captain after two years – in the first case six months, and in the second twenty-four months earlier than was usual up to then.[27] In this respect as well the example of William Calley is representative of this trend. If it was questionable enough to promote him to non-commissioned officer, his promotion to second lieutenant even before he was sent to Vietnam broke valid procedural rules. These required an assessment of competence during a minimum of four months' operational service.[28] Especially the positions of the platoon and company leaders, so critical in active deployments, were frequently occupied by prematurely promoted officers who were out of their depth – even in the ranks of the Marines who were otherwise praised for observing principles of seniority.[29] So there were frequent cases of ordinary soldiers not just looking down their noses at the 'lifers' – the career soldiers – but occasionally even considering that their lack of experience was a threat to themselves. 'The officers, you try to stay away from them, 'cause they're dangerous. They'll get you killed. 'Cause they don't know.'[30]

A 'Vietnam Only Army' emerged from the clash between personnel policies of the military bureaucracy and political decision-making by the White House – an army which differed from the armed forces of past wars principally because of its leadership personnel. At the lower level the poorly-trained and inexperienced were strongly represented, in the middle ranks the uninterested held sway and the higher ranks from brigade commander upwards had the reputation of being 'remote officers', invisible and unapproachable.[31] Faced with such a mishmash it is basically difficult – and under the constraints of a hot war virtually impossible – to get anywhere. Precisely because of this many officers saw their relief after six months as liberation from a hopeless situation heading towards disaster. Superiors either did not care about the needs and problems of their troops, were oblivious to morale and blind to situations which required corrective intervention, or wanted to make up for lack of recognition by being sociable and free and easy with their men, in so doing overlooking how fluid is the dividing line between indulgence on the one hand and indifference and indiscipline on the other. Above all, they failed to make a clear distinction between violence which is permissible in war and criminal violence which contravenes the rules of warfare.

THE RULES OF ENGAGEMENT

As already stated, the framework guidelines for deployments issued by the American headquarters in Saigon emphatically demanded that such a distinction should be made. The Rules of Engagement had been revised twice yearly since 1966 and were delivered to all units with the instruction that the men should be made fully aware of them in every detail.[32] If one wanted to summarise in one sentence the criteria for operations on the ground, in the air and on the water, which were formulated in more than forty directives up to the end of 1968, it would be an unwavering appeal for self-control and self-discipline. As stated in MACV 525-3, 'Commanders at all echelons must strike a balance between the force necessary to accomplish their missions . . . and the high importance of reducing to a minimum the casualties inflicted on the non-combatant populace.'[33] The Supreme Command had put together a compendium of those regulations which we know from the Hague Conventions of 1899 and 1907 and the Geneva Conventions of 1929 and 1949 for the protection of civilians and prisoners of war.

Various safety and control measures were designated to ensure adherence to these rules. They applied primarily to air and artillery attacks within or in the vicinity of residential areas. Such attacks were only permitted if the leaders of the Vietnamese provincial and district administration were in agreement; secondly, if the US troop leader had contacted a higher-ranking officer; thirdly, if an American forward air controller was available to observe and fine-tune the attack in compliance with the rules. Since March 1969 decisions on the American side had been assigned to either the battalion or appropriate task-force commander responsible. In principle these restrictions even applied in the event of their own troops coming under fire from villages and needing aerial support. In the Free Fire Zones or Specified Strike Zones no advance coordination with South Vietnamese authorities was indeed required; however, if settlements lay in an attack zone, US staff had to be consulted – from March 1969 either the Commanders of I or II Field Force or the senior civilian adviser in the region.[34]

To this day a distant echo of these regulations can be found in the complaints of disappointed members of the military who attribute their defeat to bureaucratic high-handedness and accuse the Supreme Command of having sent the Army into battle with one hand tied behind its back. This picture is as absurd as the allegation popular in William Peers's milieu, that the Rules of Engagement were flawless, but came to grief because of a lack of comprehension on the part of subordinates or inadequate instruction given to the men.

On closer consideration it is clear that the Rules of Engagement suffered mainly from their inherent contradictions. As they were open to opposite interpretations, it was possible to read them more as recommendations than obligations. In other words, the leadership problems can by no means be blamed solely on the middle and lower ranks. They originated at the very top – in the divisional and corps headquarters and at the summit of the Military Assistance Command Vietnam (MACV). There sat the planners responsible for the Rules of Engagement – men like Westmoreland, who were well aware of the dynamic of asymmetrical wars and, according to their circulars, knew that the strategy of attrition had led them into a grey area of unbridled violence. No doubt such an unbounded escalation was not their intention, and no doubt there were generals, too, who like their mentor Douglas MacArthur considered themselves called upon to protect the weak and unarmed. Nevertheless they adopted Rules of Engagement which were glaringly ambiguous. As the résumé of an internal review put it, 'The MACV directives were found to be clear as to intent but are unacceptably vague in certain definitions and prescribed procedures.'[35]

This freedom from obligation was called 'military necessity' or the 'preservation of operational flexibility'. Because of it, exceptions which were compatible with the rules were set out in the Rules of Engagement. Essentially they were concerned with three scenarios. Firstly, the procedure for consultation and clearance: helicopter pilots were allowed without consultation to open fire on villages as soon as they were fired at and inasmuch as 'the source of the fire could be visually identified, if the strike could be positively oriented against the source, or if the fire was of such intensity that counter-action was necessary.'[36] The guideline that heavy firing at American troops could be met with more than light fire was equally vague. If the enemy were firing from villages with heavy-calibre weapons, a deployment leader could counter-attack on the basis of exceptional circumstances without the permission of superior authority.[37] In this case fighter-jets were on standby and no conditions were placed on their use of ammunition. Anyone who wanted to could re-interpret the duty of care and protection towards his own soldiers as an operational *carte blanche* without the risk of disciplinary repercussions. Secondly, even the principle that the population must be warned before air and artillery attacks on settlements was a matter of discretion. The leaders of deployed units alone decided whether and in what circumstances such warnings were repeated.[38] 'Once warned, always warned,' soon became one of the GIs' favourite expressions.[39] What is more, the requirement to inform residents in advance ceased to apply as soon as a commanding officer believed that the element of surprise was necessary for the success of his operation.[40] Thirdly, the protection of property, houses, livestock and supplies was similarly put under a proviso: their destruction was unquestioned as 'an unavoided [*sic*] consequence of combat operations' or if by so doing support and supplies for the enemy could be damaged.[41] Yet again, powers of discretion became the general yardstick: 'Destruction of structures in areas used as VC base camps, or those obviously built by the VC to fight from, is authorized.'[42] What constituted a 'base camp' and how 'obviously' could be defined was left up to the discretion of the individual officers responsible. If in doubt, they could entrust a scorched-earth policy to someone else: 'The destruction of dwellings and livestock of non-combatants as a denial measure is to be left to GVN authorities or RVNAF [Republic of Vietnam Armed Forces] units.'[43]

There was a built-in disclaimer of the orders laid down in the Rules of Engagement in the case of the Free Fire Zones as well, the situation being that units operating in these areas had guidelines to hand which differentiated between 'friendly populated areas' and 'no friendly populace' and thus between first- and second-class civilians.[44] On the one side were 'those non-combatants who must be brought back into the fold in the course of time'[45] – people who were unable to defend themselves against the repressive measures of the Viet Cong and who deserved the protection provided for civilians in the laws of warfare. On the other, those voluntarily living in Viet Cong strongholds counted as part of the enemy and had forfeited all consideration. Where the distinction should be drawn between voluntary and involuntary support was obviously unanswered and in practice the difference between friendly and enemy civilians was anyhow irrelevant. As soon as a local South Vietnamese district official had designated an area as a Free Fire Zone, the Rules of Engagement could be interpreted by local commanders as a licence for unrestricted action. Accordingly, a circular from the headquarters of III Marine Amphibious Force dated 13 December 1966 stated, 'Specified strike zones [Free Fire Zones] will be configured to exclude populated areas except those in accepted Viet Cong bases.'[46] The Standing Operating Procedures of the same unit spoke of 'zones containing no friendly population, which are used by the VC/NVA; and wherein the civilian population in the area, if any, actively supports the VC/NVA . . . Supporting arms fire[47] may be delivered into these areas without further clearance.'[48] Daily life in the Free Fire Zones was therefore not determined by individual officers or disobedient groups of men overstepping the mark. The Supreme Command of the US Armed Forces had laid down in writing the prerequisites for total war and for ten years continued to give it the stamp of approval.

After Telford Taylor, the former American prosecutor in Nuremberg, had harshly attacked the US conduct of the war in Vietnam and had received support from countless intellectuals both nationally and internationally,[49] the US Army commissioned an internal study of the Rules of Engagement. Do they contravene the internationally recognised laws of warfare? What do the Hague and Geneva Conventions say about guerrilla warfare? And above all, what was the Nuremberg judges' verdict on right and wrong in partisan fighting? It is not surprising that the authors of the Army study were looking for justification and were even able to legitimise parts of the strategy pursued in Vietnam, for the traditional regulations for land warfare primarily deal with the parameters of normal warfare waged between regular armed forces, and only marginally with the type of confrontation typical in guerrilla warfare between 'regulars' and 'irregulars'. Moreover, Article 26 of the Hague Convention and Article 49 of the Geneva Convention permit, under certain conditions, attacks on populated areas without prior warning, or the deportation of civilians together with the subsequent destruction of militarily useful infrastructure. How these clauses are interpreted is crucial: whether they are regarded as options to be applied in exceptional cases only, or as perfectly legal standards valid at all times and therefore not requiring any further justification. The answer turned out to be as simple as it was radical. According to the résumé, violation of the international laws of warfare only occurs if a policy of deliberate mass murder is being pursued and therefore the intention of committing genocide can be proved. In the absence of any such intention, there is no question of a war strategy which contravenes law and statute.[50]

The granting of legal immunity to troop commanders could hardly have been clearer. Traditionally provided with wide discretionary powers in any case and therefore apostrophised as 'gods in the field', the field commanders' autonomy was applied even more liberally in Vietnam than in other wars. Fundamentally they could interpret the Rules of Engagement as they chose.[51] It was therefore not a question of easy self-exoneration when one soldier stated for the record on his return from Vietnam, 'Where small unit commanders have such autonomy (lieutenants and captains to a large degree run the show), an individual can make a big difference. If a man wants to burn villages, he can do it.'[52] For many years General Westmoreland either could not or would not touch this policy and it was his successor Creighton Abrams who first made some careful corrections at the beginning of 1969, without actually countermanding that passage in the Rules of Engagement which conceded complete freedom to the most aggressive among the troop leaders: 'It is absolutely essential that US forces establish the reputation of being able to move at will throughout SVN [South Vietnam] and to defeat any VC force encountered. This reputation for invincibility will produce innumerable psychological benefits and hasten the end of the war.'[53]

In fact, no encouragement to be high-handed and autocratic would have been necessary at all. No matter whether one consults journalists' reports, interviews carried out by historians or the evidence of participants, all alike confirm that the officer corps rejected the Rules of Engagement for reasons ranging from indifference to denunciation.[54] This impression is formed not only from studying those units which tarnished their reputation by committing atrocities or war crimes; a colonel of 101st Airborne Division, which at that time was considered the best-trained unit in the US Army, responded to the question of the laws of war with two dogmatic comments: 'There's no such thing . . . Well, they [Standing Operating Procedures] just simply don't apply on the battlefield.'[55] Similarly, from a captain of an artillery unit: 'There used to be a regulation in Vietnam covering everything. At the battery [artillery company] level, I ignored most of them. No one cared at battery level.'[56] Beside the quantity of almost identical definitions it is striking that, in the course of court-martial investigations, senior officers – among them the commander of 11th Light Infantry Brigade, Americal Division and the Assistant Chief of Staff for Operations of the same brigade – successfully cited the ignorance of the majority as an excuse for their own flouting of the Rules of Engagement.[57]

Two of the investigations commissioned by the Army leadership show that contempt for the laws of warfare was by no means only to be found in troops stationed in Vietnam. After a visit to the Officer Candidate School in Fort Benning in summer 1967, investigators reached the conclusion that many budding officers, like a sizeable proportion of their men, rated rapid military success significantly more highly than legal imperatives. Half of the 149 participants on one course were of the opinion that they were permitted to use torture to procure essential information and twenty per cent of those questioned said they were prepared to shoot dead prisoners of war under their control if their unit was ambushed.[58]

Considerably more comprehensive than this random sample taken at Fort Benning was a study that Secretary of the Army Stanley R. Resor commissioned in mid December 1969 after the exposure of the My Lai (4) massacre. The office of the Judge Advocate General produced a catalogue with twenty-eight questions that were answered by 4,000 officers and soldiers in individual interviews and by a further 18,000 in writing. Those interviewed were confronted with hypothetical situations which might commonly arise in war, in order to discover their understanding of illegal orders in particular. Did they know about their right to refuse and their duty to report? The results from units in the United States and Europe were available in early April 1970.[59] The fact that thirty per cent of those questioned had given incorrect answers to over half the section on the Geneva Convention was a serious finding in itself, but the response from those well-informed about the laws of warfare was even more revealing. As soon as an order was taken for granted or it was assumed that they were in an emergency situation, they too were prepared to flout the legal norm. A quarter of the officers (and half of the men) claimed unconditional legal immunity in cases when they were carrying out an order to torture or murder prisoners. It was only the giving of criminal orders which they considered to be an offence. The lower the rank, the more marked was the readiness for blind obedience – and even for taking authority themselves in the name of military necessity. The latter sanctioned criminal behaviour even when it exceeded 'acting under orders'. About twenty per cent of captains and twenty-five per cent of first and second lieutenants and warrant officers agreed that civilians caught spying or setting booby-traps could be shot dead immediately. Over sixty per cent of all captains, first and second lieutenants and warrant officers claimed that, even without being ordered to, they would use torture or the threat of it on prisoners in order to get essential information. In reply to the question of whether prisoners could be killed if their presence endangered the success of an operation, twenty-eight percent of all officers (and thirty-three per cent of the men) answered 'Yes'.[60]

In Vietnam junior officers occasionally permitted themselves not just to modify the Rules of Engagement which had been issued by the Supreme Command in Saigon, but to circulate completely divergent operational regulations – with the result that units within the same formation could quote differing directives. When, for example, 9th Infantry Division carried out a large operation near Saigon in spring 1968, the helicopter teams had a free hand, unlike the artillery and the tactical Air Force – even though they were flying their missions in populated areas.[61] An internal study of the war in the provinces of Quang Ngai and Quang Tin revealed similar differences within the 4th Infantry Division: 'One Brigade permits fire upon evading civilians, while another requires positive identification by sighting of uniforms or weapons before engaging personnel.'[62] Soldiers attached to 198th Light Infantry Brigade could kill enemy soldiers immediately on sight, whereas GIs of 3rd Brigade were urged to take prisoners and only shoot in self-defence. There were corresponding differences in the stipulations for avoiding civilian casualties.[63] Soldiers stationed in Cambodia reported that they were subject to no restrictions there whatsoever; 'Unless ARVN [Army of the Republic of Vietnam] forces are in the area it is common to get a complete (free fire) clearance anytime it is asked for, even where there are towns and villages.'[64]

Scanning the files suggests that the smaller the units, the more lax the implementation of the rules.[65] For example, at the level of companies and platoons it was usual to fire on settlements on suspicion – merely to find out whether Viet Cong were in the area in question. In the northern provinces this practice had spread to such an extent by the end of 1967 that one high-ranking civil servant sent a letter of complaint to General Westmoreland. In his role as Deputy Head of CORDS, Robert Komer wrote, 'I . . . believe that we have a serious "political problem" on our hands.'[66] The US Supreme Command in Saigon had definitively lost control over the implementation of the Rules of Engagement – or to be more precise, had given it away without resistance.

From this it can be assumed that neither the Rules of Engagement nor the laws of warfare played any part in the training of troops and their briefing before going into action. Senior officers believed they had fulfilled their duty by handing out to newly arrived soldiers, along with their uniforms, four brochures of optional reading matter without making any comment.[67] Only half the officers carried out the simple task of delivering an annual hour-long briefing on the laws of warfare and compulsory or forbidden conduct in the field.[68] Because General Peers believed that the Army leadership wanted to play down the consequences of these failings and to get out of trouble by referring to regrettable individual cases, he wrote a strongly worded letter to his superiors in the Pentagon in mid February 1970: 'Subject: Nonconcurrence . . . It should be noted that there is a dearth of written information concerning illegal orders. The phrase is not defined in the dictionary of Army terms . . . Department of the Army guidance must not only stress the individual's responsibility concerning illegal orders but must clearly and emphatically indicate that those in responsible positions must not issue or condone the issuance of such orders.'[69]

ONLOOKERS, ACCOMPLICES AND FELLOW-CRIMINALS

'Must not issue or condone the issuance of such orders': in one half-sentence William Peers was speaking about a development which damaged the command climate more than anything else. He was refer-ring to the fluid line between a disdain for the laws of warfare on the one hand and the tacit or explicit authorisation of atrocities and war crimes on the other. General Peers was comparatively restrained in his criticism. When asked about their experiences by the Army War College, the majority of officers leaving the armed forces after long years of service stated formally that they had never served in an 'honest Army' but in an institution which was more interested in bureaucratic process than in cultivating a professional ethic.[70] On the subject of 23rd Infantry Division, known as 'Americal' and notorious for its partic-ipation in the My Lai (4) massacre, there was even talk of a 'moral vacuum' and 'a moratorium on restraint and self-control'.[71] Despite the fact that the conditions in which the Americal Division found itself cannot be generalised and do not stand comparison with, for example, 1st Infantry Division, General Harry G. Summers testified to an exten-sive 'lowering [of] ethical standards' and proposed rewriting the history of the US Army since the 1950s. 'It had an effect beyond belief.'[72] This verdict is essentially about commissioned and non-commissioned offi-cers who were directly or indirectly linked with stimulating excessive violence – through toleration, complicity and ultimately even taking part. As this group was also responsible for keeping the records of their actions, the military files are of only limited worth – a problem which I shall return to in the context of the investigations of the Crim-inal Investigation Division and the conduct of court-martial cases,[73] but the outlines of the situation deplored by General Peers and others are quite clear.

Toleration means allowing culprits to operate in a tacitly protected sphere, without having to reckon with moral ostracism or being punished and with the certainty of their superiors' backing. Two examples from the daily routine of helicopter gunship teams illustrate the meaning of this. It could be proved that in early July 1969 and mid May 1971 respectively, pilots of D Troop, 1st Squadron, 1st Cavalry Regiment, 23rd Infantry Division (Americal) and of A Troop, 1st Squadron, 9th Cavalry Regiment, 3rd Brigade (Separate), deliberately deceived their operational command when they claimed they had come under enemy fire and, on being given permission to return fire, bombarded several villages, in all killing eighteen inhabitants and wounding thirty.[74] In both cases the Rules of Engagement were breached without any excuse whatever and in both cases there were a number of credible witnesses – a rare advantage for the investigators into deployments in remote areas.

The inquiries made with the help of the Criminal Investigation Division led to one clear conclusion: the teams of A Troop and D Troop had needlessly murdered obvious non-combatants. However, no court martial was convened. The guilty parties from D Troop received a verbal caution[75] and three soldiers from A Troop a written warning.[76] According to Major General Lloyd B. Ramsey of the Americal Division, 'We have to give them the benefit of the doubt . . . I don't think they should be brought to trial because of their lack of judgement and their lack of understanding of the Rules of Engagement.'[77] In the investigation report of 12th Combat Aviation Group which was operationally responsible for A Troop, the Rules of Engagement were downgraded to 'broad guidance' – non-binding guidelines which would not do justice to the reality of 'men in battle'. 'It is sadly lacking and somewhat unfair to the participants, in that the investigation failed to fully develop and explore the environment in which the incident happened. To stay alive, the aviators must react instantly and with effective and deadly firepower . . . These men must be tough, fearless, and reactive, and their actions must be so accepted . . . Men see things differently under such conditions.' The requirement that South Vietnamese authorities should give permission for the bombardment of populated areas was rejected as unrealistic: 'Some are not really proficient in the English language. Many do not have a real understanding of the situation.'[78] The commander of 3rd Cavalry Brigade (Separate) closed the A Troop file with the comment, 'It is quite clear that both men were following the Rules of Engagement as they understood them to be, however erroneous . . . Although there are technical violations, I believe that no military court would convict either man.'[79] 'Technical violations': a dismantling of the Rules of Engagement could scarcely have been more obvious.

Above all, the daily routine of the ground troops showed how closely backing and complicity were interlinked – particularly in the example of a policy which dominates memories to the present day. Major General Jim Johnson, commander of 82nd Airborne Division in the 1991 Gulf War said, 'You know, the lesson of Vietnam for me as a member of the younger generation, as a captain, was seeing my senior officers compromised and fall victim to the body-count syndrome and look the other way.'[80] The body count is not just the core of the story of the war; it is more an illustration of what the detailed discussion of leadership breakdown – of the gradual disintegration of disciplined and disciplining troop leadership – is all about. When the Army War College put the questionnaire already mentioned to officers, 'they went on and on, and all of them seemed to zero in on body-count as the root or virus that drove all this.'[81]

It was well known that the success of the war was measured by the number of dead enemy soldiers,[82] with the result that there are reports from literally all war zones and by all frontline troops on how officers incessantly spurred their teams on to optimise the body-count tally. Sometimes monthly and weekly killing targets were laid down *ex cathedra*; sometimes extended leave was granted for an improved kill ratio; sometimes those who did not reach their targets were threatened with cancellation of the popular rest and recuperation breaks in Thailand, Japan and South Korea.[83] Whether shooting pregnant women dead really earned an extra ten points, as was frequently claimed, or whether soldiers produced severed ears as proof of their efficiency are as much open questions as the reports of the body-count prayers recited by clerics.[84] What can be vouched for, however, is that one lieutenant colonel, commander of 5th Battalion, 60th Infantry Regiment, 3rd Brigade, 9th Infantry Division, awarded special performance badges for soldiers to sew onto their uniform – so-called Sat Cong or Cong Killer insignia, which they could collect and, when they reached a certain number, exchange at battalion headquarters for privileges.[85] Leaflets in English and Vietnamese circulated by the same unit indicated a policy of 'taking no prisoners'. 'Viet Cong and NVA – Beware. You are now located in the area of operations of "Cong Killer", 5th Battalion, 60th Infantry. Each member of this elite American unit is a trained killer, dedicated to the annihilation of every VC/NVA. . . . We will hunt you with our helicopters, track you down with radar, search above and below the water with boats, bombard you with artillery and airstrikes. There are no havens here.'[86]

The aforementioned insignia were taken out of circulation at the end of November 1969 after the intervention of Senator Philip A. Hart.[87] At this stage most of 9th Infantry Division was already pulling out of the Mekong Delta. John Paul Vann told the journalist David Halberstam that its soldiers had rampaged there like butchers in the course of Operation Speedy Express.[88]

The example of 1st Marine Division indicates that there is good reason to connect the mania for body count with the murder of civilians. On entering the headquarters of 1st Battalion, 7th Regiment of this division one would pass a noticeboard with the heading 'Kill Board' – a ranking list recalling the motto of the battalion, 'Get Some', and giving information about the successes of individual units. 'Get Some' also formed part of the rhetorical repertoire employed by the divisional commander, Lieutenant Colonel Frank Clark, when briefing his company commanders and platoon sergeants.[89] When asked how he interpreted his guidelines regarding women and children, one of them replied, 'If it was at night, if it moved, that's tough.'[90]

First Lieutenant Lewis R. Ambort led B Company of the 1st Battalion in this manner. Driven by ambition to make first place on the Kill Board, he put together killer teams of four to five men on his own initiative and regardless of the organisational principles applying to the Marines, with instructions to go out on patrol at night and track down Viet Cong hideouts, supplies and weapons. As has been repeatedly confirmed, it was routine for the killer teams to comb through villages with concentrated aggression, to shoot peasants dead for the slightest reason or to throw hand grenades into their homes.[91] In February 1970 Ambort prepared five Marines for a deployment south west of Da Nang in Quang Nam Province. 'Don't let them get us any more. I want you to pay these little bastards back . . . Shoot first and ask questions later.'[92] On the night of 19 February the patrol had no enemy contact; even when searching the village of Son Thang they found no sign of the Viet Cong. As a court martial later established, the soldiers forced the unarmed occupants of three huts into the open and shot them dead one after another – sixteen women and children, among them babies and a twenty-year-old blind girl. None of the usual excuses could be used in their defence – neither self-defence, nor battle stress, nor confusion. The Marines had not killed like soldiers but slaughtered like murderers – probably out of frustration, because the body count they hoped for had not materialised.[93]

Admittedly in his deployment briefing First Lieutenant Ambort had not given any explicit order to murder civilians. (No such order was given in most other cases, either, including the My Lai (4) massacre.) However, he had chosen the sort of speech which was bound to work as a direct stimulant on the most aggressive. One of the Son Thang defendants said, 'What do I care about some gook woman or child! It's them or me. If they get in my way, that's too bad.'[94] This kind of 'prep talk' was in fact widespread, detectable in deployment briefings designed to make the GIs 'hot' with claims, often plucked out of thin air, about the strengths and fighting power of enemy units or with a hint that the whole population of a target area to be cleared was without exception on the side of the Viet Cong and consequently would not deserve any mercy if they showed the slightest sign of resistance. 'Upon arrival, I was surprised to find people in the village,' one GI said of his deployment in the vicinity of Bong Son (II Corps Tactical Zone). 'Considering the tone of the orders, I had suspected a very hostile atmosphere.'[95] 'That's just the way it was,' writes the military lawyer and former Marine company commander Gary D. Solis in his investigation into Son Thang. 'Not in every unit, not in the best-led units, but in most.'[96]

This obsession with the body count prescribed from the highest level of the Pentagon was perceived in middle and lower levels of command as a choice between the frying-pan and the fire. Anyone wanting to safeguard his chances of promotion could either falsify statistics and fabricate casualty figures, or tolerate excesses of violence, if not actually encourage them, in order to avoid being found guilty of falsification. Both attitudes can be easily proved and in the latter case they indicate a more exact definition of leadership breakdown. It is a question of the deliberate or negligent acceptance of random killing – of a licence to kill as many Vietnamese as possible. In the logic of the body count, each corpse counted as a Viet Cong: 'Dead men tell no tales.'[97]

'[It was an] incentive program to instil esprit within soldiers of the unit.'[98] A captain used these words to try to excuse the Sat Cong badges. The echo of an age-old, well-known practice and the calculation which goes with it can be heard: in order to dissipate the troops' built-up aggression, the reins have to be slackened from time to time and the limits of what is allowed or tolerated relaxed. For this reason, in early modern times – to give just one example – plunder and rape was occasionally permitted for a short period after the capture of a town.[99] Troop leaders in Vietnam continued this history in countless different ways, and so talk of 'Indian Country' and its association with areas where the law does not rule was not an invention of GIs. The attacks carried out by 1st Cavalry Division between November 1968 and January 1969 were officially called Comanche Falls, Liberty Canyon, Navajo Warhorse I, Navajo Warhorse II and Sheridan Sabre.[100] Similar titles were chosen for a series of other operations. Apache Snow and Rolling Thunder brought to mind Indian mythology and underlying images of guerrilla warfare in the American frontier lands. Apparently the old soldiers from that period – from George Armstrong Custer to Samuel Sturgis – were turned into prompters: troops who are continually being ambushed and mourn more casualties from booby-traps than from open battles need the opportunity for revenge and a symbolic reckoning.

This was also the thinking of Brigadier General John W. Donaldson, who was accused during his time as commander of 11th Light Infantry Brigade, Americal Division of having personally practised target shooting on clearly unarmed civilians.[101] Donaldson said his victims were Viet Cong.[102] Conversely, the Criminal Investigation Division recorded in its concluding report in mid April 1971 that, 'on 13 separate occasions during the period October 1968 through March 1969, BG [Brigade General] (then Colonel) Donaldson . . . while flying in a helicopter over Quang Ngai Province, either fired or ordered others to fire, resulting in the apparent killing of unarmed and unresisting Vietnamese persons.'[103] Donaldson was the first general to be accused by the Army of war crimes since the proceedings taken in 1902 against Jacob Smith, commander of 6th Separate Brigade in the Philippine–American War.[104] 'We had him [Donaldson] dead to rights,' said one of the examiners in an interview carried out in 1996. 'They used to bet in the morning how many people they could kill – old people, civilians, it didn't matter. Some of the stuff would curl your hair.'[105]

However, the case against Donaldson and his co-accused, Lieutenant Colonel William J. McCloskey,[106] never came to court – two helicopter pilots had withdrawn their incriminating statements after their transfer to another base.[107]

When Lieutenant Colonel Anthony Herbert went public in summer 1971 and with the authority of an officer denounced the behaviour of his colleagues,[108] there was an almost overwhelming rush of similar accusations. A few examples must suffice. Second Battalion, 12th Infantry Regiment, 25th Infantry Division had also brought a 'Donaldson case' against Lieutenant Colonel Burton J. Walrath Jr., who had ordered helicopter pilots to target-shoot peasants in the province of Tay Ninh (III Corps Tactical Zone) for the sake of the body-count tally and was also suspected of having ordered the destruction of a village and the murder of all its inhabitants.[109] At the end of an internal investigation a company commander and a battalion commander of 47th Infantry Regiment, 3rd Brigade, 9th Infantry Division were strongly suspected of having tolerated, if not actually called for, the murder of prisoners.[110] A lieutenant colonel had admitted to having given the 173rd Aviation Company of the 11th Aviation Battalion the order for an 'aerial funeral' during a deployment in Gia Dinh Province (IV Corps Tactical Zone) – what was intended was the 'disposal' of a fallen North Vietnamese over enemy territory, in other words the desecration of a corpse, in order to intimidate the guerrillas and their supporters.[111] A company leader of 2nd Battalion, 503rd Infantry Regiment of the 173rd Airborne Brigade (Separate) had allowed the printing and sale of Christmas cards on which, next to the brigade insignia and the message, 'Peace on Earth – To Men of Goodwill', could be seen the mutilated face of a Vietnamese;[112] he had probably taken as his model Colonel George S. Patton III, son of the well-known Second World War general, who had sent greetings cards at Christmas 1968 together with colour photographs of mutilated Viet Cong piled up one on top of the other and the message, 'From Colonel and Mrs George S. Patton III – Peace on Earth.'[113] And so on and so forth, in a list to which, on the basis of the individual cases described in the following chapters, can be added countless further examples.

Herbert knew that his intervention coincided with the withdrawal of the ground troops and therefore came far too late. He was left with an emotional reckoning

We use our worst for cadre. The best go to the Pentagon looking for big jobs . . . This stuff would stop, if we'd hang a couple of senior commanders. If it's no longer condoned, then it will cease . . . When I first got to Vietnam and saw the torture that went on in my battalion, I talked to other officers about it. They all told me, 'That's the way it is. You can't rock the boat. You can't antagonize the big dragon.' That was what they said – don't antagonize the big dragons, or you're gone.[114]

He undoubtedly found favour with the Winter Soldiers and with other sections of the public but in the Pentagon those who did not want to make any further inquiries beyond My Lai (4) felt their views confirmed. Thus Herbert's criticism ultimately became one 'case' – meaning a further pretext for hushing things up behind a 'green wall of silence'.

In the light of the circumstances and developments described, Westmorelands's exhortations about the spirit and letter of the Rules of Engagement seem like something of a ritual. They appear to be acts of bureaucratic entreaty – as if the respect required could be engendered by means of repetition. Nor can a calculated intention to cover one's back be ruled out. A Supreme Command that is sufficiently well informed about the excesses of violence and war crimes committed by its troops but still allows things to take their course needs to protect its back – in this case in the form of proof, supplied by circulating files, that the commitments entered into in Nuremberg are taken seriously and that it is above any accusation of having licensed random killing. However that may be, the gulf between the claims and realities of the war, between rhetorical political doctrine and practised military strategy lay right in front of the eyes of the MACV leadership. With a catalogue of permitted violations of the rules, laid down in the definitions of exceptions to the Rules of Engagement, they had single-handedly established this gulf. In this respect, Westmoreland's appeals reflect an awareness of a carefully calculated risk: officers who do not adhere to the laws of warfare also release their men from any sense of responsibility. To quote Anthony Herbert once more, 'If you don't tell a soldier what's right, then he thinks whatever is tacitly condoned is what you want, and that's what he does.'[115]

4

Warriors

All those eyes on me – the town, the whole universe – and I
couldn't risk the embarrassment . . . In my head I could hear
people screaming at me. Traitor! They yelled. Turncoat! Pussy! I
felt myself blush. I couldn't tolerate it . . . Embarrassment, that's
all it was.

Tim O'Brien[1]

'U-U-U-U'

Abbreviation scribbled on the helmets of US soldiers in
Vietnam for 'The unwilling, led by the unqualified, doing the
unnecessary for the ungrateful'

Man Crazy is the name Joyce Carol Oates gave to her 1997 novel about
a stormy spiritual landscape in 1980s America.[2] The story revolves
around something intangible, which seems temporarily lost in the
mists of the past but at any time can erupt into the present with
destructive force, embodied in the figure of a former US Air Force
combat pilot who seems to have committed a criminal offence on his
return from Vietnam and is constantly on the run. He only appears
in person once, yet he accompanies his family at every trick and turn,
whispers to them and creeps into their dreams. The further his wife
and daughter imagine they have got away from him, the nearer he
gets to them. 'It's crazy, man' – 'This man is crazy'; whatever one

reads into the title, the book is about someone who cannot find his place in society any longer because he has lost himself.

I killed people in Nam, men, women, kids, Christ knows – water buffalo! . . . I knew I wouldn't die or if I did it didn't matter shit. A man is shit. So how can it matter? . . . If I blew the head off a man who's upright walking talking shit and everybody including his friends – including the cops – acknowledges that fact, you expect me to take it seriously? . . . Don't make me laugh. I'm shit in the eyes of God so anything I do or have done or will do isn't important.

He lives in a no man's land, surrounded by ghosts who torment all the more because beyond the memory of his shame they offer him a vain hope of salvation. Defiantly he retorts to his wife in the same breath: 'Like hell I ruined our lives . . . I'm a man of pride. I've got my pride.'[3]

'GRUNTS' AND CRACKS

In autumn 1964 184,000 US soldiers, including a variety of special units, were stationed in Vietnam; in 1969 there were 541,000 and by the time the war ended in April 1975 with the fall of the South Vietnamese capital Saigon, 3,400,000 GIs – among them a few thousand women – had served in Vietnam, Laos, Cambodia, Thailand and the South China Sea. Of them 2,600,000 had been stationed in South Vietnam over a period of barely eleven years. These figures tell us a lot about the political importance attached to the war but little about its daily routines, and to understand them one must create a picture of the jungle fighters. Trained for active service and perpetually either on the move or caught up in the fighting, they carried the main burden and ran the greatest risk of being killed, while killing other people was their principal remit. By continually putting their own lives on the line, they also had the last word over the lives of others – the fate of enemy soldiers depended on their battle morale and their conduct had the decisive influence on whether and how noncombatants survived in the war zones. But it is just when one looks at the 'grunts' or 'legs' – the American jargon for cannon-fodder –

that statistics are vague. Ask how many tons of ice cream or pizza were flown into Vietnam: the Pentagon archives will tell you; ask how many GIs were deployed at the front and actually saw action, as against the number responsible for either supplies, logistics or administration: there is no agreed or precise answer.

In the US Army order of battle an active division with an average of 16,000 men is officially designated as requiring 32,000 support troops; however, no division, brigade, regiment or battalion in Vietnam ever reached this ratio of one to two. Because the guerrillas concentrated on attacks against soft targets, the majority of the American troops were assigned to protecting bases, communication lines or centres of population. Apart from that, there was a very labour-intensive outlay to let the soldiers enjoy the amenities of civilian life so far as was possible – from air-conditioned quarters to short periods of leave in South-East Asia. Last but not least it is significant that the Americans built with their own hands a good part of the infrastructure needed for the war, from harbours to runways. An internal inventory gives a figure of only twenty per cent – that is, 520,000 out of a total of 2,600,000 soldiers – acting primarily as fighting troops, that is, in the infantry, the armoured divisions or the artillery,[4] although we do not know how they were actually deployed. On average, according to an assessment made at the end of the 1970s, only half of an Army or Marine Corps infantry battalion was assigned to rifle platoons and under combat orders, and less than half of all 'manoeuvre forces' – the classical fighting troops – were available for offensive operations.[5] Both contemporary calculations and subsequent accounts by officers point the same way and consequently we can assume that only one in ten regular Army soldiers was directly confronted with warfare in the traditional sense – that is, with killing and being killed. Accordingly the number of these jungle troops may therefore be estimated at 260,000 in all. In 1969, the year of the greatest troop concentration, it came to about 54,000.[6]

While during the Second World War and the Korean War almost all fit men reaching call-up age each year were mobilised, in the mid 1960s general conscription existed only on paper. In this matter as well the data is confusing. Depending on whether one looks at the whole duration of the war or one single year, the proportion of those exempted from military service varies between thirty-five and sixty per cent.[7] Following this trend one can assume that about half the twenty-seven million young men of military age in the 1960s benefited from deferment of some kind – either temporary postponement or making sure that they met their obligations peacefully in their home country. The selective service system had deteriorated into a selective system. In the words of the historian Christian Appy, American society had gone over to recruiting young upper and middle class males into the universities and putting children from working-class homes and the underclass into uniform.[8] Although this sociological use of 'class' and 'stratum' gives rise to the same scepticism as the Pentagon statistics, the findings are unambiguous. More than half of all the soldiers sent to Vietnam came from working-class families and a further quarter from poor backgrounds with a precarious livelihood often below the poverty line. The well-educated middle classes with above average earnings were represented by a bare quarter.[9] The all-purpose description of oneself as 'unwilling' is undoubtedly linked to this realisation of an unfair selection process.

The fact that sixty-five per cent of all GIs volunteered is not an argument against the widely documented distaste for the war.[10] In fact, anyone who did not wait for his call-up papers but enlisted in the Army ahead of time could wager on gaining certain advantages: a three-year term of service reduced to two years and above all not having to take a ticket to Vietnam. While between fifty and eighty per cent of conscripts were sent to the war, among volunteers the proportion was notably lower.[11] The paradox about this being compulsory service for volunteers also had a socio-economic background. Seventy-nine per cent of all soldiers serving in Vietnam had graduated from high school, while in the Korean War and the Second World War this proportion had been sixty-three and forty-five per cent respectively.[12] A comparatively good education guaranteed a good job and was an argument against joining the Army which, in contrast to later years, was not at that time appreciated as an attractive employment agency. From this viewpoint, Ronald Spector hits the nail on the head when he points out that the US armed forces in Vietnam 'were in many respects the finest military force the United States had ever sent abroad'.[13]

Yet whether this was 'the finest military force' is open to debate. At any rate it was the youngest. The average age of the draftees was just under twenty, that of the enlistees a few months younger. Taking into account basic training or months serving elsewhere, the typical GI was twenty-two years old when he arrived in Vietnam and therefore four to five years younger than the US soldiers serving during the American Civil War or the Second World War.[14] Even more marked is the difference in the casualties: two-thirds of those who lost their lives in Vietnam were twenty-one or younger.[15] Compared with that, a further fact that Catholics and Southerners were proportionally over-represented in the Vietnam Army is of negligible interest; what is significant is the price the political leadership paid for its indulgence towards the middle classes, or more precisely, for its refusal to call up reservists and members of the National Guard. They sent into the field the youngest sons of those who did not live in leafy suburbs, men who played an increasingly marginal role in the calculations of their electoral strategists.

This applies without exception to the 'grunts' in the narrower sense – background, age and on the whole education – and yet in comparison with the remaining ninety per cent of the Vietnam Army there are remarkable distinctions. The proverb that 'the devil takes the hindmost' seems tailor-made for them. For preference the Army put into the fighting units the men who had not volunteered, that is, those who were not familiar with the alternative opportunities within the system or did not know how to use them to their advantage. In 1970 eighty-eight per cent of all infantry riflemen were draftees[16] and despite all protestations, the directives for allocating men were not in fact colour-blind. Between 1964 and 1966 between 20 and 25 per cent of all Americans killed in action were black, while the proportion of Afro-Americans in Vietnam was 10.6 per cent, which corresponded to demographic distribution within the American population.[17] Admittedly this death rate was halved by mid 1969, because the Army was sending fewer blacks into the front line, not least influenced by the burning ghettos in some major US cities. But even then an infantry rifle company was anything but representative of America's younger generation: half of it consisted of blacks and soldiers of Latin-American and Asiatic origin.[18]

It is not clear how many soldiers recruited for 'Project 100,000' arrived among the grunts. Under the pressure of an increased need for manpower the Pentagon had in 1967 drastically lowered the entry criteria for the Army to enable it to admit 100,000 men graded as Category 4, who actually should have been rejected as unfit on grounds of mental deficiency. Thus by December 1971 354,000 unsuitable men had joined the Vietnam forces – seven per cent went to the Marines[19] and ninety-three per cent to the Army.[20] Those from Category 4 were certainly not the best soldiers, but this minority was not disproportionately responsible for the breaches of discipline at the front and elsewhere. 'Their court-martial rates did eventually decrease to levels only slightly higher than those of other mental categories,' according to a Pentagon study.[21]

No matter how one finally evaluates these details about the grunts, they are all in all only variations on the social dimension. As in no other period in American history, those from the bottom third of the social spectrum carried the main burden of the war. Social standing more than anything else determined the probability of having to fight and running the risk of dying. About thirty-two per cent of all American war dead – 18,465 men – came from the ranks of the infantry riflemen.[22] Only against this background does the grunts' definition of themselves as 'reluctant' and 'ill-used' become clear in its explosive effect. It was in the main put forward by soldiers who had the least to expect from American society[23] – and for whom, unlike the concepts of race and class, the label 'All-American boys' was meaningless.

The smallest group of frontline and jungle troops were the Special Forces, trained specifically for counter-insurgency operations. They were specialist units in the tradition of the Marines, who fought against insurgents in Latin America and the Caribbean between 1919 and 1939, or of the Army Rangers, who had become famous during the War of Independence and the Second World War. They are traditionally kept well hidden by the military secret services and their very existence is sometimes denied; official information is sometimes disinformation, to mislead their adversaries or even the public back home. Even the few special studies now available retreat into vagueness at important points, such as, for instance, how many men they comprised. If one collates the available data, at the climax of the war – that is, between 1967 and 1969 – between 3,500 and 4,000 of these elite soldiers were deployed each year in Vietnam, Laos and Cambodia. In other words, there was one member of the Special Forces to thirteen or fourteen traditionally trained jungle fighters.[24] In no previous war had so many special units been drawn on, but while it is possible to obtain an outline of the organisation's membership, allocation of duty and the soldiers' self-image, the available data is not adequate to create a socio-cultural profile.

In 1945 the Special Forces had been almost completely demobilised and they languished in the shadows until the early 1960s, though by then 5,000 Green Berets had passed through their training centre at Fort Bragg, North Carolina. But this only amounted to three below-strength battalions. The turning-point came when Kennedy, at the beginning of his term in office, authorised an increase in these special Army units from 2,500 to 10,000 men within a few months and as a mark of their new enhanced status he gave them permission for the first time to use their name of 'Green Berets' in public. The Air Force and the Marines then followed suit by starting to train their own units for 'limited warfare'. Major General Victor Krulak of the Marine Corps, the new coordinator of the anti-guerrilla programme, was fully accepted into the ranks of the Combined Chiefs of Staff. In 1964 the Pentagon set up a Studies and Observations Group (SOG), also known as the Special Operations Group, to coordinate the secret front in South-East Asia. Through the SOG the Supreme Command in Saigon could draw on elite troops of all branches of the armed forces at any time and made thorough use of this privilege until the end of the war. According to an unambiguous message from Washington, any wish of the SOG was to be treated as an order. Camouflaged as A, B or C & C teams, or Project Delta, the special units put together by the SOG even operated beyond the frontiers of South Vietnam.[25]

The Army had the largest contingent of clandestine troops in the Green Berets and the Long Range Reconnaissance Patrols (LRRP, or Lurps). Towards the end of the 1960s on a yearly average around 1,500 Green Berets were in action, most of them with 5th and the rest with 1st and 7th Special Forces Groups.[26] The Lurps, on the other hand, were represented in all divisions and all operational areas. As the war dragged on their teams were stocked not only with men trained in the Jungle Warfare School in Panama but also with volunteers who had taken a three-week Recondo School course in Vietnam.[27] Therefore the official count of 5,000 Lurps in action during the entire war[28] may well be a significant underestimate; many observers assess their numbers at around 1,800 in February 1969 alone. In any case, the

Pentagon took administrative account of the increasing number of Lurps and gave them the rank of 'ranger' companies of 75th Infantry Regiment.[29] In contrast the Navy's contribution was modest: their Sea, Air and Land Commandos (SEALs) – assigned to Task Forces 115 and 116 and predominantly active in the Mekong Delta – reached their maximum annual strength of one hundred men in 1968.[30]

The Special Forces usually operated in small groups of six, mostly under cover of darkness, in impassable terrain only accessible by helicopter, and often on their own for days or even weeks. Their most important tasks were spying out enemy installations and prison camps; marking targets for air attacks or troop landings; carrying out sabotage operations in Laos, Cambodia and North Vietnam; working in hunter-killer teams to abduct or murder Viet Cong functionaries; infiltrating agents; locating pilots who had been shot down; freeing prisoners of war; laying ambushes; laying mines; disrupting supply lines and in exceptional cases carrying out commando raids on enemy bases. Not to mention training native troops. The SEALs trained South Vietnamese police and agents who, working as Provincial Reconnaissance Units, hunted down suspects within the framework of the Phoenix programme, while the Green Berets directed the Civilian Irregular Defense Groups, a formation of about 50,000 men distributed among eighty bases in the Central Highlands, most of whom had been recruited from among the Montagnards, or hill people.[31]

Unlike the grunts, the Special Forces were not supposed to carry out attacks, but this guideline was heeded less and less the longer the war lasted. 'It became a problem to keep men from shooting,' so ran 9th Infantry Division's evaluation of the Lurps' practices in December 1967. 'On the last day of an operation when a patrol is going to be extracted anyway, the patrol can and does take advantage of a target of opportunity.'[32] In the course of ten years the Lurps made about 23,000 sorties and in over 14,000 made contact with the enemy. They claimed they had killed 10,000 Viet Cong and lost 450 of their own men, a seemingly incredible ratio of one to twenty-two – seven times the 'killing quota' of the regular troops.[33] It is hard to say what lies behind these statistics – how many enemy soldiers and how many non-combatants were among the victims. To date there are no reliable sources available about Special Force operations and no comprehensive account; at best there are snapshots which can be interpreted either as heroic tales or as illustrations of indiscriminate murder.[34] Of the largest attack ever coordinated by the SOG, all that is known is that it was carried out in Laos in early 1969 by 8,000 Montagnard troops and 2,000 elite soldiers of the US Army and aimed against bases and transport routes of the North Vietnamese Army. For every US soldier, apparently 100 to 150 North Vietnamese were killed. You can believe that or not. In any case, at the time the SOG teams had the reputation of being 'the deadliest troops'.[35] And it has also been established that more medals were awarded per head to members of the SEALs and the Army Special Commandos than to all other units in Vietnam.[36]

'I was runnin' a LURP team . . . We hiding all the time. We become the Viet Cong.' – 'Bein' a macho, strong young brother, I joined. I'm bad. It was exciting.' – 'It was a smaller group, and I had an opportunity to share my ideas and help make some decisions. With a line company, you're really just a pin on the map for sure.'[37] The Special Forces slipped into the role of guardians of the empire, forward posts on the periphery and specialists in the unconventional – loners who, if left alone to make their own decisions and choose their own methods, achieved their objectives all the more quickly. Black overalls or green camouflage suits with striped patterns were their trademark and their exotic face-paint, futuristic weapons and casual appearance ensured their reputation as 'true believers', in the long tradition of solitary heroes. One has to look far to find such a philosophical construct which so skilfully reconciles the anarchic side of the American self-image, and the anti-institutional feelings that go with it, with the official concept of a professional serviceman. Good reasons, therefore, why more volunteers applied to join the Lurps than they could take and why many 'Specials' completed several tours in Vietnam, as though war had become second nature to them. 'A Green Beret,' wrote Mark Baker about conversations with Vietnam veterans, 'was guaranteed a barstool anywhere in South Vietnam, Cambodia or Laos, as long as he wore his hat and camouflage fatigues. Specialty work held out the promise of movie star glamor.'[38]

PERSONAL TESTIMONY

There is an unusual, even unique, volume of testimony by American jungle troops about joining the Army and about their war experiences.

It was provided firstly, and mainly, in public statements after their return home, thereafter in literary publications, ranging from traditional soldiers' tales to highbrow novels and volumes of poetry. Then there are 'oral history' interviews and recorded group discussions with psychologists, which were like diaries or letters from the front and were authorised for publication in large quantities. They also even used examinations in front of the Criminal Investigation Division or statements before military tribunals as opportunities to account for themselves and their circumstances. In form these testimonies are remarkably colour-blind. It is true that whites predominate in the literary accounts, but in any case only a minority of veterans possessed this skill. For the majority, whites and blacks alike, verbal reports were the essential means of communication. Everything combines to present a picture from below, mostly from the perspective of that ten per cent of the personnel who had been sent to the invisible front lines as grunts or Special Forces.[39]

The jungle troops had spent their childhood and youth in a world crowned with the halo of the 'American Century'. As we know, American society has always tended towards dramatic stylisation of its wars – whether in the case of the Civil War, which went down in history as the Trojan War of the New World, or the First World War, which was referred to as the 'war to end all wars', America's 'exceptional status' legitimised war and renewed its legitimacy through a long series of victories. Tom Engelhardt therefore has good reason to speak of a unique 'Victory Culture'.[40] It was to be expected that this would occupy people's imaginations more strongly than ever after 1945, in view of the length and cost of the Second World War. Cinema and television made their contribution by turning war heroes into household gods. Until 1970 films of this kind, such as Patton and Tora! Tora! Tora!, reached an audience of millions – an indication, as social historians emphasise, of a gradual transformation of political culture. In the 1950s and 1960s one can see the struggle for special status changing into visions of omnipotence. That is why David Halberstam speaks of a 'toughness culture' and a 'do or die' attitude which particularly attracted the young: 'That toughness got into the blood stream.'[41] This does not imply a 'culture of violence' – a world of unbridled passion or pent-up aggression – but perhaps an attitude which fits Kennedy's own mantra: 'Conquer. Conquer at any price.' At the time of his presidency this became a kind of national doctrine, the symbolic multiplication of which – from the written word to body language – would be worth researching for its own sake. 'Losing is not an option': one must and will win, because as an American one is born to win.

On the other hand, a deep self-doubt lay within this post-Second World War triumphalism. What was victory worth, what was the point of hoping for a world freed from evil, if the next war were to be fought out with atomic weapons and America turned into a nuclear wasteland? Even if they were only interested in profit, countless media outlets cultivated fear with films about nuclear attacks on American cities, property dealers made money selling land which they claimed lay outside any potential nuclear targets and firms designing private nuclear shelters did a roaring trade.[42] Visions of a radioactive future revealed something more: that the days of the heroic warrior were over and nuclear warfare no longer required the skills of the traditional soldier. Perhaps that was why 'containment' – warding off the dangers lurking everywhere – became a national obsession. In any case the debunking of war brought a feeling of hurtful helplessness and wounded pride, based on a fear as unidentifiable as it was ever-present.

As soon as jungle fighters started talking about their childhood, their tales seemed to resuscitate heroism at a time when it had been devalued. Their visions of masculinity and the solitary fighter even have a name – 'the John Wayne thing'. 'A man stands alone against impossible odds,' writes Mark Baker about this widespread attitude, 'meets the Apache chief in single combat to protect the manifest destiny of the wagon train . . . or falls on a grenade to save his foxhole buddies and then takes a bow to thundering applause. Death threatens only pets and grandparents.'[43] From this viewpoint John Wayne's and Audie Murphy's westerns offered a promise which transfigured the future, a moment captured on celluloid in which the instructor no longer yells 'Good morning, girls', but 'Get ready, Marines'. In them true heroism was lived out – the Air Force 'sissies' in their flying machines had not earned this soubriquet, but rather the GIs cast in bronze on the Iwo Jima memorial, who had won through in a seemingly hopeless situation against a superior Japanese force. 'War fiction . . . implanted this idea in my mind that war was a place for you to discover things,' said a Vietnam veteran.[44] 'Passages to manhood' were celebrated in epic dimensions; in them the risk of dying is removed and war no longer means pain and mourning but fun, joy and adventure. And if anyone was killed, he died in the knowledge that he would always be remembered as a hero. Daniel Ellsberg, who commanded a rifle company of Marines in the 1950s, quoted as proof of this self-awareness a chance encounter with John Wayne in a restaurant in Italy: 'That was not like meeting a celebrity, that was like meeting Moses. He recruited us all.'[45]

There are plenty of entertaining parables like this. Whether more lay behind the 'John Wayne thing' than begging the question seems actually doubtful, not least because of life stories which warn against over-estimating romantic images of war and attribute essentially more down-to-earth motives to the decision to serve in Vietnam. These motives can be condensed into a single phrase: 'one just went' – because war was regarded as an unavoidable destiny in the lives of young men.[46] 'Insecure', 'disorientated', 'weak-willed' are attributes which emerge in their recollections at least as often as references to John Wayne. They indicate that the speakers are describing themselves as downright purposeless and far from having any transfiguring illusions. 'I wanted to be acted on, and it was real hard for me to make a choice of any kind.'[47] Phrases like this do not sound as though they come from the script of *Rio Bravo* but recall *American Graffiti* and the portrait it paints of that generation which experienced the social and cultural upheavals of the 1960s as both fascinating and demanding – and who did not know how to respond to the demands.

Seen like this, it was all about breaking loose from the confines of family, school or small town and finding refuge in another world of whatever kind. 'They did not have a cause,' observed veteran Tim O'Brien in his novel *Going after Cacciato*.[48] He meant the GIs who arrived in Vietnam but had actually only wanted to play in an Army band; who were sent into battle when they had hoped to get to know Europe with the Army's help; who had wanted to save their pay for college fees but ultimately squandered it in the nightclubs of Saigon or Bangkok.[49] Above all, they could not withstand the pressure of their patriotic environment. In his dreams Tim O'Brien, an infantryman with the Americal Division, heard himself being berated as a 'traitor, 'turncoat' or 'pussy'. 'They carried the soldier's greatest fear, which was the fear of blushing. Men killed, and died, because they were embarrassed not to. It was what had brought them to the war in the first place, nothing positive, no dreams of glory or honor, just to avoid the blush of dishonor.'[50] The disgrace of being ostracised as a coward and excluded from the company of 'good Americans' could even override the gnawing fear of early death. Political reservations had no chance against this. And so on and so forth in the parlance of young men who did not want to save the world like John Wayne but to save themselves from their adolescent fears.

In essence the veterans offered a pact to those who stayed behind, disguised in the plea for understanding and consideration: we were young and naïve and are of the same flesh and blood as you. 'I had no idea what I was volunteering for.'[51] And 'Son, I don't want you to go into the service, but it was your father's wish. He wanted a soldier boy and a Red Cross girl.'[52] No matter whether they are white or black, of Latin American or Native American origin, we hear this motif again and again in their individually modulated statements. These are gullible young men, treading in their fathers' footsteps and wanting to emulate or even surpass them. 'You know, the Fourth of July parades – everybody is involved,' said Captain Ernest Medina, who was prosecuted over My Lai (4), '. . . You have the flag waving and the fanfare . . . And I just think it was something that was embedded in me.'[53] Michael Bernhardt, who had refused to take part in the My Lai (4) massacre, sounded exactly the same when he spoke of war as the natural duty of a man. 'This was my bag. I've been military all the way.'[54] They wanted to be seen as trustees of American patriotism and soldiers who had been ill-used in a dirty war, but had not let themselves be ill-used as prosecution witnesses against their own country. So the Winter Soldiers called Mark Twain as their key witness. 'We have invited our clean young men to . . . do bandit's work under a flag which bandits have been accustomed to fear not to follow,' Twain had written about the soldiers returning from the Philippines. He testified for them: 'Our uniform . . . is one of our prides . . . We love it; we revere it . . . and our flag, another pride of ours, the chiefest.'[55] And this is how the message of those returning from Vietnam should be read: 'We are here to bear witness not against America, but against those policy makers who are perverting America . . . There will be no verdict against Uncle Sam.'[56]

However much the veterans were concerned with respect and

re-integration into society, their personal testimony points as much beyond this prevalent motive. Striving for an explanation for the defeat, they reported on killing and being killed, producing an account dictated by anger, which went beyond the usual hero's tales and gave – whether they wanted to or not – insights into worlds of experience which could not be ignored when they reconstructed excessive violence.

'THEM AND US'

'And we feel that they put us on the front lines abroad and in the back lines at home . . . You know, we'd say, "What the fuck are we doing in Vietnam, man?"'[57] 'Them and us' – ultimately it made no difference whether the GIs came into the country inspired with anti-Communist ideals or whether they had never given the matter any thought before. Likewise, whether they behaved aggressively from the beginning or met people openly with offers of help was ultimately of no importance, either. Vietnam was a synonym for menace. People, language, culture, geography, climate, it was all inaccessible to them, but everything pointed in the same direction: they found themselves in a 'no win' situation, in a game whose rules nobody knew, and whose outcome therefore seemed certain. The climate and terrain were so harsh that one GI proposed that the national flower of Vietnam should be an enormous thorn.[58] The only reliable companion was the feeling that their own actions were useless and pointless. 'Aimless, that's what it is . . . A bunch of kids trying to pin the tail on the Asian donkey. But no fuckin tail. No fuckin donkey.'[59]

'The World' meant the familiar universe beyond the invisible front lines. For Vietnam itself there was no tangible equivalent but it had definite attributes: unapproachable, inscrutable and dirty. The whole society could be classified like this, as one interviewee explained when talking about Vietnamese women: at the top was an elite minority wrapped in white silk as a sign of their inaccessibility. In the middle were the shimmering figures in the towns – symbolised by the prostitutes, 'Americanized, the bastardized version'. The majority living in rural areas clinched it: 'The ones who always wear the black slacks . . . And they're very flat chested, and dirty – really'[60] – faintly echoing that obsession with hygiene, which sociologists regard as part of the

'American way', or recalling the common tendency only to recognise civilisation when it mirrors one's own world. 'We felt that we was out of the fucking world. You know. Because it seemed strange. In fact, the terrain itself seemed so different and so strange, I would expect to see a dragon, half the time. Or a dinosaur or something coming. It was just like that.'[61]

Here talk about the 'oriental human beings' comes into its own. Maintaining that the Vietnamese live in filth can seamlessly metamorphose into deciding that these people *are* filth and not worth the exertions demanded from the GIs.[62] A memorandum from the Department of Defense written at the end of December 1967 stated: 'The actions of a small segment of the US military population are beginning to tarnish the favorable image created by the majority. The real impact cannot be measured nor can the frequency of occurrence be documented since many of the incidents are not observed by or reported to the military police.'[63] This is a reference to attitudes which could be observed throughout the country and which fitted easily into a pattern of daily harassment and terror. GIs made a game out of using their heavy vehicles to force Vietnamese off the road or running them over; pelting passers-by from tanks and off-road vehicles with tins of food and stones; putting food rations which had been poisoned or set with explosive charges near rubbish heaps and shooting at the Vietnamese, including children, who fell into the trap. There is even evidence of deliberate shelling of the living quarters and positions of South Vietnamese troops.[64] Burning down houses presented no problem at all: 'We don't view their homes as being as important to them as our homes are to us.'[65] Senior officers repeatedly approached the Supreme Command of MACV about this behaviour with requests for help to correct it.[66] General Peers saw it as 'the most disturbing factor' of his investigation[67] when he dealt with the culprits and accomplices of the My Lai (4) massacre. One of them described the 'orientals' as 'funny people. You can't realize what they are thinking. They seem to have no understanding of life. They don't care whether they live or die.'[68]

The speed with which incomprehension can turn into rage or arrogance into aggression is particularly evident in the troops' view of Vietnamese women. The cultural and ethical story of all wars since ancient times offers indubitable proof that women play a dual role in the fantasies of fighting men. They are both madonna and whore; they are degraded into objects of sexual desire and worshipped as Samaritans who heal wounded souls and restore the damaged male ego. The memories of Vietnam veterans illustrate this familiar pattern.

The troops wanted Vietnamese women to give them confirmation that they were still men, that fear had not taken complete hold of them, that away from the jungle and the helplessness they felt there, they could still be strong, virile protectors. 'We begged for it . . . The insanity, lies, cruelty all around us, all of the time, made us want to run to the soft gentle flesh of a woman accepting, without any hint of danger, a respite from the killing to make life intimate and worth living again . . . We needed nurturance so badly, they gave it to us so naturally. They needed a man to take care of and protect them.'[69]

'Instant sex' as the flip side to 'instant death'. GIs sound transfigured when they talk about the 'hootch-maids' whom the officers had sent to them in their quarters in the early 1960s, about women creeping past the guards into soldiers' quarters at night or women employed by the Army and therefore already in the camps, who did not dare reject the soldiers' advances for fear of being dismissed. Most popular were the brothels, bars and nightclubs or the secure 'sex camps' fenced in and guarded by the Military Police, such as 'Sin City' in An Khe, which were partly run privately, partly under the supervision of the American medical department and partly by the South Vietnamese mafia in the vicinity of military bases.[70] These were places where the border between prostitution and sex slavery was as fluid as in Thailand, Indonesia, Singapore, Taiwan, Hong Kong or Japan, where every month 32,000 soldiers arrived from Vietnam for several days' rest at the Army's expense – to boost fighting morale, so it was said.[71] Sometimes one gets the impression that this was an Army of 'sexaholics': 'In Nam you just grabbed some broad and you fucked them . . . We fucked anything that walked.'[72]

Lecherous passion lay like a thin varnish over disappointment, hatred and fear, over the frustration of those who wanted the unreasonable, expected the impossible and of course repeatedly failed in their attempt to reassure themselves of their soldierly masculinity through bought or forced sex. 'They are so cold . . . It's not to love, you're just down there fucking, man, because this bitch might read a book while you're fucking her, or eat an apple. See, no interest in the thing whatsoever

. . . And this happens to all the guys because we used to all talk about it.'[73] The 'broad' was always suspected of particular vileness, derived from the rumours which spread like a bush fire: whores who spread venereal diseases resistant to antibiotics; prostitutes who sent their punters to sleep, whereupon the hastily-summoned Viet Cong cut off their genitals; hustlers who were fighting cadres and ordinary women who were the visible face of the invisible enemy. 'It seems to me that the philosophy over there is like somehow or another we're more afraid of females than we are of males, because I don't know why, but the female was always like you never knew where you stood, so you went overboard in your job . . . You know, we didn't want to be embarrassed by getting our asses kicked by a bunch of females.'[74]

Such fantasies hint at all kinds of possibilities: fear of castration; the warped fear of feminine sexuality which is prevalent in adolescence; a tangled mixture of fact and fiction about the groups of female guerrillas that did actually exist. As Susan Brownmiller says,[75] the wildly distorted picture of the 'death angel' implies that women were not hated because they belonged to the enemy, but because they themselves were the enemy. In any case, phobias grow from these roots – and the misunderstood and ambiguous here turns into something unambiguous and easy to grasp. 'If you go into a village and there are a lot of young pregnant women and no males around, and there are only old males, that someone has to be doing it. These young ones are probably associated with them . . . If you see a young, very healthy woman, then she's probably the wife or the girlfriend of a VC.'[76] In the end each day in Vietnam turned into a mockery of the Army's prized recruiting slogan: 'In the U.S. Army you get to know what it means to feel like a man.'[77]

HATRED AND SELF-HATRED

Army training operated on the Manichaean principle. To quote the psychiatrist Frank J. Barrett, it was a question of hate training,[78] in the course of which two things were drummed in: that there is no guerrilla war without widespread support from the population and that to the insurgents and their sympathisers the political imperative is more important than their own lives. The latter explains the emotional charging of insults like 'gook', 'dink', 'dope', 'slope' and other such names for the Vietnamese in the soldiers' lingo. Because they represented an unpredictable danger they could be hunted down like 'rabbits' or 'squirrels'[79] without moral scruples, since their moral values were incomprehensible by Western standards, based on the sanctity of individual life. Otherwise children would not offer themselves as human booby-traps; no GI would have to reckon with a boy begging for chewing gum one moment and fatally stabbing him the next; pregnant women would not be prepared to set off a grenade-belt hidden under their blouses in the middle of a group of unsuspecting soldiers. Whether they did their basic training in Fort Benning, Hawaii or elsewhere, front-line soldiers and officers alike regularly tell such stories when reminiscing[80] and reveal the dynamic which derives from such generalised rumour-mongering: whoever tries to sharpen the troops' alertness, all-round circumspection and fighting morale like this runs the risk of turning the fear of death into a limitless hate against those people who seem not to fear death. 'And it made it a lot easier for us, with that kind of thinking, to kill the people – because it made sense to us.'[81]

'Making sense' is a good term for the search for constant reassurance and for the fact that everyday military life offered ample occasion for corroboration. It certainly cannot be denied that the Viet Cong had managed to gain a large part of their regular support through intimidation and terror. From time to time US soldiers even said they had seen with their own eyes the corpses of murdered village leaders put on show in the village centre as a deterrent.[82] When 'combing through' villages, they also regularly came across terrified peasants who did not take either side and were solely concerned about their own means of livelihood – but such impressions vanished in view of the quantity of weapon and food caches which had been discovered in dwellings. It was undeniable that there were also isolated cases of grenade-throwing children or that kitchen staff and cleaners were recruited to spy on American bases for the Viet Cong and even took up arms themselves, as happened in the attack on the Long Binh depot at the end of January 1968.[83] Sending civilians into battle and holding the enemy to account morally for their deaths was part of the logic of the asymmetrical war and an acknowledged practice of the Viet Cong.[84] It seems there is no way to tackle the flip side of this logic: the temptation to distrust everybody without exception, to see even minor things as potential threats and to turn fact into fantasy.

'If those people weren't all VC then prove it to me. Show me that someone was for the American forces there. Show me that someone helped us and fought the VC. Show me that someone wanted us: one example only.'[85] – 'If these people, "civilian types", could properly be termed "civilians" then every other enemy that we encountered with rifles or without would have to be also called "civilians" . . . We learned that the VC could very well be men, women, old, young, children, down to an age of about 5 years old.'[86] These are quotations from Lieutenant William Calley and another soldier in his unit which explain how hatred turns into fear and fear fuels hatred. They represent the hidden expectation which we encounter in most of the war recollections. Anyone bringing medicines to a village expected when they left to run straight into the hands of a battalion of Viet Cong. Anyone coming across booby-traps near settlements either saw the peasants as the culprits or arrested them for withholding information. Anyone cutting his way through the jungle with a machete thought he recognised in the overhanging branches a snake put there by the enemy. Nothing seemed impossible; everything was believed. Ultimately, from out of the mishmash of indoctrination, experience and rumour, ideas ran wild which normally belong in the realm of clinical insanity: that women carry razor blades hidden in their vaginas or that any baby can turn into a deadly weapon. Therefore one can take it that Paul Meadlo was giving a subjectively honest answer when he was asked about the shooting of women and children in My Lai (4): 'They might've had a fully loaded grenade on them. The mothers might have throwed [sic] them at us . . . I expected at any moment they were about to make a counter-attack.'[87]

The more thoroughly front-line soldiers talked about their time in Vietnam, the more apparent it became how closely linked are hatred and self-hatred, or contempt for others and lack of self-esteem. In other words, the rigid division between 'them' and 'us' only describes a part of their narrative which equally contains stories of humiliation, degradation if not abuse, violation of their feelings of justice and above all injury to their masculine pride. Everything centres on the self-image of the heroic soldier who suddenly finds his features mirrored in the grimacing 'disposable soldier' – administered like military equipment, pushed back and forth like cheap goods, treated as superfluous in life and degraded even in death by lack of respect. These recollections reveal that it only took a few weeks to turn naïve young men either into partly terrified, partly enraged warriors, or into madmen, in whom self-affirmation faded into giving themselves a licence to commit violence. Both types shared the description of irretrievable loss: 'By the time you get to the end of that whole process, you feel like you're the baddest thing that ever walked the earth.'[88]

One of the time-honoured facts of military history is that recruits are maltreated and 'used' in war. In regard to Vietnam the US Army certainly considered it was facing a special kind of challenge. On the one hand jungle warfare without front lines clearly made excessive demands of the soldiers. On the other hand they knew from past experience about the shortcomings of conduct in battle. According to evaluations from the First and Second World Wars only fifteen to twenty per cent of American front-line soldiers shot with precision and intent to kill when in action – not because they wanted to spare the enemy but because they could not control their panic and fired wildly all over the place. In Korea the rate of controlled shooting stood at a still unsatisfactory fifty-five per cent.[89] In Vietnam the intention was to correct this, in the words of Joanna Bourke, by activating 'savage instincts'[90] – a 'hardening-up programme', aimed at accustoming soldiers to the face of death and making killing a habit. Songs with a refrain which inevitably ended in 'kill, kill, kill' were as much a part of this as posters in which the slaughter and evisceration of the enemy were praised as proof of hardened fighting. By way of demonstration, some instructors ripped the entrails out of dead rabbits and threw them at the feet of their recruits.[91] The message was that anyone who does not get used to this will leave Vietnam in a body bag: 'This is the program for the day: You're going to get killed in Vietnam. We're in our own world here. If you don't do what I tell you, you're going to be taken out of our world.'[92] As a result there were only two kinds of soldier in Vietnam – the quick and the dead.

In Vietnam these initiation rites were continued – to what extent and intensity, we do not know. However, the persistence with which the veterans talk of relevant examples is striking. Again and again in the conversations conducted by Jonathan Shay and Robert J. Lifton they talk about the first patrol being a course in brutalisation. They speak of superiors who urged them not to take prisoners, who had civilians maltreated for trivial reasons or killed as a deterrent, who forbade them to go to the help of wounded enemies or their supposed sympathisers and who tolerated the mutilation of corpses in every conceivable way.[93] 'You walk through [that village] for weeks. All of a sudden, "It's a known VC village. Go in and burn it".'[94] Occasionally these stories remind one of scenes from horror films and one suspects that in retrospect the witnesses are muddling up real and imaginary worlds.[95] However, there are countless indisputable, documented cases, such as the practice of Ranger Team 35, H Company, 75th Ranger Battalion, 1st Cavalry Division. Its team leader presented an inexperienced GI with the severed ear of a dead North Vietnamese soldier – apparently to underline the need for constant vigilance in the jungle. Significantly, the representatives of the Criminal Investigation Division and the Inspector General did not consider this incident as a war crime but as 'shortcomings in techniques for training new patrol members'.[96] As an infantryman summarised similar experiences, 'Everybody seemed to know that this was the customary thing. I had just been in-country for a day or so. I figured that's the way things are done here.'[97]

Whether it led to resignation and cynicism, whether it met with incomprehension or even outrage and led to negative reaction, or actually did fire the desire to kill – the 'shock training' failed in its real purpose. As in the past, there was little evidence of the training being controllable or the fighting-machine controlled. According to their own evidence and the observations of third parties, the majority of the jungle fighters never came to terms with the circumstances and demands of the war. They shared this experience with veterans of other wars but, unlike their soldier fathers and grandfathers, the grunts and Special Forces from Vietnam put a name to the disquiet: fear and rage. Rage at their own army and fear of an impenetrable terrain and an invisible enemy.

'You know how they go on patrol in the dark? You're holding on to people's hands and the back of the shirt of the guy in front of you like little kids, like baby elephants in a row.'[98] GIs' experience of the jungle was of an area of extreme menace – inscrutable, impenetrable, unpredictable, something hostile whose dimensions, noises and smells they could not interpret. 'I never did really get used to it, because it was like, hell, man, like – you don't never know.'[99] The movement of every leaf, every animal noise in the undergrowth could also have come from a Viet Cong lying in wait. 'It was ghost country, and Charlie Cong was the main ghost.'[100] – 'To me Vietnam was like a nightmare for a whole year without waking up ... It gets to the point where you're just frightened all the time, and it does something to you.'[101] Nature, the elements, literally everything took on the form of the enemy. The jungle must have seemed fundamentally unassailable, for the technological superiority of modern weapons counted for little here. For the same reason Vietnam counted as 'Indian Country', terrain in which the Viet Cong slipped into the role of Indians. Only they could read the landscape, move about in it, identify with it and use it to their advantage – as in the paddy fields or the elephant grass, where it was easy to separate the advance guard from the column and to face GIs with the choice of immediate surrender or endangering the lives of their comrades standing in the firing line. 'He could be 10 feet away and you'd never know it ... He's right back down in the ground, and you don't even know where the shot came from.'[102] – 'I began to understand what fear was all about. It's just that anticipation of something happening as opposed to being in the heat of the battle. In the heat of the battle I don't think people think about getting hurt ... Nothing happened, but the fear, the fear, man.'[103]

Booby-traps and mines represented the ultimate threat of instant death, death in a second striking from nowhere. Some estimates say that a quarter of all American deaths and injuries were caused by these booby-traps – the 'Bouncing Betties' or 'Toe Poppers'.[104] This figure is probably too high. In the first half of 1967, for example, a rate of seventeen per cent was verified but there were, to an extent, striking differences between the various war zones and individual units. In some of them, especially when the direct fighting was less intense, over half of all losses happened in this way and in 1st Marine Division the average figure for 1970 and 1971 was eighteen per cent. The number of soldiers who suffered severe lower limb injuries and even amputation in the Vietnam War was about 300 per cent and 70 per cent higher than during the Second World War and the Korean War respectively, while multiple amputations had to be carried out three times more often than in the Second World War.[105] These figures say nothing about the fate of individuals but do show the general perception. Booby-traps upset everyone in the Army, whether they had actually experienced them or heard rumours about them. It was as difficult to do anything about this atmosphere of permanent fear as it was about the temptation to hold all Vietnamese morally responsible, without exception. 'When you halfstep, it may be your last step',[106] ran the description of a nervous and mental condition which verged on paranoia.

The war strategy and manner of fighting of both the Viet Cong and the North Vietnamese Army were as unpredictable as booby-traps. They dictated the action and demonstrated in their own way that the jungle was one single battlefield, where there were no opportunities for retreat and no safe areas. But it was also a terrain without places you could identify for launching an attack: a study made in early January 1969 for the National Security Council in Washington came to the conclusion that in the two preceding years companies, platoons or squads had been sent into the field approximately two million times. However, only about one per cent of these deployments had actually led to contact with the enemy – and they generally came to a halt after short, intense gun battles without any recognisable result. In three cases out of four the enemy determined the time, place, type and duration of the confrontation. The guerrillas were specialised in ambushes and also made use of the element of surprise all over the place, so keeping the upper hand in operational terms.[107] 'One of the first things you realized when you got to Nam was that you weren't going to win this war.'[108] A minority of GIs at the most may have believed in victory, particularly since the Viet Cong fighter struck them as a tough, brave soldier, convinced of his cause – as a 'real man',[109] as one GI put it. So 'Victor Charlie', 'Mr Charles' and 'Sir Charles' featured in the repertoire of nicknames. 'We were fighting against somebody we couldn't beat ... They were just kicking our asses all over the place. And even when we kicked theirs, they shocked us with their determination.'[110]

Added to the fear came rage, a rage based on the fact that in this war even people of understanding could find nothing to understand. They had supposedly come to this country to fight beside the South Vietnamese Army against the Communists. When, after years of studying the Army of the Republic of Vietnam (ARVN), the journalist Neil Sheehan spoke of an 'institutionalized reluctance to fight',[111] he had formed an accurate idea of what American soldiers had routinely observed. 'We never did get along with them ... We would call them lazy asses and stuff. We was over there fighting for them and they was scared to fight for themselves. They used to pick up and run. They never believed in fighting at night.'[112] Nepotism in officer training, a political leadership that lived in perpetual fear of a coup and was therefore intent on getting every capable soldier out of the way as quickly as possible, corruption among servicemen that was even susceptible to bribery by the enemy, petty jealousies and overt enmity in the upper ranks, knowledge of the futility of their own cause – however things may have turned out, the ARVN proved to be not so much a help as a hindrance. Even selling weapons to the Viet Cong was no rarity. Whereas in 1965 and 1966 the number of US dead and injured rose by about 400 and 1000 per cent respectively, the number of victims from among the ranks of the ARVN remained at a constantly low level – in both absolute and relative terms. Instead of 'search and destroy' the South Vietnamese practised 'search and avoid' – searching for places where they knew there were no Viet Cong.[113] To this end they treated their own rural compatriots like enemies. American observers took it for granted that on every second occasion when they were searching villages, South Vietnamese soldiers would loot, rape or even murder.[114] Basically the ARVN had the reputation of being an army of occupation and had to be constantly on their guard against being physically attacked by peasants or betrayed to the Viet Cong.[115] 'We just felt that we were being exploited,' as one GI put it.[116]

Exploited, cheated and betrayed – even the perception of their own operations boiled down to that. Up to the end of the 1960s their job was to search and destroy in nine out of ten cases. This was a description of patrols which had nothing to report other than exhausting forced marches and nerve-killing boredom. Therefore countless recollections mainly give us a picture of endlessly marching in circles, uphill and downhill, through valleys and swamps, in stifling heat with packs of up to fifty kilos on their backs, faces bitten by mosquitoes, legs and feet attacked by leeches – sometimes for two or three months on end, often without contact with the outside world and sometimes even without supplies.[117] Tim O'Brien chose *The Things They Carried* for the title of his collection of stories about serving as an infantryman with the Americal Division. In it his way of relating his own experiences and his comrades' stories is condensed in every respect:

They moved like mules. By daylight they took sniper fire, at night they were mortared, but it was not battle, it was just the endless march, village to village, without purpose, nothing won or lost. They marched for the sake of marching . . . If you weren't humping, you were waiting. I remember the monotony . . . Even in the deep bush, where you could die any number of ways, the war was nakedly and aggressively boring . . . And right then you'd hear gunfire behind you and your nuts would fly up into your throat and you'd be squealing pig squeals. That kind of boredom.[118]

The frequent reference to 'zombies' comes to the same thing – describing soldiers who have lost all sense of direction, who stagger through villages with no feel for time or space, not knowing whom or what they are looking for, who can no longer distinguish between the front and the hinterland, who have forgotten the aims and even the purpose of their task, and who above all lack one thing: the feeling that their efforts and troubles are of any use. 'The sacrifice was a lie. The war was a fraud.'[119]

Not only did the American strategy in Vietnam seem to be going nowhere; it also claimed pointless casualties among its own men without their actually encountering the enemy. 'Walk up it getting killed and walk down the other side again. We did that three times.'[120] That was the face of war apart from the dreary patrolling: scouring hostile territory, destroying underground bunkers, supplies, infrastructure and communication lines, withdrawing and waiting for the return of the enemy and then repeating it all over and over again. The only lucky ones were those assigned to sweeping and scrubbing fatigues. Vietnam impressed other units as a 'meat-mincer'– for instance those three battalions of 101st Airborne Division who in the course of operation Apache Snow in May 1969 were commanded to storm a thickly wooded and heavily defended mountain in A Shau Valley, Thua Thien Province (I Corps Tactical Zone), shown on the maps as 'Hill no. 937'. After ten days, in the course of which 56 GIs had been killed and 420 wounded, during which the Air Force had dropped 500 tons of bombs and the artillery had fired off over 20,000 salvos, the peak was finally reached – whereupon the order was given for immediate withdrawal: a decision which could only be justified by the fact that Hill 937 had never been important in the operational planning for the area close to the border with Laos, nor would it be in the future.[121]

Although 'Hamburger Hill' – as Hill 937 was called by the GIs – did not produce the heaviest losses of the war nor was it even typical of jungle warfare, the operation soon became symbolic, standing for the willingness of the military leadership to pay a higher price in human lives for retaking supposedly crucial terrain than for originally storming it. The soldiers talked about 'baiting', linking their superiors' strategy to a cynical calculation: those making contact with the enemy could reckon on a body count which was good for statistics and for their own careers – even at the cost of misusing their own troops as bait.[122] Whether or not they were right was ultimately irrelevant. They saw themselves as guinea-pigs.

'The U.S. Army [in Vietnam] was like a mother who sold out her kids to be raped by [their] father to protect her own interests.'[123] Whatever this bizarre comparison may imply, it undoubtedly expresses a permanently damaged self-image. It is about young men who lack a soldier's self-respect. As Tim O'Brien writes, many of them only went into the Army because they did not want to disappoint the patriotic expectations of their families and friends. Once in Vietnam they had to acknowledge that an even greater disgrace threatened: how could they prove themselves as soldiers in the absence of the enemy? Deprived of the opportunity for an open fight and with no control over what was happening in the war, the jungle fighters were at the mercy of their phobias about unmanliness and cowardice. Here we encounter the ever-recurring subject of wounded feelings of right and justice and it is clear that the attribute of carefully built-up manliness no longer had any bearing. Quite the reverse: it faded in the face of a fear stigmatised as 'womanly' and in particular a fear of castration. Therefore hatred for the enemy, who on occasions actually mutilated GIs and put them on display with their severed penis in their mouth,[124] always reflects self-hatred – a rage which turns into self-contempt at one's inability to cope with the menace, to convert one's superior weaponry into an expected affirmation of bravery or to earn the hoped-for recognition. 'Depressed is an understatement. We were 25 million years under depressed, man. We were so down half of the time that we didn't know what we was going to do next, we didn't care.'[125] Incomprehension, contempt both for their own lives and the lives of others, resignation, cynicism: ultimately the amalgam of negatives was greater than the sum of its parts. Or, in the words of Michael Herr, 'Entire divisions would function in a bad dream state, acting out a weird set of moves without any connection to their source.'[126]

SELF-EMPOWERMENT

In Vietnam the transformation into raging warriors of soldiers who were either indifferent, proud or reluctant was often accomplished within a few weeks. GIs who as a rule were not on active service for more than twelve months very quickly gave the impression that they had been exposed to the deprivations, cruelties and shock experiences of war for years and showed a fundamental readiness for violence even before they had experienced combat and come face to face with the enemy.

So-called 'combat fatigue' – brutalisation built up through long-lasting battle stress – can be ruled out as an explanation. While twenty-three per cent of all periods spent in hospital during the Second World War were due to 'combat fatigue', in Vietnam this figure was below six per cent. Even when the battles became more intense and the rate of losses rose, the same percentage of soldiers were under psychiatric treatment as the troops stationed far away in the United States. Psychological illness started to increase significantly when the war abated – in complete contrast to other wars.[127] Nor did this transformation need any ideological impetus geared to an exact image of the enemy. The jungle fighters had of course grown up in a society which had cultivated anti-Japanese prejudices before and especially during the Second World War, but there was no question of a virulent aversion to the Vietnamese, particularly against the background of solidarity with South Vietnam, orchestrated by politicians and the media for the purposes of resisting a common enemy.

If anything, it is classic colonial wars which offer a comparison. In both cases making a distinction between 'them' and 'us' is equally swift and fundamental; in both cases support from the home front was precarious and the reality of war constantly denied the soldiers their secretly or openly held expectations of themselves. Nothing destroys troop morale faster or more thoroughly than the feeling that one's own actions or even one's very person are pointless.[128] In these conditions attack is always preceded by panic attack and giving oneself a licence to use excessive violence.

The reports of those fighting in Vietnam stand out from the large fund of soldiers' testimony because they are trying to find explanations for giving oneself this licence. In contrast to many if not most war stories from other times and places, denial, defensiveness or apportioning of guilt and responsibility are therefore not their central theme and their retrospective views do amount to conjuring up a passive victimisation. Certainly they keep talking about compulsion, circumstances, excessive demands and lack of self-determination. But they also look for the causes and the dynamic of their own violent acts in the context of individual willpower and decision-making. Here the active dominates the passive, as can be seen from three key concepts which lend the narrative its structure: self-assurance, conquering fear and revenge. Essentially different, they describe a practice characterised by its fluid transitions and multifarious complexity. Not least they show how closely interlinked are killing in the heat of the moment and in cold blood, calculated intention and frenzy, passion and composure.

Self-assurance

'It's really tough to catch them [the Viet Cong] with a weapon. After a fire fight, they take all weapons and bodies – there's nothing to show, seems we never accomplished anything. All that was left after a fire fight was my friends' missing arms, legs, and dead bodies.'[129] It was not just a war against an invisible opponent but also a war in which one could leave no trace behind – no symbols of victory visible for miles around like conquered territory or large prisoner-of-war camps, liberated towns or destroyed armaments factories. 'I'd pray for a fire fight, just so we could stop walking for a little while.'[130] Frustration over the soldiers' honour denied to them was even expressed in handpainted placards: 'Contact – Happiness in Heavy Contact'[131] could be read at the entrance to the command post of one unit. According to Lieutenant Colonel Anthony Herbert, 'Do something physical' became a fixed idea and leitmotif for pretence action:[132] to demonstrate their presence, to prove that they themselves could seize the initiative and free themselves of the stigma of a loser secretly mocked by the enemy or a plaything in the games of anonymous powers. Basically it did not matter how you did it; the main thing was to make a point. To the annoyance of the Supreme Command in Saigon, for a time it was a ritual in some units to prove they were intrepid by wearing necklaces made out of severed ears and fingers or to display the heads of murdered Viet Cong as trophies.[133] Others left 'death cards' behind them, sometimes on the corpses of the enemy – playing-cards such as the ace of diamonds – which were meant to underline their determination and inspire fear. It is even on record that for the same purpose dead Viet Cong were thrown from helicopters over enemy country or their bodies tied to armoured vehicles and dragged through settlements: 'The placement of enemy bodies in enemy territory shows that we are aware of their presence and has a psychological effect upon the movements and actions of the enemy.'[134] If no other means are available, success is ultimately measured in this currency.

From this perspective, randomly burning down houses and shooting wildly when entering settlements appear to be staged as symbols. They were part of the repertoire of soldiers who, in the absence of real battlefields, eventually created fantasy fighting zones and in their imagination identified everything and everyone as an enemy – an enemy which they had located, confronted and destroyed.[135] 'It started with just plain prisoners,' said one member of the Americal Division, 'prisoners you thought were enemy. Then you'd go on to prisoners who weren't the enemy, and then the civilians because there was no difference between the enemy and civilians. It came to the point where a guy could kill anybody.'[136] Violence offered the promise of regaining control, it created clear conditions beyond all ambivalence and uncertainty – and above all it left behind a blood-soaked trace of their own power. Therein lay its symbolic value, its moral-productive force. It was the proof that they could create an effect – a message to themselves and a way of communicating with others, above all with those civilians who rejected their loyalty and whom they could in this way confront with the price of this continued rejection: these people had got to reckon with everything, because they themselves were ready for everything.[137]

Conquering Fear

To a certain extent, the rituals with which the jungle fighters tried to master their fear seem comic. 'We would put on sunglasses walking in the jungle. Think about it, now. It was ridiculous. But we want to show how bad we are. How we're not scared.'[138] Others dressed in the style of the Montagnards and, like the mountain folk of the Central Highlands, wore loincloths, headbands and 'Ho-Chi-Minh sandals' cut from car tyres.[139] Evidently it was only the heavy cartridge and grenade belts which distinguished them from extras in a western. This fancy-dress party was reserved for a minority, however. The majority seemed to know that one needed superficial accessories as little as archaic tests of courage, because in fact helplessness and fear went hand in hand with a power unparalleled in the history of the US Army. Every infantry soldier in Vietnam had at his disposal over six times as much fire-power as a soldier in the Korean War – they all carried M16 assault rifles with a magazine of twenty shots or alternatively M60 or M79.[140] 'It gave you a feeling of superiority. You walking through the village and you got your great big old flak jacket on. You got your helmet and bandoliers all over you. You got your rifle. You tower over most of these people.'[141] – 'You know what it's like to walk down the road with twelve guys armed to the teeth and anybody who shoots at you is in trouble?'[142]

All self-doubt seems to have been banished at such moments – which explains the seemingly paradoxical statement that they liked being in Vietnam. Jungle fighters indicate how terrorising with superior weaponry affected them. Whether slicing water-buffalo literally into small pieces with large-calibre weapons or mowing down dozens of helpless peasants in a field in the course of a 'duck shoot', executing a woman picked up at random in order to find out how big the bullet hole would be or stoning a three-year-old to death and afterwards describing it as like a 'massive orgasm'; or whether it was simply extending by one more incident the register of injuries and deaths, which went into the thousands every year, through driving with delib-erate carelessness across the country[143] – satisfaction, pleasure and fascination are positively audible. 'I guess we did it just to prove we were real tough motherfuckers.'[144] Sometimes one can detect a quite childish pleasure at having behaved as fearlessly as film heroes: 'It was right out of the movies . . . I consider myself a decent man, but I did mow those people down from my helicopter.'[145] Whatever term one might choose to describe these emotions, the psychoanalyst Robert J. Lifton hits the nail on the head when he puts forward the concept of a 'power surge', which releases one from a heavy burden and has to be repeated, because the release cannot banish the fear and is therefore always illusory.[146]

Revenge

Once the GIs are talking about their reactions to suffering directly felt or experienced, even after a lapse of several years the pitch is still distorted by fury. Alternatively, with cooler detachment violence is depicted as something natural, as an inevitable decision made by those who could not imagine ever going home again and were convinced they must die as pointless a death as many of their comrades. In this light, murder and manslaughter, rape and looting become meaningful reparation and compelling proof that they can meet the brutality of others with a mercilessness of their own, and treat other people's bodies with the violence which threatened them. This premise also led to stripping the enemy of dignity even in death, to placing bodies on rubbish heaps or piling them up and burning them in the desire to eliminate all trace of their existence: 'I have seen them burned and I have seen them left to rot . . . I saw nothing strange about this manner of disposal.'[147]

'I had to kill a VC for those guys, I just had to kill one . . . I had to help these guys that were dead, I had to do something for them, knowing that their lives weren't wasted.'[148] More than anything else the detonation of booby-traps literally set off chain reactions of revenge. 'We went into the jungle totally different from that moment on. We walked in there looking to kill, looking to get back for what had been done to us.'[149] The range of reactions covers everything from clear-sighted calculation to blind frenzy; from company commanders reducing a nearby village to ashes, to platoons building their own booby-traps and spreading them around large areas or putting out tins of poisoned food, to soldiers firing about them wildly or in their frenzy mutilating enemy corpses until they were no longer recognisable.[150] The psychotherapist Jonathan Shay described as 'Achilles in Vietnam' the type of crazed man he met repeatedly in his therapy sessions with Vietnam veterans. These were soldiers whose feeling for fairness and justice had been damaged and was transformed by the death of a comrade into unbridled rage. It was the loss of his dearest friend

Patrocles outside Troy that put Achilles into such a rage that he did not even shrink from committing the most abhorred crime of his time and violated Hector's dead body. In Vietnam it was the accumulation of insults which induced soldiers to respond to what was to them incomprehensible in a way which is difficult for us to comprehend.

Anyone who fights fire with fire and through revenge tries to re-establish 'weapon equality' with an equally uninhibited enemy needs neither justification nor excuse for his actions. On the contrary, he intentionally oversteps the boundaries and breaks the rules which he believes always cheat those who keep to them. He wants to see his actions documented, has himself photographed or uses a camera himself and sends the photos to friends and relations – something which was obviously widespread in Vietnam but which up to now has hardly been investigated.[151] This is the root of the reverence towards William Calley and everyone else accused of war crimes, which veers between comprehension, acceptance and esteem. Lieutenant Colonel Cooper of 1st Battalion, 7th Regiment, 1st Infantry Division made this point when he said: 'You could have spent three weeks talking to troops about . . . the rules of land warfare and it wouldn't have helped.'[152]

At this point the story told by Joyce Carol Oates catches up on us again. Her protagonist's life-story was the exact negation of the idea of the 'citizen soldier'. In the 'warrior dreams' still dreamt in the 1950s, the boy matured into a man in war but he was still aware that military service was dirty and should be done as a job that you wanted to put behind you as quickly as possible. This is why the heroes of the time tried to find their way back into civilian life, got married, bought land and started a family. In *Man Crazy*, the protagonist succumbed to the self-devouring dynamic of war. His destructive energy does not wear itself out and nothing assuages his need for revenge. And he has long since given up all hope of a world that might be better after all the violence. That is why he no longer wants to return to society but instead in his doubt opts for a second tour in Vietnam. He will always be the nameless man, obsessed with fulfilling a mission. He is one of those men with a lifelong 'licence to kill'.[153]

5

1967 – Death Squads in the Northern Provinces

Over the border they send us to kill and to fight for a cause
they've long ago forgotten.
　　Paul Simon, 'The Side of a Hill'

Nam was the smell of it. The smell. You smelled the napalm and
you smelled the human flesh burning . . . Nothing smells like
Vietnam smells.[1]

To the front-line American troops the provinces of Quang Ngai, Quang
Tin, Quang Nam, Thua Thien and Quang Tri were quite simply 'Indian
country'. They lay in the narrow central part of Vietnam between the
17th Parallel to the north and the Batangan peninsula to the south, with
a frontier of more than 350 kilometres with Laos on the west and the
South China Sea on the east. Most of the population – estimated at a
million – lived on the coastal plains which, with their gentle hills and
snow-white sands, now offer material for tourist brochures. In the war
years the fields growing rice, raw sugar and cassava were in fact death-
traps, honeycombed with underground tunnels and bunker systems.

Anywhere and at any time there could be fighting there and no one
was safe from booby-traps, which is why Highway No. 1 – which is
still a very important traffic artery today – was known colloquially as
'street without joy' – a euphemism for 'street of no return'. West of
it one can see with the naked eye the contours of the mountainous

landscape which makes up three-quarters of the topography of these provinces. With the exception of a few 2,000-metre high peaks, the mountains are between 300 and 500 metres high, but together they form an extremely inhospitable region, overgrown with jungle and broken up by gorges which become a sea of mud in the rainy season. In this terrain optimum visibility is about one hundred metres and even well-trained soldiers covered no more than five kilometres in a day's march.

On American military maps the region was marked as I Corps Tactical Zone (I CTZ), one of the four war zones in South Vietnam. Places and districts in this zone have become lasting bywords for the Vietnam War: Da Nang, the port where the first US fighting troops landed in spring 1965 and re-enacted a scene from the Second World War for the television cameras; Khe Sanh, the Marines' base camp, besieged for months at the beginning of 1968 and frequently referred to as 'destiny fortress', because of its proximity to the demilitarised zone; the A Shau Valley, gateway for supplies brought down from the North along the Ho Chi Minh Trail and scene of the legendary battle for 'Hamburger Hill'; Huê, the old imperial capital, in which troops of the Viet Cong and the North Viet-namese Army massacred thousands of civilians in February 1968 before the US Air Force pulverised most of the town; lastly My Lai (4), the village of 500 souls, where American soldiers took freedom to mean a licence to kill and turned into terrorists.

For both sides in the war the five northern provinces formed the battle zone with the highest troop concentrations, the most intensive fighting and therefore also the greatest losses. Here the war was carried on with B-52 bombers and bamboo traps, with napalm and handguns, between units of battalion strength and night patrols of five men, in minefields and against fortified positions, in the loneliness of the jungle and in the middle of inhabited settlements. Here special commandos with years of experience operated alongside rookies who had just finished their basic training on the M16; here 'part-time guerrillas' fought beside regular formations of the North Vietnamese Army, who based their strategy and tactics on the pattern of previous victories over Japanese and French troops and who, in spite of everything, only prevailed because of the large number of Chinese soldiers wearing their uniform. Fifty-four per cent of all GIs who fell in Vietnam lost their lives in I Corps Tactical Zone.

First Corps Tactical Zone is therefore a microcosm, in which all the characteristics of the Vietnam War were simultaneously represented: the asymmetrical scenario of guerrilla warfare, the material battles of a classical war of attrition and the Cold War logic of escalation. There, however, one can recognise one thing above all: how the war for the people turns into a war against the people and how battlefields are transformed into a boundless space for violence – the 'killing fields'.

'INDIAN COUNTRY'

From time immemorial the inhabitants of the northern provinces, like most of their countrymen, had a reputation for stubborn tenacity, even independence of mind, coupled with the will to preserve their culture and traditional lifestyle against all comers. People who want to live by the rhythm of nature, by the spirit of their forefathers and in harmony with the gods see temporal potentates as passing figures or an unavoidable evil, and generally keep their distance out of feelings of indifference. And vice versa: French colonial masters, American innovators and Communist ideologists were united in one respect: their mistrust of a people who could not be won over with money or ideas, and definitely not with weapons. Lethargic, opportunistic, cynical, underhand and unpredictable – these were the attributes everyone used to characterise these uncooperative people, but they actually said something else: that political missionaries could never be sure how much strain the patience of their potential proselytes would stand.

It was in Quang Ngai Province that the resistance against their French colonial masters began in the nineteenth century and in the 1930s and 1940s its inhabitants again mounted opposition to foreign rule. One cannot claim that the Viet Minh, acting as spokesmen for the uprising, had at the time won the hearts and minds of the local people. They were certainly acknowledged as the patriotic adversaries of the invaders, especially the most famous sons of Quang Ngai – Ho Chi Minh and Pham Van Dong, who later became prime minister of North Vietnam – and last but not least the Viet Minh's economic and social policies met with approval. They utilised the temporary absence of the French during the Second World War to introduce overdue agricultural reform. Major landowners, who had long neglected their estates, were dispossessed in favour of the peasants; corrupt tax collectors were sacked and replaced with functionaries who kept to the spirit and letter of a tax system which favoured the poor. When after 1945 France renewed its claims, Ho Chi Minh had already proclaimed Quang Ngai Province a 'liberated zone' and recruited a number of young men, some from neighbouring provinces, for armed resistance.

Yet in spite of all this, in their very moment of greatest victory it became clear how limited were the Viet Minh's power and influence. When the French troops finally withdrew and the country was divided along the 17th Parallel, every Vietnamese citizen was free to choose to live either north or south of the demarcation line. There are no reliable statistics about the population movements, but it is estimated that the number of those who turned their backs on the Communist North was ten times higher than those who emigrated from the South. Catholics in particular left the North for fear of political repression and countless adherents of the Viet Minh chose to go in the opposite direction for the same reasons – and probably also because they could not rely on the people's support.[2]

The corrupt regime in Saigon prepared the ground for another about-turn. It helped the old landlords to return, rescinded rural tax reform and even in the towns made many opponents, if not outright enemies, through its intolerant policy towards the Buddhists. This was grist to the mill for the old Viet Minh cadres, who at the end of 1959 were clandestinely regrouping and in the following months brought the Politburo in Hanoi to the point of disregarding any criticism of acting overhastily and supporting the resistance in the South with men and materials. The early period of the Viet Cong and its political arm, the National Liberation Front (NLF), has indeed not yet been thoroughly researched;[3] however, it is not disputed that they made the northern provinces – together with the Mekong Delta – into their most important operational region nor that the Saigon regime failed miserably in its anti-guerrilla programme. Its attempt to move the rural inhabitants of Quang Ngai into militarily fortified strategic hamlets started in 1962 but was discontinued in autumn 1963, because the systematic burning-down of villages not only did the Viet Cong no harm, but actually won them new supporters.[4] Against a background of spectacular attacks on police stations and other symbols of official power a stealthy revolution was accomplished between Quang Ngai

and Quang Tri in the space of three years. This was the political equivalent of later guerrilla tactics during the war: a hit-and-run race for
soft targets, cautiously and flexibly carried out but unwavering in
defence of the strongholds secured.

The journalist Richard Hammer has painted a graphic picture of
this silent coup, based on interviews with people living in the Son My
District – scene of the My Lai (4) massacre. Once a few dozen activists
who had emigrated returned to their native villages in winter 1963,
the village councils were stripped of their power within a few days. It
is uncertain whether this was due to the power of rhetoric, the trust
of relatives and old acquaintances, looking down the barrel of a gun
or simply the absence of power structure typical in that region. In any
case there was no significant resistance to the arrest of village elders
and the setting up of 'people's courts'. 'They accused us of having
worked for the . . . "puppet government" in Saigon,' recalled one of
the 'defendants'. 'They accused us of having favored the rich against
the poor. They accused us of having taken bribes and graft and on
and on . . . The V.C. killed no one in my hamlet. Some of them they
arrested and took to the jungle. They have not returned, so maybe
the VC did kill them there.'[5] As a rule, 'unreliable' people like him
were sent to re-education camps in North Vietnam or banished permanently from their villages. Of course anyone who wanted to flee had
to leave their property behind. Almost all of them stayed and came
to terms with their new masters with their familiar stoicism. 'Whoever
ruled our village, the French, the Japanese, the Viet Minh, Saigon, the
VC, it did not matter.'[6]

Adapting oneself to the Viet Cong also brought advantages. Uncul-
tivated estates and refugees' property were shared out again as they
had been in the 1950s and poor peasants could rent fields at a low rate
and also profit from a progressive tax system – if they were taxed at
all. The guerrillas also introduced variety into the peasants' daily grind.
At irregular intervals they called village meetings which may have been
overloaded with long-winded sermons on revolutionary vigilance but
did not simply amount to political emotionalism. In the official part
of the meeting village administration could be discussed; in the unofficial part there was entertainment with singing or amateur dramatics.
However transparent the political intentions may have been, these
events did not fail in their effect, even if only because of the glaring

contrast to the exploitation and lack of respect which the villagers had experienced at the hands of the Saigon government.[7]

In return the Viet Cong expected loyalty from them. That meant donating part of their crops, being ready to give them shelter, help in building tunnel systems, bunkers and roads, acting as couriers or even preparing and setting off booby-traps. Anyone failing in this compulsory volunteering might be arrested and their sons forcibly recruited into the military. In the case of point-blank refusal, villages were sometimes even laid open to destruction, by having snipers open fire on enemy patrols in the knowledge that neither the South Vietnamese nor the Americans shrank from taking reprisals against populated places. It is impossible to judge how often the Viet Cong used this terrorist style of enforcement; it is certain, though, that peasants from Son My repeatedly reported on it and that the disciplinary effect of the terrorism did not miss its target even if it was a matter of individual cases or credibly dramatised rumours. Richard Hammer reports on countless families who served both sides as need dictated. As soon as a son was recruited into the South Vietnamese Army it was a good idea to offer the guerrillas a brother or some other relative.[8]

'By the 1960s,' according to the concluding report of the Peers Commission on the My Lai (4) massacre, 'a whole generation of young people had grown up [in Quang Ngai Province] under the control of the Viet Minh and the later National Liberation Front.'[9] Only the provincial capital Quang Ngai City and its immediate environs were controlled by government troops. The extent of this control's effectiveness was apparent on 29 August 1967, when an assault party of Viet Cong stormed the civilian prison and set free 1,200 prisoners – most of them classified as 'civilian defendants' and therefore 'terror suspects'. After further incidents the Saigon government considered withdrawing completely from the town; it seems that this idea was rejected only under massive pressure from the Americans.[10] Giving up Quang Ngai would – as a small-scale application of the domino theory – have had an incalculable effect on the other, neighbouring regions which were no less unstable. Evidently all parties to the conflict regarded the northern battle zone as critical. In the northern provinces of South Vietnam the fighting was not therefore only over key military positions; much more, even primarily, the region between Quang Tri and Quang Ngai was regarded as symbolic. Whoever had the upper hand there could count on having a good chance of victory in the whole country or, conversely, ran the risk of losing control over the course of the war.

Of the 200,000 or so fighting troops summoned up on the Communist side at the beginning of 1968 and therefore at the peak of the war, a good quarter were assigned to the northern battle zone and thus to five of the then forty-four provinces and fifteen per cent of the entire territory of South Vietnam. Apart from numerous small groups, platoons and companies, sixty-five battalions were recorded there, essentially from 2nd, 324th(B) and 325th Infantry Divisions of the North Vietnamese Army.[11] There is no record of the numbers of 'self-defence forces' – informants, couriers, explosives experts and tax collectors – attached to the guerrillas or the regular Hanoi troops. Because the majority were only lightly armed, if at all, stayed where they lived and only made an appearance at irregular intervals, they do not show in official statistics. As things stood, however, helpers and accomplices were probably very numerous in this particular region.

As was their practice elsewhere, they avoided open confrontation with the far superior American manpower, weaponry and mechanised transport, preferring to lure them into ambushes or to wear them down with gun battles as unexpected as they were brief. However, it was not the fighting tactics of the enemy which put most pressure on the US troops, but the intensive mining of the terrain which faced them with the most extreme form of the guerrillas' war of attrition waged with cut-price weaponry. 'It could be a small French pressure mine,' wrote General Norman Schwarzkopf about his experiences as a young officer on the Batangan peninsula. '. . . or a 1940s-vintage U.S. Army Bouncing Betty . . . or a dud bomb or artillery shell rewired by the VC . . . We . . . plotted the sites of mine incidents on the map . . . It ended up showing lethal little red dots from one end of the peninsula to the other.'[12] In other words, the mines proved to be a classic 'force multiplier' – a means of multiplying one's fighting strength with comparatively little outlay.

As soon as a battle zone is turned into a minefield, the enemy has to regroup his logistical and manpower resources. He can no longer move freely over the land, he needs additional patrols for preventive security and equipment to remove booby-traps and is compelled to keep changing his routes and clear new trails away from well-known, well-trodden paths. Ultimately American units took lengthy detours or only advanced at a snail's pace, to the delight of the snipers spread out over wide areas. They also repeatedly fell into the trap of the so-called 'sucker tactic' – guerrillas showing themselves for a moment when out of range, in the certainty that the GIs would pursue them by the most direct route and head straight for disaster. This wiped out one of the US troops' decisive advantages: mobility. Their head start in the air with helicopter transport was thrown away again on the ground. Of course these disadvantages could be offset with tactical circumspection, but shrewd troop leaders were fairly rare in Vietnam – another reason why many units suffered very heavy losses from booby-traps. The 1st Battalion, 52nd Infantry Regiment of the Americal Division, for instance, deployed in Quang Ngai between autumn 1967 and spring 1968, suffered twenty-three dead and seventy-seven wounded in the space of five months: eighty-seven of them were victims of mines. Beset with similar experiences, 5th Battalion, 46th Infantry Regiment of the Americal in effect failed in their military task. 'When patrols were sent out at night,' according to Norman Schwarzkopf, 'they'd go two hundred yards outside their perimeter and stop, and the next morning they'd come in and report that they'd completed their mission and encountered nothing.'[13]

Hampered in their use of manpower and resources of materiel and time, American units changed to having the artillery and the Air Force literally shoot the way clear for the infantry. The tactic of clearing mines and neutralising booby-traps from the air became a Standing Operating Procedure after III Marine Amphibious Force landed the first US fighting troops in the northern battle zone in May 1965. Helicopters or fighter-planes blanketed the ground troops' forward zones with 'harassment and interdiction' fire without any regard for collateral damage, and heavy artillery was called up in order to keep the enemy on the move and ultimately force him to break cover – and therefore to keep within tolerable limits costly operations by their own men. According to an Air Force memorandum, they were shooting on suspicion over wide swathes of land, under orders based on unreliable information and carried out under considerable time constraints: 'These factors, combined with the fact that almost all of the target areas were covered by thick jungle canopy, presented a serious target identification problem to the FAC [Forward Air Controllers].'[14]

When the ominous entry 'Events not confirmed' appeared in an operational report, it can be assumed that shots were being either fired into the void – or aimed at civilian targets. The latter was the rule, rather than the exception, in Quang Ngai and the neighbouring provinces. Sometimes it is documented in after-action reports – for instance in the case of Operation Starlight in August 1965, in the course of which 688 Viet Cong were claimed as killed, but only 109 weapons were seized.[15] Admittedly the only detailed account from this early period comes from the journalist Neil Sheehan, who visited a fishing village in Quang Ngai in November 1965 and found that within a few weeks at least 180 and possibly 600 civilians had been killed in air raids. In the eyes of the US Army the fishermen had asked for it – because they had not abandoned their homes in an operational area of the Viet Cong. 'The five hamlets that composed that village, once a prosperous community of 15,000 people, had been reduced to rubble.'[16] It seems that Sheehan was describing just one example from among a host of other cases.

There could certainly be no question of success in the struggle against the insurgents. Since 1966 the US Marines had of course been supported by 1st and 2nd Infantry Divisions of the South Vietnamese Army and a brigade of South Korean Marines, but gloomy prognoses came from the American Headquarters in Saigon: if infiltration by North Vietnamese soldiers along the demilitarised zone on the 17th Parallel was not halted, the whole of Quang Tri Province would fall into the hands of the Communists in the foreseeable future. And if the guerrillas in Quang Ngai were not decisively weakened, a strategic disaster even threatened: a defensive belt in the hands of the enemy from the Laotian frontier to the South China Sea, which would effectively cut South Vietnam in two.[17] 'One of the most critical areas in the RVN today is Quang Ngai Province,' wrote Westmoreland to the supreme commander of the American forces in the Pacific, Admiral Ulysses S. Grant Sharp, in March 1967. 'Even if a major operation were conducted in this area during 1967, the relief would be no more than temporary. A force is needed to maintain continuous pressure on the enemy, to eliminate his forces and numerous base areas, and to remove his control over large population and food reserves.'[18]

In the following months there was indeed a massive troop reinforcement. At the beginning of 1968 there were no longer 20,000 but 170,000 men in I Corps Tactical Zone – a third of all the American soldiers then stationed in Vietnam.[19] Of the 'manoeuvre battalions' – the fighting units of battalion strength – more than half had been moved in, which meant that fifty per cent of all mobile US fighting troops in Vietnam were in I Corps Tactical Zone in January 1968.[20] They were supported by about 33,000 soldiers from the 1st and 2nd Infantry Divisions of the South Vietnamese Army and 44,000 'regional' and 'popular forces', mainly on security duties.[21] 'Indian Country' had become, as Westmoreland remarked, a 'real battle zone'.[22]

TASK FORCE OREGON

In the view of the US leadership this re-grouping was too long drawn-out. Determined as they were on rapid success, in April 1967 they conjured out of thin air an improvised fighting formation called Task Force Oregon which consisted of three brigades detached temporarily from their mother divisions. Comprising 196th Light Infantry Brigade of 23rd Infantry Division, 1st Brigade of 101st Airborne Division and 3rd Brigade of 25th Infantry Division[23] under the operational control of III Marine Amphibious Force, units of the US Army were deployed for the first time in the theatre of war in the northern provinces, primarily in Quang Ngai but partly also in Quang Tin. Westmoreland gave Task Force Oregon 'maximum operational independence'. It was left to the brigade commanders to decide whether to consult those in charge of their three mother divisions before mounting operations. In case of doubt, 'brigades could conduct operations in their own AO [area of operation] without prior approval'.[24] The greatest expectations rested on 1st Battalion, 327th Infantry Regiment, 1st Brigade of 101st Airborne Division and on the three companies of this battalion, which had been deployed repeatedly as 'fire-fighters' in six different provinces since 1965. They had the reputation of being able to compensate for lack of manpower with high motivation and operational ruthlessness – characteristics which were more than ever in demand by the Supreme Command in spring 1967.

'Clear the land!' – 'Take the fight to the VC!' – 'Wear down the enemy! They will surrender!'[25] – 'There's nothing of ours out there; there are no friendlies in the area.'[26] In such terms the senior officers fired up the troops of Task Force Oregon. If the soldiers had been thinking of the 48th Local Force Battalion of the Viet Cong in those terms, they were destined to be disappointed. Undoubtedly it was part of their remit to wipe out these legendary phantom troops once and for all, but for the moment something more important arose.

Westmoreland wanted first of all to resettle as many inhabitants as possible or, to be more precise, to drive them out of their villages at a day's notice and confine them in refugee camps for the duration of the war. There were sixty-eight of these camps in Quang Ngai Province, fortified with concrete walls, barbed wire fences and armed patrols – effectively prisons, in which the inmates passed their days under corrugated iron roofs, only provided with the bare necessities of life, in unspeakable sanitary conditions and riddled with disease. They had no work and those who had a pass which allowed them to go outside for an hour or two during the day counted themselves lucky. At night these displaced people were shut in again because, in the logic of this policy, spelt out in an internal study, 'The population is totally hostile towards the GVN and is probably nearly in complete sympathy with the NLF movement . . . a militant, well disciplined, VC oriented population . . . Every boy and girl has a military duty in the hamlet. Total involvement and total commitment is the rule.'[27] Anyone thinking like this can only envisage one solution: total quarantine. Diem's government had already foundered on its resettlement policy. Westmoreland ignored this lesson. Task Force Oregon was now given the task, in which even the Marines had failed a few months before, of accommodating in short order up to 300,000 people, or half the entire rural population of Quang Ngai, in 'relocation centers'.

Secondly, most of the enemy's lines of retreat were to be made unusable over a wide area. 'Every house,' continued the expert opinion already mentioned, 'was part of a well planned defensive system. Houses were sometimes only camouflage for bunkers and "spider holes".'[28] In plain English, an evacuated village could be burnt down at will and the rice paddies poisoned with herbicides as well. With the people went the livestock, in order to deprive the guerrillas of their life-blood – living off the land – even at the expense of completely destroying all the agriculture of Quang Ngai and having to supply the refugee camps with imported rice. 'This is as important as anything else we can do,' said Westmoreland in conversation with his staff.[29]

The consequences of these operational guidelines were predictable. 'The whole thing felt like pushing waves back into the ocean.'[30] As in previous years, the peasants would soon find their way back to their villages; that a task force of three brigades or 9,000 men could not stop them was as obvious as the idea that devastating settlements and cultivated land was a poor argument in the struggle for hearts and minds. Westmoreland ignored such objections unflinchingly, in the belief that in spite of everything he had a way out – to wit, a psychological war of attrition.

On the material side Westmoreland's strategy reckoned on the effects of progressive impoverishment. Depite the exorbitant extent of the economic and ecological damage and the fact that the scorched-earth policy backfired, the guerrillas would gain no advantage from the situation, because the Viet Cong could only make good the loss of foodstuffs and difficulties in stockpiling by increasing the pressure on the remaining or returning peasants, that is, by demanding more tribute in worsened conditions – if necessary even by force. In these conditions it was only a matter of time before irreplaceable political sympathies were exhausted and even the most favourably disposed could no longer be convinced about the point of the war. No guerrilla war could be carried on indefinitely with a populace both disillusioned and worn down by American firepower. Removing the fish from the water therefore seemed a realistic goal, provided that the 'black psychology' of punishment was well understood and any talk of a 'struggle for hearts and minds' was left to the political propagandists on the American home front.[31]

From the psychological view point it was, in the terminology of the US forces, a matter of 'shock and awe'. If the rural populace could not be convinced about the American cause, they should still be made to understand that solidarity with the Viet Cong paid off even less. An escalation of the war, as Westmoreland remarked as early as 1965, 'will bring about a moment of decision for the peasant farmer. He will have to choose if he stays alive. Until now the peasant has had three alternatives: he could stay put and follow his natural instincts to stay close to the land, living beside the graves of his ancestors. He could move to an area under government control. Or he could join the VC. Now if he stays there are other dangers.'[32] In other words, the peasants had to grasp that it was lethally dangerous not to agree to being moved to the camps and that they could never again feel safe in their houses and fields. At the end of June 1967 Westmoreland presented a colour theory of deterrence to soldiers of 1st Battalion, 327th Regiment, 1st Brigade of 101st Airborne Division: 'If the people are in relocation camps, they're green, so they're safe. We leave them alone. The Vietcong and NVA are red, so we know they're fair game. But if there are people who are out there – and not in the camps – they're pink as far as we're concerned. They're Communist sympathizers. They were not supposed to be there.'[33]

Westmoreland could even have said: we shall bomb the peasants out of solidarity with the Viet Cong, find out the people's breaking-point and destroy their stubbornness by terrorising them. The logic of a psychological war of attrition is not about the inability to distinguish between combatants and non-combatants, but the refusal to make that distinction in certain circumstances and at a decisive point in the war. No matter whether they were on the Viet Cong's side or not, the price the people paid for the war had to be raised to an intolerable level, but anyone wanting to threaten the living with the dead oversteps the borderline into total war. Westmoreland never put down on paper this aspect of the war in the northern battle zone – probably from motives of political 'image management' and definitely with the aim of protecting himself from the legal consequences.[34] In the event, however, he gave his troop leaders to understand that the price he had quoted was unavoidable if defeat was to be averted.

As a result, in practice the entire province of Quang Ngai was declared a Free Fire Zone. It was well known that in areas so designated the regulations applying to the protection of civilians could be ignored on the grounds of military necessity – provided that South Vietnamese civilian or military authorities agreed to the choice of place and time for an operation.[35] Most notably in the northern provinces the Americans' allies were not very cooperative – not because of fundamental operational reservations, but because American commanders treated their partners like second-class soldiers and irritating appendages. In the words of Norman Schwarzkopf: 'We also tended to lose sight of the fact that we were in somebody else's country.'[36] In protest at being incapacitated like this and as a reminder that Task Force Oregon was acting in the operational territory of 2nd South Vietnamese Infantry Division, they repeatedly refused requests to set up Free Fire Zones, with the result that the Americans just threw their weight around like lords and masters.[37] They asked for permission less and less often and went so far as to claim they had a licence to kill indiscriminately, not in exceptional cases but as the accepted rule – Standing Operating Procedure.[38]

This SOP required no special justification nor any specific command. It was self-explanatory, according to statements from soldiers and officers who were engaged in the war in the North over a period of six years: 'I suppose given a free choice, they would not have left their hamlets. [It took] a hell of a lot of artillery . . . after which their attitude about relocation improved,'[39] said an officer responsible for the 'pacification' of the plains near Da Nang in 1965. 'It didn't matter if they were civilians. If they weren't supposed to be in an area, we shot them. If they didn't understand fear, I taught it to them,'[40] said a GI stationed in the Song Ve Valley in 1967. 'The pilots are hard boiled, unconcerned professionals. While not actually violating the current rules, they tend to take maximum license within those rules. If there aren't supposed to be friendlies in an area, then all people – regardless of what they are doing – are enemy,'[41] ran an internal memo on the practices of forward air controllers, who pinpointed bombing targets in Quang Ngai in 1967. 'We would call in on the radio – "seven VC running from hut. Shot and killed" – Hell, they weren't running. We didn't know if they were VC,'[42] said one GI about his experiences in the Song Ve Valley in summer 1967. 'It [Free Fire Zone] was used by everyone during my tour and it meant to open up and kill everything that moved,'[43] said a doctor serving with 1st Brigade, 101st Airborne Division. 'If a Vietnamese was killed in a free fire zone, he was considered a combatant,'[44] said a soldier stationed in the Song Ve Valley in 1967. 'Under questioning during the Army investigation, at least eight officers with authority [from 1st Battalion, 327th Regiment, 1st Brigade, 101st Airborne Division] – mostly captains and majors – swore that free-fire zones gave the men the right to "kill anything that moved",'[45] ran an investigation report of the Army CID. '[Do] not to worry about it, we can always get the weapons later,'[46] said a Tiger Force soldier who with his unit repeatedly shot dead unarmed people in the Song Ve Valley in 1967. 'The company followed that policy with lust. We went from hutch to hutch in that sparsely settled area. Any man found was shot, with little or no questions asked. It was the policy that no one should be living in that area,'[47] said a soldier seconded to the Americal Division in autumn 1968. 'Sir, we have permission to kill anyone in this area if we want to,'[48] said a Marine who was stationed near My Lai (4) in spring 1970 and was accused of murdering a woman.

It seems that the opportunities opened up in this way also gave a chance to apply unofficial Standing Operating Procedures, that is, the unspoken understanding not to take prisoners in the course of operations and to rape at random while combing through villages. It is impossible to say how often and to what extent such infringements occurred; at any rate a quantity of verbal accounts – and to a lesser extent the transcripts of military judicial investigations – indicate that this was a widespread, if not commonplace, practice of Task Force Oregon.

'Take no prisoners': this all-embracing slogan of American soldiers points precisely and fundamentally to a peculiarity of guerrilla wars. As opposed to conventional warfare, set-piece battles are the exception and therefore there is less chance of subsequently disarming defeated opponents. As guerrillas attack at unexpected moments and, equipped with detailed knowledge of the area, withdraw equally quickly, the risk of being taken prisoner is greatly lessened; instead, there is a danger of being blanketed with preventive fire. The term 'indiscriminate fire' is given to this attempt to cut off the enemy's retreat. Like most troops confronted with insurgents on the colonial periphery, American units had also made a habit of firing indiscriminately on suspects as soon as they spotted them, or calling up large-scale artillery and air bombardment against what they believed to be the Viet Cong's positions. Because there was no clearly defined order of battle and because no one wanted to take risks in the impenetrable tracts of country, other methods and possibilities of neutralising enemy forces did not as a rule enter into the calculations. Nevertheless, as can be gleaned from official US Army statistics and the South Vietnamese authorities, between the beginning of 1966 and the end of 1972 a total of 37,451 POWs was logged,[49] of whom 13,073 were captured by American units.[50] In comparison, during the Korean War the allied forces took about 170,000 North Korean and Chinese prisoners in just three years.

Yet these numbers do not help in reconstructing everyday events during the war; instead of giving answers, they raise more questions. How was it that the US forces, who were known to be bearing the main burden of the war in Vietnam and had by far the largest number of soldiers at the front, were only responsible for capturing thirty-five per cent of all prisoners? Why do the internment files give no information about how many prisoners were taken in combing through villages – that is, in the course of raids and evictions – and how many in the aftermath of fighting?[51] However much the suspicion persists that the murder of prisoners in the field was deliberately concealed, it cannot be proved. The official correspondence indicates rather that the Americans did not keep detailed records at any time. Prisoners of war fell under the jurisdiction of the South Vietnamese. The main point is that they were transferred into their custody after ten, or at most ninety, days. Where they came from and what became of them was of no interest to anybody.[52]

Above all it was the small groups of between five and twenty-five soldiers who tended to torture and murder prisoners. Because of their low numbers, they avoided any risky attempts to take prisoners and fired immediately at real or imagined enemies: 'Shoot first and ask questions later.'[53] In justification members of these squads and platoons raised operational objections against guarding or flying out enemies – in one case, because prisoners would handicap their mobility and flexibility; in another, because it would have meant giving away carefully camouflaged hide-outs and trails. Apart from such tactical considerations and logistical constraints, many of the men were not prepared to feed additional mouths with a share of their scantily apportioned rations, intended to last them without replenishment while they were out on an operation, often for weeks on end.[54] Others murdered for a variety of reasons: in order to spread 'shock and awe' in the enemy ranks; to ensure that no prisoners, once released, rejoined either the Viet Cong or the North Vietnamese Army; in order to give rein to their desire for revenge on an enemy with whom they could otherwise hardly ever engage.[55] The commanders' role was not insignificant, either, as they incited their men to kill indiscriminately with an eye to a high body count. 'You know what to do', 'Take care of them', 'What do you do with a horse with a broken leg?' were the veiled instructions; in many cases orders to murder prisoners were even explicit.[56] 'Remember, out in the jungle, there were no police officers. No judges. No law and order,' said a soldier of Task Force Oregon. 'Whenever somebody felt like doing something, they did it.'[57]

Violating women was regarded as an unofficial Standing Operating Procedure among jungle warriors – a custom which certainly not everyone took part in but almost everyone knew about and which rarely aroused protest.[58] Only in the smallest number of cases did disciplinary action before a military tribunal ensue, as this would have required victims to give evidence and identify their assailants beyond doubt, and a prosecutor to take on their cases. One can hardly imagine a more unlikely set of circumstances in this war. The number of victims will therefore always be in doubt but it is certain that the culprits were capable of anything, as is well documented: individual acts of violation and gang rape; ritual staging in front of an audience and secret rapes by individuals; spontaneous decisions and planned abductions, in the course of which young girls and women were drugged and often abused for days on end.[59] It was also reported that company doctors examined the selected victims for infectious venereal diseases and advised against rape when the results were positive.[60]

Corroborative documentation from the northern battle zone and from the ranks of Task Force Oregon combine to produce this pattern and also illustrate the significance of the term 'a double veteran': a title of honour given everyone who had both survived an attack and committed rape – and who may have murdered the violated woman as well.

In Vietnam, as in all wars since ancient times, rapes were linked to a hope for strategic gains: to punish collaboration with the enemy and to emphasise that collaborators were defenceless and outside the law; to confront the enemy with his inability to protect the weakest members of his community whom he has to abandon as spoils of war; to deprive the victim demonstrably of her right to self-determination; to break the will to resist or to stake a claim by making any prospect of regeneration and reproduction after the war doubtful, if not impossible. 'Destroy the eggs the boys come from', ran a saying in common use in modern times.[61] This was a standard variation on 'shock and awe' – a further attempt to force intimidated and literally overmastered people to abandon strategically important areas. In these circumstances rape was part of the job to be done, even if you didn't feel like it. 'Two of them said they couldn't get a hard on. [Another one] was standing there with his penis out trying to get an erection,' reported an article dealing with violations carried out by soldiers of

2nd Platoon, B Company, 1st Battalion, 5th Regiment, 1st Marine Division in Xuan Ngoc, Quang Tin Province at the end of September 1966.[62] It fell to other men to perform this important duty or task for the war effort.

'The body of a raped woman', said Susan Brownmiller, 'becomes a ceremonial battlefield, a parade ground for the victor's trooping of the colors.'[63] This ceremony of deterrence was performed in a variety of ways in Vietnam. As though they wanted to show everybody that their victim was dead and to substitute non-combatants for the invisible Viet Cong, soldiers carved a capital 'C' in the skin of murdered women – shorthand for 'Charlie', Army slang for the male enemy. They left their company's insignia on the disfigured corpses, mutilated the sex organs of their victims in every imaginable way – with kicks, tracer ammunition and rifle butts.[64] 'Women suspected of supporting the VC had their vaginas sewn shut or their breasts branded with heated bayonets.'[65] And finally, according to one jungle fighter, rape in public was part of the ritual, often committed in front of relatives 'because it makes a lasting impression on some guy . . . that's watching his daughter worked over . . . You doubled whatever you would do for a male.'[66] 'Redoubled violence': the exaggerated symbolism and emotional charge of abusing women can hardly be described more accurately. Reducing rapes and violations to crucial consequences of civilians being part of a battle zone, and reducing them and toleration of them to forming part of a rational calculation of war objectives, would mean understanding only half of the matter.

Perhaps the most important thing for 'double veterans' was to certify their power and virility as individuals, or more precisely, to demonstrate those characteristics which had been jeopardised during a 'no-win' war. Setting up brothels did not serve this purpose: 'You don't want a prostitute. You've got an M-16. What do you need to pay for a lady for? You go down to the village and you take what you want'[67] – in fact, with the help of those weapons which they treated as synonyms for a penis and saw as a promise of sexual satisfaction. 'This is a rifle and this is a gun,' ran the refrain of one song sung in basic training, accompanied by holding one's own member: 'This is for shooting and this is for fun.'[68] Where pleasure in power ends and sexual pleasure begins is one of those questions which are frequently asked, and rightly so, but are difficult to answer.[69] The GIs' personal testimonies at least point to the fact that tormenting and inflicting pain gave a pleasurable sensation. 'To some people carrying a gun constantly was like having a permanent hard on.'[70] One man talked about a 'godlike feeling' which came over him when raping. 'Nobody could say nothing to you.'[71] For another rape meant having 'made love' for the first time like a regular guy – 'with his boots on'.[72] There is no shortage of further examples. They describe moments in which all self-doubt seemed banished, moments of strength, ascendancy and omnipotence – and a freedom they had never known before. That these were fleeting fantasies, already exposed as such in the course of the next operation, did not alter their persistent, thrilling fascination. On the contrary, the desire for a hyper-virile reincarnation seemed all the stronger the more illusionary it was.[73]

As soon as a battle zone was regarded as a zone of instant death, the borderline between sexual violence and sexual murder was blurred. This was confirmed in reports from the northern battle zone – a region where the enemy was invisible and yet death was ever-present: in the form of mines not shown on any map, of snipers who could be hidden anywhere or of fire from one's own ranks ordered on mere suspicion and all too often hitting the wrong target. 'But you better sure as hell be scared, it's gotta happen. One or two of you men, your ass is grass,' wrote Tim O'Brien, quoting a fellow-soldier.[74] And Jonathan Shay recorded that 'It was to let you know you're still a human being . . . Sex proves you're not a fucking animal. Picture this – you come in off an operation, . . . some of your friends are dead . . . You know you stunk of fear . . . – you had to get laid . . . The only release was fucking.'[75] This was the way the soldiers talked, believing when they saw any woman 'that [she] would be the last one any of us would ever screw'.[76] So did men who were trying to overcome their fear of sudden death in the act of rape and who afterwards took the life of their victim in order to reassure themselves that they were still alive. Killing as triumph over death, killing out of despair as well as pleasure – the 'double' in 'double veterans' described this as well.

QUANG NGAI AND QUANG TIN

Wheeler, Malheur I and II, Hood River, Benton, Cook and Dragon Head V were the names of Task Force Oregon's main operations between spring and late autumn 1967 – operations which in many respects anticipated the events in the northern provinces in the following four years of war. Hardly anyone explicitly demanded that civilians be killed, but the vote for a scorched-earth policy also meant that hardly anyone inquired about the consequences or warned about consideration for civilian life – and many went so far as to interpret the implementation of their strategic superiority as an opportunity to demonstrate personal omnipotence. This link between strategy from above and individual decisions from below set in motion a dynamic of its own. In more precise terms, it turned into a setting of excessive violence which ultimately led to massacre.

Supreme Commander William Westmoreland pinned special hopes on 1st Battalion, 327th Regiment, 1st Brigade of 101st Airborne Division. He repeatedly called it 'my fire brigade' and told the officers and men that they were the hard core of the 101st.[77] These words were echoed in a variety of ways. Colonel Gerald E. Morse had just taken over command of 1st Battalion when he had four unidentified persons in a rice paddy, who he thought looked suspicious, fired on from his command-and-control helicopter. Two of them were listed in his logbook as Viet Cong killed, with the comment that 'the battalion [must show it] was deadly at any echelon of the command'.[78] During Operation Wheeler, which took place between 11 September and 27 November 1967, Colonel Morse gave the three companies in his formation new names: from then on A Company was called Assassins, B Company, Barbarians and C Company, Cutthroats; his personal recognition signal for radio traffic was Ghost Rider and the commander of B Company was Barbarian Bear. 'We decided that nice stateside names didn't make much sense out there,' said one of the officers responsible.[79] Ten thousand aces of spades were ordered from a playing-card manufacturer in the States and regularly left behind in operational areas, sometimes pinned on the bodies of dead Vietnamese as death symbols and proof of exceptional aggression. 'We had a lot of them and you just grabbed some.'[80]

Organising a competition for the highest body count was a natural ingredient of troop motivation. Dissatisfied with the results achieved to date, in November 1967 Colonel Morse radioed an order to his units that they should reach a final total of 327 to show that they were worthy of their regiment's number. 'Do you want them before or after breakfast?'[81] – this reply from a subordinate still does not prove that 1st Battalion was actually setting out on a determined manhunt, but a reconnaissance section called Tiger Force did announce within ten days a body count of fifty-four. Two weapons were seized.[82] This ratio of twenty-seven to one may at first glance seem very high, but it is normal throughout the battalion, whose after-action reports at the end of Operation Wheeler give a ratio of Vietnamese killed to weapons seized as twenty to one.[83] One of the GIs involved maintained that in the whole of 1967 they had taken only four or five prisoners. 'It probably instilled a small amount of pride that they never brought in prisoners because I believe that there [sic] manner of fighting was to ask no quarter and to give none.'[84]

Thanks to contemporary reporting by the journalist Jonathan Schell, we know what price was paid by the people of Quang Ngai and Quang Tin for this type of warfare.[85] Operation Dragon Head V: almost total eviction of inhabitants and up to forty per cent of houses destroyed. Operation Benton, officially a 'medium-sized' operation: 282 tons of bombs and 116 tons of napalm released over an area of 200 square kilometres in the space of 14 days; over 130,000 20mm-calibre shells and 8,500 artillery shells fired; sixty-five per cent of houses or dwellings for 17,000 people completely destroyed. Operation Wheeler: a repeat of this tally with slightly different figures. In total, by the end of 1967 almost seventy per cent of all settlements in Quang Ngai Province were in ruins, with regions like Duc Pho completely pulverised; forty per cent of the populace of Quang Ngai had fled, either temporarily or permanently.[86] How many dead and wounded there were can only be roughly estimated. Doctors in the Quang Ngai City hospital put the annual number at 50,000, among them many who had been deliberately gunned down from helicopters.[87] Jonathan Schell spoke of a degree of devastation beyond one's powers of imagination and in an internal assessment of his reports the Army came to this conclusion: 'The descriptions of destruction . . . are overdrawn but not to such a degree as to discredit his statements . . . Mr Schell's estimates are substantially correct.'[88]

Something which Jonathan Schell could not know about at the time and which also escaped the attention of historians for four decades were the events taking place in the shadow of these major operations. First and foremost comes a reconnaissance platoon recruited from the three companies of 1st Battalion, 327th Regiment, 1st Brigade of 101st Airborne Division. Between May and November a total of 120 parachutists, all battle-hardened volunteers, served in this platoon. For individual operations, however, they operated with a maximum of forty-five men – under a name which did not appear in any official troop register: Tiger Force.

Tiger Force was the Special Forces Unit of 101st Airborne Division. It was founded at the end of November 1965 by Major David H. Hackworth and ordered 'to outguerrilla the guerrillas'. Together with 1st Brigade of the 101st, they were seconded to Task Force Oregon just for this purpose. Invisible, blending into the landscape, they were to seek out enemy positions, mark targets for air attack and ground operations, carry out sabotage, cut supply lines and abduct Viet Cong cadres, murdering them when in doubt. It was left to the Tigers to decide how to fulfil their tasks. In the words of a Task Force Oregon soldier, 'the unit was an "ass kicking outfit" that fought their war as they saw fit . . . They didn't condone or associate with any outsiders.'[89] They were supplied with rations for thirty days, operated on their own initiative, were told to keep radio communication to a minimum and had a licence to improvise, including permission to act in the grey area between self-reliance and self-empowerment. 'If they needed to kill, then they could do so without telling anyone.'[90]

The Tigers showed off their special status for all to see. Instead of regular uniforms they wore battledress in striped tiger patterns without any rank or platoon badges, exchanged their steel helmets for wide-brimmed weather-proof hats, were the only ones allowed to grow beards and, as a special status symbol, to carry handguns openly. In their own estimation they were the elite of the elite; in the eyes of their comrades, 'the men to do the dirty work' – partly admired, partly feared – who had no time for the discipline of a regular company and were only bound by their own rules. Most of those selected for this unit were old hands – soldiers who had volunteered to prolong their service in Vietnam or for whom war had long since become a way of life. 'They developed a he-man image of being effective fighters . . . Looking at it now you'd say they sound like blood thirsty nuts but at that time we were looking for aggressive fighters and these guys developed the initiative to be aggressive fighters.'[91]

Within Task Force Oregon the Tigers performed much more than classic reconnaissance duties. They were assigned predominantly to 'pacification' and 'cleansing' duties in the northern provinces, partly with the purpose of clearing the way for larger fighting units, partly as a rearguard, to continue where others had run out of means and possibilities. For the men of Tiger Force it was an attractive job, which they fulfilled in the style of death squads.

Tiger Force's doings can be reconstructed in detail, thanks to a chain of coincidences. In early 1971 Gary D. Coy, a GI from C Company (Cutthroats) of the 1st Battalion, contacted the Army Criminal Investigation Division to report on his unit's atrocities during Operation Wheeler.[92] Under pressure from the then impending My Lai (4) case, the accusations were followed up promptly and with comparatively substantial effort. In any case the decisive factor seems to have been that the investigation was undertaken by Gustav Apsey, a lawyer known for his unerring judgement and even more for his tenacity.[93] Apsey, underestimated because of his awkward appearance and derided by his colleagues as the 'Columbo of the CID', unearthed a similar case long since discarded, the so-called Stout Allegation. Dennis Lee Stout, a former press officer, had reported in the *Phoenix Arizona Gazette* at the end of 1969 on rape, torture, murder of prisoners and mutilations carried out by B Company (Barbarians) of the 1st Battalion, but was unable to convince the Army investigators. Despite a host of similar witness statements, the investigators had dropped the matter on the grounds of an alleged lack of proof.[94] Apsey, however, pressed for further research, not least because Gary D. Coy had talked about a beheaded baby and a soldier strutting around with the child's necklace. A painstaking comparison of the Coy and Stout Allegations actually led Apsey onto the track of that infamous unit, which officially did not exist and about which nobody in the Pentagon had been able or willing to tell him: Tiger Force.

The investigations dragged on for almost three years, longer than researches into any war crimes before or since. Between May 1972 and early 1975, 100 agents from the Criminal Investigation Division conducted 137 interviews worldwide with former Tigers. About one-third of those questioned were willing to cooperate and to their surprise gave precise details of culprits and the circumstances of their misdeeds.[95] 'I know that since I am a civilian now, the Army can't touch me.'[96] Using the same argument, however, two-thirds of them

– including almost all the officers of the unit – refused to say anything.[97] In spite of this conspiracy of silence and although members of the CID who were against the investigation had at times encouraged their interviewees to refuse to talk,[98] in July 1975 Gustav Apsey was able to compile a dossier with overwhelming proof. But when the war ended, the Army leadership saw that they now also had an opportunity to close the chapter on war crimes. 'Nothing beneficial or constructive could result from prosecution at this time,'[99] ran the internal verdict. Apsey was transferred to a post in South Korea and the Tiger Force files vanished into the archives.

The Coy and Stout Allegations have in fact been available since the 1990s, but no complete history of Tiger Force could have been written on the basis of these documents alone. The picture only filled out when in 2002 the former director of the CID, Henry Tufts, donated the files in his possession to the University of Michigan and two reporters of the daily newspaper *Toledo Blade* were able to have a look at them before they were archived. Whether historical interest or the current controversy about war crimes in the Iraq War was the decisive factor, the two journalists – Michael Sallah and Mitch Weiss – were able to convince their editors-in-chief of the need to make an investment which would normally lie beyond the bounds of possibility. For almost twelve months Sallah and Weiss were released from their normal duties; they tracked down forty-three former Tigers and conducted thorough interviews, visited Vietnam, talked to survivors and finally persuaded Gustav Apsey, who had always kept silent out of loyalty to the US Army, to give his views on the background to his investigations for the first time. It was the perpetrators and collaborators in particular who gave answers to questions which would probably never have been cleared up otherwise, including alluding to about a dozen previously unknown war crimes committed by the Tigers.[100] A synoptic study of the now completed sources underlines why Tiger Force must be called a death squad.

Between June and November 1967 Tiger Force was stationed in the Song Ve Valley and in Quang Tin Province. Song Ve, a river basin in Quang Ngai Province seven kilometres wide and ten kilometres long, was one of the most fertile regions of Vietnam. In the eyes of the US Army that was just the problem. Although the peasants there were not known to support the Viet Cong and – as they themselves said –

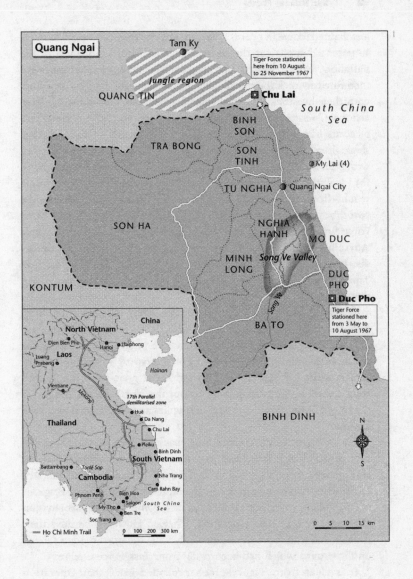

Quang Ngai

Tam Ky

Jungle region

QUANG TIN

Tiger Force stationed here from 10 August to 25 November 1967

■ **Chu Lai**

South China Sea

BINH SON

TRA BONG

SON TINH

My Lai (4)

TU NGHIA

Quang Ngai City

SON HA

NGHIA HANH

MO DUC

MINH LONG

Song Ve Valley

DUC PHO

KONTUM

Song Ve

■ **Duc Pho**

Tiger Force stationed here from 3 May to 10 August 1967

BA TO

BINH DINH

N
S

0   5   10   15 km

China

North Vietnam

Dien Bien Phu

Hanoi   ● Haiphong

Laos

Luang Prabang ●

Hainan

Vientiane ●

17th Parallel demilitarised zone

Mekong

Huế
● Da Nang

Thailand

■ Chu Lai

● Pleiku

● Binh Dinh

South Vietnam

Battambang ●   *Tonlé Sap*

Cambodia

● Nha Trang

Phnom Penh ●   Bien Hoa
●   ● Saigon   *South China Sea*
My Tho ●● Ben Tre

Cam Rahn Bay

Soc Trang ●

— Ho Chi Minh Trail

0   100 200 300 km

just wanted to live in peace,[101] the surplus rice they produced counted as potential spoils for the insurgents. The three companies of 1st Battalion, 327th Regiment, 1st Brigade, 101st Airborne Division were therefore to wreck the rice paddies and to evacuate the 7,000 peasants with their livestock into the Nghia Hanh camp. Like most of these actions, Operation Rawhide only resulted in anarchy.[102] About 2,000 peasants had either gone into hiding or returned to their villages soon after and the commanders of Task Force Oregon responded with their notorious 'shock therapy': burning down houses and giving the inhabitants a clear signal that everyone outside the refugee camps would from then on be treated as fair game. In other words, two-thirds of the region was declared a Free Fire Zone[103] and Tiger Force turned into an assault troop, instilling fear wherever it went. 'Anything in this valley is ours,' were Lieutenant James Hawkins's instructions to the Tigers. 'There are no friendlies. Do you hear me? There are no friendlies. No one is supposed to be here. Shoot anything that moves!'[104]

In Quang Tin Tiger Force found completely different conditions. In a mountainous region covered with dense jungle they were no longer dealing with civilians or scattered Viet Cong, but with sections of the feared 2nd Infantry Division of the North Vietnamese Army. So far as the US Supreme Command knew, 7,500 soldiers a month were streaming into the province from the North on the fringes of the Ho Chi Minh Trail, bringing in supplies and establishing new base camps.[105]

For William Westmoreland time was therefore pressing. For the sake of rapid success he had Task Force Oregon reorganised at the end of September 1967 and exchanged 3rd Brigade of 25th Infantry Division for two new brigades – 11th and 198th Light Infantry Brigades of 23rd Infantry Division. Under the new name of Americal Division they were to take over Operation Wheeler. However, because their training and transfer took unexpectedly long, the main burden still fell on those units which had been taken from Task Force Oregon.[106]

It is clear from Tiger Force's expanded brief that Operation Wheeler had priority in Quang Tin. They were not only to seek out the base camps of the Viet Cong and the NVA, but to destroy them and to annihilate as many small pockets of the enemy as possible. 'You're the Tigers. I expect you to be the Tigers,'[107] their battalion commander told them. The Tigers themselves spoke of a new opportunity: 'balls to the wall'. 'It was standard practice,' said one participant, 'for the Tiger Force to kill everything that moved when we went out on an operation . . . With a few exceptions I think that is correct.'[108]

For seven months Tiger Force laid a trail of blood through Quang Tin and the Song Ve Valley. They shot peasants in the fields without any pretext and murdered anyone who happened to cross their path; they tortured prisoners and executed them singly or in groups; they raided villages in the late evening or early morning and mowed down with machine gun fire everyone they could find – peasants who had gathered for a meal or were sleeping, children playing in the open, old people taking a walk. 'We knew they were civilians, not VC,' said one GI interviewed by Sallah and Weiss.[109] They stole and pillaged, beat their victims to death or raped them until they fainted; they shot dead inhabitants who minutes before had been holding in their hands leaflets dropped from the air and were prepared to obey the evacuation order; they used for target practice people who happened to be in the wrong place at the wrong time. They spared neither the wounded nor the sick; they shot at long range with M16s and at close range with hand weapons; sometimes, when they had split up into groups of five to go out separately on patrol, they could hear each other's salvos.[110] Gustav Apsey counted forty-nine murders in eleven days by analysing radio traffic;[111] however, the Tigers only kept sporadic radio contact with battalion operational headquarters and anyhow they had given up counting their victims. 'We'll never know how many were killed,' said one of them,[112] hinting at the unseen side of their marauding – murdering people who were sheltering in cellars and bunkers. In Quang Tin Province, which was regularly subjected to air attack, most of the inhabitants had built themselves primitive shelters which just became death-traps as soon as Tiger Force arrived in the village and threw hand grenades into the entrances without warning. Therefore in addition to the dozens of mass graves where the dead are remembered to this day, there is also an unknown number of unidentified death chambers.[113]

It is realistic to think in terms of several hundred dead; even a four-figure total is within the realms of possibility. At the end of November 1967 the first phase of Operation Wheeler was concluded and Tiger

Force, together with the other sections of 1st Brigade, 101st Airborne Division, was transferred further south to II Corps Tactical Zone. However the inhabitants were only allowed a brief respite before the Americal Division was fully operational and continued on the same course with new teams under the name of Operation Wheeler/Wallowa.

SCALPHUNTERS

'It was something that no one really talked about out in the open and it was something that you just kept trying to "sweep under the rug" and forget because you really didn't want to know if it was true or not.'[114] In fact the rumours which came to the ears of the 1st Battalion surgeon were true: the Tigers had made a habit of mutilating their murder victims and putting body parts on display. Sam Ybarra even had a collection of pickled ears to replace rotting and stinking necklaces at any time.[115] Twenty-seven members of the platoon are recorded as stating under interrogation by the Criminal Investigation Division that cutting off ears was an 'accepted practice'. 'There was a period when just about everyone had a neckless [sic] of ears, but as the men were wounded, they thought it was bad luck and got rid of them. Scalps were a kick for a time also, but there were lice in the hair and they got rid of those too, and it didn't last long.'[116] Gold taken from teeth, however, was carefully hoarded. Whether the tales were true of them gouging out eyes and taking them away in their baggage, sticking heads on spikes, amputating sexual organs and sewing them back between the victims eyes,[117] slicing off breasts and testicles and throwing them at the feet of their owners' relatives,[118] we can put to one side in this context. Reality was reflected in the wildest of imaginings – another reason for the proliferation and peddling of rumours .

At first sight these reports do not seem very surprising. Outside the northern battle zone too soldiers mutilated their victims and collected body parts as well.[119] There are photographs of soldiers posing in front of disfigured bodies, as though they wanted to demonstrate their courage and recklessness or give a proof of their work; members of secret commandos who hunted down Communist cadres during the Phoenix programme were called 'heads and ears guys' as a title of honour; in many places they could barter severed ears for drinks or prostitutes.[120] 'Even in the hospitals, they're passing out pictures of mutilated bodies,' said one soldier during the Winter Soldiers hearings, 'showing this is what we do to the Gooks, this is what's fun to do with the Gooks.'[121] In random checks US customs officers came upon dozens of parcels of human skulls, bones and dried ears, often addressed to friends, relatives or wives. Perhaps the senders were also the perpetrators; perhaps like tourists they had obtained their trophies on the black market in Vietnam. All this is reminiscent of those mavericks who roamed through the American West in the second half of the nineteenth century in the shadow of the Indian wars, and particularly those GIs who were fighting in Asia in the Second World War.[122]

On the other hand the tales of members of Tiger Force indicate an unusually extreme attitude. In interrogations carried out at the time by the Criminal Investigation Division and talking to journalists after an interval of thirty-six years they always come down to the same formula: the Tigers had decided not to concern themselves about anybody or anything. 'I ain't taken anyone to any relocation camp . . . You don't have to worry about anyone who's dead,' said Sergeant William Doyle at the end of an exchange of fire with North Vietnamese troops.[123] For Sam Ybarra the Song Ve Valley was a vast hunting ground: 'That's were [sic] the gooks are . . . I'll kill all these gooks.'[124] The theme is fear, rage and hatred – and above all, revenge. 'Everybody was blood thirsty at the time, saying "We're going to get them back . . . We're going to even the score".'[125] They wanted to avenge the deaths of fallen comrades retrospectively and their own death in anticipation. 'We were living day to day. We didn't expect to live. No one out there with any brains expected to live. We were surprised to be alive next week . . . I'm not saying you give up and die. You struggle to live. But the way to live is to kill.'[126] However you read these words, they do not simply bear witness to emotion but also to cold reasoning – to the deliberate intention to kill, violate and mutilate in any circumstances and at any time.

Routine murder. In fact the Tigers did not care where they were and in what circumstances they went into action. Certainly some comrades were ambushed in the Song Ve Valley, wounded or killed, but Song Ve could not be compared with the 'hell of Quang Tin'. In the former the losses were substantially smaller, they did not have to be on the alert for mines at every step and in early summer 1967 there were only a few of the well-trained and battle-hardened soldiers from the North around. In Song Ve they were moving over ground with relatively good visibility, not in country which seemed to be the enemy's silent accomplice, and in this valley the Tigers were not left alone for days on end without any prospect of speedy rescue or relief. In other words, Song Ve was not a setting of extremes and yet even there they stabbed, scalped, bayoneted, strangled and executed, and hunted down people who were fleeing or in hiding, just as they did in Quang Tin. Their behaviour was more reminiscent of killer commandos, doing a job and waiting for the next one, rather than of gangs and lynch mobs. And the longer the murdering went on, the easier it seemed to get.

It is well known that routine and wild violence are not incompatible. After his old and only friend, Kenneth 'Boots' Green was shot dead in an ambush at the end of September 1967, Sam Ybarra changed from a murderous arsonist into a madman. Once, disdaining any protection from his flanks, he rushed at a suspect target, drowning the noise of his M16 with wild screams, as though he wanted to demonstrate simultaneously his will to kill and his invulnerability.[127] On another occasion in the course of a raid Ybarra beheaded with his bush knife a baby whom he had found crying beside its mother in a hut.[128] Others whipped themselves up into a frenzy and went on beating dead bodies; furious men became blind with rage, took no more scalps or ears as trophies but stabbed corpses as though they were out of their minds.[129] Even their leaders had to be on their guard against these soldiers, who repeatedly threatened to kill them for issuing risky orders or after unforeseeable accidents.[130] These Tigers even gave their comrades in the same company a feeling of threat and unpredictability.

It is hard to judge how often the violence changed from one form to the other. In interrogations and interviews only casual questions were asked about the moments when they 'snapped' and the Tigers themselves did not speak about that problem, either because they could no longer put themselves into the situation any more after an interval of weeks or sometimes years, or because losing self-control did not fit the image of a poised, elite warrior. Consequently their stories in general and the suggestion of calculated actions in particular could even have been a retrospective rationalisation and therefore a refusal to admit that a Sam Ybarra lurked within everyone. The suspicion that they were being deceitful, consciously or unconsciously, will remain a suspicion, given the lack of convincing evidence to the contrary.

Equally sparse are hints at the pleasure they took in killing or, to be more precise, at the physical excitement which tormenting and desecrating the bodies of strangers aroused. As in most soldiers' tales, this factor is so overlaid with stories of fear, hatred, rage and revenge as to be non-existent. Yet even when the Tigers couldn't find the words, their deeds spoke for themselves. It is proved that one Tiger wagered that he could strike a prisoner unconscious with one blow, but failed at the first attempt and waited to strike the second blow until a comrade had aimed at the victim's neck with his bayonet. 'The prisoner bled to death and everyone present thought this was funny.'[131] The killer could from then on award himself the nickname 'one-punch Varney'. There is also proof of soldiers betting on the number of shots needed to hit a human target.[132] Whether practising with 'turkey-shot', slitting throats or hacking off limbs, the sight of blood was always greeted with yells and laughter.[133] There is proof, too, of shooting at point-blank range into people's faces or inflicting wounds in such a way that the victim died a slow and painful death.[134] It was even fun to leave behind explosives they had assembled themselves and hidden in food rations, which then blew to pieces the bodies of the hungry people who found them.[135] There is a suggestion that abusing helpless bodies was fun and done for fun's sake. A GI stationed elsewhere in Vietnam added his opinion: 'I know what killing is, and I know what the relief is when you kill somebody . . . They're just doing that for kicks.'[136]

About a dozen Tigers stayed apart from these practices – a quarter of the forty-five men mobilised for an operation. They temporarily moved away, put down their weapons or expressed their contempt in some other way.[137] There are no more exact descriptions, apart from those of three GIs, who actively tried to stop their comrades. Bill Carpenter had a noisy argument with his platoon leader who was taking aim at a peasant, though he could not prevent the murder.[138] Donald Wood urged some GIs to defy the order given by Lieutenant James Hawkins to shoot two old women – but in vain. 'You don't countermand my orders. This is my platoon.'[139] And Gerald Bruner aimed his M16 at two comrades who had already shot a peasant who was prepared for evacuation and wanted to kill his younger brother as well.[140] 'If you fire up that kid, I'll do the same to you, damn it.'[141] The young man was shortly afterwards flown out by helicopter with the rest of his family. It seems that in the course of seven months this was an isolated case: there was not enough courage among individuals to save any other lives.

The three examples of active resistance also illustrate why it was difficult for these abstainers or resisters to keep utilising their options and why they finally gave up during an operation.

'You chicken shit son of a bitch. If you don't shut up, I'll shoot you,' Bill Carpenter was told by Lieutenant Hawkins, a platoon leader with Tiger Force from mid August to the end of October 1967.[142] Such invective was no empty threat. Donald Wood was knocked down by a comrade and his commander fired a warning shot at him as he lay dazed on the ground.[143] 'The only reason you're still alive,' Wood was told, 'is that you're a medic and we need you.'[144] 'To make him [Ybarra] angry with you and then go into combat with him, you would just end up on the short end.'[145] It was also reported from the ranks of other units that soldiers who rebelled were risking their lives. They talked of the 'to whom it may concern round', meaning shots which hit one's own comrades – seemingly tragically, but in fact aimed at unreliable men or suspected traitors: another but largely unknown form of fragging. 'Keep your mouth shut about this,' said a 'comrade in arms' to Dennis Lee Stout, who was temporarily attached to the Tigers as an Army journalist. 'Remember, you don't have to return from the next operation.'[146]

The bullies – three or four soldiers full up with testosterone, who let everyone know that they were capable of anything – made sure everyone kept to the rules of the game. Anyone who in their eyes was showing too much restraint was made to commit murder in the presence of witnesses, regularly by Lieutenant Hawkins[147] and repeatedly also by Sam Ybarra or Harold Trout. 'Break your cherry' or 'grease her', the latter used to say.[148] Whatever the motives were of those who kept pace, sometimes hesitantly, sometimes willingly, it is clear that soldiers like Ybarra, Trout, William Doyle or James Barnett did not keep the troop together with fear and forced complicity alone; alongside the solidarity based on violence and compliance came trust and respect, which were perhaps the main prerequisites for a voluntary following. Newcomers, drafted in to replace fallen members of Tiger Force, wanted to be accepted into the ranks of the aggressive, battle-hardened and supposedly fearless. The platoon leaders, replaced on an eight-week rotation,[149] could not produce such credentials – not even Hawkins, who was mocked for a while for his tactical incompetence and in the end had to realise that his orders were being ignored.[150] As so often, 'jungle rank' counted for more than formal rankings. The bullies were the de facto commanders of Tiger Force.

Scepticism, aversion and of course being prepared to mount an active opposition were eroded in this milieu, but the lack of verbal or written records make it impossible to reconstruct this process in detail. It can only be substantiated that Bill Carpenter did go so far as to shoot a Vietnamese who had been seriously wounded by another Tiger. 'Mercy killing', more or less; no one who knew him would have thought Carpenter capable of doing this. Two other soldiers, who had at first refused to take part in marauding, also joined the ranks of the murderers and it seems that newcomers to the group were the least able to resist being caught up in the maelstrom. They were the ones who would have been relying on discipline and the example of troop leaders; instead they found themselves dealing with sergeants to whom the life of a Vietnamese was worthless. One after the other abandoned their scruples and even Wood and Bruner kept silent. There was no way to rise above a mixture of shame, incomprehension, resignation and fear. One has to record how quickly they adjusted and that their compliance grew in intensity.[151]

In this way Tiger Force was perpetuating a tradition in the history of warfare – that small armed groups do not just extend the latitude for people who commit atrocities; they create a special setting for violent actions, because in this microcosm people are allowed to live by their own rules, and because in principle everyone is free to indulge in violence away from the battlefield. 'We really got a chance to act it out,' said one Special Forces soldier, 'and there was no mommy to scold us, no principal's office to be sent to.'[152] Military training was forgotten; the restraints of civilian life were suspended. A soldier stationed in Quang Ngai maintained: 'What matters is what people here and now think about what you're doing . . . This group of people . . . was the whole world. What they thought was right was right.

And what they thought was wrong was wrong. The definitions for things were turned around. Courage was seen as stupidity . . . and cruelty and brutality were seen sometimes as heroic.'[153] This is not to say that opportunities for murder and manslaughter were actually seized; in the final analysis it was the character of each individual which alone decided the matter. The temptation, however, was great: 'There are just four or five of you together,' a member of Tiger Force recalls. 'If you trust the guys you're with, if you have good men with you, you don't have to worry about what you do. You can do any damn thing you want to, anywhere you want to. Who's going to check you? What's the checks and balances? There's not any. You're calling all the shots.'[154]

In Vietnam an unknown number of small groups turned into rampaging mobs. Some cases that are recorded bear a resemblance of one kind or another to Tiger Force. Before a platoon of Marines carried out a night raid on the village of Xuan Ngoc in Quang Tin Province at the end of September 1966, the lieutenant in charge had given nine of his men permission to take out their anger on the peasants. 'We wanted to get some V.C. so we could more or less prove that we were as good as anyone else, because we had a lot of pride, our platoon and we wanted real bad to get some V.C. that day.'[155] The only condition was that they did it on their own responsibility and in his absence. 'The people wouldn't turn the V.C. in,' said the two self-appointed leaders of the group. 'But if we created enough fear they would.'[156] They left four people dead including a baby, its skull smashed with a rifle butt, several rape victims and a village largely in ruins. In 'Indian Country' no one needed to bother about anything. 'I just said as we looked down at the baby that I was glad this wasn't in the United States.'[157]

Assault troops of other units who were sent out in the late 1960s to lay ambushes or spy out the land and in the course of so doing took prisoners, cast votes to be the executioner. 'I want to shoot the man, I want to kill the man.' – 'Save one for me.'[158] – 'I always wanted to shoot a gook between the eyes . . . "Western Style".'[159] One reconnaissance platoon of E Company, 4th Battalion, 503rd Infantry Regiment of 173rd Airborne Brigade (Separate) rampaged for four weeks at the end of 1970, unobserved and left to their own devices in a remote corner of I Corps Tactical Zone, destroying crops, torturing suspects and using prisoners as mine dogs. 'If anyone was going to get it, it would be them.'[160] Referring to the officer in charge, an investigation report of the Criminal Investigation Division read: 'LT [Lieutenant] Ambrose appears to have become a power unto himself in the area.'[161]

In the film *Apocalypse Now* Colonel Kurtz, who is holed up in the jungle with a handful of trusted men – a doomed quasi-religious leader awaiting his end literally in a fever – comes from this background. Like this fictional character, most of his historical precursors are also shadowy men, silhouettes whose contours unfailingly fade into a blur.

Undoubtedly small groups were in a better position to conceal their excesses than other formations. The abductors who took a young woman around with them for days on end, raping her as they went, only moved about at night to hide from helicopter patrols.[162] 'Make the ambush side look good' meant burning down a sacked village, scattering Soviet or North Vietnamese cartridge cases around the scene, putting weapons from enemy stock in the lifeless hands of corpses or rendering them unrecognisable by blowing them up with hand grenades.[163] This last idea was hatched up with his Marines by the platoon leader responsible for the attack on Xuan Ngoc; in addition they had agreed to report to battalion headquarters that they had been hunting Viet Cong who had taken refuge in peasant huts, that they had heard cries and had opened fire partly in self-defence, partly in panic, and by accident had hit some non-combatants as well.[164] Anyone operating in a remote area could radio any lies to their leaders and if asked awkward questions they could always destroy their radio and enter 'enemy fire' in the logbook as the cause – there are many examples[165] to show why one investigation after another had to be aborted.

On the other hand the tales of deceit and secrecy only tell half the story, for in spite of all their criminal enterprise even small groups left behind telltale traces; even Tiger Force's misdeeds came to light in summer and autumn 1967. By spring 1967 so many rumours and reports of mutilation had reached 1st Brigade, 327th Regiment, 101st Airborne Division that the brigade commander felt the need to send a directive to all sections of his troops with the threat of harsh punishment. Yet no investigation into the incidents took place.[166] The directive did not succeed in deterring them, either, or Tiger Force would have taken greater care with their radio traffic. It was unusual even in the northern battle zone to report up to eight contacts with the enemy in a day and to include 'Viet Cong shot while trying to escape' in the body count. They could feel safe, however, because after completely destroying a village they could rely on not having to face critical questioning but on being praised by their superiors for a successful operation: 'That's why you're the Tigers!'[167] were the words of Lieutenant Colonel Gerald E. Morse, who had taken over command of 1st Battalion from Austin in summer 1967 – an officer known for his supervision and precision. 'He . . . insisted,' said one of his junior colleagues, 'upon being knowledgeable of all aspects of the operations of his battalion . . . Morse expected exceptional standards from his staff . . . Morse had a C&C Ship [command and control helicopter] at his disposal and made exceptional use of the ship for observing his battalion's tactical situations on the ground.'[168] Even if there is no proof that Morse knew of Tiger Force's crimes, at least his closest colleagues were in the know. While the Tigers were still rampaging through the Song Ve Valley and Quang Tin, Donald Wood and Gerald Bruner had made contact with three battalion staff officers and made detailed reports. They were both withdrawn from Tiger Force and transferred to another unit. Bruner, who had threatened a fellow-soldier with a gun, so preventing yet another murder, was sent to a psychiatrist by his company commander and Wood was told by an officer at headquarters: 'We're in the middle of a war, Lieutenant. And you want me to take our best unit out of action because a few guys are killing gooks?'[169]

The quintessence of the American strategy in the northern battle zone in 1967 could hardly have been described more tellingly. Troops like Tiger Force were needed and their atrocities were the eggs broken to make an omelette. Without units able and willing to terrorise, the intention to inflict shock and awe on the peasants of Quang Ngai and Quang Tri would have remained an implausible threat. As early as the mid 1960s, some officers at MACV had been concerned about the Special Forces' tendency to use excessive force and thereby to take the war into their own hands, but the critics were put in their place at the time by having the peculiar nature of guerrilla warfare pointed out to them – even by William Westmoreland himself.[170] This remained the situation, in spite of the fact that special units sometimes claimed 100 to 150 enemies killed for the loss of only one of their own men – a ratio which seems crazy in comparison with the action figures of regular units and which can only be explained by assuming that a high percentage of the dead were non-combatants.[171] Even when recruiting for Tiger Force only the most aggressive applicants were accepted: soldiers who had demonstrated a determined readiness to kill during their training. The unwritten rule of thumb for its deployment was certainly not to allow execution commandos and death squads to get out of hand, but to keep them on the longest possible leash. The same applied to the bullies within the units, as Captain Harold McGaha indicated when he took over the command of Tiger Force, learnt about Sam Ybarra threatening to kill one of his comrades and watched him mutilating a corpse: 'We need him, but just don't let him go off crazy.'[172]

At the end of 1967 the war in 'Indian Country' entered its decisive phase.

6

16 March 1968 – The Massacres of My Lai (4) and My Khe (4)

Evidence is not truth. It is only evident.
   Tim O'Brien[1]

Oderint, dum metuant. –
They may hate me so long as they fear me.
   Caligula, Roman emperor

At the start of 1968 both sides seemed to be running short of what they most urgently needed – the moral resource of the war. Neither could reckon on exhausting the enemy in material terms but the motivation of the troops and support on the home front clearly left much to be desired. American officers read in captured documents that the political leaders of the Viet Cong were complaining not only about the planning and coordination of military operations, but also about waning enthusiasm, untimely hesitation and even timidity in the face of the enemy – indications that the rumours of a dramatically increased number of Communist deserters were credible.[2] Last but not least, the US Supreme Command in Saigon reckoned on growing tensions between the guerrillas and the rural population, because demands for taxes and food were continually rising and the enemy forces were not in a position to protect from attack the areas where their clients lived. 'The Viet Cong obviously is in trouble and is looking for a way out,' so ran one expert report. '. . . It appears that the struggle that lies ahead will be one that will test the staying power, the determination of both sides.'[3]

Given the domestic political disputes in the United States, Hanoi and the National Liberation Front for South Vietnam came to similar conclusions. William Westmoreland was thwarted in his demand for additional troops in autumn 1967 and the president, entering the election year of 1968 handicapped by an unpopular war, had categorically ruled out mobilising the Reserves. The United States appeared to be militarily vulnerable because it had overplayed its hand politically: 'The U.S. ground troops are now short of personnel, the negroes have risen up to oppose the government . . . We must intensify attacks in cities and towns and simultaneously seek to liberate all the areas in the vicinity of these urban zones.'[4] Basically both sides saw that the opportunity had come for a decisive breakthrough: the Communists, because they could use the Americans' political predicament to force their withdrawal, and the American masters of war, because they had to make use of the enemy's military weakness to restore the credibility of their war policy. In these conditions everything pointed to an intensification of the war. The only question was when.

GENERALS

The Viet Cong and the North Vietnamese Army opened the battle for American public opinion. During the 'winter–spring offensive' at the turn of the year in 1967–68, they repeatedly tied up American units in skirmishes on the borders with Laos and Cambodia. When 325th (C) and 304th Infantry Divisions of the NVA prepared to storm a US Marine base in Khe Sanh on 21 January 1968, a phase of classic set-piece battles or sieges seemed on the cards. The US Supreme Command even feared an encirclement battle, as had happened at Dien Bien Phu, and moved 15,000 additional troops into Quang Tri Province. General Giap, however, had no positional war in mind but stepped up the psychological war of attrition. At the start of the Buddhist New Year Festival on 31 January 1968, 80,000 guerrillas attacked town centres throughout South Vietnam – thirty-six out of forty-four provincial capitals, sixty-four regional administrative centres and the capital city Saigon.[5] It was clear that they would not be able to hold out for any length of time, but in any event the offensive promised to pay moral dividends. The unprepared US Armed Forces had disgraced themselves and could only retake the towns at the cost of civilian casualties – thereby doing further damage to the image of the United States.

In the event, political America was shocked. No one had expected the Viet Cong to be capable of shelling the presidential palace and the headquarters of the US Armed Forces in Saigon – not to mention storming the American Embassy. The optimistic prognoses from both the White House and the Pentagon sounded at best naïve and at worst like deliberate deception. In the words of a contemporary witticism, the light at the end of the tunnel was just a guerrilla miner's lamp. Themes which up to then had been a preserve of the anti-war movement now became part of the repertoire of leading politicians such as Eugene McCarthy or Robert Kennedy, who were preparing to fight President Johnson's re-election from within the ranks of his own party. As the journalist Peter Braestrup writes, 'The [New York] Times reader found little but dismay, despair, or disapproval in the paper's analyses and commentaries.'[6] Walter Cronkite expressed the same reactions when he presented his evening news broadcast on CBS: 'What the hell is going on? I thought we were winning this war!'[7] When Cronkite, according to many opinion polls the most trustworthy man in America, had finished his broadcast, Johnson realised that the end of his presidency had come. '[He] told his press secretary . . . that it was a turning-point, that if he had lost Walter Cronkite he had lost Mr Average Citizen.'[8]

Meanwhile in South Vietnam Communist troops were stepping up their terrorism against civilians. After freeing some 600 prisoners from the provincial prison in Quang Ngai City at the end of January 1968, the guerrillas stormed the undefended civilian hospital in the town, murdering patients, nurses and doctors indiscriminately.[9] At the same time the old imperial town of Huê also became the scene of a massacre: 12,000 soldiers – mostly members of the NVA – had invaded the town on the night of 31 January and put into action a plan to murder the political and intellectual elite, which had evidently been prepared by the Communist Party of North Vietnam and the National Liberation Front in December 1967.[10] According to one captured deployment report, 'Huê was the place where reactionary spirit has existed for over ten years. However, it only took us a short time to drain it to its root.'[11] Out of roughly 150,000 inhabitants, 5,700 were assumed to have been executed or abducted. Later exhumations proved that these people – among them French priests and four West German doctors – were beaten to death, shot dead, decapitated or buried alive. A few were found in groups of ten or fifteen, killed in front of mass graves they had dug themselves, their mouths stuffed with dirt or scraps of cloth.[12] A reliable reconstruction of the event has yet to be made and if such a study were still possible decades afterwards, it would have to refer to the hypotheses Douglas Pike made in 1970. He claimed that the murders were all committed according to a plan; there is nothing to indicate either uncontrolled killing in the heat of battle or panic and it appears that the perpetrators were without exception local Viet Cong. Finally, most of the victims were murdered shortly before the enforced withdrawal from the town and therefore with the intention of clearing as many witnesses as possible out of the way.[13]

In Huê Communist terrorism claimed the majority of victims at that time; however the town was by no means the only scene of terror. One Viet Cong leadership document captured by American units implies that in the wake of Tet, repression and arbitrary behaviour in Quang Ngai Province was escalating, and threatening to get out of the control of their originators: 'We failed to conduct a careful investigation before abusing or arresting a suspected person. We did this without evidence or sufficient grounds, but only out of personal hatred.'[14] The writers are complaining that any of the functionaries could arrest and imprison anyone they did not like without consulting a higher authority – an opportunity which they used to settle personal quarrels, to enrich themselves with other people's property and not least to remove political rivals.

Some prisoners became ill and died due to the lengthy confinement . . . Detainees were ill-treated. Sometimes, they were even beaten by armed security personnel . . . In some areas, the party secretaries in charge of the villages even denounced their opponents as being dangerous tyrants or spies. Then the local party unit secretly arrested and executed these people without trial and without asking for instructions from their superiors. In some areas 12-year old children were killed, together with their parents and relatives.

It was a question of routine terror encompassing the whole province and a population which as a consequence was noticeably keeping its distance from the Viet Cong. 'As a result, we were unable to gather the people's forces together to defeat the enemy and oppress the guilty reactionaries.'[15]

The US Supreme Command in Saigon also feared for the steadfastness of its ally. Certainly the urban solidarity which the Viet Cong had hoped for did not materialise and there was absolutely no question of the peasants rising up against the 'American puppets'. However, Tet cost the lives of 13,000 civilians, 20,000 were wounded and a million people had become refugees.[16] Local home security troops – 'regional forces' and 'popular forces', assigned to support the South Vietnamese Army – had mostly taken flight; some units still existed only on paper; deserters could no longer be traced. With the exception of Quang Tin, American observers in all provinces in I Corps Tactical Zone certified that by April 1968 there was 'almost a total collapse of security',[17] in view of villages having been left unprotected. Even in the hinterland of large towns there was no evidence that things had calmed down: 'The population of metropolitan Saigon has become quite jumpy and whole neighborhoods pick up and move toward Saigon at the drop of a VC sandal.'[18] In the US Embassy, and even more in the circle around William Westmoreland, the reaction was of alarm if not panic. It seemed that the defeatism prevalent everywhere had even gripped the South Vietnamese political and military leadership,[19] but an ally which no longer believed in its own prospects would have completely destroyed American credibility. In other words, the enemy had won yet another round in the political race against time.

On the other hand, in military terms Tet ended in a disaster for the Viet Cong. In the battles for Quang Tri City 900 guerrillas were allegedly killed, and during the attacks on Quang Ngai City 640 – mostly from well-equipped and experienced units. According to American estimates, between January and March 1968 in I Corps Tactical Zone alone, the Viet Cong and the NVA lost sixty-five per cent of their men either through death, serious injury or capture. From April to June – during the second wave of the Tet Offensive – 4,000 Communist fighters were killed each week, eight times more than from the American forces. The total number of guerrillas and North Vietnamese soldiers killed cannot be extrapolated from these figures, nor is it known how quickly and to what extent the North recruited fresh troops. However, by and large one can assume that they lost between 50,000 and 100,000 men.

The drain on the Viet Cong was so drastic in 1968 that the insurgents would not have been able to continue the war without support from the North.[20]

A politically exhausted ally on one side and a militarily severely weakened enemy on the other: under the influence of these conflicting results of Tet William Westmoreland pressed for seizing the initiative. In several letters to all commanding generals in Vietnam between early February and mid April 1968 he called for an intensification of the course followed since mid 1967. 'We must now take maximum advantage of the current situation, and put relentless pressure on the enemy to achieve what could be a major turn in the course of the war ... The challenge is now ours. We cannot let it slip ... We can achieve a decisive victory and we must do so at once ... We must demonstrate by our actions that we are, in fact, winning the war.'[21] Within South Vietnam, Westmoreland identified I Corps Tactical Zone and the Mekong Delta as the main geographical focal points of the roll-back, while simultaneously playing with the idea of extending the war to the retreat lines of the Viet Cong in Cambodia, Laos and the demilitarised zone.[22] However this last only seemed to make sense given a double prerequisite: destroying most of the Viet Cong bases in advance and eliminating as many Viet Cong political leaders as possible. 'Base areas determined to be habitual safe havens for the enemy will be selected for total destruction when warranted ... Several base areas may be clustered in the same general area; even though one may be considered more important than the others, it is desirable to neutralize the entire cluster.'[23] In I Corps Tactical Zone, 114 primary targets of this sort were identified[24] and 120 additional experts in counterinsurgency were sent into Quang Ngai Province alone, with the remit of stepping up the hunt for guerrilla functionaries, their helpers and auxiliaries.[25] The implications were clear: the Army had to cooperate from then on more closely with the CIA and with all the South Vietnamese police authorities responsible for the Phoenix programme. In inhabited areas the population could reckon less than ever on operative consideration – especially if they lived in Viet Cong 're-generation zones'. The asymmetrical war stood at the threshold of symmetrical escalation.[26]

In the 'Indian Country' between Quang Tri and Quang Nam William Westmoreland wanted as quickly as possible to achieve successes which would point the way forward. This was where the Tet offensive had started, in these provinces the guerrilla leaders had temporarily broken cover and only here was it possible to disrupt effectively the supplies of men and materiel from the North. For this reason the senior commander gave his troops in I Corps Tactical Zone unparalleled freedom of action, by temporarily countermanding the regulations for the protection of civilians, their homes and their possessions. Deviating from Directive 525-18, troop leaders were permitted to attack villages and towns at any time without prior consultation and with weapons and formations of their choice.[27] In any case there was certainly a host of exceptional provisions in the Rules of Engagement with which one could get round the order to use fire-power with restraint,[28] but to date there had been no official backing for such manipulation of operational freedom. As William Peers stressed in his report on the My Lai (4) massacre, since Tet commanding officers no longer had to worry about sanctions – not even if they had unduly strained the limits of their powers of discretion or completely ignored the Rules of Engagement,[29] Westmoreland's temporary permission amounted to an open invitation to behave as arbitrarily as one liked.

Ninety-eight fighting battalions stood ready for the new offensive in I Corps Tactical Zone: fifty-seven American, thirty-seven South Vietnamese and four South Korean. The US units belonged to 1st and 3rd Marine Division, 1st Cavalry Division, 101st Airborne Division, 4th Infantry Division and 23rd Infantry Division (Americal) – the last-named being the strongest formation with 24,000 men. Of the numerous tasks assigned to them since the end of 1967, Operations Wheeler/Wallowa[30] and Muscatine[31] are of particular significance in the present context – classic search-and-destroy deployments in the provinces of Quang Tin, Quang Nam and Quang Ngai, which were carried out essentially by units from the Americal Division.[32]

On their return from Vietnam a handful of soldiers went public or complained to Secretary of Defense Melvin Laird and the Criminal Investigation Division of the Army about the behaviour of the Americal Division in the wake of the Tet offensive. Taken together, their statements painted a picture of a division, all the subordinate sections of which could be linked to atrocities.

An interrogation specialist of 1st Military Intelligence Team, 11th Light Infantry Brigade claimed that over a lengthy period he had observed between twenty and forty incidents of torture daily – often even on women and children. 'In one case, I saw a girl brought back and tortured to the point where she menstruated on the floor.'[33] According to Richard H. Brummett, his unit – A Troop, 1st Squadron, 1st Cavalry Regiment (Airmobile) – used violence not just deliberately but as a habit. 'This was done with the full knowledge, consent and participation of our Troop Commander.'[34] In other words, in Quang Tin Province between January and March 1968 civilians were harassed and tormented in every imaginable way, their livestock was indiscriminately slaughtered and their villages reduced to ashes at the slightest provocation. After examining witnesses over several months Army investigating officers confirmed the truth of Brummett's complaints in almost every point.[35] However, no charges were brought – not even against one sergeant who had thrown an old man into a well and then let off a hand grenade in the shaft. 'It could not conclusively be determined if the unidentified Vietnamese National died as a result of this incident,' ran a letter from the Department of Defense dated 11 February 1972 to Richard H. Brummett. 'Your interest in the military service is appreciated.'[36] Although Richard Dell, among others, had made serious accusations against B Company, 1st Battalion, 6th Infantry Regiment, 198th Light Infantry Brigade, it was also left in peace. It was claimed that in the course of deployments in Quang Tin Province many prisoners were murdered and women raped and one troop doctor deliberately caused the death of a wounded woman by injecting her with an overdose of morphine. The unit allegedly made a habit of laying out ammunition of Soviet origin in burnt-out villages to pretend that Viet Cong had been there. In deployment briefings it was reputedly impressed on the squad leaders that they should basically shoot anyone trying to escape and thus improve the battalion's killing tally.[37] The company commander was accused of radioing an explicit order to murder a prisoner: 'What do I have to do, spoon feed you people, don't bring him back.'[38] In spite of serious circumstantial evidence and corroborative witness statements the Criminal Investigation Division showed no interest in examining the Dell Allegation in detail. Its final report even suppressed incriminating evidence against officers.[39]

It is an open question whether and how this chapter in the history of the Americal Division can be reconstructed at all; it also remains to be established whether it represented an example of exceptional violence, even within the parameters of the Vietnam War.

'On February 8, 1968, 19 women and children were murdered in Viet-Nam by members of 3rd Platoon, B Company, 1st Battalion, [3rd Brigade], 35th Infantry Regiment, [4th Infantry Division]. The details are set forth in the first issue of *Scanlan's* magazine. There is little I can add to that article.' With these words James D. Henry, an Army doctor, opened a press conference at the Los Angeles Press Club on 27 February 1970. 'I would like to emphasize that the murders of February 8, 1968 were not isolated incidents, nor was "B" company composed of abberant [*sic*] individuals . . . Incidents similar to those I have described occur on a daily basis and differ one from the other only in terms of numbers killed.'[40] Almost four years later the investigation report of the Criminal Investigation Division came out[41] – and with it, the proof that Henry's unit had followed in the footsteps of Tiger Force. Therefore this unit was not the first to carry out a massacre of civilians but was in fact continuing the series of terror actions carried out within the framework of the operations Wheeler/Wallowa and Muscatine and on the part of the Americal Division.

None of the atrocities reported by James D. Henry were connected with actual combat. 'There was never any fire fights the day that they occurred.'[42] On 8 October 1967 B Company was deployed to the west of Chu Lai in Quang Tin Province when a few GIs seized a child. The leader of 2nd Platoon, a first lieutenant, asked for volunteers to execute the unarmed boy who was only wearing summer shorts. A radio operator and an Army doctor came forward; the former maltreated the 'prisoner' by kicking him in the stomach, the latter took him behind a rock and shot him dead with his M16 set on automatic. The company commander received a report of a dead Viet Cong whose body could not be found as he was shot while escaping through a river. Three days later other members of the unit maltreated an old man suspected of collaborating with the enemy and threw him off a cliff. On 15 October two members of 2nd Platoon – a non-commissioned officer and a GI – came upon a peasant sleeping in his hut. They murdered the man, radioed the company leader for permission to test shoot and used as a target the corpse which they had leant against a cave wall. 'Everybody was taking pot shots at him seeing how accurate they were.'[43] On 22 October GIs from 1st Platoon lured five women into an ambush and murdered them. Presumably the victims had first been raped. Enemy contact and a body count of five male enemies, said the report. 'I personally know of at least 50 civilians executed by our company . . . ,' stated Henry, 'not in the heat of battle or from air or artillery strikes – deliberate murder. And then there were the rapes and the cases of torture (without even the pretext of trying to gain information).'[44] Henry's comrades obviously enjoyed killing, mutilating corpses and collecting body parts.[45]

The fifty victims also included those killed on 8 February 1968. On that day B Company combed through rural Quang Nam, with the intention of avenging five colleagues who had been killed the previous day in an exchange of fire with snipers. Initially they took out their anger on a peasant. 'He was Vietnamese and he was there – that was sufficient to mark him for death.'[46] After a few GIs had discussed how to murder him, they pushed the man in front of an armoured troop carrier which ran him over several times – in the presence of Captain Donald C. Reh, the company commander.[47] Shortly afterwards 3rd Platoon marched into a village fifteen miles east of Hoi An. The soldiers found nineteen people there, all women and children. The platoon leader Lieutenant Johnny M. Carter radioed Captain Reh to ask how he should deal with the – literally speaking – 'civilians'. According to James D. Henry, 'The Captain asked the Lieutenant if he remembered the Op Order [Operation Order] that came down that morning and he repeated the order which was "kill anything that moves".'[48] The reference to higher authorities probably meant Lieutenant Colonel William W. Taylor Jr., the commander of 1st Battalion who was watching the operation from a helicopter.[49] The rest was played out within minutes: a young woman, clearly a victim of rape, was dragged naked out of her hut and thrown at the feet of the villagers who were cowering in a circle. Lieutenant Carter asked for volunteers to form a firing-squad and four or five soldiers, among them the platoon leader, released the safety catches of their weapons and shot the whole group dead at close range. The captain went up to the observers who were standing around with expressionless faces and according to James D. Henry made a brief announcement: 'I forget exactly what it was, but it didn't concern the people who had just been killed. We picked up our stuff and moved on.'[50]

At the same time South Korean units were rampaging in the deployment area of the Americal Division – four battalions of mercenaries and reserve units who were paid from American funds and were under the command of 2nd Republic of Korea Marine Corps Brigade. Since they arrived in Vietnam in 1965 they were reputed 'to burn everything down, to destroy everything, to seize everything and kill everyone,' stated a study by the RAND Corporation.[51] According to a platoon leader of 198th Light Infantry Brigade, Americal Division, South Korean troops attacked a village near My Lai (4), forced thirty-six inhabitants to dig graves and executed them one after another by shooting them in the head.[52] After one operation in the same area in December 1967 they recorded in their war diary the loss of 20 of their own men and 700 Viet Cong dead – a ridiculous assertion, given that a mere 500 Viet Cong were believed to be there, but one which leads to the supposition that South Korean soldiers had carried out the second massacre of civilians within ten months in the settlement area around My Lai (4).[53] The number of victims is unknown. There is no doubt whatever about the events of 12 February 1968 in the villages of Phong Nhi and Phong Nhut (2) in the Bien Ban district: the Korean Marines murdered seventy-nine inhabitants and destroyed the settlements down to the last building.[54] The senior American civilian adviser in Quang Nam Province wrote on 18 March 1968, 'The Vietnamese peasants are, of course, deathly afraid of the Koreans. Many say that they prefer the VC to the Koreans . . . [This] may actually be causing an increase in VC sympathizers throughout the Korean TAOR [tactical area of operations].'[55] As one situation report from the CORDS office in Quang Nam Province dated 25 March 1968 stated, 'The peasants do not even want to work during the days in their fields for fear of Korean attacks.'[56]

The escalation of violence in the context of operations Wheeler/Wallowa and Muscatine had been known about at the highest level since November 1967. The commanding officer of 196th Light Infantry Brigade, Americal Division, spoke of 'instances of mis-behavior'.[57] Westmoreland's deputy, Creighton W. Abrams, complained about 'an increasing number of allegations and complaints . . . These incidents reportedly include harassment of innocent civilians travelling on Route 1, illegal confiscation of property and serious assaults committed by military personnel.'[58] Lastly, Americal Commander Major General Samuel W. Koster referred in his command report to rape, looting, pilfering and brutality. Incidents which provoke such allegations are destructive to our mission and to the image of our great Nation and can not be tolerated within this command. This is a subject for prompt attention by commanders at all levels and must become a matter of personal concern by every man in the chain of command. I will not tolerate anyone in authority looking the other way when an incident, mischievous or discourteous act is perpetrated on a Vietnamese citizen.[59]

These were letters for the file, full of grand gestures but devoid of any follow-up – and the same applied to the South Korean Marines. Since March 1968 top American civil servants, the head of CORDS and his representative in the Quang Nam office had been calling for measures to discipline these units. The officer in command of III Marine Amphibious Force, Lieutenant Colonel Rosson, even commissioned a special study group to draw up appropriate suggestions.[60] William Westmoreland was not impressed. He informed his South Korean opposite number, 'After a limited investigation [of the massacres of Phong Nhi and Phong Nhut (2)] it was recognized that this matter is more properly a concern of your country . . . Our investigation was terminated.'[61] Westmoreland wouldn't hear of withdrawing 2nd Republic of Korea Marine Corps Brigade from Quang Nam, even though this had been repeatedly demanded since July 1968 both by the South Vietnamese leaders of the province and by CORDS.[62] Just as with Tiger Force, the most aggressive units were obviously indispensable both strategically and tactically – and even at the price of them turning their deployment zones into killing fields.[63]

OFFICERS

Since the Tet Offensive the US Supreme Command had focused more than ever on fighting the war with small teams. Special commandos, companies, platoons and squads were considered the suitable means for tracking down the guerrillas who had scattered in all directions, driving them out of their back-up areas and preventing them from regrouping. Small groups required less logistical effort, were more mobile than other formations and could also risk attacking the greatly weakened enemy units with small numbers of men. On 10 March 1968

William Westmoreland spoke about his plans: 'Assign specific villages as objectives and specify times when objectives will be occupied. Task forces will occupy objective areas, clear them of enemy forces, and apprehend infrastructure members which identified themselves with VC during Tet-offensive.'[64] For Westmoreland it was important to incorporate South Vietnamese troops into these ad hoc units. This was a question of combined 'show-the-flag' operations which were needed as a political symbol after Tet and were essential for motivating a demoralised ally. Dissatisfied with the previous efforts, Westmoreland put heavy pressure on his officers, demanding 'intensive . . . immediate measures.'[65] If at all, the race against time could only be won with small units.

This initiative came at exactly the right time for those responsible for the Americal Division. Since autumn 1967 they had been waging their war predominantly in small groups and under the impact of Tet had put together new special commandos at the beginning of February 1968 – among others the 500-man strong Task Force Barker. They were to be deployed in an area of 150 square miles north-east of Quang Ngai City within the framework of Operation Muscatine, to 'pacify' an area known to be a Viet Cong stronghold within eight weeks. They would be facing 48th Viet Cong Local Force Battalion and three guerrilla companies. Three companies of 11th Light Infantry Brigade, Americal Division were earmarked for Task Force Barker: A Company (3rd Battalion, 1st Infantry Regiment), B Company, (4th Battalion, 3rd Infantry Regiment) and C Company (1st Battalion, 20th Infantry Regiment). According to the brigade commander 'Alpha', 'Bravo' and 'Charlie' were the best fighting companies of their respective 'parent battalions'.[66] Their new commanding officer, Lieutenant Colonel Frank Barker, had trained at the Special Forces School in Fort Bragg in the early 1960s and then spent fourteen months as an adviser with the Green Berets. He was considered to be an officer who had little time for bureaucracy, who led his troops in an unconventional fashion and was occasionally inclined to 'shoot from the hip'. Troop leaders in this mould were now in more demand than ever before. The fact that the men under his command renounced their traditional name of 'Jungle Warriors' in favour of 'Barker's Bastards' was intended as a sign of great respect.[67]

As regards background and education, the Task Force Barker soldiers fitted the average profile of the US Armed Forces in Vietnam. The particulars available for C Company, as an example, apply equally to the other two companies, with only slight variations: on average the non-commissioned officers were 22 years old and the enlisted men 21.6. Eighty-seven per cent of the total of twenty-three non-commissioned officers had graduated from high school and twenty-five per cent had been to college. They were therefore – at least on paper – much better educated than the average non-commissioned officer in the American Armed Forces in the 1960s. Among the enlisted men the number of high school graduates stood at seventy per cent – slightly above the statistical average. Only eight per cent of the GIs in C Company had been recruited under the notorious 'Project 100,000', thus falling within drastically reduced criteria for qualifying – four per cent less than in all other units of the Vietnam Army. The fact that half the GIs in C Company were black was not out of the ordinary, either, as all the fighting units in Vietnam had a similarly high proportion of ethnic minorities. If anything, C Company, like the whole of Task Force Barker, stood out only in one respect: its comparatively high educational level.[68]

The deployment area of Task Force Barker resembled a gigantic minefield. Apart from the guerrillas, South Korean units had also laid quantities of mines, without keeping records or informing the Americans. 'The papers were highly unreliable,' commented the former commander of 11th Light Infantry Brigade, Americal Division. 'We weren't sure whether we were running into Viet Cong mines or ROK [Republic of Korea forces] mines.'[69] There were of course dead and wounded men to mourn as a result of gun battles. Alpha and Bravo had repeatedly run into well-armed Viet Cong in the Son My settlement area, and hence in the vicinity of the villages of My Lai (1) and My Lai (4), and Charlie now and then had to deal with scattered snipers. However, it was the phantom war which put most pressure on the GIs: not knowing where the enemy lay, having no target to attack, having no recognisable gains to aim for – and yet within a short space of time having to absorb considerable losses from hidden traps. 'Being forced at every moment to have to face a decision, from one step to the next, demands a high mental price. And from time to time it paralyses,' writes Tim O'Brien about his experience in this operational area. 'He walks like a wooden man, a toy soldier . . . He walks with his eyes pinned to the dirt, spine arched and he's shivering, shoulders hunched . . . It's more than the fear of death that chews on your mind. It's an absurd combination of certainty and uncertainty.'[70]

Four GIs from C Company met their deaths in the minefields and thirty-eight were wounded. On one single day, 25 February, three soldiers bled to death within a few minutes and a further twelve were very seriously wounded. 'I brought the doctor to the soldier,' said company commander Captain Ernest Medina, describing the chain of explosions. 'He was split from his crotch to his chest: I've never seen anything so unreal. The intestines, the liver, the stomach looked just like plastic. The medic started to pick him up, I reached under his arms, and we set him on top of another mine: I fell backwards. The medic was starting to go to pieces on me.'[71] In the course of a few weeks C Company lost one-third of its men like this; by mid March only 105 men out of the original 150 were still fit for action. Task Force Barker as a whole had by then lost one hundred men, at least twenty per cent of its original complement. As with C Company, in the vast majority of cases they were GIs who had trodden on mines and often came away with lasting injuries.[72]

'Dear Dad,' wrote Gregory Olsen of C Company on 14 March 1968,

. . . One of our platoons went on a routine patrol today and came across a 155-mm artillery round that was booby trapped. It killed one man, blew the legs off two others, and injured two more. And it all turned out a bad day made even worse. On their way back to 'Dottie' [base camp of C Company] they saw a woman working in the fields. They shot and wounded her. Then they kicked her to death and emptied their magazines in her head. They slugged every little kid they came across. Why in God's name does this have to happen? These are all seemingly normal guys; some were friends of mine. For a while they were like wild animals. It was murder, and I'm ashamed of myself for not trying to do anything about it. This isn't the first time, Dad. I've seen it many times before.[73]

Private First Class Olsen described in a few lines the everyday routine of Task Force Barker, whose soldiers behaved like their colleagues in Tiger Force or in 1st Battalion, 35th Infantry Regiment, to name just two examples from I Corps Tactical Zone. Soon it was scarcely worth even mentioning peasants being harassed and tormented by having their beards and hair cut off.[74] Atrocities were far more frequently reported by GIs from A, B and C Companies: women violated and murdered, civilians shot dead at random, artillery bombardment of villages for the sake of revenge, prisoners executed, corpses mutilated and their ears severed, suspects tortured, villages and fields burnt down, wells poisoned with the corpses of animals and old and young alike maltreated just for the fun of it.[75] The war diary of C and B Companies lists eighty dead guerrillas, referring to an operation from 13 to 16 February, in the course of which not one single weapon was captured. On 24 February 1968 A Company reported seventy-five Viet Cong killed – and six weapons captured. Task Force Barker boasted of 300 enemy dead up to 15 March 1968. Weapons captured: 20.[76] After the explosion of a booby-trap on 14 March Lieutenant William Calley had shouted out, 'Kill Nam' and then shot at the trees around him. 'Grease the place. Kill it.'[77]

One striking feature merits particular consideration: hardly any troop in Vietnam which stood out as excessively brutal had brutalised itself in such a short time. From the very beginning the men of Task Force Barker emerged as violent criminals and by the end as mass murderers. They had landed in Vietnam between 5 and 22 December 1967, committed their first atrocities a few weeks later and on 16 March massacred the inhabitants of three villages in Son My. There is little doubt about the stages by which they reached this extreme so fast: many had come to the country full of prejudice after their basic training in Hawaii; virtually all of them had been taught to be ruthless by instructors in Vietnam – among them veterans of the notorious Task Force Oregon.[78] Last but not least, they had discovered a climate of extreme violence surrounding operations Wheeler/ Wallowa and Muscatine and had themselves been victims of attacks. On the other hand one should bear in mind that many other units were likewise stationed in killing fields or had suffered heavy losses from booby-traps and mines. Yet by no means all of them rampaged across the country like murdering arsonists and only a few adopted this behaviour literally overnight. It seems that, together with the multitude of possible explanations,[79] a further factor must be considered: the role of officers who could not or would not break free from the operational pressures or time constraints placed on them by their superiors.

A unit such as Task Force Barker would have needed to be rigorously controlled at all levels of command, but the officers responsible had other things on their minds than disciplining men who were prepared to use violence. The example of C Company shows what mattered to them more. Their commanding officer, Captain Medina, described the deployment zone of Task Force Barker as a 'permanent Free Fire Zone'[80] and talked about a region which the Viet Cong had ruled for twenty-five years. In other words, his soldiers were to understand that all inhabitants who had not yet left their villages either supported the Viet Cong or were fighting with them – especially those who had already been deported and had repeatedly returned home in spite of all the warnings. However, where political education did not work, educational violence was called for. This could even be described as deterrence through targeted terror or as a policy of threatening the living with the dead. Anyone entering 'off-limit' villages had to understand that they had forfeited their lives.[81] Such an 'education programme' was clearly only possible if, like Tiger Force, one was committed to the principle of zero tolerance and made no allowances for anyone. The main concern was to encourage aggression and reward violent actions.

According to the Peers Commission report on the My Lai (4) massacre, 'A dangerously permissive attitude toward the handling and safeguarding of Vietnamese and their property existed within elements of the 11th Brigade chain of command prior to the Son My operation.'[82] This applied to all those in command in Task Force Barker, from brigadier down to platoon sergeant. During their entire training the soldiers in Task Force Barker had been told nothing about international laws of warfare or the Geneva Convention and had not been acquainted with the Rules of Engagement of their division and the conditions set out in them for the protection of civilians.[83] On the contrary, Medina gave them to understand from the first day on that Vietnamese life was cheap. 'He didn't ever talk about the gooks,' said one GI from C Company, 'He didn't call them any names, just didn't seem to care one way or another about them. I mean, it seemed to a lot of us that he sometimes didn't ever know they were there, didn't pay any attention to them, didn't know they were people. Except, of course, when some guy got hit, then Medina'd get real angry and talk about how we'd get ours back at them. That's all he ever called them where I heard him – them.'[84]

Several witnesses confirmed unanimously that Captain Medina criticised soldiers who in his opinion treated prisoners too considerately, suggested they should murder prisoners because otherwise they would have to be responsible for guarding them and share their rations with them; also that he personally tortured suspects on several occasions.[85] The Criminal Investigation Division heard sworn declarations that Medina explicitly gave the order to murder two fishermen: a C Company patrol had asked over the radio for instructions on how they should deal with the men they had seen on a lake. 'You know what to do with them,' answered Medina and repeated the order to shoot them dead after the platoon leader had pointed out that they could easily arrest these unarmed men. Medina is alleged to have watched his orders being carried out through binoculars.[86] Whatever wrong the C Company soldiers did, they were never reprimanded or even held to account. Of the eleven GIs from Americal Division who were court-martialled between September 1967 and June 1968 for rape or murder, not a single one belonged to Task Force Barker.[87]

The platoon leaders of C Company were putty in the hands of their superiors and a plaything to their subordinates. The Peers Commission came to this conclusion about those very leaders who bore disproportionate responsibility in a war waged with small units: 'Each platoon leader was, to an extent, fearful of his men and hesitant in trying to lead. Instead, they attempted to become "buddies" with their noncommissioned officers and men and, in more than one instance, allegedly joined with their men in immoral and illegal acts against Vietnamese prior to the Son My operation.'[88] Justifiably, in this context it always comes back to Lieutenant William Calley. Responsible for C Company, 1st Platoon, he wanted to ingratiate himself with Captain Medina through instant obedience and haughty behaviour and to the GIs to look like a hard-bitten officer – with the result that neither side took him seriously. Medina repeatedly mocked him in front of others as 'sweetheart'.[89] Among the soldiers scorn turned to contempt. A few were said to have even put a price on Calley's head. 'He messed up, he just wasn't cut out for the job,' said his former radio operator. 'He was easily excited. Most of the people in the company considered him a "dud" . . . He was moved around. Nobody wanted to work with him.'[90] Lieutenant Calley was one of those officers in C Company who sometimes put up with defiance of their own orders for the sake of the GIs' goodwill: 'His authority could have been encroached upon without too much trouble.'[91] On the other hand, when it came to instructions from Captain Medina Calley demanded exaggerated compliance.

Chumminess with the troops meant keeping them happy by giving them a free rein. Or to be exact, for the sake of holding the group together and releasing their frustrations he gave them a licence to use violence even beyond the battlefield. Therefore rapists in C Company could assume that they would not be punished even if they did it again. '[The squad leader] would say, "It's not all right", and then sometimes he would say, "They've got to get it someplace". He says, "They might as well get it in the village" . . . With Charlie Company to me they do that practically – almost, well, they try to do it in every village they go through.'[92] For the same reason they could treat prisoners of war as they pleased. 'As we went on, more and more prisoners would be executed. I would say it was a regular occurrence.'[93] In one case Calley watched one of his soldiers hitting an old man several times during questioning and then pushing him into a well. The old man clung tightly to the walls so Calley raised his M16 and shot the man dead.[94] One of the soldiers who refused to take part in these acts of violence was Gregory Olsen: 'I was in the village . . . You start losing your sense of what's normal. You don't give up your morals, but you become a lot more tolerant . . . I didn't think we were doing anything different from any other unit. You really do lose your sense . . . not of right or wrong, but your degree of wrong changes.'[95]

Evidence of Lieutenant William Laws Calley, Jr., Leader of 1st Platoon, C Company, Task Force Barker:

December 1967: 'A shanty land, the houses of cardboard and tin . . . I felt superior there. I thought, I'm the big American from across the sea. I'll sock it to these people here . . . I had promised myself, I'll act as if I'm never secure. I hollered, I yelled, I threw rocks, I threw little kids in the river – yes! I was afraid of Vietnamese kids. At OCS [Officers Candidate School], I had heard enough of kids putting things in a gasoline truck or a GI's hootch.'

January 1968: [Calley had just given the order for extensive shooting of flares.] '"Charlie One. This is Charlie Six". [It was Captain Medina.] "You nitwit! You're without a doubt the most stupid second lieutenant on the face of this earth".'

February 1968: 'He [Colonel Frank Barker] kept asking us, "Any body count?" – "No, Sir." – "No Body Count?" – "Nobody there to shoot at." . . . "You better start doing the job, Lieutenant, or I'll find someone who can." . . . It was getting ridiculous there. I couldn't keep the GIs awake now. In one platoon, the GIs went without helmets on: a T-shirt and shower shoes on . . . I couldn't bring the GIs' spirits up: I wondered too, Now where in the goddamn hell are the VC here? Or aren't there any?'

Presumably February 1968, deployment in the vicinity of 'My Lai (1)': 'Sure enough there was a *click click click* from the other side of the river . . . I used up every artillery shell on Uptight [Landing Zone] that day . . . I used up one million dollars of artillery shells that day . . . It didn't bother me. I had troops getting shot at. If it took fifty million dollars of artillery to save a PFC's [Private First Class] life, I'd have poured it on. I'd have dropped a hydrogen bomb if I'd had it! Because: one million dollars didn't do. A rifle shot got my RTO . . . "Charlie Six. This is Charlie One . . . I got an elephant here." A dead man . . . "Okay, sweetheart! And keep fucking around, and you'll get the others killed too!" And some soldiers blamed it on me . . . The GIs were calling it Calley's stupidity that we had just walked on the levee, rather than in the river near it. I admit it: I was stupid that day.'

Late February 1968: 'My soldiers said, "God, am I dreaming? Or going mad?" We had been in Vietnam three months: we were losing men, were being nickel-and-dimed away, we were being picked off. We were in Vietnamese villages daily, and we still hadn't seen one VC . . . I couldn't talk to the soldiers under me: I was a very inadequate leader, I think . . . I acted big: I tried to let everyone think, We accomplish things here. I tried to keep up the esprit de corps. I didn't. I let those doubts show, and the GIs saw through me.'

Probably early March 1968: 'I once saw an intelligence man, a Vietnamese who just stepped off a helicopter and everyone there went limp. Because god! He was bad, and the Vietnamese knew it . . . I was impressed . . . I told myself, This man! He just stands here and people cry, As for me, I didn't care to make people cry, but I was an Army officer and I had to get that intelligence. I would pop a Vietnamese in the mouth, sometimes. If it threw him, I stepped on his ankle bone and I started to grind it. I may have killed a Vietnamese once.'

Probably early March 1968: 'Nothing worked ever . . . I've been foolish. I had been asking everyone where the VC were: I had been talking to VC myself! That is why everyone said, "I don't know." They weren't about to tell me, "I surrender." At last it dawned on me, These people, they're all the VC . . . Everyone there was VC. The old men, the women, the children – the babies were all VC or would be VC in about three years. And inside of the VC women, I guess there were a thousand little VC now. I thought, Damn it, what do I do? Hack up all these damned people? Pull a machete out and kkk-? Chop up all of these people? That's what the VC themselves will do. Kill the rear echelon people: ones in the quartermaster corps, the transportation corps, the ordnance corps.'

March 1968: 'And if a squad suddenly blew its mind: if it kicked a Vietnamese kid or killed a damn innocent woman that he hadn't any compassion for – god! Medina was going to criticize them? . . . Hell, Medina wasn't about to lose those men. He had to keep a combat-effective unit.'

16 March 1968, 7 a.m.: 'Medina yelled, "Get your goddamn people down to that helicopter pad!" – "I don't think they'll start the firefight without us." – "Get your people down, or I'll get someone who can!"'

16 March 1968, morning hours: 'I had been alone at a big brick house, and I had looked inside. In the fireplace there was a Vietnamese man. At the window another one – and I shot them, I killed them. And strange, it just didn't bother me . . . I thought, Sonofabitch's dead, and I got a body count now.'[96]

The behaviour of Task Force Barker between early February and mid March 1968 was generally described as 'leadership breakdown' or compared with a 'machine out of control'.[97] Without doubt faults in leadership – apparent elsewhere in the Vietnam Only Army[98] as well – stood out clearly in this unit. Yet talk of 'disintegration of military leadership' does not go far enough. As it concentrates on incompetence and negligence, it obscures the calculations of the US Supreme Command or, to be exact, the decision taken in early 1968 to allow troops in I Corps Tactical Zone a tactical free rein, in order to win strategic control over the course of the war. For this very reason Task Force Barker was not called to order for weeks. Troop leadership was not lightly given away but handled in a supposedly appropriate manner in the special circumstances.

This was the background against which Task Force Barker received a special commission at the beginning of March 1968: the immediate 'pacification' of Son My village in Quang Ngai Province. Lying at the south-easterly end of Son Tinh district and nine kilometres from the provincial capital of Quang Ngai City, Son My was a favourite travel destination before the war. Its beaches on the South China Sea were considered the most beautiful in Vietnam, and with two rice crops a year and abundant fishing the area had become very prosperous. Many of the simple peasant huts had grown over the years into spacious thatched-roofed houses with several rooms. In 1968, however, the region looked more like a poorhouse. One third of the 130,000 inhabitants of Son Tinh district had fled; villages lay abandoned or had been devastated in the course of search-and-destroy operations; 25,000 people were in refugee camps behind barbed-wire entanglements.[99] A particular casualty of the war was the village of Son My – an extensive settlement complex which had been an operational area for strong Viet Cong formations for a long time and had been held by the guerrillas before the Tet offensive. From there the enemy attacks against Quang Ngai City had been carried out at the end of January 1968.[100] Since that time the American military had kept an eye on the four administrative districts of Son My – also commonly known as hamlets: Tu Cung, My Lai, My Khe and Co Luy. None of the twenty villages in these administrative districts was marked on US military maps with its Vietnamese name. Instead they were named after their administrative district and were given numbers – so the villages Kho Truong and My Khe (not to be confused with the eponymous administrative district of My Khe) appeared as My Lai (1) or *'Pinkville'*, Xom Lang[101] and Binh Tay appeared as My Lai (4) and the village of My Hoi as My Khe (4).[102] It is certain that the special operation was directed at the villages of My Lai (1), My Lai (4) and My Khe (4), which lay a few kilometres apart. Opinons clearly differ as to the meaning and purpose of the operation.

There is much evidence to suggest that the plan was to catch the 48th Local Force Battalion of the Viet Cong. This unit, in December 1967 estimated at 500 men, had suffered severe losses during the battles for Quang Ngai City at the time of the Tet offensive. Its commanding officer, Nguyen Tram, was killed and South Vietnamese troops dragged his corpse for kilometres through villages, chained to a jeep. When attempting to withdraw into the Son My area, the 48th LF Battalion was trapped by US troops. An American secret service officer said, 'American helicopter gunships struck, slaughtering the Viet Cong, as one aviator later described it, "like hogs".'[103] The extent of the guerrillas' losses is unclear; American estimates varied between 250 and 450 dead. However strong 48th LF Battalion might be, it was thought to be split up into squads and platoons scattered over the whole Son My area and temporarily non-operational.[104] In other words, the enemy could not defend most of Son My until manpower reinforcements arrived. 'The Song My complex was defenseless,' wrote Jesse Frank Frosch, then US secret service officer in Quang Ngai and later head of the Phnom Penh office of the news agency UPI. 'Psychologically, the villagers of Song My were staggered; they had suffered first the Korean massacre and then the Tet losses.'[105] It was the most favourable opportunity for finally wiping out a severely hit Viet Cong formation and the attack was to be aimed at inhabited villages, for that was where the various small groups of 48th LF Battalion were presumed to be.[106]

At the same time there are indications that Task Force Barker had not been aiming for the armed wing of the insurgents as much as for their civilian leaders – the so-called Viet Cong Infrastructure (VCI). According to various Army and CORDS memoranda, the highest priority since Tet was given to fighting the VCI and hence to the Phoenix programme. Thus on 22 February 1968 Project TAKEOFF of III Marine Amphibious Force (MAF) – which was responsible operationally for both the Americal Division and Task Force Barker – was told: 'Mount Attack on VC Infrastructure . . . The Sector S-2 Advisor is currently preparing a master black list [of all suspects] and will forward it to all districts and allied units operating in the province as soon as it is completed.'[107] In a balance sheet for the first half of 1968 the general commanding III MAF wrote to William Westmoreland: 'Special emphasis was given to the attack on the VCI and despite the difficulties of February and March, results have been impressive with some 2,000 VCI eliminated against an annual target of 4,000.'[108] There is certainly some reason to believe that this 'announcement of success' was grossly exaggerated; as a rule only insignificant functionaries were caught. Many of those allegedly 'eliminated' were freed after brief interrogation.[109] On the other hand it cannot be disputed that the military responsible for Quang Ngai had a marked interest in the Viet Cong Infrastructure.[110]

The CIA also transferred 120 additional 'insurgency fighters' from their training centre in Da Nang to rural Quang Ngai at the beginning of 1968. The province was obviously a primary target area for Phoenix operations in I Corps Tactical Zone[111] and there were undoubtedly close ties between Task Force Barker and the new CIA team.[112] Jesse Frank Frosch goes a step further. According to him the Secret Service made all the relevant information for the Son My Village operation available and convinced Frank Barker that there were only enemy fighters left in My Lai (4) – either armed members of 48th Local Force Battalion or Viet Cong political leaders. Two-thirds of the inhabitants of My Lai (4) had supposedly been marked off on a black list as 'VCI'. 'In effect, Company C was doing no more and no less than following CIA directives, by putting the inhabitants of My Lai to the wall . . . Indisputably, Lieutenant Colonel Barker was spoon-fed the CIA estimate of the area.'[113] In fact in such cases the operational order generally read, 'Kill anything that moves.'

Neither interpretation of Task Force Barker's special assignment is convincing. In fact the intelligence wing of Americal Division as well as the CIA produced black lists for Son Tinh District and Son My Village. However, it is uncertain whether these lists were already available in mid March 1968, to which units they were passed – and in particular, whether Task Force Barker was in possession of these documents and what use they made of them.[114] During the My Lai (4) trials various defence counsels brought up the subject and several journalists and historians followed it up – and in the end they all only offered arguments with a conspiracy theory slant.[115] Jesse Frank Frosch, who was thought to be the most authoritative source of information, was killed in an ambush in Cambodia at the end of October 1970.[116] He had persistently refused – most recently before the Peers Commission – to add any further information to his statement. Speculation over the influence of the secret service on Task Force Barker was raised again and again because the operational reasons for the deployment are questionable in military terms. Certainly the intention was to elim-inate the Viet Cong 48th Local Force Battalion once and for all, but no one knew the exact whereabouts of this formation in mid March 1968. Many secret service officers in Americal Division and its 11th Light Infantry Brigade placed the unit somewhere in the Quang Ngai hills, a long way from My Lai (4). Whether, when and in what form this information was passed on to Task Force Barker is unclear – and will probably always remain so, because the deployment plan for the Son My operation was never written down.[117] The most plausible assumption is therefore that Task Force Barker assumed they would be able to wipe out parts of 48th LF Battalion and probably also intended to eliminate some Viet Cong civilian functionaries. However, in neither case did they have even half-way reliable information. Rural Quang Ngai was a world as alien as the far side of the moon. 'At that point in time,' said an American adviser in Son Tinh District, '. . . the intelligence capability of many of these districts was almost nil.'[118] Task Force Barker were carrying out an operation based on suspicion.

On the other hand, Operation Song My Village fitted the mood in March 1968. The message from William Westmoreland's Supreme Command was an emphatic call for immediate action. Tet had opened a window of opportunity, giving a unique chance to 'show the flag' and eliminate Viet Cong strongholds. Success in Son My, so they reckoned, would not just change the constellation in Quang Ngai Province but shine out across the whole country, thus improving the prospects of turning the war around. To show initiative, expose the guerrillas' vulnerability, 'emphasize those aspects of pacification which will have greatest short-term impact'[119] – this was what it was all about. Hence poorly planned and hastily initiated attacks were accepted – the main thing being to correct the disastrous image that had followed in the wake of the enemy 'Winter Offensive'. 'Do battle!' This was the slogan adopted by both Colonel Oran Henderson, newly installed as commander of 11th Light Infantry Brigade in mid March, and by Lieutenant Colonel Frank Barker – even though for different reasons. For them, the Son My operation offered an opportunity to attract attention to themselves as capable soldiers and to improve the previous poor fighting tally of their units. They both demanded more aggression, just for the sake of the reputation of Americal Division and Task Force Barker.[120] For everyone involved an operation of great symbolic value lay in store – an operation in which the end justified any means.

The directives given by the officers responsible for the operation on 16 March 1968 were drawn up on this basis. Fundamentally Task Force Barker could make its plans in any way it wished. 'Destruction of fortified villages, structures in VC base camps, or structures that are obviously VC fighting positions is authorized without approval from this headquarters,' ran Regulation 525-1 of 11th Light Infantry Brigade dated 30 January 1968.[121] Son My Village fitted effortlessly into this target profile. In addition, Regulation 525-1 left it to their discretion whether to disregard two essential points in the otherwise customary deployment guidelines: officers were neither obliged to urge their soldiers to protect civilian life and property, nor did they have to produce in advance a 'civic action plan' – in other words, measures for possible evacuation or emergency medical care.[122] If in doubt, Barker could also refer to III Marine Amphibious Force guidelines, which explicitly allowed populated areas to be treated as Free Fire Zones, provided they were known to be places either to which the Viet Cong withdrew or where the civilian population supported the enemy.[123] To Major Charles C. Calhoun, the S-3 officer responsible for the coordination of the operational plan, it was clear – as it was to his colleagues – that they would come across unarmed civilians between My Lai (1) and My Khe (4). They had repeatedly had this experience in earlier deployments and all officers in charge made this assumption.[124] However in their eyes they were dealing with second-class – that is, enemy – civilians. Calhoun apparently asked South Vietnamese officials about spare capacity in nearby refugee camps. It is an open question whether the negative answer actually turned the scales or not;[125] in any event it was decided not to take any precautions which would have served to avert or minimise harm to civilians.[126] Naturally, no advance leaflets or loudhailer announcements told the inhabitants to leave the area. 'We would have lost the element of surprise,'[127] said Major Calhoun; they would thus have ruined their prospects of catching enemy troops or political functionaries. There was therefore no question of omissions, oversights or faulty coordination. Planning for the deployment corresponded in all details with the planners' intentions.

In the early afternoon of 15 March 1968 Oran Henderson, Frank Barker, Major Calhoun and Captain Eugene Kotouc summoned the company leaders of Task Force Barker to Firebase Dottie. There is no transcript of the discussion and probably none was made.[128] As in countless other cases, what happened can only be reconstructed from the recollections of those involved. The remit of the three companies is undisputable: C Company was to approach My Lai (4) from the west, occupy and comb through it. Major Calhoun's words were: 'If I was quoted as stating that this was a search and destroy operation I could nor would not deny it.'[129] B Company was assigned the task of tracking down suspected Viet Cong in the area around My Lai (1) and cutting off the retreat of enemies who might be fleeing from C Company. A Company was responsible for overall security in the whole deployment zone. The Americal Division had been asked for helicopter support from B Company (Aeroscout), 123rd Aviation Battalion and 174th Assault Helicopter Company, 14th Aviation Battalion.[130] Finally, each of the landing zones on the edges of villages were to be bombarded with artillery fire for five minutes immediately before the attack, as were the western and south-western part of the villages in My Lai (4). 'I am not saying that I could [not] care less,' said the commanding officer of the artillery regiment responsible. 'But, I am saying that if a ground commander requests fire . . . I have a responsibility to question it if I know it is on a populated area, yes, sir, but if the commander on the ground still insists that he needs it, it is my responsibility to fire.'[131] All the participants unanimously confirmed that Colonel Henderson warned that they should not be tempted to stop even in the event of losses and should 'aggressively pursue the enemy and move on out'. [132]

For the rest, the briefings given to the troop commanders provided a glint in a grey area where they were explicitly non-explicit. Referring to the frustrating deployments of the previous weeks, Barker reminded them that they had already been 'booted out of there once'. According to Medina, he said, 'It is the last time we are going into that place and we want it cleared out.'[133] Not even the reconnaissance officer, Captain Kotouc, was able to say exactly where the Viet Cong 48th Local Force Battalion was located; but anyhow its headquarters was assumed to be in My Lai (4). Medina therefore expected to be dealing with 200 to 250 enemy fighters on the following morning.[134] It is not clear whether Barker also reckoned on enemy resistance but in any case that had no effect on the operation. Barker wanted the place to be completely destroyed. C and B Companies were to burn down all the houses, kill or drive away all working animals, destroy provisions and poison wells.[135] 'I didn't think we made war that way,' one soldier is supposed to have replied, provoking Barker to reply, 'It's a tough war.'[136] Anyone who chose to could assume that meant a scorched-earth policy with no strings attached.

Equally equivocal were statements about the inhabitants of Son My village. Henderson and Barker gave no direct orders to murder; in contrast to the usual deployment briefings, however, they did not answer questions about who was responsible for the interrogations usual elsewhere or how to proceed with transporting suspects to the collection points.[137] Instead they sought ways to give pointers which, taken by themselves and certainly as a whole, could legitimise indiscriminate murder, not just speaking of 'sympathizers with the VC' but of 'active sympathizers'. This insinuated, contrary to the truth, that the people were still staying in their villages despite previous warnings and that anyone who was found still at home at 7 a.m. was presumably not living like a farmer, since in that case he would long since have been in his fields or on the way to market.[138] Colonel Oran Henderson is said to have warned them against repeating the mistakes of previous operations but told them instead to watch how 'men, women, or children, or other VC soldiers' gathered up their weapons and ran away.[139] Admittedly only Captain Medina remembers Henderson making this remark but even if he misquoted him, Medina's recollection is revealing; it explains how those responsible in Task Force Barker could be understood – and probably wanted to be understood. As the Peers Commission report states, Henderson and Barker alike gave their company leaders ample reason to assume 'that they were authorized to kill any persons found there'.[140]

How the leaders of A, B and C companies passed on these instructions was up to them. Ernest Medina called the soldiers of C Company together for half an hour's briefing on the afternoon of 15 March. It was unusual for the whole company to be informed of the details of an operation; usually such instructions were only given to the platoon leaders. Certainly on this occasion Medina wanted to be in direct contact with his men. Most of them had just come back from the funeral of the universally popular Sergeant George Cox, who had been fatally wounded by a booby-trap during a patrol on Highway One on the previous day. Many were still affected by the acts of revenge committed after this attack – those atrocities which the eye-witness Gregory Olsen described in a letter to his father. In this situation Medina's word carried particular weight. As the son of a Mexican immigrant from a poor background he was not suspected of being a socially privileged career officer. As a commander he was highly rated on all sides. The official appraisal of him said that 'His manner of performance has consistently placed him in the exceptional/outstanding category with no identifiable weaknesses.'[141] Among the men he enjoyed more than respect; they admired and revered him. 'He was a damn good officer. You were convinced you were going to be about as safe as a soldier can be with Medina around. Sure he was looking for action, but you felt he wasn't going to go throwing somebody's life away just for a couple of medals, for a chance to be a hero and get a promotion.'[142] 'I believe that he was the greatest.'[143] They called him 'mad dog Medina'. It was meant as a compliment.

On that day Medina had only one thing in mind: firing his men up, which is why he wanted to address them all. 'Everybody was pretty down in the dumps. We had lost a lot of guys and hadn't had a chance to fight yet. And all we had been doing – he [Medina] kind of got to you like, "now's our big chance".'[144] The talk was of 'a hell of a good fight'.[145] Medina played on the frustrations of those who saw themselves as second-class soldiers and failures; he held out the prospect of being able to get even with the Viet Cong and manipulated the fantasies of those who wanted to take revenge on the peasants – on people whom they held responsible for deaths in ambushes or for the fact that they had to suffer in the jungle at all. As can be gathered from the statements of those involved, Medina catered for a whole range of expectations:

love of fighting, avenging their sufferings, giving full expression to their aggression. Above all he offered the prospect of justifying themselves, of confirming their masculinity, superiority and power. 'Your adrenalin started to flow just thinking about the next day. We were going to get into it – and this is what we're here for. Finally, at last, it was gonna happen.'[146]

Medina made much use of a method which was already a favourite in basic training: he made the GIs afraid; he filled them with the fear of death. Up to then C Company had had no battle experience worth mentioning, though they were aware of the enemy's presence. Only a few weeks before, A and B companies had discovered an extensive tunnel complex six metres underground, filled with three tonnes of military equipment.[147] Medina was not in a position to say how many enemy troops were around or where. He did, however, describe the deployment zone as a 'hot place', surmised that My Lai (4) could prove to be a fiercely defended stronghold, would not even exclude the possibility of Viet Cong numerical superiority and got the GIs to expect 'heavy losses' in their own ranks.[148] Medina also told them to take additional ammunition with them – with the result that more than double the usual 16,000 rounds of ammunition per hundred men was assembled, as well as additional shells for M79 and 81mm mortars.[149] 'We really thought that we were going into "hell".'[150] Medina seems to have wanted to stimulate this reaction or, more precisely, to reach the point at which fear no longer paralyses but releases an excess of aggressive energy and transforms the fear of death into contempt for death. The punchy refrain from the boot camp had caught up with them all again: 'Kill, kill, kill – or you'll come home in a body bag.'

Medina was asked explicitly how they should deal with women and children. The exact wording of the questions is unclear. 'A couple of times they asked if they could shoot anything they saw,' recalls Michael Terry.[151] According to other witnesses, some GIs wanted to know whether Medina classified civilians as the enemy.[152] No matter how the question was formulated, it was simply asking whether they were *allowed* to shoot women and children or whether they *had* to kill them – that is, whether they had a licence or an order to murder civilians. In short, whether they had powers of discretion and how far they went. Some GIs seem to have found this scenario unusual.[153] However, no one voiced his irritation, no one contradicted, no one was outraged.

A cool, business-like tone reigned: do we kill women and children too? So spoke warriors who had long since become accustomed to murder – soldiers to whom nothing scandalous was worth making a scandal about any more.

By refusing to give a definite answer, Medina's message was unambiguous. This operation did not call for any scruples: 'I told them we had permission . . . that the village could be destroyed since it was a VC stronghold, to burn the houses down, to kill all the livestock, to cut any of the crops that might feed the VC, to cave the wells, and destroy the village.'[154] The fact that civilians were to be spared did not get a mention. In the way Medina looked at it, either there were no non-combatants around or they were simply irrelevant.[155] Out of 104 soldiers of C company questioned under oath only one, Gregory Olsen, remembered Medina's address as requiring the evacuation of civilians – albeit with the proviso that anyone looking like an enemy should be killed.[156] During the case against William Calley twenty-one soldiers and non-commissioned officers spoke of an explicit order to murder all the inhabitants indiscriminately.[157] The rest gave a taste of Medina's semantic hair-splitting: 'Medina said there were no innocent civilians in the village.'[158] – 'I remember him saying, "If you see a man, woman, or a child, he probably will be carrying a weapon, equipment or supplies".'[159] – 'Captain Medina . . . told the men to destroy everything that gave aid and comfort to the enemy.'[160] The exact words do not really matter. 'He didn't actually say to kill every man, woman, and child in My Lai,' said Michael Bernhardt. 'He stopped just short of saying that. He gave every other indication that that's what he expected.'[161] Whether he did it by encouraging or suggesting, what is important is that Medina left it up to his soldiers to loot or murder. They were to kill every enemy. It was left up to each individual to decide whom he regarded as an enemy.[162]

'They were looking for an excuse and they got it.'[163] In these words Michael Bernhardt described the mood at the end of the briefing and many GIs in C Company admitted he was right. 'To me some of them looked happy about it, because it seemed like some of them wanted revenge for the casualties suffered in this area on a prior date. This is what the company wanted mostly.'[164] The fact that Medina took the time to speak to them all told them another thing: they could feel safe. Medina was basically promising that they could carry on as they had done in the past. Regardless of whether someone abused civilians or shot prisoners, he could be certain of his company commander's backing.

In contrast to Medina, Captain Earl Michles, commanding B Company, briefed only his platoon leaders. He also gave the order to raze to the ground their target area, My Lai (1).[165] Michles was in fact known as an officer who did not tolerate attacks on civilians and repeatedly threatened severe punishments,[166] but there is argument about whether he did insist even in this case on bystanders being spared or if in doubt treated as prisoners of war.[167] The fact that Michles harboured no fantasies about revenge did not seem to impress his soldiers. 'The men figured,' one participant recalls, 'that after days of walking and of stepping on mines this was the chance to get into Pinkville and let the people there know how it felt to be hurt.'[168] Whether and how A Company was prepared for the operation is not known.

On the evening of 15 March most of the GIs in Task Force Barker retired early to their quarters as usual, though more soldiers than normal wanted to distract themselves with porn films or alcohol. 'I visited two or three squads. Virtually all of them were drinking as if they were having a party; a lot more than normal, a lot more than usual . . . This was, in my experience, somewhat unusual.'[169] To quote Michael Bernhardt, 'It just didn't hit me. I didn't think there was going to be any big difference in the attitude of the men. It was just that, well, OK, now they had permission. The difference was nothing. I figured there was always the possibility that these guys won't be so bad.'[170]

WARRIORS

At about 7.30 a.m. on 16 March ninety-nine soldiers from C Company were landed from helicopters in the immediate vicinity of My Lai (4) – that is, the villages of Xom Lang and Binh Tay. The first platoon comprised twenty-eight soldiers, the second twenty-four and the third thirty. In addition there were eight GIs from Captain Medina's staff and nine men of the mortar platoon.[171]

Immediately beforehand, their landing zone and the western edge of Xom Lang had been bombarded for five minutes with 'preparatory fire' – a common practice since early 1966, aimed at setting off mines and forcing enemy fighters to flee into underground hideouts. The final report on an operation of this kind carried out in the area of Bong Son (Binh Dinh Province, II CTZ) in early 1966 contained these words: 'We cannot allow the Viet Cong the opportunity to engage us from prepared, well fortified positions near a landing zone which has not been subjected to preparatory fires, humanitarian reasons not withstanding.'[172]. In the case of My Lai (4), Lieutenant Colonel Barker carried ruthlessness to the extreme. 'The artillery was the most severe that I heard in 28 months of Vietnam service,' said one GI from C Company. 'The volume of fire was so great that all of us had our notions of violent resistance confirmed.'[173] On average an artillery shell exploded every one and a half seconds and on top of that, Barker had instructed the gunners in the transport and fighting helicopters to make unrestricted use of their shell and rocket launchers and miniguns.[174] 174th Assault Helicopter Company alone fired 13,500 7.62mm shells in the hours of the early morning.[175] On the subject of the effect of the miniguns which were used simultaneously, William Calley said, 'A minigun: a super machine gun, in a minute it can have holes in every square foot of a football field.'[176] No one knows how many houses in Xom Lang were set alight during these five minutes; in any event, the columns of smoke could be seen from a distance.

Shortly before 8 a.m. the three platoons split up. The 1st Platoon occupied the southern part of Xom Lang, 2nd Platoon stormed the northern half of the village, went on to Binh Tay (about 400 metres away) at around 8.45 a.m. and came back to Xom Lang an hour later. The 3rd Platoon and the mortar platoon first secured the rear deployment zone and began a mopping-up operation in Xom Lang shortly before 9 a.m.[177] At about 10.30 a.m. all C Company platoons ceased fire.

Their tally after two and a half hours stood at about 350 civilians murdered in Xom Lang and over 50 in Binh Tay. Reliable facts are hard to ascertain. As no soldier in C Company had an overview of the entire action, the Criminal Investigation Division of the Army consulted population statistics and compared these equally unreliable details with the statements of survivors and the tax registers of the provincial administrators. This yielded an overall figure of between 400 and 430 victims in Xom Lang and Binh Tay – the villages known as My Lai (4).[178]

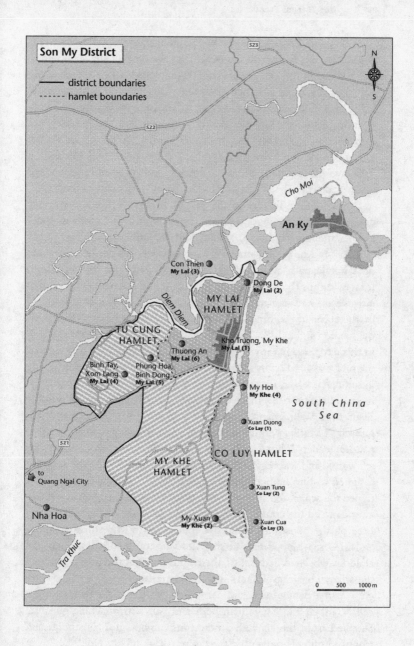

At 8.15 a.m. B Company reached Landing Zone Uptight, which lay two kilometres further to the west. They were originally supposed to comb through the villages of Kho Truong and My Khe – that is, My Lai (1) or 'Pinkville'. As they advanced, a 2nd Platoon lieutenant was killed by a mine and seven GIs were wounded by booby-traps. Consequently Lieutenant Colonel Barker withdrew 2nd and 3rd Platoons from My Lai (1) and sent the units into Thuong An village, or My Lai (6), under the supervision of company commander Earl Michles. In Thuong An people, animals, houses and provisions remained unscathed. The inhabitants simply had their identity papers checked.[179]

One kilometre further to the east of My Lai (6) there were very different scenes. At about 9.30 a.m. 1st Platoon of B Company under First Lieutenant Thomas K. Willingham surrounded the village of My Hoi, or My Khe (4), a hamlet of a mere twenty houses on either side of a jungle path. Many of its inhabitants had only returned from refugee camps the previous day, trusting in the government representatives who had named their village a safe area.[180] The order radioed by the company commander Michles was unambiguous: 'Don't hurt the women and kids!'[181] The order was not obeyed – for reasons which to this day remain a mystery. Some of those taking part claimed that the unit was fired on by snipers in the village and was therefore acting in self-defence, but it seems they were using a very familiar excuse.[182] It is highly improbable that Captain Michles revoked his order; possibly Lieutenant Willingham ignored his superior and countermanded it himself.[183] Mutiny with murderous intent is even a possibility: neither platoon leader Willingham – who had only been with B Company for a few days and was regarded by his men as a 'flop'[184] – nor the sergeant assigned to him had control over their unit.[185] Whatever it was that tipped the scales, ten soldiers – the 'point team' and 1st Squad – thereafter dictated the course of events. From the edge of the village they fired on the houses for about five minutes with M16 storm weapons and M60 machine guns and shot dead several terrified women and children who had fled out of their houses. Then the group stormed the village, blew up shelters with hand grenades, even levelling their guns at the people who had complied with the order to leave their cellars, raped and cut human bodies in half with machine gun fire. Supplied from the air with a new consignment of TNT, the assault troops ultimately pulverised the entire village of My Hoi.[186]

According to the Peers Commission, the tally of 1st Platoon, B Company after a bare hour was ninety civilians probably murdered in My Hoi, or My Khe (4); own losses: none; weapons captured: none.[187] When questioned eighteen months later, Lieutenant Willingham spoke of twenty-three Viet Cong killed.[188]

From the deposition made by a survivor of My Hoi, Nguyen Thi Bay, put together by the CID investigator Andre C. R. Feher:

'Approximately 20 U.S. soldiers entered her hamlet . . . According to Bay, there were no VC or Vietnamese troops in the hamlet. The U.S. troops were not fired upon. Prior to this day when American troops entered the hamlet, the population always went into bunkers. After the troops had entered, they came out of the bunkers and were given candy and food by the U.S. troops. On this particular day, however, when they came out of the bunkers the soldiers opened fire and shot them. According to Bay, most of the people were shot as soon as they came out of the bunkers . . . At the time of the incident the population of My Hoi was approximately 100 people . . . According to Bay, 90 people were shot and only 10 of the sub-hamlet survived. The survivors, at the time, were fishing at the ocean . . . Bay came out of the bunker with Mrs Be, Mrs Bo, and three children, Tuong, Chau, and Hung . . . They were forced into a hootch by 2 or 3 U.S. white soldiers . . . At this time there were 4 women and 3 children in the hootch. After that, two other colored soldiers entered the hootch . . . The 2 colored soldiers . . . started to take off their pants, and instructed the women to lay on the floor so they could have sexual intercourse with them. By this time only the 2 colored soldiers were in the hootch. The other soldiers had departed . . . The women refused and one of the colored soldiers struck the women with the butt of his rifle. One of the soldiers put his pants back on. This was the one that beat the women with the butt of his rifle . . . At this time they did not bother the women any more. A short time later, the women related to the soldiers that the children needed some food. One of the soldiers took two rounds of ammunition and told them that this was food for the children. The same soldier hit the women a few more times with the butt of his rifle. After this the two soldiers raped Bay. She does not remember how many times but she was told by the other women she was raped by both of the soldiers. After this a white soldier came in and told the two colored soldiers to leave. Then the white soldier took the whole group to another hootch near the sea. After that, Bay's hands were tied and she was taken by the white soldier to another hootch about 3 or 4 hootches away. At this hootch, there were five white soldiers and one of them showed her two spent cartridges which were tied together with a rubber band and she was then called a VC which she denied. This was about noon time. One of the soldiers threatened Bay with a knife because the soldier thought the cartridges had been used by the VC. She also denied this. She then was given 2 bags to carry and went with the soldiers. She was taken to a field and spent the night with the soldiers. That night nothing happened to her. The next morning she was told by the soldiers to take them back to My Hoi sub-hamlet . . . At this time she met some ARVN's . . . She was then asked by the ARVN soldiers information concerning the VC and she was told if anything happened to them that they would kill her. She was then released . . . Bay, at the time of the incident, was 2 months pregnant and subsequently she lost her baby the following day that she was raped . . . This statement was . . . taken at Bay's bedside at the hospital in Chu Lai.'[189]

In the course of their attack on the Son My area, Task Force Barker killed about 500 villagers on the morning of 16 March 1968 between 8.00 a.m. and 10.30 a.m. The precise figure could be anywhere between 490 and 520. Some were only a few weeks old, many were elderly, most were middle-aged peasants.[190] The number of Viet Cong present in Xom Lang, Binh Tay and My Hoi at this moment was claimed to be ten, four of them armed.[191]

The massacre raises numerous questions. *Under what circumstances did the murdering begin?* What conditions did the soldiers find in the place they were attacking? How did they see the situation? Is there a connection between the dynamic of the situation on the one side and the violence on the other? *How were the murders committed?* How did the perpetrators act? What means did they use? Can any distinction be drawn between dominant and marginal ways of behaving? *What did the graph of the violence look like?* Were there stages in the escalation or periods of pause? Were certain individual or groups spared, at what point in time and under what circumstances? *How large was the group of culprits; who refused to take part in the violence?* Was there a hierarchy in the group? Who acted voluntarily and who against his will, under pressure or under orders? Were any opportunities for active and passive resistance either created or made use of? *Why did the slaughter last so long?* Who intervened and when? What gave them an incentive to intervene?

As in most cases of atrocities and war crimes in Vietnam, these questions can only be answered inadequately in the case of the Son My operation. In the after-action report there is not the slightest hint of the massacre in My Khe (4) by 1st Platoon, B Company of Task Force Barker and subsequent questioning of those involved was not carried out with the necessary vigour. Moreover, because half of the suspects refused to testify and the other half gave depositions of some-times contradictory recollections, basically all that can be established is that the murders really did take place. Exactly what happened in My Hoi will probably never be known.[192]

The slaughter in My Lai (4) and the behaviour of C Company, on the other hand, can still be reconstructed comparatively accurately. Forced into action by Ronald Ridenhour's letter,[193] the Criminal Investigation Division carried out well over one hundred interviews with people who took part, interrogated perpetrators and recorded the impressions of survivors months before the report was published and eighteen months before the cases against Lieutenant Calley and Captain Medina opened. The soldiers' evidence merits particular attention. In contrast to their officers, most of the GIs had not worked out stories of defence or denial in advance. On the contrary, most of them were willing to give information and around a dozen of them[194] even gave the impression of having waited for an opportunity to make a state-ment, either because they had not come to terms with the events of 16 March 1968, because they had been discharged from the Army and no longer needed to worry about legal consequences or perhaps also because they had no idea of the public repercussions of the case. The witnesses made their statements under oath, if necessary had to comment on the their comrades' differing accounts and were called back whenever needed. Apart from these topical accounts there were dozens of photographs taken during the operation by the army photographer Ronald Haeberle – pictures which could be produced to check individual statements and above all allowed countless victims to be identified. As a result, the story of C Company of Task Force Barker stands out. It is one of those exceptional cases in which culprits, observers and abstainers not only gave information about themselves but opened up a view over the execution and the dynamic of a massacre.

The starting point

The first death squad came from the air. A few dozen inhabitants of Xom Lang had put together a few essentials under the impact of the intensive artillery fire and were trying to leave the village in a south-westerly direction, carrying a few cooking utensils and some food. 'They didn't seem to be in any great hurry. They were just walking down the road.'[195] They did not get far because helicopters from 174th Assault Helicopter Company, 14th Aviation Battalion immediately sighted them. For a short time they circled three metres above the fugitives, trying to drive them into the arms of the advancing infantry.[196] The rest of the story was described in a letter to his wife by Brian W. Livingston, one of the door-gunners not involved in the shooting. 'A gun team from the sharks [Shark assault helicopters], a notorious killer of civilians, used their minny [sic] guns, people falling dead on the road. I've never seen so many people dead in one spot. Ninety-five per cent were women and kids . . . I can also see why they hate helicopter pilots. If I ever here [sic] a shark open his big mouth I'm going to shove my fist into his mouth.'[197] On an estimate, thirty to fifty people died in this attack. Some of the Shark pilots had previously served in a supply unit with obsolete equipment. Being sent on a fighting mission was, in the opinion of one of them, their cherished goal – and a task in which they wanted to excel in their own way. 'They really thought they should kill a whole lot of people.'[198] Besides, these pilots had not been present at Medina's briefing.

'We heard the gunships firing, so I for one thought there must be resistance,' said one GI, describing the moment when he and other C Company soldiers were put down in the landing zone, '. . . Once a firefight starts, you cannot tell if the fire is outgoing or at you.'[199] The landing zone was in actual fact 'cold': not one single shot was fired at the advancing American troops either at this point or in the following hours. However for a short time Captain Medina's worst predictions seemed to be proving true. And for a short time there came no clear word about the situation from the officers – whether they themselves were confused, negligent or deliberately wanted to make the troops believe in a strong enemy presence is unclear. William Calley said, 'The fear now: I was saturated with it. I felt it, I kept running . . . to Mylai Four.'[200] The nearer they came to Xom Lang, the more indiscriminately the GIs loosed off their guns in all directions. Several of those involved spoke of a 'chain reaction'. 'Everyone except a few of us were shooting.'[201] 'It just happened and started to mushroom and everybody was shooting at everybody . . . There was a lot of confusion and everything moved pretty fast.'[202] 'We were at such close range we were afraid we would hit each other.'[203] 'There was "on-line fire", which means that almost everyone armed with an M-16 was walking and shooting at the same time.'[204] 'Everyone was just shooting at everything and anything, like the ammo wouldn't ever give out.'[205]

Their M16 storm rifles set on automatic fire, C Company simulated a battle situation, staged a killing field and surrounded themselves with an impenetrable shield of noise and lead. In short, they imagined themselves into the world of real warfare and therefore into a universe where they were allowed to kill. Some may have succumbed to this suggestion and imagined that they really were facing opponents. Fear probably took its toll, distorting perspectives or triggering additional aggression. One other thing cannot be excluded – that many of them, who did not want to make any distinction between armed and unarmed people anyway, in the given circumstances believed that they did not actually have to do so any more. Even before they entered Xom Lang, the soldiers of C Company were firing on everything and everyone. They took aim at water-buffalo, shot dead a peasant in his field who had raised his hands – either in greeting or because he wanted to show that he was unarmed. One woman who had tried to protect herself from the artillery fire died in agony, as did two children begging for their lives and twenty other civilians who had accidentally got in the way.[206] Including the victims of the helicopter attacks, between fifty and seventy victims lost their lives in the first quarter of an hour of the operation alone. Imaginary numbers of Viet Cong victims were passed on over the radio.

When they had reached Xom Lang and shortly after, Binh Tay, the three platoons of C Company divided into squads – small groups of between five and eight men. A few soldiers also went on through the villages alone or with just one comrade. They all acted on their own initiative and sometimes they got lost in the dense groves of bamboo and banana trees.[207]

It was now, at the latest, that the GIs realised who they were faced with. Despite the artillery fire many of the inhabitants were not at all suspicious. In mid January and early February American troops had come to their villages, asked for water, given the children chocolate and the adults cigarettes and had cared for the sick. Lieutenant Calley remembered peasants who were even now standing expectantly in front of their huts, a few of them waving at the soldiers.[208] Another GI saw three children, about nine years old, crawling out of some bushes. 'They had their hands out hollering "chop chop" which means they wanted food.'[209] It seems that to begin with only a few people took refuge in their cellars and underground bunkers. Those who did not dare leave their own plots stayed in their houses and gardens. Others had learned their lesson about dealing with GIs from their own experience or from acquaintances' stories. Anyone running away was suspected of being Viet Cong and was shot. The same applied to anyone who approached too quickly, because he might have a grenade on him. Consequently it was advisable to go up to the soldiers slowly with arms out stretched. Whatever the inhabitants of Xom Lang and Binh Tay decided to do, their behaviour gave no reason to panic.[210]

Without any appreciable incentive from elsewhere, the small groups of C Company soldiers advancing from the north and south simultaneously opened fire immediately and all over the place. Many of them shot from a distance, others used single shots aimed at close range, some put their M16s on automatic or sprayed bullets in a semicircle holding their M60 machineguns on their hips. Now and again they also threw hand grenades at groups crouching terrified on the ground. Bodies were torn to pieces, brains forced out of skulls by the shock waves from the M16 bullets, scraps of cloth and splinters of bone flew through the air, people lay in pools of blood, mutilated by bayonets and knives: GIs had cut off ears or heads, slit throats, cut out tongues and taken scalps.[211] They murdered not just with their steel killing machines but with their hands too. Within minutes C Company had transformed an imaginary battle zone into an actual slaughterhouse.

On the way they murdered

Ronald Haeberle and Jay A. Roberts called the behaviour of C Company 'businesslike'.[212] In their respective capacities of Army photographer and press officer both men accompanied the unit and could observe events from close by, including a scene in Binh Tay, when six GIs of 3rd Platoon rounded up a group of about ten women and children. They clearly wanted to rape one of the young women. They tore at her clothes, shouted, 'VC boom, boom' – meaning that 'Viet Cong whores' could service them as well. 'Let's see what she's made of.' – 'Jesus, I'm horny.'[213] Haeberle took a photo of the Vietnamese women after an older woman had placed herself protectively in front of the molested woman who was finishing buttoning her blouse. 'Watch it, he has a camera.' – 'What are we going to do with them now?' – 'Well, the order's to kill them anyway. Might as well go ahead and kill them now.'[214] Seconds later they were all dead, shot by two soldiers with an M6o machine gun.[215] Haeberle remembers: 'I asked some soldiers: "Why?" They more or less shrugged their shoulders and kept on with the killing. It was like they were fixed on one thing – search and destroy, and that meant killing civilians . . . That was their job. It was weird, just a shrug of the shoulder. No emotional reaction.'[216]

In the reports of the Criminal Investigation Division and the Peers Commission on My Lai (4) there are dozens of examples of 'businesslike killing' – of murder that seems to be routine, calculated and detached. Shortly before members of 1st Platoon proceeded to execute a group in the centre of Xom Lang, they made certain that their comrades left the expected field of fire – 'that any soldiers behind the hut should come out "because we were going to commence firing into the Vietnamese".'[217] Soldiers are reported to have fired in a kneeling position like a sporting marksman and brought children down like game.[218] GIs exchanged weapons in order to proceed as effectively as possible,[219] reached agreement about who had shot dead how many people in how long and which victim should be chalked up to whose account.[220] In this context an occurrence described by Lieutenant Calley is revealing. Calley had just ordered the murder of several dozen people when he discovered a soldier trying to force a woman to perform oral sex.

He had hold of her hair to keep holding her to her knees . . . I ran right over. "Get on your goddamn pants," I screamed. "Get over where you're supposed to be!" . . . Why was I being saintly about it? Because: if a GI is getting a blow job, he isn't doing his job. He isn't destroying Communism . . . Our mission in Mylai wasn't perverted though. It was simply, "Go and destroy it" . . . If a GI is getting gain, he isn't doing what we are paying him for. He isn't combat-effective.[221]

Calley was one of the few who did not just describe their behaviour but also interpreted it – and in the process revealed something fundamental: the murdering in Xom Lang and Binh Tay was seen in many ways as 'killing work'.

'Killing work'[222] was distinguished primarily by its systematic calculation. The culprits made a big effort to discover the hiding places of their victims, trawling from hut to hut, from bunker to bunker. As Michael Bernhardt described it, 'They were doing it in three ways. They were setting fire to the hootches and huts and waiting for the people to come out and then shooting them. They were going into the hootches and shooting them up. They were gathering people in groups and shooting them.'[223] They indiscriminately butchered women with small children in their arms, groups of adults begging on their knees for mercy or old people whom they found alone in their huts.[224] Anyone seeking refuge in bunkers stood absolutely no chance. 'In the center of the village the men were criss-crossing, running in different directions, and throwing grenades into bunkers.'[225] Sometimes people were forced into the bunkers at gunpoint and then blown up.[226] 'When Vietnamese did respond most of them were shot down as they exited the bunkers.'[227] They did not even spare the children, who ran about, confused and sometimes wounded, between the lifeless bodies of their relatives.[228] 'Mercy killings' meant that no one received medical attention or was even evacuated, but was killed without regard to his or her injuries.[229] 'We were making sure no one escaped from the village.'[230]

As if they wanted to certify their work symbolically, the perpetrators left their insignia behind on bodies they had abused. The words 'C Company' or the outline of an ace of spaces was carved into the skin of some victims. They were playing with Vietnamese superstition, for to them the ace of spades was an omen of bad luck.[231] The soldiers of C Company – like countless other units in Vietnam – saw in disfigurement and mutilation maximum cultural punishment for peasants deeply rooted in Buddhist beliefs, according to which the souls from such bodies are perpetually searching for their scattered body parts and never find peace.[232] In this way the dead could always be used as a message to deter the living. A well-known photo – not generally understood – taken by Ronald Haeberle on a path at the edge of Xom Lang village bears particular witness to this. It shows a group of murdered people, in the midst of them a young woman with her legs bent up and spread wide, her hands placed protectively over her vulva. One could almost think she was giving birth. Yet at her feet lies not a baby but a child of about two years old. The language and position of her body differ strikingly from the others lying crumpled around her – as if a picture of mother and child had been deliberately arranged. And this was highly visible on a path that led directly to the devastated village and which anyone would have to take if they wanted to bury their dead.

William Calley wrote about that day when he was summoned to the Pentagon on account of his impending court martial: 'I pictured the people of Mylai: the bodies, and they didn't bother me. I had found, I had closed with, I had destroyed the VC: the mission that day. I thought, it couldn't be wrong or I'd have remorse about it.'[233] If everyone had still thought like that, months after the event, the story of Xom Lang and Binh Tay would probably never have come to light. But at the time of the slaughter and immediately afterwards many GIs from C Company shared this attitude, according to the observation of soldiers who were posted to the unit shortly after the massacre. 'They say, "if we kill the mothers, the women, they will not produce any more VC. And if we kill the kids then they won't become VC. So if we kill them all there won't be no more VC left".'[234] On 16 March 1968 they imagined themselves to be in the right because as soldiers they had done a dirty piece of work which in their opinion had been demanded of them. And because they saw nothing unlawful in it, they praised each other for having done an efficient job.[235]

The fact that in the reports on My Lai (4) there is only passing mention of men going berserk fits into the picture of controlled killing. There were of course soldiers who worked themselves up into a killing frenzy and fired off one magazine after the other while laughing

hysterically.[236] 'But honest to Christ, at first I didn't even recognize him
. . . I don't know what you'd call it, a smile or a snarl or something,
but anyway, his whole face was distorted. He was covered with smoke,
his face streaked with it, and it looked like there was blood on him,
too.'[237] GIs like that filled even their own comrades with fear when
they went at their victims with a Bowie knife or bayonet as though
they were out of their minds; slit throats or pulled out entrails; threw
themselves at water-buffalo, stabbing them dozens of times; tore the
M16 out of the hands of another soldier and, yelling, 'Kill them all!
Don't turn them over to the company! Kill them all!' literally shot the
brains out of the skulls of four unarmed men.[238] Yet the much-repeated
talk of unbridled murderous frenzy and the image of the monstrous
killer miss the mark. Massacres do not need them. In My Lai (4) those
who ran amok could be counted on the fingers of two hands.

On the other hand, countless soldiers availed themselves of the
craft of these excessively brutal criminals without going into a killing
frenzy, as they did. The GI who went up to a small boy and, laughing,
shot a bullet into the base of his neck from a few centimetres away,
seemed completely relaxed. 'Did you see me shoot that son of a
bitch?'[239] The murderer is recorded as having said in retrospect, 'At
the time I would say . . . I couldn't tell you exactly how I felt, except
to prove to myself I could kill someone because that was the first
time I had ever killed anyone.'[240] Frederick Widmer was not alone in
this. Others also wanted to try it out on the 'dinks' – as they disparag-
ingly called the Vietnamese – to see how far they could go.[241] Some
tortured their victims before they fired their M16s; others tormented
animals to take delight in their slow death.[242] In none of these cases
was it reported that the culprits had gone on raging wildly, but for
one moment they seem to have adopted the behaviour of madmen
and so demonstrated how frail the boundaries are between cold-
blooded and hot-blooded killing; to be more precise, how the
majority's controlled killing and the minority's uncontrolled slaughtering define and reinforce each other. Although they were terrifying,
excessively brutal criminals therefore always exerted a certain fascination as well. As is reported, they could always be certain of a grinning
audience – and an audience ready to learn.[243]

It is almost impossible to differentiate between routine, delight and
murderous fever in the countless sexual attacks on women. As in all

previous C Company deployments, in My Lai (4) there was individual and gang raping – even when the commanders had declared that the operation was at an end.[244] In contrast with the previous weeks and months, the rapists did not stop at violation but also murdered and mutilated their victims. After they had finished with one young woman, three men seized all the weapons they could lay their hands on – M16s, M60s and .45-calibre pistols. 'Her face was just blown away and her brains were just everywhere.'[245] In Binh Tay one GI from 3rd Platoon forced seven women to undress. Because they would not let him go any further he decided to test out the effectiveness of his M79 mortar which he had not used before – at a distance of thirty metres because the shells would only be effective after travelling that distance. His comrades who were standing by, wanting to watch the rape, took over murdering some of the seriously wounded women.[246] Elsewhere in My Lai (4) dead women lay with their vaginas slit open and in one case the perpetrators had pushed in a rifle barrel and pulled the trigger.[247]

'And once you start, it's very easy to keep on. Once you start.'[248] On his own admission, Varnado Simpson felt no emotion. Others were said to be clearly enjoying themselves. Some had to force themselves. Paul Meadlo was in tears as he emptied his M16 into dozens of people who had been rounded up into an irrigation ditch and in one case a GI is said to have told his victims, 'I don't want to do it, but I have to because we were ordered to do it.'[249] Whether they enjoyed the power of killing or saw it as a denial of their image of themselves as damaged losers, whether they were pursuing cravings for revenge or living out sadistic desires, whether they were trying to conquer fear or could not resist the pressure from a group of men doing the same thing, each case must be decided on its own merits.[250] However, Simpson's comment that murdering came all the more easily the longer the operation lasted applies to everyone. 'No direction. I just killed.' As long as the slaughter lasted they were free of all restraints, at that moment the unreasonable demands of a war they did not understand were of no importance, simple truths and clarity of purpose took the place of confusion and complexity. In the chaos of massacre lay the prospect of order and in murder, the promise of freedom – because nothing else mattered any more.[251]

The progression of violence

Within an hour about 240 villagers from Xom Lang and Binh Tay had met their deaths: 70 or so even before the villages were stormed and thereafter about 170 in their houses, shelters or nearby. At least 170 others spent the time between hope and fear before they, too, were murdered by the execution commandos.

The actions of 1st Platoon were at first strikingly different from those of 2nd and 3rd Platoons. While the latter literally shot at everything that moved, 1st Platoon divided up the tasks. Some of its members murdered, others rounded up the people in Xom Lang and neighbouring Binh Dong and drove them into a rice paddy or an irrigation ditch.[252] How many they were is a matter of dispute. Taking an average of the widely differing accounts, there were probably about 60 in the rice paddy and 110 in the irrigation ditch, amongst them a significant number of old people.[253] While the bloodbath raged all around them, both groups were guarded by a few soldiers from 1st Platoon. 'Take care of them,' Lieutenant Calley had told his men.[254] 'Meadlo and Carter were playing with the kids, telling the people where to sit, and giving the kids candy.'[255] – 'And we sat there and watched them like we usually do.'[256]

'Like we usually do.' Some soldiers from 1st Platoon probably expected that in this operation, as in the course of many others, they would just check papers or fly suspects out as detainees to be questioned in the camps provided for that purpose. 'We did not know what was to be done with these people, so we brought them together and made them sit down.'[257] This explanation cannot be dismissed, as the GIs who were split into many small units could act independently of each other and at their own discretion. Detaining 190 people within an hour lay wholly within the capabilities of two or three squads. It makes sense that some soldiers wanted to await events. After all, the previous evening they had been given no precise instructions on how to deal with civilians and the investigation reports do not show whether Captain Medina had briefed his platoon leaders differently. Strangely enough, the investigators only looked into this question very casually. William Calley was the only one who talked about a clear instruction: 'One squad at Mylai wasn't supposed to kill everyone there. We had those mines to go through, and the Vietnamese people would know the way . . . Medina had told me, "Save some of the people". I'd said to Sergeant Mitchell, "Save some".'[258] Neither Mitchell nor Medina confirmed this version.

The further chain of events is also mired in uncertainty – as always when one comes to the role of officers in this operation. Calley testified that he had been suddenly been heavily pressurised by Medina. According to him, 1st Platoon was to get into position for a further advance. '"Why did you disobey my damn order?" – "I have these bunkers here –" – "To hell with the bunkers!" – "And these people [in the rice paddy], and they aren't moving too swiftly." – "I don't want that crap! Now damn it, waste all those goddamn people! And get in the damn position!"'[259] What tells against Calley's version is that from the first day he built his defence on the assertion that he was 'acting under orders'. On the other hand, as a subsequent analysis of the radio traffic proved, Medina had been in contact with Calley at least twice at about this time.[260] What he discussed with his platoon leader and what words he chose are not recorded. Calley was certainly as well known for his obsequious approach towards Medina as for his tendency towards pre-emptive obedience. The idea cannot therefore be dismissed that he wanted to advance as quickly as possible as requested – and that, knowing Medina's contempt for the Vietnamese, he regarded the peasants in the rice paddy as irritating leftovers from the operation.

However, it is clear that shortly before 9 a.m. Lieutenant Calley returned to the rice paddy. Three witnesses confirmed under oath the following dialogue: '"I thought I told you to take care of them." – "We're taking care of them." – "I mean kill them . . . Come on, we'll line them up here, we'll kill them . . . When I say fire, fire at them."'[261] At least two men from 1st Squad, 1st Platoon, Calley and Meadlo, possibly even five, stepped a few metres back and mowed the people down. The witness Dennis Conti said: 'A lot of the women had thrown themselves on top of the children to protect them, and the children were alive at first. Then the children, who were old enough to walk got up and Calley began to shoot the children.'[262] Calley alone is said to have used up four or five magazines of twenty rounds each.[263] Conti said: 'He [Calley] turned around, and said, "Okay, let's go." We turned around, and walked away.'[264] At that moment they discovered ten more people – women and children who had escaped from Xom Lang and were fleeing into the jungle. 'Get 'em! Get 'em! Kill 'em!' yelled Calley.

The group survived because the squad had no time to go after them. Sixty-one of the corpses in the rice field could be identified.[265]

Calley went on with his soldiers to the irrigation ditch, where by now over 100 people had been driven together, most of them from Xom Lang and some from Binh Dong, 500 metres away.[266] Calley greeted the guards with the words, 'We have another job to do.'[267] Several GIs pushed the people into the ditch or beat them in with their rifle barrels. Calley shot dead a two-year-old child who had scrambled up to the edge of the ditch, hit and shot dead a monk who was unable to give any information on the Viet Cong's whereabouts and killed an old woman who had been brought to the ditch on a stretcher.[268] The people screeched and begged for their lives. At least eight GIs put their M16s on automatic, one used a machine gun, another threw hand grenades, one squad leader tried to line up the marksmen in a row, someone ordered single fire to save ammunition, Paul Meadlo alone fired over 400 bullets.[269] One hundred and ten of the corpses in the irrigation ditch could be identified.[270]

In the rice paddy and the irrigation ditch the murders were committed to order; in Binh Tay it took one radioed order and the murdering stopped. Captain Medina told Lieutenant Stephen Brooks, the officer responsible for 2nd Platoon, to 'cease fire' or 'stop the killing' at about 9.30 a.m. His exact wording is disputed but in any event the people in Binh Tay who had survived until then were spared. About fifty peasants were taken to a field and ordered to abandon their village which was then burned to the ground. 2nd Platoon started on its way back to Xom Lang.[271]

On the eastern edge of Xom Lang 2nd Platoon met the other sections of C Company who had set up a makeshift post there. Together they unpacked their field rations and ate their lunch. William Calley said, 'I had some fruit, and I made small talk. "How is everything going?" – "Fine." – "Getting beer in?" – "Yeah. I guess I'll request it".'[272] On the way one soldier had come across two orphaned girls, both between three and four years old, and brought them with him. The children were given sweets and piggyback rides, played with and eventually entrusted to some survivors.[273] Even William Calley was one of those men who looked after the children.[274] Or should that read: those men who now understood how to show the flip side of the absolute power to kill and were prepared to make use of their licence to reprieve?

Away from this group and near the irrigation ditch two GIs from 1st Platoon had sat down. They heard seriously wounded people groaning, went over, shot them dead and then carried on with their lunch.[275] Helicopter pilot Hugh Thompson watched the scene from the air. 'They were just casually, nonchalantly sitting around smoking and joking with their steel pots off just like nothing had happened. There were five or six hundred bodies less than a quarter of a mile from them, and I just couldn't understand it.'[276]

Testimony of Lieutenant William Laws Calley, Jr., Leader of 1st Platoon, C Company, Task Force Barker:

Probably autumn, 1968: It's almost unreal there, and I had been there for months without seeing it. I knew, I can win if I make these people aware of their prospects. Of the comforts that a democracy offered them . . . I felt alive now, as I never had in America. I felt helpful, even if I couldn't build an SST, a spaceship, or something spectacular. I built wells, I showed the Vietnamese movies: I even showed them *The Green Berets*, and I went out to medcap them too . . . To compete with: I was teaching the Vietnamese free enterprise. And giving the Vietnamese desires and telling them, "See, I can better your life." And taking the Vietnamese from the itty-bitty little paddies there. I saw some tremendous possibilities now: I saw a tremendous force of Americans say, 'We can help you', I saw the Vietnamese tell us, 'You're right. You're treating us now like human beings. And you're not racists.' . . . And we're going to win their hearts and minds.[277]

Perpetrators, onlookers and abstainers

After sixteen months of investigative work by the Criminal Investigation Division of the Army and the Peers Commission, 49 out of 99 soldiers of C Company were deemed to be suspects, 44 of murder and 5 of rape. Out of about fifteen GIs who were present during the execution at the irrigation ditch, according to the Criminal Investigation Division at least eight had committed murder. Four of them confessed.[278] In percentage terms the figures for the rice paddy were probably similar. Taken together, these details only give a rough idea but the few reports on other massacres available give a similar picture: for every murderer there was one abstainer or in exceptional cases one soldier who raised an objection.[279] It therefore seems realistic to assume that about half of C Company belonged to the group of culprits and the other half comprised onlookers and those who condoned what was happening. It is not always possible to differentiate clearly between them; now and then soldiers who had already committed murder on earlier occasions abstained, or abstainers turned elsewhere into accomplices if not actually culprits.

'If they are going to be killed, I'm not doing it,' shouted Dennis Conti during the execution in the rice paddy and pointed to William Calley: 'Let him do it.'[280] At the irrigation ditch the following argument was heard between Calley and a private first class: '"Maples, load your machinegun and shoot these people." – "I'm not going to kill those people. You can't order me to do that." – "I'll have you court-martialed."'[281] Calley pointed his M16 at Maples but gave up when others soldiers put themselves in front of their comrade to protect him. James Dursi also refused to obey Calley's order.[282] It was reported that Herbert Carter, one of the soldiers posted as a guard, could not bear to stand by and watch the shooting any longer and forced his evacuation by shooting himself in the foot. Whether Carter's injury was inflicted deliberately or – as he himself says – was an accident while he was cleaning his weapon,[283] is still a contested question. Carter refused to obey any longer, along with a handful of other GIs, among them a notorious rapist and soldiers who, on their own admission, while combing through Xom Lang and Binh Tay had fired at random and blown up bunkers as if it were all a matter of course. From their point of view, the mass execution went too far.[284]

Although known to be a weak troop leader, William Calley could get his own way. There must be some doubt whether incessant shouting and threats against those who were out of line were any help, and his big-mouthed 'I'm the boss here'[285] can have impressed hardly anyone, either. He asserted himself in a different way: to the willing amongst his men, Calley was an accomplice. He had executed a woman with his pistol at close range and in front of everybody he had maltreated and killed a Buddhist priest: 'You sonofabitch. And bam: . . . He had frustrated me.'[286] The insecure in his unit – such as Paul Meadlo – did not know how to stand up to him. In both the rice paddy and at the irrigation ditch Meadlo was the weakest member in the ranks of the potential executioners. Calley was after this man who played with children while guarding them, threatened him with orders and stood next to him as an accomplice with his M16. James Dursi said, 'Calley noted Meadlo's reluctance and bore down on Meadlo . . . Calley took it upon himself to personally observe Meadlo's performance during the ditch incident, insuring Meadlo "participated", during which time Meadlo continued weeping loudly.'[287] While he, together with Calley and probably five others, fired into the irrigation ditch, Meadlo shouted to a comrade standing near, 'Why aren't you firing? Fire, why don't you fire?'[288] And in the rice paddy he tried to press his weapon into another man's hands. 'You shoot them.'[289] In this case there is no question of group pressure; because the onlookers held back, officer William Calley had the last word.

Only one individual risked a confrontation in order to help these distressed people out of the death zone: Hugh Thompson, helicopter pilot and Warrant Officer in B Company (Aeroscout), 123rd Aviation Battalion, Americal Division. His company had been called in to support the operation in Son My, and with two helicopter gunships to provide him with cover, Thompson was to act as an observer. Circling at low altitude he had a good overview of events on the ground.[290] Immediately after the start of the operation he and his air gunner Lawrence Colburn called for medical assistance for injured civilians. The response was murder: when Thompson and his crew flew once again over the spot they had marked out with smoke flares they could make out the corpses and watched a captain approach to within a few paces of a seriously injured woman and shoot her dead – it was, they were later to learn, Ernest Medina. An hour later Thompson discovered the crowd of people in the irrigation ditch. He landed his helicopter and spoke to a 1st Platoon sergeant and to Lieutenant Calley. Both gave him to understand that rather than evacuating the people, they intended to shoot them.[291] Thompson thought this was a bad joke and left. Scarcely was he in the air before his air gunner informed him that they were shooting at the people in the ditch.

A third time Thompson held his nerve. On seeing a group of soldiers from 2nd platoon, who emerged from Binh Tay to continue their manhunt in Xom Lang, and had taken aim at a dugout holding about sixteen women, children and old men, Thompson placed his helicopter in between the attackers and their targets. His request for help for the civilians was turned down by the platoon leader, Lieutenant Stephen Brooks, in the manner already familiar to Thompson: 'The only way to get them out [is] with a hand grenade.'[292] Thompson summoned up help from the helicopter gunships escorting him, fetched the doomed people from their hiding-place and had them flown out in the larger machines.[293] Throughout, the air gunners in Thompson's helicopter kept their murderous comrades from 2nd Platoon in check with their machine guns. Thompson had instructed his men to shoot instantly if American soldiers tried to prevent the rescue operation by force of arms.[294] Thompson then flew once more to the irrigation ditch where they were able to rescue and bring to safety an uninjured eight-year-old. The commander of one of the helicopter gunships said, 'On the radio Thompson told me that if he saw the ground troops kill one more woman or child he would start shooting [the ground troops] himself.'[295]

There were reports of four other cases besides Hugh Thompson in which villagers in My Lai (4) owed their lives to American soldiers. At the beginning of the operation three GIs took a family to the edge of Xom Lang and enabled them to escape to a neighbouring village.[296] A member of 1st Platoon, Harry Stanley, and another soldier – probably from the same platoon – independently of each other ensured that children were not discovered in their hiding-places.[297] According to one peasant from Binh Tay, two GIs stopped their comrades who wanted to shoot survivors dead despite the order to cease fire.[298] There may very well have been other rescue operations of this sort.[299] If the story from Binh Tay is correct and if one includes the fifty people whose lives were spared there, it is likely that abstainers amongst the GIs saved the lives of about eighty people. In total, rather more than 200 people probably survived the operation in Son My village.[300]

The question why there were not more Hugh Thompsons was repeatedly put to active and passive abstainers. 'I wasn't really violently emotionally affected,' replied Michael Bernhardt who was later to play an important part in the exposure of the massacre. 'I just looked around and said, "This is all screwed up".'[301] Others seemed to be similarly resigned: 'You can't do nothing about it.'[302] – 'I didn't want to get involved and walked away.'[303] Others talked about their fear of 'fragging' – the possibility of being murdered by their own people out of revenge.

'You got to remember that everybody there has a gun . . . It's nice to face your accuser, but not when he's got a gun in his hand.'[304] – 'You got rocks or something? . . . I think if I had even said a word to him at all, he would have turned and killed me and not thought a damn thing about it.'[305] This was why Michael Bernhardt kept in the background[306] and why Ronald Haeberle refrained from photographing the murderers in flagrante.[307] The soldiers did not appear in his pictures like culprits but like GIs going about their normal wartime work – burning down huts, interrogating villagers and checking bunkers. Haeberle did not even record the deaths in the rice paddy and the irrigation ditch. The same unwritten rule applied to him as to everyone else in C Company: 'When you're in Vietnam, you don't do things like that.'[308] – 'That would have been encouraging your own sudden death. These are the guys who get in fire fights with you. It would have been too easy to get blown away.'[309]

On the duration of the slaughter

There is still the question why the slaughter was not stopped by the officers in charge at an early stage. Which troop leader would have had the opportunity to step in and when? Why were such opportunities either not taken at all, or only hours later?

The artillery bombardment on Xom Lang had just begun when the commanding officer of Task Force Barker, Lieutenant Colonel Frank Barker, and the Commander of 11th Light Infantry brigade, Colonel Oran Henderson, accompanied by four other senior officers flew over the deployment zone in their command-and-control helicopters. As their pilots assured the Peers Commission, two things were clearly visible from an average altitude of 300 metres: firstly, that those fleeing from Xom Lang were predominantly women and children; secondly, that countless civilians had fallen victim to artillery fire and the ruthless attacks of the Shark helicopter gunships – corpses lined the route of C Company as it advanced. The officers took in what was happening – their own statements and the observations of the people with them leave no doubt about that.[310] The Peers Report states that, 'Despite these observations, no action was taken to provide relief or assistance to the noncombatant casualties.'[311] Barker and Henderson returned to Firebase Dottie between 8.35 a.m. and 8.45 a.m. and therefore may have also observed the beginnings of the bloodbath in Xom Lang itself.[312] Frank Barker at any rate had the most accurate overview. He only stayed for a short time in Dottie and then, according to the Peers report, 'had been orbiting over the operational area for most of the morning.'[313] Whether Major General Koster, commanding the Americal Division, was also in the picture is debatable. He arrived at Dottie at about 9.35 a.m. and had probably flown over the Son My area. His exact flight path and altitude could not be subsequently established. However there is no convincing evidence to absolve the two-star general from the suspicion of having been an eye-witness.[314]

The fact that the troop leaders knew about the events which followed the operation and still allowed them to take their course also emerges from a contemporary action report. When Barker and Henderson had returned to Firebase Dottie they found the following entry in the Task Force Barker log book, timed at 8.40 a.m.: '69 VC KIA [killed in action] within My Lai (4).' Shortly after that, sixty-nine fallen Viet Cong 'at a location [600 metres] north of My Lai (4)' were reported to the Tactical Operations Center of 11th Light Infantry Brigade, suggesting that the supposed Viet Cong were victims of the artillery or helicopter bombardment. The Peers Commission was unable to ascertain who was responsible for the falsification but the investigators raised the point that four officers – amongst them Barker and Henderson – 'either participated in or condoned the making of fictitious reports to higher headquarters and false entries in official records',[315] their purpose certainly being to deflect attention from the events in Xom Lang and Binh Tay and prevent anyone asking questions 'that could not readily have been answered.'[316] Among other things, an explanation would have had to be given for how the sixty-nine enemy soldiers in Xom Lang lost their lives, seeing that there was not the slightest indication of any fighting in the village and at a time when the artillery support had long since been withdrawn.[317]

Shortly before 9.00 a.m. Lieutenant Colonel Barker once more boarded his observation helicopter. At this time 3rd platoon of C Company was moving in on its 'clearance operation' in Xom Lang, followed by the company commander, Captain Ernest Medina, and a seven-man strong staff team.[318] Now at least Medina should have stepped in as officer in charge on the spot. The opposite happened. The Peers Commission came to the conclusion that Medina himself committed murder at least once and in two instances incited his soldiers to murder or condoned their misdeeds without comment. He may well have committed three murders himself.[319] Among other things four witnesses confirmed independently of each other and under oath that Medina shot and seriously injured a woman from about 150 metres, went up to her and shot several volleys into her body at close range – this being the scene which Hugh Thompson had also observed. 'It was a pure out and out murder,' according to the eye witness Herbert Carter.[320] A few GIs stated that two disoriented children aged two and six running about among the bodies of their murdered relatives were shot dead in Medina's presence. Ordered to take a lie detector test in the course of the court martial proceedings, Medina conceded 'that he also mistakenly ordered the shooting of a small boy.'[321] In at least one other case he accepted with indifference that soldiers committed murder in his immediate vicinity.[322] When the captain was asked about the fate of an old man who had been dragged out of his house, one soldier who had taken part said about the situation, 'Appearing not to care and as though this were not the type of decision he was supposed to make, Medina said nothing. However, it seemed as if he had no desire to keep the old man and did not want to be bothered with him . . . The soldiers shot the old man . . . Medina did not stop walking.'[323]

Up until Lieutenant Calley's trial Medina maintained his ignorance of the large number of dead. Under pressure from the prosecutor, he admitted this to be a lie.[324] As countless observers had asserted, Medina had come across several groups of murdered civilians, without asking a single question or expressing disapproval.[325] A Vietnamese interpreter serving with C Company recorded the following exchange between a sergeant in the South Vietnamese Army and Medina: 'Why did you kill the women and children like this?' – 'That was the orders, don't ask why.'[326] Ronald Haeberle had a similar recollection of the scene.[327] Yet during Medina's court martial this statement was of no more importance, because when the Vietnamese witnesses were asked in cross-examination about their knowledge of English at the time, they had answered, 'Not very good.'[328]

The fact that the first order to cease fire was given after about two hours is known simply and solely from the helicopter pilots' radio messages, because radio traffic was monitored and recorded. 'From up here it looks like a blood-bath. What the hell are you doing down there?'[329] 'They're killing innocent civilians out here.'[330] 'I just got a call from the dustoff chopper and he said he spotted a lot of bodies all over the place.'[331] Even after intensive research by the Peers Commission the exact time frame cannot be pinpointed. However, it is without question that the radio traffic was known about in the Tactical Operations Center of Task Force Barker, that there was then contact with Medina, Captain Michles and Frank Barker and that the company commanders were warned to hold back.[332] It is also recorded that at around 9.30 a.m. Medina instructed 2nd Platoon to stop the shooting. Why 1st and 3rd Platoons, however, carried on with murdering and pillaging for another full hour and whether they also had been notified by Medina cannot be answered.[333] It appears that Lieutenant Colonel Frank Barker tuned in once more at about 10.30 a.m. and shortly afterwards Medina made contact with 1st and 3rd Platoons. Statements vary as to his exact words: 'Stop the shooting; the party's over.'[334] – 'They want the shooting stopped.'[335] – 'Stop the killing.'[336]

Task Force Barker spent another two days in the area around Son My village. On the afternoon of 16 March C Company and platoons from B Company combed through villages to the northeast of My Lai (4). In Phung Hoa and Binh Dong – My Lai (5) – ten of the inhabitants were arrested and about sixty-five others told to leave their villages immediately.[337] According to one Vietnamese interpreter, 'Captain Medina instructed me to tell the people they had to get out of this area because this area was a Communist area, and when they returned the next time on an operation in this area, anybody left in this area would be all killed just like in the area they had just left.'[338] The suspects from Phung Hoa and Binh Dong, together with another twenty supposed Viet Cong, waited until evening – tied up and hooded – to be interrogated. This was carried out by South Vietnamese policemen and the secret service officer from Task Force Barker, Eugene Kotouc, using a 'black book' on Viet Cong infrastructure. Kotouc tried to break the silence of one prisoner by cutting off his little finger with a bush knife and inflicting a ten centimetre cut in the nape of his neck. The man, along with another prisoner, was subsequently shot dead by members of the South Vietnamese National Police.

The following day Paul Meadlo trod on a mine and lost his left foot. 'This is what God did to me for what you made me do,' he roared at William Calley. 'God is going to get you.'[339] His unit moved on, burning down abandoned villages and isolated houses on Medina's orders, surprising three Viet Cong – two men and a woman – and taking them prisoner. The notorious rapist Dennis Conti only left the woman un-molested because after 'examining' her closely he said she was 'too dirty to screw'.[340] On 17 March Ernest Medina personally took over the role of torturer. He beat up one of the suspects, acted out a mock execution with an unloaded pistol to entertain his men, finally positioning the man against a tree and firing two shots with his M6, which hit the trunk just centimetres above his head. After that the suspect confessed to being a Viet Cong political leader and named the position of the long-sought 48th VC Local Force Battalion: the guerrilla troops were allegedly to be found in a mountainous region outside the Son My area.[341] On 18 March two GIs of C Company were wounded by booby-traps and had to be flown out. Apart from B Company shooting up a boat on the evening of 17 or 18 March, killing eight unarmed people[342] – according to the recollection of one witness – evidently no further civilians were killed. On 8 April 1968 Task Force Barker was disbanded.

It was eighteen months before the world was to learn of the events in My Lai (4) but the Communists had won an important round in the psychological war of attrition under the impact of the Tet offensive. On 10 March the *New York Times* caused excitement with the announce-ment that Westmoreland had asked for a further 206,000 men and two days later Senator Eugene McCarthy, the 'peace candidate' running for the Democratic presidential nomination, won forty-two per cent of the votes in the New Hampshire Primary. Shortly afterwards Senator Robert Kennedy also announced his candidature for the White House. At long last Lyndon B. Johnson's circle of foreign policy advisers, the 'wise men', rejected a recommendation made only a few months previ-ously for an undiminished continuation of the war. On 31 March the President drew the obvious conclusion and declared in a televised address that he would not seek a further term of office.[343] Months before the November election, the post of president was empty and the war entered an ambivalent transitional phase.

With an improvement in the prospects for a diplomatic solution and a gradual withdrawal of US ground troops, the risk of military escalation increased, because during this uncertain period both sides wanted to gain as much political advantage as possible on the battlefield. Whichever side was now able to inflict further substantial material damage on the enemy could count on optimising its negotiating position. For the USA, this meant strengthening the South Vietnamese armed forces as quickly and as sustainably as possible and stepping up the 'roll back' of territory held by the Viet Cong. With this in mind, Westmoreland played with the idea of occupying North Vietnamese territory above the demilitarised zone. For Hanoi, the time had come to send increased numbers of regular troops to the South, because otherwise disaster threatened the guerrillas in terms of casualties and logistics. In the following months the war claimed more victims on both sides than at any other time between the landing of American ground troops in March 1965 and the ceasefire in January 1973. Between April and June 1968 alone 800 GIs and 1,600 South Vietnamese soldiers were killed every week, while the losses of the Viet Cong and the North Vietnamese Army at this time were said to have amounted to 4,000 a week.[344] For soldiers and civilians alike, 1968 was the bloodiest year of the war.

7

1968–71
War of Attrition in the
Southern Provinces

Dear Abe, you and I know that the really crucial stage of both diplomatic and military operations is now upon us. If we are to win the kind of peace in Paris we want, you must keep the enemy on the run – in South Vietnam and in Laos . . . Your President and your country are counting on you to follow the enemy in relentless pursuit. Don't give them a moment's rest. Keep pouring it on. Let the enemy feel the weight of everything you've got.

Lyndon B. Johnson: handwritten letter to Creighton Abrams, commander of the US troops in South Vietnam, end October 1968[1]

Once Task Force Barker had completed its operation in Son My district, there were unusual verbal attacks on officers in several debriefings at the base. '[You mean] four VC and a hundred and twenty-four women and kids,' was the response to a secret service officer about a body-count of 128 dead Viet Cong recounted with pride.[2] 'They didn't look like they could do much to us,' several pilots added. Their company commander had to intervene to get them to keep quiet.[3] GIs of B Company were still angry about it days later in their headquarters and named the murderers in the presence of staff officers; others laughed at the official talk of a successful operation or speculated that Medina would be hanged for mass murder and that they themselves would finish up in prison.[4] Door-gunner Brian Livingston wrote to his wife about the daring rescue of some civilians in Xom Lang: 'We had to do this while *we* held machine guns on our own troops – American troops. I'll tell you something it sure makes one wonder why we are here.'[5] Apparently helicopter pilots of the 123rd Aviation Battalion wanted to give their account in writing to the Inspector General of the Americal Division: 'They were all excited and mad . . . Everyone was upset that night [16 March 1968]. It was talked about, the following days it was talked about.'[6]

It seems that some soldiers did not let themselves be shaken off by their immediate superiors telling them that an investigation was pending. One member of C Company made contact with the legal department of the Americal Division and informed a captain working there not only about the events of 16 March 1968 but also about other instances of excessive violence by the unit and the part played by Ernest Medina. Neither the captain nor his superior tried to pursue the matter. They seem to have thought they were dealing with a 'grass' or a busybody: 'There were frequently rumors about various excesses during operations.'[7] GIs from B Company told the Peers Commission about a number of written submissions to senior officers. They were puzzled as to why these documents were not to be found in the divisional files.[8]

There are only two contemporary written submissions in existence. John Ebinger, a private first class in B Company, 4th Battalion, 3rd Infantry Regiment, 11th Light Infantry Brigade, Americal Division, sent a comprehensive handwritten letter to President Johnson on 30 July 1968. He claimed to have seen with his own eyes a prisoner, who had already been maltreated as a 'mine-dog', being tortured again and described some of his comrades as serial rapists. 'There are many things like this and *worse* going on . . . Can you or anyone higher up do anything about this kind of conduct in this war?'[9] Ebinger was serving with B Company at the time of their operation in My Khe (4) but it is not clear whether he had actually taken part in the attack or for whatever reason was not in action that day. His letter was forwarded anyhow to the office of the Inspector General of the US Army in Vietnam and filed with the comment that interviews with seven commissioned and non-commissioned officers from Ebinger's unit had apparently given no indication of the validity of his accusations.[10]

Private First Class Tom Glen, of A Company, 4th Battalion, 3rd Infantry Regiment, 11th Light Infantry Brigade, Americal Division was in fact not a member of Task Force Barker. However the letter he sent to General Creighton Abrams on 17 November 1968 was written in the knowledge of the atrocities committed by the Americal Division in general and of the My Lai (4) massacre in particular. 'The average GI's attitude towards and treatment of the Vietnamese people all too often is a complete denial of all our country is attempting to accomplish in the realm of human relations . . . Far beyond merely dismissing the Vietnamese as "Slopes" or "Gooks" . . . too many American soldiers seem to discount their very humanity.' Glen continued that not individual soldiers but whole units should be held responsible for acts of violence. He implied that many of his comrades murdered civilians for the fun of it and indulged their sadistic leanings by torturing prisoners. 'Does his presence in a combat zone and his possession of a rifle so absolve a soldier from moral responsibility? American soldiers . . . perhaps more significantly practice here the intolerance which is so divisive of our country. What has been outlined here I have seen not only in my own unit, but also in others we have worked with, and I fear, it is universal.'[11] Creighton Abrams forwarded this lengthy letter to the headquarters of the Americal Division. 'Who is Glen? . . . What is he talking about?' Glen's superior officer, Lieutenant Colonel Albert L. Russell, brought the matter to a close in December 1968 with these words: 'That he [Tom Glen] should write a letter, charging violations coached [*sic*] in vague generalities after he had rotated makes his charges suspect and casts doubt on the moral courage he must possess to weather the onslaughts against the idealistic convictions he purportedly advocates.'[12]

Nine months after the mass murder there is no reason to conclude that those responsible were likely to be in any trouble. Nebulous accusations such as those which John Ebinger or Tom Glen had written about gave no cause for alarm. Moreover, none of those who started out by being angry tried to find out what had happened to their submissions and whether an investigation was actually going to take place. Even Hugh Thompson, who had repeatedly demonstrated extraordinary moral courage, withdrew. When he and his fellow crew members Glenn Andreotta and Lawrence Colburn were decorated weeks later for the rescue of civilians, the citation read: '[The evacuated were] located between friendly forces and hostile forces engaged in a heavy fire fight.'[13] Thompson made no comment on this fantasy image of My Lai (4); he even accepted that the citation had been composed without his knowledge and that someone had forged his signature certifying an eye-witness report.[14] In effect abstainers, onlookers, accomplices and culprits had mutually resigned themselves to remaining silent.

'We felt we were not going to break this story because we were part of it.'[15] With these words Ronald Haeberle expressed the mood which Private First Class Thomas Partsch had described in his diary while the Son My operation was going on: 'I didn't think it was right but we did it. At least I can say I didn't kill anybody. I think I wanted to but in another way I didn't.'[16] Feelings of guilt over help denied or fears of having to face up to one's own capacity for violence: compared with these, the pressure exerted by officers seems less important. Of course there were attempts at intimidation, particularly by Captain Medina; he tackled Michael Bernhardt, who was known as an abstainer, and warned him with veiled threats against contacting his congressman.[17] And the hint that incautious speech could be regarded as pre-trial publicity and therefore have a negative effect on the legal evaluation of the investigation's findings obviously did not miss its mark.[18] Ultimately, however, the culprits could rely on one thing above all: the team spirit and solidarity in their unit: 'We were like a family';[19] – 'I wouldn't tell the names because if people don't stick together in a war like this, man, they're no good, telling on each other, no good in my book.'[20] And Hugh Thompson's gunner, Lawrence Colburn, said: 'I can't see a man going to Vietnam and risking his life for his country and doing what he probably thinks is best and then getting punished for it.'[21]

If we say something, nothing will happen anyhow, because atrocities like those in My Lai (4) go on all the time – this was the common denominator of all those whose silence was not based on loyalty or shame. 'Well, I'm sure it has happened before, and I am sure it has happened since My Lai . . . Maybe not such a great number, but there are civilians being killed.'[22] This sort of statement was remarkably often produced by members of Task Force Barker – both officers and men. 'His [the witness's] only surprise in relation to the matter was that such a big fuss was made about it. The witness recalled an instance in which A Company killed two four or five year old children because it was thought the children had weapons.'[23] At this point their reports fall into the familiar pattern of stories about the Vietnam War. 'It was trifling.' – 'Vietnam taught you to be a liar. To be a thief. To be dishonest. To go against everything you ever learned.'[24] Certainly those who talked like that were not always thinking of massacres; as a rule they were talking about the harassment which had become habitual in routine search-and-destroy operations and the fact that killing came easily, in a land where the smell of death was everywhere and among people whose lives they held cheap. At the same time a three-week-long poll among 244 soldiers returning from Vietnam showed that it was actually the front-line fighters of My Lai (4) who were hardly or only moderately surprised. Twenty-three per cent believed that something like that had happened a few times and fifteen per cent spoke about 'many similar incidents'. Twenty-six per cent – notably fewer – regarded My Lai (4) as an isolated case and the remaining third did not want to commit themselves. 'It became obvious,' said the interviewers, 'that the more combat experience a man had the more easily he acknowledged that such incidents are possible.'[25]

SEVERAL 'MY LAIS'?

The National Liberation Front (NLF) in Quang Ngai Province, in its role as the political arm of the Viet Cong, repeatedly drew attention in March and April 1968 to the massacres carried out by Task Force Barker. Backed by survivors' reports, leaflets and a three-page proclamation were circulated. As was only to be expected, the NLF wanted to make political capital out of the murders, praised the resilience of the rural populace and exhorted the South Vietnamese Army to mutiny. 'The American Devils Divulge Their True Form . . . When the red evil Americans remove their prayer shirts they appear as barbaric men. When the American wolves remove their sheepskin their sharp meat-eating teeth show. They drink our peoples blood with animal sentimentality . . . Can you accept these criminal friends who slaughter our people and turn Vietnam into red blood like that which runs in our veins? There is no better time than now. The American Rifle is in your hands. You must take aim at the American head and Pull the trigger.'[26] – 'Shamefully defeated, confused, the enemy is like a wild animal just before dying, due to our thunderous Spring attack.'[27] Viet Cong soldiers from then on wore red armbands bearing the words: 'Resolved to avenge the atrocity at Son Tinh.'[28] At the end of April two demonstrations took place on Highway 521 with two to three hundred people taking part in each. The South Vietnamese regional and provincial troops barred their way into Quang Ngai City.[29]

In April 1971 the Provisional Revolutionary Government (PRG) of South Vietnam Information Bureau based in Paris produced a fourteen-page list compiled by a 'Committee to Denounce U.S. War Crimes in South Vietnam', cataloguing sixty-five terrorist acts allegedly committed by South Vietnamese, South Korean and American units between April 1968 and the end of 1970, causing the deaths of about 16,000 civilians. Three-quarters of the cases concerned ground operations and the rest air attacks on inhabited areas. The South Vietnamese infantry was held responsible for seventeen massacres, South Korean ground troops for eleven and American GIs and Marines were said to have committed mass murder in the course of twenty-one operations, either on their own or together with their allies.[30]

Most cases prove very difficult to check and evaluate. In the case of attacks by bomber squadrons, helicopter formations or artillery it is impossible to know whether there was deliberate firing, negligence or a chain of chance events. Were these places undefended? Or had the guerrillas taken hostage some of the villages and towns in question for operational reasons? Were they bombed by B-52s from a great height or from low-flying helicopter gunships? These are open questions, too. In the case of ground operations, times, locations and the numbers of dead and wounded are in fact given precisely and sometimes even the number of men deployed and their type of weaponry. But whether these were combat operations or unprovoked attacks is often as unclear as is the identity of the units being accused. Mostly they are described as 'enemy troops' (Americans), 'puppet troops' (South Vietnamese) or 'mercenaries' (South Koreans). It also looks as though the Viet Cong were using different place names from those used by the Americans or even the South Vietnamese. When joint operations by the American and South Vietnamese infantry are discussed, one cannot make out who is supposed to have committed the alleged atrocities, who was assigned to operational security in the area and who was possibly only giving logistical support and therefore was not anywhere near the scene of the crime.

The assertions of the PRG Information Bureau about the conduct of American infantrymen or airborne troops should be read with these reservations in mind. It is alleged

- that units of the 9th US Infantry Division devastated wide swathes of countryside and murdered 3,000 people, mainly the old, women and children between 1 December 1968 and 1 April 1969 in the course of 'accelerated pacification' in the provinces of Kien Hoa and Dinh Tuong (IV Corps Tactical Zone) (Case 9);[31]
- that allied troops under the command of General Cooksey (probably meaning Howard Harrison Cooksey, brigadier general in the Americal Division) on the Batangan Peninsular, Quang Ngai Province (I Corps Tactical Zone) and mostly in the districts of Binh Son and Son Tinh between mid January and early February 1969 burned down a number of villages, executed 300 peasants in the village of Chau Binh, 15 in Khanh My and 10 in Phuoc Hoa, forcibly resettled 11,000 inhabitants in the Van Thanh refugee camp and in March murdered 1,300 of these refugees suspected of being Viet Cong sympathisers. The details given are that 400 refugees were driven into the Co Luy River and drowned on 9 March; more than 100 people were killed when US helicopters shot up the Van Thanh camp on 18 March and 800 people, mostly from the Van Thanh camp together with some inmates of the Quang Ngai City prison, were crammed into sailing boats, put out onto the open sea and left to die of drowning in the second half of March (Case 10);[32]
- that four US battalions destroyed the village of Ty Se in Phuoc Son District, Quang Nam Province (I Corps Tactical Zone) between 15 and 27 January 1969 and executed 200 people in groups of 20 to 30 (Case 11);[33]
- that between 9 and 12 May 1969 three battalions of 5th Infantry Regiment, 1st US Marine Division with strong air and artillery support annihilated the villages of Loc Phuoc, Loc Hoa and Quang Doi in Quang Nam Province (I Corps Tactical Zone), killing 300 civilians (Case 16);[34]
- that at the beginning of October 1969 American and South Vietnamese units in Tu Nghia District, Quang Ngai Province (I Corps Tactical Zone) while combing through three settlement complexes, shot dead seventy-seven people in the village of Nghia Thang alone

and that on the orders of a South Vietnamese officer poisoned drinks were distributed in the Go Su refugee camp, killing 197 people (Case 25);[35]

- that American officers during Operation Sea Tiger[36] between 11 and 16 November 1969 commanded a 350-man force of 'pacification agents' who, together with South Vietnamese and South Korean troops, within a few days transformed twelve villages in the districts of Thang Binh and Que Son, Quang Nam Province (I Corps Tactical Zone) into a dead area. In detail: they burned down more than 1,000 houses and destroyed crops and cattle over a wide area; removed thousands to refugee camps; in the settlement complexes of Binh Duong, Binh Giang, Binh Trieu, Binh Hoa and Binh Dao killed more than 700 civilians, among them a large number of small children and frail old people, either with artillery fire, by having them executed by death squads or having patrols shoot them dead in their refuges or slaughter them in their houses (Case 26);[37]

- that from the end of September 1969 to early February 1970 American patrols together with South Vietnamese soldiers were stationed in An Xuyen Province (IV Corps Tactical Zone) and in two villages of the Bien Bach and Tri Phai settlement complex murdered 162 people, maimed 36 and seriously wounded a further 52 (Case 31);[38]

- that on 15 and 21 January 1970 American and South Vietnamese troops in the course of Operation Mekong Sacred Waves went through villages in Kien Phong Province (IV Corps Tactical Zone), plundering and raping, and executed thirty-six inhabitants in a hamlet in the An Long settlement (Case 28);[39]

- that between 22 and 25 February 1970 in Kien Hoa Province (IV Corps Tactical Zone) fifty civilians were killed and dozens tortured when US and South Vietnamese troops carried out a 'pacification operation' in several villages in Ho Cay District (Case 32);[40]

- that Marines of the 7th US Marine Regiment on 19 February 1970 in the villages of Son Thang and Son Thach, Quang Nam Province (I Corps Tactical Zone), shot dead sixteen women and children and slit the throats of eight adults and children with their bayonets (Case 33);[41]

- that from 1 to 6 April 1970 US soldiers, together with South Korean troops, in the course of a search-and-destroy operation in the districts of Vinh Son and Khanh Son, Khanh Hoa Province (II Corps Tactical

Zone) killed more than thirty peasants and drove eighty-four out of their villages (Case 38);[42]

- that in April 1970 a battalion of the 198th Light Infantry Brigade, Americal Division, together with a battalion of the 6th South Vietnamese Infantry Regiment, carried out several 'cleansing' actions in the east of Binh Son District, Quang Ngai Province (I Corps Tactical Zone), set fire to the villages of Binh Woa, Binh Phu, Binh Tan and Binh Thanh, deported the inhabitants to refugee camps and murdered thirty-six people (Case 39);[43]

- that on 1 April 1970 two infantry battalions and six companies of security police fired on the village of Tam Phoung in Vinh Binh Province (IV Corps Tactical Zone) with heavy artillery in the course of a joint American and South Vietnamese operation and in the raid which followed killed 140 inhabitants (Case 40);[44]

- that between 1 and 19 April 1970 US and South Vietnamese troops repeatedly attacked villages in the An Bien and Vinh Thuan Districts in Kien Giang and An Xuyen Provinces respectively (IV Corps Tactical Zone) and murdered 109 inhabitants (Case 42);[45]

- that on 15 April 1970 a company from 5th US Marine Regiment in Duy Xuyen District, Quang Nam Province (I Corps Tactical Zone), attacked the village of Le Bac and had thirty-seven people executed by death squads (Case 43);[46]

- that on 7 May 1970 American and South Vietnamese troops descended on three villages in the Dam Doi District, An Xuyen Province (IV Corps Tactical Zone), killing or wounding more than seventy inhabitants (Case 45);[47]

- that between June and August 1970 US troops murdered about fifty civilians in Phong Dinh Province (IV Corps Tactical Zone) (Case 48);[48]

- that on 26 June 1970 American low-flying helicopters attacked several fishing boats off the coast of Kien Giang Province (IV Corps Tactical Zone), killing 70 people and wounding more than 200 (Case 49);[49]

- that between 26 and 30 July 1970 American soldiers in the To Cay and Giong Trom Districts, Kien Hoa Province (IV Corps Tactical Zone) executed seventy-eight civilians in the course of a 'cleansing' action (Case 50);[50]

- that on 19 July 1970 1,500 US Marines and 5,000 South Vietnamese troops began Operation Pickens Forest and in attacks on dwelling

houses near Da Nang, Quang Nam Province (I Corps Tactical Zone),
killed about three dozen inhabitants (Case 52);[51]

- that in September 1970 units of 4th US Infantry Division in the
mountain village of Ma Nham, Phu Yen Province (II Corps
Tactical Zone), murdered or seriously wounded thirty-three civilians (Case 55).[52]

Twenty-one operations between April 1968 and September 1970
alone and more than 6,500 civilian victims, for whose deaths American
ground troops were supposed to be directly or indirectly responsible.
When the Provisional Revolutionary Government of South Vietnam
Information Bureau published these assertions in April 1971, Lieutenant
William Calley was having to answer for the My Lai (4) massacre
before a court martial, the Winter Soldiers of the Vietnam Veterans
Against the War were making similar accusations – and in Paris the
diplomats were arguing over terms for a ceasefire in Vietnam. The
Pentagon and the White House, bent on damage limitation on all
fronts, ignored the new accusations and filed the PRG's document
under 'Enemy Allegations' without checking it. The incriminated units
were not asked for their reaction nor was the Army Criminal
Investigation Division instructed to mount an investigation. On the
other hand, the Peers Commission and the Vietnam War Crimes
Working Group, set up by the Army in the wake of the My Lai (4)
scandal, had already assembled a fund of corroborative material,
which can be drawn on for critical examination of the wartime events
between 1968 and 1970.

The majority of these American files concerned the Army and
Marine units stationed in I Corps Tactical Zone and therefore give
information about the war in Quang Ngai, Quang Tin, Quang Nam,
Thua Thien and Quang Tri – those provinces which, in the black book
of the Provisional Revolutionary Government of South Vietnam, were
singled out (together with IV Corps Tactical Zone in the Mekong
Delta region) as the principal scenes of massacres.

As for I Corps Tactical Zone, this operational region had since April
1968 consisted of two combat zones, in which the war was waged in
different ways and with different objectives. In Quang Tri Province in
the extreme north, on the border with the demilitarised zone, the aim
was to put a stop to the supply of troops and materiel from North

Vietnam and in particular to eliminate the regular troops of the NVA. First and 3rd Marine Divisions, 3rd Airborne Brigade (Separate), 101st Airborne Division and units of the Americal Division – 196th Light Infantry Brigade from the end of April 1968 and some formations of 198th Light Infantry Brigade – bore the brunt of the fighting, which was the hardest and most costly of the entire war. Examples are the A Shau Valley and Hamburger Hill – places which recall the battles of attrition in the First World War rather than guerrilla warfare. Further to the south – in the provinces of Quang Ngai, Quang Tin and Quang Nam – General Creighton Abrams, who became US supreme commander in Vietnam in summer 1968, wanted to step up the 'pacification' of the countryside, bearing in mind Lyndon B. Johnson's directive: 'Dear Abe, you and I know that the really crucial stage of both diplomatic and military operations is now upon us . . . Your President and your country are counting on you to follow the enemy in relentless pursuit. Don't give them a moment's rest. Keep pouring it on. Let the enemy feel the weight of everything you've got.'[53] Norfolk Victory, Burlington Trail, Wheeler/Wallowa, Russell Beach/Bold Mariner, Nantucket Beach and Brave Armada were the names of some of the operations carried out for this purpose mainly by units of the Marines, by 11th and 198th Light Infantry Brigade, Americal Division, 3rd Brigade of 1st Cavalry Division and 2nd Infantry Division of the South Vietnamese Army. Once again it was a matter of making whole swathes of countryside unusable for the Viet Cong, by moving the people into refugee camps, destroying crops, letting fields go to waste and, especially, by hunting down the political cadres of the guerrillas. Even if – as Johnson implied – a military victory could no longer be counted on, there might still be a chance of negotiating an advantageous ceasefire. The crucial area for this objective lay also, if not primarily, in I Corps Tactical Zone.

It cannot be proved from the divisional files that in this phase of the war American units were carrying out massacres in I Corps Tactical Zone but it would be premature, if not negligent, to dismiss out of hand the reports published by the NLF or the North Vietnamese Communist Party about atrocities and war crimes as enemy propaganda and deliberately misleading. The report of the My Lai (4) massacre, for example, was remarkably precise: facts about the circumstances and the course of the crimes agreed substantially with later researches by American investigators and were in part better researched than those publicised in the US media. Only the troop classification ('3rd Brigade of the 82nd Paratroops Division') was plucked out of thin air. Above all, however, they refrained from dramatising the numbers of victims for political ends – 502 dead and 50 wounded are not estimates to argue with.[54] Moreover, this and all further information was disseminated even through the affected regions by leaflets and radio broadcasts. Deliberate distortion would have therefore rebounded onto its originators and would have played into the enemy's hands in the psychological war of attrition. Even if these indications of the credibility of the Communist charges are not adequate, they still raise doubts about the American military record-keeping, which seems strikingly normal and untroubled.

At the end of 1967 the American journalist Jonathan Schell had already described the war waged in the south of I Corps Tactical Zone as calculated terrorism against civilians[55] – a finding which also applied to the following years. Formations of the Americal Division murdered and pillaged even after My Lai (4) and they carried on raping and murdering prisoners. So ran a report sent by a soldier of C Company, 3rd Battalion, 21st Infantry Regiment, 196th Light Infantry Brigade to his Congressman: 'He [the Company Commander] told us that we may not understand why it was the policy to kill all males over 15 years of age, but we should go along with it. The company followed that policy with lust. We went from hutch to hutch in that sparsely settled area. Any man found was shot, with little or no questions asked. It was the policy that no one should be living in that area.'[56] Similar accusations were levelled at units of 11th and 198th Light Infantry Brigade. 'The captain liked you better if you were a rough mother[fucker] who hated dinks.'[57] C Company of 1st Battalion, 20th Infantry Regiment, 11th Light Infantry Brigade, which was responsible for the massacre in Xom Lang and Binh Tay, was after that event sent on patrol in uninhabited jungle areas for weeks on end. They rarely entered villages and hardly saw any civilians, yet as soon as opportunity arose, they lashed out. The entry for 3 May 1968 in GI Thomas Partsch's diary notes: 'We went down to the valley . . . saw some gooks running they shot but missed . . . down further into the villey [sic] some huts were there. We all ransacked the places and messed with the girls tore there [sic] clothes off and screwed them.'[58]

When Operation Wheeler/Wallowa was terminated in November 1968 and with it one of the longest operations of the entire war, the US forces in the provinces of Quang Ngai, Quang Tin and Quang Nam had by their own account killed 10,020 enemies, captured 2,053 weapons and lost 682 of their own men.[59] This means that only one in five Viet Cong or NVA soldiers was carrying a weapon and that for every GI killed there were fifteen from enemy ranks. Explanations for these remarkable ratios are sought in vain; it can and must be inferred that they conceal a high death-toll of non-combatants. There is more data to support this inference. Out of 600,000 inhabitants in Quang Nam Province 270,000 were still refugees a year later – significantly more than in all the other provinces. At the beginning of 1972 between two-thirds and three-quarters of the population had left their native villages and forty-six per cent of all settlements in the province were ghost towns or no longer existed.[60] This meant that almost every second village had become the target of military operations which all followed one operational principle: to evacuate across the board, when in doubt to use violence against those who did not want to be moved and to ensure that those who wanted to return home no longer had any incentive to do so. 'Go Noi Island,' read the after-action report on Operation Pipestone Canyon, 'had been converted from a densely populated, heavily wooded area into a barren wasteland, a plowed field. In that, the operation was a success.'[61]

Among the accusations of the PRG Information Bureau one which carried most weight concerned the forced deportations in the train of operation Russell Beach/Bold Mariner. Between mid January and mid July 1969 units of the US Marines and Navy and the American and South Vietnamese Army carried out a 'massive pacification effort' on the Batangan Peninsula, which lay to the north-east of Quang Ngai City,[62] with the aim of evacuating all civilians from the island and getting rid of the political cadres of the guerrillas. Under the heading 'Enemy Situation', the 'Spot Report' of 13 February 1969 issued by the 4th Battalion, 3rd Infantry Regiment, 11th Light Infantry Brigade, Americal Division read as follows: 'The area is VC dominated and their control was uncontested by GVN [Government of Vietnam] until operation Russell Beach. Everyone should be considered as either a VC or VC sympathizer and all men of military age must be considered as members of VC forces in the area.'[63] In the course of this operation some 12,000 people were evicted, 9,000 from the area of the Son My district alone, through which Task Force Barker had rampaged nine months before and carried out the massacres of My Lai (4) and My Khe (4). Some of the inhabitants were taken by boat to the island of Trai Thien An and some were accommodated in Binh Duc village. The remainder were sent into the corrugated-iron huts of the Van Thanh refugee camp, only provided with the bare necessities of life, surrounded by several rows of barbed wire and guarded by three companies of American and South Vietnamese infantrymen.[64] After a few months thousands of hectares of the peninsula resembled a moonscape. Anything not burnt down with fire from ground troops, artillery or from the air fell victim to the bulldozers and levellers. A quarter of the evacuees were, however, able to return to their villages.[65]

Did 1,600 civilians in fact pay for this operation with their lives between January and the end of March 1969? Three hundred peasants are said to have been executed in the village of Chau Binh, fifteen in Khanh My and ten in Phuoc Hoa and one hundred refugees are said to have died as a result of helicopter attacks on the inmates of Van Thanh Camp when they revolted. It was claimed that 1,200 suspected Viet Cong sympathisers were driven into the Co Luy river or the open sea and drowned – according to the PRG in the résumé of American war crimes after My Lai (4) already quoted.[66] Even before the PRG presented the Western public with these accusations, the Army found that it needed to question witnesses, the decisive factor being the unexpectedly negative headlines back home. On 28 November 1969 CBS television reported in its evening news about the 1,200 Vietnamese supposedly drowned by American soldiers, citing a Viet Cong deserter.[67] Shortly afterwards a woman from Chau Binh contacted the international press in Paris, in May 1970 *Scanlan's* magazine – part of the Californian 'counterculture' – published a corroborative article,[68] and in addition the attack on Van Thanh was mentioned during the investigation into the My Lai (4) massacre. Private First Class Theodore Blauveldt accused 11th Light Infantry Brigade of having carried out a massacre in a refugee camp near Quang Ngai City and another GI confirmed that this was Van Thanh Camp.

Because neither witness had belonged to a unit which had taken part in Russell Beach/Bold Mariner at the time in question and were only relying on hearsay accounts gleaned while serving in Vietnam, no further investigations were ordered;[69] neither was there any reaction to the alleged massacre in the village of Chau Binh. The Army, according to a recommendation from the Criminal Investigation Division, would only have to take action about it if the Marine Corps, which was operationally responsible in the area, should come across anything suspect.[70] With regard to the mass drownings, the Pentagon said this was nothing to do with them and forwarded the file – to the State Department. It is not clear whether anyone felt any responsibility whatever by the end of this game of bureaucratic ping-pong; unless something should be found by chance in some remote part of the archives, the last recorded word on the subject is the following Army résumé: 'This conclusion [to refrain from further investigation] is based on the absence of complaint or substantiation from sources other than the NLF radio . . . Information obtained during interviews of U.S. and Vietnamese officials at that time *tend to refute* the NLF story concerning the alleged drownings.'[71]

With regard to I Corps Tactical Zone, only one of the Communist accusations was officially confirmed: the Son Thang massacre.[72] In that village to the south west of Da Nang a five-man 'killer team' of B Company, 1st Battalion, 7th Regiment, 1st Marine Division slaughtered five women and eleven children on 19 February 1970 – partly in revenge for recent losses in their own ranks, partly to improve their body-count tally and partly because in the 'Indian Country' of Quang Nam they had a licence to shoot at anything which moved.[73] If the PRG had ever drawn attention to this crime, it would probably have been denied. Thanks to Lieutenant Colonel Richard E. Theer, Operations Officer (S3) of that battalion, it was investigated. Informed by devious routes about an eye witness's complaint, he ordered the suspects to be questioned, charged them with the murder and the attempted cover-up on the grounds of their contradictory statements and in the face of strong resistance convened a military tribunal.[74]

Because American soldiers broke their silence, three further massacres – carried out since April 1968 in I Corps Tactical Zone but not even mentioned in the PRG document – came to light:

- Quang Ngai Province, Operation Iron Mountain, 18 April 1969: a squad from E Company, 4th Battalion, 21st Infantry Regiment, 11th Light Infantry Brigade, Americal Division were instructed by their platoon leader to storm the village of Truong Khanh (2), twenty kilometres from My Lai (4), and to take revenge on the inhabitants for a comrade killed the evening before by a booby-trap. 'There's a village over there, and there's people in it, and they're responsible for it. I want some kills.'[75] Of the ten men in the squad, half opened fire and killed thirty civilians who were recorded in the body-count statistics as thirteen Viet Cong killed. This was the description of E Company's operation given by Private First Class Danny S. Notley, supported by two other witnesses, before the Dellums Committee, an ad hoc body convened by members of the House of Representatives in April 1971.[76] Five women from Truong Khanh (2) confirmed Notley's statement[77] and two soldiers of the 4/21 accused their unit of further war crimes before the Pentagon Counter Intelligence Force, consisting of attacks on undefended villages, desecration of corpses, using peasants as mine dogs and routinely torturing prisoners with electric shocks – and accused the torturers of taking photos of their actions.[78] In the event the Criminal Investigation Division ceased their investigations on account of contradictory evidence,[79] but there is little doubt that there was a mass murder in Truong Khanh (2), whether by the squad mentioned or by the helicopter gunships also deployed, which burnt the whole village down and used their own methods to destroy all existing evidence.[80]

- Quang Nam Province, end September/beginning October 1969: a reconnaissance platoon of E Company, 4th Battalion, 31st Infantry Regiment, 196th Light Infantry Brigade, Americal Division carried out a search-and-clear operation in Que Son Valley and were to track down so-called 'stragglers' – peasants who had refused to be moved to the Hiep Duc refugee camp. In order to lend emphasis to their orders, the platoon set fire to a hamlet near Phu Binh. 'We were burning their huts as we went to insure they wouldn't return after we left.'[81] The inhabitants – a dozen old men, women and small children – stayed there all the same. The following day they were all shot dead by the unit in question.[82] The platoon leader told his men 'not to worry about it' and recorded in his daybook a successful operation against armed Viet Cong.[83] 'It is also indicated,' according to the examiners from the Criminal Investigation Division, 'that the incidents were not reported to anyone above company level.'[84] Private First Class Davey V. Hoag, who went public in May

1972, had immediately brought the murder to the attention of his superior, with the result that a lieutenant got him involved in a brawl and he was immediately transferred to another unit.[85]

• Quang Tin Province, 1 July 1969: four helicopter gunships of D Troop, 1st Squadron, 1st Cavalry Regiment, Americal Division pretended to have been under continuous enemy fire during an operation north-west of Chu Lai and as a result received permission to fire from their operational command and attacked the village of Phu Vinh with 2,000 rounds from 7.62mm weapons and 74 aerial rockets. Another helicopter, without getting advance permission, shot up the neighbouring village of Diem Pho. In Phu Vinh ten inhabitants were killed and fifteen wounded.[86] The episode could be reconstructed, because a Combined Action Platoon in the neighbourhood was ordered to the village and refuted the culprits' statements: they found neither enemy ammunition nor any trace of the weapons dump they had allegedly blown up.[87] 'It also appears', according to the final report, 'that this was not an isolated case but that these young men were following the Rules of Engagement as they understood them to apply in their unit.'[88]

In fact there are further indications of dozens of people killed by helicopter fire in I Corps Tactical Zone. A gunner from D Troop, 101st Assault Helicopter Battalion, 2nd Brigade, 101st Airborne Division stated, both in an interview with the Illinois daily newspaper *Courier News* and shortly afterwards to examiners from the Criminal Investigation Division, that during an operation near Can Thien, Thua Thien Province, in mid August 1968, he and his comrades had shot dead seven civilians and that murders of this kind were regularly committed by his formation.[89] According to another GI, in autumn 1969 helicopter gunships of 71st Assault Helicopter Company fired several times on large groups of unarmed people from the air over Barrier Island, to the south of Hoi An, Quang Nam Province. The report of the Criminal Investigation Division states that 'U.S. Forces . . . did use weapons aboard helicopter gunships to fire upon Vietnamese on the ground, believed to be hostile forces.'[90] In neither case were the responsible authorities anxious to pursue an investigation, an additional reason being that the divisional files in question had by then already been transferred to Okinawa.[91]

OPERATION SPEEDY EXPRESS

Apart from I Corps Tactical Zone and the northern provinces, most of the accusations of the PRG Information Bureau concerned the provinces to the southwest of Saigon or IV Corps Tactical Zone. In that region American ground troops were said to have carried out ten massacres between December 1968 and July 1970[92] and their South Vietnamese allies seventeen between May 1968 and August 1970.[93]

Between Kien Tuong Province on the Cambodian frontier and An Xuyen Province on the Gulf of Thailand lay the most economically productive region of South Vietnam. With an area of over 14,000 square miles – about twice the size of New Jersey – the region represented a mere quarter of the country's landmass; in it there lived close to six million people – a third of the population – and from here came three-quarters of the rice production and about eighty per cent of all the country's meat products. According to an internal study by the US Army, 'The prevailing attitude is one of fatalism and indifference to political events that occur around it.'[94] This only applied to a certain extent to the Mekong Delta – Dinh Tuong and Kien Hoa Provinces – where the National Liberation Movement had been founded and from which came some of the Viet Cong leaders. In the eyes of the American secret services, Kien Hoa was reckoned to be the province with 'perhaps one of the most highly organized infrastructures of any province in SVN [South Vietnam].'[95] The daily lives of the inhabitants demonstrated that the guerrillas were widely recognised as the legitimate political authority in the Delta. Many sent their children to NLF schools and used hospitals funded from the coffers of the resistance movement. The services of the South Vietnamese government were neither wanted nor needed and nearby Saigon was as alien as the seat of a foreign government. In the problematic provinces of Dinh Tuong and Kien Hoa the American Army, as was the case in all the other war zones, faced serious logistical problems. Unlike the rest of Vietnam, which was covered with mountains and hills, the Mekong Delta was of course open country. There was no rampant jungle, though near the shores there were thickets of mangrove, coconut and banana trees, yet the terrain was quite unsuitable for large combat formations. Rivers, canals and irrigation ditches made up in all a meander of 3,500 kilometres while stagnant pools, brackish water and marshes inhibited any freedom of movement even in the dry season from December to mid April and effectively ruled out the use of heavy equipment. Infantrymen regularly waded up to their knees or sometimes their shoulders through polluted water full of leeches, or cut their way through elephant grass with stems like razor blades which slit their clothing. Unlike I Corps Tactical Zone, here it was impossible to keep patrols operating for weeks on end. After two days at the most the soldiers had to be recalled and replaced. The three brigades of 9th Infantry Division, which were stationed from January 1967 in Dinh Tuong, Long An and Kien Hoa, resorted to operating sporadically in small groups and larger formations were not introduced until the end of 1968.[96] Even the Viet Cong and the North Vietnamese Army only kept a few of their well-armed and mobile formations in the Delta and until the Tet Offensive they were waging a classical guerrilla war in this region with stationary, locally-based assault troops who needed no supply lines, managed with minimal equipment, could live effortlessly off the land and above all through skirmishing and harassing offered no identifiable target for attack. 'The VC are still able to roam at will through much of the area [the Delta],' ran an expert analysis produced by the RAND Corporation in 1967.[97]

Since spring 1968 the American planning staff in Vietnam had been discussing the terms and conditions for a countrywide 'enhanced pacification campaign'. From the military viewpoint the prospects seemed promising. Admittedly they had suffered substantial reverses in all forty-four provinces in the course of the Tet Offensive. In a CIA situation report of March 1968 there had even been mention of going back to the time before 1965: 'Evidence already indicates that the enemy action has greatly increased the apathy and passivity of many rural residents toward government programs and personnel.'[98] In Kien Hoa the South Vietnamese Army had not even been able to hold their twenty-seven defensive positions round the provincial capital of Ben Tre. On the other hand, during Tet and the subsequent offensives of May and August 1968 the Viet Cong had lost a substantial number of men which, in the opinion of many observers, they would have difficulty in making good. At US Headquarters reports were coming in from all parts of the country of demoralised, badly organised and fleeing guerrilla units. Allegedly a quarter of prisoners captured in IV Corps Tactical Zone between January and October 1968 were between fourteen and seventeen years old – child soldiers who gave the impression of a last-ditch stand. 'The enemy does not have the ability to withstand sustained combat,' ran a situation analysis regarding the southern provinces.[99] It was in these areas most of all that the Viet Cong seemed to be having difficulty in making good their losses, because the North Vietnamese Army was concentrating its supply of personnel on I Corps Tactical Zone in the north and only wanted to spare inexperienced and less qualified forces for operations elsewhere.[100] This presented to the US armed forces an invitation to turn the south of the country as well into a zone of intensive action after years of reluctantly holding back.

Primarily political considerations lay behind the actual military upgrading of IV Corps Tactical Zone. As can be gleaned from the fragmentary surviving files, the decisive impetus came from civilian and military advisers – the senior management of CORDS in collaboration with the US Army Advisory Group, Advisory Team 96, IV CTZ. In numerous submissions to the Headquarters of the American Forces in Saigon they pointed out the symbolic importance of IV Corps Tactical Zone. The key words were 'Paris' and 'Vietnamisation'. However the ceasefire talks in the French capital might develop, one thing seemed crucial: to make sure that on the day it was signed the provinces immediately around Saigon were not under enemy control. This simultaneously defined the essence of successful 'Vietnamisation'. The way had not yet been paved for the withdrawal of American troops, but in the foreseeable future the South Vietnamese Army would bear the main brunt of the war and above all had to guarantee winning back prestige and recognition in their own country. Beyond all operational considerations, 'Vietnamisation' also stood for the struggle for the psychological assets of the war. 'The war started in the Delta, and this is where it will end,' was a much-quoted view directed mainly at the Vietnamese. In other words, whoever had the upper hand in the grassroots country of the Viet Cong had made his determination to establish himself look credible; whoever controlled this region made a lasting improvement to his negotiating position. Hence the pressure and impatience of the American advisers; in their eyes it was militarily possible and politically imperative to create a breach for the South

Vietnamese forces in IV Corps Tactical Zone. 'Except for Saigon, the Delta in many ways is the most important area in Vietnam to both the VC and the GVN [Government of Vietnam] . . . It is recommended that the decision be made now to commence the necessary preparations so that by 1 December 1968 a well organized, dry-weather offensive may be launched that will dramatically improve the security situation in IV CTZ by 1 June 1969.'[101]

The input of the US Army Advisory Group, IV CTZ forced the issue. At the beginning of September 1968 the planning staff at US Headquarters spoke in favour of the proposed offensive and on 14 October Operational Plan 1 68 (OPLAN 1 68) was passed. It did in fact reject the idea of bringing in an additional airborne brigade from III Corps Tactical Zone, but this did not affect 9th Infantry Division's task. Before their departure from Vietnam – already decided on and scheduled for mid 1969 – they were to carry out one more major operation and implement 'the first overall long range plan developed for the elimination of all Vietcong forces in the Delta.'[102] This meant eliminating about 20,000 stationary guerrillas, about 6,000 mobile Viet Cong and North Vietnamese Army troops and 11,000 political leaders or 'Viet Cong infrastructure'.[103] This brought the 9th Infantry Division directly into the Phoenix programme:

The importance of taking aggressive action against the Viet Cong Infrastructure cannot be overemphasized . . . If their main force military units are defeated, the VC can always fall back on their political structure and rely upon guerrilla warfare. If we are to successfully deal with the enemy, great effort must be given to eliminating both the enemy's military and political organization. Once the political infrastructure has been neutralized . . . the Viet Cong cannot survive.[104]

This meant winning back at least 400 villages by the end of January 1969 and placing them under the control of the South Vietnamese authorities, even at the cost of widespread destruction and eviction of the inhabitants.[105] In the words of Major General Harris W. Hollis, commander of 9th Infantry Division from April to August 1969: 'Military operations of the 9th Infantry Division were carried out to achieve a broader goal than the simple elimination of Viet Cong and North Vietnamese infiltrators. The overriding goal was total pacification.'[106]

The operation, concentrated on the provinces of Dinh Tuong, Kien Hoa, Kien Tuong, Kien Phong and Vinh Long, began on 1 December 1968 and ended on 1 June 1969. Its code name was Speedy Express.

On the allied side 19,000 soldiers were in operation: seven combat battalions of 1st and 2nd Brigades of 9th US Infantry Division,[107] units of the US Air Force and Marines and parts of 7th, 9th and 21st South Vietnamese Infantry Divisions. Supporting ground troops with squadrons of helicopters, tactical aircraft and patrol boats was routine in Vietnam. In Speedy Express, however, the 'air cavalry troops' played an exceptionally major role.[108] If there was mention in the operational plans of their 'maximum participation', this had less to do with transport helicopters than gunships, whose sole remit it was to destroy enemy formations or supposed positions in surprise attacks.[109] The difficult and often impassable terrain facing the infantry suggested this policy, but there was also the matter of further operational training for the ARVN, a force which had still not recovered from the shock of the Tet Offensive and which, in view of its shattered morale, could not cope with any substantial losses on the ground.[110] Side by side with 9th Infantry Division, the South Vietnamese were to be made familiar with the advantages of a combined ground-air operation in the Mekong Delta and prepared for independent operations in IV Corps Tactical Zone. In the words of Julian J. Ewell, Commander of 9th Infantry Division: 'Long-run success depends on getting the ARVN forces in high gear. Though US units can help out by taking on the hardest nuts, there just aren't enough US troops to carry the main load.'[111] In view of this, Speedy Express – as an internal memorandum noted – was to be 'a valuable training vehicle for ARVN and Territorial Forces'.[112] It could even be described as a laboratory for the imminent 'Vietnamisation' of the war or, to be more precise, for a war which, in view of the impending withdrawal of the American infantry, would essentially be fought in the air.

'The 9th Infantry Division conducted a series of pre-emptive operations against an elusive enemy in the Upper Mekong Delta, which was unprecedented in the history of the US Army in Vietnam.'[113] A letter of commendation to President Nixon described Speedy Express in these terms, forming the basis for an application to confer on 9th Infantry Division the honorary title of 'Presidential Unit'. Whether and in what way the war in the Delta was actually 'unprecedented' remains to be proved in the light of closer examination but, in any

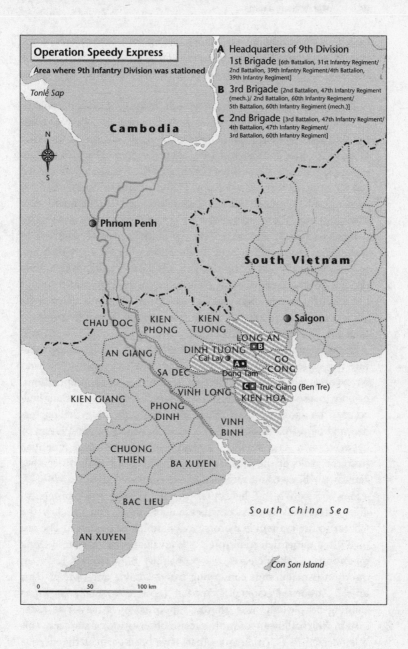

case, those responsible were among the extreme interpreters of the war of attrition who were therefore uncompromising advocates of maximised firepower. The combat tactics to which Speedy Express was committed speak for this.

Deviating from usual practice, 9th Infantry Division took to mounting operations round the clock. Within their 24/7 concept night fighting also counted as a Standing Operating Procedure. At least half of their 'surprise and shock actions' against supposed Viet Cong hide-outs or the alleged whereabouts of their political leaders were carried out after sunset and forty per cent of the victims of Speedy Express were logged under night attacks. Bushmaster and Checkerboard were the names of these operations by ground troops, assembled in company strength and swarming out under cover of darkness in platoons or squads, either lying in wait motionless for thirty-six hours or systematically combing through the countryside, which they divided up like a chessboard. Helicopter crews were sent on night hunter, night raid or night search missions and as a rule flew sorties with two or three Cobras, escorted by a Huey helicopter to direct their fire. Armed for the proverbial 'power punch', fifty-two rockets, a machine gun firing 6,000 shots a minute and a quick-firing shell-thrower were part of the Cobras' standard equipment.[114] It was innovations which had previously not been used at all in operations, or only to a small extent, which explained the crews giving their heli-copters the name of 'killer machines'. Firstly, the Huey helicopters had on board sharpshooters – specialists in deadly fire at a range of between 150 and 600 metres who had been recruited since June 1968 from the ranks of the infantry. They alone accounted for fifteen per cent of the body count recorded in the course of night search oper-ations.[115] Secondly, the helicopters carried CS tear gas canisters, to drive actual or suspected enemies out of hiding and to allow the Cobras to fire at them in a broad area illuminated by flares. 'The use of CS in a target detection role . . . is a valuable innovation in Delta operations . . . It increases the probability of a contact *before* an insertion is made, thus conserving troop stamina and time.'[116] This official 'Airborne Personnel Detection' tactic, colloquially known as 'sniffing people out' was, thirdly, supported by a new-style radar system which allowed for more precise observation of surfaces. This was referred to as '[techniques that] have been particularly effective in engaging enemy forces travelling [*sic*] at night near or through populated areas where artillery cannot be fired.'[117]

With these operational directives the relevant provisions for protecting civilians and their dwellings were so much waste paper from the outset. In the case of Speedy Express there can be no talk of junior commanders and isolated groups of soldiers having gone off the rails or that such guidelines had been ignored under the pressures of unexpected situations. From the planning stage on the Rules of Engagement were treated as antiquated relics by the operational leadership, who pointed out the allegedly new kinds of opportunities for coordinating superior firepower, and the need to act pre-emptively to stop an enemy who was difficult to locate from regrouping his units. As well as the people living in combat zones, enemy troops were obviously affected by this new thinking. Encirclement, destruction and annihilation were the key terms for dealing with the Viet Cong.[118] In other words, they were not expected to surrender. The operational directives did not just amount to a policy of taking no prisoners; they required it. Basically an unofficial practice long in use by some parts of 9th Infantry Division was now declared to be officially sanctioned: 'The first rule of engagement,' said a company leader about his experiences with a killer patrol in August 1967, 'is to kill *at the first opportunity* whether it is by SA [small arms], claymore, or hand grenade. The second rule is to use claymore, hand grenades, and SA in that order.'[119] Any member of the Viet Cong entering the Mekong Delta at the time of Speedy Express was in a 'general kill zone'[120] and in an area beyond all laws of warfare. In effect, civilians living there found themselves once again in an extensive Free Fire Zone and might at any time, even during the evening or at night, be aimed at by units who neither made nor tried to make any distinction between combatants and non-combatants. 'After 1900 hours in the 1st Brigade AO [area of operation] anything that moved – anywhere – was considered enemy, and was engaged.'[121] 'A review of available documents,' according to an internal evaluation of Speedy Express, '. . . failed to identify any specific actions which were actually taken to avoid unnecessary civilian casualties.'[122] The same happened often enough in other combat zones but it was relatively rare for the highest authorities – brigade and divisional commanders – not only to accept but to authorise in advance a blanket licence to kill.

From February 1968 to the end of March 1969 the 9th Infantry
Division was under the command of Major General Julian J. Ewell,
who was known as the 'Butcher of the Delta'. In fact Ewell only
oversaw the first phase of Speedy Express,[123] but he had made his expectations and guidelines for the entire operation abundantly clear.
How Ewell briefed his troop leaders and men was explained by three
West Point graduates, all with the rank of captain, to the AP news
agency, CBS television and a commission of the House of Representatives led by Ronald V. Dellums in April 1971. According to them, Ewell
demanded of the brigade and battalion commanders a substantial
increase in the monthly 'hit quota'. 'He said that we were only killing
2,000 of these little bastards a month . . . He assigned the division a
quota, the division assigned brigades quotas . . . He constantly referred
to them [the Vietnamese] that way – gooks, slants, slopes, bastards; and
he talked about shooting fish.'[124] Ewell confirmed the accusations in
principle[125] and repeated in public the evaluation of the war in the Delta
which he had put on record when he left 9th Infantry Division: 'I guess
I basically feel that the "hearts and minds" approach can be overdone.
In the Delta the only way to overcome VC control and terror is by
brute force applied against the VC.'[126] On 1 April 1969 Ewell took over
command of II Field Force[127] and six weeks later was promoted to
lieutenant general. After his return from Vietnam he was the American
delegation's chief military adviser at the ceasefire talks in Paris.[128]

How the operational planning for Speedy Express was implemented
and what the battle routines in the Mekong Delta looked like between
December 1968 and the end of May 1969 is still one of the unwritten
chapters of the Vietnam War. Unlike Tiger Force or Task Force Barker,
we know hardly anything about the mental and psychological state
of the troops involved, their combat experiences and previous conduct,
the dynamic of the situation or their freedom of action. In other
words Speedy Express is probably the largest 'black hole' of the
Vietnam War.

To this day there is only one reliable source of information on the
events in Dinh Tuong and Kien Hoa Provinces – the report of an anony-
mous GI, who at the time was in the 4th Battalion, 39th Infantry
Regiment, 1st Brigade, 9th Infantry Division, stationed in Dinh Tuong
Province. At the end of May 1970, prompted by the debate over My
Lai (4), he wrote a letter to William Westmoreland from his new posting

in West Germany. On 30 March 1971 he sent a slightly modified version
to the Commander of Fort Benning, Major General Orwin C. Talbott
and finally on 30 July 1971 turned to Major General William A. Enemark,
Inspector General of the US Army. The fifteen-page handwritten letter
was full of orthographic and grammatical mistakes but the factual
precision and both objective and forceful arguments of the writer made
it compelling. The letter was signed: 'Very truly yours, Concerned Sgt.'
The author would only give his name on condition that the Army
mount an investigation into the events he described. 'I would not be
afraid to talk to CID if I was one of a big bunch of dudes being talked
to.' To begin with at least the writer did not think of going public. 'I
like the Army because I think the Army has been fair to me and given
me a decent life in return for my hard work and so I don't want to see
the Army get in more trouble.' However he reserved the right to take
further steps. 'And if you don't do something you better be ready to
tell Senator [sic] Dellums why not because on September first he is
gona [sic] get a big envelope with copies.' His reason was that 'I have
been trying for a year now to tell somebody about a bunch of little
things that add up to bad as My Lay [sic] or worse.'[129]

'It is about nobody giving a damn about the Vietnamese, no mind
[sic] which side they are on.'[130] During Operation Speedy Express the
'Concerned Sergeant' claimed to have seen with his own eyes hundreds
of cases of deliberate terror attacks – primarily against civilians but
also against enemy soldiers.

In these ambushes we killed anything or anybody and a lot of these weren't
VC. We used Claymores on any people or any boat that passed and sometimes
it would be a sampan with a load of bannanas [sic] and a couple of women
or sometimes a papasan [male Vietnamese] with a hoe. No big thing, they
were VC as soon as we killed them. This was most times in the early morning
when the Vietnamese might be going to work in the fields or to the market
... I asked my platoon leader about this and he said it was ok to zap them
if they move during curfew. But he couldn't answer when I asked if they
knew it was curfew. He just said hardcore ... to zap them ... This thing
happened 15 or 20 times in my platoon.

Since the ground troops knew about the enhanced role of the Air
Force during Speedy Express, the witness went on to say, many platoons

did not even bother to follow their combat instructions. 'Any time we got shot at from a tree line we'd always call for artillery or gunships or airstrikes. And lots of times it would get called for even if we didn't get shot at. And then when we'd get in the village there would be women and kids crying, and sometimes hurt or dead.' The 'Concerned Sergeant' said that Speedy Express was an operation in which every method of terrorising was used simultaneously and with particular unscrupulousness – in addition to the Air Force and artillery, there was random shooting from helicopters at anything moving on the ground, tear gas was even released in settlements and prisoners were used as mine dogs. 'The snipers was [sic] the worst killers.' He said the snipers of his battalion were alone responsible for at least 600 murders a month. 'He [the Battalion Commander] told my company comander [sic] that pretty soon there wouldn't be any rice farmers left because his snipers would kill them all. And he laughed.'

The battalion commander in question was Lieutenant Colonel David H. Hackworth, who commanded 4th Battalion, 39th Infantry Regiment, 9th Infantry Division from 1 February 1969.[131] According to the description given by the 'Concerned Sergeant' Hackworth, together with a number of unidentified senior officers, unceasingly urged his men to forget about the Rules of Engagement and the comments of the South Vietnamese advisers, made no distinction between military and civilian targets and did not consider the appropriateness of the methods he was using, while most of his subordinates were clearly unable to resist his pressure. 'The FO [Air Forward Observer][132] and my company comander [sic] would do anything to get the COL [Colonel] off there [sic] backs.' In mid March 1969 Hackworth apparently gave a specific order to murder civilians: 'I don't give a shit. Shoot them anyway, women or not,' and soon after he allegedly maltreated prisoners with his own hands. 'His body count fever . . . made lots of guys do things that they could end up like LT [Lieutenant] Calley . . . The point of all this is to tell you like I tried to tell the other Gens [Generals] that it is not the EM [enlisted men] and the company officers alone that did wrong in Vietnam . . . Trouble has gotta be stopped at the head like COL [Colonel] Hackworth, not at the bottom.'

With regard to the helicopter war, the 'Concerned Sergeant's' statements were indirectly confirmed by Jeffrey Record. Record was working for the Agency for International Development from September 1968 to August 1969 and during that period was Assistant Province Advisor for Psychological Operations in Bac Lieu Province. In several internal memoranda and finally in an article for the *Washington Monthly* magazine he described his experiences with helicopter gunships during so-called 'night raids'. In Bac Lieu, at the southwest extremity of IV Corps Tactical Zone, helicopters were originally only used for troop transport, but from October 1968 on the aerial warfare was intensified throughout the region, with the aim of preventing the rural populace from leaving the refugee camps.

From his own observations Record described how Cobra pilots did not concentrate on Free Fire Zones at all during their 'phantom missions'. Without being attacked themselves, without being able to identify their target as a military objective and without having received permission to fire, the crews started 'indiscriminate killing and terror-ization of the uncommitted and non-combatant population'. According to Record, it was not the 3,000 Viet Cong fighters thought to be there, but mainly the peasants of Bac Lieu who suffered under these attacks – children and young people guarding the water-buffalo, adults travelling on the rivers in sampans, people taking refuge behind trees from low-flying Cobras, inhabitants of villages which happened to lie in the vicinity of their flight paths. 'Approximately 85% of the targets assaulted in this province by Phantom flights have been outside the Free Fire Zones.'[133] Even water-buffalo were included in the body-count statistics as enemy losses, because they served the Viet Cong as means of transport.[134]

Most of the opposition to restrictions came from the older officers, many close to retirement, for whom Vietnam provided their first and last chance to see real combat . . . Others appeared troubled by the suggestion that military effectiveness was not commensurate with simply the amount of firepower at one's disposal . . . He [the senior provincial advisor] failed to grasp that the problem lay not in their *indiscriminate* use but in the very nature of the gunships themselves. *Any* use of Cobras in a densely populated province . . . would be indiscriminate . . . What had started out as a program designed to hamper Viet Cong military operations had become an unmanageable and monstrous terror directed against the entire rural population.[135]

Repeated protests from political advisers were fruitless. Like Jeffrey Record, they returned from Vietnam embittered and knowing '[that] there were indeed terrible numbers [in Bac Lieu] of civilians killed and wounded in these attacks.'[136]

In spring 2001 the excesses carried out in the hunt for political leaders of the Viet Cong within Operation Speedy Express came into the public arena, when an article appeared in the *New York Times Magazine* about Delta Platoon, 'SEALs' Team One, Fire Team Bravo, Task Force 115 – a special naval unit, which was assigned to the Phoenix programme and was operating against the Viet Cong infrastructure in Kien Hoa Province at the beginning of 1969.[137] Task Force 115 was commanded by Captain Roy Hoffmann, who had already succeeded in gaining permission to suspend the Rules of Engagement at his own discretion during operations in the Mekong Delta in summer 1968. His soldiers did not have to wait for contact with the enemy, but could open fire when they personally felt they were under threat – a ruling which suited the commander of Delta Platoon fine. According to this twenty-five-year-old lieutenant, he was ready to storm Hanoi 'with a knife in my teeth'. Twenty years later Robert (Bob) Kerrey was representing the State of Nebraska in the US Senate and was regarded as a candidate for the White House. In early 2001 he was made president of the New School University in New York, better known under its former name of New School for Social Research. His platoon in Vietnam called itself unofficially 'Kerrey's Raiders' or 'Takeout Mission'.

In February 1969 half-a-dozen villages in Kien Hoa, seventy-five miles southeast of Saigon, were on Kerrey's Raiders' list, as Viet Cong political functionaries were believed to be there. The village elder of the 150-soul community of Thanh Phong was supposedly planning to meet local guerrilla leaders in secret, on which occasion he was to be 'neutralized', that is, either abducted or murdered. There is controversy over what actually happened in Thanh Phong just before midnight on 25 February. Of the seven soldiers in Kerrey's team four refused to say anything and one kept contradicting himself. Kerrey himself and two of his men confirmed that their team crept into the village and stabbed five people in the first hut – a man, a woman and three children, who were in the wrong place at the wrong time, because they could have warned the people the soldiers were actually looking for. 'Standard [*sic*] operating procedure,' said Kerrey, 'was to dispose of the people we made contact with. Kill the people we made contact with, or we have to abort the mission.'[138] One of the men said Kerrey was lying when he stated that the group was shot at shortly after and returned fire in self-defence. Instead he claimed that they had driven about fifteen villagers, mostly women and children, into the middle of the village, questioned them about the village elder and then shot them from a range of two to three metres. This version of events was confirmed by two former Viet Cong to CBS television in 2001.

'I'm not going to make this worse by questioning somebody else's memory of it,' said Kerrey when asked about it. 'You were authorized to kill if you thought that it would be better . . . We were instructed not to take prisoners.'[139] What is certain is that Kerrey claimed a body-count of twenty-one Viet Cong in his after-action report, that on the following day survivors raised the matter of the massacre in public and that the American military advisers in the province were informed immediately. 'Thus far it appears,' ran the transcript of Army radio traffic on 27 February 1969, 'that 24 people were killed. 13 were women and children and one old man. 11 were unidentified and assumed to be VC. Navy Seals operating in the area. Investigation continues.'[140] Instead of a subpoena, Kerrey's Raiders received a letter from the superior authorities, congratulating them on a successful operation. Kerrey himself was awarded a bronze star.

When the murders in Thanh Phong became public knowledge, David H. Hackworth came out of retirement to defend Kerrey, speaking of the routine life of warriors in Vietnam and pointing out that 'there were thousands of such atrocities'. He said that his own unit, 4th Battalion, 39th Infantry Regiment was responsible for 'at least a dozen such horrors'[141] in the Mekong Delta – a belated confirmation of the 'Concerned Sergeant's' account, which was not followed up, however. Unlike in the case of Tiger Force, no retrospective investigation was undertaken, and the name 'Speedy Express' was not even mentioned.

As a result we know no more about Speedy Express than we did in the early 1970s. The 'Concerned Sergeant' had spoken of about 1,500 dead a month and gave a possible figure for civilian dead of at least 200 a month – in his own opinion an extremely low estimate.[142] The PRG Information Bureau accused 9th Infantry Division of having killed 3,000 unarmed people with no involvement in the war in the provinces of Dinh Tuong and Kien Hoa in April 1971.[143] In June 1972 the journalist

Kevin P. Buckley published an article in *Newsweek* about 9th Infantry Division, under the title 'Pacification's Deadly Price'. Buckley had travelled through the Mekong Delta for months, talked to inhabitants, studied hospital records and evaluated statements from members of 9th Infantry Division. Since the end of November 1971 he had also been in contact with US Headquarters in Saigon and asked several times for a response to the data he sent in.[144] 'Defenseless villagers are bombarded from the air, the inhabitants driven out into the countryside, the cattle machine gunned, the huts set afire with incendiary bullets: this is called pacification,' said Buckley, summarising his researches in *Newsweek*. 'In my opinion, the U.S. military has been guilty of more than recklessness. It can, I believe, be documented that thousands of Vietnamese civilians have been killed deliberately by U.S. forces.' Strong words, which Buckley justified by referring to the data explicitly confirmed to him, according to which the figure of 10,899 enemies appeared in the body-count statistics of 9th Infantry Division; the same records give the number of weapons seized as 748. This ratio means that only one in every fifteen of the dead was armed. 'The Viet Cong were shot before they could get to their weapons,' was the reply Buckley received from officers of 9th Infantry Division. The *Newsweek* correspondent drew the different and more probable conclusion: that of the nearly 11,000 dead 5,000 were probably civilians.[145]

Buckley's estimate may possibly be too low. This was the conclusion reached by Colonel Maurice L. Clouser, head of the Investigation Department of the Inspector General, MACV. 'It would appear,' he maintained in a memorandum with various attachments a few days after the *Newsweek* article was published, 'that the extent of these casualties was in fact substantial, and that a fairly solid case can be constructed to show that civilian casualties may have amounted to several thousand (between 5,000 and 7,000) ... US air strikes were conducted against areas of suspected enemy concentrations. As the entire Delta is a region of high population density, these strikes inevitably resulted in some noncombatant deaths.'[146] Clouser based this on the files of 1st and 2nd Brigades, 9th Infantry Division at US Headquarters which were available at the time. According to them, 30,300 people in all were killed during Speedy Express – at least 11,000 resulting from American attacks and more than 19,000 from operations by the South Vietnamese Army.[147] In the light of this information the total number of civilian victims has to be corrected and was probably way above the estimated 5,000 to 7,000. Everything else is speculation, because corroborative operation reports of the ARVN are either not available or have so far not been evaluated.

According to American data, a maximum of 300 GIs lost their lives during Speedy Express;[148] this means that for every US soldier, 37 Viet Cong were killed – if we assume that the 11,000 enemy losses actually were combatants.[149] If, however, there were 5,000 civilian victims, the ratio would stand at 1:20 rather than 1:37. Major General Harris W. Hollis, Ewell's successor as commander of 9th Infantry Division, described the killing quota as 'a feat unprecedented in the history of United States Army combat in the Republic of Vietnam'.[150] No infantry unit stationed in Vietnam had in fact produced such a tally. Comparing the 9th Infantry Division figures from the period before Speedy Express, the ratio was 1:10 in 1966 and 1967 and 1:11 in 1968;[151] when the 3rd Brigade of that division was assigned the task of 'pacification' in Long An Province between February 1967 and March 1968, eight Viet Cong were claimed to have been killed for each GI lost.[152] The South Vietnamese Army itself lost 3,411 dead – eleven times as many as the Americans – with a poor ratio of 1:5.5 in comparison.[153]

However you move the figures around, they still illustrate one and the same point: only troops who had relatively little direct contact with enemy forces on the ground could arrive at a ratio of 1:37 or 1:20 killed in action. From the 9th Infantry Division combat statistics it is clear that US infantrymen only had any contact with the enemy during a third of their operations at most and were only responsible for half of all recorded Viet Cong dead.[154] In other words, the ratio praised by Hollis as a 'feat' was primarily due to the excessive aerial warfare – that is, to the Air Force, which flew about 6,500 tactical sorties,[155] the artillery, which was called up 6,300 times[156] by 1st Brigade alone, and the helicopter gunships. How often the last-named were called into action cannot be gleaned from the records, but ten per cent of the enemy victims were ascribed to the sharpshooters on board the Cobras alone.[157]

Taken as a whole, Speedy Express does indeed seem to have been without precedent. The written sources available and the statements of participants and observers, together with a host of pointers, give no reason to doubt the general content of the 'Concerned Sergeant's' letter to William Westmoreland and the following passage in particular: 'Sure, there was some real big fights with a hard core unit, but *very* few . . . If I am only 10% right . . . then I am trying to tell you about 120–150 murders, or a My Lay [*sic*] each month for over a year.'[158] Only one thing in this statement is obviously wrong: Speedy Express lasted for six months, not twelve and, unlike in My Lai (4), in most cases the perpetrators probably did not come face to face with their victims but killed them from a distance – except in places like Thanh Phong – but in any case we have no knowledge of their numbers.

COVERING UP THE TRACKS

The Pentagon realised it needed to find an explanation for the weapons seized in the course of Speedy Express. According to Kevin P. Buckley's officially confirmed information, the figure was 748. At the time no other operational report had given such an absurd ratio as 748 weapons to 11,000 enemy casualties[159] – apart from My Lai (4) with a ratio of 3:128.[160] In the 9th Infantry Division files for the period before Speedy Express there was no mention of a ratio even approaching 1:15; 1:2.3 was recorded for 1966 and 1967 and 1:4.2 for the first eleven months of 1968,[161] all of which are still below the usual average statistic for other units.[162] When replying to Buckley, the press spokesman of MACV fell back on a written explanation which followed word for word 9th Infantry Division's after-action report. This said that, since many victims died during night operations and as a result of aerial attacks, their weapons could not be seized; that many Viet Cong did not carry individual weapons; that in the Mekong Delta it was particularly easy for the enemy to dispose of weapons in canals, rivers and rice paddies; that the Viet Cong is better trained in concealing than the average GI in searching out; that in heavily mined terrain in particular American soldiers could not be required to look for armaments which had been thrown away or left behind.[163] Months later Senator Jacob K. Javits was fobbed off with the same answer by an assistant defense secretary.[164] 'It takes some special kind of historical naivete and nerve to offer such comic lies as a serious rationale for our death toll,' commented Garry Wills in the *Washington Post* on 3 July 1972. 'Only one character in a Western keeps piling up a record like that –

the hired gun, the man whose motto reads "Death is my business, and business is good".'[165] Kevin Buckley had also quoted this motto in his *Newsweek* article. He had seen it painted in gigantic letters at a helicopter squadron's base.

In principle it would have been easy to raise more questions about Speedy Express on the basis of Buckley's article. How was it that the South Vietnamese Army seized ten times as many weapons?[166] Is the fact that the Americans preferred aerial combat an adequate explanation for this discrepancy? What is the relevance of talking about weapons hidden in rivers when an operation was conducted as a 'dry weather campaign' and was therefore popular with the soldiers, because most of the land was parched and even the canals often had no water in them? What sense can be made of 11,000 Viet Cong recorded as killed and only 550 taken prisoner[167] and of the fact that this ratio of 20:1 lay vastly lower than that of 9:1 or 10:1 normally claimed by 9th Infantry Division?[168] How does the number of 11,000 Viet Cong killed fit with the estimate of roughly the same number of enemy soldiers (45,000) in IV Corps Tactical Zone before and after Speedy Express, although the North Vietnamese Army had made no appreciable effort to reinforce the guerrillas with fresh troops from the North?[169] What was happening with the refugees, officially recorded as 250,000 in IV Corps Tactical Zone at the end of February 1969?[170]

In summer 1972 the public interest in further controversy over atrocities and war crimes had waned. According to the press office of the US Army Chief of Staff, eight weeks after the publication of the *Newsweek* article about Speedy Express not a single journalist had made an inquiry.[171] Even Buckley did not pursue the matter any further. 'Apparently, *Newsweek* received no derogatory letters from actual participants in SPEEDY EXPRESS since discharged from the Services,' ran an internal interim assessment from the Pentagon. 'It is surprising that the Vietnam Veterans Against the War (VVAW) has not located former 9th Div soldiers who support Buckley's conclusions with observations of their own.'[172] By the end of November 1972 the Pentagon had received seventeen requests for a reaction from Congress. 'Considering the serious nature of Buckley's charges, the number of queries and interest-level to date have been surprisingly light.'[173] Even more surprising is the information which congressmen and senators were prepared to accept. The Department of the Army maintained that they temporarily had no access to the files of 9th Infantry Division and that 'an examination of the Rules of Engagement would jeopardize continuing U.S. and Allied military operations in RVN', and lastly that the terms of a ceasefire published in October 1972 – in particular the withdrawal of American troops within sixty days – 'would greatly hinder the conduct of an investigation of the scope requested'.[174] Rarely was a policy of cover-up made so easy for the Army.

In view of the existence of the 'Concerned Sergeant's' complaints, which had been known about since 1970, this can only be called deliberately covering their tracks. Army Secretary Stanley R. Resor was informed about the complaints and asked his department's legal division for its reaction in June 1970. 'On reading this letter . . . I was impressed by its forcefulness and by the sincerity of the feelings which give rise to the author's theory of command responsibility for the body count system,' replied a senior official. Resor was also told that the anonymous GI's criticism

has a certain inescapable logic. It is common knowledge that an officer's career can be made or destroyed in Vietnam. A command tour there is much sought after and generally comes only once to an individual, who may have anywhere from six months to a year to prove himself in the 'crucible of combat'. The pressure to excel is inevitably tremendous; and it is my impression that a primary indication of such excellence has in the past been the unit's enemy body count . . . Under such circumstances . . . the pressure to kill indiscriminately, or at least to report every Vietnamese casualty as an enemy casualty, would seem to be practically irresistible.

The Army Secretary was in fact advised to commission a study and to examine possible ways and means to put a stop to the body-count excesses. Scrutiny of 9th Infantry Division was, however, not the intention; the best possible preparation for the Calley trial was far more important. 'I am convinced . . . that there is a good possibility that we are vulnerable to attack in this area, and that arguments such as those expressed in the anonymous letter may be made as part of the defense in some of the Son My court-martial cases.' Last but not least, there was a request for briefing on how to deal with the press. 'What can be done to diminish press interest in the body count as an indicia [*sic*] of our "success" in Vietnam?' The concluding recommendation was that the 'Concerned Sergeant's' letter should be filed – allegedly because it lacked details of times, places and principal participants.[175]

This last statement was plucked out of thin air. The 'Concerned Sergeant' had mentioned two units he knew about personally – 4th Battalion, 39th Infantry Regiment and 6th Battalion, 31st Infantry Regiment – and identified the officers responsible by name: Lieutenant Colonel David H. Hackworth of 4th/39th and Colonel Ira A. Hunt, commander of 1st Brigade, 9th Infantry Division. Most importantly he gave the date of one particularly brutal attack as 18 March 1969.[176] In a host of other cases – for example that of Tiger Force – vaguer references than this were enough to kick-start the Criminal Investigation Division's researches. The CID had indeed been told in August 1971 to find the 'concerned sergeant' but it is not clear whether he was actually contacted.[177] What is indisputable, however, is that in the following months investigations into Speedy Express were blocked at the highest level. 'Do not develop investigation plan at this time,' ran the concluding handwritten comment on a memorandum which went round the Investigations Division of MACV in June 1972.[178] At the end of July 1972 a note composed by employees of the Army Chief of Staff was sent to Defense Secretary Melvin Laird, reading as follows: 'An investigation in itself guarantees "news" and heightens suspicion that the military has acted improperly in SVN. Any investigative results short of admission of guilt and appropriate punitive action would probably be attacked as a whitewash . . . An investigation would be detrimental to Army morale.' Should the accusations be proved correct, 'our ability to effectively translate the findings into meaningful cleansing measures is questionable.'[179]

Lieutenant Colonel David H. Hackworth had by that time been prematurely retired. Without any mention of the 'Concerned Sergeant's' accusations, the Criminal Investigation Department and the Inspector General of MACV had assembled an eight-volume dossier which urgently called for his early discharge. According to the accusations, Hackworth had carried on currency transactions for his own advantage, involving others in his illegal dealings, promoted prostitution and gambling, smoked marijuana with officers and men under his command and secured the loyalty of his subordinates with medals they had not earned, using forged certification.[180] Evidently the Army did not want a legal investigation. An internal assessment mentioned 'persuasive indications that sufficient evidence of serious criminal misconduct by Hackworth was unlikely to be developed by the ongoing investigation.'[181] The Army preferred to come to a tacit agreement with Hackworth to their mutual advantage: he would return to private life, proceedings damaging to his reputation would be discontinued and he would be protected against any renewed examination of atrocities or war crimes, because anyone retired from the services could no longer be summoned before a military tribunal. Hackworth accepted the deal, the Army discharged him on 30 September 1971 with full honours and handed over his files to the tax authorities for further assessment. A year later Hackworth answered in his own way – with a withering article on the degenerate condition of the American Army, which he alleged was not battle-worthy, heading his suggestions for reform with the words: 'Forget Vietnam as if it were a bad dream.'[182]

On the other hand it would be over-hasty to associate our fragmentary knowledge of operations like Speedy Express only with political skulduggery in suppressing evidence. Other, no less important, factors entered into the matter, as is shown by the complaints lodged by Jeffrey Record, for example. Eighteen months after the publication of his article about helicopter terror tactics in IV Corps Tactical Zone, the Criminal Investigation Division halted its work on the pretext of 'insufficient evidence'. Apathy and delaying tactics undoubtedly went hand in hand: as the concluding report shows, precise information about those who took part in the crimes was set aside or suspects' denials were accepted as credible refutations of the charges without checking them,[183] yet even with greater effort and well-motivated investigators the researches would have turned out to be difficult. As Record rightly remarked in a hearing, no reliance could be placed on the written documentation of the operations in question. Either the filing systems of the units involved had been carelessly maintained or no transcripts whatever had been required. 'The exact location of the incident will perhaps never be known since this particular "airstrike" was not recorded in the flight log of Bac Lieu's Tactical Operations Center, even though detailed records were required of all airstrikes in Bac Lieu.'[184] This kind of thing did not only apply to IV Corps Tactical Zone or Speedy Express; one and the same conclusion can regularly be reached when looking at other war zones. The manner in which war records in Vietnam were classified, dealt with and filed away diametrically opposes any reconstruction of wartime events. The bureaucratic records accumulated no 'institutional memory' but fostered an institutionalised amnesia. The question is not whether deliberate calculation or routine carelessness predominated. We rather witness an *interplay* of calculation and routine; covering up the tracks had become an accepted custom.

'There appears to be a tendency among units to destroy records rather than to retire them in accordance with established procedures,' announced the Peers Commission.

Files transferred to records holding areas were poorly selected, poorly organized and, in some cases, inaccurately identified . . . In the records holding areas, files appear to have been consolidated in boxes without consideration as to headquarters, time, or subject matter; there was no index system or cross referencing available to facilitate the rapid identification and location of documents. In the retirement process, general lack of supervision was obvious, especially at the unit level, where apparently each unit wrote its own rules.[185]

No matter whether in daily messages, action and after-action reports, field commander reports, G-3 journals or unit histories, there are serious gaps in documentation everywhere. Haphazard record-keeping was one thing; exploiting loopholes in MACV directives another. For example, files on aerial attacks, including information on the purpose of the operation, the type and amount of ammunition used, the target area and the time of the operation only had to be kept for three months. What was done with the records thereafter was a matter of choice.[186] Ground troops were not required to file after-action reports if the participants had given provisional interim reports – so-called 'on the spot investigations'; if artillery units used 'unobserved fire' on supposedly small targets, they were not obliged to submit a supplementary account of the damage done.[187] It is therefore not very surprising that Kevin Buckley got no information when he inquired about aerial operations and Free Fire Zones during Speedy Express; however it cannot be taken as read that the answers about missing facts repeated time and again were just cheap excuses.[188] In this scenario even Lieutenant Colonel Douglas A. Huff's assertion 'that an incident of the type alleged to have occurred at My Lai could actually occur and not be recorded anywhere in the Army system' does not seem far-fetched.[189] However that may be, a working group commissioned by the Army Chief of Staff to examine the files echoed the criticism of the Peers Commission in every respect.[190]

Even the operational reports actually composed, preserved and classifiable are of only limited use, though they were set down on paper because of expectations formulated in Washington. It was known that Defense Secretary Robert McNamara only used one yardstick by which to judge society, politics and war – statistics. By them success and failure were measured and on the basis of them target guidelines were formulated. He judged his subordinates by their willingness and ability to translate problems into numbers, diagrams and visual aids. He found his soul-mates in his immediate entourage, in the young mathematicians and cybernetic whizz kids of the Herman Kahn school, but since the 1950s a training and administration orientated towards industrial management had been accepted in the military organisation as well. The operational reports from Vietnam reflect this underlying feature to the point of absurdity: the fighting strength of the Viet Cong or the number of its political leaders were specified in every imaginable order of magnitude down to the last man; the relative proportion of 'friendly' or 'hostile' villages in the entire inhabited area of South Vietnam was calculated to the second percentage point; the amount of rice seized given in pounds and grams and the number of requisitioned chickens was as painstakingly written down as the trans- action of an enormous sum of money.[191] Routine production of a pointless wilderness of data in the end added up to a reconstruction of virtual reality. 'Duplicity became so automatic,' commented one major, 'that lower headquarters began to believe the things they were forwarding to higher headquarters. It was on paper, therefore, no matter what might have actually occurred, the paper graphs and charts became the ultimate reality.'[192]

It seems that manipulated body-count statistics lay at the heart of this fictitious numbers universe. The more dead Viet Cong appeared in the books, the more favourably did Washington view the chances of victory and the better were the prospects for commanding officers and soldiers alike of leave, medals and promotion. 'In the entire year I was there, my platoon actually killed maybe five VC,' said one GI from 1st Infantry Division. 'We turned in a body-count of close to a hundred from my platoon alone. And I know the other platoons were doing the same thing.'[193] In the after-action report on one attack on the Fire Support Base Crook (Tay Ninh Province) in early June 1969, the commander of 3rd Battalion, 22nd Infantry Regiment, 25th Infantry Division reported 312 North Vietnamese soldiers killed for the loss of one GI. In fact only about thirty dead and a few wounded had been found in the combat area. 'It was later a joke throughout the division TOC [Tactical Operations Center] that the 3/22 Inf had surged forward on the body count chart.'[194] After Lieutenant General Julian J. Ewell had taken over command of II Field Force, Vietnam and with it the responsibility for 25th Infantry Division, the statistics were doctored in that division until they met the requisite monthly quota of 2,000 dead Viet Cong.[195] In other units which could not meet the inflated body-count expectations because the lack of enemy contact, there were reports of exhumations – fetching corpses from graveyards and listing them as dead Viet Cong.[196] Not for nothing was the term 'body-count fairytales' one of the terms used by American soldiers.

On the other hand, when in doubt the body count was also consciously kept low. There were repeated reports by GIs that their superiors wanted to protect themselves against critical inquiries or even investigations, particularly when there had been a large number of civilian victims or when an implausible ratio of enemies killed to weapons seized might arouse suspicion of war crimes.[197] Therefore in the case of My Lai (4) only 128 dead Viet Cong were mentioned and in many other after-action reports the standard ratio of dead enemies to weapons seized was 3:1 or 5:1 – a margin which was accepted as genuine by senior authorities. Even the reports on Speedy Express which fall outside the parameters in this respect seem to have been corrected downwards. 'Probable enemy casualties, or VC KIA (POSS),' according to an internal assessment, 'are not estimated in the 9th Infantry Division, although there is convincing evidence that actual casualties are significantly higher than body count figures.'[198] In other words, respect for the laws of warfare and the Rules of Engagement were only demonstrated by the vigour with which the documents were falsified.

It is evident that breaches of the laws governing warfare, atrocities and war crimes were not voluntarily recorded in operational reports and therefore all officers and men were obliged by MACV's Directive 20-4 to report personally any obvious or presumed infringements. At any rate, until MACV 20-4 was revised in 1970 GIs had to go through the official channels usual in other cases, their only recourse being to their immediate superior officer. If either he showed no interest or was one of the culprits or accomplices himself, any complaint was to all intents and purposes pointless.[199] Anyone who still went higher was usually rebuffed and moreover laid himself open to a suspicion of 'grassing'. In the final analysis it was those operationally responsible – from platoon leader to company commander – who controlled as they pleased how incident reports from within their jurisdiction were formulated.

In the event the superior officers made ample use of this invitation to cover things up. If a village had been burnt down for no reason, the after-action report turned the cellar where the civilians took shelter into a military bunker and the village in question into a 'fortified hamlet'.[200] If there were indications of civilian casualties, it spoke of gun-battles with snipers and victims unavoidably caught in the subsequent cross-fire.[201] When the officers of Tiger Force had to account for an exaggerated body count and explain away the lack of enemy weapons, they described the victims as unarmed Viet Cong on the way to their arms depot or said that poor visibility in the jungle was responsible for mistaken identity.[202] And so on and so forth in a string of distorted accounts and lies with countless variations but all coming to the same thing: that the culprits' stories found their way into the files unsifted and unchecked. This deplorable state of affairs had been known about for years[203] but only came into the open in the wake of the My Lai (4) scandal. Of course as a result guidelines were issued for monitoring after-action reports and new conditions given out for reporting war crimes[204] but whether in practice anything changed is doubtful. In any case these modest reforms only came into force when the ground troops withdrew from Vietnam.

In regard to your letter of 20 November 1972 we regret to tell you that we have destroyed our war crimes files in anticipation of a cease fire ... As a substantial amount of our classified files consisted of war crimes which are rarely if ever referred to in the normal course of business, permission was requested for their immediate destruction. Permission was granted on 3 Nov. 1973 [sic]. War crimes files for the years 1965 through 1971 were destroyed between 9 and 13 November 1972 ... As we have regularly sent you copies of every war crime completed by the Army, your files should not lack any information. However, the great majority of war crimes records were microfilmed by MACV History and forwarded to the U.S. Army Archives at Carlisle Barracks, Pennsylvania. Further assistance might be available from that source.[205]

From this perspective it becomes clear why even mass murder received no attention for some time, or in some circumstances is still awaiting disclosure. The My Lai (4) massacre remained undetected for fourteen months and only came up after GI Robert Ridenhour, who had second-hand information, had written dozens of letters to the White House, to ministers and to congressmen. When the inspector general went into action in spring 1969, the first likely impression was that the investigations were being deliberately sabotaged. Staff officers of 11th Light Infantry Brigade had pre-empted the investigators days before and purged the record office.[206] Retrospective destruction of files was, as soon became apparent, only a marginal problem. Those responsible for Task Force Barker had anyhow not made use of this crude cover-up in March 1968 but instead relied on the unquestioned authority of the operational commanders. 'On this operation the civilian population supporting the VC in the area numbered approximately 200,' wrote Lieutenant Colonel Frank Barker on 28 March 1968 in his combat action report for My Lai (4). 'This created a problem in population control and medical care of those civilians caught in fires of the opposing forces. However, the infantry unit on the ground and helicopters were able to assist civilians in leaving the area and in caring for and/or evacuating the wounded.'[207]

The entries in the Army Operations Center Daily Summary, the

Daily Journal of the American Division and the Daily Staff Journal of 11th Light Infantry Brigade, all composed on 16 and 17 March 1968, were also pure invention.[208] Their authors wrote in the certainty that even glaring deficiencies would not give rise to critical inquiries, and in fact nobody demanded an explanation as to why these reports mentioned 'intensive combat actions', although the troops involved had not at any time radioed in reports of enemy contact. No staff officer inquired why a unit which claimed to have come under heavy fire had omitted to call up artillery and air support, as was usual in such situations.[209] No interest was shown in the units of the fallen 'enemies'. Did they really belong to the legendary 48th Local Force Battalion of the Viet Cong? Or had the North Vietnamese sent in fresh troops? Had they been able to seize any documents which threw light on the state of the enemy forces and their future deployment? The superior authorities were as unconcerned with such questions as they were with criticising the manipulated body-count figures. As expected, the tally of 128 dead Viet Cong and a handful of weapons seized was rated a splendid success and praised personally by General William Westmoreland. In other words, the cover-up of My Lai (4) did not break with the norms of bureaucratic practice; it observed the rules of a system common to all units.

Nevertheless, in the aftermath of My Lai (4) a relatively vigorous effort had to be made to cover up the tracks, for the witness Hugh Thompson had fulfilled his duties according to service regulations and immediately reported to a senior officer. He flew back to Firebase Dottie from Quang Ngai City, where he had left a two-year-old boy rescued from the irrigation ditches of Xom Lang in medical care. He then, in the presence of several witnesses, sought out Major Frederick W. Watke, company commander of B Company (Aeroscout), 123rd Aviation Battalion, American Division around midday and described to him his experiences that morning.[210] The 'Thompson Report' left it in no doubt that there had been no fighting in Xom Lang and Binh Tay but rather that hundreds of civilians had been murdered. For his part, Watke informed Lieutenant Colonel Frank Barker and Lieutenant Colonel John L. Holladay and, together with Holladay, went to see Brigadier General George M. Young on the staff of the American Division on the following day. According to the researches of the Peers Commission, on 17 March Young informed the divisional commander,

Major General Samuel W. Koster. So within twenty-four hours five senior officers knew about the Thompson Report.[211]

The top leadership's dilemma was obvious. According to MACV Directive 20-4, they were bound to inform Headquarters in Saigon about war crimes as well as the unintentional killing of a large number of civilians. In the present case not conforming to this obligation involved a high element of risk, because Thompson could in the end have acted on his own initiative and informed MACV himself. They had no option, therefore, but to follow the agenda but it was more important to protest their ignorance. In the words of George M. Young, 'One must be aware that a war crime has been committed before it can be reported.'[212] In other words, it had to be proved that care had been taken over Thompson's statement and that there were good reasons not to take it seriously. This task was entrusted to Colonel Oran Henderson, Commander of 11th Light Infantry Brigade, Americal Division.

The Peers Commission were unable to find out what Henderson's detailed instructions were, even after a week-long interrogation, but the inferences drawn by the investigations were that Brigadier General George M. Young and Major General Samuel W. Koster called the tune and made their colleagues Watke and Holladay toe the line, although they were initially sceptical.[213] Henderson was neither to examine witnesses under oath nor produce transcripts of statements.[214] The so-called investigation came up to expectations. No item of the detailed information which Henderson had received in his conversations with Hugh Thompson and his crew was included in his final report[215] and instead he passed on Medina's lie about twenty to twenty-eight civilian victims killed in cross-fire with enemy units.[216] The 'interrogation' of thirty to forty soldiers of C Company became a farce. Having just arrived at Firebase Dottie after the end of the Pinkville operation, Henderson congratulated them on their success and asked just one question: '[Does any of you have knowledge of] anybody killing civilians during this operation?' A sergeant broke the silence with 'no comment'.[217] Henderson saluted and dismissed the group without asking any further questions. No GI from C Company was ever to see him again about this matter. 'Their appearance and demeanor were not that of men who had just killed a great many women and children,' explained Henderson some months later.[218] It is almost superfluous to mention that Henderson had no village inspections carried out in Xom Lang and Binh Tay. As his masters wished, seventy-two hours later he reported to Samuel W. Koster that the matter had been concluded. The divisional commander expressed his satisfaction in a verbal summary. 'It seems clear,' said the Peers Commission, 'that in his reports Henderson deliberately misrepresented both the scope of his investigation and the information he had obtained.'[219]

A written version of the Henderson Report was first drawn up as a result of a complaint from the South Vietnamese. In mid April 1968 the Headquarters of the American Division learned that the head of Son Tinh District, Tran Ngoc Tan, had gone to the South Vietnamese administrator of Quang Ngai Province to complain about the 'atrocious attitude' and the 'insane violence' of the American troops.[220] On the recommendation of Major General Koster, Henderson produced a two-page report of investigation on 24 April 1968, reinforcing his well-known style and adding a rebuttal implicitly directed at Hugh Thompson: 'At no time were any civilians gathered together and killed by US soldiers.' In conclusion the report quoted high-ranking South Vietnamese sources, according to whom contradictory assertions from the propaganda department of the Viet Cong had been made. 'It is recommended,' said Henderson, 'that a counter-propaganda campaign be waged against the VC in eastern Son Tinh District.'[221] The assertion which Koster made to the Peers Commission, to the effect that he had commissioned a further investigation, because he was dissatisfied with the Henderson Report, and would be able to prove that he had no knowledge of any massacre on the basis of a quantity of authenticated handwritten statements, was demonstrably a lie. The alleged researches were nowhere documented, because no one had commissioned them.[222] This revelation was the final stone in the structure of the Peers Commission's crushing findings: 'Within the American Division, at every command level from company to division, actions were taken or omitted which together effectively concealed the Son My incident.'[223]

When the official investigations into the American Division began in early summer 1969, the unit was in an advanced state of disintegration. 'There was no discipline whatsoever,' said a GI who had been posted to 3rd Platoon, C Company, 1st Battalion, 20th Infantry Regiment – that very company responsible for the My Lai (4) massacre – in April 1968. '... Everybody was doing everything individually ...

The higher commanders didn't care.'[224] Many of the men had given up on the war, drank alcohol during operations, applied for transfer, reported sick, defied marching orders or just went on 'search and evade' patrols, on which they did not go into action but spent the time in hiding. In effect, self-styled 'group leaders' had taken over command. Their superiors who wanted to do their job met at best with contempt and mockery. 'What are you doing tonight at 10 o'clock? You come by my bunk anytime, I will be ready for a blow job.'[225] In the worst case a price was put on their heads and death threats were made – against Lieutenant William Calley, among others. During an inspection Lieutenant Colonel Edwin Beers, the commander of the 1/20, found to his cost that such threats were made in earnest when shots were aimed at him and only missed him by good luck.[226] When Norman Schwarzkopf took over command of 1st Battalion, 6th Infantry Regiment, American Division in December 1969, he too found his worst fears confirmed: soldiers going out on night patrol without steel helmets, weapons or ammunition but probably carrying rusty guns, letting the Viet Cong slip past them and thus not even defending their own base camp. 'The bottom line was that they had no security. The enemy could have strolled in, opened fire, and killed dozens of men.'[227]

In actual fact that did happen, repeatedly. For example, in the early hours of the morning of 28 March 1971 forty to fifty Viet Cong stormed Fire Support Base Mary Ann, a post of 1st Battalion, 46th Infantry Regiment, 196th Light Infantry Brigade, American Division in the west of Quang Tin Province. 'The alert status of the base,' it was said in the subsequent enquiry, 'approached zero on the night in question. The defense . . . can best be described as inattentive and grossly unprepared.'[228] The few night guards were not at their posts, did not know where the ammunition supplies were kept and in case of need would certainly not have been able to make use of them, because stocks had not been replenished. The guerrillas occupied the camp undetected and within forty-five minutes had destroyed the most important installations, including the Tactical Operations Center of the 1/46. Thirty GIs were killed and eighty-two wounded. Army inspectors and the Criminal Investigation Division gave damning testimony about the officers responsible, right up to the top of the American Division – particularly because they had either ordered or allowed the bodies of five Viet Cong killed in the attack to be burnt in a rubbish pit. 'Troop indiscipline [was caused] through lack of close supervision.'[229]

'The foregoing facts point to widespread conditions among American forces in Vietnam that have only been exceeded in this century by the French Army's Nivelle mutinies of 1917 and the collapse of the Tsarist armies of Russia in 1916 and 1917,' wrote Colonel Robert D. Heinl in 1971 in the *Armed Forces Journal*.[230] The news from all parts of Vietnam gave little cause to reach any other conclusion. Well over half of the GIs returning home claimed to have used marijuana, heroin or opium in Vietnam.[231] In 1970, 60 out of 1,000 soldiers deserted from the ranks of the Marines alone, while the highest ratio in the Second World War had been 17:1,000 and in the Korean War 30:1,000. The number of Marines who deserted the flag either permanently or temporarily every day in 1971 would have made up a complete infantry battalion.[232] When Robert D. Heinl spoke of mutiny, he was mainly thinking of acts of self-destruction which had never before been known in this form in the American Army. 'Fragging' – attacks on superiors and comrades with fragmentation grenades which had a wide scatter effect – caused deaths, though how many is still unknown. The official number of attempted murders of commissioned and non-commissioned officers for 1969 stands at 126 and in 1971 333 cases were confirmed, but the actual numbers may be many times higher and includes GIs who had made themselves unpopular for one reason or another as well as hated superiors.[233]

Even more widespread and far more lasting in their effect were the violent racial confrontations. At first confined mainly to support troops, from 1969 on they occurred increasingly among soldiers on active duty. Sometimes they even affected readiness for action. In 1970, 1,060 violent quarrels between black and white soldiers were recorded in the Marine Corps files alone and there were very probably similar numbers in other units.[234] The riots in the military prisons of Long Binh and Camp Baxter, where blacks were in the majority, which broke out in August 1968 and December 1970 respectively, were only brought under control after several days. It appears they were not only in protest against the irksome prison conditions but that some of the rioters saw the time had come to give a signal to incite their comrades at the battle-front to disobey commands – among other things because they believed the Viet Cong were sympathetic to their cause.[235] 'Today's American Army is fighting its most threatening battle,' said the *Washington Post* in September 1972, 'a struggle for survival as an institution.'[236] In part the disciplinary problems were bound up with the horror and shame men felt about their own capacity for violent actions. Seymour M. Hersh made this observation for example about C Company, 1st Battalion, 20th Infantry Regiment, Americal Division. One of its soldiers wore an armband with the words 'ashamed of the Americal Murders' on it, others took every opportunity to challenge their superiors. It was said of one GI that he wanted to murder all the officers responsible for My Lai (4). 'They were uncontrollable.'[237] The actual cause of the passive and active resistance lay in the expectation of an impending withdrawal. Since the end of 1968 it was well known that the war could not be won with the means available and that Washington could not invest in any further materiel for political reasons. The GIs drew their own conclusions: 'Who the hell wants to be the last man killed in a retreat?'

The 9th Infantry Division was the first major formation to be ordered home, two months after the end of Operation Speedy Express. In August 1969 all the American combat battalions in IV Corps Tactical Zone had gone and by the end of December 1969 68,000 GIs had left Vietnam. During the following year another 140,000 left the country and on 1 December 1971 the US military presence had shrunk to 184,000 men.[238] Instead of carrying out active missions, they were mainly concerned with training and supplying Vietnamese troops. Hardly anything is known about the routines of the 'Vietnamisation of the war'. In the lists of war crimes and massacres published by the Viet Cong the South Vietnamese Army was held responsible for the majority of all such actions since mid 1969. In twenty-two attacks they had apparently acted alone and murdered thousands of civilians.[239] As similar accusations levelled at US troops could only be proved in few cases, the 'civil war' entirely escapes any critical evaluation. Here, again, it is hard to discover the truth.

8

Judges

It [My Lai (4)] was covered up because it was in the interest of the country . . . We know why it was done. These boys being killed by women carrying that stuff in their satchels . . . Let's get it out of the way.

Richard Nixon [1]

The Vietnam debate often turned into a fascination with issues that were, at best, peripheral . . . The 'Phoenix' program became a subject of attack although North Vietnamese and Viet Cong tactics were infinitely more brutal. The Mylai incident tarnished the image of the American Army that had generally – through [*sic*] not always – been compassionate in dealing with the civilian population.

Henry Kissinger [2]

Apart from the My Lai (4) massacre, the Criminal Investigation Division (CID) of the Army dealt with 244 serious contraventions of the laws of warfare up to the end of 1972; by the end of October 1971 examinations were concluded in 172 cases against 216 defendants. On the basis of their investigations the CID recommended instigating criminal proceedings against 152 GIs and officers. Eighty-four actually had to face a military tribunal, thirty of them were sentenced in the first instance, a further thirty were acquitted and twenty-four released unpunished, either because they had turned state's evidence or for other unspecified reasons.[3] The fact that forty-eight Marines were also found guilty of murder or manslaughter of Vietnamese is only mentioned here for the sake of completeness; this fact is not meaningful, because the statistics of the Naval Investigative Service (NIS) give no information on how many accusations had been made against Marines and whether the culprits had committed criminal offences during operations or in their free time.[4]

Although considerably more detailed than those of the Marines, the facts about Army personnel should also only be seen as rough indications. They relate exclusively to cases which had been reported by GIs since autumn 1969 and mostly date from the period between summer 1967 and autumn 1969. It is unclear how many further proceedings were pending and this can hardly be ascertained in retrospect, because the Army did not consistently maintain records over preliminary inquiries and criminal proceedings, nor was a corroborative central register covering the entire period of the war kept by either the Judge Advocate General – the highest judicial authority for all the armed services – or anywhere else in the Pentagon.[5] Consequently most transcripts for military tribunals, inasmuch as they were preserved, are difficult to locate. Our knowledge about the period before the My Lai (4) scandal is based on chance discoveries in the files of individual divisions or regiments. Putting together the available facts, it emerges that – with reference to all the war years – forty-seven per cent of all accused were charged before military tribunals and a mere twenty-five per cent of them sentenced in the first instance.[6]

THE LAWS OF WARFARE AND THE CULTURE OF MILITARY LAW

In principle, American troops in Vietnam were subject to the international laws of warfare – though admittedly war was never declared by either side. Whether in such a case the rules and regulations covering the conduct of land warfare apply unreservedly has been since time immemorial as contentious an issue as the status of irregular fighters: can guerrillas and insurgents, who contrary to military practices do not carry their weapons openly and cannot be identified either by uniform or rank insignia, lay claim to the protection clauses in the Hague and Geneva Conventions? From March 1966 on, however, such questions were irrelevant. By no longer defining the Vietnam War as a civil war but as an international conflict, the US political leadership also clarified this legally and entered into a commitment which was explicitly accepted by the military: in Vietnam as elsewhere, both the written and the generally respected rules on the containment of a war applied – that is, both the spirit and the letter of all commitments which had been recognised by the international community since the Hague Agreement of 1907. Every military court was constrained to reach its judgments on the basis of international law.[7]

The vetoes set out in the canon relating to the laws of warfare were crucial: the deliberate killing of civilians and prisoners of war, attacks on undefended settlements or buildings, any kind of inhuman treatment towards anyone, torture, hostage-taking, destruction without military justification, plunder, deportation for the purpose of enslaving or forcing people into military service, depriving civilians or prisoners of war from an enemy state of their rights.[8] The fact that non-combatant civilians were often victims of air attacks had no bearing on the restrictions applying to ground troops. As it states in the often-quoted formula of the Nuremberg trials of the Nazi *Einsatzgruppen*: 'The bomb falls, it is aimed at the railroad yards, houses along the tracks are hit and many of their occupants killed. But that is entirely different, both in fact and in law, from an armed force marching up to these same railroad tracks, entering those houses abutting thereon, dragging out the men, women, and children and shooting them.'[9]

Over and above this, the precepts of the laws of warfare were also accepted as binding – legal guidelines which were comparatively open to interpretation and offered more latitude for subjective discretion, but underlined in their own way that warfare was not a law-free sphere and that even exceptional circumstances could not be interpreted as legitimising arbitrary action. The best known and, at the same time, most contentious of these precepts concerns the appropriateness of means. Against the background of the trials held after 1945, it can be established in relation to Vietnam that each side in the war could claim the right to deprive the enemy of their sources of materiel reproduction. Nevertheless, not every kind of destruction of infrastructure, whether by defoliation, the poisoning of streams, or the establishment

of Free Fire Zones, could automatically be excused as 'military necessity'. In case of doubt, a commanding officer had to answer for his
decisions just as he had to answer for disproportionate deployment of
firepower against military targets in populated areas or strategically
irrelevant locations.[10] Above all, however, the precepts of the laws of
warfare were geared to a principle universally proclaimed after 1945 –
the principle of the individual responsibility of officers and men.

The principle of *'respondeat superior'* applied to officers: 'let the
superior answer' should be taken to mean 'takes responsibility' and
implies liability for any harm caused by subordinates. The prerequisites
and complications linked with this were negotiated for the first time
in the case of the Japanese General Tomoyuki Yamashita. As general
commanding 14th Army Group of the Imperial Army, Yamashita was
charged with the murder of 25,000 Filipino civilians during the capture
of Manila between October 1944 and August 1945. Having been
condemned to death by hanging by a US military judicial commission
at the beginning of December 1945, Yamashita lodged an appeal,
relating first and foremost to the fact that he had demonstrably not
been in the Philippines at the time in question. The reasons given for
rejecting his appeal entered the annals of the international laws of
warfare. According to the prosecution, Yamashita must have been well
aware of the events in the Philippines, because a quantity of people
were murdered by a very large number of perpetrators and because
the crimes were spread over a period of almost eleven months. Pleading
ignorance lacked any plausibility in concrete terms. To make allowances
for the general, it was possible that the murders might have been
committed against his specific orders. Hence the verdict did not imply
that a commanding officer can be held responsible at all times and in
all circumstances for the conduct of the troops under his command;
the decisive factor was more that Yamashita had deliberately and with
gross negligence not fulfilled his duty of supervision. In other words,
superiors are guilty in the sense of *respondeat superior* the moment they
fail to utilise means and opportunities available to them for the control
and discipline of their subordinates.[11]

The Yamashita judgment was subsequently confirmed by the US
Supreme Court and played an important role in the Nuremberg trials
of the Supreme Command of the German Armed Forces (Case 12)
and in the international military tribunal for the Far East. In Nuremberg

the criteria for the liability of superiors were more narrowly defined as follows: 'The offenses committed [by the troops] must be *patently* criminal. There must be a *personal dereliction* [of the commander] . . . amounting to a *wanton, immoral* disregard of the action of his subordinates amounting to *acquiescence*.'[12] We do not know whether Yamashita would have been found guilty if the prosecution had been obliged to prove that he had given his approval of the crimes through producing 'recognisable' information – that is, information which identified war crimes beyond all doubt.[13] On the other hand, in the Tokyo trial the range of litigable neglect was extended: even a commanding officer who had repeatedly insisted on compliance with the laws of warfare could be found guilty: '*His duty is* to take such steps and issue such orders as will prevent thereafter the commission of war crimes and *to satisfy himself that such orders are being carried out.*'[14] The fact that the litigable interpretation of these guidelines are wrangled over to this day demonstrates the complexity of the subject.[15] In this context it should be enough to say that troop commanders in Vietnam had to be prepared to be measured against the criteria of the Yamashita judgment. According to the Army Field Manual 27-10, which was binding at the time, 'the commander is also responsible if he has actual knowledge, or should have knowledge, through reports received by him or through other means, that troops or other persons subject to his control are about to commit or have committed a war crime and he fails to take necessary and reasonable steps to insure compliance with the law of war or to punish violators thereof.'[16]

Simple soldiers have repeatedly demanded a general pardon for their own conduct by referring to *respondeat superior* – in other words, claiming 'orders from a superior' or alternatively 'acting under orders'. Although in the mid nineteenth century American military and civil judges had already stressed the unlimited responsibility of the subordinate and had even spoken of a duty of disobedience in the case of illegal orders,[17] for decades GIs could be certain of immunity. There are judgments in favour dating from the time of the war in the Philippines[18] and particularly the Rules on Land Warfare issued by the US War Department in 1914: 'Individuals of the Armed Forces will *not* be punished for these offenses in case they are committed under orders or sanction of their government or commanders.'[19] Until well into the Second World War unconditional acquittals were handed down on these grounds and even the radical amendment to the US Army Field Manual dated November 1944 at first met with considerable opposition. 'Superior Orders will bar conviction,' it stated, 'if the accused did not know and could not reasonably be expected to know that the order was illegal.'[20] No institution committed to obedience can easily accept this last concept. In America the traditional obsession with command tactics made matters worse. Subordinates were drilled to keep strictly to their superiors' instructions and to forgo that freedom of interpretation which is desirable, if not essential, when the tactics of a mission call for improvisation. In such a scenario the only people tolerated are those who ask no questions.[21]

On the other hand the lasting effect of the Nuremberg Trials and in particular of the trial of the Task Forces (Case 9) must be taken into account, and with it the Latin legal maxim of *mens rea*: '*Actus non facit reum nisi mens sit rea.*' It translates – problematically – like this: in order to substantiate a responsibility punishable by law, the subjective aspect of the matter or its 'inner aspect' must be primarily appreciated, that is, the spirit of the matter, meaning an attitude of mind of which the culprit can be accused.[22] A written statement dating from 1954 clarifies the context relevant to the purpose here. In appeal proceedings the experts had to deal with a plea for clemency from a GI who had murdered a civilian in Korea and had cited orders given by his superior. Updating the Nuremberg arguments, the judges maintained that

a soldier or airman is not an automaton but a reasoning agent who is under a duty to exercise judgement in obeying the orders of a superior officer to the extent, that where such orders are manifestly beyond the scope of the issuing officer's authority and are so palpably illegal on their face that a man of ordinary sense and understanding would know them to be illegal, then the fact of obedience to the order of a superior officer will not protect a soldier for acts committed pursuant to such illegal orders.

In other words, according to criminal law only clinical unsoundness of mind can clear a defendant of guilt in the legal sense; otherwise anyone obeying an order to murder would himself face the charge of murderer: 'This is the law in regard to superior orders.'[23] This judgment also entered the Field Manual 27-10 of the US Army as a binding principle from 1956.

The adoption of the Uniform Code of Military Justice (UCMJ) in 1951 was of crucial importance for the implementation of the international laws of warfare within the American armed forces. Not only were the Rules of Land Warfare confirmed in their entirety – including the principles derived from *respondeat superior* and *mens rea* – as fundamental and compulsory basic principles for military tribunals but moreover, new principles on legal procedures were established. Up till then the American military legal system had seemed to illustrate Georges Clemenceau's famous saying, that military law is to law as military music is to music. Both internal and external observers had for decades criticised the inadequacy of legal advice and in particular the practice, which had become commonplace, of imposing different if not actually arbitrarily calculated sentences for one and the same offence. They also asserted with good reason that in such cases it was not a matter of establishing the facts and administering justice, as of rigorously enforcing discipline above all else.[24] The UCMJ put an end to all that. From then on the rules of civilian criminal proceedings applied to military ones. Defendants had the right to legal representation from the first examination to sentence, could choose between a military and civilian defending counsel and, if the sentence was dishonourable discharge or a prison sentence of a year or more, could automatically appeal. That appeal had to be determined by a Board of Review, called the Court of Military Appeals, the most senior military judge or the secretary of state for his branch of the armed services. It was also possible, however, to appeal to a civilian court. All in all, care was taken to ensure that the lawyers representing all those involved, who had up to that point only been on the periphery, now stepped into the centre of military criminal proceedings. On the basis of these guarantees of procedure alone, the UCMJ must qualify as the most enduring reform in the history of American military law.[25]

The fact that this very reform in reality went hand in hand with a devaluation of military tribunals is one of the little-noticed aspects of American military justice. While during the First World War 19 out of every 1,000 soldiers appeared each year before a General Court Martial (the authority responsible for serious criminal offences) in the 1970s there were only 2 per 1,000. Apart from an insignificant interruption in 1968 and 1969, the statistical curve fell sharply after the introduction of the UCMJ. After 1951 less than five per cent of all court martial cases were conducted by a General Court Martial, while the remaining ninety-five per cent were dealt with by Special or Summary Courts Martial, though these were only responsible for trying less serious offences.[26] As there are no grounds for suggesting that the rate of serious crimes had fallen dramatically and that consequently there was hardly any reason to convene General Courts Martial, another presumption suggests itself: serious crimes were either redefined as routine offences or in by far the majority of cases did not even come to court; however, in either case one would be looking at a deliberate blockade of the course of law.

In the event the originators of the UCMJ had made available both the means and the opportunity for their own work to be annulled, because of the traditionally strong position of commanding officers in military jurisdiction and the decision to establish their autocratic dominance in the UCMJ. The divisional commanders were investigators, prosecutors and appeal judges in their own cause. It was they who decided when and whether examinations would be instigated into whether a soldier from their unit should be accused of a war crime or exonerated in view of the special military circumstances of the operation; as the convening authority they were entrusted with choosing between a General, Special or Summary Court Martial, or abandoning a trial altogether and imposing administrative penalties instead; they appointed the judges and selected the jury; immediately after a case had finished they had the power to lower the penalty or to cancel the verdict altogether. For Telford Taylor, the prosecutor at the Nuremberg Trials, this personalisation – which flew in the face of all legitimisation through process – was simply a 'fiasco'[27] and the military lawyer Gary D. Solis spoke of an institutionalised erosion of the culture of law.[28]

Why most commanding officers used their discretionary powers to the full and called a General Court Martial only in exceptional cases would require an investigation of its own. Basic reservations concerning the international laws of warfare were perhaps the decisive factor in some cases and there are ample grounds for this suspicion,[29] but it seems that there were plenty of other possible motives, first and foremost being consideration for the Army as an institution. Granting a defendant the rights provided for in civil law was seen to enhance individuality and therefore call into question subordination, discipline and obedience, which is hard to reconcile with military values, particularly at a time of cultural and social upheaval. And not least, the clause about advocates embodied in the UCMJ aroused disapproval. The presence of civilian defence lawyers inevitably led to greater publicity concerning the proceedings and threatened both control over internal processes and the public face of the armed forces. Evidently, the more unpopular the war in Vietnam became, concern for reputation and prestige carried ever-increasing weight and officers had no interest in sitting in judgement over their own people, which would inevitably lay them open to the suspicion of having poor leadership qualities. However, there would have been no basic need for circumstances influenced by war; the causes of the obstruction had nothing to do with cases being dismissed for current political ends and point towards the will to defend itself of an institutional milieu, which rewarded those who resisted reforming initiatives.[30]

Institutional obstructiveness with regard to prosecuting crimes according to the UCMJ came to light equally clearly in another matter, namely arguments about whether soldiers could still be brought before a military court after they had been discharged from the service. This too was a legal minefield that invited contradictory interpretations. According to Articles 3a and 18 of the UCMJ, the armed forces were authorised to launch retrospective prosecutions and administer justice. By invoking this clause which had been in force since the First World War, even in the 1950s former GIs were held to account for infringements dating from their time in uniform. If they had undertaken to serve for an additional term after their standard military service or had even chosen a service career, this condition applied at any time. In fact retired soldiers had not only pension rights but also an obligation to be at the disposal of their former employer at any time – even as defendants or witnesses before a military court.[31] In arguing against this clause, critics drew attention to a nineteenth-century precedent: none of the members of the Colorado Volunteers who had slaughtered Cheyenne women and children during the Sand Creek massacre in November 1864 was ever prosecuted, because they had left the Army immediately after the event.[32]

Not even the intervention of the Supreme Court in 1955 brought any legally binding clarification. In the case of Toth vs. Quarles the Supreme Court judges upheld the habeas corpus petition of a GI

who was to be court-martialled five months after his discharge from
the Air Force for a murder committed in September 1952. The
Supreme Court rejected UCMJ Article 3a as being contrary to the
Constitution and asserted '[that] ex-servicemen, like other civilians,
are entitled to have the benefit of safeguards afforded those tried in
the regular courts authorized by Article III of the Constitution'.[33] At
first glance the official version seems unequivocal. However, Robert
W. Toth had been charged not with a war crime, but with the murder
of a South Korean civilian inside a military restricted area – and thus
with a criminal offence completely unrelated to any military operation. Consequently the Supreme Court did not mean its decision to
be regarded as a legally binding guideline for the treatment of crimes
which broke the international laws of warfare. On the other hand,
in a personal comment on the decision the presiding judge denied
the armed forces any jurisdiction over discharged soldiers, 'no matter
how intimate the connection between their offense and the concerns
of military discipline'.[34] Army legal experts were unimpressed and
continued to claim the validity of UCMJ Article 3a in the case of
serious violations of the laws of warfare.[35] Thus only one thing was
agreed: that the legislators were called upon to close a loophole in
interpretation.

In principle, Congress had two alternatives: either to endorse the
contentious UCMJ passages in their original version or to ensure, by
way of a new law, that soldiers accused of war crimes after discharge
from active service had to answer to a civilian court. In the light of
the 1949 Geneva Convention which had been ratified by the United
States, one of these alternatives would have to be decided on. The
relevant passage stated that 'Each High Contracting Party shall be
under the obligation to search for persons alleged to have committed,
or to have ordered to be committed, such grave breaches, and shall
bring such persons, regardless of their nationality, before its own
courts.'[36] In this sense and for the purposes of relieving military jurisdiction, the most senior lawyers in the US armed forces, represented
by the Judge Advocate General, had by the early 1950s already thrown
their weight behind the jurisdiction of civil courts.

Certainly the subject was not raised again for decades. The armed
forces left Toth vs. Quarles alone and politicians were clearly not interested. Senators Thomas Hennings and Sam J. Ervin, who were the

only ones working on drafts for an appropriate law and in favour of prosecuting former GIs through the civil courts, never succeeded in even having their drafts considered by the plenary Senate, their applications being repeatedly blocked by the Senate Justice Committee.[37] Not even the debate over the My Lai (4) massacre provoked any reaction. In early April 1971 a Pentagon spokesman announced that, 'after eighteen months of study, the Department of Defense and the Department of Justice have been unable to agree on a method of prosecuting former servicemen for atrocities committed in Vietnam, and that, as a practical matter, the problem is not being studied any further'.[38] With regard to My Lai (4), the consequence was that of the twenty-six members of C Company who, in the eyes of the Criminal Investigation Division and the Peers Commission and also demonstrably because of the weight of evidence against them, should have been put before a court martial, fifteen escaped the long arm of the law.[39] The custom of not prosecuting criminals who had been discharged from the Army, which Toth vs. Quarles had made the norm, was not corrected until 1996, with the passing of the War Crimes Act. Since then, such cases can be dealt with by the civil courts – with the exception of Vietnam veterans. For them and for all others who left military service before 1996, the retrospective ban applies.[40]

INVESTIGATIONS

Besides the hurdles thrown up by legal dogma and institutional obstructions, the criminal prosecution faced a further series of problems. Unlike police authorities concerned with clearing up crimes committed in civilian life, Army and Marine investigators could not as a rule rely on either forensic evidence, ballistics expertise or clues left behind at the scene of the crime – if indeed it were at all possible to establish the precise time and place of the alleged offence. Also, since military operational logs gave no reliable information about the events to be investigated, they had to look almost exclusively to the statements of participants or observers and consequently depended on the willing cooperation of individual witnesses. The results are in the transcripts: in countless interviews, those questioned either maintained that they could no longer remember anything, gave monosyllabic answers which could only be taken to mean that they were not going to provide any information, refused to make statements out of consideration for their comrades or demanded in advance complete immunity and the assurance that no proceedings would be taken against them personally.[41] Even comparatively fruitful examinations repeatedly failed to do justice to legal requirements, because either statements contradicted each other, witnesses retracted their testimony or refused to speak under oath, or it turned out that supposedly eye-witness accounts were in fact only hearsay.[42]

Summoning Vietnamese witnesses fell outside the authority of the American military. They had to rely on the cooperation of the South Vietnamese authorities, who repeatedly met such requests with a mixture of indifference, reluctance and incomprehension – or refused them, because damage to the image of their ally was seen as endangering their alliance. This last explains why, for example, political functionaries in South Vietnam and senior ARVN officers did everything they could to denounce the victims of My Lai (4) as fellow-travellers of the Viet Cong and the investigations into the massacre as a waste of time.[43] The fact that US investigators for their part treated the rural population with distrust and allowed themselves to be blinded by deep-rooted prejudices still comes out in the reports subsequently compiled. 'The people ... were filthy personally, and many were covered with scales and sores ... Considerable patience was required during the conduct of the investigation in a primitive area.'[44] 'Fear, apprehension, illiteracy, and a total lack of sophistication marked the interviewees encountered by the Special CID Team in Son My Village. The people ... were unimpressed when they were told that the CID Team had come from Washington to talk to them; their knowledge of the world in many cases did not extend as far as Quang Ngai, only 5–6 miles away.'[45] Equally counter-productive were the interview techniques which conformed to American standards. Having to recite the same story again and again, with even minimal deviations arousing the suspicion of lying, bordered on humiliation to the Vietnamese mind, as did the notion that their own credibility should depend on their ability to read a compass, identify aerial photographs or calculate time with the help of the Gregorian calendar. The differences were insuperable when Vietnamese witnesses insisted that what they had themselves experienced and what they had learnt at second-hand were of equal value. In these circumstances even those investigators who respected the mentality of a people whose culture was alien to them found their hands were tied.[46]

Last but not least, enquiries were blocked by refusals to give evidence for political and ideological reasons. After the Winter Soldiers had finished their three-day conference in early February 1971, the Criminal Investigation Division followed up forty-six of their accusations. In twenty-three cases the investigations yielded no helpful result because the veteran complainants refused to cooperate in any way with the military authorities.[47] 'It's against the policy of the Winter Soldiers to name any names of any officers or NCOs because we're trying to avoid scapegoating . . . We don't want these people to just jump on them; we want the government policy changed; we don't want them scapegoating more Calleys.'[48] – 'I wanted to indict the U.S. Army, more specifically the Pentagon . . . My sole motivation was and is to stop the atrocities . . . This can't be done by singling out a few individuals for punishment, for they are as much the victims as those they murdered.'[49] – 'If I were to testify . . . as is the desire of the Army, my testimony would not only confirm the process of scapegoating to the lowest levels of command responsibility, but would legitimate an already established policy of genocide in Viet Nam . . . It would divert attention away from those most responsible for deciding policies and direct attention towards those forced to carry out policy.'[50] A genocidal war as a reflection of a racist society, Vietnam as nemesis for 'AmeriKKKa': some of them were basically not interested in clearing matters up with legal means, and had their lawyers circulate political statements about class justice which is poisoned from its roots up or the political 'system' being corrupt. Others attached political conditions to taking the witness stand – ranging from public debate to a Congressional Committee to investigate the war as a whole. A third and final group was unwilling to give details about units and people involved for fear of affecting mobilisation: only those who could be certain of immunity from criminal prosecution would join the Winter Soldiers and their campaign against the war.

However it would be precipitate to place responsibility for failed investigations on adverse circumstances or unwilling witnesses alone.

The government turned around, the Nixon administration turned around, and in defense of what we were all saying, they said 'These guys weren't willing to come forward and give facts.' That's bullshit. They got everything except the names . . . And I told Naval Intelligence that they had access to the unit logs, they could find out who participated in the unit, . . . who was in command and who ran the operations, but that I wasn't going to help them make a scapegoat out of any more officers like they did Calley . . . They had ample opportunity to subpoena other people who were involved, and to find out whether I was lying or whether I was telling the truth.[51]

Deciding whether in this case such reproaches are really justified is impossible through examination of source material. However it is not in dispute that a great many GIs did not give the names of culprits known to them but did specify units, times and locations. The Criminal Investigation Division, on the other hand, often seemed just to be waiting for a pretext to save them having to follow up incriminating material. It was by no means the case that the investigating authorities could not have done anything because the information they had was inadequate; in many cases they did not want to take advantage of the possibilities. When in doubt, 'image-management' and public damage limitation weighed more heavily than the interests of criminal justice.

'This report is full of discrepancies and contradictions . . . If the papers got this bum report of investigation, the Army would . . . be crucified again. This indifference to individual life is intolerable. Such terms as "eligible male" are gobbledygook – but they are reflected by every "witness". The statement that the helicopter personnel asked him to show ID card but he refused is ridiculous. I could go on.'[52] This letter dated 30 October 1969 from a senior officer to the general in command of 25th Infantry Division is a rare instance of internal criticism of the CID. It concerns the crew of a UH-1 'Huey' helicopter from D Troop, 3rd Squadron, 4th Cavalry Regiment, 25th Infantry Division, who had pursued a civilian for no apparent reason, shot him dead and recorded him in their deployment report as a dead Viet Cong. As the CID investigators had clearly adopted the logic and language of the perpetrators, the divisional commander endorsed the transfer of the case to the MACV Inspector General – and invited a further cover-up in anticipation. 'IG [Inspector General] inquiry should be low key, balanced, taking into account the dynamics of the situation.'[53]

Whenever possible, the Criminal Investigation Division also endorsed the versions of events given by the accused. 'The circumstances indicated that the individuals attacked were VC, or VC supporters or sympathizers,' read a constantly recurring résumé. [54] Of one unit which, after a gun-battle, abused two dead Viet Cong by displaying their corpses on a tank, it read, 'It was noted that the actions appeared to have been motivated primarily by battle-field necessity, curiosity, and ignorance of the laws of war and applicable regulations rather than a desire to desecrate the dead. Furthermore, disciplinary action . . . would be of negligible value.' [55] Whether murder, torture or desecration of corpses was being investigated was immaterial. When it came to pleading extenuating or exculpating circumstances, the repertoire of excuses seemed inexhaustible. For example, sexual assaults committed in the course of active deployments were generally only seen as punishable on one condition: if morale or control of the unit suffered. [56] Even when victims reported rape and asked for a medical examination, they were thwarted in the face of a blanket suspicion that they were Viet Cong prostitutes. In one of these cases the CID agents did not even correctly identify the accused. In their memoranda they constantly muddled up '2nd brigade' with '2nd battalion'. [57] When investigators were meant to ascertain why children who had been looking for anything they could use in the neighbourhood of a base had had hand grenades thrown at them, the case was closed with a six-line statement: 'The children had come from a village from which hostile fire had come, and it was possible that they may be terrorists.' [58]

Whether or not serious investigations were undertaken depended on the public scandal value of a case. As is evident from the meticulous dossiers of press cuttings and letters from voters, the risk of the repercussions getting out of hand was assessed in the Pentagon from week to week – 'public affairs pitfalls', as a memorandum from the Department of the Army's press office called them. [59] When Congressman Morris Udall, who had repeatedly called for war crimes to be investigated, came forward again at the end of September 1969 to demand a statement on the murder of a deserter from the South Vietnamese Army, the Pentagon reacted immediately and tracked down those responsible. [60] On the other hand statements which were made to an ad hoc committee formed by the comparatively obscure Congressman Ronald Dellums, who was stigmatised as a left-wing deviator, got nowhere [61] – unless they found their way into the daily press or into high-circulation magazines such as *Esquire, Playboy* or *Life*. The crimes which were addressed in the wake of the My Lai (4) scandal were dealt with decisively, on occasion involving hundreds of detectives. Yet public interest had scarcely abated when things changed. Thereafter, even mass murders were dealt with in a dilatory fashion and always along the same lines: investigations were either dragged out or prematurely abandoned, the evidence of their own discoveries was devalued in the final reports or conclusive evidence was set aside.

'[He] came on very strong and very rowdy and gave me the impression that he was distinctly after me and not after the incident.'[62] This was how James D. Henry remembers the manner of an Army lawyer in Fort Hood in September 1968, when he tried to report to him the murder of over fifty civilians in the provinces of Quang Tin and Quang Nam.[63] Investigations only started eighteen months later, after Henry had given a press conference in Los Angeles and had published his experiences in the magazine *Scanlan's*. Normally it might have been possible to ignore this insignificant magazine but as this issue coincided with the imminent Calley trial its contents were explosive. If Henry was correct, My Lai (4) had to be seen in a different light – as a continuation of brutality practised for months in the northern provinces and a further example of the murderous teamwork between officers and men.

The final report which was produced in January 1974 conceded that Henry was correct in all essential points and it could have formed the basis of murder charges against nine suspects.[64] The fact that nevertheless no case was brought was due in large measure to the CID's assessment of the evidence. The battalion commander had indeed instructed his soldiers to shoot dead captured civilians if they moved. However, because the suspects had been killed for other reasons and in other circumstances, a tortuous exoneration of those in command was built up: 'If this remark was made by [the battalion commander], it does not constitute an order to kill the prisoners in the manner in which they were executed.'[65] The case of the company commander was dealt with in similar fashion: in military criminal law someone could only be held responsible if he had given an order to murder which went into detail about how to carry it out.[66] It would theoretically have been possible to demand a legal examination on the *respondeat superior* principle, but in view of the fact that all ground troops had been withdrawn from Vietnam some time before, such requests were made less than ever. 'No action was taken against any member of the unit, specifically identified, because of insufficient evidence,' stated the concluding file entry dated 21 February 1975.[67] Henry learned just as little about it as the press, which was anyhow busy with other issues.[68]

Danny S. Notley had also informed the authorities of a mass murder: the massacre of thirty civilians in Truong Khanh (2).[69] Other members of the unit claimed in their defence that they had been shot at from the village; they were presumably making use of a common ploy to justify their behaviour. According to another witness, 'As they left the village, the squad leader ordered . . . to fire over the heads of the lead element, apparently in an effort to deceive the platoon leader, who was positioned some distance away, into thinking that the patrol was being fired upon by the enemy.'[70] The Criminal Investigation Division ignored this information and spoke with certainty of the presence of enemy troops. The investigators produced as proof the Daily Staff Journal Log of the battalion in question – a written source composed by the suspects themselves. They declared that contradictions in the transcripts of a survivor's statement amounted to a refutation of the accusation – contradictions which may well have been provoked by leading questions and extreme intimidation: 'There were quite a few guerrillas, weren't there? Think about it. There were quite a few.'[71] Scant public reaction played a major role in the decision not to summon either the battalion commander or any other additional witnesses and to close the case on account of lack of evidence. Initially only the *Washington Post* had reported on Notley's public appearance and his demand that Congressman Dellums should be brought into discussions with the CID.[72] Thereafter press interest faded. In early June 1971 a memorandum mentioned the investigation's 'low priority treatment in the news media. Any statement by the Army at this time would only serve to recall the story and perhaps give it additional news mileage. As of noon today neither the DOD [Department of Defense] nor the DA [Department of the Army] has received a single press inquiry about the story.'[73]

In the case of Tiger Force there is clear evidence of deliberate sabotage by several members of the CID.[74] This death squad was investigated because in spring 1971 Gustav Apsey, the military lawyer well known for his impartiality and persistence, was not prepared to put up with the usual excuses. In view of the fact that there was no mention in Army files of any special unit called Tiger Force, it would have been easy to reject the statements by GIs Gary D. Coy and Dennis Lee Stout sight unseen. Investigations had been stopped in dozens of other cases on account of trivial discrepancies in date and location. Apsey, however, took the initial suspicions seriously – not least because they referred to a beheaded baby – and just eighteen months after Dennis Lee Stout's public appearance he made the CID take action.[75] However, he was not in control of the proceedings which dragged on until 1975. A considerable number of CID agents viewed their task as having to kowtow to conscientious objectors and anti-war protestors and consequently conducted their interviews with reluctance. They worked from a standard list of questions and only asked for comments on those assertions which came directly from Coy and Stout. They did not take up any information which might have led further, including indications of formerly unknown crimes and perpetrators.[76] Even witnesses who got tangled up in a web of contradictions or were patently lying did not have to fear being questioned any further and survivors were simply not summoned. Moreover, it is known that two agents specifically told former Tigers – among them a murder suspect – to keep quiet: 'Hey, just do me a favor. Say that you don't remember anything, so I can get the thing over with.' – 'There is a faction of CID agents . . . trying to protect you guys.'[77]

Accordingly the final report on Tiger Force produced in early 1975 contributed more to a cover-up than to clarification. The sworn statements by four GIs who had reported the murder of several peasants working in their fields were not taken into account, because the witnesses disagreed on the number of dead – grounds enough for the CID to have doubts about the crime itself. Those victims who had been killed by hand grenades thrown into their bunkers were not even mentioned. Although several Tigers had spoken of women and children, the CID described the murder victims as enemy fighters and finished with the standard formula: 'The investigations yielded insufficient evidence to prove or disprove the accusations.' Two statements originally classified as 'proved' were not even mentioned in the summary; likewise the names of five serious suspects. Who knows whether the production of the final report was deliberately delayed in the knowledge that most of the accused were about to be discharged? By the end of the investigations into eighteen alleged culprits, who were supposed to have taken part in about two dozen war crimes, only two of them were still serving in the Army – one of them a Tiger Force officer, Lieutenant James Hawkins. In the circumstances it was almost inevitable that the authorities responsible should decide not to put in motion any court-martial proceedings.[78]

Even the investigations into My Lai (4) hung by a thread for a long time. The impetus came from a soldier – Private First Class Ronald Ridenhour – who knew about the massacre only from hearsay. From December 1967 to the end of 1968 he was attached to various units of the Americal Division – partly as air gunner with a helicopter formation and partly as infantryman with a Long Range Reconnaissance Patrol (LRRP) – and had several times seen his comrades murdering civilians and prisoners of war and in one case skinning a suspect alive.[79] Since April 1968 soldiers from C Company who had meanwhile been transferred to Ridenhour's LRRP told him about My Lai (4) and their part in the bloodbath:

The people who were involved in this . . . were not just friends, but good friends. I was on deep jungle reconnaissance missions with them while I was trying to track down what happened in My Lai. Within these five- or six-man LRRP teams these were the people that, in theory at least, were ready to lay down their lives for me and I was prepared to do the same. At the same time I was tracking down the truth about My Lai, I was going to report it. It was a hard choice but I had to make the one that I had to live with.[80]

His decision was made easier when Michael Bernhardt – one of the abstainers in My Lai (4) – suggested a pact: if Ridenhour made the first move, he would also testify. Although many friends and relatives strongly advised him against it,[81] at the end of March 1969 Ridenhour sent a letter giving a thorough, detailed account of My Lai (4) to President Nixon, the chairman of the Joint Chiefs of Staff, the secretary of state and the secretary of defense, together with twenty-nine congressmen. 'I somehow feel that investigation and action by the Congress of the United States is the appropriate procedure, and as a conscientious citizen I have no desire to further besmirch the image of the American serviceman in the eyes of the world.'[82]

Mr Ron Ridenhour
1416 East Thomas Road # 104
Phoenix, Arizona
March 29, 1969

Gentlemen:

It was late in April, 1968 that I first heard of 'Pinkville' and what allegedly happened there. I received that first report with some skepticism, but in the following months I was to hear similar stories from such a wide variety of people that it became impossible for me to disbelieve that something rather dark and bloody did indeed occur sometime in March, 1968 in a village called 'Pinkville' in the Republic of Viet Nam . . .

When 'Butch' told me this I didn't quite believe that what he was telling me was true, but he assured me that it was and went on to describe what had happened. The other two companies that made up the task force cordoned off the village so that 'Charlie' Company could move through to destroy the structures and kill the inhabitants. Any villagers who ran from Charlie Company were stopped by the encircling companies. I asked 'Butch' several times if all the people were killed. He said that he thought they were, men, women and children . . .

When I arrived at 'Echo' Company, 51st Infantry (LRP) the first men I looked for were Pfc's Michael Terry and William Doherty. Both were veterans of 'Charlie' Company, 1/20 and 'Pinkville'. Instead of contradicting 'Butch' Gruver's story they corroborated it, adding some tasty tidbits of information of their own . . .

If Terry, Doherty and Gruver could be believed, then not only had 'Charlie' Company received orders to slaughter all the inhabitants of the village, but those orders had come from the commanding officer of Task Force Barker, or possibly even higher in the chain of command . . .

Exactly what did, in fact, occur in the village of 'Pinkville' in March, 1968 I do not know for <u>certain</u>, but I am convinced that it was something very black indeed. I remain irrevocably persuaded that if you and I do truly believe in the principles, of justice and the equality of every man, however humble, before the law, that form the very backbone that this country is founded on, then we must press forward a widespread and public investigation of this matter with all our combined efforts . . .

Sincerely,

/a/ Ron Ridenhour

A TRUE COPY[83]

Although initially Ronald Ridenhour did not want to go public, the Pentagon had to act. In any case, a handful of congressmen and senators had reacted to his letter, asking the military for an explanation and saying that their temporary silence would depend on the result of internal investigations.[84] Since no useful information was to be expected to come out of MACV Headquarters in Saigon,[85] the Inspector General of the Army passed the investigation over to Colonel William V. Wilson. Although Wilson had been decorated during the Second World War and later as an officer with the Green Berets, he was not familiar with the practices of criminal investigation work and so took it on reluctantly. With only a stenographer to help him, he travelled around the country for weeks, talking to Ronald Ridenhour and numerous members of Task Force Barker, including Michael Terry, Larry LaCroix, Charles Gruver, William Doherty, Ernest Medina, Hugh Thompson, Michael Bernhardt, Oran Henderson, Paul Meadlo and lastly Thomas K. Willingham, who was platoon leader of B Company in My Khe (4) on 16 March 1968.[86] 'There was no doubt in my mind that a massacre had been committed at My Lai (4),' Wilson remembered later. 'Something in me had died as I watched Meadlo regress to the revulsion . . . I had prayed to God that this thing was fiction, and I knew now it was fact.'[87]

Either Colonel Wilson still believed in the possibility of preventive damage limitation or he simply did not want to draw the obvious conclusions from what he had heard: in any event, in early August 1969 he wrote a summary to accompany the 1,000 pages of interrogation transcripts which reads like a modified extension of the prevailing cover-up. According to it, strong guerrilla units were occupying My Lai (4) and My Khe (4) and paid for their intensive resistance with the lives of 128 men. In addition Wilson embellished the supposed incident with comments which were complete figments of his imagination. In no official document of Task Force Barker was there any mention of the Viet Cong having taken up 'fighting positions' on the outskirts of My Lai (4); none of the GIs he questioned had even claimed such a thing. The same applies to his claim that an unknown number of the enemy was able to escape to safety at the end of a gun-battle lasting several hours, 'by infiltrating with civilians leaving the area or by going down into the extensive tunnel systems throughout the area'.[88] In Wilson's description the massacre by two companies sounded like a fighting deployment in the course of which one participant, namely William Calley, was out of order. Wilson adjusted conflicting statements until they were unrecognisable. Out of the wide circle of witnesses Paul Meadlo was the only one he believed. 'All testimony referring to groups being killed by LT [Lieutenant] Calley is hearsay with the exception of the testimony of Meadlo which provides an eyewitness account of LT Calley firing on one group of assembled villagers.'[89]

In mid August 1969 the Criminal Investigation Division took over the ongoing enquiry from Wilson, who was clearly not up to the job, with a so-called 'task force' of three agents[90] led by Chief Warrant Officer Andre C.R. Feher, who were to track down an entire company. From the very first day the investigators were mostly dealing with willing witnesses, amongst them GIs who had been waiting for a chance to unburden themselves about their experiences and – unlike the majority of the Winter Soldiers – harboured no reservations about the CID. 'Now I know I am going to say things against friends of mine,' said Herbert Carter, 'but this is the time for the truth.'[91] However, even this task force achieved much less than it could have done. According to the files passed on to Washington, for the most part the agents carried out their task by the book. This is the only explanation of their lack of interest in information on culprits other than Calley or of their not digging any deeper, even when a member of C Company personally confessed to murder.[92] Internal evaluations months later spoke of a 'lack of an investigative orientation' and 'myriad leads without firm direction from the task force headquarters'.[93]

On the other hand, those interviewed by the task force recorded for the tape forty-seven sworn but unsigned depositions, giving all essential information about the lead up to and the course of the My Lai (4) massacre: who committed murder, who abstained and who actively intervened.[94] But most importantly, on 25 August a clearly worried Andre C.R. Feher learnt of the existence of incontrovertible evidence when he talked to Army photographer Ronald Haeberle: 'I was the photographer on this mission and had as a camera a Leica M3 and a Nikon (personal).' – 'If I'm correct you do have about 20 color slides depicting the entire operation in question.' – 'Yes . . . And after the duplicates have been made, I will turn them over to the Government against receipt. They are my personal property. I took them with my own camera.' Haeberle also mentioned that he had shown these slides several times at presentations in Ohio. 'I estimate a total of 600 people or more has seen the slides.'[95]

This information obviously caused considerable internal anxiety. A few days later, in consultation with the Pentagon, the White House Press office prepared 'an appropriate press plan', because 'the incident will almost surely find its way into the public press' or in case congressmen went public because of the Ridenhour letter.[96] How the Department of the Army thought it could deal legally with this new situation can only be gleaned in outline from the files. It is certain that on the basis of the Wilson reports William Calley had been summoned to Washington in early June and informed that a murder charge was being drawn up against him.[97] In the first week of September the press was informed in general terms about a forthcoming court martial. It is also certain that if at all possible the intention was only to charge Calley. No embargo was placed on the discharge of any other suspects, so that most of the officers and men of C Company could count on being able to leave the service promptly and thus slip through the net of the protracted proceedings. One piece of information which the journalist Seymour M. Hersh reported still remains unproven: 'I am telling you, however, that it is my belief – there is no evidence and I am just talking about a feeling – that if Calley had copped a plea on a manslaughter charge, they would have closed the case. He was being offered a manslaughter charge in the fall of 1969, or at least that is what his lawyer Judge George Latimer told me.'[98]

If that really had been so, Hersh confounded the Army's plan. He was by no means the first reporter to be passed information about My Lai (4). Ronald Ridenhour – disappointed over the behaviour of the Army which was keeping him in the dark about the progress of the promised investigations – with the help of a middleman had approached major newspapers in Boston and New York and several leading television companies on a number of occasions, but each time had to put up with the same answer: 'What are you associating yourself with something like this for?'[99] Being fobbed off in this way was alien to Hersh. In the course of research for a book on biological warfare and as Pentagon correspondent with Associated Press he had also built up good contacts with moles in the Pentagon, who saw themselves as conservative opponents of an increasingly corrupt organisation. After one of these confidants had told Hersh about William Calley's imminent court martial and the former had satisfied himself of the substance of the accusations through laborious and painstakingly detailed work, it may have taken weeks for him to find a publisher,[100] but in view of the high profile of the newspapers which eventually published the story and the global coverage of their reports, the Army was no longer able to indulge in internal damage limitation. After 13 November 1969, when My Lai (4) first hit the headlines, all that was left to the Pentagon was to mount a positive defence.

On 26 November 1969, Secretary for the Army Stanley Resor and the Chief of Staff of the US Army, William Westmoreland, announced in a joint communiqué that the My Lai (4) investigations were being opened up. William R. Peers had been given the task of uncovering the nature and the extent of the cover-up immediately after the event. This three-star general had the reputation of subscribing to old-school conservative values; he was independent, awkward and incorruptible. Although he was not a West Point Military Academy graduate, Peers had made his way up step by step since the Second World War. He had been stationed in Burma and China as a member of the secret body OSS (Office of Strategic Services), worked for the CIA and during the 1960s been an expert adviser on counterinsurgency to the Joint Chiefs of Staff. He knew the war in Vietnam from his own experience, as in early 1967 he had been appointed to the command of 4th Infantry Division and from March 1968 to March 1969 had commanded 1st Field Force, which comprised over 50,000 troops stationed in II Corps Tactical Zone.[101] Peers's My Lai (4) team originally consisted of thirteen people, among them the lawyers Jerry Walsh and Robert MacCrate – a partner in the New York firm of Sullivan & Cromwell. Like his colleagues,

Peers was determined not to allow himself to be influenced or restricted by anyone during the investigations. The decision to include in their reconnaissance trip to Vietnam the helicopter pilot Hugh Thompson, who had taken a stand during the events at My Lai (4), also sent a symbolic message to those who had given him this commission: glossing things over was to stop.

At the same time as William Peers's appointment, the Criminal Investigation Division's task force was increased from three agents to fifteen and augmented with an administrative staff.[102] At the end of November 1969 they went to Vietnam for the first time, visited the location of the massacres, sought out survivors in refugee camps and conducted over a hundred interviews. After initial difficulties with translators, and facing resistance from South Vietnamese officials who said the murder victims had brought it on themselves, the breakthrough came. On the basis of a household count, the villagers had calculated the number of dead at 370 and a CID agent was told by two women from My Khe (4) that there had been a further massacre, committed by B Company from Task Force Barker, on the morning of 16 March 1968.[103] After Terrence Reid, a GI from B Company, had also reported on the murders in My Khe (4) in an interview with a provincial Wisconsin newspaper on 28 November 1969 and both Associated Press and the *New York Times* had published his report, the investigators really were under strong pressure. On 8 December 1969 Henry Kissinger wrote to Secretary of Defense Melvin Laird, 'The President has asked if there is any factual basis to Reid's story and if you expect similar stories to surface which have some veracity.'[104] Kissinger said to Alexander Haig, Chief of Staff at the White House, 'Al – make sure we get a reply as soon as possible.'[105] In view of the wide dissemination of the Reid interview, William Peers was instructed on 10 December 1969 to follow up the accusations.[106] Whether and how the investigations would be broadened in the light of these new discoveries was up to the leaders of the CID task force to decide.

Once he was back from Vietnam, William Peers pre-empted their decision. He put the Department of the Army under pressure by asking for a revision of his remit. In addition to the investigation into the cover-up, he also wanted to reconstruct the course of events on 16 March 1968 in all its aspects, including My Khe (4). With the agreement of Stanley Resor and William Westmoreland, Peers recruited an additional seventy people to his staff. He had a race against time to win. According to the Uniform Code of Military Justice, a case could only be laid against officers for dereliction of their duties of service and supervision if the offence in question was set out in writing and the files were presented to the prosecuting authorities for examination within a maximum of two years after the event. In this case the deadline was 15 March 1970. Crucial to Peers's progress was the fact that from that point onwards the Criminal Investigation Division no longer had the power to analyse the evidence and interviews it had collected: 118 interviews about My Lai (4) and My Khe (4) were placed at the disposal of Peers and his colleagues in the following weeks, together with a large quantity of sources taken from the archives of Americal Division and other units. In addition, the Peers Commission carried out inde-pendent interviews with suspects, witnesses and survivors. Doubtless because of the immense time pressure, many questions could not be addressed in the desired way. Nevertheless, when the several volumes of the Peers Commission's final report was completed in mid March, it was the most thorough piece of documentation ever prepared about any single war crime in Vietnam:[107] over 20,000 pages of witness state-ments and about 10,000 pages of evidence – a gold mine for historians and above all a solid foundation for bringing charges against Task Force Barker.

Had it been up to William Peers, the My Lai (4) tribunals would have taken place as a mass trial in a prominent location on the Nurem-berg model, with thirty-seven members of Task Force Barker sitting together in the dock. Peers knew that he was still groping in the dark about many things. Out of the group of senior officers alone, six of those summoned had refused to make any statement. 'There is evidence that an even larger number of witnesses either withheld information or gave false testimony,' ran Peers's summary.[108] As neither time nor resources were available for the clarification of contentious cases, Peers concentrated on those which were legally substantiated in all respects. The accused must not have left military service and each charge was to rely not on circumstantial evidence but on a large number of state-ments certified under oath.

In the case of eleven GIs Peers argued that there was a strong suspi-cion of multiple murder, one officer was accused of torture and twenty-five other officers – from two-star general to lieutenant – were to be called to account for other serious contraventions of the international laws of warfare. From among commanders and troop leaders of Task Force Barker only two names were absent: Lieutenant Colonel Frank Barker, who had died in a helicopter crash in June 1968 and Lieutenant Stephen Brooks, who had died in action shortly after My Lai (4).[109]

The decision on what measures were set in motion on contraventions of the laws of warfare normally fell to the divisional commanders of the accused. In accordance with the Uniform Code of Military Justice these generals were free to close the file on a case without involving further authorities, and either grant the person concerned exemption from punishment or impose a disciplinary penalty – a so-called 'administrative sanction' under UCMJ Article 15. The list of possible punishments ranged from written warnings – placed on personal files as 'letters of censure', 'letters of admonition' or 'letters of reprimand' – to fines and imprisonment not exceeding one month. Such administrative sanctions could have a negative effect on promotion but did not count as previous convictions in the UCMJ sense. Since the early 1950s Article 15 summary proceedings, held in camera, had virtually replaced the Summary Courts Martial – a type of court martial originally envisaged for minor or fairly serious offences.[110]

Alternatively, with recourse to UCMJ Article 32 commanding officers could call for an examination of evidence – a common, well-known practice in civilian law. However, unlike in civilian legal proceedings, the accused was permitted to be present and had the right to be defended by a lawyer, to see the evidence against him, to bring evidence in his own defence and to have witnesses for the prosecution questioned or cross-examined.[111] At the end of an Article 32 hearing a commanding officer had to decide between two alternatives: if the accused were not to be let off unpunished, he could abandon the investigations and impose a disciplinary penalty at his own discretion, or he could pass the case on to be dealt with by a military tribunal and await the decision of the jury – whilst retaining his right of appeal against the judgment at any time.

Deviating from normal practice, the divisional commanders of the accused were not entrusted with legal supervision of the proceedings relating to My Lai (4); instead this fell to Lieutenant General Jonathan O. Seaman, General Commanding, 1st US Army, Lieutenant General

Albert O. Connor, Commander of 3rd US Army and Major General Orwin C. Talbott, head of the Fort Benning training camp. Seaman was responsible for the officers accused, Connor for non-commissioned officers and other ranks and Talbott was initially responsible for William Calley, who had been ordered back to Fort Benning.

Of the thirty-seven cases which William Peers had strongly recommended to be brought before a court martial, it was accepted that twenty-five should be taken further. The reason for twelve suspects – all officers – being excluded from the outset, and whether Seaman, Connor and Talbott were involved in this decision, cannot be found in the files. In spring 1970 the following cases were waiting to be decided on:

- Eleven members of Task Force Barker were suspected of several instances of murder and physical assault with intent to murder: William Calley, Ernest Medina, David Mitchell, Charles Hutto, Esequiel Torres, Kenneth Schiel, William F. Doherty, Robert W. T'Souvas, Gerald Smith, Max Hutson and Kenneth Hodges.[112]
- Captain Eugene Kotouc was suspected of torture. The Peers Commission considered it proven that, hours after the My Lai (4) massacre, he cut off the finger of a prisoner during interrogation and incited members of the South Vietnamese security police to shoot two prisoners dead. Kotouc himself disputed the charge of complicity to murder but admitted the mutilation.[113]
- Against thirteen officers accusations were brought on the *respondeat superior* principle, following to the letter the Uniform Code of Military Justice: contravention of the laws of warfare, disregard of the Rules of Engagement applicable to Vietnam, dereliction of their duty of supervision, the subsequent covering up of a war crime and perjury. Some of the officers were charged with multiple offences in concomitance. In the case of Colonel Robert P. Luper, Major Charles C. Calhoun and Captain Dennis H. Johnson the central matter was deliberately ignoring the Rules of Engagement.[114] Those primarily accused of contraventions against MACV Directive 20-4, which makes it an obligation to report a war crime immediately, and of a concerted cover-up were: Major General Samuel Koster, Brigade General George H. Young, Jr., Colonel Nels A. Parson, Lieutenant Colonel David C. Gavin, Lieutenant Colonel William D.

Guinn, Major Robert W. McKnight, Major Frederick W. Watke, Captain Kenneth W. Boatman and Colonel Oran Henderson.[115] Lieutenant Thomas Willingham was under suspicion of having issued unlawful orders during the operation in My Khe (4).

Jonathan O. Seaman, Albert O. Connor and Orwin C. Talbott made their rulings between June 1970 and July 1971 as follows:

- In the case of nine of the accused they exercised their right not to open proceedings and instead to decide at their own discretion whether and how they should be punished: the officers Luper, McKnight, Boatman, Gavin, Guinn and Willingham were released without reservation. Their colleagues received written warnings as follows: Young (letter of censure), Parson (letter of censure) and Calhoun (letter of reprimand).[116] The reason alleged for this was insufficient proof. One searches the files in vain for any balanced analysis of the findings resulting from its investigations put forward by the Peers Commission.
- Sixteen times Article 32 hearings were called but in ten instances further investigations were stopped after final reports were received – again with the standard reference to supposedly unconvincing incriminating evidence. Frederick W. Watke was confirmed as having behaved in all respects in accordance with the law, Dennis H. Johnson received a letter of reprimand and Samuel Koster – by then superintendent of the West Point Military Academy – a letter of censure.[117] consequently even those GIs suspected of several murders – Torres, Schiel, Doherty, Hutson, Smith, T'Souvas and Hodges – could only be given administrative penalties. Based on the relevant recommendation from the Judge Advocate General, they were discharged from the Army and permanently exempted from recall.[118]
- In accordance with the results of the Article 32 investigations, six suspects were to answer to a General Court Martial: Henderson, Kotouc, Medina, Mitchell, Hutto and Calley.

William Peers had good reason to talk about 'a horrible thing'.[119] Taking as a benchmark the legal assessments of the recommendations of the Peers Commission, which were drawn up by various military lawyers – some on the staff of 1st and 3rd US Army, some on that of the Judge Advocate General – the evidence against Seaman and Connor offered no justification for terminating the proceedings prematurely. As in the case of Oran Henderson and Eugene Kotouc, not a single charge against twelve other officers was cleared up. Like Medina, Mitchell, Hutto and Calley, six other members of Task Force Barker were also strongly suspected of murder: Esequiel Torres in between six and fifteen instances, Kenneth Schiel and William F. Doherty in a countless number of instances, Robert W. T'Souvas in two, Gerald Smith in at least seven and Max Hutson in ten.[120]

Only the charges set out against Kenneth Hodges raised doubts about legally pursuing his case: in the course of the Article 32 examination several witnesses had revised or even completely retracted their original statements implying murder. So far as the charge of sexual violence was concerned, Hodges, like most of the suspected rapists, benefited from the fact that victims had not brought charges and that military lawyers were inclined to redefine rape as a 'sexual frolic' or 'kicking over the traces'. 'He [the witness] testified that he . . . saw SSG [Special Sergeant] Hodges on top of the girl. SSG Hodges . . . was moving in an up-and-down manner normally associated with sexual intercourse. He [the witness] did not see SSG Hodges' private parts and could not tell whether any penetration had been made.'[121] Faced with the choice of believing a statement claiming that the victim lashed out and screamed or of taking at face value the insinuation that the woman was enjoying an orgy with three men, the experts plumped for the latter.[122] Even if one chooses to regard Hodges's case as exceptional, the issue remains that the guilt or innocence of not just six but twenty-four of the total twenty-five accused should have been dealt with by a court martial.

Granting procedural privileges to commanding generals proved to be a serious obstacle to the administration of justice, particularly in the case of My Lai (4). Originally envisaged as a counterweight to the unlawful interference of politicians and bureaucrats, it encouraged the blocking of legal processes on another level – a 'reverse command influence' as it was euphemistically called in the internal jargon of the armed forces. Since there was no possibility of an internal review, one could even regard it as overextending individual discretionary powers, or even offering an opportunity for subjective, arbitrary actions.

TRIALS

Although Jonathan Seaman and Albert Connor acted up to the very limit of their authority, it would be wrong to hold them solely responsible for the crimes committed in My Lai (4) effectively going unpunished. The available sources certainly provide no proof that they had personally been put under pressure; however, there is no doubt that the prevailing political and professional environment facilitated or suggested their decision; that is, that politicians, senior officers and bureaucrats wanted to put My Lai (4) behind them as quickly as possible and to this end urged legal minimalism. The early decision of the Pentagon not to conduct a mass trial based on the Nuremberg model was made on this basis and there is a great deal of further evidence for the contemporary criticism summed up by independent observers in one catchphrase: 'Politics reigns.'[123]

Ever since autumn 1969 there was talk in the Pentagon about military tribunals possibly having a negative influence on the Paris peace negotiations and manipulating the domestic political climate in favour of the anti-war activists.[124] Out of choice, top priority was given to the working atmosphere within the armed forces and in particular to protecting its officer elite from negative publicity. 'Serious considerations must be given to needs of the Army as an institution . . . That factor played an important part in the decision to start full investigation after the Ridenhour letter and to form the Peers–MacCrate Inquiry,' noted an Army Department file dated 10 January 1970, weeks before the Peers investigation was concluded.

However, SA [Secretary of the Army] feels that whatever short-term public relations benefits might follow from punitive action against commanding officers would be outweighed in the long run by the corrosive effect of such action upon the Army interest in its reputation for dealing fairly and justly with individual members. The SA concludes that the actions at My Lai are isolated; forces in Vietnam operate under detailed directives prohibiting killing or mistreating prisoners or civilians.[125]

The Chief of Staff of the Army introduced another argument: one neither could nor should bow before critics like Telford Taylor or their

demand for unrelenting military justice. In response to Taylor's book
Nuremberg and Vietnam General Westmoreland therefore commissioned
a study with a conclusion formulated a priori:

Since Taylor has also questioned the effectiveness of U.S. control of combat
operations, the Task Force <u>must establish</u> the fact of such control beyond
any doubt . . . The Task Force <u>must establish</u> that criminal or inhumane
behavior in combat in Vietnam, has been, in fact, so rare that it merits specific
attention in each instance of a reported or suspected violation . . . Thesis of
the project is to show that never in the history of warfare has a war been
fought with more concern for civilians and humane treatment of noncombatants than the counterinsurgency waged by U.S. Forces in RVN.[126]

'Dirty tricks – not too high level; discredit one witness, get out facts
on Hue; admin line – may have to use a senator or two, so don't go
off in different directions; keep working on the problem.'[127] These
notes on a conversation with Richard Nixon on 1 December 1969 were
written by Presidential Advisor Harry R. Haldeman. They are among
the few papers in the archives to throw light on the relevant discussions
in the White House and they show a President with a premonition
that My Lai (4) represented a direct threat to his entire Vietnam policy.
Nixon's fear was that if the opposition were able to make capital out
of the case and stir up further support for an unconditional withdrawal,
his medium-term calculations would be thrown into the melting-pot
– that is, his resolve to escalate the war despite the withdrawal of
ground troops (which had already started) and to force Hanoi into
submission within a year by means of extensive air strikes.[128] Scarcely
anything was missing from the repertoire of the propaganda counter-
offensive. Nixon repeatedly demanded an attack against media he
disliked; he tried to threaten with cartel law and the tax authorities
the 'dirty rotten Jews in New York'[129] – as he called the publishers and
chief editors of the *New York Times* and others he suspected were
behind the reporting on My Lai (4); he demanded inquiries into Ronald
Ridenhour and covert surveillance of Seymour M. Hersh by agents of
the National Security Agency.[130] Nixon evidently feared that not
just the C Company murderers but the whole Vietnam policy of his
government would be on trial. If circumstances demanded it, Henry
Kissinger agreed, 'we should execute a program . . . which could not

be attributable to the White House'.[131] Even if a covertly orchestrated intervention in the court-martial proceedings still cannot be proved, such a measure would fit neatly into the catalogue of 'dirty tricks'.

William Peers was soon to discover how the My Lai (4) investigations were being politically manipulated when he presented his concluding report in public on 17 March 1970. On that day 225 pages were made available to the press, about one-tenth of the complete report. Despite Peers's vehement disagreement, Secretary of the Army Stanley Resor and a major general responsible for public relations first of all imposed a new ruling: the term 'massacre' was replaced with 'major tragedy'; 'victims amongst non-combatants' replaced the reference to murdered women, children, babies and old people; rapes became 'sexual molestations'. Apart from these semantic adjustments, the relevant authorities in the Pentagon also insisted on a complete cover-up of the My Khe (4) massacre. Reporters wanted to know whether the rumours about a second mass murder were true, going back to the statements made months before by Terrence Reid. The Pentagon spokesmen did not repudiate the suspicion, following Westmoreland's line that the events of 16 March 1968 were a one-off deviation from the broad path of a properly conducted war; they shifted the blame for the murders at My Khe (4) onto a South Vietnamese unit. Just hours before William Peers had tried to object to this deliberate attempt to confuse and wanted to withdraw from taking part in the press conference. It is not clear why he nevertheless gave way. Presumably he did not want to play into the hands of those who were hoping anyway that he would voluntarily withdraw – unidentified leading figures in the Pentagon who, according to Peers, had been determined to put the kibosh on all trials, including the Calley court martial.[132]

In such a scenario ample grounds therefore exist for assuming that at least in the case of My Khe (4) direct influence was exerted on the decisions of Jonathan Seaman and Albert Connor and that there was external pressure to close the Thomas Willingham file. At the time of the press conference the charges made against the platoon leader of B Company, Task Force Barker, which was deployed in My Khe (4), had by no means been cleared up – quite the reverse. A memorandum dated 11 March 1970 and produced by lawyers who had examined the Peers Report at the behest of the Judge Advocate General states: 'Evidence indicated that Cpt Willingham's platoon killed 15 to 90 civilian inhabitants of My Khe (4) on 16 March 1968. Witnesses indicated the dead were mostly women and children . . . That Cpt Willingham was aware of felonies committed by soldiers under his command and attempted to conceal these by submitting false reports to his commanding officer is indicated by the available evidence.'[133] The head of the Criminal Investigation Division, Colonel Henry Tufts, had made a similar comment on 12 February 1970 and together with the Provost Marshal General – the most senior authority responsible for disciplinary measures – had demanded that the scope of the investigations be broadened.[134] Some files suggest that this led to internal controversy. Colonel Tufts was informed by the Headquarters of the US Army, Vietnam: 'Note: The "innocent" civilians [at My Khe (4)] were violating RVN law by living with the VC. Differentiation between "innocent" civilians and VC was therefore purely academic.'[135] Months later a dossier on the Thomas Willingham case was drawn up in a similar vein by the Pentagon's legal department: 'It would not comport with reality to limit "Viet Cong" to only males of military age. There is ample evidence that Viet Cong combatants could include women, and possibly children. Thus, it would be difficult to conclude that CPT Willingham knew that all 38 Vietnamese he reported as Viet Cong were in fact noncombatants.'[136] It can no longer be established from the files available which individuals took part in the discussion nor how the debate was conducted; however, one is struck by the speed with which Seaman and Connor hastened to exonerate Thomas Willingham. While no evidence in his favour had been produced in the interim, all charges against him were lifted on 8 June 1970. Seaman and Connor had even dispensed with a presentation of evidence in accordance with UCMJ Article 32.[137]

It is also worth mentioning that the Pentagon meanwhile resorted to a policy of waiting on events and of 'dirty tricks'. These involved publicly discrediting Seymour M. Hersh and Richard Hammer who had produced the first books on the massacre of 16 March 1968 in spring 1970: 'As with the Hersh book, we are pointing out privately to interested correspondents and writers some of the weaknesses and inaccuracies . . . In Hammers's case, I am searching out the people in control of the publishing firm and . . . we will point out privately the terrible inaccuracies and provable distortions in the hope that we can further damage Hammer's not-so-good reputation.'[138] Whatever they achieved by this, delaying tactics were always the key to the cover-up of My Khe (4). On the one hand the combined silence of the suspected perpetrators could be relied upon: of the forty people interviewed up to April 1970, nearly thirty claimed not to have seen or heard anything. Not even Terrence Reid wanted to give any further information: 'The guilt, I believe, is not with them alone but with the people who helped train their minds with regard to the invincibility of one's race, color and creed.'[139] As long as people were prepared to accept this refusal to give evidence and to forgo the examination of further South Vietnamese witnesses there was nothing to fear – especially as Hersh was still groping in the dark. According to an internal memorandum dated 20 April 1970: 'Analysis of the content of the article reveals that Mr Hersh's knowledge is apparently confined to the events which occurred in My Lai (4) on 16 March 1968. No mention is made of the events of B Company 4/3 Inf or of the actions by commanders or staff officers. It would appear that Mr Hersh does not possess any substantive information concerning the suppression or cover-up aspects of the Son My incident . . . The need to terminate . . . assistance to Mr Hersh becomes increasingly important when consideration is given to the use Mr Hersh would make of any information he obtained concerning command reaction and efforts of suppression relating to the Son My incident.'[140] A dossier of 8 July 1971 drawn up by General Westmoreland's staff reads: 'LTG [Lieutenant General] Kervin indicated that we have no basis at this time to reopen this phase of the investigation of the My Lai Incident, and Hersh must come up with any new evidence before it would be appropriate to do so . . . Concluding guidance: . . . OSA [Office of the Secretary of the Army] may want to inform OSD [Office of the Secretary of Defense] and the White House on this matter.'[141] Seen in this light, Hersh's suggestion that the investigations into My Khe (4) fell victim to a concerted intervention by the military leadership and the White House[142] is not so much speculation as well-grounded suspicion.

With this the legal chapter on My Lai (4) neared its end. On 5 June 1972 Seymour Hersh reported for the first time on My Khe (4) on the basis of unpublished parts of the Peers Report which had been leaked to him by a confidant in the Pentagon.[143] In contrast to November 1969, there was no public reaction and anyway the Army only had limited public relations damage to fear by this time; opening a trial was out of the question, since all those in B Company who were involved had already left the service.[144] The six pending courts martial – against Oran Henderson, Eugene Kotouc, Ernest Medina, David Mitchell, Charles Hutto and William Calley – were also long since finished: Henderson, Kotouc, Medina and Mitchell had been acquitted without a stain on their honour and Hutto had been dishonourably discharged.

The only person who had to pay the price was William Calley, albeit not behind prison bars. Hours after he was sentenced to life imprisonment on 31 March 1971 – on the grounds of deliberate murder in no less than twenty-two cases and one assault with intent to murder – President Nixon decreed that Calley could spend the time under house arrest until the appeal lodged by the defence was concluded. Besides, Nixon said, he would personally take charge of the case and make the final decision.[145] This intervention of politics in the judicial process, which contravened both the spirit and the letter of the separation of powers though it was only mildly criticised in public,[146] set out in advance the course of future decisions. Just five months later Albert Connor revoked the original judgment and imposed a sentence of twenty years' imprisonment with hard labour, which was upheld by the Court of Military Appeals in December 1973. In mid April 1974 the Secretary of the Army reduced the sentence to ten years and at the end of September a civilian court in Columbus, Georgia ordered Calley to be released under caution – on account of the 'unfairness' of the court-martial proceedings. Judge Robert Elliott said, 'Keep in mind that war is war and it is not at all unusual for innocent civilians to be numbered among its victims. It has been so throughout recorded history. It was so when Joshua took Jericho in ancient Biblical times . . . Now Joshua did not have charges brought against him for the slaughter of the civilian population of Jericho. But then "the Lord was with Joshua" we are told.'[147] Secretary of the Army Howard H. Callaway protested against the intervention of a civilian judge: 'We in the military take the normal view that we would like to control our own discipline through the UCMJ .'[148] However, Callaway raised no objections on this point and acceded to Calley's plea for clemency in November 1974. After forty-four months of house arrest, the mass murderer of My Lai (4) was once again a free man.[149]

On the one hand the My Lai (4) investigations are exceptional, in that only twenty-five per cent of those accused were brought before a court martial – significantly less than the statistical average of forty-seven per cent. Just one defendant in every six was convicted, whereas the long-standing average was one conviction for every four defendants. Regardless of this, the legal handling of My Lai (4) should be seen as pars pro toto for military jurisdiction at the time of the Vietnam War. This is based on three observations:

Firstly, commanding generals made constant and far-ranging use of their right to prevent a charge being laid at all or to bring proceedings to a premature close by imposing administrative penalties. This may be illustrated by some cases which were investigated by the Criminal Investigation Division at considerable expense and which have already been discussed in another context – examples from an airborne brigade, an infantry unit and a helicopter formation. Out of twenty-nine elite soldiers from 173rd Airborne Brigade (Separate) who were strongly suspected of torture, fifteen had admitted their crimes but only the four prime suspects were punished – one with a verbal and three with written cautions. A fifth appealed and escaped without any penalty whatsoever.[150] Article 32 proceedings were in fact started against a soldier from 196th Light Infantry Brigade, Americal Division, who was suspected of taking part in the murder of twelve people, but after eight weeks they were stopped again despite the lack of defence evidence – on condition of a dishonourable discharge from the Army.[151] Even the helicopter pilots who had indiscriminately murdered dozens of peasants in Binh Long and Quang Tin Provinces during 1969 got away with warnings.[152] Because the files repeatedly throw up similar occurrences over and above these arbitrarily chosen examples, it may be said with good reason that even in the face of the most serious violations of the laws of warfare – the so-called 'grave breaches' – commanding officers refrained from starting criminal proceedings against the majority of suspects. It can be presumed from the available, albeit incomplete, data that just over half of those accused were exonerated in this way – and it cannot be ruled out that the actual numbers were possibly much higher.

Secondly, instances of manipulation of the criminal justice process were by no means limited to My Khe (4). Solving the murders committed by the Green Berets and Tiger Force was also blocked at the instigation of the highest authorities. Presidential Advisor

Haldeman's diary reveals that in late summer 1969 – when they already knew about the massacre perpetrated by Task Force Barker – Richard Nixon and Henry Kissinger insisted that the pending trial of eight soldiers from the Green Berets and one CIA employee should be cancelled.[153] According to the results of an investigation ordered by MACV, the accused had executed a South Vietnamese double agent and thrown the corpse into Nha Trang Bay for the sharks to eat. Despite – or because of – the widespread publicity about the case, Secretary of the Army Stanley Resor decreed at the end of September 1969 that proceedings should be abandoned.[154] The role played by President Nixon in the cover-up of the Tiger Force crimes[155] is not clear. For two years – from 1971 to 1973 – the White House received weekly summaries on the progress of all investigations into war crimes, among them ten dossiers on the death squad Tiger Force, and the final report which came out in 1973 was sent directly to the offices of the secretary of state for defense and the secretary of the Army. It is possible that they urged for the matter to be put right.[156] If not, senior Pentagon officials took matters into their own hands in 1973, by summoning a former platoon leader of Tiger Force, the regular officer Lieutenant James Hawkins, and informing him in confidence that he would not have to face trial.[157] It seems that in other proceedings witnesses were heavily pressed to retract their former statements[158] and investigating officers were threatened with a premature end to their careers.[159] The official military files leave no clues about the number and the effect of such interventions.

Thirdly, exceptionally lenient sentences were passed in courts martial. Soldiers who had been found guilty of murder, manslaughter and rape in Vietnam received notably smaller sentences than their comrades charged with the same crimes elsewhere. In Europe or the United States an average sentence for murder was twenty-nine years, whereas in Vietnam it was sixteen years. The prison sentence for the manslaughter of Vietnamese people was usually reduced by almost a quarter – ten instead of thirteen years.[160] The fact that a notoriously violent criminal like Sergeant Roy E. Bumgarner, found guilty of triple murder beyond doubt, was merely demoted by one rank, made to pay a fine of 600 dollars and then allowed to serve for a further twelve months in Vietnam,[161] might at first glance seem an extreme example – were there not countless other cases like his.[162] Severe sentences were also doubtless imposed. The rapists and murderers of the young girl Phan Thi Mao were sentenced to life, fifteen, ten and eight years imprisonment;[163] the Marines who took part in the attack on the village of Xuan Ngoc in September 1966 were given prison sentences of several years, including one life sentence,[164] and two defendants found guilty of the massacre at Son Thang were sentenced respectively to life and five years in prison.[165] Whatever sentences were imposed by courts of first instance, in the mandatory appeal proceedings laid down by the Uniform Code of Military Justice they were regularly adjusted downwards, if not revoked altogether, with the result that most of the culprits sentenced to terms of imprisonment generally only served a few months and lifers a maximum of seven years.[166] The indication that even civilian courts in the 1960s and 1970s were committed to a generous interpretation of the law and pardoned criminals prematurely is not without foundation,[167] but this misses the central point – or, more precisely, the fact that in by far the majority of cases protection of the culprits was carried to the limit.

Why that was so cannot be answered as precisely as one might wish in view of the inadequacy of the existing court files. However on the basis of well-documented individual cases it is possible to describe the technical, staffing and ideological backgrounds which in themselves or where they coincided gave an unmistakable profile to the current military jurisdiction.

Trials which were held in Vietnam itself took place in extremely poor material circumstances. The military lawyer Gary D. Solis, who was appointed Chief Prosecutor in 450 cases by 1st and 3rd Marine Divisions, pointed out that as a rule prosecutors were thrown back on their own resources, were not provided with the requisite technical equipment nor could rely on being given any assistance. On occasion they had to hitch-hike to their hearings because no one was responsible for providing them with transport. Under such conditions the idea of examining crime scenes or interviewing Vietnamese witnesses was virtually unthinkable. 'Even the production of Marine witnesses was problematic – they were often transferred, wounded, or killed before trial, and there is no provision in the UCMJ for such occurrences. A missing crucial witness simply meant a failed defense or prosecution.'[168] Solis was unable to say how many acquittals were obtained because the units concerned did not produce any of the documents necessary for the presentation of evidence, because the electricity supply to the court was cut off during the session or the equipment necessary for making transcripts went wrong for some other reason. Such things probably happened regularly, however, and countless observers rightly estimated that the harm caused by the trials was considerably greater than their effectiveness. 'It's totally unworkable in a combat environment.'[169]

Apart from unfortunate technical mishaps, the staffing policy at the Pentagon had considerable influence on the preparation and implementation of military tribunals. Three-quarters of the lawyers dispatched to Vietnam were fresh from university and at best they had learnt about murder trials from textbooks; only a minority had specialised in the international laws of warfare or received appropriate training in preparation for this job. Solis writes, 'Its cost was measured in failed prosecutions and unpunished criminality,'[170] even in the case of the proceedings against the Son Thang murderers which had been scheduled to take place in I Corps Tactical Zone in summer 1970 and was frequently described as a test case.[171] In this case the evidence was clear: the Marines had not been fired on by enemy units nor could they find other excuses for the slaughter of sixteen people, among them babies and a young blind woman. Although the judge called for the maximum punishment prescribed in the indictment and instructed the jury accordingly, two out of the four accused left the court as free men. They had been defended by experienced civil lawyers who made maximum capital out of the technical mistakes of the prosecutors – for example in instructing state witnesses – and won the acquittals on the grounds of legally unacceptable shortcomings in procedure.[172] The fact that the very same defence counsel drew their fees from citizens' action groups, and saw themselves as political attorneys in the service of an ideological war against the supposedly arbitrary justice of the armed forces, had nothing to do with it, at least in the eyes of the jury. They had allowed themselves – as some of their number admitted – to be dazzled from day one by the commanding and unyielding manner of the professional counsel.[173] As one general assigned to observe the Song Thang case put it, 'If you want to beat the court-martial, get yourself a prestigious, high-pressure civilian and he'll tie the young judge advocate captains into knots.'[174]

However, the culprits benefited above all from the contempt for the international laws of warfare. Whether proceedings were held in

Vietnam or at bases in the USA, one continually comes across judges and jurors who acted demonstrably against the letter and the spirit of the Uniform Code of Military Justice. Solis quotes a juror who had to reach a verdict on rapists as saying: 'We're not going to ruin the lives of these young Marines for some Vietnamese.'[175] The so-called 'jury nullification' allowed jurors to put their subjective feelings above the law and even to release convicted defendants. It is uncertain how often this privilege was exercised; however during long years of practising in court Solis had experienced it many times – even in the case of judges themselves: 'More often than one would care to acknowledge, when the victims were Vietnamese, courts-martial acquitted or imposed light sentences out of sympathy for the frustrations experienced by the infantryman dealing with a hostile indigenous population.'[176] It is an open question how often racist motives were a decisive factor – the proverbial 'mere gook rule'. In fact, one could even do without them. The killing-field bonus was justification enough at any time – independent of the type and severity of the offence and irrespective of whether the accused had been guilty in the course of an operation or outside the battlefield.

The example of the cases against officers Eugene Kotouc and Ernest Medina reinforces the impression that the presiding judges had been intent on a symbolic refutation of the letter and spirit of the laws of warfare. In both cases they made use of the so-called 'jury instruction' – judicial directions on the legal position, to which the jurors had to adhere when giving their verdict – crucial guidelines which could be challenged by neither the prosecution nor the defence. Although the 'jury instructions' had no binding effect beyond the trial in question, they nevertheless gave out a signal, especially since the jurisdiction in the general courts martial concerning Task Force Barker and the My Lai (4) massacre had a strong public impact .

The Uniform Code of Military Justice and the Geneva Convention would have had to apply to Eugene Kotouc, who was convicted on witness statements and his own admission of the torture and physical mutilation of a prisoner. Article 17 of the Geneva Convention left no latitude for leniency towards culprits: 'No physical or mental torture, nor any other form of coercion, may be inflicted on prisoners of war to secure from them information of any kind whatever. Prisoners of war who refuse to answer may not be threatened, insulted, or exposed

to unpleasant or disadvantageous treatment of any kind.'[177] Yet the
judge instructed the jury not to reach a verdict in accordance with the
national and international laws of warfare but instead to take as a
guiding principle a handbook of the American Army, the Field Manual
30-15 on Intelligence Interrogation,[178] which contravened law and
statute:

I advise you that regulations and directives of the United States Army with
respect to intelligence interrogation in force at the time of the alleged incident
could well have led Captain Kotouc to believe it was lawful for him to use
harsh and abusive language toward the victim and to threaten violence in an
attempt to get information . . . Therefore, in this case I instruct you that if
you find Captain Kotouc was merely offering to do violence to the alleged
victim such an act by Captain Kotouc would be legally justified in this case.[179]

The fact that the accused had cut off his victim's finger was of no
more importance to the jury's decision. On 29 April 1971 Eugene
Kotouc was released.

In the trial of Ernest Medina the judge had to decide whether and
in what way the legal principle of *respondeat superior* should apply or,
to be more precise, whether Medina was guilty of the 'involuntary
manslaughter' of one hundred civilians, because he had neglected his
duty of supervision over C Company, Task Force Barker, in a criminal
and punishable manner. The prosecutors had asserted that Medina
was in constant radio contact with his unit, that he was aware of the
absence of enemy troops and that he knew, or must have known,
about the mass murder of civilians at an early stage. Reference was
therefore made to paragraph 501, US Army Field Manual 27-10 and the
clause on culpability embodied in it: 'The commander is also responsible if he has actual knowledge, *or should have knowledge* . . . that troops
or other persons subject to his control are about to commit or have
committed a war crime.'[180] In his 'jury instruction' Judge Kenneth A.
Howard gave this legally binding guideline in an abbreviated and
misleading manner: he instructed the jury only to find Medina guilty
if they were convinced that he 'had actual knowledge'. Howard made
no mention of the equally vital criterion that he 'should have had
knowledge', ignoring the duty of commanding officers to keep themselves up-to-date with events at all times during an operation: 'Mere

presence at the scene without knowledge will not suffice.'[181] Secondly, according to Judge Howard the jury should make any guilty verdict dependent on proof that the killing continued after Medina had learnt about it. Thirdly, he left it to them to decide on 'negligent manslaughter' rather than 'involuntary manslaughter' in one hundred cases and so to give the court grounds for imposing a prison term reduced from three years to twelve months.[182]

Whatever intentions Judge Kenneth A. Howard may have had, it is clear that he allowed the jury no opportunity of returning a guilty verdict on the basis of *respondeat superior*. Had he stuck to the letter of American military law, Medina might possibly have been found guilty – for the 'should have been informed' clause was a significant factor in the conviction of commanding officers, because of the lasting improvement in the quality and more comprehensive use of battlefield communications in Vietnam in comparison with other wars. Moreover the second judicial instruction was, as Telford Taylor notes, unrealistic: 'Since no one was holding a stopwatch on the morning's doings in Mylai, it is hard to see how a conscientious jury could have made any such finding.'[183] In fact the jury returned a verdict of 'not guilty' on the most important charges – one hundred cases of 'involuntary manslaughter'. In so doing they had established a precedent in favour of all those who had not fulfilled their duty of supervision or had not tried to fulfil it. To quote Telford Taylor again, 'It is clear that Medina's acquittal effectively immunized all those above him in the chain of command, for if the company captain, within earshot of the killings and in radio communication with the guilty unit, could not be found liable, how could colonels and generals overhead in helicopters?'[184]

For the sake of completeness, it should be mentioned that Medina was also exonerated on all other charges. The alleged murder of a young boy was not even put to the jury after a private first class, Gene Oliver, had admitted guilt in cross-questioning and a further witness, Frederick Widmer, had refused to give evidence. It seems that in this trial, too, the prosecutors were no match for their defence opponents, who were all experienced civilian criminal lawyers. They were helpless to prevent their chief witnesses being discredited: Michael Bernhardt, pressed by Medina's attorney, would not rule out telling a lie for the sake of a just verdict. Gerald Hemin forfeited all credibility by confessing to using alcohol and drugs. Why in their place other soldiers who had strongly discredited Medina since autumn 1969 were not called to the witness stand is still known only to the prosecutors. This failure harmed their cause even more than the mistakes in procedure for which Major William Eckhardt and his colleagues were repeatedly censured by the court.[185] Under these conditions it was only to be expected that the jury would not find Medina guilty of the murder of a woman which allegedly took place in a rice field. The accusation of torture was likewise rejected. Medina had indeed confessed to having hit a prisoner and threatened him with a mock execution a few hours after the operation in My Lai (4) but the court – as before – accepted the defence argument that such interrogation methods were covered in Field Manual 30-15 and hence the Geneva Convention could not be applied.[186]

On 21 September 1971 Ernest Medina left the courtroom a free man and assured the waiting reporters that his unbroken faith in military justice had never been shaken. Three weeks later he left the Army of his own volition, on condition that he could never seek to re-enlist and would surrender the medal awarded to him for the My Lai (4) operation. Months later his evidence was a decisive factor in the acquittal of Colonel Oran Henderson, commander of 11th Light Infantry Brigade, Americal Division, when Medina admitted for the first time that he had been aware of the massacre and had lied to both his superior officers and the Army investigators out of consideration for the armed forces. He himself had nothing to fear. He could not be tried again for the same crime and no accusation of perjury could be considered because he had already left the service.[187]

It therefore can be concluded that the responsibility of commanding officers and the legal principle of *respondeat superior* was never made to apply in any military tribunal. Aside from the Medina case, this cornerstone of the laws of warfare and of the Uniform Code of Military Justice was rejected as irrelevant during preliminary investigations or at the end of Article 32 proceedings. As a consequence, accused officers were held to account not for participating in or condoning a war crime but rather for failing to pass on information subsequently received or hindering investigation proceedings. Such minor offences attracted administrative penalties – letters of caution or small fines. Five hundred dollars and a letter of reprimand were the price Lieutenant Lewis R. Ambort had to pay for inciting his 'killer team' to random murder in

Son Thang.[188] Telford Taylor alone was responsible for a passing moment of unease in the Pentagon, when he drew attention to the fact that General Westmoreland knew about war crimes as his repeated warnings to the troops proved, but had nevertheless imposed no penalties and had thus shared in the blame. However the denials which had already been prepared internally proved to be superfluous. Outside academic circles Taylor's statements fell on deaf ears.[189]

As a rule, soldiers appearing before courts martial pleaded superior orders and 'acting under orders' in their defence. Alternatively, they used as excuses the body-count policy, the strategy of search and destroy or lack of instruction in the laws of warfare in basic training. Judges and jurors were therefore required to confine themselves to the second fundamental legal principle of the Uniform Code of Military Justice – *mens rea* or the maxim that soldiers of sound mind and understanding could refuse to obey an order in so far as it could be seen, at face value, to be illegal. In the words of the prosecutor in the Son Thang case, 'An order to rob a bank is inherently illegal on its face, and the government contends that an order to shoot down a group of unarmed women and children is inherently unlawful on its face.'[190]

Mens rea was confirmed in a precedent set by a verdict returned in 1969. On the basis of the right and duty to refuse to obey unlawful orders, a military tribunal in 'United States vs. Keenan' convicted a Marine accused of a double murder. The verdict set a precedent, because the jurors had taken into account the war conditions prevailing in Vietnam and yet did not accept them as mitigation. Apart from that, judgments which set precedents have a particular status in the pragmatic culture of American law which is open to interpretation for situational appeals – a further reason for the adoption of the Keenan Instruction in countless general courts martial.[191] The bottom line was that the defence strategy based on 'acting under orders' could apply only in cases of clinically proven unsoundness of mind.

William Calley, however, insisted on 'acting under orders': 'We had political clearance to burn and destroy anything in the area ... He [Medina] said that meant everything.'[192] His defence counsel even tried to introduce neurological examinations to prove that their client did not have the necessary mental capabilities to differentiate between right and wrong. The fact that they failed utterly was not just due to the incontrovertible evidence which incriminated the defendant – jurors in other cases had ignored this kind of thing often enough – but Calley was represented by incompetent (and at times ridiculed) lawyers around George W. Latimer, who changed their strategy umpteen times during the course of the trial and at decisive phases of it arrived in court completely unprepared. The contrast with Medina's defence counsel could hardly have been greater: Calley was, in Michael Belknap's words, literally undefended;[193] unlike their normal practice, the prosecution retained a well-versed, unusually eloquent and aggressive prosecutor in Aubrey Daniel. What the life sentence handed down in the first instance might have been, had the positions been reversed, could form the subject of a major legal dispute over the significance of the subjective factor in the administration of justice. So far as Calley was concerned, it added up to the most unfavourable possible combination of circumstances.

In fact *mens rea* and the Keenan Instruction became meaningless when there were different people involved. At the same time as Calley, Charles Hutto – another suspected My Lai (4) murderer – was brought before a General Court Martial accused of the rape and murder of a young woman and a criminal assault on a group of civilians with intent to murder. In the course of the preliminary investigation Hutto had admitted under oath that he had killed between eight and ten people with an M60 machine gun – admittedly under orders, but knowing that those orders were disgraceful: 'It was murder . . . I was firing at the people and shooting into the houses.'[194] During his trial Hutto confirmed this statement. His defence counsel, a civilian lawyer from Miami, then presented a psychological expert opinion, which described Hutto as an easily led personality, fixated on figures of authority and fundamentally incapable of making his own decisions. The court accepted this plea and acquitted Hutto on 14 January 1971 – on the basis of one single expert's report and without looking into who had actually given him the orders that he allegedly took as law. In a legal expert's report subsequently produced by the Army Department the verdict was criticised as unfounded in all respects.[195] What the report did not mention was the attitude of the judge and the jurors. The judge accepted as foreman of the jury a colonel who, when asked in the course of the preliminary selection process for his opinion on how to treat prisoners of war, had replied, 'This is not a conventional war. We have to forget propriety.'[196] At the beginning of the trial the prosecutor William Eckhardt overheard a conversation in the officers' mess at Fort McPherson: 'How in the world could such a fine, upstanding officer be charged with such a horrible incident?' The man referred to was William Calley and the speakers were members of the jury sitting in judgment on Charles Hutto.[197]

The Hutto sentence was treated as a precedent for all My Lai (4) murder cases awaiting rulings. When Hutto was acquitted, Lieutenant General Albert O. Connor had to decide whether, on the basis of the Article 32 proceedings in the cases of Esequiel Torres, Kenneth Schiel, William Doherty, Robert W. T'Souvas, Gerald Smith and Max Hutson, six more trials should be held. In all cases he refused further legal proceedings in spite of serious suspicious factors – referring explicitly to Hutto – the interests of justice and 'the convenience of the Government'.[198] He probably also anticipated that the jurors would anyway disregard all litigable evidence out of sympathy for the accused. This had been the jury's attitude not just in the Hutto case, but also in the tribunal against David Mitchell in mid October 1970.[199] The massacre of My Lai (4) itself was taken as a pretext to annul the most important axiom of American and international laws of warfare after *respondeat superior*– the guideline that any defence based on 'acting on orders' is to be rejected as unlawful.

The other rulings laid down in the laws of warfare about what must and must not be done were not even once discussed during the Vietnam trials: attacks on undefended locations, militarily unjustified destruction, excessive deployment of firepower, appropriateness of methods, the expulsion of civilians and destruction of their means of livelihood, deployment of cluster bombs and other anti-personnel weapons – just to name the most important points. This is not to say that the laws of warfare would have had no place in the US military legal culture. As the Uniform Code of Military Justice and the submissions of various lawyers demonstrate, the relevant commitments were understood. Nevertheless the legal methods have to be described as self-release from law and statute – or to put it another way: the will, capability and mechanisms for self-correction within the military were greatly damaged in the course of the war in Vietnam. This was what Seymour M. Hersh meant when he described the verdict on William Calley as 'strictly public relations'.[200] This was also Mary McCarthy's view when she angrily described America as a country 'where scarcely anybody believes in a higher law'.[201]

Conclusion

You are the reason we lost the Vietnam War.[1]

'They're not going to get by with this. I had a little something to do with stopping the Green Beret business and I'm going to have something to do with stopping this.'[2] These words were addressed by one of the most influential members of the House of Representatives to an enthusiastic audience of 600 in Altus, Oklahoma on 10 April 1970. Mendel Rivers, chairman of the House Armed Services Committee and acting as liaison for the legislature with the Pentagon and the White House in all questions concerning the armed forces, was promising no less than a premature cessation of investigations into William Calley – and thus confirmed a public statement given a few weeks before. In mid March 1970 he had declared: 'We are not going to sit idly by and see men indicted for crimes of war when you have no Rules of Engagement; when the enemy is savage in treatment of prisoners of war, and where men, women, children – everybody is attacking their benefactors with hand grenades.'[3] Instead of humiliating the fighting men, the Pentagon should concentrate on its actual task and demonstrate strong leadership. 'I still think we should win. We should turn loose our air force. Nobody on earth can stand what we can do from the air.'[4]

For a whole year Mendel Rivers used Congress as a forum for denouncing the current proceedings of the military courts. A sub-

committee of the House Armed Services Committee set up by him
and led by F. Edward Hebert of Louisiana summoned William Peers
and Hugh Thompson to a hearing on My Lai (4) in December 1969.
Although this was not an official session and all those present were
committed to confidentiality, Rivers immediately went to the press
and discredited the eyewitness Thompson as a denigrator and liar:
'From his testimony nobody can be charged in my opinion with having
massacred anybody.'[5] Others taking part in the hearing contradicted
this assertion and criticised Rivers for a deliberate whitewash, but would
not give their names for fear of reprisals.[6] In fact there was no redress
against Rivers's smear campaign. He and some of his colleagues accused
Defense Secretary Melvin Laird of undermining troop morale and the
defence of the country by bringing William Calley before the courts;
on the subject of the Peers inquiries, they spoke of a 'frivolous policy'
and 'nose-in-air investigations' and an unacceptable contempt for the
will of the people. 'If you could see the My Lai incident as Chairman
[of the House Armed Services Committee]', said Rivers to Laird,

the American people are just very unhappy about the whole business . . .
There has to be a determination date . . . I remember very vividly our bombing
Germany, and brother, they killed them there by the tens and tens of thousands. I was in Pforzheim, and the Germans told me, I know a lot of Germans,
they said one Saturday afternoon we had about 60,000 people killed by your
wonderful bombers . . . Now, war is war, we are very upset about this, since
they brought it [My Lai (4)] up.[7]

The agenda of Rivers and Hebert became clear in the course of the
hearings of the Hebert Committee which had been sitting since mid
April 1970. Thirty-nine witnesses testified about My Lai (4), among
them thirteen soldiers and officers who were facing accusations of
war crimes or of hindering investigations.[8] They were all as certain of
moral acquittal by the representatives of the people as was Ernest
Medina, who at the end of his testimony was roundly applauded by
the whole committee, all of whom shook his hand as he left.[9] Three
months later Hebert published his report or, more exactly, a memorandum, which called in populist language for soldiers to be protected
from the imposition of the international rules of warfare: 'We are like
the policeman on the beat . . . They [the Pentagon bureaucrats] don't

know where we will strike next, but when we strike we know what we are talking about.'[10]

The first blow was aimed at Hugh Thompson and Ronald Haeberle, who were belaboured with insults to their honour and made to look like liars and con men. The sub-committee did not challenge the Criminal Investigation Division's confirmation of the authenticity of Haeberle's photographs months before. 'There were bodies in a ditch – they could have been in any ditch.'[11] Hebert did not want any talk about a massacre. 'Well if everyone of those people [defendants] killed as many as they say were killed obviously somebody killed somebody three or four times.'[12] Therefore just a minority of C Company of Task Force Barker could be considered to be responsible for the shootings – but not, significantly, for committing a crime. 'I would say some people [soldiers of C Company] are unfortunate victims of the dereliction of duty of some officials of the Army.'[13]

For this reason Rivers and Hebert felt themselves obliged to obstruct military justice. When the prosecutors and defenders preparing several cases demanded to see the statements of suspects recorded by the Hebert Committee, the latter refused to release the files. 'Frank and complete statements from some of our witnesses,' he told the Army Secretary Stanley Resor on 27 April 1970, 'could not be obtained without first assuring them that their testimony would not be disclosed voluntarily to anyone outside the Subcommittee.'[14] Whether this stipulation would have stood up to a legal challenge is more than doubtful, and why Stanley Resor did not take legal action can only be explained by speculation that he himself had reservations about the proceedings. The House of Representatives as a whole also kept quiet; out of well over 400 Congressmen – a quarter of whom were officers in the reserve[15] – only eighteen called on their colleague Hebert to rethink his policy of obstruction.[16]

One beneficiary was Private First Class David Mitchell, who was accused of an attack aimed at killing thirty civilians in May Lai (4). Because the Hebert Committee kept their records under lock and key, Mitchell's defence team were successful in their demand for four main prosecution witnesses, including Hugh Thompson, not to be called before the court. Due to lack of evidence the defendant was acquitted on 20 November 1970.[17] A similar disaster would also have been possible in Calley's case, if the presiding judge, Colonel Reid W. Kennedy, had not used his powers of discretion and ordered all the witnesses in question to be summoned.[18] However, in their ideological crusade nothing played more into Rivers's and Hebert's hands than the Calley conviction. 'It is the Army system itself that is on trial,' declared Congressman Samuel Stratton on 8 February 1972, looking back on his involvement in the Hebert Committee, 'and Congress and the American people require a resolution, a verdict, in that trial.'[19]

Rivers and Hebert had already anticipated this view after completing their hearings in July 1970, by calling for a substantial revision of the Uniform Code of Military Justice. Firstly, every GI should be able to cite in his defence 'binding orders'; secondly, they wanted the legal principle of *mens rea* to be deleted, without anything put in its place, and soldiers' conduct not to be measured against the criterion of individual responsibility, but on the basic assumption of a temporarily 'disturbed mind', due to battle stress; thirdly, a psychiatric assessment was to be ordered at the stage of preliminary investigations. Defendants would therefore only face a military court if the experts had demonstrated beyond any doubt that at the time of the deed they were psychologically accountable.[20] However controversial the political discussions about international military law had been since 1945, such radical pleading for soldiers' immunity from prosecution when in action has no equal.

The intervention of the two congressmen reflected the mindset of a public which had within a few weeks forgotten its horror at the media reports about My Lai (4) of November 1969. In the vehement criticism of military tribunals some strange bedfellows shared a common language – citizens who in other circumstances could only agree to disagree: left-wingers, liberals and conservatives, hawks and doves, Democrat and Republican supporters, rednecks and peaceniks, country people with no interest in politics and politically active city-dwellers, old and young, men and women, rich and poor, white and black. Even the anti-war movement – with the exception of a few activists – removed the subject of war crimes and their legal punishment from its agenda and, like the protesting soldiers of the Vietnam Veterans Against the War, resorted to general criticism of a criminal 'system' alone responsible for all transgressions.[21] Thus the loud cry of 'peace now' was not only to bring the war to an end, but with its conclusion get rid of an unwanted debate which could only be conducted at the cost of social self-isolation. The editors of *Time* viewed America as a country prepared to 'accept the unacceptable',[22] gripped in a 'horrendous confusion' and 'an astounding, indeed sickening distortion of moral sensibility'.[23] In any case it looked as though a nation which had for years been torn apart and unsure of its future wanted to reconstitute itself – in collective agitation over war crimes prosecutions on the one hand and communal refusal to face the problems they dealt with on the other.[24]

Instant opinion polls by newspapers and surveys by professional bodies like Gallup or Harris Polls consistently resulted in a majority of two or more to one in favour of the accused GIs. In a survey of 600 people in December 1969 the *Minneapolis Tribune* established that forty-nine per cent regarded the news items about My Lai (4) as media lies, while the rest just shrugged their shoulders and said 'war is war'.[25] Research among 1,600 households commissioned by *Time* found that sixty-five per cent regarded massacring civilians as a normal event not worthy of further comment and dismissed the suggestion of putting legal limitations on war as 'absurd'.[26] People in twelve towns questioned by the *Wall Street Journal* answered in the same vein: 'If people here could see what the Vietcong do, no one would be saying our soldiers are such bad guys.' – 'It was good. What do they give soldiers bullets for – to put in their pockets? That's the way war is.' – 'It sounds terrible to say we ought to kill kids, but many of our boys being killed over there are just kids, too.' – 'I think we should drop a few bombs over there and clean them out.'[27]

'When soldiers of other nations did such things, our outrage was clear and strong, and we had no trouble finding the words of condemnation,' wrote Jonathan Schell. '. . . When others committed them, we looked on the atrocities through the eyes of the victims. Now we find ourselves . . . looking through the eyes of the perpetrators, and . . . the victims are indistinct – almost invisible. A death close to us personally seems unfathomably large, but their deaths dwindle in our eyes to mere abstractions.' That Schell went on to speak of a kind of pride in sinning – 'as if we had gone through an initiation ceremony into adulthood as a nation, or as if committing great crimes were part of being a great nation, like having a huge gross national product, or going to the moon'[28] – might seem at first glance like far-fetched polemics, were it not that a week before Schell's article was published in the *New Yorker* a large advertisement which looked like an illustration of his thesis appeared in another prominent publication: in *Time*, on 12 December 1969, appeared the following 'yes, but' statements in facsimile handwriting, suggesting that they embraced all Americans: 'I have died in Vietnam. But I have walked the face of the moon . . . I have beat down my enemies with clubs. But I have built courtrooms to keep them free . . . I have watched children starve from my golden towers. But I have fed half of the earth . . . I am ashamed. But I am proud. I am an American.'[29]

As soon as a military tribunal was convened, plebiscites demonstrating support for the accused were regularly organised. From Oklahoma came a petition signed by 160,000 people showing their solidarity with Randell Dean Herrod, who was charged with the murders in Son Thang. 'I felt they were picking on some people who didn't have a helluva lot to say about their destiny,'[30] said one supporter. In Herrod's home town of Calvin money was collected to enable his grandfather to visit him in Vietnam, where he was being held on remand; congressmen from the region came down on the side of the protesters and vied with each other in their denunciation of the military justice system – probably even expecting the proceedings to be terminated because of inadmissible influence on the jury by the media.[31] In Brownsville, Texas, an 'Esequiel Torres Day' was celebrated in July 1970, after it became known that the said Torres was facing prosecution for a number of murders in My Lai (4). That the man of the moment got into a quarrel with some customers in a bar and fired several shots was recorded by the authorities as excusable behaviour in the circumstances and they dropped the case.[32]

> My name is William Calley. I'm a soldier of this land.
> I've tried to do my duty and to gain the upper hand.
> But they've made me out a villain. They have stamped me with a brand.
> . . . As we go marching on.

> While we're fighting in the jungles, they were marching in the street.
> While we're dying in the ricefields, they were helping our defeat.
> While we're facing VC bullets, they were sounding a retreat.
> . . . As we go marching on.[33]

In just the first week after Calley's conviction the record firm of Singletons in Nashville, Tennessee received half a million orders for this ballad about William Calley, sung by country singer Tony Nelson to the tune of 'The Battle Hymn of the Republic'. 'It looks like it's going to be a bigger hit than Harper Valley P.T.A.,' said the publisher and pointed out that the low profile kept by the big broadcasting stations like NBC was more than compensated for by programmes from local rock and country music transmitters, which played the song round the clock.[34] In the event the words conveyed all the emotions which were drummed up in defence of Calley and others – the image of a conscientious patriot who is stigmatised and has to suffer for the faults of others; the brave warrior who sees his comrades die in night ambushes and can only survive by paying back the enemy for his lawlessness in the same coin; the man betrayed by his homeland, who puts his life on the line, while demonstrators leading sheltered lives in New York or Santa Fe open a second front. And not least, a point of view was established which, in spite of all the detailed media reports, unshakably maintained that My Lai (4) was a fortress held by the Viet Cong: 'We responded to their rifle fire with everything we had.'

Responding with everything one had even became the watchword when the Calley case entered its decisive phase. According to a survey, ninety-six per cent of those questioned were following the court proceedings – an unparalleled proportion, even in times of blanket media coverage.[35] The American Legion and the Veterans of Foreign Wars – veterans' associations representing the interests of twenty-nine million surviving servicemen and women who had served in the American forces since the First World War – once more proved to be the most powerful lobby organisation in the country.[36] They organised 'Rallies for Calley', collections of funds, protests and demonstrations all over the country. At the invitation of the American Legion the Governors of Alabama and Mississippi, George Wallace and John Bell Williams, addressed a meeting in Columbus, Georgia, the co-organiser of which, a local clergyman, offered the press a remarkable headline: 'There was a crucifixion 2,000 years ago of a man named Jesus Christ. I don't think we need another crucifixion of a man named Rusty Calley.'[37] Jimmy Carter, at the time still governor of Georgia, called for an 'American Fighting Men's Day' and asked the citizens of his state to put on their headlights as a sign of support for Calley and to 'honor the flag as "Rusty" had done'.[38]

'He only did what he was told to do, what he was asked to do, what he was trained to do, and what millions of the rest of us did in World War One, Two and the Korean War,' said one member of the American Legion during a demonstration in Waterloo, Illinois,[39] thereby giving a prompt to countless veterans who in the following weeks sent their medals back to the Pentagon, confessed to their own war crimes or – like Audie Murphy, America's most highly deco- rated soldier of the Second World War – declared that in a situation like My Lai (4) they would probably have acted as Calley did.[40] Serving soldiers chose more drastic means of expression. Some sprayed 'Kill a Gook for Calley' on a house wall in Saigon; a unit stationed in Khe Sanh set up a board at their base with the words 'A Troop, 1st Cav, Salutes Lt. William Calley' on it; artillerymen in A Shau Valley baptised a gun with the name 'Calley's Avenger'; in Fort Benning recruits wrote a new marching song: 'Calley, Calley, he's our man. If he can't do it, Medina can.'[41] To speak out in favour of military tribunals was, in the view of the journalist David Halberstam, refer- ring to his colleague Neil Sheehan and his rousing piece in the *New York Times Book Review*, a bolder thing to do than publishing secret Pentagon papers.[42]

One can easily go on chronicling the public uproar: death threats against the family of one of the jury on the Calley case; flags flying at half-mast in front of private firms in Florida and public buildings all over other southern states; the little goat which arrived at the Wash- ington, DC National Airport by air freight addressed to the White House, wearing a uniform jacket with SCAPEGOAT written on it.[43] Angry mothers wrote protest letters to newspapers and magazines which had printed Ronald Haeberle's photos from My Lai (4), enraged that naked people could be seen in them.[44] The abstainer and airman rescuer of My Lai (4) was treated as the actual guilty party: when Hugh Thompson returned to his home in Louisiana, he also received death threats over the telephone. 'He was treated like a traitor for thirty years,' said Thompson's biographer Trent Angers. 'So he was conditioned to just shut up and be quiet. Every bit of information I got from him, I had to drag it out of him.'[45] 'Dead animals on your porch, mutilated animals on your porch some mornings when you get

up. So I was not a good guy,' Thompson recalled in the CBS broadcast
'Sixty Minutes' in 2004.[46]

The Vietnam Veterans Against the War wanted to be numbered
among the 'good guys'. For months the Winter Soldiers were busy
strengthening the opposition to military tribunals and exculpating war
criminals as victims of the system. Their spokesman John F. Kerry
said:

We are all of us in this country guilty for having allowed the war to go on.
We only want this country to realize that it cannot try a Calley for something
which generals and Presidents and our way of life encouraged him to do.
And if you try him, then at the same time you must try all those generals
and Presidents and soldiers who have part of the responsibility. You must in
fact try this country.[47]

We ask here and now: where are McNamara, Rostow, Bundy, Gilpatric and
so many others? . . . These are commanders who have deserted their troops,
and there is no more serious crime in the law of war. The Army says they
never leave their wounded. The Marines say they never leave even their dead.
These men have left all the casualties and retreated behind a pious shield of
public rectitude . . . Finally, this Administration has done us the ultimate
dishonor. They have attempted to disown us and the sacrifices we made for
this country.[48]

And when Kerry during a televised discussion broadcast by ABC was
asked for his opinion on a co-protester who had poured scorn on the
rules of warfare as a romantic illusion and described Calley's murders
as normal behaviour in wartime, he replied: 'I agree with what Mr
Reel is saying.'[49]

The campaign of publicity which verged on the hysterical produced
a political effect countrywide. In the state legislatures of North
Carolina, Colorado, Kansas, Alabama and Michigan petitions to
reprieve Calley immediately were introduced in spring 1971 and the
Senate of the State of Georgia supported this demand in mid February
1974.[50] Months before the case opened the Florida House of Representatives and the Oklahoma Senate had spoken out strongly in favour
of halting the proceedings. 'Much of the publicity attributable to the
charges suggests that convictions of these men are necessary to acquit

the Army from any guilt in the happenings,' according to the petition drawn up in Tallahassee,[51] and the legislators in Oklahoma City argued categorically that the statutory civil law offence of murder could not be applied in wartime – without making any mention of the international laws of warfare. 'Murder trials resulting from the normal incidents of the war,' it went on, 'would have the effect of demoralizing our troops and interfering with the maximum safety with which it is possible for us to provide our troops.'[52] President Nixon discussed with his advisers whether to make a public declaration addressing 'the obsolete idea that war is a game with rules and [that] you cannot during this crisis of war follow this line [of prosecution] unless there's a direct clear breach of orders.'[53] Nixon rejected this intervention but the mere consideration of the option made clear how far support for the campaign initiated by Congressmen Mendel Rivers and F. Edward Hebert on Capitol Hill had reached.

Describing such events is simple; explaining them is difficult for historians and social scientists alike. Essentially we encounter two models here which make use of arguments from psychoanalysis and the history of mentalities and differ in many ways. In a conversation with US News & World Report in 1969 Robert J. Lifton had already linked his concept of 'psychic numbing' – well known in later years – with My Lai (4). According to his theory, American society was practising a kind of self-defence: under the illusion of being superior to other nations not only in material terms but morally, too, and of representing the avant-garde of an enlightened culture, the news of My Lai (4) was regarded as a denial of this exceptionalism in general, and of the emphatic idea from the 1960s that through good education the nation had armed itself against incursions of violence.[54] In the words of the historian Stephen Ambrose: 'My Lai was the single most shocking thing to come out of the Vietnam War for me . . . I have spent a lot of time since trying to understand how this could happen – how American boys could do what SS boys did, how Boy Scouts could do what the Nazi Youth did.'[55] Should guilt feelings and self-images which had become questionable therefore be eradicated or protected respectively by aggressive defensiveness? Was it even possible that a consciousness of guilt was absolved through identification with the culprits? For John F. Kerry the answer was obvious: 'I think that what the country is really saying through Calley is . . . that it can't accept the destruction of the illusion, and that it can't accept all the contradictions.'[56]

In this context the historians Tom Engelhardt and Gabriel Kolko refer to a myth engraved on the collective memory: America, according to the 'master narrative' prevalent since the Indian Wars, does not conduct its wars of its own volition or for self-seeking motives, but always finds itself caught in a surprise ambush. Its troops face enemies who avoid open battle and instead attack the unarmed and the weak – women and children – so demonstrating that they are striking at the roots of freedom and safety. This contempt for the lives of others is reflected in belittling the value of their own lives: faced with the choice between capitulation and defeat, the fanatical enemies of civilisation opt for the latter, but anyone confronting kamikaze warriors in the service of evil is involuntarily forced into a war without rules. In order to save himself from barbarism he occasionally has to use barbaric methods himself – including the counter-attack which will cause total annihilation. Thus the story of betrayal and initial defeat, of revenge and final triumph, is also always a tale of self-victimisation imposed from without – of self-sacrifice in the cause of cultural progress – and therefore a story which is above moral criticism.[57]

However one may like to evaluate in detail these differing explanations, they all seem to share one weakness: they become vague as soon as one enquires about what is specifically American. As well as Vietnam, Lifton's 'psychic numbing' is applied with identical arguments to the perception and treatment of many other events: Nazi crimes, Hiroshima, the gulags, the Cuban missile crisis, nuclear escalation, the Gulf War. It is put forward as a catch-all model of contemporary history, throwing up umpteen new questions for each one it answers. Engelhardt's 'self-sacrifice discourse' serves little better. We meet it in strikingly similar form in Germany, Japan, Turkey, Austria, France, Sweden, the Netherlands, Rwanda, Cuba and Indonesia. One is almost tempted to speak of a standard repertoire of societies at war, no matter whether tribal warlords or atomic controllers have the say and independently of whether they fought with handheld weapons or long-range bombers.

All the more astonishing is how little scientific effort has been applied for a long time to close the gaps in our knowledge. The My Lai (4) debate itself, measured by the number of people involved and the emotional intensity, offered a unique opportunity for a social science field study, but hardly any representative or empirical data suitable for making comparisons were produced – with two exceptions. In May and June 1971 Herbert Kelman and a sociology team from Harvard University conducted a national survey immediately after Calley had been convicted, on the basis of a block quota sample. Dwelling units in 'block size' were randomly selected from all over the country. From them 990 people were chosen as representative of the national spread of gender and age and were asked to answer the question whether orders to murder civilians should be obeyed. (We will return later to the results.) Five years later the University of Massachusetts commissioned a follow-up study based on a similar method but restricted it to the Boston area and to interviewees who were considerably above the average in terms of education and income and also showed other significantly differing characteristics – for instance religious convictions. Such deficiencies are no coincidence. Long after the 1970s the relationship between war and civilian society was not a favourite subject for social scientists.

A scientific historical approach is possible with the help of those letters and petitions which American citizens wrote to their congressmen, to secretaries of state and to the president around the time of Calley's conviction – declarations of solidarity which in nine out of ten cases called for the convicted man to be released at once. No one knows how many in all were dispatched but probably somewhere in the hundreds of thousands. F. Edward Hebert alone received 2,000 letters a week from the end of 1969 to the middle of 1970; after Calley was sentenced 6,000 citizens telephoned Fort Benning in the space of two days and 1,500 others sent telegrams and letters to the commandant of the training camp.[58] The Pentagon was inundated with 12,500 communications in the first two weeks of April 1971[59] and the White House post-room recorded 335,000 – a record unsurpassed by any other event to date.[60] Because of the sheer volume, it was not possible to answer many of the letters and the Army filed about 30,000 unanswered. Written in the last two days of March and during the first week of April 1971, they allow us to look into the mindset of their authors and to recognise in the way they write about war and war crimes their images of themselves and of society, but above all the motives for their emotional outbursts.

The following analysis is based on a representative selection of 907 letters about William Calley's case – 811 massive denunciations of the verdict and 96 in favour.[61] Thirty-one per cent of the 907 were standard chain letters or petitions with up to 8,000 signatures, twenty-four per cent were telegrams consisting of just a few lines and other brief communications. On the other hand, about half the writers took a lot of time and trouble to write sophisticated, well-reasoned letters, mostly one page long and in 113 cases between two and four pages. Common to all of them is a tense tone, sometimes resorting to crude language: 'It is illegal to print language strong enough to express our feelings over this.'[62] They came from all parts of the country and reflected the geographical distribution of the population. We can establish neither regional groupings nor differentials between town and country which deviate from the norm. Age brackets and membership of professional bodies cannot be identified because of insufficient data. If, however, one takes as a basis the five per cent of letters sent by business post, one finds a significantly broad spectrum, from clergy through textile industrialists to gastronomes. The handwriting – 262 of them were in manuscript – leads one to assume a similarly wide age range. Judging by syntax, grammar and literacy, almost all the writers had at least an average level of education. Three or more orthographic mistakes only occur in about a dozen of the letters. If one ignores the lists of signatories and those letters with illegible signatures, forty-seven per cent of the contributors were women and fifty-three per cent were men; many of the women tended to express themselves more emphatically, if not more crudely, than the men.[63] One hundred and fifteen people, mostly men, said they had served in the war or were former members of the armed forces. In this case the grey area may probably be small, because they gave their military experience as proof that they were especially well qualified to form a judgement. From that we could infer that well over eighty per cent of the writers had never been in uniform.[64]

'We have had some quit the American Legion and V.F.W. [Veterans of Foreign Wars],' said one letter, 'because they didn't do more about this case.'[65] In the event only thirty-one per cent of the contributions – chain letters and petitions – lead one to conclude that they represented organisations with political or military interests. Well over two-thirds were therefore written by citizens following a spontaneous impulse on their own initiative. Their language was different from the rhetoric of parties and associations; no clichés, no formulae, no ritualistic metaphors – instead, vigorous images and arguments, backed up by a range of colloquial swearwords and abuse. Many considered politics an alien country, even a minefield, which they were only prepared to enter in an emergency such as the Calley case clearly was. 'The silent majority is beginning to speak and we beg the officials to listen.'[66]

As though the Calley verdict had opened a valve, many people were airing their displeasure about the 1960s – a period which in their eyes stood for chaos, anarchy and humiliation: 'The country in which we live now, it is slowly being broken down.'[67] The letters about Calley's case proclaim an inability or unwillingness to face up to the challenges of a world in upheaval or even as proof of a 'collective weariness'. Assassination of a president, burning ghettos, escalating criminality, drug-dealing, youth in revolt, a war which had never been officially declared, whose aims no one really understood, which never came to an end in spite of all the promises and which claimed more victims every day – and to crown it all a verdict which seemed to make a mockery of their own experiences of life. 'See, Calley should have done this in the U.S. Here, kill a "cop", murder an actress [Sharon Tate] & three friends, what the heck. I'll probably go free.'[68] It was not accepted as an objection that the military judges were trying to counter this development in their own way but rather that an army which sat in judgment on itself was to be regarded as the ultimate symbol of powerlessness – a symbol which led to seeking refuge in panic metaphors: sometimes talk of tying their own hands, sometimes of fascination with their own downfall and repeatedly of self-emasculation. In one case the writer addressed the Pentagon as 'patsygon' – the mother of all castrati. 'Dear sirs, you all have just created the greatest patsy in the history of the United States.'[69] A political culture dominated by images and rituals of masculinity was damaged in many sensitive spots.[70]

Behind the rage at the 1960s also lay hidden the fear of a repetition of history. The racial disturbances at home and the war overseas had divided American society as deeply as only the Civil War had done before – and with recollections of the Civil War resurfaced the spectre of a society collapsing on itself. From everywhere rang out the imploring cry for 'unity'. An immigrant society's traditional and most cherished ritual, celebrating the sense of community, was being transformed into a slogan for political battle: all or nothing, 'One nation under God' or farewell to the American dream.

Anyone looking for proof can take the Calley letters as a key. Their authors worked relentlessly on the symbolic restoration of national unity, whether by formulating a collective guilt, as a result of society as a whole having welcomed the Vietnam War and therefore having to take collective responsibility for the crimes committed there, or by opposing Calley's judges with a united voice: 'Please intervene we ask as AMERICANS!'[71] Solidarity with the soldiers still fighting in Vietnam could hardly have been expressed more emphatically. They were to be sure of returning to a society which did not punish, but rewarded, them for their service to the community. The appropriate description of this self-therapy comes from the 1860s: 'To heal a nation'.[72]

'Don't misunderstand us,' wrote four citizens to Secretary of the Army Stanley Resor, 'we realize a massacre has actually taken place . . . and we also realize certain individuals were directly responsible for this tragic destruction of lives.'[73] However they insisted on William Calley being immediately released – with arguments which lead us to the heart of the problem, beyond any current political reservations. This was a question of the relationship between the military and civilian society or, to be more precise, the range of civil liberties: how far should the arm of the military be allowed to reach out and where must a line be drawn to protect the citizen? What material, and above all non-material, price should the individual and society pay for maintaining a costly standing Army? Can the norms and laws which bind civilian society be extended to apply to the military? The argument over these questions is one of the classical conflicts in American democracy, fought over for longer and above all more passionately there than anywhere else. To ignore it means being incapable of either deciphering the Calley letters or discovering what is specifically American in them.[74]

Reduced to ideal types, we see here the attack on the Calley verdict pointed towards basic and human rights in the following form: those liable for military service do not go to war of their own accord; the military either compels them to do so or they respond to a government appeal out of patriotic conviction. In either case they have to subject themselves to an institution which may have been called into being for the defence of liberty, but gives no liberty to its members. For the duration of his term of service the soldier is therefore literally disenfranchised and, moreover, he is required to relinquish the attributes of his civilised existence. Only by suppressing his memory of morals and ethics will he fulfil the expectations inherent in a fighting machine: 'Kill, kill, kill'. In war this 'expropriation' of individuality is taken to the limit. Fighting means deprivation, stress, pain and facing death – experiences which as a rule lead to losing control, if not to psychological regression. 'Our country has taught my brother that he must take life in order to preserve it. This has been constantly pounded into his thinking. Our country has formed him into a machine, to fight, to suffer, to kill, without question. Will our country now punish him because this machine did not stop where we thought it should?'[75] An individual thus distorted and stripped of his autonomy, dignity and free will is, however, no longer a legally responsible person and consequently the ground is cut from under the dictates of the criminal law: they apply to free people in peace, not to those compelled to go to war.

Following this logic anyone who wants to cite the criminal law must, in the case of soldiers, at least take into account the catalogue of mitigating circumstances and abandon in principle any accusation of 'deliberate murder'. If it is nevertheless brought and – as in the case of Calley – punishment is based on it, the state threatens to deprive its subjects of their liberty not only temporarily, but also for life. Then the borderline with despotism has definitely been crossed and citizens may and must dissociate themselves from their government. 'Loyalty is a two-way street – down as well as up.'[76] The notion of civil disobedience was articulated in a way as if one had the right to take the law – or what was seen as the law – into one's own hands. Or as if one wanted to signal to the government that in future it could not count on the loyalty of the 'silent majority', whether in domestic or foreign policy. 'I don't know how you people feel about this, but around here anyone who would promise to reverse Lt. Calley's sentence could run for President on Republican or Democratic Party and win.'[77] Such a statement of mistrust is unique, at least during the period of the Cold War.[78]

'Free Calley' came easily to the lips of those who saw in the verdict on him an abuse of the judicial office. In their view a battlefield was always and everywhere an anarchic, lawless zone. A 'law of warfare', as laid down in the Hague Rules for Land Warfare and the Geneva Convention for the protection of civilians, seemed from this perspective like the brainchild of bureaucrats out of touch with reality. 'After all, look at Japan, wasn't that pre-meditated, and how many did we kill?'[79] Or: 'One of the largest cases of human disaster was the dropping of the atom bomb on Japan to end World War II. The United States did not need to drop the bomb to defeat the Japanese who were on the edge of surrender anyway.'[80] The Indian wars, the First and Second World Wars, Korea and repeated references to Hiroshima and Nagasaki: the history of modern warfare could be read as irrefutable proof that for a long time there had been no distinction between combatants and non-combatants – nor would there be in the future.

Vietnam was seen as a temporary climax of this development – a war in which old men, women and children were allegedly the worst enemies, because they lay in wait with hand grenades and booby-traps. Mixing fact and fiction in this context may be a reproach to a historian but not to Calley's supporters, because in the past the borderline with the inconceivable had been crossed so often that even surreal exaggerations looked like fitting descriptions of reality. In other words, the twentieth century and its wars were seen as the norm which cancelled out all other norms. 'War is war' – many letter-writers penned a dialogue with themselves as proof of this thesis. They demolished ethical or moral reproaches either by referring to the immutable laws of history or to chances regularly gambled away in the past. 'Now is a little late to try to correct the atrocities that have taken place since the turn of the century.'[81]

'Free Calley' was also a demand from those who clung in principle to putting legal limitations on war. In any case – to use their own phraseology – the judges had killed the wrong pig, by disregarding the standards the United States set itself at the end of the Second World War, for example in the Yamashita case: 'If we set these legal precedents, why do we now choose to ignore them?'[82] There was no lack of justification for extending the principle of *respondeat superior* as the legal yardstick to apply to everything: in contrast to simple soldiers, political strategists and senior officers operate at a distance from zones of fighting and death; they are therefore exposed to neither the physical nor the psychological pressures of battle and have much greater freedom of action; in Vietnam the initiative to radicalise the war and shift moral standards came from on high – with blanket bombardment, defoliation, napalm and body count. 'What I trying [sic] to say is that maybe no actual orders were given but Lt. Calley could have interpreted the feelings of senior officers and acted accordingly.'[83] Only after the massacre became known did the Army command consider introducing ethics courses. In the final analysis does that not demonstrate that Calley should have been acquitted and that his superiors were involuntarily condemning themselves? 'Calley represents that part of our past which has become unacceptable in the present, but in the interim society neglected to bring him up to date . . . At My Lai, as far as a portion of public opinion is concerned, he [Calley] was at least one war too late.'[84] Therefore the Pentagon could only legally set new standards for its soldiers' conduct on condition that a fresh evaluation of the military establishment was accepted in advance.[85]

'When there is blame to take the whole Army should bear this blame. Not just one man. I say Lt. Calley should be freed of this blame. And the whole damn Army condemned, and on trial.'[86] The deep distrust of the top brass echoed a persistent tradition going back to the early days of a republic which rejected the formation of a standing army by pointing to Europe which had been militarily ruined. It also brings to mind the 1920s and 1930s – the last time when it was possible to cut back drastically the armed forces which had been inflated during a war. Even in the Cold War this legacy had not been entirely exhausted. So we come to a conclusion as paradoxical as it is compelling: that the case of a war criminal could be legally defended with anti-militaristic arguments – alternatively, even with anti-institutional feelings against the State as it appears as co-prosecutor, that necessary evil which has always counted as the greatest threat to a freedom-loving individual. 'They shoot student's [sic] . . . Don't They??' was written on one photograph which was sent in, showing a young man lying on the ground, killed by the National Guard during an anti-Vietnam demonstration on the campus of Kent State University.[87] The ten per cent of correspondents who welcomed the Calley verdict had to give in to this mood. The more the struggle on Calley's behalf started to look like a battle against the treacherous 'big government', the less they were listened to. David against Goliath, omnipotence against powerlessness, State against the common man, special interests against the common weal: the politics of emotion in the United States live off even this sort of material.

And seen like this, in the end the burning controversy over My Lai (4) no longer revolved around war crimes. It can even be seen as the Calley sympathisers symbolically fighting for their political identity and their role in the social system; also as a conflict sparked off by a violent event but with only an indirect connection, if any, with the violence generated by society at large.[88] In his research Herbert C. Kelman came to strikingly similar conclusions. In contrast to the Harris or Gallup Poll interviewers, he was not primarily interested in views on the Calley verdict, but wanted to trace how those questioned saw themselves as citizens. In essence the answers record a distorted concept of law and circle continuously around variations on the same reproach: 'The My Lai prosecutors damaged a contract.' What they meant was a 'political contract' between rulers and ruled, specifying what a citizen may expect of his government and what demands a government can make on its citizens.

When asked by Kelman and his colleagues after My Lai (4), members of the lower classes defined themselves as a group without political influence, at the mercy of the whims of others – yet still in principle citizens prepared to make sacrifices. They were ready to bear the costs of policies imposed on them and valued loyalty as the prime political virtue, though admittedly only on condition that those in power met their own obligations. As regards military service, it follows that the State can compel its citizens to take up arms but must assume responsibility for the consequences of this enforced action. To try to call the individual to account for the consequences of a misguided policy would cancel the morally binding contract and legitimise civil disobedience. To call Calley a scapegoat therefore expressed the defiance of those who had been led by the nose and who had only gathered up the crumbs of the American dream, but fundamentally did not want to stop dreaming that dream.[89]

This is how Paul Meadlo's mother defended her son when he was accused of the murders in My Lai (4): 'I raised him up to be a good boy and I did everything I could. They come along and . . . made a murderer out of him.'[90] And this is how a non-commissioned officer confronted his instructor at Fort Benning: 'Sir, in all your examples, the nation seems to have less responsibility than individual soldiers . . .

Sir, what you're saying is you have the right to hang us, but we don't have the right to question the nation.'[91]

Representatives of the middle classes – well educated and better placed socially and economically – also spoke of betrayal though with the use of different arguments. Their premise was not exclusion or political estrangement, but an engagement which even extended to identifying with the nation. The majority of those who replied to Kelman's questionnaire, whether office workers, the self-employed or small business people, showed themselves inclined to rank civil obedience as the highest and therefore the crucial moral value. My Lai (4) confronted them with a dilemma: in their eyes Calley was guilty of damaging national values – primarily the principle of individual responsibility – and in that respect was justly arraigned. On the other hand this example could not be allowed to create a precedent without risking the respect for institutions which represented the State and with it the nation's prestige. This last would have inevitably been the case if the accusation had been extended to those symbolic figures of national integrity – the officers who were suspected of participation or covering up. The fear of unpredictable repercussions, however, was the underlying motive for joining their voices, if necessary, with those who uncompromisingly rejected any legal proceedings – in spite of all their reservations about Calley.[92] A commentator on the *Philadelphia Inquirer* was considering this middle-class attitude when he wrote: 'Lt. Calley has been lionized by the people to whom "my country, right or wrong" means that any suggestion of ugliness within American institutions is an assault on their own loyalties and personal senses of being.'[93]

'The silent majority is beginning to speak and we beg the officials to listen,' one writer wanted the Joint Chiefs of Staff to know.[94] This was not only intended as a contribution to the Calley affair; rather, the silent majority was indicating that they were looking beyond it. This was a question of what price people were prepared to pay for America's wars and where were the limits of what was tolerable. In other words, that seventy per cent of the population which in the following years described the Vietnam War as wrong and morally reprehensible had made no pacifist about-turn.[95] The victory which had eluded them was the only unacceptable factor and it was unforgivable that the nation's leaders had apparently shown a lack of political decisiveness to give the fighting troops the necessary support. 'Get out or win': in that lay the core of the so-called 'Vietnam syndrome'. There was no question of dignified reserve, but a refusal to accept defeat; no question of self-restraint, but an aversion to handicapping oneself militarily, politically and legally.[96] Seen like that, the Vietnam syndrome was a perpetuation of the traditional 'victory culture'. Anyone arguing from that vantage point could dismiss the Vietnam War as amoral, without raising the amorality of atrocities or the suffering of others. Telford Taylor was thinking of this normative self-obsession and insistence on the United States' lofty special position above everything and everybody, when at the end of his book *Nuremberg and Vietnam* he wrote: 'Somehow we failed ourselves to learn the lessons we undertook to teach at Nuremberg, and that failure is today's American tragedy.'[97]

Acknowledgements

Faced with many thousands of archive boxes, it was an attractive – and in every way exciting – challenge not to lose confidence in the feasibility of this task. Whether the author has done justice to it, is for the public to decide.

This does not affect my gratitude to everyone who has accompanied me in my work on the manuscript in different ways and contributed to its publication. This sentence or something similar is to be found in most introductions to books which are time and labour intensive; it is therefore easy to overlook what the purpose actually is: no less than to point out that a piece of work attributed to one individual represents far more than the result of that individual's labour.

My first and most grateful thanks go to my daughter Lena. Richard Boylan of the military history department of the National Archives, College Park (Maryland) has given indispensable help in the search for relevant documents. I have Gar Alperovitz to thank for years of encouragement, advice and support, Peter Weiss for the use of his private archives, Seymour M. Hersh and Daniel Ellsberg for stimulating conversations and the urge not to lose the impetus to publish speedily without sacrificing scientific meticulousness. Stig Förster has stood by me as friend and colleague not only with this project – a further reason to look forward to the next. I would like to thank Gaby Zipfel and Martin Bauer not only for their good cooperation, but also for always being ready to publish the initial thoughts and early results of this work in *Mittelweg 36*. The same applies to Thomas Neumann, to whom I am much indebted even after his premature death. Jörg Nagler,

Michael Hochgeschwender, Wilfried Mausbach, Frank Schumacher, Fabian Hilfrich, Ann-Kathrin Colomb and Annette Jander have enriched my reflections on this subject in several workshops on the history of Vietnam. For this I thank both them and also their colleagues in the study field of 'Theory and History of Violence' at the Hamburg Institute for Social Research: Cornelia Berens, Birthe Kundrus, Regina Mühlhäuser, Klaus Naumann, Christian Th. Müller, Reinhard Müller, Jan Philipp Reemtsma, Dierk Walter and Michael Wildt. Ingwer Schwensen, Christoph Fuchs and Paula Bradish have helped me further with research into small details; Birgit Otte, Jürgen Determann and Hannes Sieg together with Wilfried Gandras have, from the editing to the publicity, ensured that the manuscript has finally reached the German market in book form. Last but not least, I want to express my thanks and gratefulness to my translator, Anne Wyburd, and to Jörg Hensgen at the Bodley Head for a marvellous cooperation.

It will not detract from the contributions of all of these people if I say that this is not the place for expressing one special vote of thanks in appropriate words. So I shall borrow the lyrics of 'New Beginning': 'Another day over, and all I ask is to share the next with you' – for you, Betsy.

Berlin, 10 June 2009

Abbreviations

AAI	After-Action Interviews
ACoS	Assistant Chief of Staff
AMH-CF	Alexander M. Haig Chronological File
AMH-SF	Alexander M. Haig Special File
AOC	Army Operations Center
AO-CGR	Administrative Office Security Classified General Records
ARVN	Army of the Republic of Vietnam
AS	Army Staff
BM-68	Background and Draft Materials for 'US Marines in Vietnam The Defining Year 1968'
CaFi	War Crimes Allegations Case Files
CAP	Combined Action Platoon
CC	Calley Correspondence Unanswered Letters, 1971
CCI	National Committee for a Citizens' Commission of Inquiry on United States War Crimes in Vietnam
CF	War Crimes Allegations Central File
CGR	Security Classified General Records
CH	Command Historian, United States Army Vietnam
CINUSARPAC	Commander in Chief, United States Army, Pacific
COHRO	Columbia University Oral History Research Office
COMUSMACV	Commander in Chief, United States Military Assistance Command Vietnam
CORDS	Civil Operations and Revolutionary Development Support
CSO-CGR	Assistant Chief of Staff for Operations (G 3) Plans Division Security Classified General Records
DCSO	Deputy Chief of Staff for Operations
DRAC	Delta Regional Assistance Command
FFV	Field Force Vietnam

FRUS	US Department of State, Foreign Relations of the United States, Diplomatic Papers, Annual Volumes
G-3	Assistant Chief of Staff for Operations
GVN	Government of Vietnam
HAK	Henry A. Kissinger Papers
HBF	Historian's Background Files
HD22-CR	Headquarters Detachment, 22. United States Army, Prisoner of War/Civilian Internee Information Center Confidential Records
HD22-SR	Headquarters Detachment, 22. United States Army, Prisoner of War/Civilian Internee Information Center Secret Records
HD22-UR	Headquarters Detachment, 22. United States Army, Prisoner of War/Civilian Internee Information Center Unclassified Records
HMC-HDPT	Headquarters United States Marine Corps, Historian's Department
HMC-HMD	Headquarters United States Marine Corps, History and Museum Division
IA	Interservice Agencies
ICD	Investigation and Complaint Division
ID	Investigations Division
IG	Inspector General
LRRP	Long Range Reconnaissance Patrols
MACV	Military Assistance Command Vietnam
MHD	Military History Detachment
MLM	Records Pertaining to the My Lai Massacre, 1969–1974
NA	National Archives, College Park (Maryland)
NLF	National Liberation Front
NPMP	Nixon Presidential Materials Project
NSC	National Security Council
NVA	North Vietnamese Army
OCMH	Office of the Chief of Military History
ODCS-PER	Office of the Deputy Chief of Staff for Personnel
OSA	Office of the Secretary of the Army
OSE-BF	Operation Speedy Express Background Files
PI-AC	Peers Inquiry Records Created after the Completion of the Peers Inquiry, 1969–1975
PI-CI	Peers Inquiry Administrative and Background Materials Files – Closed Inventory, 1967–1970
PI-FR	Peers Inquiry Final Report, Edited Version, 1970–1975 (Report of the Department of the Army Review of the Preliminary Investigations into the My Lai Incident)

PI-OI	Peers Inquiry Administrative and Background Materials Files – Open Inventory, 1967–1970
PM	Provost Marshall Section
PRG	Provisional Revolutionary Government of South Vietnam
PSOT	Plans and Security Operations and Training Division
RG	Record Group
RICF	Reports of Investigation Case Files
ROE	Rules of Engagement
ROI	Reports of Investigations
RVNF	Republic of Vietnam Armed Forces
S 3	Assistant Chief of Staff for Operations
SEALs	Sea, Air and Land Commandos
SGR	Administrative Office Security Classified General Records
SJA	Staff Judge Advocate
SJA-GR	Staff Judge Advocate General Records
SOP	Standing Operating Procedure
SVN	South Vietnam
TF	Trial by Fire 1968–1969 NA, 127-94-0012
TRAC	Third Regional Assistance Command
UCMJ	Uniform Code of Military Justice
USA-AG	United States Army, Advisory Group
USA-CH	United States Army, Commands Headquarters
USAV	United States Army Vietnam
USCR	United States Congress, Congressional Record Veterans' Testimony on Vietnam
USFSEA	United States Forces in Southeast Asia
USMC	United States Marine Corps
VC	Viet Cong
VCI	Viet Cong Infrastructure
VWCWG	Vietnam War Crimes Working Group

Notes

Introduction

1. Schell, *Observing the Nixon Years*, p. 20. • 2. 'Song [*sic*] My Details and Photos Shock, Sicken Congressmen', *New York Times*, 27 Nov. 1969. For the impact of these photos see Thompson, Clarke and Dinitz, *Reactions to My-Lai*. • 3. 'Ex-GI Tells U.S. He Killed Women, Babies at Song [*sic*] My', interview in *International Herald Tribune*, 26 Nov. 1969. • 4. This refers to the reports of Orville Schell, 'Cage for the Innocents'; Schell, 'Quang Ngai and Quang Tin'; Shepherd, 'Incident at Van Duong'; Lang,. *Casualties of War* and 'An American Atrocity', *Esquire*, Aug. 1969; and countless texts and photos in the daily press by Malcolm W. Browne, Homer Bigart, Charley Mohr and Herbert Faas. See also Prochnau, *Distant War*, pp. 26, 72ff., 81. • 5. Quoted in Prochnau, *Distant War*, p. 483. See ibid., pp. 109, 139, 410, 457. • 6. Department of State, Department of Defense, United States Information Agency, Cable 1006, 20 Feb. 1962, quoted in Wyatt, *Paper Soldiers*, p. 92. • 7. For a discussion of this background see Hallin, *Uncensored War*, pp. 6, 20, 45, 54–8, 61, 77, 83ff., 93ff., 96–101, 119ff., 129ff., 137–48, 155ff., 161, 176; Wyatt, *Paper Soldiers*, pp. 92, 129, 138–55, 164; Halberstam, *Powers*, pp. 442–8, 475ff., 529; and Braestrup, *Big Story*, pp. 475–84, 497, 515. • 8. 'Civilized Warfare', *Washington Post*, 15 Aug. 1965. • 9. Wyatt, *Paper Soldiers*, pp. 153–6. • 10. Hallin, *Uncensored War*, pp. 119ff., 161, 176. • 11. For the genesis and durability of this position see Greiner, 'Der kurze Sommer der Anarchie'. • 12. See Hallin, *Uncensored War*, pp. 61, 83–5, 93–5, 146ff., and Braestrup, *Big Story*, pp. 500, 510. • 13. Falk, *Nuremberg*. See also Braestrup, *Big Story*, p. 495. • 14. Wyatt, *Paper Soldiers*, p. 129. See ibid., pp. 138–42, 146–8, 168, 174ff.; Braestrup, *Big Story*, pp. 466ff., 475–84, 497, 509, 511–27; and Hallin, *Uncensored War*, pp. 6, 108, 161ff., 168, 174, 197ff. • 15. For availability of relevant reports see Prochnau, *Distant War*, pp. 26, 72ff., 81, 112; Hersh, 'Story Ignored'; and Unger, 'NLF Radio'. 'We did have

a very big problem with apathetic press', a GI also maintained retrospectively: Larry Rottman, quoted in USCR, 7 Apr 1971, p. E2911. • **16**. Braestrup, *Big Story*, pp. 516, 519, 520. • **17**. At a hearing of the foreign policy committee of the Senate in mid April 1971, John F. Kerry, then spokesman for the 'Vietnam Veterans Against the War', claimed to know a correspondent of *Time* who did not publish his knowledge of the massacre of 150 Cambodians for fear of losing his accreditation: OSA, Memorandum for the Record, Subject: Resume of Congressional Hearings, 23 Apr 1971, in NA, RG 319, AS, ODCS-PER, VWCWG, CaFi, Box 9, Folder: Rottman Allegation (CCI), Case 63. • **18**. Sheehan, 'War Crime Trials?' • **19**. The *Columbus Inquirer* was the first newspaper to report on the impending charge against Calley: 'Fort Benning Soldier Charged with Murder', 6 Sep. 1969. • **20**. Quoted in Eszterhas, 'Toughest Reporter', p. 73. See also Hersh, 'Story Ignored', p. 55ff. • **21**. Quoted in Halberstam, *Powers*, p. 682. • **22**. Halberstam, *Powers*, p. 679. See ibid., p. 680. James Reston confirmed Halberstam's views and described his paper in those years as 'not a risk taker – by tradition opposed to crusading reporters': quoted in Prochnau, *Distant War*, p. 450. See also Hersh, 'Story Ignored', p. 55ff. and Eszterhas, 'Toughest Reporter', Part I, p. 8off. • **23**. A commission of social scientists set up by the government in the wake of the political murders and racial unrest in the 1960s, which studied the background and causes of everyday violence in the United States. • **24**. 'On Evil: The Inescapable Fact and My Lai: An American Tragedy', *Time*, 5 Dec. 1969, pp. 4, 26–7. See also 'GIs in Battle: The "Dink" Complex', *Time*, 1 Dec. 1969, p. 37; 'Conscience and the War and An American Nightmare', *International Herald Tribune*, 24 Dec. 1969; 'My Lai 4', *International Herald Tribune*, 27 Nov. 1969; James Reston, 'Who is to Blame for Song [*sic*] My?', *International Herald Tribune*, 27 Nov. 1969; 'Abhorrent to Conscience', *International Herald Tribune*, 28 Nov. 1969; 'Songmy Boy Pantomimes Slaying of Mother', *New York Times*, 4 Dec. 1969; 'My Lai Scapegoating', *International Herald Tribune*, 4 Dec. 1969; and 'Atrocities and Politics', *Wall Street Journal*, 1 Dec. 1969. • **25**. Reinhold Niebuhr, quoted in Bilton and Sim, *Four Hours*, p. 364. • **26**. Schell, *Observing the Nixon Years*, p. 20. • **27**. 'U.S. Lawyers Criticize Army on Green Beret, My Lai Case', *International Herald Tribune*, 29 Dec. 1969; 'Mansfield Asks Congress Study into Alleged Vietnam Massacre', *New York Times*, 23 Nov. 1969. • **28**. Alexander Haig, Memorandum for Henry A. Kissinger, Secret/Sensitive, Subject: My Lai Atrocities, 4 Dec. 1969, in NPMP, NSC, AMH-SF, Box 1004, Folder: My Lai Incident (2 of 2). • **29**. Henry A. Kissinger, Memorandum for the President, Secret/Sensitive, Subject: My Lai Atrocities, 4 Dec. 1969, in NPMP, NSC, AMH-SF, Box 1004, Folder: My Lai Incident (2 of 2). See also Bryce N. Harlow, Memorandum for the President, Subject: My Lai Atrocities, 3 Dec. 1969, in ibid. See also NPMP, NSC, AMH-SF, Box 1004, Folder: Possible My Lai Commission; Henry A. Kissinger, Memorandum for the President,

Secret/Sensitive, Subject: My Lai Atrocities, 6 Dec. 1969, in NPMP, AMH-CF, Box 960, Folder: Haig Chron. 17–20 Dec. 1969 (1 of 2); ibid., Box 961, Folder: Haig Chron. 21–31 Dec. 1969 (1 of 2) and NPMP, NSC, Staff Files – Lake Chron. Series, Box 1046, Folder: T. Lake Chron. – December 1969. • **30**. Varnado Simpson, Michael Bernhardt and Michael Terry were amongst the witnesses to the first hour. • **31**. See amongst many others, 'The Killings at Song [sic] My', *Newsweek*, 8 Dec. 1969, pp. 33–41. • **32**. Amongst others on the CCI Board were Noam Chomsky, professor of Linguistics at the Massachusetts Institute of Technology; Ralph Schoenman, former secretary to Bertrand Russell; comedian and political activist Dick Gregory; Melvin L. Wulf as representative of the American Civil Liberties Union; and Eric Seitz as representative of the National Lawyers Guild. • **33**. 'Unofficial Atrocities Attributed to Pentagon', *Christian Science Monitor*, 10 May 1970. The 'National Veterans' Inquiry into US War Crimes', which was held at the beginning of December 1970 in the Du Pont Plaza Hotel in Washington, DC, was amongst the best known hearings carried out by the CCI. • **34**. The 'Concerned Officers Movement' was an opposition group of active officers claiming to have 600 members, of whom twenty were still stationed in Vietnam at the beginning of 1971: 'Five Officers Seek War Crimes Inquiry', *Washington Post*, 13 Jan. 1971 and Neil Sheehan, 'Five Officers Say They Seek Formal War Crimes Inquiries', *New York Times*, 13 Jan. 1971. In spring 1971 forty young officers who had received posting orders to Vietnam, sent a petition to the White House and threatened to refuse to obey orders if the war, pursued half-heartedly in their opinion, were not ended forthwith: Bilton/Sim, *Four Hours*, pp. 311–13. • **35**. In summer 1971 representatives of the 'Vietnam Veterans Against the War' (VVAW) said they had 15,000 members; outside observers said 7,000: 'Confessions of "The Winter Soldiers"', *Life*, 9 Jul. 1971, p. 25; Fact Sheet, in NA, RG 127, HMC-HDPT, TF, Box 4, Folder: Command Concerns: Drugs, Racial Strife, Fragging; Moser, *New Winter Soldiers*; and Nicosia, *Home to War*. • **36**. 'Confessions of "The Winter Soldiers"', *Life*, 9 Jul. 1971, p. 25. See also Vietnam Veterans Against the War, *Winter Soldier Investigation* and Stacewicz, *Oral History*. The transcripts of the 'Winter Soldier' hearing in Detroit are reprinted in USCR, 7 Apr. 1971, pp. E28252–936. • **37**. Lewy, *America in Vietnam*, pp. 316–17. • **38**. For criticism of Mark Lane's *Conversations with Americans: Testimony from thirty-two Vietnam Veterans*, New York, 1970, see the well-regarded article by Sheehan, 'War Crime Trials?' • **39**. OSA, Memorandum for the Record, Subject: Resume of Congressional Hearings, 23 Apr. 1971, in NA, RG 319, AS, ODCS-PER, VWCWG, CaFi, Box 9, Folder: Rottmann Allegation (CCI), Case 63. In the 1990s John F. Kerry was actually elected to the Senate. In November 2004 he lost the election to the presidency to George W. Bush. • **40**. Elmer E. Snyder, Interoffice Memorandum, For: Acting Chief, Field Assistance Division, Subject: Desk Sheets, 1 Feb. 1971, in NA, RG 319,

AS, ODCS-PER, VWCWG, CF, Box 4, Folder: Reporting and Investigating War Crimes Allegations – Procedures and Regulations. See also ibid., Folder: Action File – 'Winter Soldier Investigation' Hearings, 1971 (Part 1 of 2). • **41**. NA, RG 319, ODCS-PER, VWCWG, CaFi, Box 3, Folder: War Crimes Allegations Index (For Allegations Other than My Lai); NA, RG 319, ODCS-PER, VWCWG, CF, Box 3, Folder: War Crimes Allegations Working Papers (1); ibid., Folder: SGS Tasking for Monitoring of War Crimes Allegations. • **42**. At the end of 2005 Nicolas Turse handed in to the Department of Epidemiology of Columbia University, New York City, a hitherto unpublished dissertation about war crimes in Vietnam which makes use of material from the files of the Vietnam War Crimes Working Group. Based on these files, in summer 2006 Turse presented a handful of cases and perpetrators in a series of articles for the *Los Angeles Times*: see Deborah Nelson and Nick Turse, 'A Tortured Past', *Los Angeles Times*, 20 Aug. 2006. See now also Deborah Nelson, *The War behind Me: Vietnam Veterans Confront the Truth about US War Crimes*, New York, 2008. The journalists Michael Sallah and Mitch Weiss used the Tiger Force files of the VWCWG in their Pulitzer Prize-winning history of the Commando unit Tiger Force: see Sallah and Weiss, *Tiger Force*, London 2006. • **43**. For relevant preliminary work see Greiner, 'Spurensuche'; id., '"First To Go, Last to Know"'; id., 'Sexuelle Gewalt'; id., '"Silent majority"'; id., 'Blutpumpe'. • **44**. See Mühlhäuser, 'Sexuelle Gewalt'. • **45**. Peers, *My Lai Inquiry*. • **46**. See Bilton and Sim, *Four Hours*; Lewy, *America in Vietnam*; Olson and Roberts, *My Lai*; Hersh, *Report on the Massacre* and id., *Cover-Up*. The files had been passed on to Hersh by an informant in the Army Department before their official release. • **47**. Amongst the most important exceptions are Schell, *Real War*; Schulzinger, *Time for War*; Moyar, *Phoenix*; and Prados, *Blood Road*. • **48**. This criticism can also be applied to the various accounts of the My Lai (4) massacre. Fixed on a narrow time frame and a single event, important questions about the dynamic and course of a ten-year war were left out of consideration. • **49**. Lewy, *America in Vietnam*, p. 345. • **50**. Spector, *After Tet*, p. 202; Resic, *American Warriors*, pp. 212–13; Oliver, *My Lai in History*, p. 13. • **51**. In official studies put forward since the 1990s by the Vietnamese side there is absolutely no reference to this dimension of the war: see Military History Institute, *Victory*. The Viet Cong type of warfare is raised in Diem, *Jaws of History*. In American files the brutality of the 'fratricidal war' is repeatedly mentioned: see Sworn Testimony, Anthony B. Herbert, 28 Sep. 1970, in NA, RG 319, AS, ODCS-PER, VWCWG, CaFi, Box 8, Folder: Herbert Allegation (Part 2 of 2), Case 58. • **52**. NA, RG 319, AS, ODCS-PER, VWCWG, CaFi, Box 4, Folder: Bentley Allegation, Case 12 (1). • **53**. Investigator's Statement, Interview John P. Casey, 14 Dec. 1970; Sworn Statement John P. Casey, 6 Jan 1971; Sworn Statement Walter F. Berninger, 6 Jan. 1971; Sworn Statement Joseph E. Benham, 13 Jan. 1971; Sworn Statement John Robert Heintzelman,

22 Jan. 1971; Sworn Statement Bruce A. Sprague, 18 Feb. 1971; Sworn Statement Charles H. Boss, 16 Dec. 1970, in NA, RG 472, USFSEA, MACV, DRAC, IG, Preliminary Inquiry Re: Colonel Franklin, Box 2, Folder: Preliminary Investigation Re: Col. Franklin Vol. IV (Pt. 1 of 3) 1971. • **54**. Quoted in Lewy, *America in Vietnam*, p. 369. See also Friedman (ed.), *Law of War*, p. 804–9, and Kramer, 'Race-Making'. • **55**. See Klein and Schumacher (eds), *Kolonialkriege*; Walter, 'Symmetry and Asymmetry'; Münkler, *Wandel des Krieges*. • **56**. See Tuchman, *Torheit*. • **57**. Anderson (ed.), *Facing My Lai*, p. 47. • **58**. See NA, RG 319, AS, PI-AC, Box 7, Folder: Conduct of the War, MACV Directives, ROE, Chron. File # 2 (1 of 2) and (2 of 2); Army Response to Recommendation C of the Peers Inquiry, in NA, RG 319, AS, PI-AC, Box 21, Folder: Peers Report Fallout; ibid., Box 22, Folder: Psychological Aspect of Son My Incident – Chron. File # 1; ODCS-PER, Memorandum For: Secretary of the General Staff, Subject: Lessons Learned from the Son My Incident, in NA, RG 319, AS, ODCS-PER, VWCWG, MLM, Box 6, Folder: Release of My Lai Documents under FOIA and ibid., Box 7, Folder: Congressional Correspondence My Lai: Correspondence with Rep. Samuel S. Stratton. • **59**. See Kitfield, *Prodigal Soldiers*. • **60**. Carl Rippberger, quoted in USCR, 7 Apr. 1971, p. E2926; see ibid., pp. E2924 and E2909: 'I was that tiny premature baby – born Christmas, 1942 at St Mary's Hospital . . . When I question the policies and the decisions and the people that made me a killer – When I ask you why you never asked why – You treat me like a stranger – Hey! Remember me?' • **61**. Jim Weber, quoted in USCR, 7 Apr. 1971, p. E2929; see ibid., 7 Apr. 1971, pp. E2828, E2857; Gross, 'Lieutenant Calley's Army' and James D. Henry, 'Men of "B" Company'. Myrtle Meadlo expressed herself in similar vein after her son Paul had confessed to taking part in the massacre of My Lai (4) on television: 'He wasn't raised up like that. I raised him up to be a good boy and I did everything I could. They come along and took him to the service. He fought for his country and look what they done to him – made a murderer out of him, to start with.' Quoted in Bilton and Sim, *Four Hours*, p. 263. • **62**. James D. Henry, quoted in USCR, 6 Apr. 1971, p. E2851; see ibid., 6 Apr. 1971, pp. E2826, E2861–2, E2865; ibid., 7 Apr. 1971, pp. E2929–30; James Higgins, 'Horror Takes the Stand', *The Nation*, 4 Jan. 1971, pp. 6–8. • **63**. Thomas Paine, *The American Crisis*, Whitefish, Mont., 2004, p. 3. • **64**. See the interviews conducted by *Life* journalists: Donald Jackson, 'Confessions of "The Winter Soldiers"', *Life*, 9 Jul. 1971, pp. 23–8. • **65**. Major General Kenneth J. Hodson (Judge Advocate General, US Army), 'From Nuremberg to Mylai', lecture to the Minnesota State Bar Association, 18 Jun. 1971, quoted in *Congressional Record*, Senate, 29 Jun. 1971, p. S10210. • **66**. Slotkin, *Gunfighter Nation*, pp. 88–124. • **67**. Bilton and Sim, *Four Hours*, pp. 366–7. • **68**. NA, RG 319, AS, PI-FR, Vol. II: Testimony, Box 18, Book 11, Haeberle: SUM APP T-174, p. 4; ibid., Vol. IV: CID Statements, Box 57, Sworn Statement Ronald L. Haeberle, 25 Aug. 1969, p. 5. • **69**. Ronald Haeberle quoted in Bilton

and Sim, *Four Hours*, p. 242. • **70**. The authors dealing with the reactions to My Lai (4) concentrate on an analysis of opinion polls: see Belknap, *War on Trial*, pp. 191–216. Michael S. Foley's collection of source material refers to the Vietnam War in general and only touches in passing on the subject of war crimes: Foley (ed.), *Dear Dr Spock*. • **71**. Richard Rorty, *Achieving Our Country: Leftist Thought in Twentieth-Century America*, Cambridge, Mass. and London, 1998, pp. 39–73. • **72**. See Bacevich, *New American Militarism*.

1 Masters of War

1. Lyndon B. Johnson in an interview with Doris Kearns, quoted in Karnow, *Vietnam*, p. 485. • **2**. Bernard B. Fall, 'This Isn't Munich, It's Spain', *Ramparts*, Dec. 1965. • **3**. Lewy, *America in Vietnam*, p. 99; Spector, *After Tet*, p. 11; Anderson (ed.), *Facing My Lai*, p. 220; Olson, *Vietnam War*, p. 103. • **4**. The conservative estimates are sourced from Lewy, *America in Vietnam*, pp. 442ff., 448–53. Lewy works with the problematic hospital statistics. Other data can be found in Anderson (ed.), *Facing My Lai*, p. 220; Spector, *After Tet*, p. 207; Olson, *Vietnam War*, p. 112; Tucker, *Encyclopedia*, pp. 64, 140. • **5**. 'How North Vietnam Won the War', interview with Colonel Bui Tin, *Wall Street Journal*, 3 Aug. 1995. • **6**. For the debate over asymmetrical wars, see Mack, 'Why Big Nations Lose Small Wars'; Daase, *Kleine Kriege – Große Wirkung*; Arreguin-Toft, *How the Weak Win Wars*; Münkler, *Wandel des Krieges*; Gilbert, *Why the North Won*. • **7**. See Walter, *Symmetry and Asymmetry*. • **8**. Situation report of the US Army, quoted in Sheehan, *Bright Shining Lie*, p. 688. • **9**. For the political and social acceptance of the Viet Cong, see Schell, *The Real War*. Schell's observations were also shared by many Pentagon analysts: Headquarters Pacific Air Force, Directorate, Contemporary Historical Examination of Current Operations, Project Report: Air Support in Quang Ngai Province, Secret, 25 Feb. 1970, p. 3ff., in NA, RG 319, AS, PI-AC, Box 27, Folder: RVN Trip Report Information – Folder #3; Debriefing Report, Major General Charles M. Gettys, Commanding General, Americal Division, 19 May 1969, p. 1ff., in NA, RG 319, AS, PI-AC, Box 5, Folder: Background Americal Division; PI-FR, Vol. I: Analyses, Chapter 3, p. 3, in NA, RG 319, AS, PI-FR, Box 1, Vol. I. • **10**. The dossier of 25 Feb. 1968 ('Plan for Political Struggle from February to April 1968') was captured by US troops in the south (IV Corps Tactical Zone), in NA, RG 127, USMC, HMC-HMD, BM-68, Box 5, Folder: Enemy Plans 29 May 68. • **11**. The demand for the total liquidation of all 'agents' can be found in a stolen document belonging to the Current Affairs Party Committee dated 5 Feb. 1968, in NA, RG 127, USMC, HMC-HMD, BM-68, Box 10, Folder: PRP Assessment of Tet 68. See ibid., Box 10, Folder: Strategy – 12/67 (Pike Assessment: Dec. 1967). • **12**. Quoted in Schell, *Real War*, p. 17. • **13**. Radio Hanoi, quoted in Office

Chief of Staff Army, Office Memorandum: Huê Massacres, 31 Dec. 1969, p. 3, in NA, RG 319, AS, PI-AC, Box 12, Folder: Huê File (1 of 2). • **14**. See Valentine, *Phoenix Program*, pp. 43, 59; Lewy, *America in Vietnam*, pp. 88, 109, 272–5. Similar details of those murdered and kidnapped may be found in US military files: see Army Report: Law of Southeast Asia Rules of Engagement, Law of War, undated, Annex B, pp. 6–9, in NA, RG 319, AS, ODCS-PER, VWCWG, CF, Box 4. For attacks on refugee camps and villages, see Lewy, *America in Vietnam*, pp. 245, 276; NA, RG 319, AS, ODCS-PER, VWCWG, CF, Box 4, Folder: Army Report – Law of Southeast Asia Rules of Engagement, Law of War, undated, p. 96 and Annex B, p. 5. • **15**. See Beckett, *Modern Insurgencies and Counter-Insurgencies*; James, *Savage Wars*; Vandervort, *Wars of Imperial Conquest*; Klein and Schumacher, *Kolonialkriege*; Walter, *Symmetry and Asymmetry*. • **16**. Quoted in Fall, *Street Without Joy*, p. 34. The comment coined by Giap on the French Army was, in his view, no less relevant to the US armed forces: see Giap, *People's War*. • **17**. From a North Vietnamese Army document captured by US troops on 9 Sep. 1968 (Unit 500, Number: 154/L. 12, p. 31), in NA, RG 127, USMC, HMC-HMD, BM-68, Box 5, Folder: PLAF/PAVN Assessment of Strategy 1965–68. For the background to this strategy see Fall, *Street Without Joy*, pp. 15, 65, 130. Fundamental in this context is Münkler, 'Guerillakrieg und Terrorismus'. • **18**. 'How North Vietnam Won the War', interview with Colonel Bui Tin, *Wall Street Journal*, 3 Aug. 1995. See Cheng Huan, *The Vietnam War from the Other Side*. • **19**. For Viet Minh handling of French prisoners, see Fall, *Street Without Joy*, pp. 71, 100, 219. • **20**. Hoang Phan An, quoted in NA, RG 319, AS, ODCS-PER, VWCWG, CF, Box 4, Folder: Army Report – Law of Southeast Asia Rules of Engagement, Law of War, undated, Annex B, p. 4. • **21**. See Fall, *Street Without Joy*, pp. 16, 113ff., 146ff., 151, 162; Hammer, *One Morning*, pp. 53–4; Lewy, *America in Vietnam*, pp. 59, 71ff., 102; Neil Sheehan, 'Not a Dove, But No Longer a Hawk', *New York Times Magazine*, 9 Oct. 1966, p. 137. • **22**. MACV Briefing on Enemy Order of Battle, Nov. 1967, in NA, RG 127, USMC, HMC-HMD, BM-68, Box 5, Folder: MACV Order of Battle Briefing and Folder: Order of Battle – Statistics of Forces, Dec. 67–Jan. 68. These figures do not include the so-called 'Self-Defence Forces'. They included all those who provided support services in any way for the regular troops and the guerrillas who were engaged in fighting – informants, couriers, tax collectors, explosive experts. It is not known how many people this involved. Estimates vary between hundreds of thousands and one and a half million. As most of them were at best lightly armed, if at all, and did not leave their permanent homes, they were also not classified as enemy armed forces by American analysts. • **23**. Spector, *After Tet*, p. 315. • **24**. Quoted in NA, RG 319, AS, ODCS-PER, VWCWG, CF, Box 4, Folder: Army Report – Law of Southeast Asia Rules of Engagement, Law of War, undated, Annex B, p. 4. • **25**. Quoted in Fall, *Street Without Joy*, p. 35. • **26**. MACV Briefing on Enemy Order of Battle, Nov. 1967, in NA, RG 127, USMC,

HMC-HMD, BM-68, Box 5, Folder: MACV Order of Battle Briefing. For the Viet Minh war experiences, see Fall, *Street Without Joy*, pp. 33–48, 54, 70, 186ff., 234ff. For the role of the USSR and the People's Republic of China, see Gaiduk, *The Soviet Union and the Vietnam War*; Zhai, *China and the Vietnam Wars*. • **27**. The jargon of the aerial war planners is taken from the Pentagon Papers: see Ellsberg, *Secrets*, p. 364. • **28**. Quoted in ibid., p. 82. • **29**. For Edward Lansdale, see ibid., pp. 99, 138. • **30**. Quoted in Sheehan, *Die Große Lüge*, p. 383; see ibid., p. 528. • **31**. Robert S. McNamara to Lyndon B. Johnson, Nov. 1966, quoted in Lewy, *America in Vietnam*, p. 82 and Bilton and Sim, *Four Hours*, p. 42. • **32**. Quoted in Ellsberg, *Secrets*, p. 83. • **33**. George F. Ball, quoted in Ellsberg, *Secrets*, p. 82. See Head, 'Counterinsurgency in Vietnam', in Olson, *Vietnam War*, pp. 125–43; Berman, *Planning a Tragedy*; Gardner, *Pay Any Price*; Kaiser, *American Tragedy*; Logevall, *Choosing War*; Jones, *Death of a Generation*; Ball, *The Past Has Another Pattern*; Di Leo, *Rethinking of Containment*. • **34**. Quoted in Schlesinger, *Thousand Days*, p. 547. See Jones, *Death of a Generation*, pp. 232, 261, 267. • **35**. Richard Nixon on 15 Feb. 1973, quoted in The White House, Memorandum of Conversation, Secret, 15 Feb. 1973, p. 2, in NA, NPMP, NSC, Presidential/HAK MemCons, Box 1026, Folder: MemCons – Jan.–Mar. 1973, Presidential/HAK. See Ellsberg, *Secrets*, p. 216. • **36**. McNamara, Blight and Brigham, *Argument Without End*. • **37**. Ellsberg, *Secrets*, p. 192. See ibid., pp. 188–92, 274ff. The 'quagmire' theory refers chiefly to the works of Arthur Schlesinger Jr. and David Halberstam. • **38**. See Schlesinger, *Imperial Presidency*; Greiner, 'Zwischen "Totalem Krieg" und "Kleinen Kriegen"'. • **39**. For Harry Truman and Dean Acheson, see Tuchman, *Torheit*, pp. 302ff. • **40**. Quoted in Tuchman, *Torheit*, p. 283. For Kennedy's fears, see Jones, *Death of a Generation*, pp. 12, 238, 352; for Khrushchev, see Fursenko and Naftali, *One Hell of a Gamble*, p. 73. • **41**. Quoted in Tuchman, *Torheit*, p.319. • **42**. Quoted in Kolko, *Anatomy of a War*, p. 113. For the influence of the Vietnam Lobby, see Morgan, *Vietnam Lobby*. • **43**. Quoted in Gibson, *Perfect War*, p. 76. • **44**. Quoted in Halberstam, *Best and Brightest*, p. 76. See also Jones, *Death of a Generation*, p. 120. See ibid., pp. 14, 39ff., 67, 117, 173ff., 355. • **45**. Henry Kissinger made the most emphatic argument of that time in favour of 'small wars' at the end of the 1950s in his book *Nuclear Weapons and Foreign Policy*. See also Taylor, *The Uncertain Trumpet*. For the obsession with the anti-guerrilla war, see Lewy, *America in Vietnam*, p. 85; Greiner, '"First To Go, Last to Know"'. • **46**. For Kennedy's ambivalent stance, see Jones, *Death of a Generation*, pp. 45–50, 55, 59, 63, 112, 120ff., 145, 159, 189ff., 233ff., 243ff., 314ff., 318–21, 338, 348, 355ff., 377ff., 426; Newman, *JFK and Vietnam*. • **47**. Quoted in Jones, *Death of a Generation*, p. 449. See ibid., pp. 444ff. • **48**. Robert Komer, head of the Civil Operations and Revolutionary Development Support Programme (CORDS) in Vietnam, quoted in Ellsberg, *Secrets*, p. 178. Countless other Pentagon employees expressed themselves in similar vein to Komer: see ibid., pp. 53, 56, 60.

• **49**. Tuchman, *Torheit*, pp. 346–7. • **50**. Quoted in Jones, *Death of a Generation*, p. 445. • **51**. Quoted in Memorandum of Conversation (Participants: President Nixon, Elliot Richardson, the Joint Chiefs of Staff, Brent Scowcroft), Secret/Nodis/XGDS, 15 Feb. 1973, p. 2, in NA, NPMP, NSC, Presidential/HAK MemCons, Box 1026, Folder: MemCons, Jan.–Mar. 1973, Presidential/HAK. • **52**. Quoted in ibid. • **53**. Richard Nixon on 4 May 1972, quoted in Kimball, *War Files*, pp. 219–20. • **54**. Quoted in *Foreign Relations of the United States* (FRUS), 1964–68, Vol. XV, p. 402. • **55**. Tuchman, *Torheit*, p. 365; Leslie H. Gelb, 'Vietnam: Nobody Wrote the Last Act', *Washington Post*, 20 Jun. 1971. • **56**. Quoted in Berman, *No Peace*, p. 55. • **57**. Tuchman, *Torheit*, p. 312. • **58**. Gelb, 'Last Act'. • **59**. Tuchman, *Torheit*, p. 282. For Kennedy's Vietnam policies, see Jones, *Death of a Generation*, pp. 27, 52, 74ff., 79, 89, 138, 146, 197, 201, 220; Shultz, *Secret War*; Greiner, 'Der "Alice in Wonderland"-Präsident', pp. 74–9. For the background and repercussions of the coup against Diem, see Jones, *Death of a Generation*, pp. 277ff., 310–15, 343–70, 386–406, 422–8, 439ff., 454ff. For criticism of Robert Kennedy, Theodore Sorensen and William Bundy, see Jones, *Death of a Generation*, p. 452. • **60**. Quoted in Kimball, *War Files*, pp. 43–4. • **61**. Quoted in documentary film by Erroll Morris, *In the Fog of War – Robert S. McNamara and Vietnam*, 2004. • **62**. Richard Nixon on 17 Oct. 1969, quoted in Kimball, *War Files*, p. 45. • **63**. Henry Kissinger on 18 Sep. 1971, quoted in Kimball, *War Files*, p. 45. See also Memorandum of Conversation (Participants: John McCormack, Carl Albert, Bryce Harlow, Henry A. Kissinger, William Watts), Limited Official Use, 6 Nov. 1969, in NA, NPMP, NSC, Presidential/HAK MemCons, Box 1026, Folder: MemCons Jun.–Dec. 1969, Presidential/HAK (1 of 2). • **64**. For Johnson's obsession with his own image in history, see Tuchman, *Torheit*, pp. 388, 398; Ellsberg, *Secrets*, pp. 49, 197ff.; Jones, *Death of a Generation*, p. 443; Gardner, *Any Price*, p. 513ff. For Nixon, see Berman, *No Peace*, pp. 56, 80; Kimball, *War Files*, pp. 27ff., 133ff., 148ff., 168, 174, 187, 197, 221ff. For the 'GI Generation', see Kaiser, *American Tragedy*; Engelhardt, *Victory Culture*; and Cuordileone, *Manhood and American Political Culture*. • **65**. For Nixon's pontificating on a 'profile in courage', see Harry Robbins Haldeman, diary entry of 27 Jan. 1973 and id., 'Vietnam White Paper', undated, quoted in Berman, *No Peace*, pp. 236, 238. • **66**. Richard Nixon on 19 Mar. 1971 to Henry Kissinger, quoted in Kimball, *War Files*, p. 146. • **67**. Richard Nixon on 27 Apr. 1971 to Henry Kissinger, quoted in Kimball, *War Files*, p. 159. • **68**. Richard Nixon on 23 Jun. 1971 to Henry Kissinger, quoted in Kimball, *War Files*, p. 167 (my emphasis). • **69**. Richard Nixon to Harry Robbins Haldeman, quoted in Haldeman, *Ends of Power*, p. 82. See Kimball, *War Files*, pp. 90, 124, 140, 149, 162–5, 169, 226ff. • **70**. Quoted in Haldeman, *Ends of Power*, p. 96. See Sagan and Suri, 'Madman Nuclear Alert'; Burr and Kimball, 'Nuclear Ploy'; Ellsberg, *Secrets*, p. 344: Kimball, *War Files*, pp. 15–19, 54–64, 175, 206. • **71**. For Nixon's interpretation of Eisenhower's Korea policies, see Memorandum of Conversation (Participants: President Nixon, Elliott Richardson, the Joint Chiefs of Staff, Brent Scowcroft), Secret/Nodis/XGDS, 15 Feb. 1973, p. 2, in NA, NPMP, NSC, Presidential/HAK MemCons, Box 1026, Folder: MemCons, Jan.–Mar. 1973, Presidential/HAK. Discussions with Henry Kissinger on this matter are documented in Kimball, *War Files*, pp. 63, 117, 183ff. Berman, *No Peace*, p. 49. • **72**. See Kimball, *War Files*, pp. 27ff., 133ff., 148ff., 168, 174, 187, 197, 221ff.; Berman, *No Peace*, p. 80; Greiner, 'Die Falle des Nicht-aufhören-Könnens'. • **73**. Richard Nixon on 2 Jun. 1971, quoted in Kimball, *War Files*, p. 163. • **74**. Richard Nixon on 2 Jun. 1971, quoted in Kimball, *War Files*, pp. 163, 165; see ibid., pp. 151, 169. • **75**. Henry Kissinger on 23 Jun. 1971, quoted in Berman, *No Peace*, p. 58. • **76**. For the background to the 'Christmas Bombardment', see Berman, *No Peace*, pp. 174ff., 187, 196–206, 212, 215, 218ff. and Kimball, *War Files*, pp. 262, 272–9.

2 Generals

1. Quoted in Anderson (ed.), *Facing My Lai*, p. 132. • **2**. William DePuy, quoted in Bilton and Sim, *Four Hours*, p. 33 and Sheehan, *Bright Shining Lie*, p. 568. • **3**. See Spector, *After Tet*, p. 220. For the characteristics of 'total warfare', see Chickering, Greiner and Förster (eds), *World at Total War*, pp. 1–19, 375–85. • **4**. William Westmoreland during a press conference on 14 Apr. 1967, quoted in Lewy, *America in Vietnam*, p. 73. See Sheehan, *Bright Shining Lie*, p. 642; Anderson (ed.), *Facing My Lai*, p. 132. For the part played by search and destroy in all combat operations see Lewy, *America in Vietnam*, p. 63. Leepson, *Dictionary*, p. 363. • **5**. Department of State, outgoing telegram, Dean Rusk for American Embassy Saigon (Ambassador Lodge), 27 Aug. 1968, p. 2, in NA, RG 338, USAC, HD22-CR, Box 16, Folder: Confidential 511-02 Vietnam, US Operation of PoW Camps in SVN (1965–66). Dean Rusk compares the costs quoted with what he considered to be the totally inadequate expenditure on POW camps. • **6**. For the cross-over point, see Lewy, *America in Vietnam*, pp. 68, 74. For the unrealistic expectations of the strategies supporting a war of attrition, see Tuchman, *Torheit*, p. 415; Berman, *Lyndon Johnson's War*; Krepinevich, *Army and Vietnam*. • **7**. Sheehan, *Die Große Lüge*, p. 631. See ibid., pp. 83, 114–20, 149ff.; Tuchman, *Torheit*, p. 432; Olson, *Handbook*, pp. 115, 128, 133; Lewy, *America in Vietnam*, p. 116; Spector, *After Tet*, p. 282. For the Combined Action Platoons, see Peterson, *Combined Action Platoons*; Cable, *Counterinsurgency Doctrine*. For the allocation of tasks within the CAPs, see MACV, Handbook for Military Support of Pacification, Feb. 1968, p. 53ff., in NA, RG 319, AS, PI-FR, Vol. III: Exhibits, Box 54, Book 4: Miscellaneous Documents. • **8**. George S. Patton III, quoted in Department of the Army, Office of the Secretary of the Army, Memorandum for the Record, 27 Apr.

1971, p. 2, in NA, RG 319, AS, ODCS-PER, VWCWG, CF, Box 5, Folder: Memorandums for Record – Summaries of Congressional Hearings on War Crimes, Apr. 1971. • **9**. An unnamed senior officer, quoted in Lewy, *America in Vietnam*, p. 138. • **10**. Ibid. • **11**. Between 1965 and 1971 114 Combined Action Platoons operated in the five provinces in the battle zone of I Corps. In 1969 the United States had assigned to them 1,735 Marines; in 1970 the figure was 1,949 – or two per cent of the 100,000 Marines then stationed in Vietnam. In the same two years the South Vietnamese Army had posted 3,875 and 4,330 soldiers respectively to the CAP: Dunnigan and Nofi, *Secrets*, p. 91; Spector, *After Tet*, p. 34. • **12**. An unnamed member of a CAP, quoted in Spector, *After Tet*, p. 195. • **13**. For details on the financial expenditure, personnel and casualty rates of the CAPs, see Spector, *After Tet*, pp. 188, 192ff.; Lewy, *America in Vietnam*, pp. 89, 116; MACV, Handbook for Military Support of Pacification, Feb. 1968, pp. 52–4, in NA, RG 319, AS, PI-FR, Vol. III: Exhibits, Box 54, Book 4: Miscellaneous Documents. Fundamental to this subject is the study by Blaufarb, *Counter-Insurgency Era*. • **14**. Robert Komer, quoted in Sheehan, *Die Große Lüge*, p. 667. See Tuchman, *Torheit*, p. 360. • **15**. MACV, Memorandum: Phung Hoang (Phoenix) Program, 24 Dec. 1969, pp. 1, 3, in NA, RG 338, USAC, HD22-UR, Box 43, Folder: S11-02 Vietnam. Phung Hoang (Phoenix) Program (1969). See also Republic of Vietnam, Central Pacification and Development Council, Guidelines: Pacification Campaign 1969, 15 Dec. 1968, in NA, RG 472, USAV, II FFV, CSO-CGR, Box 5, Folder: Pacification Files 1969. • **16**. An unnamed member of a counter-terrorism team, quoted in Valentine, *Phoenix Program*, p. 109. • **17**. See Valentine, *Phoenix Program*, pp. 44ff., 61ff., 107ff., 115, 119, 126, 151, 154, 170ff., 214, 221ff., 230, 359, 365ff., 381; Lewy, *America in Vietnam*, pp. 281ff., 291; Head, 'Other War', in Olson, *Handbook*, p. 129ff. For the military operational interest in Phoenix, see 'Operation Dragnet', *Newsweek*, 24 Jul. 1967, p. 25; NA, RG 338, USAC, HD22-UR, Box 50, Folder: S11-04: 'Operation Dragnet' Newsweek Article (1967); Bilton and Sim, *Four Hours*, p. 88ff.; Valentine, *Phoenix Program*, pp. 91, 138, 141, 145, 151, 161, 203–11, 284ff. • **18**. Sheehan, *Die Große Lüge*, p. 731ff. • **19**. In the Matter of the Application of Lieutenant Francis Theodore Reitemeyer (Petitioner) vs. Lieutenant Colonel Hector McCrea, Commanding Officer, Troop Command, Fort Holabird, Maryland and United States Army (Respondents), 29 Jan. 1969, p. 5, in NPMP, NSC, AMH-SF, Box 1004, Folder: My Lai Incident (1 of 2). • **20**. Michael Uhl, statement before the Subcommittee on Foreign Operations and Government Information, US House of Representatives, Committee on Government Operation, 2 Aug. 1971, pp. 1101, 1104, in NA, RG 319, AS, ODCS-PER, VWCWG, CF, Box 4, Folder: House Hearings: Currency Exchange in Southeast Asia, 2 Aug. 1971 (Includes War Crimes Allegations). For a similar statement from Kenneth B. Osborn, see ibid., pp. 1111, 1119. Further recollections of Phoenix have been drawn up by Cook, *Advisor* and Herrington, *War in the Villages*. • **21**. Michael Uhl, statement before the Subcommittee on Foreign Operations and Government Information, US House of Representatives, Committee on Government Operation, 2 Aug. 1971, p. 1176, in NA, RG 319, AS, ODCS-PER, VWCWG, CF, Box 4, Folder: House Hearings: Currency Exchange in Southeast Asia, 2 Aug. 1971 (Includes War Crimes Allegations). For the deployment of artillery and Air Force against the Viet Cong infrastructure, see also Colby, *Lost Victory*, pp. 247–50. • **22**. Valentine, *Phoenix Program*, pp. 171, 188ff., 257, 381ff., 420. For the estimated death toll, see Moyar, *Birds of Prey*, pp. 235–41; Dunnigan and Nofi, *Secrets,* p. 196; Tucker (ed.), *Encyclopedia*, p. 67; Lewy, *America in Vietnam*, p. 281.ff.; Gibson, *Perfect War*, p. 302ff. • **23**. MACV, Strategic Objectives Plan, Spring 1969, quoted in Lewy, *America in Vietnam*, p. 78. • **24**. The inability to change course is also the subject of Isaacs, *Without Honour* and of Joseph, *Cracks in the Empire*. • **25**. See Krepinevich, *Army and Vietnam*; Weigley, *American Way of War*; Greiner, 'Der "Totale Krieg" im Spiegel amerikanischer Militärzeitschriften'. • **26**. Sheehan, *Die Große Lüge*, p. 285; Loren Baritz, *Backfire,* pp. 17–55, 233–82. • **27**. Tuchman, *Torheit*, p. 471. • **28**. Colonel Frank Barker, quoted in Bilton and Sim, *My Lai*, p. 192. Whether and how the experts' reports drawn up within the Army in the 1950s on guerrilla and anti-guerrilla warfare during the Second World War were received remains an open question for military historiography. • **29**. Showalter, 'The War That Was Never Fought', p. 16. For the institutional crisis, see also Sheehan, *Die Große Lüge*, p. 66; Olson, *Handbook*, pp. 95–124. • **30**. For details, see Cable, *Counterinsurgency Doctrine*; Lewy, *America in Vietnam*, pp. 98, 119; Sheehan, *Die Große Lüge*, p. 122; Spector, *After Tet*, p. 220. Under this pressure even a resolute advocate of pacification strategy such as John Paul Vann eventually became a supporter of the bombing with B-52s. As his biographer Neil Sheehan writes, Vann derived an almost erotic pleasure from being able to direct the B-52 attacks: Sheehan, *Die Große Lüge*, p. 784. • **31**. Quoted in Sheehan, *Die Große Lüge*, p. 636. For McNamara's criticism of the Marine Corps's pacification proposals, see also Tuchman, *Torheit*, pp. 288, 297, 308–17. • **32**. This quote by McNamara is not included in the primary sources. However, as well as Tuchman, *Torheit*, p. 326, other authors vouch for its authenticity: see Rosenberg, 'Arms and the American Way', p. 170 and Summers, *On Strategy*, p. 18. • **33**. For a full discussion of the connection between political lies, the legitimation crisis and the escalation of the war, see Ellsberg, *Secrets*. • **34**. Gelb and Betts, *The System Worked*. • **35**. Charles Sweet to Edward Lansdale, 12 May 1968, Visit to Districts 6 and 8, in NA, RG 472, USFSEA, MACV, IG, ID, RI, Box 5, Folder: MIV-16-68 Damage in Saigon, Part 1 of 4. • **36**. MACIG, Report of Investigation Concerning Destruction Resulting from the VC Offensive of 5–13 May 1968, p. 24, in NA, RG 472, USFSEA, MACV, IG, ID, RI, Box 5, Folder: MIV-16-68

Damage in Saigon, Part 1 of 4. • **37**. A captain in the US Air Force, quoted in Valentine, *Phoenix Program*, p. 216. • **38**. During the course of the debate over My Lai Neil Sheehan spoke about this early experience: Sheehan, 'War Crimes Trials?' • **39**. See NA, RG 319, AS, ODCS-PER, VWCWG, CaFi, Box 12, Notley Allegation (CCI), Part 1 of 2, Case 85; USCR, 7 Apr. 1971, p. E2885. • **40**. An unnamed infantryman, quoted in Baker, *Nam*, p. 212. See ibid., p. 277. • **41**. See Cooling (ed.), *Air Support*; Sheehan, *Die Große Lüge*, p. 116; Showalter, 'The War That Was Never Fought', p. 17; Schell, *Real War*, pp. 220, 313, 318–22, 351, 359–62, 366. For the internal investigations by the US Army, see NA, RG 319, AS, ODCS-PER, VWCWG, CaFi, Box 10, Dell Allegation, Part 1 of 6, Case 70. • **42**. Headquarters, 3rd Brigade, 1st Air Cavalry Division, Combat Operations After Action Report, Masher/Whitewing, Binh Dinh Province, 10 Mar. 1966, p. 11, in NA, RG 319, AS, ODCS-PER, VWCWG, CaFi, Box 4, Folder: Applegate Allegation, Case 22. Binh Dinh Province was blanketed with this type of warfare up to the end of 1967: see Lewy, *America in Vietnam*, pp. 58, 71. • **43**. An unnamed lieutenant, quoted in Ellsberg, *Secrets*, p. 165. See Schell, *Real War*, pp. 114, 220, 236. • **44**. Spector, *After Tet*, pp. 197–8; Schell, *Real War*, p. 68. • **45**. See Schell, *Real War*, p. 214. • **46**. See ibid., pp. 274, 301, 349; Ellsberg, *Secrets*, p. 135ff. • **47**. Quoted in Lewy, *America in Vietnam*, p. 104. • **48**. Serious accusations, which were not investigated, often crop up in the files. See the complaint, typical of many others, made by Alison Palmer, a Foreign Service employee, who sought in vain an explanation as to why the refugee camp Khiem Chan in Khanh Hoa Province (II Corps Tactical Zone) was destroyed in early December 1968: NA, RG 319, AS, ODCS-PER, VWCWG, CaFi, Box 2, Folder: Khiem Chan Incident. • **49**. Army Chief of Staff, G 3, 20 May 1969, Artillery, Mortar, Army Aviation Accidents and Incidents, in NA, RG 472, USAV, DCSO, PSOT, AOC, Accident Case Files, Box 1, Folder: Accident Case Files Oct. 1968. See ibid., Box 1, Folder: Accident Case Files Sep. 1968; Box 2, Folder: Reports of Investigations (General) 1969; NA, RG 472, USAV, II FFV, S 3, Reports of Artillery Accidents and Incidents, Box 1, 2, 3, 4, Folders: Volume Aug. 1966–May 1968. • **50**. Lieutenant Colonel Douglas A. Huff, Change to USARV Regulations Pertaining to Investigations of Friendly Fire Incidents, undated memorandum, in NA, RG 472, USAV, DCSO, PSOT, AOC, Accident Case Files, Box 2, Folder: Reports of Investigations (General) 1969. For internal criticism of this practice, see letters to the Commanding General of II Field Force, 20 Aug. 1966, in NA, RG 472, USAV, II FFV, S 3, Reports of Artillery Accidents and Incidents, Box 1, Folder: Volume August 1966; Lieutenant General Jonathan O. Seaman, Errors in Artillery and Mortar Fires, 21 Mar. 1967, in ibid., Box 2, Folder: Volume IV, Mar. 1967. • **51**. For misunderstandings, lack of training and violation of rules, see NA, RG 472, USAV, DCSO, PSOT, AOC, Accident Case Files, Box 1, Folder: Accident Case Files, Oct. 1968; ibid., Box 2, Folder:

Reports of Investigations (General) 1969. • **52**. Criticism of South Vietnamese provincial administrators comes up repeatedly in both the records and internal memoranda of the US Army. See Sheehan, *Die Große Lüge*, pp. 117ff.; NA, RG 472, USAV, DCSO, PSOT, AOC, Accident Case Files, Box 1, Folder: Accident Case Files Oct. 1968; NA, RG 472, USAV, II FFV, S 3, Reports of Artillery Accidents and Incidents, Box 1, Folder: Volume Aug. 1966; ibid., Box 2, Folder: Volume IV, Mar. 1967; ibid., Box 3, Folder: Volume XIV, Nov. 1967. • **53**. For indifference to friendly-fire incidents, see NA, RG 472, USAV, DCSO, PSOT, AOC, Accident Case Files, Box 1, Folder: Accident Case Files Sep. 1968 and Accident Case Files Oct. 1968. • **54**. No protection for civilians could be expected from this quarter; their loyalty was to central government not the local populace. Accordingly, American observers repeatedly complained of a policy which set the fox to keep the geese: see van den Haag, 'War Crime?', p. 1230. • **55**. Elliott L. Meyrowitz, letter to General Creighton Abrams, 8 Nov. 1972, in NA, RG 319, AS, ODCS-PER, VWCWG, CaFi, Box 18, Folder: Meyrowitz Allegation, Case 210.2. See ibid., Box 16, Folder: Torres Allegation, Case 161 and ibid., Box 6, Folder: Senning-Wilson Allegation. • **56**. An advisor to 25th Infantry Division, quoted in Sheehan, *Die Große Lüge*, p. 542. Similar comments are to be found in the Army's internal correspondence: see NA, RG 472, USAV, II FFV, S 3, Reports of Artillery Accidents and Incidents, Box 3, Folder: Volume XV Oct.–Dec. 1967 and ibid., Box 4, Folder: Mar. 1968. • **57**. Army Report: Law of Southeast Asia Rules of Engagement, Law of War, undated memorandum, pp. 35, 43, in NA, RG 319, AS, ODCS-PER, VWCWG, CF, Box 4, Folder: Army Report: Law of Southeast Asia Rules of Engagement, Law of War (Undated). • **58**. Quoted in Schell, *Real War*, p. 386. See ibid., pp. 271, 286, 302, 350. For the practice of identifying even populated areas as Free Fire Zones, see Headquarters, III Marine Amphibious Force, Standing Operating Procedure for Ground and Air Operations (SOP), 10 Nov. 1967, Section 4, p. 4, in NA, RG 319, AS, PI-AC, Box 8, Folder: Conduct of the War, MACV Directives, ROE – Chron. File # 3; NA, RG 472, USAV, II FFV, S 3, Reports of Artillery Accidents and Incidents, Box 2, Folder: Volume V, Apr. 1967; ibid., Box 2, Folder: Volume VI, May 1967; ibid., Box 3, Folder: Vol. VIII, Jul. 1967; ibid., Box 3, Folder: Volume IX, Aug. 1967; ibid., Box 3, Folder: Volume XV, Oct.–Dec. 1967. See Lewy, *America in Vietnam*, p. 106; Solis, *Son Thang*, pp. 8, 30. • **59**. For the official interpretation of the Free Fire Zones, see Westmoreland, *A Soldier Reports*, p. 152; according to this the aim was 'to remove the people and destroy the village. That done, operations to find the enemy could be conducted without fear of civilian casualties.' • **60**. Leaflets dropped over Quang Ngai Province, quoted in Schell, *Real War*, pp. 205–7. For example, between May and August 1967 twenty-three million leaflets were dropped over Quang Ngai Province during Operation Malheur: Lewy, *America in*

Vietnam, p. 69. • **61**. Tucker, *Encyclopedia*, pp. 64, 140. • **62**. See NA, RG 319, AS, ODCS-PER, VWCWG, CaFi, Box 13, Folder: Record Allegation (Congressional Inquiries and Background Information) Case 90; ibid., Box 13, Folder: New York Times Allegation (Part 1 of 2), Case 92 and Folder: New York Times Allegation (Correspondence, Congressional Inquiries and Background Information), Case 92. See Lewy, *America in Vietnam*, p. 102; Schell, *Real War*, pp. 157, 212ff., 235, 272, 284, 337ff., 342ff.; Spector, *After Tet*, p. 198. • **63**. Report of Facts Concerning Artillery Firing Vicinity Grid XT 1674, 23 Jan. 1968, in NA, RG 472, USAV, II FFV, S 3, Reports of Artillery Accidents and Incidents, Box 4, Folder: Jan. 1968. • **64**. Report of Investigation – Firing Incident Involving Vietnamese Nationals During Combat Operations by Elements of Company A, 2nd Battalion, 60th Infantry Regiment, 25th Infantry Division, 5 Sep. 1970, in NA, RG 472, USFSEA, MACV, IG, ID, Miscellaneous Reports of Investigations, Box 9, Folder: ROI – Firing Incident Involving Vietnamese Nationals during CBT OPS by Elements of Co A, 2nd BN, 60th Inf, 1 of 2. This concerned an operation carried out at the end of August 1970 in Binh Long Province, Chon Thanh District, III Corps Tactical Zone, on the Cambodian border. • **65**. See Schell, *Real War*, pp. 158, 375–84; Lewy, *America in Vietnam*, p. 259; Terry, *Bloods*, pp. 24, 94; Witness Statement Richard T. Altenburger, 31 Dec. 1970, in NA, RG 472, USFSEA, MACV, DRAC, IG, Preliminary Inquiry Re: Colonel Franklin, Box 2, Folder: Preliminary Investigation Re: Col. Franklin, Vol. IV, Pt. 1 of 3. • **66**. See Valentine, *Phoenix Program*, pp. 36, 50; Sheehan, *Die Große Lüge*, pp. 294, 315. • **67**. An employee of the Agency for International Development, quoted in Schell, *Real War*, p. 136. See ibid., pp. 122–59, 187ff., 262, 356. • **68**. For Operation Masher/Whitewing, see NA, RG 319, AS, ODCS-PER, VWCWG, CaFi, Box 4, Folder: Applegate Allegation, Case 22; Sheehan, *Die Große Lüge*, p. 583. For Operation Russell Beach/Bold Mariner, see NA, RG 319, AS, PI-AC, Box 29, Folder: Sensitive Material – My Lai – Folder # 6; Lewy, *America in Vietnam*, p. 141. For the destruction in Quang Ngai Province from 1965 to 1967, see Schell, *Real War*, p. 198. • **69**. USCR, 6 Apr. 1971, p. E2838. Such figures can only be regarded as estimates. The same applies to the official information on the amount of defoliant used. • **70**. See Draper, *Abuse of Power*; Kahin and Lewis, *United States in Vietnam*; Lewy, *America in Vietnam*, pp. 59, 65, 70, 108, 111; Spector, *After Tet*, pp. 207–10; Schell, *Real War*, pp. 133–59, 198, 215, 246–9, 254–8, 368, 375–93; Schell, 'Cage for the Innocents', p. 32; Sheehan, *Die Große Lüge*, p. 620; USCR, 6 Apr. 1971, p. E2895. Philip Jones Griffiths has captured the destruction of rural life in impressive pictures: see Greiner, 'Gesellschafts-Bilder'. • **71**. See Headquarters, III Marine Amphibious Force, Overall Status of the Pacification Effort, 14 Jul. 1968, in NA, RG 319, AS, PI-OI, Box 4, Folder: MACV Reports (2). • **72**. James A. May, senior advisor in Quang Ngai Province, quoted in Schell, *Real War*, p. 386. • **73**. An unnamed officer, quoted in Schell, 'Cage for the Innocents',

p. 29. • **74.** Michael Uhl, statement before the Subcommittee on Foreign Operations and Government Information, US House of Representatives, Committee on Government Operation, 2 Aug. 1971, p. 1103; see ibid., pp. 1155, 1172, in NA, RG 319, AS, ODCS-PER, VWCWG, CF, Box 4, Folder: House Hearings: Currency Exchange in Southeast Asia, 2 Aug. 1971 (Includes War Crimes Allegations). • **75.** See Schell, 'Cage for the Innocents'; Schell, *Real War*, p. 241ff. • **76.** 94,000 people were arrested by US soldiers during this period, 126,000 by troops from South Vietnam, Australia, New Zealand, South Korea and Thailand. For this information and the subdivision of prisoner categories, see NA, RG 338, USAC, HD22-CR, Box 32, Folder: Confidential 511-05 Vietnam. Office of the Provost Marshal General (1970); ibid., Box 32, Folder: Confidential 511-05 Vietnam. Office of the Provost Marshal General (1968); NA, RG 338, USAC, HD22-UR, Box 23, Folder: S11-02 Vietnam EPW/CI/D Gen Info Files (1973). At that time South Vietnam had a population of *c.* 17.5 million. • **77.** The fact that between 1967 and 1970 the Viet Cong carried out a total of seventy liberation attacks on civilian prisons also suggests that prisoners of war were detained in them. • **78.** Schell, 'Cage for the Innocents', p. 29. • **79.** See Lewy, *America in Vietnam*, p. 294ff. • **80.** NA, RG 338, USAC, HD22-CR, Box 28, Folder: Confidential 511-04 Vietnam. Reports on Con Son (1970); ibid., Box 32, Folder: Confidential 511-05 Vietnam. Office of the Provost Marshal Gen. (1970). See also U.S. Assistance to the Vietnam Corrections System, in NA, RG 338, USAC, HD22-UR, Box 43, Folder: S11-02 Vietnam. Misc. Correspondence VN (1966). • **81.** Embassy Saigon to Secretary of State, Washington D.C., Subject: Conditions at Con Son Prison, Confidential, 16 Dec. 1970, in NA, RG 338, USAC, HD22-CR, Box 28, Folder: Confidential 511-04 Vietnam. Reports on Con Son (1970). • **82.** After repeated inspections of the Phu Quoc POW camp the Red Cross spoke of routine torture: NA, RG 338, USAC, HD22-CR, Box 27, Folder: Confidential 511-04 Vietnam. ICRC Visit to Phu Quoc Camp (1970–1971); ibid., Box 27, Folder: Confidential 511-04 Vietnam. ICRC Visit to Phu Quoc Island (1970); ibid., Box 27, Folder: Confidential 511-04 Vietnam. ICRC Visit to Phu Quoc Island (1971); ibid., Box 28, Folder: Confidential 511-04 Vietnam. Conditions at Phu Quoc PW Camp (1970, 72). See 'Prisoners of War Protest Conditions in S. Vietnam Camp', *Washington Post*, 8 Jun. 1972 and 'Thieu's Political Prisoners', *Newsweek*, 18 Dec. 1972. • **83.** *Washington Star*, editorial, 8 Jul. 1970. The paper also compared the conditions in Con Son with a Nazi concentration camp. • **84.** J. William Doolittle, General Counsel, Memorandum for Major General Thomas N. Wilson, Deputy Director of Plans, DCS/P&O, 5 Dec. 1967, in NA, RG 319, AS, PI-AC, Box 5, Folder: Background Info; U.S. Assistance to the Vietnam Corrections System, in NA, RG 338, USAC, HD22-UR, Box 43, Folder: S11-02 Vietnam. Misc. Correspondence VN (1966); Secretary of State, Washington, DC to Embassy Saigon, Secret, 11 Oct. 1966, in NA, RG 338, USAC,

HD22-SR, Box 3, Folder: S11-04 Vietnam Prisoners of War (1966); Joint Embassy/MACV Message to Secretary of State, Washington, DC, Secret, 1 Sep. 1966, in ibid., Box 3, Folder: S11-02 Vietnam, Joint Embassy/MACV MSG (1966). See also 'Saigon: "Tiger Cage" Case Poses Bigger Problem', *Sunday Star* (Washington, DC), 12 Jul. 1970. • **85.** Joint Chiefs of Staff, Memorandum for the Secretary of Defense, Subject: Phu Quoc PW Camp, 16 Oct. 1970, in NA, RG 338, USAC, HD22-CR, Box 28, Folder: Confidential 511-04 Vietnam. Conditions at Phu Quoc PW Camp (1970, 72). • **86.** Roy W. Johnson, Information Department of the US Embassy in Saigon, quoted in 'U.S. Denies Responsibility for "Tiger Cages" at Conson', *Washington Post*, 8 Jul. 1970. Congressman Philip M. Crane also spoke in similar vein: News from Congressman Philip M. Crane (13th District Illinois), undated, in NA, RG 338, USAC, HD22-CR, Box 28, Folder: Confidential 511-04 Vietnam. Reports on Con Son (1970). Congressmen Hawkins and Anderson referred to the fact that in appointing Frank E. Walton as adviser to the South Vietnamese Security Forces, the US State Department had chosen a senior Los Angeles police officer known for his contempt for civil rights: 'Choice of Police Aide to S. Viet Prison', *Washington Post*, 9 Jul. 1970. • **87.** NA, RG 338, USAC, HD22-CR, Box 26, Folder: Confidential 511-04 Vietnam. ICRC Visits to PW Installations (1968–69); RG 338, USAC, HD22-UR, Box 23, Folder: S11-02 Vietnam. EPW/CI/D Gen Info Files (1973). • **88.** NA, RG 338, USAC, HD22-CR, Box 26, Folder: Confidential 511-04 Vietnam. ICRC Visits to PW Installations (1968–69). RG 338, USAC, HD22-UR, Box 4, Folder: S11-01 Vietnam. Report of Detainee Incident 1967. RG 319, AS, PI-AC, Box 19, Folder: Other Allegations/Incidents – Unreported Allegations; ibid., Box 53, Folder: War Crimes Allegations – 124: De John Incident. RG 319, AS, ODCS-PER, VWCWG, CF, Box 1, Folder: War Crimes Allegations Talking Papers – September 1971; ibid., Box 5, Folder: Memorandums for Record – Summaries of Congressional Hearings on War Crimes, Apr. 1971; ibid., Box 5, Folder: Congressional Correspondence – War Crimes Allegations, 1971–1972; ibid., Box 5, Folder: Public Correspondence – White House, A –L: War Crimes and other Topics, 1971. RG 319, AS, ODCS-PER, VWCWG, CaFi, Box 3, Folder: War Crimes Allegations Index (For Allegations Other Than My Lai). RG 472, USFSEA, MACV, DRAC, IG, Preliminary Inquiry Re: Colonel Franklin, Box 3, Folder: Preliminary Investigation Re: Col. Franklin, Vol. IV (Pt. 3 of 3). USCR, 7 Apr. 1971, pp. E2837, 2867ff., 2874–8. Gross, 'Lieutenant Calley's Army', p. 154ff. • **89.** NA, RG 319, AS, ODCS-PER, VWCWG, CaFi, Box 6, Folder: Rottman-Uhl Allegation; ibid., Box 7, Folder: Barbour-Drolshagen-Morton Allegation (CCI), Case, 55.1: ibid., Box 9, Folder: Rottman Allegation (CCI), Case 63; ibid., Box 11, Folder: Hale Allegation, Case 71; ibid., Box 11, Folder: Lloyd Allegation (VVAW-WSI), Case 81; ibid., Box 15, Folder: Somers Incident, Case 144. RG 319, AS, PI-AC, Box 19, Folder: Other

Allegations/Incidents – Unreported Allegations. Similar accusations were also made against South Vietnamese units: RG 319, AS, ODCS-PER, VWCWG, CF, Box 5, Folder: Memorandum for Record – Summaries of Congressional Hearings on War Crimes Apr. 1971. • **90**. Sworn Testimony of Anthony B. Herbert, 28 Sep. 1970, p. 8, in NA, RG 319, AS, ODCS-PER, VWCWG, CaFi, Box 8, Folder: Herbert Allegation (Pt. 2 of 2), Case 58. See Statement Franklin T. Booth, in ibid., Box 8, Folder: Herbert Allegation (Pt. 2 of 2), Case 58 and Folder: Herbert Allegation (Part 1 of 2). • **91**. Commanding General, US Army (Vietnam), Long Binh to CINUSARPAC, COMUSMACV, 8 Oct. 1968, Info: CG 173rd Abn Bde, Confidential, in NA, RG 338, USAC, HD22-CR, Box 29, Folder: Confidential 511-04 Vietnam. Treatment of EPW/D and Reports of Maltreatment Allegations (1968). See RG 319, AS, ODCS-PER, VWCWG, CaFi, Box 15, Folder: Swain Allegation, Case 143; ibid., Box 15, Folder: Kneer Incident, Case 148; RG 472, USFSEA, MACV, DRAC, IG, Box 1, Folder: Preliminary Investigation Re: Col. Franklin, Vol. I (Pt. 1 of 3, 1971); ibid., Box 3, Folder: Preliminary Investigation Re: Col. Franklin, Vol. IV (Pt. 3 of 3, 1971). • **92**. Lieutenant General Connor, Deputy Chief of Staff for Personnel, Capture Point Handling of PW, undated memorandum, in NA, RG 338, USAC, HD22-CR, Box 29, Folder: Confidential 511-04 Vietnam. Treatment of EPW/D and Reports of Maltreatment Allegations (1968). • **93**. From Chief of Staff Army (Harold K. Johnson) to CGUSARV (Commanding General US Army Vietnam) Long Binh, Subject: Repeated War Crimes at Capture Point, 24 Jan. 1968, in NA, RG 338, USAC, HD22-CR, Box 29, Folder: Confidential 511-04 Vietnam. Treatment of EPW/D and Reports of Maltreatment Allegations (1968). • **94**. Lieutenant General Bruce Palmer Jr., letter to General Harold K. Johnson, 15 Jun. 1968, in NA, RG 319, AS, PI-FR, Vol. III: Exhibits, Box 55, Book 5; Information Officer, Provost Marshal, Treatment of Captured Enemy Personnel, 11 Jun. 1968, in NA, RG 472, USFSEA, USAV, PM, AO-CGR, Box 2, Folder: Correspondence File – Outgoing Apr.–Jun. 1968. See RG 319, AS, PI-FR, Vol. II: Testimony, Box 21, Book 13, Summary of Testimony: Witness John L. Pittman, SUM APP T-191, p. 3. • **95**. Brigadier General Edward Bautz Jr. to Deputy Chief of Staff for Personnel, Fact Sheet: Torture of PW by U.S. Officers, in NA RG 319, AS, PI-AC, Box 53, Folder: War Crimes Allegations – 124: De John Incident. The addressee of this letter, the Deputy Chief of Staff for Personnel, was responsible for prisoners of war. For accusation of torture against Co A, Detachment B-36, 1st Special Forces, 5th Special Force Group (Airborne), see RG 338, USAC, HD22-CR, Box 26, Folder: Confidential 511-04 Vietnam. ICRC Visits to PW Installations (1968–69). For the role of the instructors returning from Vietnam see USCR, 6 Apr. 1971, p. E2874; Department of the Army, Memorandum for the Record: Resume of Hearing, 28 Apr. 1971, p. 2, in RG 319, AS, ODCS-PER, VWCWG, CF, Box 5, Folder: Memorandums for Record – Summaries of

Congressional Hearings on War Crimes, Apr. 1971; 'Veteran of Special Forces Denounces U.S. Policy in Vietnam as "a Lie"', *New York Times*, 10 Feb. 1966 and Duncan, *New Legions*. An intelligence officer who served with the rank of captain with a battalion of 9th Infantry Division claimed that during their training at Fort Benning US recruits were tortured for up to seven hours – by veterans playing the role of the Viet Cong who wanted to prove to the novices that any prisoner could be made to talk: Ronald Dellums, Vietnam War Crimes Hearings, quoted at http://members.aol.com/warlibrary/vwch1g.htm, 31 Aug. 2004. • **96**. Administrative Review of Son My Cases, 17 May 1971, in NA, RG 319, AS, ODCS-PER, VWCWG, MLM, Box 4, Folder: Administrative Review – Cpt. Eugene M. Kotouc and Memorandum of Law (Cpt. Kotouc), undated, p. 11, in ibid. • **97**. Two unnamed GIs, quoted in Schell, *Real War*, p. 230. • **98**. William J. Simon, letter to the Editor, *New York Times*, 3 Jun. 1971. In 1970 Simon was US military adviser in the Mekong Delta. For the complaints mentioned, see also NA, RG 319, AS, PI-AC, Box 54, Folder: War Crimes Allegations – 219: Brooks Incident. RG 319, AS, ODCS-PER, VWCWG, CF, Box 4, Folder: Helicopter Incident. CID Reports – Testimony # 1, Case 8 (2); ibid., Box 5, Folder: Memorandums for Record – Summaries of Congressional Hearings on War Crimes, Apr. 1971; ibid., Box 13, Folder: Jackson Allegation. RG 472, USFSEA, MACV, IG, ID, IR, Box 12, Folder: Hai Dong (Part 1 of 2). • **99**. NA, RG 472, USAV, II FFV, S 3, CGR, Box 1, Folder: Accident/Incident Report 69. RG 472, USFSEA, USAV, IG, ICD, RICF, Box 14, Folder: Case # 69-65. • **100**. David Bressem, 1st Cavalry Division, quoted in OSA, Memorandum for the Record, Subject: Resume of Hearing, 29 Apr. 1971, p. 2, in NA, RG 319, ODCS-PER, VWCWG, CF, Box 5, Folder: Memorandums for Record – Summaries of Congressional Hearings on War Crimes, Apr. 1971. • **101**. Hersh, *Cover-Up*, p. 48. • **102**. An unnamed pilot, quoted in Schell, *Real War*, p. 293. • **103**. Schell, *Real War*, pp. 233–4, 303, 321, 329–30. Many of these operations were carried out in the presence of senior officers: see NA, RG 319, AS, ODSC-PER, VWCWG, CF, Box 4, Folder: Helicopter Incident – CID Reports, Testimony # 1, Case 8 (2). • **104**. Seymour M. Hersh, quoted in transcript of the television broadcast 'Firing Line', WETA-TV, 7 Jul. 1971, p. 9, in NA, RG 319, AS, PI-AC, Box 38, Folder: Son My Chron. File # 20 (1 of 2). • **105**. Joseph S. Lelyveld, 'Most Helicopter Pilots are Eager for Duty in Vietnam', *New York Times*, 26 Apr. 1971. • **106**. Some relevant files have been reclassified since early 2000, with no explanation given: see NA, RG 472, USFSEA, USAV, IG, ICD, RICF, Box 33, Folder: Case # 71-6. • **107**. Witness Statement Paul Duane Halverson, 24 Nov. 1970 and Investigator's Statement, Ralph R. Scott, 11 Mar. 1971, in NA, RG 472, USFSEA, MACV, DRAC, IG, Preliminary Inquiry Re: Colonel Franklin, Box 2, Folder: Preliminary Investigation Re: Col. Franklin, Vol. III, Pt. 2 of 4 (1971). • **108**. William J. Patterson, quoted in Patterson Allegation, in NA, RG 319, AS, ODCS-PER, VWCWG, CaFi, Box 12, Folder: Patterson Allegation, Case 87. • **109**. NA, RG 319, AS, ODCS-PER, VWCWG, CaFi, Box 6, Folder: Bressem Allegation. • **110**. NA, RG 319, AS, ODCS-PER, VWCWG, CaFi, Box 7, Folder: Rice Allegation, Case 50. • **111**. NA, RG 319, AS, ODCS-PER, VWCWG, CaFi, Box 7, Folder: Murphy-Patton-Uhl Allegation (National Citizens' Commission), Case 52. RG 472, USFSEA, USAV, IG, ICD, RICF, Box 22, Folder: Case # 70-18: Alleged Killing of 100 Innocent Montagnards; Joseph S. Lelyveld, 'Most Helicopter Pilots are Eager for Duty in Vietnam', *New York Times*, 26 Apr. 1971. • **112**. Headquarters USAV, Memorandum for: USARV Inspector General, Subject: MACIG Inquiry into Activities Vicinity of Fire Base Oasis . . . o/a 1 Feb. 1968, in RG 472, USFSEA, USAV, IG, ICD, RICF, Box 22, Folder: Case 70-18 Alleged Killing of 100 Innocent Montagnards. • **113**. NA, RG 319, AS, ODCS-PER, VWCWG, CaFi, Box 10, Folder: Connelly Allegation. • **114**. Robert Komer to General Eckhardt, 7 Apr. 1968, in NA, RG 319, AS, PI-OI, Box 3, Folder: MACV Directives (3). • **115**. NA, RG 319, ODCS-PER, VWCWG, CaFi, Box 8, Folder: Helicopter Gunship Incident, Case 57. • **116**. A lieutenant interviewed by Jonathan Schell, quoted in Schell, *Real War*, p. 327. • **117**. Statement of a soldier from 9th Infantry Division on the occasion of the Winter Soldier investigation in Detroit, 31 Jan.–1 Feb. 1971, quoted in USCR, 7 Apr. 1971, p. E2919; see ibid., p. E2881. See also NA, RG 472, USFSEA, MACV, DRAC, IG, Preliminary Inquiry Re: Colonel Franklin, Box 2, Folder: Preliminary Investigation Re: Col. Franklin, Vol. III (Part 1 of 4) 1971 and RG 319, AS, ODCS-PER, VWCWG, CaFi, Box 10, Folder: Dell Allegation (Part 1 of 6), Case 70. • **118**. Sworn Statement Ross L. Cowan, 1 Jun. 1970, p. 5, in NA, RG 319, AS, OCMH, Records Relating to the Courts Martial of 1st Lt. W. Calley, Capt. V. Hartman, 1st Lt. R. Lee, and Capt. O. O'Connor, Box 25, Folder: 708-07 Adverse Information File – Vincent N. Hartman (Folder 221) (1 of 2). • **119**. Sworn Statement David Jay Startzer, 1 Dec. 1969, p. 1, in NA, RG 319, AS, OCMH, Records Relating to the Courts Martial of 1st Lt. W. Calley, Capt. V. Hartman, 1st Lt. R. Lee, and Capt. O. O'Connor, Box 22, Folder: CID Report of Investigation – Hartman and Lee (Folder 206) (2 of 3). Both the Criminal Investigation Division and the military lawyers of II Field Force, Vietnam recommended that those responsible for deliberate murder should be brought before a court martial. However, nothing came of this because the chief witnesses withdrew their evidence at the last moment on flimsy pretexts: NA, RG 319, AS, OCMH, Records Relating to the Courts Martial of 1st Lt. W. Calley, Capt. V. Hartman, 1st Lt. R. Lee, and Capt. O. O'Connor, Boxes 22, 23, 25, 33 and RG 319, AS, ODCS-PER, VWCWG, CaFi, Box 3, Folder: Hartman Incident (Sugarman Allegation). • **120**. Duncan, *New Legions*, p. 169. See also Schell, 'Cage for the Innocents', p. 32ff.; Terry, *Bloods*, pp. 2, 91ff.; Solis, *Son Thang*, pp. 33, 82ff.; NA, RG 472, USFSEA, MACV, IG, ID, RI,

Box 14, Folder: MIV-30-68 Harbor Patrol. • **121**. Schell, *Real War*, p. 192. • **122**. Caputo, *Rumor of War*, Introduction, pp. xix–xx. See also David Halberstam, in Anderson (ed.), *Facing My Lai*, pp. 124, 132; Schell, *Real War*, pp. 240, 326, 365ff. • **123**. Schell, *Real War*, p. 231. • **124**. An unnamed major, quoted in Hammond, *Military and the Media*, p. 355.

3 Officers

1. General Douglas MacArthur in his reaction to the death sentence on the Japanese general Tomoyuki Yamashita: General Headquarters, United States Army Forces, Pacific, 7 Feb. 1946, in NA, RG 319, AS, ODCS-PER, VWCWG, CF, Box 6, Folder: Background Information – History of War Crimes. • **2**. Telford Taylor, 'The Course of Military Justice', *New York Times*, 2 Feb. 1972. • **3**. COMUSMACV, Subject: Relationship between US Military and Vietnamese, 18 Nov. 1966, in NA, RG 319, AS, PI-FR, Vol. III: Exhibits, Box 53, Book 1: Directives. • **4**. Quoted in *Congressional Record*, 6 Apr. 1971, p. E2826. • **5**. Ibid. For Westmoreland's criticism, see 'Obey P.O.W. Code, U.S. Soldiers Told', *New York Times*, 1 Dec. 1965; Army Report – Law of Southeast Asia Rules of Engagement, Law of War (Undated), pp. 30–8, 86–92, in NA, RG 319, AS, ODCS-PER, VWCWG, CF, Box 4, Folder: Army Report – Law of Southeast Asia Rules of Engagement, Law of War (Undated); Summary of Remarks by COMUSMACV Relating to Noncombatant Casualties, 28 Aug. 1966, in NA, RG 319, AS, PI-FR, Vol. III: Exhibits, Box 53, Book 1: Directives; ibid., Vol. III: Exhibits, Box 55, Book 5: Miscellaneous Documents, Overlaps, Sketches and Statements; Memorandum MACV Commanders' Conference 3 Dec. 1967, in RG 319, AS, PI-AC, Box 6, Folder: Conduct of the War in Vietnam, Chron. File # 2 (Part 2 of 2); Fact Sheet, MACV Actions – Proper Treatment of Noncombatants, undated, in ibid., Box 6, Folder: Conduct of the War in Vietnam, Chron. File # 2 (Part 2 of 2); Message, For All Commanding Officers, Jan. 68, p. 2, in ibid., Box 10, Folder: Documents Obtained in Vietnam by Peers Inquiry (Part 2 of 2): Mistreatment of Detainees and PW, in ibid., Box 48, Folder: Untitled – 22 Sep. 1972 (Part 2 of 2); Letter to Lieutenant General Bruce Palmer Jr., 16 Oct. 1967, in RG 319, AS, PI-OI, Box 13, Folder: Americal Division, Miscellaneous (1). • **6**. MACV 525-3, Combat Operations Minimizing Noncombatant Battle Casualties, 14 Oct. 1966 and 2 Mar. 1969, in NA, RG 319, AS, PI-AC, Box 8, Folder: Conduct of the War, MACV Directives, ROE – Chron. File # 3. See Rules of Engagement in Republic of Vietnam, in RG 319, ODCS-PER, VWCWG, MLM, Box 7, Folder: Congressional Correspondence My Lai: Hebert Subcommittee Investigation. • **7**. William Peers, Leadership Requirements in a Counterinsurgency Environment, 18 Mar. 1970, in NA, RG 319, PI-AC, Box 11, Folder: General

Correspondence: Security Classified Review – Peers Report. • **8**. US Army Aviation Group (Provisional), Command Memorandum No. 1, 4 Aug. 1965, quoted in Army Report – Law of Southeast Asia Rules of Engagement, Law of War (Undated), p. 40, in NA, RG 319, AS, ODCS-PER, VWCWG, CF, Box 4, Folder: Army Report – Law of Southeast Asia Rules of Engagement, Law of War (Undated). Further on in this memorandum it states, 'I also expect each commander to have a soul-searching session with his aviators and gunners. Army aviation units have no unilateral hunting license and will not take these decisions onto themselves. There will be no tolerance of "zap happy" aviators or gunners in this command.' • **9**. Solis, *Son Thang*, p. 26; Lewy, *America in Vietnam*, p. 330ff. • **10**. Results of the United States Army War College Study on Military Professionalism, Annex E, p. 38, in NA, RG 319, PI-AC, Box 21, Folder: Peers Report Fallout. The Army War College published the study in October 1971 under the title 'Leadership for the 1970's: USAWC Study of Leadership for the Professional Soldier'. • **11**. Aspects of Army War College Study on Military Professionalism, Enclosure 3, p. 1, in NA, RG 319, PI-AC, Box 21, Folder: Peers Report Fallout. See Cincinnatus, *Self-Destruction*, pp. 130ff., 167, 175 and Kitfield, *Prodigal Soldiers*, pp. 107–113. • **12**. David H. Hackworth was the model for Lieutenant Colonel Bill Killgore in the film *Apocalypse Now*. • **13**. King, 'Making It'. King expanded this article into the book *The Death of the Army*. • **14**. David H. Hackworth, 'The War Was Winnable. Army Leadership Is Ineffective', *Washington Post*, 29 Jun. 1971. • **15**. King, 'Making It'. Colonel Lucian K. Truscott III chose almost identical wording in a contribution for the *New York Times*: 'Duty, Honor (and Self)', *New York Times*, 4 Feb. 1972. See Palmer, *The 25-Year War*; Hackworth, *About Face*. • **16**. Herbert, *Soldier*. See the interview with Anthony B. Herbert in *Life*, 9 Jul. 1971 and NA, RG 472, USFSEA, MACV, DRAC, IG, Preliminary Investigation Re: Col. Franklin, Box 2, Folder: Preliminary Investigation Re: Col. Franklin, Vol. III (Pt 2 of 4), 1971. • **17**. Hackworth, 'Soldier's Disgust'. • **18**. Quoted in Anderson (ed.), *Facing My Lai*, p. 125. • **19**. Department of the Army, Office of the Deputy Chief of Staff for Personnel, Subject: Lessons Learned from the Son My Incident, 19 May 1972, Enclosure 5: The Officer Personnel Management System, in NA, RG 319, AS, ODCS-PER, VWCWG, MLM, Box 6, Folder: My Lai Lessons Learned Reports (Drafts and Working Papers). See Lewy, *America in Vietnam*, p. 118; Sheehan, *Bright Shining Lie*, p. 649; Gabriel and Savage, *Crisis in Command*; Dunn, *Modern Counterinsurgency*. • **20**. Lieutenant Colonel Edward L. King had this experience in 1969: see King, 'Making It'. • **21**. Solis, *Son Thang*, p. 18. • **22**. Janowitz, *Professional Soldier*; Janowitz and Little, *Military Establishment*. • **23**. Brigadier General Edwin H. Simmons, U.S. Marine Corps, Debriefing, 24 May 1971, p. 10, in NA, USMC, HMC-HDPT, TF, FRC, Box 4, Folder: Command Info Notebook; 1st Mardiv; Apr. 1971 Debriefing; 3rd MAB; May 1971. • **24**. Belknap, *War on Trial*, p. 33. •

25. Department of the Army, Office of the Deputy Chief of Staff for Personnel, Subject: Lessons Learned From the Son My Incident, 19 May 1972, Enclosure 3: Personnel – Officer Records, in NA, RG 319, AS, ODCS-PER, VWCWG, MLM, Box 6, Folder: My Lai Lessons Learned Reports (Drafts and Working Papers). See Department of the Army, Office of the Chief of Staff, Subject: Survey of Policies Concerning Personnel Records Systems, 1 Oct. 1971, in RG 319, AS, PI-AC, Box 10, Folder: Fire Support Base Mary Ann File # 1 (Part 2 of 2, 4 Jul. 71–9 Feb. 72); Spector, *After Tet*, p. 33ff. • 26. An unnamed colonel, quoted in Lewy, *America in Vietnam*, p. 330. • 27. Department of the Army, Office of the Deputy Chief of Staff for Personnel, Subject: Lessons Learned From the Son My Incident, 15 Jun. 1972, § 5 (b), in NA, RG 319, AS, ODCS-PER, VWCWG, MLM, Box 6, Folder: Release of the My Lai Documents under FOIA. • 28. 'Army's Records Dispute My Lai Findings', *Sunday Oklahoman*, 14 May 1972. • 29. Solis, *Son Thang*, pp. 20, 26; Lewy, *America in Vietnam*, p. 118. • 30. An unnamed GI, quoted in Terry, *Bloods*, p. 123. • 31. Spector, *After Tet*, pp. 45, 313. • 32. MACV Directives Nos: *20-4*, Inspections and Investigations, War Crimes and Similar Prohibitive Acts, 20 Apr. 1965; *95-2*, Aviation: Employment of and Operational Restrictions on US Military Air Delivered Firepower in RVN, 20 Dec. 1965; *95-4*, Aviation: US Air Operations in RVN, 28 Jun. 1966; *525-3*, Combat Operations: Minimizing Non-Combatant Battle Casualties, 7 Sep. 1965, 14 Oct. 1966 and 2 Mar. 1969; *525-4*, Tactics and Techniques for the Employment of US Forces in the Republic of Vietnam, 17 Sep. 1965; *525-9*, Safeguarding VN Property and Food Supplies, 2 Feb. 1966; *525-13*, Combat Operations: Rules of Engagement in the RVN for Use of Artillery, Tanks, Mortars, Naval Gunfire and Air and Armed Helicopter Support, 12 Oct. 1968 and 9 Mar. 1969. See Department of the Army, Office of the Deputy Chief of Staff for Military Operations, Subject: An Analysis of the Evolution of MACV Rules of Engagement Pertaining to Ground Operations 1965–1969, in NA, RG 319, AS, PI-AC, Box 7, Folder: Conduct of the War, MACV Directives, ROE, Chron. File # 1 and Talking Paper: Air Operations Rules of Engagement – South Vietnam and Laos, 14 Apr. 1971, in ibid., Box 7, Folder: Conduct of the War in Vietnam, Chron. File # 4 (Part 1 of 2); Headquarters III Marine Amphibious Force, Subject: Standing Operating Procedure for Ground and Air Operations 10 Nov. 1967, in ibid., Box 8, Folder: Conduct of the War, MACV Directives, ROE – Chron. File # 3; ibid., Box 6, Folder: Conduct of the War in Vietnam, Chron. File # 2 (Part 2 of 2); ibid., Box 10, Folder: Documents Obtained in Vietnam by Peers Inquiry (Part 2 of 2). • 33. MACV Directive *525-3*, 2 Mar. 1969, p. 1, in NA, RG 319, PI-AC, Box 8, Folder: Conduct of the War, MACV Directives, ROE – Chron. File # 3. The directives issued by the divisional commands were also based on this premise: see Headquarters III Marine Amphibious Force, 13 Dec. 1966, Subject: Minimizing Noncombatant Battle Casualties, in NA, RG 319, AS, PI-FR, Vol.

III: Exhibits, Box 53, Book 2: Directives. • **34**. Department of the Army, Office of the Deputy Chief of Staff for Military Operations, Subject: An Analysis of the Evolution of MACV Rules of Engagement Pertaining to Ground Operations, 1965–1969, in NA, RG 319, AS, PI-AC, Box 7, Folder: Conduct of the War, MACV Directives, ROE, Chron. File # 1. See ibid, Box 6, Folder: Conduct of the War in Vietnam, Chron. File # 2 (Part 2 of 2). • **35**. MACV, Office of the Inspector General, Subject: Report of the Investigation Concerning Destruction Resulting from the VC Offensive of 5–23 May 1968, 2 Jun. 1968, p. 40, in NA, RG 472, USFSEA, MACV, IG, ID, RI, Box 5, Folder: MIV-16-68 Damage in Saigon (Part 1 of 4). This criticism refers to MACV *95-4* and *525-18* but fundamentally can be applied to the Rules of Engagement in their entirety: see James D. Hataway, Memorandum to the Ambassador, 26 Jan. 1968, Subject: Destruction in Quang Ngai and Quang Tin, in NA, RG 319, AS, PI-CI, Box 5, Folder: LTG Peers' Notes # 4: Colonel Henderson Interrogation (Part 2 of 2). • **36**. Department of the Army, Office of the Deputy Chief of Staff for Military Operations, Subject: An Analysis of the Evolution of MACV Rules of Engagement Pertaining to Ground Operations 1965–1969, p. 7, in NA, RG 319, AS, PI-AC, Box 6, Folder: Conduct of the War in Vietnam, Chron. File # 2 (Part 2 of 2). • **37**. Department of the Army, Office of the Deputy Chief of Staff for Military Operations, Subject: An Analysis of the Evolution of MACV Rules of Engagement Pertaining to Ground Operations 1965–1969, p. 18, in NA, RG 319, AS, PI-AC, Box 6, Folder: Conduct of the War in Vietnam, Chron. File # 2 (Part 2 of 2). The definition of 'larger caliber fire' is open to interpretation. See MACV, Office of the Inspector General, Subject: Report of the Investigation Concerning Destruction Resulting from the VC Offensive of 5–23 May 1968, 2 Jun. 1968, p. 43, in NA, RG 472, USFSEA, MACV, IG, ID, RI, Box 5, Folder: MIV-16-68 Damage in Saigon (Part 1 of 4). • **38**. An attack was allowed to proceed 'once the inhabitants of a preplanned target area have been adequately warned that the area has been selected as a target and given sufficient time to evacuate.' That was not to say that the warning had to be given shortly before an attack: Department of the Army, Office of the Deputy Chief of Staff for Military Operations, Subject: An Analysis of the Evolution of MACV Rules of Engagement Pertaining to Ground Operations 1965–1969, p. 8, in NA, RG 319, AS, PI-AC, Box 6, Folder: Conduct of the War in Vietnam, Chron. File # 2 (Part 2 of 2). • **39**. James D. Hataway, Memorandum to the Ambassador, 26 Jan. 1968, Subject: Destruction in Quang Ngai and Quang Tin, in NA, RG 319, AS, PI-CI, Box 5, Folder: LTG Peers' Notes # 4: Colonel Henderson Interrogation (Part 2 of 2). • **40**. MACV *525-18*, Conduct of Artillery, Mortar and Naval Gunfire, 21 Jan. 1968, § 4 d (e), quoted in Report of the Department of the Army Review of the Preliminary Investigation into the My Lai Incident (Peers Report), Chapter 9: Policy and Directives as to Rules of Engagement and

Treatment of Noncombatants, in NA, RG 319, AS, PI-AC, Box 8, Folder: Conduct of the War, MACV Directives, ROE – Chron. File # 3. • **41**. MACV 525-9, Combat Operations: Control, Disposition, and Safeguarding of Vietnamese Property, Captured Materiel and Food Supplies, 10 Apr. 1967, § 4 a (2, 3), in NA, RG 319, AS, PI-AC, Box 8, Folder: Conduct of the War, MACV Directives, ROE – Chron. File # 3. • **42**. MACV 525-13, Combat Operations: Use of Artillery, Tanks, Mortars, Naval Gunfire and Air and Armed Helicopter Support, 9 Mar. 1969, § 6 (C): Rules Governing Destruction of Dwellings by Ground Forces, quot. Rules of Engagement in Republic of Vietnam, in NA, RG 319, AS, VWCWG, MLM, Box 7, Folder: Congressional Correspondence My Lai: Hebert Subcommittee Investigation. • **43**. MACV 525-9, Combat Operations: Control, Disposition, and Safeguarding of Vietnamese Property, Captured Materiel and Food Supplies, 10 Apr. 1967, § 4 a (3), in NA, RG 319, AS, PI-AC, Box 8, Folder: Conduct of the War, MACV Directives, ROE – Chron. File # 3. • **44**. MACV 525-3, Military Operations: Minimizing Noncombatant Battle Casualties, 2 Mar. 1969, § 4 (1), in NA, RG 319, AS, PI-AC, Box 8, Folder: Conduct of the War, MACV Directives, ROE – Chron. File # 3 and Department of the Army, Office of the Deputy Chief of Staff for Military Operations, Subject: An Analysis of the Evolution of MACV Rules of Engagement Pertaining to Ground Operations 1965–1969, pp. 16, 17, in NA, RG 319, AS, PI-AC, Box 6, Folder: Conduct of the War in Vietnam, Chron. File # 2 (Part 2 of 2). • **45**. MACV 525-4, Tactics and Techniques for Employment of U.S. Forces in the Republic of Vietnam, 17 Sep. 1965, II General, § 4, in NA, RG 319, AS, PI-AC, Box 8, Folder: Conduct of the War, MACV Directives, ROE – Chron. File # 3. See MACV 525-9, Combat Operations: Control, Disposition, and Safeguarding of Vietnamese Property, Captured Materiel and Food Supplies, 10 Apr. 1967, § 2 a (1), in ibid.; MACV 525-3, Combat Operations: Minimizing Noncombatant Battle Casualties, 14 Oct. 1966, § 2 a, in ibid. • **46**. Headquarters III Marine Amphibious Force, Subject: Minimizing Noncombatant Battle Casualties, 13 Dec. 1966, § 4 a (7), in NA, RG 319, AS, PI-FR, Vol. III: Exhibits, Box 53, Book 2: Directives, Exhibit D-21. • **47**. This includes heavy weapon fire such as artillery. Air attacks were supposed to be observed by a Forward Air Controller. • **48**. Headquarters III Marine Amphibious Force, Subject: Standing Operating Procedure for Ground and Air Operations, 10 Nov. 1967, Section IV, § 405 (2), in NA, RG 319, AS, PI-FR, Vol. III: Exhibits, Box 53, Book 2: Directives, Exhibit D-22. • **49**. Taylor, *Nuremberg and Vietnam*; id., 'Nuremberg and Son My', *New York Times*, 21 Nov. 1970. • **50**. Army Report – Law of Southeast Asia Rules of Engagement, Law of War, undated, pp. 33–5, 43–4, 52, 95, in NA, RG 319, ODCS-PER, VWCWG, CF, Box 4, Folder: Army Report – Law of Southeast Asia Rules of Engagement, Law of War (Undated) and ibid., Legal Annex, Annex A, pp. 1–14. Townsend Hoopes, secretary for the

Air Force, also put forward this argument in an article published in 1970: 'The Nuremberg Suggestion'. • **51**. Lewy, *America in Vietnam*, p. 114. See also Marshall, *Battles in the Monsoon*. • **52**. Sam Bunge, 1st Lieutenant, B Company, 3rd Battalion, 187th Regiment, 101st Airborne Division, 1968/69, quoted in USCR, 7 Apr. 1971, p. E2913. • **53**. MACV *525-3*, Combat Operations. Minimizing Noncombatant Battle Casualties, 14 Oct. 1966 § 3 a (11), in NA, RG 319, AS, PI-AC, Box 8, Folder: Conduct of the War, MACV Directives, ROE, Chron. File # 3. This passage was also adopted by the Marines, with identical wording. See Headquarters, III Marine Amphibious Force, Subject: Minimizing Noncombatant Battle Casualties, § 4 c, in ibid. • **54**. Lewy, *America in Vietnam*, p. 234. The army magazine *Soldiers* reported on the resistance to instruction in the laws of warfare in its August 1971 edition, pp. 4–8. See William Greider, 'Teaching of War Law Revitalized by Army', *Washington Post*, 14 Feb. 1971. • **55**. An unnamed colonel, quoted in Anderson (ed.), *Facing My Lai*, p. 45. See Captain William A. Beinlich, Statement, 15 Jan. 1971, in NA, RG 319, AS, PI-AC, Box 7, Folder: Conduct of the War in Vietnam, Chron. File # 4 (Part 2 of 2); 'Who Else is Guilty?', *Newsweek*, 12 Apr. 1971, p. 32. • **56**. An unnamed captain, quoted in Gibson, *Perfect War*, p. 148. See Michael Erard, 3rd Battalion, 503rd Infantry Regiment, 173rd Airborne Brigade (Separate), 1969/70, in USCR, 7 Apr. 1971, p. E2916. • **57**. NA, RG 319, AS, PI-FR, Vol. II: Testimony, Box 20, Book 12, Henderson: APP T-1, pp. 61–2; ibid., Box 21, Book 13, McKnight: SUM APP T-2, p. 4; Pittman: SUM APP T-191, p. 2. • **58**. The journalist William Greider spoke of this 1967 investigation in a report published a year later: 'Teaching of War Law Revitalised by Army', *Washington Post*, 14 Feb. 1971. • **59**. William Westmoreland, Memorandum for Secretary of the Army, Subject: Training Concerning the Geneva Conventions, 6 Apr. 1970, in NA, RG 319, AS, PI-AC, Box 7, Folder: Conduct of the War, MACV Directives, ROE – Chron. File # 1; ibid., Folder: Conduct of the War, MACV Directives, ROE – Chron. File # 2 (Part 1 of 2); ibid., Folder: Conduct of the War in Vietnam, Chron. File # 4 (Part 2 of 2); Department of the Army, Survey of Opinions of Army Personnel Concerning the Rules of Land Warfare as of 31 Jan. 1970, OPOPM Report 3-70-E, Apr. 1970, in ibid., Box 22, Folder: Personnel Appearing Before Congressional Committees. • **60**. A similar atmosphere amongst officers was recorded by a colonel from the Legal Department of the Army, who in April 1970 was given the task of reporting to units in Vietnam, South Korea, Japan and Hawaii on the state of investigations into William Calley. He came across officers who called for other measures in a war like the one in Vietnam and moreover were of the opinion that courts martial proceedings eroded the morale and battle-readiness of the troops: Robert E. Miller to Lieutenant General Walter T. Kerwin, Jr., Deputy Chief of Staff for Personnel, Department of the Army, 14 Apr. 1970, in NA, RG 319, AS, PI-AC, Box 35, Folder: Son My Chron. File # 10 (2 of 2). • **61**. MACV, Office of the Inspector

General, Subject: Report of the Investigation Concerning Destruction Resulting from the VC Offensive of 5–23 May 1968, 2 Jun. 1968, pp. 13, 20–3, 40, 43–4, in NA, RG 472, USFSEA, MACV, IG, ID, RI, Box 5, Folder: MIV-16-68 Damage in Saigon (Part 1 of 4). • **62**. James D. Hataway, Memorandum to the Ambassador, 26 Jan. 1968, Subject: Destruction in Quang Ngai and Quang Tin, p. 1, in NA, RG 319, AS, PI-CI, Box 5, Folder: LTG Peers' Notes # 4: Colonel Henderson Interrogation (Part 2 of 2). • **63**. Ibid., pp. 3–4. • **64**. Headquarters, Third Regional Assistance Command, Subject: Report of Investigation – Firing Incident in Cambodia, 23 Oct. 1971, p. 8, in NA, RG 472, USFSEA, MACV, TRAC, SJA, RI, Box 1, Folder: ROI (Law of War/Rules of Engagement). • **65**. Policy and Directives as to Rules of Engagement and Treatment of Noncombatants, p. 23, in NA, RG 319, AS, PI-AC, Box 8, Folder: Conduct of the War, MACV Directives, ROE – Chron. File # 3 and Department of the Army, Office of the Deputy Chief of Staff for Military Operations, Subject: MACV Directives Concerning Treatment of Vietnamese Civilians, 16 Dec. 1970, § 6, in ibid. • **66**. Quoted in Lewy, *America in Vietnam*, p. 113. • **67**. 'The Enemy in Your Hands', 'Nine Rules', 'Code of Conduct' and 'Geneva Convention'. • **68**. Such was the result of an inspection carried out in Vietnam in May and June 1969: Lewy, *America in Vietnam*, p. 366. • **69**. William Peers, Memorandum for Secretary of the General Staff, Subject: Nonconcurrence, 16 Feb. 1970, § 3 c (1, 4), in NA, RG 319, ODCS-PER, VWCWG, CF, Box 6, Folder: Publicity – War Crimes and Other Sensitive Topics, 1973. • **70**. Anderson (ed.), *Facing My Lai*, p. 134; see ibid., pp. 21, 45, 137, 157. • **71**. Bilton and Sim, *Four Hours*, p. 79. • **72**. Harry G. Summers, quoted in Anderson (ed.), *Facing May Lai*, p. 134. See Karlin, *Rumors and Stones*; Hauser, *Army in Crisis*; Cincinnatus, *Self-Destruction*. • **73**. See below, pp. 288–334 • **74**. For the deployment of D Troop see below, p. 255ff. For the deployment of A Troop, see NA, RG 319, AS, PI-AC, Box 54, Folder: War Crimes Allegations – 219: Brooks Incident. • **75**. NA, RG 319, AS, PI-AC, Box 20, Folder: Other Than Son My. Ky Trong Incident: Subject/Suspects: Bell, Barnhart, Herron, Applegath. • **76**. NA, RG 319, AS, PI-AC, Box 54, Folder: War Crimes Allegations – 219: Brooks Incident; Hersh, 'The Reprimand'. • **77**. Quoted in 'Hersh Says U.S. Copters Killed 10 in Friendly Vietnam Villages in '69', *Washington Post*, 6 Oct. 1971, p. A3. • **78**. Headquarters, 12th Combat Aviation Group, Subject: Report of Investigation – Firing Incident in Cambodia, 11 Dec. 1971, § 2 (a, b, c), in NA, RG 319, AS, PI-AC, Box 54, Folder: War Crimes Allegations – 219: Brooks Incident. • **79**. James F. Hamlet, Brigadier General, Report of Investigation – Firing Incident in Cambodia, 24 Feb. 1972, § 5, in NA, RG 319, AS, PI-AC, Box 54, Folder: War Crimes Allegations – 219: Brooks Incident. • **80**. Quoted in Anderson (ed.), *Facing My Lai*, p. 157. • **81**. Harry G. Summers, quoted in ibid., p. 135. • **82**. See above, pp. 55–85. • **83**. Gibson, *Perfect War*, pp. 113ff., 120. See Baker, *Nam*, pp. 232, 198; NA, RG 319, AS, ODCS-PER, VWCWG, CaFi, Box 3, Folder: Duffy – Lanasa Incident; ibid., Folder: Keck Allegation – Rep. Schneebeli Letter (Keck Letters Incl.); ibid., Box 18, Folder: Meyrowitz Allegation (Correspondence and Messages), Case 210. 2. • **84**. The news agency AFP reported on the ten 'extra points' on 26 Nov. 1969: NA, RG 319, AS, ODCS-PER, VWCWG, CaFi, Box 3, Folder: Hartmann Incident – Messages. See ibid., Box 17, Folder: Shepard Allegation (VVAW-WSI), Case 190. At a public hearing in Washington D.C. a veteran claimed that the regimental chaplain of 11th Armored Cavalry regularly said the following prayer: 'Help us, O Lord, to fulfill the standing order of this regiment. Give us the wisdom to find the bastards – and the strength to pile it on!' An unnamed GI, quoted in *The Nation*, 4 Jan. 1971, p. 6. • **85**. NA, RG 319, AS, ODCS-PER, VWCWG, CaFi, Box 17, Folder: Shepard Allegation (VVAW-WSI), Case 190 and Franklin Shepard, 5th Battalion, 60th Infantry Regiment, 9th Infantry Division, 1968/69, in USCR, 7 Apr. 1971, p. E2923. • **86**. Cong Killer Leaflet from 5th Battalion, 60th Infantry Regiment, 3rd Brigade, 9th Infantry Division, in NA, RG 319, AS, ODCS-PER, VWCWG, CaFi, Box 17, Folder: Shepard Allegation (VVAW-WSI), Case 190. • **87**. Investigator's Statement, 5 Oct. 1971, in NA, RG 319, AS, ODCS-PER, VWCWG, CaFi, Box 17, Folder: Shepard Allegation (VVAW-WSI), Case 190. • **88**. David Halberstam on John Paul Vann, quoted in Anderson (ed.), *Facing My La*i, p. 124. • **89**. Solis, *Son Thang*, pp. 22, 78, 96, 153ff., 177. • **90**. An unnamed company commander of 1st Battalion, 7th Regiment, 1st Marine Division, quoted in Solis, *Son Thang*, p. 98. Other soldiers of this unit expressed themselves in similar vein: see ibid., p. 40. • **91**. Ibid., pp. 20–2, 29, 150ff. • **92**. 1st Lieutenant Lewis R. Ambort, quoted in ibid., p. 27; see ibid, p. 94. • **93**. Ibid., pp. 31, 45–8. • **94**. The accused Samuel Green, quoted in ibid., p. 73; see ibid., p. 27. • **95**. James Robert Barrett, Sworn Statement, p. 1, 13 Dec. 1970, in NA, RG 472, USFSEA, MACV, DRAC, IG, Preliminary Inquiry Re: Colonel Franklin, Box 2, Folder: Preliminary Investigation Re: Colonel Franklin, Vol. IV (Pt 1 of 3) 1971. See also Dugan Robert Ersland, Sworn Statement, p. 3, 31 Dec. 1970, in ibid. • **96**. Solis, *Son Thang*, p. 14. • **97**. An unnamed GI about his superior officer's deployment order, quoted in Baker, *Nam*, p. 198. See ibid., pp. 191, 232 and NA, RG 319, AS, ODCS-PER, VWCWG, CaFi, Box 1, Folder: Concerned Sergeant Allegation. • **98**. Statement Philip Francis Kearns, Company Commander, 5th Battalion, 60th Infantry Regiment, 3rd Brigade, 9th Infantry Division, 1968, in NA, RG 319, AS, ODCS-PER, VWCWG, CaFi, Box 17, Folder: Shepard Allegation (VVAW-WSI), Case 190. • **99**. Lynn, *History of Combat*, p. 134; Best, *Humanity in Warfare*, pp. 61–7; Rogers, 'Hundred Years' War', in Grimsley and Rogers (eds), *In the Path of War*, pp. 60–2. • **100**. Headquarters, 1st Cavalry Division (Airmobile), Subject: Operational Report for Quarterly Period Ending 31 Jan. 1969, 15. Feb. 1969, in NA, RG 127, USMC, HMC-HMD, BM-68, Box 8, Folder:

1st Cavalry Div, Lessons Learned, 6 Jun. 1969. • **101**. NA, RG 319, AS, ODCS-PER, VWCWG, CaFi, Box 12, Folder: Notley Allegation (Appearances of Danny S. Notley and LTC Anthony B. Herbert at a CCI News Conference, 2 Jun. 1971), Case 85. These accusations against Brigadier General Donaldson had also been made by others: see ibid., Folder: Seger Allegation (Talking Papers, Fact Sheet), Case 86. • **102**. 'General, Ex-Aide Accused of Murdering Vietnamese', *New York Times*, 3 Jun. 1971. • **103**. Talking Paper, Subject: BG Donaldson and LTC McCloskey Case, in NA, RG 319, ODCS-PER, VWCWG, CaFi, Box 12, Folder: Seger Allegation (Talking Papers, Fact Sheet), Case 86. • **104**. 'Donaldson Case First in 70 Years', *Washington Post*, 3 Jun. 1971. • **105**. An investigator preserving his anonymity in the Donaldson Case, quoted in Robert Parry and Norman Solomon, 'Behind Colin Powell's Legend – Pentagon-Man', in *The Consortium*, quoted at http://www.consortiumnews.com/archive/colin4.html. • **106**. The CID considered it proven that Lieutenant Colonel William J. McCloskey had given the order in January 1969 to shoot dead a peasant who was thought suspicious on account of his bicycle and that he had had a captive thrown out of a helicopter in flight: NA, RG 319, ODCS-PER, VWCWG, CaFi, Box 12, Folder: Seger Allegation, Case 86. • **107**. In mid June 1970 a patrol leader from B Company (Aeroscout), 123rd Aviation Battalion, Americal Division was acquitted by a court martial although the CID had confirmed that he had deliberately and without provocation murdered two young boys: NA, RG 319, AS, ODCS-PER, VWCWG, CaFi, Box 5, Folder: SP 4 Miller Allegation. • **108**. Nine months previously Herbert had presented his complaints through the official channels: NA, RG 319, ODCS-PER, VWCWG, CaFi, Box 8, Folder: Herbert Allegation (Part 1 of 2) and (Part 2 of 2), Case 58. • **109**. No criminal proceedings resulted from this case either: NA, RG 319, ODCS-PER, VWCWG, CaFi, Box 21, Folder: Crowe Allegation, Case 237. • **110**. NA, RG 319, AS, PI-AC, Box 5, Folder: Army Staff Monitor Summary and Backup Material and Box 29, Folder: Sensitive Material – My Lai – Folder # 6. • **111**. NA, RG 319, ODCS-PER, VWCWG, CF, Box 4, Folder: Helicopter Incident, Case 8 (1); ibid., Folder: Helicopter Incident CID Reports – Testimony # 1, Case 8 (2); ibid., Folder: Helicopter Incident CID Reports Testimony # 2, Case 8 (3). For the desecration of corpses, see also NA, RG 319, ODCS-PER, VWCWG, CaFi, Box 19, Folder: Potter Incident (FSB Mary Ann Incident), Case 226. • **112**. Anthony B. Herbert, Sworn Testimony, 28 Sep. 1970, in NA, RG 319, AS, ODCS-PER, VWCWG, CaFi, Box 8, Folder: Herbert Allegation (Part 2 of 2), Case 58 and RG 472, USFSEA, MACV, DRAC, IG, Preliminary Inquiry Re: Colonel Franklin, Box 1, Folder: Preliminary Investigation Re: Col. Franklin, Vol. 1 (Part 1 of 3), 1971. • **113**. Hersh, *My Lai 4*, p. 9. • **114**. Anthony B. Herbert, interview with *Life*, 9 Jul. 1971, p. 24. • **115**. Ibid. Herbert C. Kelman speaks in this context of the switching off of 'moral authority':

Kelman, 'Context of Torture', in Crelinsten and Schmid (eds), *Politics of Pain*.

4 Warriors

1. O'Brien, *Things They Carried*, p. 59. • **2**. Oates, *Man Crazy*. • **3**. Ibid., pp. 88–9 • **4**. Fact sheet, undated, in NA, RG 127, USMC HMC/HDPT, TF, FRC Box 4, Folder: Command Concerns: Drugs, Racial Strife, Fragging. See Spector, *After Tet*, pp. 40, 43. • **5**. Lewy, *America in Vietnam*, p. 175. • **6**. In 1969 an additional *c*. 34,000 frontline fighters were added from troops of the United States' allies: Lewy, *America in Vietnam*, p. 175; Dunnigan and Nofi, *Secrets*, pp. 91, 168, 181; Tucker (ed.), *Encyclopedia*, pp. 74, 241, 249, 371, 435; Gibson, *Perfect War*, p. 189ff. • **7**. Baritz, *Backfire*, pp. 277–81 and Spector, *After Tet*, p. 29. • **8**. Appy, *Working-Class War*, pp. 6, 18, 37. • **9**. Fact Sheet, undated, in NA, RG 127, USMC HMC-HDPT, TF, FRC Box 4, Folder: Command Concerns: Drugs, Racial Strife, Fragging. See also Baskir and Strauss, *Vietnam Generation* and Appy, *Working-Class War*, p. 27. For the difficulties in dealing with the numerical material, see Resic, *Warriors*, p. 53ff. • **10**. Fact Sheet, undated, in NA, RG 127, USMC HMC-HDPT, TF, FRC Box 4, Folder: Command Concerns: Drugs, Racial Strife, Fragging; Dunnigan and Nofi, *Secrets*, p. 3. • **11**. Dunnigan and Nofi, *Secrets*, p. 5; Spector, *After Tet*, p. 32. • **12**. Fact Sheet, undated, in NA, RG 127, USMC HMC-HDPT, TF, FRC Box 4, Folder: Command Concerns: Drugs, Racial Strife, Fragging and Fact Sheet: Company C, 1st Battalion, 20th Infantry Division, 21 Dec. 1969, in NA, RG 319, AS, ODCS-PER, VWCWG, MLM, Box 1, Folder: My Lai Army Staff Monitor. Summaries, Jan. 1970; Dunnigan and Nofi, *Secrets*, p. 4; Spector, *After Tet*, p. 36. The most detailed study of family backgrounds and levels of education comes from Baskir and Strauss, *Vietnam Generation*. • **13**. Spector, *After Tet*, p. 26. See also p. 38 and Moskos, *Enlisted Man*. • **14**. Spector, *After Tet*, p. 35; Dunnigan and Nofi, *Secrets*, pp. 3–7; Gibson, *Perfect War*, pp. 214–17. • **15**. Fact Sheet, undated, in NA, RG 127, USMC HMC-HDPT, TF, FRC Box 4, Folder: Command Concerns: Drugs, Racial Strife, Fragging. • **16**. Resic, *Warriors*, p. 77. • **17**. Gibson, *Perfect War*, p. 215; Spector, *After Tet*, p. 37; Lewy, *America in Vietnam*, p. 154 and Fact Sheet, undated, in NA, RG 127, USMC HMC-HDPT, TF, FRC, Box 4, Folder: Command Concerns: Drugs, Racial Strife, Fragging. • **18**. Spector, *After Tet*, p. 37; Dunnigan and Nofi, *Secrets*, p. 7; Lewy, *America in Vietnam*, p. 155; Appy, *Working-Class War*, p. 18ff.: forty-eight per cent of all soldiers of Latin American origin were detailed to fighting units, thirty-four per cent of black, but only twenty-nine per cent of white GIs. • **19**. Solis, *Son Thang*, p. 118. • **20**. Dunnigan and Nofi, *Secrets*, p. 4; Gibson, *Perfect War*, p. 217 and Fact Sheet: Company C, 1st

Battalion, 20th Infantry Division, 21 Dec. 1969, in NA, RG 319, AS, ODCS-PER, VWCWG, MLM, Box 1, Folder: My Lai Army Staff Monitor. Summaries, Jan. 1970. • **21**. Quoted in Solis, *Son Thang*, p. 117. • **22**. Dunnigan and Nofi, *Secrets*, pp. 3, 7; Gibson, *Perfect War*, p. 215; Resic, *Warriors*, p. 54ff. • **23**. Spector, *After Tet*, p. 37. • **24**. Dunnigan and Nofi, *Secrets*, pp. 91, 168, 181; Tucker (ed.), *Encyclopedia*, pp. 74, 241, 249, 371, 435; Gibson, *Perfect War*, p. 189ff; Shultz, *Secret War*. • **25**. The smallest units were the Recon Teams with up to twelve soldiers, followed by the Hatchet Forces that operated in platoon strength of up to thirty-five men. Lastly, the Slam Forces were of company strength. See USCR, 6 Apr. 1971, p. E2884; Dunnigan and Nofi, *Secrets*, p. 171 and Tucker (ed.), *Encyclopedia*, p. 386. For the history of the Special Forces, see Marquis, *Unconventional Warfare* and Greiner, 'Amerikanische Guerilla'. • **26**. Dunnigan and Nofi, *Secrets*, p. 168ff.; Leepson (ed.), *Dictionary*, p. 375; Tucker (ed.), *Encyclopedia*, pp. 74, 241, 249, 386. • **27**. MHD, 9th Infantry Division, Subject: Combat After Action Interview 12–67, p. 2, in NA, RG 472, USAV, MHD, AAI, Box 9, Folder: Folder I, AA Interviews (68). • **28**. Tucker (ed.), *Encyclopedia*, p. 241. • **29**. Dunnigan and Nofi, *Secrets*, p. 81ff., estimate the number of 'Lurps' at 15 companies at this point, giving a figure of 1,800, based on the average company strength of 120 men. • **30**. Tucker (ed.), *Encyclopedia*, p. 371. • **31**. Ibid., pp. 67, 75 and Dunnigan and Nofi, *Secrets*, p. 181ff. • **32**. MHD, 9th Infantry Division, Subject: Combat After Action Interview 12-67, p. 5, in NA, RG 472, USAV, MHD, AAI, Box 9, Folder: Folder I, AA Interviews (68). • **33**. Dunnigan and Nofi, *Secrets*, pp. 80ff.; Tucker (ed.), *Encyclopedia*, p. 241. • **34**. Perhaps the scandal of the Democrat senator and later president of the New School for Social Research in New York City, Robert Kerrey, who served in Vietnam with the SEALs, belongs here: see below, p. 268–9. • **35**. Dunnigan and Nofi, *Secrets*, pp. 170ff., 199ff.; Tucker (ed.), *Encyclopedia*, pp. 74, 241, 249, 386. • **36**. Marquis, *Unconventional Warfare*, p. 26. • **37**. Three unidentified Special Force soldiers, quoted in Terry, *Bloods*, pp. 251, 239, 91. See also USCR, 6 Apr. 1971, p. E2884. • **38**. Baker, *Nam*, p. 148. See ibid., p. 174 and Terry, *Bloods*, pp. 260–1. • **39**. For public reactions, see Stacewicz, *Winter Soldiers* and Nicosia, *Home to War*. For literary contribution see, as representative, the books of Philip Caputo, Tim O'Brien and Michael Herr. For veterans' literature as a whole, see Lewis, *Tainted War*; Herzog, *War Stories*; Myers, *Walking Point*; Appy, *Patriots*; Kindsvatter, *American Soldiers*. For oral history interviews, see COHRO: Interviews conducted for the Oral History Research Office by Professor Clark Smith; Maurer, *Strange Ground*; MacPherson, *Long Time Passing*. For conversations with psychologists, see Lifton, *Home from the War*; Shay, *Achill in Vietnam*. • **40**. Engelhardt, *Victory Culture*, pp. 73ff., 86ff., 236. See also Bates, *Conflict and Storytelling*, pp. 9–48 and Goodwin, *Remembering America*. • **41**. Quoted in Anderson (ed.), *Facing My Lai*, p. 123. See also Cuordileone, *Manhood and Political Culture*. • **42**. Engelhardt, *Victory Culture*, pp. 9, 13, 56ff.,

157. See Rose, *Nation Underground* and Lutz, *Homefront*. • **43**. Baker, *Nam*, p. 23. • **44**. An unnamed GI, quoted in ibid., p. 27; see ibid., p. 52. • **45**. Quoted in Appy, *Patriots*, p. 432. See Wills, *John Wayne's America*; Slotkin, *Gunfighter Nation*; Suid, *Guts and Glory*; Murphy, *To Hell and Back* and Kovic, *Fourth of July*. • **46**. See Appy, *Working-Class War*, p. 61ff. • **47**. An unnamed GI, quoted in Baker, *Nam*, p. 33. • **48**. O'Brien, *Cacciato*, p. 321. • **49**. Terry, *Bloods*, pp. 4, 174, 229–37. See also Baker, *Nam*, pp. 23, 56, 27–31, 34–9. • **50**. O'Brien, *Things They Carried*, pp. 21, 59. See ibid., pp. 39–61. • **51**. An unnamed GI, quoted in Baker, *Nam*, p. 56. • **52**. An unnamed GI, quoted in Terry, *Bloods*, p. 145. See ibid., pp. 4, 119. • **53**. Ernest Medina during an appearance on the David Frost Show, WTTG TV, Washington, D.C., 5 Oct. 1971, quoted in WTTG TV, An Interview with Captain Ernest Medina & F. Lee Bailey, 5 Oct. 1971, 8.30 p.m., p. 4, in NA, RG 319, AS, ODCS-PER, VWCWG, MLM, Box 4, Folder: Administrative Review – Cpt. Ernest L. Medina. • **54**. Quoted in Lelyveld, 'A Soldier Who Refused to Fire'. • **55**. Mark Twain, 'To The Person Sitting In Darkness', *North American Review*, 172, Feb. 1901. • **56**. 1st Lieutenant William Crandell, 199th Light Infantry Brigade (Separate), quoted in USCR, 6 Apr. 1971, p. E2826. See also 'The Voice of the Winter Soldier', *Playboy*, Aug. 1971, pp. 48–9. • **57**. COHRO, Sanders Interview, pp. 222–3. • **58**. An unamed GI, quoted in Anderson (ed.), *Facing My Lai*, p. 97. • **59**. Quoted in O'Brien, *Cacciato*, p. 48. See also the dense description of this mood in the autobiographical writings in Caputo, *Rumor of War* and Herr, *Dispatches*. • **60**. COHRO, Lemke Interview, pp. 56–7. • **61**. COHRO, Sanders Interview, p. 104. See also Baker, *Nam*, pp. 51ff., 254. • **62**. Terry, *Bloods*, pp. 83, 264; Spector, *After Tet*, p. 200ff.; Schell, *Real War*, p. 230ff.; Bilton and Sim, *Four Hours*, p. 21; Lewy, *America in Vietnam*, p. 310 and Solis, *Son Thang*, pp. 33, 82ff. • **63**. Headquarters, USAV, Memorandum, 31 Dec. 1967, in NA, RG 472, USFSEA, USAV, PM, AO-CGR, Box 1, Folder: Crime Prevention Program File (Pt 2 of 2) 1968. • **64**. NA, RG 472, USAV, II FFV, G3, CGR, Box 1, Folder: Friendly Casualty Report 69 and Folder: Accident/Incident Report 69. • **65**. Gregory J. Hayward, letter to Major General Ellis W. Williamson, 2 May 1971, p. 2, in NA, RG 319, AS, ODCS-PER, VWCWG, CaFi, Box 12, Folder: Hayward Allegation (reported separately), Case 84. • **66**. Lieutenant General Walter T. Kerwin, Jr. to Lieutenant General Frank T. Mildren, undated, in RG 472, USFSEA, USAV, PM, SGR, Box 1, Folder: Provost Marshal Instruction File 1968 and RG 472, USAV, II FFV, G3, CGR, Box 1, Folder: Accident/Incident Report 69. • **67**. Quoted in Solis, *Son Thang*, p. 104. • **68**. Garry Crossley, quoted in Hammer, 'Interviews with My Lai Veterans', p. 56. • **69**. An unnamed GI, quoted in Shay, *Odysseus in America*, p. 71. • **70**. Sworn Statement, Richard D. James, 1 Dec. 1970, p. 2 and Sworn Statement, David W. Hoh, 2 Dec. 1970, p. 1, in NA, RG 472, USFSEA, MACV, DRAC, IG, Preliminary Inquiry re: Colonel Franklin, Box 2, Folder: Preliminary Investigation Re: Col. Franklin, Vol. III (Pt. 2 of 4),

1971 and USCR, 6 Apr. 1971, p. E2855 and 7 Apr. 1971, p. E2934. See also Schell, *Real War*, pp. 164–5 and Bilton and Sim, *Four Hours*, pp. 80–1. • **71**. Spector, *After Tet*, p. 272. See ibid., p. 268ff.; Terry, *Bloods*, pp. 26, 262ff.; Valentine, *Phoenix Program*, p. 229; Shay, *Odysseus in America*, p. 115ff. Four of the sixteen verses of the divisional song of 9th Infantry Division ('Try Harder') have an explicit sexual content: NA, RG 472, USAV, 9th Infantry Division, Organizational History, Box 1, Folder: Unit Song. • **72**. An unnamed GI, quoted in Shay, *Odysseus in America*, p. 115. • **73**. COHRO, Sanders Interview, p. 150. • **74**. An unnamed GI, quoted in USCR, 6 Apr. 1971, p. E2831. • **75**. Brownmiller, *Against Our Will*. • **76**. Sworn Testimony of Captain Thomas K. Willingham, 8 May 1969, p. 19, in NA, RG 319, AS, PI-AC, Box 47, Folder: Son My – Other Individuals (1 of 3) and Sworn Statement, Max D. Hutson, 28 Oct. 1969, p. 2, in RG 319, AS, PI-FR, Vol. IV: CID Statements, p. 262, Box 57. See also Bilton and Sim, *Four Hours*, pp. 54, 61, 76; Hammer, *Court-Martial of Lt. Calley*, pp. 161–2; Shay, *Odysseus in America*, p. 116; Gibson, *Perfect War*, p. 29; Baker, *Nam*, pp. 70, 73, 75. • **77**. Advertising slogan of the US Army, quoted in Gibson, *Perfect War*, p. 216. • **78**. Barrett, 'Hegemoniale Männlichkeit', in: Eifler and Seifert (eds), *Soziale Konstruktionen*, pp. 71–94. • **79**. According to Gibson, instructors made use of this comparison: Gibson, *Perfect War*, p. 181. • **80**. See Bilton and Sim, *Four Hours*, p. 74ff.; Baker, *Nam*, pp. 36-45, 81, 119; Anderson (ed.), *Facing My Lai*, p. 173; Anthony B. Herbert interview, *Life*, 9 Jul. 1971, p. 24; 'An Old Man's Death Haunts State GI', *Detroit News*, 11 Dec. 1969; Captain Jerry L. Cooper, letter, 6 Apr. 1971, p. 3, in NA, RG 319, AS, PI-AC, Box 37, Folder: Son My Chron. File # 17 (2 of 2). In a reader's letter to *Look* dated 2 Jun. 1970 Lieutenant General Ira C. Eaker, US Air Force, put this rumour about as a reality of the war. • **81**. COHRO, Camil Interview, p. 79. See also Terry, *Bloods*, pp. 90, 166. • **82**. COHRO, Sanders Interview, p. 130. • **83**. See Terry, *Bloods*, p. 121ff. • **84**. Solis refers to corroborative statements by captured Viet Cong: Solis, *Son Thang*, p. 144ff. and Spector, *After Tet*, p. 75. • **85**. William Calley, quoted in Sack, *Leutnant Calley berichtet*, p. 62. • **86**. Sworn Statement, Stephen R. Glimpse, private first class, 3rd Platoon, Company C, Task Force Barker, 13 Dec. 1969, p. 6, in NA, RG 319, AS, PI-FR, Vol. IV: CID Statements, p. 218, Box 57. • **87**. Paul Meadlo, quoted in Hammer, *Court-Martial*, p. 161. For the fear fantasies, see Edelmann (ed.), *Letters Home*; Bilton and Sim, *Four Hours*, pp. 40, 54, 61, 74–6, 85; Spector, *After Tet*, p. 308; Baker, *Nam*, pp. 70–5; and COHRO, Camil Interview, p. 79; Hemple Interview, p. 34; Heiden Interview, p. 34 and Sanders Interview, pp. 91, 99. • **88**. An unnamed GI, quoted in Baker, *Nam*, p. 40. See also pp. 36–9 and Spector, *After Tet*, p. 261. • **89**. Grossman, *On Killing*, pp. 3ff., 333ff. • **90**. Bourke, *History of Killing*, p. 153. • **91**. USCR, 6 Apr. 1971, p. E2829; Department of the Army, Memorandum for the Record: Resume of Hearing, 29 Apr. 1971, p. 1, in NA, RG 319, AS, ODCS-PER, VWCWG, CF, Box 5, Folder: Memorandums for

Record – Summaries of Congressional Hearings on War Crimes, Apr. 1971; 'Confessions of "The Winter Soldiers"', *Life*, 9 Jul. 1971, p. 24. • **92**. An unnamed instructor, quoted in Baker, *Nam*, p. 81. See ibid., pp. 23, 27–36, 56, 119; Spector, *After Tet*, p. 60; COHRO, Sanders Interview, pp. 33ff., 55, 72. • **93**. Shay, *Achill in Vietnam*, pp. 58–76, 119–51 and Lifton, *Home From the War*, pp. 135–89. Similar accusations had already been made during the war by Donald Duncan: Duncan, *New Legions*. • **94**. An unnamed GI, quoted in Baker, *Nam*, p. 110. • **95**. See ibid., p. 78 and Terry, *Bloods*, p. 45ff. • **96**. Report of Investigation Concerning Alleged Violations of the Law of Land Warfare, 27 Feb. 1970, in NA, RG 472, USAV, II FFV, SJA, RI, Box 1, Folder: ROI (Maltreatment of Dead Body, 1st Cav. Div.). The same unit was accused of other mutilations. However, the investigations came to a halt due to serious discrepancies between sworn and unsworn statements. • **97**. An unnamed GI, quoted in Baker, *Nam*, p. 83. This 'acclimatisation' was also repeatedly mentioned in the course of William Calley's trial: see Engelhardt, *Victory Culture*, pp. 195, 209, 220ff. • **98**. An unidentified GI, quoted in Baker, *Nam*, p. 129. See ibid., pp. 98, 100, 102ff., 108; Terry, *Bloods*, p. 55; Gibson, *Perfect War*, pp. 108ff., 151; O'Brien, *Things They Carried*, p. 220ff. • **99**. COHRO, Sanders Interview, p. 73. See ibid., p. 207ff. and COHRO, Branham Interview, p. 6. • **100**. O'Brien, *Things They Carried*, p. 202. See ibid., p. 205. • **101**. COHRO, Sanders Interview, p. 108. • **102**. Ibid., p. 114. • **103**. An unnamed GI, quoted in Terry, *Bloods*, pp. 92–3. See also Spector, *After Tet*, pp. 46–7. For a vivid description of an operation in a paddy field, see Ellsberg, *Secrets*, p. 155ff. • **104**. Lewy estimates about twenty-five per cent for the peak period of the war between January 1967 and September 1968: Lewy, *America in Vietnam*, p. 309. • **105**. Ibid., p. 101; United States Marine Corps, Headquarters, 3rd Marine Amphibious Brigade, Subject: Brigadier General Edwin H. Simmons, Debriefing Viet Nam Service, 24 May 1971, p. 7, in NA, RG 127, HMC-HDPT, TF, Box 4, Folder: Command Info Notebook; 1st Mardiv; Apr. 1971 Debriefing; 3rd MAB; May 1971 and Fact Sheet, in ibid., Folder: Command Concerns: Drugs, Racial Strife, Fragging. • **106**. COHRO, Sanders Interview, p. 113. See also Gibson, *Perfect War*, p. 29; Baker, *Nam*, p. 101 and Lewy, *America in Vietnam*, p. 309. • **107**. National Security Study Memorandum # 1, Jan. 1969, in Ellsberg, *Secrets*, p. 240. See also Gibson, *Perfect War*, p. 108ff.; Lewy, *America in Vietnam*, p. 82ff.; Spector, *After Tet*, p. 54. • **108**. An unnamed GI, quoted in Baker, *Nam*, p. 112. • **109**. An unnamed GI, quoted in Terry, *Bloods*, p. 61. • **110**. An unnamed GI, quoted in Gibson, *Perfect War*, p. 151. See also Baker, *Nam*, pp. 98, 100, 102ff., 108, 112, 129 and COHRO, Sanders Interview, pp. 114, 209. • **111**. Sheehan, *Die Große Lüge*, p. 90. • **112**. COHRO, Sanders Interview, p. 90. See also Terry, *Bloods*, pp. 67, 169. • **113**. Spector, *After Tet*, pp. 105ff., 116, 190ff., 293; Ellsberg, *Secrets*, pp. 115ff., 172; Sheehan, *Die Große Lüge*, p. 131. • **114**. Lewy, *America in Vietnam*, pp. 178, 181; Sheehan, *Die Große Lüge*, p. 118; Ellsberg, *Secrets*, pp. 128–31. • **115**.

Spector, *After Tet*, p. 110ff. For the history of the ARVN as instrument of domestic repression, see Sheehan, *Die Große Lüge*, p. 195ff. • **116**. COHRO, Sanders Interview, p. 90. See also Spector, *After Tet*, p. 62. • **117**. COHRO, Sanders Interview, pp. 67, 85, 92ff., 96 and Solis, *Son Thang*, p. 11. • **118**. O'Brien, *Things They Carried*, pp. 15, 34. • **119**. An unnamed GI, quoted in Baker, *Nam*, p. 310. See ibid., pp. 100–4, 112, 189, 240, 291; COHRO, Sanders Interview, p. 92ff.; Lewy, *America in Vietnam*, p. 150ff. and Bilton and Sim, *Four Hours*, p. 70. • **120**. An unnamed GI, quoted in Baker, *Nam*, p. 233. See also Terry, *Bloods*, p. 21. • **121**. Zaffiri, *Hamburger Hill* and Lewy, *America in Vietnam*, p. 144ff. Those involved from 101st Airborne Division were: 1st Battalion, 506th Infantry Regiment, 2nd Battalion, 501st Infantry Regiment and 3rd Battalion, 187th Infantry Regiment. They were supported by two battalions from 1st South Vietnamese Infantry Division. The North Vietnamese allegedly lost 633 soldiers at Hamburger Hill. In any event it is entirely unclear how many of them were killed by hand grenades and bombs in the wide-spread tunnel systems. • **122**. Ronald Dellums, Vietnam War Crimes Hearings, at http:// members.aol.com/warlibrary/vwch1g.htm, 31 Aug. 2004. • **123**. An unnamed GI, quoted in Shay, *Achill in Vietnam*, p. 35. • **124**. NA, RG 319, AS, ODCS-PER, VWCWG, CaFi, Box 14, Folder: APC Incident, Case 109; COHRO, Sanders Interview, pp. 136ff, 208ff. and Terry, *Bloods*, p. 241. • **125**. COHRO, Sanders Interview, p. 207. See also Baker, *Nam*, pp. 60, 94, 112, 189, 240. • **126**. Herr, *Dispatches*, p. 55. • **127**. Spector, *After Tet*, p. 63; Solis, *Son Thang*, p. 247ff.; Bourne, *Men, Stress, and Vietnam*. • **128**. Manning, 'Esprit de Corps', in Mangelsdorff et al. (eds), *Military Psychology*. • **129**. Marine Lance Corporal Denzil R. Allen, Co A, 1st Battalion, 27th Regiment, 1st Marine Division, who, with a few colleagues, lured three Vietnamese into an ambush east of Huê in early May 1968 and murdered them in a kind of shooting competition, quoted in Shepherd, 'Incident at Van Duong', p. 31. For this case, see also Memorandum: An Analysis of Misconduct in Combat in Vietnam, Jun. 1968, in NA, RG 127, HMC-HDPT, TF, Box 4, Folder: War Crimes – Copies of Items in Mr Bill Anderson's File. For 'self-authorisation', see also USCR, 7 Apr. 1971, pp. E2915–16 and James D. Henry, 'The Men of "B" Company', pp. 26–31. • **130**. An unnamed GI, quoted in Baker, *Nam*, p. 97. • **131**. Ronald Dellums, Vietnam War Crimes Hearings, at http:// members.aol.com/warlibrary/vwch1g.htm, 31 Aug. 2004, p. 5. • **132**. Interview with Anthony B. Herbert, 'Confessions of the "Winter Soldiers"', *Life*, 9 Jul. 1971, p. 24. • **133**. NA, RG 319, AS, ODCS-PER, VWCWG, CaFi, Box 15, Folder: Ulysses Williams Incident; Statement of Franklin D. Massey, 1 Sep. 1972. See also ibid., Box 19, Folder: Goodwin Allegation, Case 227; Report of Investigation Concerning C/3/17 Air Cavalry Incident, 5.2.1971, in RG 334, IA, MACV, DRAC, SJA, Box 1, Folder: War Crime Investigation – LTC Lowell K. White (1 of 2) 1971 and RG 319, AS, PI-AC, Box 53, Folder: War Crimes Allegations – 129: Ashbaugh

Incident: this case refers to an officer who had the corpse of a prisoner decapitated and who subsequently cooked the head for eighteen hours in boiling water. For the ritual of mutilations, see also 'Ex-Pilot Alleges Civilian Slayings', *New York Times*, 7 Apr. 1970; COHRO, Sanders Interview, p. 138; Baker, *Nam*, pp. 84, 174ff., 199; Gibson, *Perfect War*, p. 147; Lewy, *America in Vietnam*, p. 329; Terry, *Bloods*, p. 244. • **134**. Statement of CW2 Randall Bert Cassels, 23 Sep. 1970, p. 3, in NA, RG 319, ODCS-PER, VWCWG, CF, Box 4, Folder: Helicopter Incident, CID Reports, Testimony # 2, Case 8 (3). See also ibid., Folder: Helicopter Incident, CID Reports, Testimony # 1, Case 8 (2); Terry, *Bloods*, p. 207. • **135**. Robert Jay Lifton before the Veterans' Subcommittee, U.S. Senate, 27 Jan. 1970, in *UPI Wire Service News*, UPI-91, 27 Jan. 1970. See also Ellsberg, *Secrets*, p. 167. • **136**. Michael Bernhardt, quoted in Bilton and Sim, *Four Hours*, p. 78. • **137**. This point of view will be revisited in connection with the My Lai (4) massacre. See also Oliver, *My Lai in History and Memory*, p. 184. • **138**. An unnamed GI, quoted in Terry, *Bloods*, p. 35. • **139**. Ibid., p. 244. • **140**. Schell, *Real War*, p. 153. • **141**. An unnamed GI, quoted in Baker, *Nam*, p. 195. • **142**. An unnamed GI, quoted in ibid., p. 301. • **143**. These excesses are reported (in the order given) in Terry, *Bloods*, p. 129; O'Brien, *Things They Carried*, p. 78ff.; Baker, *Nam*, pp. 152ff., 196; Memorandum: An Analysis of Misconduct in Vietnam, Jun. 68, in NA, RG 127, HMC-HDPT, TF, Box 4, Folder: War Crimes – Copies of Items in Mr Bill Anderson's File; Gross, 'Lieutenant Calley's Army', p. 158; Statement of Joseph Norbert Konwinski, 26 Oct. 1969, p. 2, in NA, RG 319, AS, PI-FR, Vol. IV: CID Statements, p. 288, Box 57; Lewy, *America in Vietnam*, p. 311; RG 472, USFSEA, USAV, PM, SGR, Box 1, Folder: Provost Marshal Instruction File 1968; ibid., Folder: Crime Prevention Program File (2 of 2) 1968 and RG 472, USAV, II FFV, S 3, CGR, Folder: Accident/Incident Report 69. • **144**. An unnamed GI, quoted in Baker, *Nam*, p. 197. See also pp. 126, 170, 203, 226, 301. • **145**. An unnamed GI, quoted in ibid., pp. 152, 154. • **146**. Lifton, *Home from the War*, pp. 135–61. • **147**. Sworn Statement Murray L. Cable, 10 Nov. 1970, p. 2, in NA, RG 319, AS, ODCS-PER, VWCWG, CF, Box 4, Folder: Helicopter Incident, CID Reports Testimony # 2, Case 8 (3) and ibid., Folder: Helicopter Incident, Case 8 (1). • **148**. Lance Corporal Frank C. Schultz, quoted in William T. Anderson, Misconduct in Combat and Mental Responsibility. A Case Study, p. 10, in NA, RG 127, HMC-HDPT, TF, Box 4, Folder: War Crimes – Copies of Items in Mr Bill Anderson's File. See also Shay, *Achill in Vietnam*, p. 93. • **149**. Baker, *Nam*, p. 90. See ibid., pp. 114–15, 197. • **150**. USCR, 6 Apr. 1971, p. E2836; Sworn Statement McNeil Rigby, Jr., 30 Apr. 1971, in NA, RG 319, AS, ODCS-PER, VWCWG, CaFi, Box 4, Folder: Bentley Allegation – Case 12 (1); Sworn Statement Norman Ryman, 4 Mar. 1970, p. 1, in ibid., Box 5, Folder: Ryman Incident; ibid., Box 16, Folder: Hunter Allegation (VVAW-WSI), Case 168; ibid., Box 16, Folder: Mallory Allegation (VVAW-WSI), Case 169; ibid., Box 16, Weber Allegation (VVAW-WSI), Case

170; ibid., Box 16, Folder: Duffy Allegation (VVAW-WSI), Case 171; ibid., Box 16, Folder: Stephens Allegation (VVAW-WSI), Case 173; Baker, *Nam*, p. 203. • **151.** In the files indications of the habitual photographing of atrocities repeatedly crop up: NA, RG 319, PI-FR, Vol. II: Testimony, Box 28, Book 18, Dahner: SUM APP T-152, p. 4; Box 31, Book 20, Michener: SUM APP T-209, p. 12; Box 33, Book 21, Duff: SUM APP T-268, p. 3; Box 35, Book 22, Harlow: SUM APP T-295, p. 3; Box 38, Book 24, Carter: SUM APP T-53, p. 3; Vol. III: Exhibits, Box 54, Book 4: Miscellaneous Documents, p. 301 (Exhibit M-86); Vol. IV: CID Statements, Box 57, pp. 204, 381, 427; RG 319, AS, PI-AC, Box 47, Solder: Son My – Other Individuals (3 of 3); RG 319, AS, ODCS-PER, VWCWG, CF, Box 4, Folder: Helicopter Incident, Case 8 (1) and Folder: Helicopter Incident, CID Reports – Testimony # 1, Case 8 (2); Conduct of the Men of Charlie Company, 1/20, during the Assault on My Lai 4 on 16 March 1968, p. 30, in: RG 319, AS, ODCS-PER, VWCWG, MLM, Box 5, Folder: Administrative Review – SSG Kenneth L. Hodges (Part 3 of 4); RG 319, AS, PI-CI, Box 1, Folder: Vol. III – Chronology; ibid., Box 8, Folder: Admin. File – Feb.; ibid., Box 11, Folder: Admin. – Secret # 1. See also Schell, *Real War*, pp. 378–9. • **152.** Quoted in Solis, *Son Thang*, p. 58. • **153.** See Gibson, *Warrior Dreams*, pp. 31, 41, 44, 48ff., 81ff., 89, 107–17, 161, 285, 305. Slotkin has worked out in detail the parallels and differences in comparing this with the 'gunfighter Western' of the 1950s: see Slotkin, *Gunfighter Nation*, pp. 389–405, 461–90.

5 1967 – Death Squads in the Northern Provinces

1. An unnamed GI, quoted in Baker, *Nam*, p. 84. • **2.** Hammer, *One Morning*, pp. 28–53. • **3.** Most of the relevant studies date from the 1970s and 1980s. See Duiker, *The Communist Road to Power*; Pike, *Vietnamese Communism*; Fitzgerald, *Fire in the Lake*; Trullinger, *Village at War*; Moise, *Land Reform*; Diem, *In the Jaws of History*; Chanoff and Toia, *People at War*. A recent publication is Duiker, *Ho Chi Minh*. • **4** According to the head of Quang Ngai Province, Ton That Khien, in a memorandum dated 30 Nov. 1969: Results of the Investigation of the Case of the American Operation in the Son My Area (East of Son Tinh), 30 Nov. 1969, p. 1, in NA, RG 319, AS, PI-OI, Box 56, Folder: Exhibits: Reports (4). See also Headquarters Pacific Air Force, Contemporary Historical Examination of Current Operations Report, Air Support in Quang Ngai Province (U), 25 Feb. 1970, Secret, p. 6, in RG 319, AS, PI-AC, Box 27, Folder: RVN Trip Report Information – Folder # 3. • **5.** An unnamed contemporary witness, quoted in Hammer, *One Morning*, pp. 43–4. • **6.** An unnamed contemporary witness, quoted in ibid., p. 39. • **7.** Ibid., pp. 46, 51–3. • **8.** Ibid, pp. 47–9. • **9.** NA, RG 319, PI-FR, Vol. 1: Analyses, Box 1, Chapter 3, p. 3. See also Debriefing Report, Major General Charles M. Gettys, Commanding

General, Americal Division, Jun. 1968–May 1969, p. 1, in RG 319, AS, PI-AC, Box 5, Folder: Background Americal Division. • **10**. Bilton and Sim, *Four Hours*, p. 57ff. • **11**. MACV Briefing on Enemy Order of Battle, Nov. 1967, in NA, RG 127, USMC, HMC-HMD, BM-68, Box 5, Folder: MACV Order of Battle Briefing. See also ibid., Folder: Order of Battle – Statistics of Forces, Dec. 67–Jan. 68 and RG 319, PI-FR, Vol. I: Analyses, Box 1, Chapter 3, p. 1; Debriefing Report, Major General Charles M. Gettys, Commanding General, Americal Division, June 1968–May 1969, pp. 1-2, in RG 319, AS, PI-AC, Box 5, Folder: Background Americal Division. See also Pearson, *War in the Northern Provinces*, p. 97ff. • **12**. Schwarzkopf, *Autobiography*, pp. 163–4. • **13**. Ibid., p. 163. • **14**. Headquarters Pacific Air Force, Contemporary Historical Examination of Current Operations Report, Air Support in Quang Ngai Province (U), 25 Feb. 1970, Secret, p. 35; see also pp. 32, 36, 39, 58, in RG 319, AS, PI-AC, Box 27, Folder: RVN Trip Report Information – Folder # 3. For the Standing Operation Procedure described see also Schwarzkopf, *Autobiography*, p. 129. • **15**. Hersh, *My Lai 4*, p. 4 and Lewy, *America in Vietnam*, p. 54ff. For Westmoreland's view on the I CTZ, see also the memoirs of his longstanding Secret Service Chief, Lieutenant Phillip Davidson, *Vietnam at War*. • **16**. Neil Sheehan, quoted in Bilton and Sim, *Four Hours*, p. 36. Sheehan's report appeared in the *New York Times* on 9 Oct. 1966. • **17**. Sallah and Weiss, *Tiger Force*, p. 28ff. • **18**. William Westmoreland to Ulysses S. Sharp, Mar. 1967, quoted in Bilton and Sim, *Four Hours*, p. 58. • **19**. Hammer, *One Morning*, p. 88. • **20**. Spector, *After Tet*, p. 109. • **21**. Intelligence Estimate of the Situation in I Corps Tactical Zone (I CTZ), Republic of Vietnam, Secret, 8 Jan. 1968, p. 1, in NA, RG 127, USMC, HMC-HMD, BM-68, Box 5, Folder: Order of Battle – Statistics of Forces, Dec. 67–Jan. 68. • **22**. Quoted in Hammer, *One Morning*, p. 88. • **23**. 3rd Brigade of 25th Infantry Division was shortly afterwards renamed 3rd Brigade of 4th Infantry Division. • **24**. NA, RG 319, PI-FR, Vol. II, Testimony, Box 4, Book 2, Granger: SUM APP T-367, p. 2; see ibid., Granger: APP T-367, pp. 5–10, 16–18. • **25**. Sallah and Weiss, *Tiger Force*, pp. 27, 29. • **26**. Sworn Statement Kenneth A. Smith, 15 Mar. 1975, p. 4, in NA, RG 319, AS, ODCS-PER, VWCWG, CaFi, Box 19, Folder: Coy Allegation (CID ROI 72 – CID 46-27852; Exhibits 260–350; Part 5 of 7), Case 221. See also Sworn Statement Anthony J. Curcio, Jr., 24 Jan. 1975, p. 4 and Sworn Statement Joseph A. Westbrook, 19 Jan. 1975, p. 5, in ibid. • **27**. Comments on the Schell Manuscript, Secret, undated, pp. 1–3, in NA, RG 319, AS, PI-CI, Box 11, Folder: Admin.-Secret # 2. This text is an internal expert's report on an article that Jonathan Schell had published on 9 and 16 March 1968 in the *New Yorker* under the title 'Quang Ngai and Quang Tin'. As well as an empirical examination of Schell's statements the operational guidelines for the war in I Corps Tactical Zone were recapitulated. • **28**. Comments on the Schell Manuscript, Secret, undated, p. 2, in NA, RG 319, AS, PI-CI, Box 11, Folder: Admin.-Secret # 2. • **29**. Quoted in Sallah and Weiss, *Tiger Force*, p. 36. • **30**. Ibid., p. 54. • **31**. AB 143, Combined Campaign Plan 1968, Annex L (Neutralization of VC/NVA Base Areas), undated, Confidential, p. L1, in NA, RG 319, AS, PI-AC, Box 17, Folder: (OCLL) Miscellaneous Documents from Peers. Even in retrospective observations on the war American soldiers stressed this benefit of the psychological war of attrition: see Pearson, *War in the Northern Provinces*, p. 94. • **32**. William West-moreland, quoted in Bilton and Sim, *Four Hours*, p. 35. • **33**. Quoted in ibid., p. 30. • **34**. See above, p. 110. • **35**. See above, pp. 72–4, 96–8. • **36**. Schwarzkopf, *Autobiography*, p. 126. • **37**. Hammer, *One Morning*, p. 58. • **38**. See below, pp. 196, 205. The fact that the question of whether and when this area had been declared a Free Fire Zone could not be clarified in the investigations into the My Lai (4) massacre, points to the now normal practice of no longer differentiating between No Fire Zones and Free Fire Zones. • **39**. An unnamed officer, quoted in Bilton and Sim, *Four Hours*, p. 35. • **40**. William Doyle, Reconnaissance Platoon (Tiger Force) 1st Battalion, 327th Infantry Regiment, 1st Brigade, 101st Airborne Division, quoted in Michael Sallah and Mitch Weiss, 'Demons of Past Stalk Tiger Force Veterans', *Toledo Blade*, 22 Oct. 2003. • **41**. Comments on the Schell Manuscript, Secret, undated, p. 14, in NA, RG 319, AS, PI-CI, Box 11, Folder: Admin.-Secret # 2. • **42**. Rion Causey, Reconnaissance Platoon (Tiger Force), 1st Battalion, 327th Infantry Regiment, 1st Brigade, 101st Airborne Division, quoted in Michael Sallah and Mitch Weiss, 'Day 1: Rogue GIs Unleashed Wave of Terror in Central Highlands', *Toledo Blade*, 22 Oct. 2003. • **43**. Sworn Statement Bradford E. Mutchler, 21 Jan. 1975, p. 4, in NA, RG 319, AS, ODCS-PER, VWCWG, CaFi, Box 19, Folder: Coy Allegation (CID ROI 72 – CID 46-27852; Exhibits 260–350; Part 5 of 7), Case 221. • **44**. Sworn Statement Joseph A. Westbrook, 19 Jan. 1975, p. 5, in NA, RG 319, AS, ODCS-PER, VWCWG, CaFi, Box 19, Folder: Coy Allegation (CID ROI 72 – CID 46-27852; Exhibits 260–350; Part 5 of 7), Case 221. • **45**. Michael Sallah and Mitch Weiss, '"Free Fire" Situation Set Stage for Abuses', *Toledo Blade*, 22 Oct. 2003. See also Sworn Statement Larry J. Cottingham, 24 Jan. 1973, p. 2, in NA, RG 319, AS, ODCS-PER, VWCWG, CaFi, Box 18, Folder: (CID ROI 72 – CID 46-27852; Exhibits 1–60; Part 2 of 7), Case 221. • **46**. Harold Trout, Reconnaissance Platoon (Tiger Force), 1st Battalion, 327th Infantry Regiment, 1st Brigade, 101st Airborne Division, quoted in Gustav A. Apsey, Sworn Witness Statement by James Robert Barnett, 3 Dec. 1974, p. 2, in NA, RG 319, AS, ODCS-PER, VWCWG, CaFi, Box 18, Folder: Coy Allegation (CID ROI 72 – CID 46-27852; Exhibits 151–259; Part 4 of 7), Case 221. Sallah and Weiss, *Tiger Force*, p. 197, ascribe the quotation to Lieutenant James Hawkins. • **47**. Robert L. Keck, C Company, 3rd Battalion, 21st Infantry Regiment, 196th Light Infantry Brigade, 23rd Infantry Division (Americal), in a letter to his congressman, Herman T. Schneebeli, 27 Nov. 1969, in NA, RG 319, AS, ODCS-PER, VWCWG, CaFi, Box 3, Folder: Keck

Allegation – Rep. Schneebeli Letter (Keck Letters Incl.). • **48**. The accused Marine belonged to a Combined Action Platoon and was deployed together with troops from Troop H, 17th Cavalry Regiment, 198th Light Infantry Brigade, 23rd Infantry Division (Americal): Sworn Statement Edwin B. Jackson, 4 May 1971, p. 2, in NA, RG 319, AS, ODCS-PER, CaFi, Box 13, Folder: Jackson Allegation, Case 91. • **49**. Seven in every ten prisoners were interned on the island of Phu Quoc in the Gulf of Thailand, the remaining thirty per cent were divided between five other camps. About a quarter of the prisoners of war were members of the North Vietnamese Army and three quarters were Viet Cong: Report of EPW/Detainee Data and Information Relative to EPW/Detainee in RVN, Tab B: Enemy PW/Detainee Totals, p. 5, in NA, RG 338, USAC, HD22-UR, Box 23, Folder: S11-02 Vietnam EPW/CI/D Gen Info Files (1973). For the social profile of these prisoners, see Stephen T. Hosmer (RAND Corporation), Profiles of Communist Prisoners of War in South Vietnam, 22 Dec. 1971, in RG 338, USAC, HD22-UR, Box 13, Folder: Unclassified, S11-02, Korea. Student Study – 'Name, Rank + Serial Number', 1956. For the conditions in the camps, see RG 338, USAC, HD22-CR, Box 27, Folder: Confidential 511-04 Vietnam. ICRC Visit to Phu Quoc Camp (1970–1971); ibid., Folder: Confidential 511-04 Vietnam, ICRC Visits to PW Camps (1970); ibid., Folder: Confidential 511-04 Vietnam, ICRC Inspections of Phu Quoc Island (1970); ibid., Folder: Confidential 511-04 Vietnam, ICRC Inspection rpts of Phu Quoc Island (1971) and ibid., Box 28, Folder: Confidential 511-04 Vietnam, Conditions at Phu Quoc PW Camp (1970, 72). • **50**. Office of the Provost Marshal General, Memorandum, 31 Jan. 1973, Subject: PW/Detainee Activities, Incl. 1: Enemy Prisoner of War Camp Population (as of 31 Dec. 72), in NA, RG 319, AS, PI-AC, Box 23, Folder: PW/Detainee Activities Report, Aug. 67–Jan. 73 (1 of 3). Most of the prisoners were captured in 1967 and 1968: see Headquarters MACV, Command History 1970, Vol. II, Secret NOFORN, pp. 4, 45, 51, in NA, RG 127, USMC, HMC-HDPT, TF, FRC Box 4, Folder: MACV Command Histories – Extracts; RG 338, USAC, HD22-CR, Box 29, Folder: Confidential 511-05 Vietnam, COMUSMACV (1966) and Box 16, Folder: Confidential 511-02 Vietnam, UCSA Memo PW Activities Rpt. 1971 (Folder 1 of 2). • **51**. See above, pp. 75–80. • **52**. For the lack of interest in the origins of prisoners and their treatment, see NA, RG 338, USAC, HD22-UR, Box 51, Folder: S11-05. Rpt. of Proceedings by Board of Officers 'Classification of Detainees' (1972); RG 338, USAC, HD22-CR, Box 1, Folder: Confidential – 511-01 – Vietnam (Request for List of EPW who died in captivity); ibid., Box 3, Folder: Confidential – 511-02 – Vietnam Civil Prison Conditions (1967–71); ibid., Box 4, Folder: Confidential 511-02 Vietnam Proposed DoD Directive on PW Program (1969); ibid., Box 4, Folder: Confidential 511-02 Vietnam DoD Task Group Indochina War (1971); ibid., Box 5, Folder: Confidential 511-02 Vietnam EPW/D Program (Gen Info + Requirements); ibid., Box 5, Folder: Confidential 511-02 Vietnam

Identification + Classification of EPW (1965–71); ibid., Box 5, Folder: Confidential 511-02 Vietnam Accountability of EPW (1966–70); ibid., Box 5, Folder: Confidential 511-02 Vietnam Reclass/Rescreening of EPW (1967); ibid., Box 5, Folder: Confidential 511-02 Vietnam Movement Plan – Finalized Copy (EPW) 1972; ibid., Box 7, Folder: Confidential 511-02 Vietnam Trip Report Chief PW Br. To Vietnam (1968); ibid., Box 17, Folder: Confidential 511-02 Vietnam Talking Paper – Central PW Camp Phu Quoc (1969). • **53** For a typical case, reconstructed in detail by the CID, see NA, RG 472, USFSEA, MACV, IG, ID, Miscellaneous Reports of Investigation, Box 9, Folder: ROI – Firing Incident Involving Vietnamese Nationals during CBT OPS by Elements of Co A, 2nd BN, 60th Inf (1 of 2). • **54**. GIs repeatedly spoke of this aspect in the context of the Winter Soldiers hearings: see USCR, 7 Apr. 1971, pp. E2914–16. • **55**. For dealings with prisoners in II, III and IV CTZ, see NA, RG 319, AS, ODCS-PER, VWCWG, CaFi, Box 3, Folder: Duffy – Lanasa Incident; an article also refers to this in *Scanlan's*, 1 (1970) 3, p. 77. In this text Captain Turner, C Company, 2nd Battalion, 47th Infantry Regiment, 3rd Brigade, 9th Infantry Division is quoted as saying, 'Bullet the guy – don't give him a chance . . . You couldn't get the people back here to classify them. They were released to come back and fight you again.' For incidents from other units, see RG 319, AS, ODCS-PER, VWCWG, CaFi, Box 10, Folder: Connelly Allegation; ibid., Box 11, Folder: Carmon Allegation, Case 79. Susan Sheehan published a book in 1967 on the torture and murder of prisoners of war: *Ten Vietnamese*. • **56**. Sworn Statement Stanley R. Newton, 18 Mar. 1971, in NA, RG 472, USFSEA, MACV, DRAC, IG, Preliminary Inquiry Re: Colonel Franklin, Box 1, Folder: Preliminary Investigation Re: Col. Franklin Vol. 1 (2 of 3), 1971; ibid., Box 2, Folder: Preliminary Investigation Re: Col. Franklin Vol. II (4 of 4), 1971; ibid., Box 3, Folder: Preliminary Investigation Re: Col. Franklin Vol. IV (2 of 3), 1971; RG 319, AS, ODCS-PER, VWCWG, CaFi, Box 3, Folder: Brown Allegation – Brown Letter; Coy Allegation – Investigative Summary, p. 7, in ibid., Box 18, Folder: Coy Allegation (CID ROI 72 – CID 46-27852, Part 1 of 7), Case 221 and Sworn Statement Leland W. Carpenter, 18 Jan. 1973, in ibid., Folder: Coy Allegation (CID ROI 72 – CID 46-27852, Exhibits 1–60, Part 2 of 7), Case 221. See also Sallah and Weiss, *Tiger Force*, pp. 112, 162. 'Take care of them' ran Lieutenant Calley's famous instruction in My Lai (4). Calley intended that to be understood as an order to murder: see below, p. 227. • **57**. Ken Kerney, 1st Battalion, 327th Infantry Regiment, 1st Brigade of 101st Airborne Division, quoted in Sallah and Weiss, *Tiger Force*, p. 210. See also Sworn Statement Joseph N. Konwinski, 26 Oct. 1969, p. 2, in NA, RG 319, AS, PI-FR, Vol. IV: CID Statements, Box 57, p. 288 and Alexander Casella, 'The Politics of Prisoners of War', *New York Times Magazine*, 28 May 1972. For the dealings with prisoners in I CTZ, see RG 319, PI-AC, Box 55, Folder: War Crimes Allegations – 221: Coy Allegation, Part

III; RG 319, AS, ODCS-PER, VWCWG, CaFi, Box 9, Folder: Halverson Allegation II (Investigation Reports), Case 65; ibid., Box 10, Folder: Dell Allegation (Part 1 of 6), Case 70; ibid., Box 18, Folder: Coy Allegation (CID ROI 72 – CID 46-27852, Part 1 of 7), Case 221; ibid., Folder: Coy Allegation (CID ROI 72 – CID 46-27852, Exhibits 1–60, Part 2 of 7); ibid., Box 19, Folder: Coy Allegation (CID ROI 72 – CID 46-47852, Exhibits 151–259, Part 4 of 7); ibid., Box 19, Folder: Coy Allegation (CID ROI 72 – CID 46-47852, Exhibits 260-350, Part 5 of 7). • **58**. Representing an unmanageable amount of documentary evidence, see Bilton and Sim, *Four Hours*, p. 80ff; Baker, *Nam*, pp. 191–3, 206–11, 237; Terry, *Bloods*, pp. 8, 82 and countless statements made during the Winter Soldiers hearings: USCR, 6 Apr. 1971, pp. E2837, E2880–2. • **59**. Subject: Alleged War Crimes, in NA, RG 319, AS, ODCS-PER, VWCWG, CF Box 4, Folder: Reporting and Investigating War Crimes Allegations – Procedures and Regulations; ibid., Box 4, Folder: Brooks Allegation, Case 23; RG 472, USFSEA, MACV, DRAC, IG, Preliminary Inquiry re: Colonel Franklin, Box 1, Folder: Preliminary Investigation Re: Col. Franklin Vol. III (1 of 4), 1971; RG 472, USFSEA, USAV, IG, ICD, RICF, Box 12, Folder: Case # 69-16, Alleged Misconduct of US Military Personnel. A case of abduction and murder which came to light by chance – committed by soldiers from C Company, 2nd Squadron, 8th Cavalry Regiment, 1st Cavalry Division – is documented in Lang, *Meldung*. Lang's book was filmed in 1989 by Brian De Palma, starring Michael J. Fox and Sean Penn, under the title *Casualties of War*. • **60**. See United States vs. John D. Potter, Jr., Board of Review, US Navy, 21 Jan. 1967, in NA, RG 127, USMC, HMC-HDPT, TF, FRC Box 1; Baker, *Nam*, pp. 90, 211 and Greiner, 'Sexuelle Gewalt'. • **61**. Description of the battle of Zernsdorf, 25 August 1758, in Christian Wilhelm von Prittwitz and Gaffron, *Under der Fahne des Herzogs von Bevern: Jugenderinnerungen*, Breslau 1935, p. 213ff. • **62**. 'An American Atrocity', *Esquire*, Aug. 1969 and Department of the Navy, Office of the Judge Advocate General. United States vs. John D. Potter, Jr., Board of Review, US Navy, 21 Jan. 1967, p. 3, in NA, RG 127, USMC, HMC-HDPT, TF, FRC Box 1. • **63**. Brownmiller, *Against Our Will*, p. 38. See also Seifert, 'Geschlechtsspezifische Gewalt'. • **64**. NA, RG 319, PI-FR, Vol. II: Testimony, Box 21, Book 13, Lackey: SUM APP T-389, p. 1 and ibid., Box 22, Book 14, Ridenhour: SUM APP T-266, p. 5. • **65**. Tucker (ed.), *Encyclopedia*, p. 30. • **66**. USCR, 6 Apr. 1971, p. E2831. • **67**. An unnamed GI, quoted in Baker, *Nam*, p. 206. • **68**. O'Brien, *Combat Zone*, p. 48. • **69**. See Stuhldreher, 'Rape in Viet Nam'. • **70**. An unnamed GI, quoted in Baker, *Nam*, p. 206. • **71**. An unnamed GI, quoted in ibid., p. 191; see ibid., pp. 193, 211, 237; Bilton and Sim, *Four Hours*, pp. 81, 128ff, 131ff; Gilkes, 'Missing from History', p. 63. • **72**. Heinemann, *Paco's Story*, p. 180. See also Lang, *Meldung*, p. 44ff. • **73**. See Seifert, 'Krieg und Vergewaltigung'; Zipfel, '"Blood, Sperm and Tears"'; Neill, 'Duty, Honor, Rape'. • **74**. O'Brien, *Combat Zone*, p. 72. • **75**. An unnamed GI, quoted in Shay, *Odysseus*

in America, pp. 115–16. • **76**. An unnamed GI, quoted in Terry, *Bloods*, p. 211.
• **77**. Sallah and Weiss, *Tiger Force*, p. 28. • **78**. Colonel Gerald E. Morse's
Logbook, quoted in ibid., p. 143. • **79**. Sworn Statement Lawrence M. Jackson,
17 Jan. 1975, p. 22, in NA, RG 319, AS, ODCS-PER, VWCWG, CaFi, Box 19,
Folder: Coy Allegation (CID ROI 72 – CID 46-27852, Exhibits 260–350, Part 5
of 7), Case 221. For naming see ibid., Sworn Statement Gerald E. Morse, 17
Mar. 1975, p. 6; ibid., Sworn Statement Kenneth A. Smith, 11 Mar. 1975, p. 6
and ibid., Box 18, Folder: Coy Allegation (CID ROI 72 – CID 46-27852, Exhibits
61–150, Part 3 of 7), Case 221: Sworn Statement James W. Alexander, 5 Feb.
1975, p. 2. • **80**. Sworn Statement Lawrence M. Jackson, 17 Jan. 1975, p. 10, in
NA, RG 319, AS, ODCS-PER, VWCWG, CaFi, Box 19, Folder: Coy Allegation
(CID ROI 72 – CID 46-27852, Exhibits 260–350, Part 5 of 7), Case 221. See ibid.,
Sworn Statement, Bradford E. Mutchler, 21 Jan. 1975, p. 2; ibid., Box 18, Folder:
Coy Allegation (CID ROI 72 – CID 46-27852, Exhibits 61–150, Part 3 of 7),
Case 221; Sworn Statement John J. Colligan, 22 Nov. 1972, p. 3 and ibid., Box
19, Folder: Coy Allegation (CID ROI 72 – CID 46-27852, Exhibits 151–259, Part
4 of 7), Case 221: Statement of Gustav A. Apsey, prepared on 3 Dec. 1974. •
81. Sworn Statement Leland W. Carpenter, 18 Jan. 1973, p. 13, in NA, RG 319,
AS, ODCS-PER, VWCWG, Box 18, Folder: Coy Allegation (CID ROI 72 –
CID 46-27852, Exhibits 1–60, Part 2 of 7), Case 221 and ibid., Folder: Coy Alle-
gation (CID ROI 72 – CID 46-27852, Exhibits 61–150, Part 3 of 7), Case 221:
Sworn Statement John J. Colligan, 22 Nov. 1972, p. 3. • **82**. Coy Allegation,
Investigative Summary, p. 7, in NA, RG 319, AS, ODCS-PER, VWCWG, Box
18, Folder: Coy Allegation (CID ROI 72 – CID 46-27852, Part 1 of 7), Case
221. • **83**. Sworn Statement Lawrence M. Jackson, 17 Jan. 1975, p. 8, in NA,
RG 319, AS, ODCS-PER, VWCWG, CaFi, Box 19, Folder: Coy Allegation (CID
ROI 72 – CID 46-27852, Exhibits 260–350, Part 5 of 7), Case 221. See ibid,
Sworn Statement Bradford E. Mutchler, 21 Jan. 1975, pp. 2–4. • **84**. Sworn
Statement Bradford E. Mutchler, 21 Jan. 1975, p. 3, in NA, RG 319, AS, ODCS-
PER, VWCWG, CaFi, Box 19, Folder: Coy Allegation (CID ROI 72 – CID
46-27852, Exhibits 260–350, Part 5 of 7), Case 221. See ibid., Box 18, Folder:
Coy Allegation (CID ROI 72 – CID 46-27852, Exhibits 1–60, Part 2 of 7), Case
221: Sworn Statement James R. Barnett, 27 Apr. 1973 and Statement taken by
Gustav A. Apsley, 21 Aug. 1974, in ibid., Box 18, Folder: Coy Allegation (CID
ROI 72 – CID 46-27852, Exhibits 61–150, Part 3 of 7), Case 221. • **85**. Schell,
'Quang Ngai and Quang Tin'. • **86**. See Headquarters Pacific Air Force,
Contemporary Historical Examination of Current Operations Report, Air
Support in Quang Ngai Province, Secret, 25 Feb. 1970, p. 10, in NA, RG 319,
AS, PI-AC, Box 27, Folder: RVN Trip Report Information – Folder # 3; Bilton
and Sim, *Four Hours*, p. 44; and USCR, 6 Apr. 1971, pp. E2895–7. • **87**. Bilton
and Sim, *Four Hours*, p. 44. • **88**. Comments on the Schell Manuscript, Secret,
undated, p. 1, in NA, RG 319, AS, PI-CI, Box 11, Folder: Admin.-Secret # 2.

See ibid., p. 7 and US House of Representatives, Hearing Held before Subcommittee on Foreign Operations and Government Information of the Committee on Government Operation, Currency Exchange in Southeast Asia, 2 Aug. 1971, p. 1176, in RG 319, AS, ODCS-PER, VWCWG, CF, Box 4, Folder: House Hearings: Currency Exchange in Southeast Asia, 2 Aug. 1971 (Includes War Crimes Allegations). • **89**. Gustav A. Apsley, Agent's Statement, 28 Mar. 1975, in NA, RG 319, AS, ODCS-PER, VWCWG, CaFi, Box 18, Folder: Coy Allegation (CID ROI 72 – CID 46-27852, Exhibits 1–60, Part 2 of 7), Case 221. • **90**. Sallah and Weiss, *Tiger Force*, p. 277; see ibid., p. 13. • **91**. Sworn Statement Lawrence M. Jackson, 17 Jan. 1975, p. 4, in NA, RG 319, AS, ODCS-PER, VWCWG, CaFi, Box 19, Folder: Coy Allegation (CID ROI 72 – CID 46-27852, Exhibits 260–350, Part 5 of 7), Case 221. See ibid., p. 5 and Box 18, Folder: Coy Allegation (CID ROI 72 – CID 46-27852, Exhibits 61–150, Part 3 of 7), Case 221: Sworn Statement James W. Alexander, 5 Feb. 1975, p. 3; ibid., Box 19, Folder: Coy Allegation (CID ROI 72 – CID 46-27852, Exhibits 260–350, Part 5 of 7), Case 221: Sworn Statements Gerald E. Morse, 10 Aug. 1972 and 17 Mar. 1975, Sworn Statement Bradford E. Mutchler, 21 Feb. 1975, p. 2 and Sworn Statement Joseph A. Westbrook, 19 Jan. 1975, p. 1. • **92**. NA, RG 319, ODCS-PER, VWCWG, Box 18, Folder: Coy Allegation (CID ROI 72 – CID 46-27852, Part 1 of 7), Case 221. • **93**. See Sallah and Weiss, *Tiger Force*, pp. 217–34. • **94**. NA, RG 319, AS, PI-AC, Box 51, Folder: War Crimes Allegations – 13: Stout Allegation (1 of 2). In his outrage at the case against William Calley, Dennis Stout had gone public to draw attention to the fact that it was not soldiers such as Calley but the type of warfare prescribed by the Pentagon which was responsible for atrocities. • **95**. See NA, RG 319, AS, PI-AC, Box 55, Folder: War Crimes Allegations – 221: Coy Allegation, Part III. • **96**. Sworn Statement James R. Barnett, 27 Nov. 1974, p. 1, in NA, RG 319, AS, ODCS-PER, VWCWG, CaFi, Box 19, Folder: Coy Allegation (CID ROI 72 – CID 46-27852, Exhibits 151–259, Part 4 of 7), Case 221. • **97**. See NA, RG 319, AS, ODCS-PER, VWCWG, CaFi, Box 19, Folder: Coy Allegation (CID ROI 72 – CID 46-27852, Exhibits 151–259, Part 4 of 7), Case 221 and Folder: Coy Allegation (CID ROI 72 – CID 46-27852, Exhibits 260–350, Part 5 of 7). • **98**. Michael Sallah and Mitch Weiss, 'Day 2: Inquiry Ended without Justice. Army Substantiated Numerous Charges – Then Dropped Case of Vietnam War Crimes', *Toledo Blade*, 22 Oct. 2003, and 'Comment: Uncovered', *New Yorker*, 22 Jan. 2004. • **99**. Memorandum on the Apsey Report, quoted in Sallah and Weiss, *Tiger Force*, p. 306. • **100**. Michael Sallah and Mitch Weiss published their results firstly in the daily newspaper *Toledo Blade* in October 2003 and in the form of their book *Tiger Force* in 2006. • **101**. Lu Thuan, quoted in Michael Sallah and Mitch Weiss, 'Day 1: Rogue GIs Unleashed Wave of Terror in Central Highlands', *Toledo Blade*, 22 Oct. 2003. • **102**. The attempted evacuation was vividly described by Schell, *Real War*, pp. 189–398. • **103**. Sworn Statement, Lawrence M. Jackson, 17 Jan. 1975,

p. 16, in NA, RG 319, AS, ODCS-PER, VWCWG, CaFi, Box 19, Folder: Coy Allegation (CID ROI 72 – CID 46-27852, Exhibits 260–350, Part 5 of 7), Case 221. • **104.** Lieutenant James Hawkins, quoted in Sallah and Weiss, *Tiger Force*, p. 108. • **105.** Ibid., pp. 134, 170. • **106.** 196th Light Infantry Brigade, 23rd Infantry Division remained an integral part of Americal Division until the latter was disbanded in November 1971; 1st Brigade, 101st Airmobile Division split away from Americal at the end of the first part of Operation Wheeler, end November 1967. • **107.** Colonel Gerald E. Morse, quoted in Sallah and Weiss, *Tiger Force*, p. 179. • **108.** Sworn Statement, Leland W. Carpenter, 18 Jan. 1973, p. 7, in NA, RG 319, AS, ODCS-PER, VWCWG, CaFi, Box 18, Folder: Coy Allegation (CID ROI 72 – CID 46-27852, Exhibits 1–60, Part 2 of 7), Case 221. Similar statements were made by nearly all 'tigers' who spoke over the years about their deployments. See ibid., Folder: Coy Allegation (CID ROI 72 – CID 46-27852, Exhibits 260–350, Part 5 of 7), Case 221: Sworn Statement Bradford E. Mutchler, 21 Jan. 1975, p. 4; Michael Sallah and Mitch Weiss, 'Day 3: Pain Lingers 36 Years after Deadly Rampage', *Toledo Blade*, 22 Oct. 2003. • **109.** Rion Causey, quoted in Sallah and Weiss, *Tiger Force*, p. 360. • **110.** See NA, RG 319, AS, ODCS-PER, VWCWG, CaFi, Box 18, Folder: Coy Allegation (CID ROI 72 – CID 46-27852, Part 1 of 7), Case 221: ibid., Folder: Coy Allegation (CID ROI 72 – CID 46-27852, Exhibits 1–60, Part 2 of 7); ibid., Folder: Coy Allegation (CID ROI 72 – CID 46-27852, Exhibits 61–150, Part 3 of 7); Michael Sallah and Mitch Weiss, 'Witness to Vietnam Atrocities Never Knew About Investigation', *Toledo Blade*, 22 Oct. 2003 and id, '"Free Fire" Situation Set Stage for Abuses', ibid. Gary D. Coy and Dennis Lee Stout reported on attacks on twelve villages. For a more detailed description of the killing, see also Sallah and Weiss, *Tiger Force*, pp. 96–104, 112–14, 141, 146, 150ff., 162, 184, 199, 208ff, 223, 238, 244–50, 256, 301ff., 382ff. • **111.** Ibid., p. 279. • **112.** Rion Causey, quoted in ibid., p. 212. See also the interview with a former member of the Tiger Force: 'U.S. Reportedly to Probe Charges of Vietnam Killings', *Washington Post*, 16 Feb. 2004, p. A13. • **113.** Coy-Allegation, Investigation Summary, p. 9, in NA, RG 319, AS, ODCS-PER, VWCWG, CaFi, Box 18, Folder: Coy Allegation (CID ROI 72 – CID 46-27852, Part 1 of 7), Case 221. • **114.** Sworn Statement, Bradford E. Mutchler, 21 Jan. 1975, p. 3, in NA, RG 319, AS, ODCS-PER, VWCWG, CaFi, Box 19, Folder: Coy Allegation (CID ROI 72 – CID 46-27852, Exhibits 260–350, Part 5 of 7), Case 221. • **115.** Sallah and Weiss, *Tiger Force*, pp. 202–3. • **116.** Sworn Statement Larry J. Cottingham, 24 Jan. 1973, p. 3, in NA, RG 319, AS, ODCS-PER, VWCWG, CaFi, Box 18, Folder: Coy Allegation (CID ROI 72 – CID 46-27852, Exhibits 1–60, Part 2 of 7), Case 221. See ibid., Sworn Statement Leland W. Carpenter, 13 Jan. 1973, p. 2; ibid., Sworn Statement James R. Barnett, p. 5; and ibid., Folder: Coy Allegation (CID ROI 72 – CID 46-27852, Exhibits 61–150, Part 3 of 7), Case 221: John R. Espy, Agent's Statement; Folder: Coy Allegation (CID ROI 72 – CID

46-27852, Exhibits 151–259 Part 4 of 7), Case 221: Sworn Statement Frederick E. Tomlin, p. 1: RG 319, AS, PI-AC, Box 55, Folder: War Crimes Allegations – 221: Coy Allegation, Part III: Investigative Summary, p. 21. See also Sallah and Weiss, *Tiger Force*, pp. 202ff., 207, 383. • **117**. Sworn Statement Leland W. Carpenter, 18 Jan. 1973, p. 12, in NA, RG 319, AS, ODCS-PER, VWCWG, CaFi, Box 18, Folder: Coy Allegation (CID ROI 72 – CID 46-27852, Exhibits 1–60, Part 2 of 7), Case 221. • **118**. According to the statement by David B. Johnson in 'Deserter, Ashamed of U.S. is an Escapee from USDB', *Leavenworth Times*, 8 Jan. 1972. • **119**. See NA, RG 319, ODCS-PER, VWCWG, CaFi, Box 16, Folders: Hunter Allegation – Case 168; Mallory Allegation – Case 169; Weber Allegation – Case 170 and Stephens Allegation – Case 173. See also Sworn Statement Franklin D. Massey, 1 Sep. 1972, p. 3, in ibid., Box 19, Folder: Goodwin Allegation – Case 227. • **120**. From a multitude of examples see: 1st Platoon, B Troop, 3rd Squadron, 4th Cavalry Regiment, 25th Infantry Division after an operation in Binh Duong Province north of Saigon, III CTZ in June 1967: NA, RG 319, AS, ODCS-PER, VWCWG, CaFi, Box 14, Folder: Esquire Allegation – Case 113; B Company, 1st Battalion, 503rd Infantry Regiment, 173rd Airborne Division after an operation close to Landing Zone Uplift, II CTZ in early May 1970: ibid., Box 19, Folder: Goodwin Allegation. See also Baker, *Nam*, pp. 82ff, 164, 174ff., 199, 213; Gibson, *Perfect War*, p. 147; Tucker (ed.), *Encyclopedia*, p. 29. • **121**. John Geymann, quoted in USCR, 6 Apr. 1971, p. E2857. See ibid., p. E2828. See also CID Report of Investigation: 70-CID 448-37587, 20 Jun. 1970, p. 3, in NA, RG 319, AS, ODCS-PER, VWCWG, Box 4, CF, Folder: Helicopter Incident, Case 8 (1) and Sworn Statements Robert A. Gebhardt, 31 Mar. 1970; Robert L. Asplin, 2 Dec. 1969, p. 3; Randell B. Cassels, p. 7; Julian P. Bellak, 15 Dec. 1969, p. 20, in ibid., Folder: Helicopter Incident. CID Reports – Testimony # 1, Case 8 (2); RG 319, AS, ODCS-PER, VWCWG, CaFi, Box 15, Folder: Ulysses Williams Incident, Case 136. • **122**. See John Dower, *War Without Mercy*. • **123**. William Doyle, quoted in Sallah and Weiss, *Tiger Force*, pp. 92, 120. • **124**. Sam Ybarra, quoted in ibid., pp. 60, 120. • **125**. William Carpenter, quoted in Michael Sallah and Mitch Weiss, 'Day 1: Rogue GIs Unleashed Wave of Terror in Central Highlands', *Toledo Blade*, 22 Oct. 2003. • **126**. William Doyle in a telephone interview with Mitch Weiss, quoted in Sallah and Weiss, *Tiger Force*, p. 316; see ibid., p. 149. Jonathan Shay quotes similar comments by one of the veterans from another unit whom he interviewed: *Achill in Vietnam*, p. 93. • **127**. Sallah and Weiss, *Tiger Force*, p. 197. • **128**. Sworn Statement Robert W. Ledbetter, 19 Jan. 1973, in NA, RG 319, AS, ODCS-PER, VWCWG, CaFi, Box 18, Folder: Coy Allegation (CID ROI 72 – CID 46-27852, Exhibits 260–350, Part 5 of 7), Case 221. See also Sworn Statement Harold E. Fischer, 30 Nov. 1972, p. 1 and Sworn Statement Larry J. Cottingham, 24 Jan. 1973, pp. 1, 3, in ibid., Folder: Coy Allegation (CID ROI 72 – CID 46-27852, Exhibits 1–60, Part 2 of 7), Case 221. See also

Sallah and Weiss, *Tiger Force*, pp. 212–14, 255, 265, 360–4, 372. • **129**. Ibid., p. 203. • **130**. Ibid., pp. 182–3. • **131**. CID Report of Investigation 72-CID046-27852, 10 Jun. 1974, p. 15, in NA, RG 319, AS, PI-AC, Box 55, Folder: War Crimes Allegations – 221: Coy Allegation, Part III and Sworn Statement Leland W. Carpenter, 18 Jan. 1973, p. 11, in RG 319, AS, ODCS-PER, VWCWG, CaFi, Box 18, Folder: Coy Allegation (CID 72 – CID 46-27852, Exhibits 1–60, Part 2 of 7), Case 221. • **132**. CID Report of Investigation 72-CID046-27852, 10 Jun. 1974, pp. 17–24, in NA, RG 319, AS, PI-AC, Box 55, Folder: War Crimes Allegations – 221: Coy Allegation Part III and Sworn Statement Gerald W. Bruner, 12 Feb. 1974, p. 7, in RG 319, AS, ODCS-PER, VWCWG, CaFi, Box 18, Folder: Coy Allegation (CID ROI 72 – CID 46-27852, Exhibits 61–150, Part 3 of 7), Case 221. • **133**. Sallah and Weiss, *Tiger Force*, pp. 64, 184, 238ff., 255ff. • **134**. Michael Sallah and Mitch Weiss, 'Day 1: Rogue GIs Unleashed Wave of Terror in Central Highlands', *Toledo Blade*, 22 Oct. 2003. • **135**. Sworn Statements Robert P. Mohs, 20 Jun. 1974, p. 3 and Cecil L. Peden, 25 Jun. 1974, p. 4, in NA, RG 319, AS, ODCS-PER, VWCWG, CaFi, Box 19, Folder: Coy Allegation (CID ROI 72 – CID 46-27852, Exhibits 151–259, Part 4 of 7), Case 221. The following report was made about a Marine unit stationed near Dong Ha, I CTZ: 'We'd take C-ration crackers and put peanut butter on it and stick a trioxylene heat tap in the middle and let a kid munch on it . . . The effect more or less of trioxylene is to eat the membranes out of your throat.' Bill Hatton, USMC, quoted in Gross, 'Lieutenant Calley's Army', p. 158. • **136**. COHRO, Branham Interview, pp. 29, 44. See Baker, *Nam*, p. 153. • **137**. Sallah and Weiss, *Tiger Force*, pp. 77, 124, 127. • **138**. Ibid., p. 96. • **139**. Ibid., p. 99. See also CID Report of Investigation 72-CID046-27852, 10 Jun. 1974, p. 9, in NA, RG 319, AS, PI-AC, Box 55, Folder: War Crimes Allegations – 221 and Sworn Statement Lee J. Heaney, 28 Jun. 1974, p. 1, in NA, RG 319, AS, ODCS-PER, VWCWG, CaFi, Box 19, Folder: Coy Allegation (CID ROI 72 – CID 46-27852, Exhibits 151–259, Part 4 of 7), Case 221. • **140**. Investigative Summary, 72-CID 046-27852, p. 8, in NA, RG 319, AS, ODCS-PER, VWCWG, CaFi, Box 18, Folder: Coy Allegation (CID ROI 72 – CID 46-27852, Part 1 of 7), Case 221. • **141**. Gerald W. Bruner, quoted in Sallah and Weiss, *Tiger Force*, p. 167. • **142**. James Hawkins, quoted in ibid., p. 96 and Sworn Statement Leland W. Carpenter, 18 Jan. 1973, pp. 5, 14, in NA, RG 319, AS, ODCS-PER, VWCWG, CaFi, Box 18, Folder: Coy Allegation (CID ROI 72 – CID 46-27852, Exhibits 1–60, Part 2 of 7), Case 221. • **143**. Sallah and Weiss, *Tiger Force*, p. 97. • **144**. This is how Dennis Stout recalls the incident: Dennis Stout, 'Exposing Atrocities', letter to the Editor, *Playboy*, Apr. 1972. • **145**. Sworn Statement Larry J. Cottingham, 24. Jan 1973, p. 4, in NA, RG 319, AS, ODCS-PER, VWCWG, CaFi, Box 18, Folder: Coy Allegation (CID ROI 72 – CID 46-27852, Exhibits 1–60, Part 2 of 7), Case 221. See ibid., Sworn Statement Harold E. Fischer, 30 Nov. 1972, p. 2. • **146**. Dennis Lee Stout, quoted in 'Vietnam "Acts" Reported, Tempe Veteran Claims', *Phoenix*

Arizona Gazette, 12 Dec. 1969. See also Michael Sallah and Mitch Weiss, 'Day 4: Demons of Past Stalk Tiger Force Veterans', *Toledo Blade*, 22 Oct. 2003; id., 'Day 1: Rogue GIs Unleashed Wave of Terror in Central Highlands', ibid. • **147.** In addition to this Hawkins personally murdered several people: CID Report of Investigation 72-CID046-27852, 10 Jun. 1974, pp. 8–10, in NA, RG 319, AS, PI-AC, Box 55, Folder: War Crimes Allegations – 221 and Sworn Statement Leland W. Carpenter, 18 Jan. 1973, pp. 5, 14, in NA, RG 319, AS, ODCS-PER, VWCWG, CaFi, Box 18, Folder: Coy Allegation (CID ROI 72 – CID 46-27852, Exhibits 1–60, Part 2 of 7), Case 221. • **148.** Sworn Statement James R. Barnett, 27 Nov. 1974, p. 2, in NA, RG 319, AS, ODCS-PER, VWCWG, CaFi, Box 19, Folder: Coy Allegation (CID ROI 72 – CID 46-27852, Exhibits 151–259, Part 4 of 7), Case 221; Sallah and Weiss, *Tiger Force*, pp. 101, 156, 202, 251. • **149.** Sworn Statement James W. Alexander, 5 Feb. 1975, p. 3, in NA, RG 319, AS, ODCS-PER, VWCWG, CaFi, Box 18, Folder: Coy Allegation (CID ROI 72 – CID 46-27852, Exhibits 61–150, Part 3 of 7), Case 221. • **150.** Sallah and Weiss, *Tiger Force*, pp. 83, 202. • **151.** Ibid., pp. 156/157, 210/211. • **152.** An unnamed GI, quoted in Baker, *Nam*, p. 163. • **153.** Michael Bernhardt, quoted in Bilton and Sim, *Four Hours*, pp. 18–19. See Spector, *After Tet*, pp. 59–60. • **154.** William Doyle, quoted in Joe Mahr, 'Why did Some Troops Target Civilians but Others did not?', *Toledo Blade*, 22 Oct. 2003. • **155.** The leader of 2nd Platoon, B Company, 1st Battalion, 5th Regiment, 1st Marine Division, quoted in 'An American Atrocity', *Esquire*, Aug. 1969, p. 22. • **156.** Two unnamed Marines, quoted in ibid., p. 23. The reporting in *Esquire* was confirmed in an investigation by the Office of the Judge Advocate General: Department of the Navy, Office of the Judge Advocate General. United States vs. John D. Potter, Jr., Board of Review, US Navy, 21 Jan. 1967, pp. 1–13, in NA, RG 127, USMC, HMC-HDPT, TF, FRC Box 1 and ibid., FRC Box 4, Folder: War Crimes – Copies of Items in Mr Bill Anderson's File. • **157.** An unnamed Marine from 2nd Platoon, B Company, 1st Battalion, 5th Regiment, 1st Marine Division, quoted in 'An American Atrocity', *Esquire*, Aug. 1969, p. 23. • **158.** Charles D. Wilkerson, 3rd Marine Division, quoted in William T. Anderson, Memorandum, Subject: An Analysis of Misconduct in Combat in Vietnam, June '86, p. 8; see ibid., p. 5, in NA, RG 127, USMC, HMC-HDPT, TF, FRC Box 1 and ibid., FRC Box 4, Folder: War Crimes – Copies of Items in Mr Bill Anderson's File. See ibid., William T. Anderson, Misconduct in Combat and Mental Responsibility: A Case Study, Chapter 3, p. 8. • **159.** John R. Lanasa, quoted in 'Tan am Base Vietnam, Feb 12, 1000 Hrs', *Scanlan's*, 1 (1970) 2, p. 2. This murder was thoroughly investigated and documented by the CID: see NA, RG 472, USFSEA, MACV, IG, ID, Miscellaneous Reports of Investigations, Box 3, Folder: ROI – Shooting of an Alleged ARVN Soldier near Bin Phuoc, RVN (USARV). • **160.** Warren Ambrose, quoted in Report of Investigation Concerning Allegations Made Against 2Lt Warren Ambrose,

561-60-8722, for Possible War Crimes, 14 Jan. 1971, p. 5, in NA, RG 319, AS, ODCS-PER, VWCWG, CaFi, Box 16, Folder: Ambrose Incident, Case 157. • **161**. Report of Investigation Concerning Allegations Made Against 2Lt Warren Ambrose, 561-60-8722, for Possible War Crimes, 14 Jan. 1971, pp. 12/13, in NA, RG 319, AS, ODCS-PER, VWCWG, CaFi, Box 16, Folder: Ambrose Incident, Case 157. Lieutenant Warren Ambrose was brought before a Special Court Martial in March 1971 and acquitted. • **162**. Lang, *Meldung*. • **163**. During the court martial of Sergeant Roy E. Bumgarner from 1st Cavalry Division who had murdered three peasants at the end of February 1969 and was suspected of countless other murders, this practice was discussed in detail. Bumgarner was only convicted of manslaughter and escaped with demotion and a fine of $600. See NA, RG 319, AS, ODCS-PER, VWCWG, CaFi, Box 15, Folder: Bumgarner Incident, Case 147 and ibid., CF, Box 5, Folder: Congressional Correspondence – War Crimes Allegations, 1971–1972. • **164**. Department of the Navy, Office of the Judge Advocate General. United States vs. John D. Pottter, Jr., Board of Review, US Navy, 21 Jan. 1967, pp. 4, 13, 14, in NA, RG 127, USMC, HMC-HDPT. TF, FRC, Box 1. • **165**. See NA, RG 319, ODCS-PER, VWCWG, CaFi, Box 7, Folder: Hooks-Miller Allegation (Armstrong-Mackler Incident), Case 49; Sworn Statement Leland W. Carpenter, 18 Jan. 1973, p. 11, in NA, RG 319, AS, ODCS-PER, VWCWG, CaFi, Box 18, Folder: Coy Allegation (CID 72 – CID 46-27852, Exhibits 1–60, Part 2 of 7), Case 221 and Sworn Statement Franklin D. Massey, 1 Sep. 1972, p. 3, in ibid., Box 19, Folder: Goodwin Allegation. See also Sallah and Weiss, *Tiger Force*, p. 110; Baker, *Nam*, p. 91. • **166**. Sworn Statement James W. Alexander, 5 Feb. 1972, p. 4, in NA, RG 319, AS, ODCS-PER, VWCWG, CaFi, Box 18, Folder: Coy Allegation (CID ROI 72 – CID 46-27852, Exhibits 61–150, Part 3 of 7), Case 221 and Investigative Summary, 72-CID046-27852, p. 10, in ibid., Folder: Coy Allegation (CID ROI 72 – CID 46-27852, Part 1 of 7), Case 221. • **167**. Lieutenant Colonel Gerald E. Morse, quoted in Sallah and Weiss, *Tiger Force*, p. 198. For the 'Tigers'' radio messages, see ibid., pp. 199, 208, 210. • **168**. Sworn Statement Kenneth A. Smith, 15 Mar. 1975, p. 5, in NA, RG 319, AS, ODCS-PER, VWCWG, CaFi, Box 19, Folder: Coy Allegation (CID ROI 72 – CID 46-27852, Exhibits 260–350, Part 5 of 7), Case 221 and Sworn Statement Joseph A. Westbrook, 19 Jan. 1975, pp. 2–6, in ibid. • **169**. An unnamed officer on the staff of 1st Battalion, 1st Brigade, 101st Airmobile Division, quoted in Sallah and Weiss, *Tiger Force*, pp. 128–9. For reactions to Wood's and Bruner's complaints, see ibid., pp. 137ff., 172, 193, 258. See also Investigative Summary, 72-CID046-27852, p. 8, in NA, RG 319, AS, ODCS-PER, VWCWG, Box 18, Folder: Coy Allegation (CID ROI 72 – CID 46-27852, Part 1 of 7), Case 221; Sworn Statement Gerald W. Bruner, 12 Feb. 1974, p. 8, in ibid., Folder: Coy Allegation (CID ROI 72 – CID 46-27852, Exhibits 61–150, Part 3 of 7), Case 221 and CID Report of Investigation 72-CID046-27852, 10 Jun. 1974, pp. 24–5, in RG 319, AS, PI-AC, Box 55, Folder: War Crimes Allegations

– 221: Coy Allegation, Part 3. • **170**. Sallah and Weiss, *Tiger Force*, p. 52. • **171**. Marquis, *Unconventional Warfare*, p. 117. • **172**. Captain Harold McGaha, quoted in Sallah and Weiss, *Tiger Force*, p. 207. For the strategic thinking about Killer Commandos, see ibid., pp. 14, 278. This also fits in with the decision about Sergeant Roy E. Bumgarner, which was taken in February 1970. Bumgarner was known to be extremely aggressive and had been convicted for multiple manslaughter (see Note 164), but he was taken back into the Army and sent out to Vietnam again: NA, RG 319, AS, ODCS-PER, VWCWG, CF, Box 5, Folder: Congressional Correspondence – War Crimes Allegations, 1971–1972.

6 16 March 1968 – The Massacres of My Lai (4) and My Khe (4)

1. O'Brien, *Lake of the Woods*, p. 30. • **2**. PRP Assessment of TET, 68, 2/68, in NA, RG 127, USMC, HMC-HMD, BM-68, Box 10, Folder: PRP Assessment of Tet 68. • **3**. Pike Assessment: December 1967, p. 3, in NA, RG 127, USMC, HMC-HMD, BM-68, Box 10, Folder: Strategy – 12/67; see ibid., pp. 1, 2 and Neil Sheehan, 'Westmoreland Predicted Big 1968 Gains in Vietnam', *New York Times*, 21 Mar. 1968. • **4**. Directive to all military and political leaders, undated, quoted in Spector, *After Tet*, pp. 24–5. To date the internal discussions about the strategy of the Viet Cong and the NVA is known about only in outline: see Duiker, *Ho Chi Minh*; Gilbert, *Why the North Won*; Lanning and Craig, *Inside the VC and NVA*; Military History Institute of Vietnam, *People's Army*. • **5**. See Frey, *Geschichte des Vietnamkriegs*, p. 160ff. • **6**. Braestrup, *Big Story*, p. 495. See Greiner, 'Sommer der Anarchie'. • **7**. Quoted in Wyatt, *Paper Soldiers*, p. 168. • **8**. Halberstam, *Powers That Be*, p. 514. See Hallin, *Uncensored War*, pp. 108, 168 and Wyatt, *Paper Soldiers*, pp. 168, 174ff. • **9**. Hammer, *One Morning*, pp. 95–6. • **10**. For the clean-up plan of December 1967, see Hosmer, *Viet Cong Repression*, p. 70. • **11**. 'Information on the Victory of Our Armed Forces in Hue from 31 January to 23 March 1968', 29 May 1968, quoted in ibid., p. 77. • **12**. Ibid., p. 75. • **13**. Pike, *Strategy of Terror*, pp. 52–61. See United States Senate, The Human Cost of Communism in Vietnam. A Compendium prepared for the Subcommittee to Investigate the Administration of the Internal Security Act and other Internal Security Laws of the Committee on the Judiciary, 92nd Congress, 2nd Session, Washington, DC 1972. • **14**. NV71 (possibly Security Agency, Security Section, Quang Ngai Province, Region 5), 21 Oct. 1969, p. 1, in NA, RG 319, AS, PI-OI, Box 6, Folder: MACV Reports (14). • **15**. NV71 (possibly Security Agency, Security Section, Quang Ngai Province, Region 5), 21 Oct. 1969, p. 2, in NA, RG 319, AS, PI-OI, Box 6, Folder: MACV Reports (14). • **16**. Operation Recovery, 26 Dec. 1968, p. 1, in NA, RG 319, AS, PI-OI, Box 5, Folder: MACV Reports (8). • **17**. Quang Ngai, Territorial

Security, 13 Mar. 1968, p. 1, in NA, RG 319, AS, PI-OI, Box 5, Folder: MACV Reports (6); William Westmoreland, letter to the US Supreme Command in the Pacific and all Commanding Generals in Vietnam, Subject: Pacification in South Vietnam during February 1968, Confidential NOFORN, 6 Apr. 1968, p. 3, in ibid., Folder: MACV Reports (7). See also Office of the Province Senior Advisor, Quang Ngai Province, CORDS, Subject: Province Monthly Report, 31 Mar. 1968, p. 1, in ibid., Box 55, Folder: Exhibits: Reports (2) and Headquarters Pacific Air Force, Contemporary Historical Examination of Current Operations Report, Air Support in Quang Ngai Province, 25 Feb. 1970, p. 11, in NA, RG 319, AS, PI-AC, Box 27, Folder: RVN Trip Report Information – Folder # 3. • **18**. C.E. McManaway, Office of the Assistant Chief of Staff, CORDS, letter to Deputy Assistant Administrator for Viet Nam, Agency for International Development, 28 May 1968, Limited Official Use, p. 2, in NA, RG 319, AS, PI-OI, Box 5, Folder: MACV Reports (8). • **19**. See the MACV correspondence of February 1968, in NA, RG 319, AS, PI-OI, Box 5, Folders: MACV Reports (6) and MACV Reports (7); Situation Report from Ambassador Ellsworth Bunker, Pacification, Secret, 17 Apr. 1968, p. 3, in ibid., Box 65, Folder: Admin.-Secret (Open) # 2 and Robert Komer, Memorandum for General Westmoreland, Subject: Meeting with Sir Robert Thompson and Desmond Palmer, 16 Mar. 1968, p. 1, in ibid., Box 5, Folder: MACV Reports (6). • **20**. Statistical Highlights, January 1968, Enemy Order of Battle, I CTZ/DMZ Summary, Secret, p. 84, in NA, RG 127, USMC, HMC-HMD, BM-68, Box 5, Folder: FMF Repro Order of Battle Enemy and Department of the Navy, Headquarters USMC, Chief of Staff, Memorandum, Subject: Symposium Book, 1968 General Officers Symposium, p. 8, in RG 127, USMC, HMC-HDPT, TF, FRC Box 4, Folder: General Officer Symposia, 1965–1971, Extracts. See also Pike, *Strategy of Terror*, pp. 45–6 and Frey, *Geschichte des Vietnamkriegs*, p. 165. • **21**. William Westmoreland, letter to the Commanding Generals of the US Armed Forces in Vietnam, 11 Apr. 1968, Confidential, pp. 2, 4, in NA, RG 319, AS, PI-OI, Box 3, Folder: MACV Directives (4). See also William Westmoreland, letter to the Commanding Generals of the US Armed Forces in Vietnam, 1 Feb. 1968, Confidential, p. 2, in ibid.; William Westmoreland, letter to the US Senior Province Advisors, 9 Feb. 1968, Confidential NOFORN, pp. 1, 2, in ibid., Box 5, Folder: MACV Reports (6). Similar reports were issued by the high command of CORDS, the civil authority responsible for the 'pacification': ibid., Box 5, Folder: MACV Reports (8). See also Spector, *After Tet*, p. 282. • **22**. Neil Sheehan, 'Westmoreland Predicted Big Gains in Vietnam', *New York Times*, 21 Mar. 1968 and Ellsberg, *Secrets*, p. 200. • **23**. Combined Action Plan AB 143 – 1968, Annex L (Neutralization of VC/NVA Base Areas), Confidential, p. L-2, in NA, RG 319, AS, PI-AC, Box 17, Folder: (OCLL) Miscellaneous Documents from Peers. • **24**. Combined Action Plan AB 143 – 1968, Annex L (Neutralization of VC/NVA Base Areas), Confidential,

p. L1-1, in NA, RG 319, AS, PI-AC, Box 17, Folder: (OCLL) Miscellaneous Documents from Peers. See also CINCPAC, Measurement of Progress in Southeast Asia, 31 Mar. 1968, Secret NOFORN, in RG 319, AS, PI-OI, Box 65, Folder: Admin.-Secret (Open) # 1. • **25**. Bilton and Sim, *Four Hours*, p. 201. • **26**. NA, RG 319, PI-FR, Vol. I: Analyses, Box 1, Vol. I, Ch. 3: Background, p. 6. • **27**. NA, RG 319, PI-FR, Vol. I: Analyses, Box 1, Vol. I, Ch. 9: Policy and Directives as to Rules of Engagement and Treatment of Noncombatants, p. 7. • **28**. See above, pp. 96–9. For the MACV Directives valid in early 1968, see NA, RG 319, AS, PI-FR, Vol. III: Exhibits, Box 53, Book 2, Directives, pp. 587–792; ibid., Vol. I: Analyses, Box 1, Vol. I, Ch. 9: Policy and Directives as to Rules of Engagement and Treatment of Noncombatants, pp. 20–7; RG 319, AS, PI-AC, Box 8, Folder: Conduct of the War, MACV Directives, RoE – Chron. File # 3, especially pp. 475–82 and Department of the Army, IG, Subject: Report of Investigation Concerning Alleged Atrocities Committed by Members of Co C, 1/20th Infantry, Task Force Barker, Americal Division, in the Republic of Vietnam, 19 Sep. 1969, p. 14, in ibid., Box 12, Folder: IG Report – My Lai Task Force Copy. • **29**. NA, RG 319, PI-FR, Vol. I: Analyses, Box 1, Ch. 8: Significant Factors which Contributed to the Son My Tragedy, p. 5. • **30**. The 196th Light Infantry Brigade of the 23rd Infantry Division (Americal), 3rd Brigade, 1st Cavalry Regiment, 1st Cavalry Division and B Troop, 1st Squadron, 9th Cavalry Regiment, 1st Cavalry Division, were responsible for Operation Wheeler/Wallowa. • **31**. Operation Muscatine was carried out by a battalion of 11th Light Infantry Brigade and 198th Light Infantry Brigade, 23rd Infantry Division (Americal) and a battalion of 3rd Brigade, 4th Infantry Division. At the end of February 1968 3rd Brigade, 4th Infantry Division was transferred to II Corps Tactical Zone. Thereafter 11th Light Infantry Brigade, 23rd Infantry Division (Americal) was responsible for the operative direction of Operation Muscatine. • **32**. Americal Division comprised three originally independent brigades: 11th Light Infantry Brigade, 196th Light Infantry Brigade and 198th Light Infantry Brigade. From early January 1968 1st Squadron, 9th Cavalry Regiment, 1st Cavalry Division also belonged to Americal. From October 1967 operational control over 3rd Brigade, 1st Cavalry Regiment, 1st Cavalry Division was the responsibility of Americal. From 16 February to 12 March 1968 3rd Airborne Brigade (Separate) was also attached to Americal, without however being under its operational control. Americal was formed in May 1942. Its name derives from its first place of operation: 'American Troops in New Caledonia'. In December 1954 the Division was reactivated under the double name 23rd Infantry Division/Americal. See NA, RG 319, PI-FR, Vol. I: Analyses, Box 1, Ch. 4, Organization, Operations, and Training of US Units, p. 2, and Fact Sheet, Subject: TF Oregon, Americal Division and the 11th Light Infantry Brigade, 21 Mar. 1970, Confidential, in RG 319, AS, PI-AC, Box 5, Folder: Army Staff Monitor Summary and Backup

Material. • **33**. Michael Uhl, 1st Military Intelligence Team, 11th Light Infantry Brigade, Americal Division, quoted in James Higgins, 'Horror Takes the Stand', *The Nation*, 4 Jan. 1971, p. 7. See also NA, RG 319, AS, ODCS-PER, VWCWG, CaFi, Box 6, Folder: Rottman-Uhl Allegation and ibid., Box 11, Folder: Hale Allegation. • **34**. Richard H. Brummett to Secretary for Defense Melvin Laird, 27 Oct. 1970, in NA, RG 319, AS, ODCS-PER, VWCWG, CaFi, Box 9, Folder: Brummett Allegation, Case 61. A Troop, 1st Squadron, 1st Cavalry Regiment (Airmobile) was under the operative control of Americal Division. • **35**. NA, RG 319, AS, ODCS-PER, VWCWG, CaFi, Box 9, Folder: Brummett Allegation, Case 61. See also ibid., Box 10, Folder: Dell Allegation (Part 1 of 6), Case 70. • **36**. Henry H. Tufts, Colonel, MPC, to Richard H. Brummett, 11 Feb. 1972, in NA, RG 319, AS, ODCS-PER, VWCWG, CaFi, Box 9, Folder: Brummett Allegation (Correspondence), Case 61. • **37**. CID Report of Investigation, 31 Oct. 1973, pp. 1, 5–7, 12–15, 17, 19–25, 30–3, 41; Sworn Statement Richard W. Dell, Jr., 8 Feb. 1971; Jesse E. Day, Investigator's Statement, 27 Dec. 1972, in NA, RG 319, AS, ODCS-PER, VWCWG, CaFi, Box 10, Folder: Dell Allegation (Part 1 of 6), Case 70. See also Sworn Statement Milbon J. Batiste, Jr., 28 Feb. 1973, p. 2, in ibid., Box 11, Folder: Dell Allegation (Part 5 of 6), Case 70; Sworn Statement John Charles Sistrunk, 5 Apr. 1973, p. 2, and Louis Golden, Agent's Statement, 11 Jun. 1973, in ibid., Box 11, Folder: Dell Allegation (Part 6 of 6). • **38**. CID Report of Investigation, 31 Oct. 1973, p. 41; see ibid., p. 19, in NA, RG 319, AS, VWCWG, CaFi, Box 10, Folder: Dell Allegation (Part 1 of 6), Case 70. • **39**. CID Report of Investigation, 31 Oct. 1973, p. 41; CID Report of Investigation, 18 Dec. 1972, p. 1; Jesse E. Day, Investigator's Statement, 27 Dec. 1972, p. 1, in NA, RG 319, AS, VWCWG, CaFi, Box 10, Folder: Dell Allegation (Part 1 of 6), Case 70 and Sworn Statement Walter L. Young, 2 Mar. 1972, p. 2, in ibid., Box 11, Folder: Dell Allegation (Part 5 of 6), Case 70. • **40**. Press Statement by James D. Henry, 27 Feb. 1970, in NA, RG 319, AS, ODCS-PER, VWCWG, Box 5, Folder: Henry Allegation (Part 1 of 3) and Henry, The Men of 'B' Company. For Henry's sworn statement to the Criminal Investigation Division, see RG 319, AS, PI-AC, Box 52, Folder: War Crimes Allegations – 32: Henry Allegation (Vol. I). • **41**. CID Report of Investigation 72-CID056-29559, 16 Jan. 1974, in NA, RG 319, AS, ODCS-PER, VWCWG, Box 5, Folder: Henry Allegation (Part 1 of 3). • **42**. Sworn Statement James D. Henry, 28 Feb. 1970, p. 10, in NA, RG 319, AS, ODCS-PER, VWCWG, Box 5, Folder: Henry Allegation, CID Reports. The following account is based on this sworn statement. • **43**. Sworn Statement James D. Henry, 28 Feb. 1970, p. 2, in NA, RG 319, AS, ODCS-PER, VWCWG, Box 5, Folder: Henry Allegation, CID Reports. • **44**. Henry, 'The Men of "B" Company', p. 30. • **45**. Ibid., p. 29. • **46**. Ibid., p. 28. • **47**. Sworn Statement James D. Henry, 28 Feb. 1970, p. 2, in NA, RG 319, AS, ODCS-PER, VWCWG, Box 5, Folder: Henry Allegation, CID Reports. See ibid, p. 6. • **48**. Sworn Statement James

D. Henry, 28 Feb. 1970, p. 2, in NA, RG 319, AS, ODCS-PER, VWCWG, Box 5, Folder: Henry Allegation, CID Reports. • **49** According to the statements of two GIs who took part: Jonathan Peter Coulson, Agent's Statement, 31 Dec. 1973, p. 8, in NA, RG 319, AS, ODCS-PER, VWCWG, Box 5, Folder: Henry Allegation (Part 3 of 3). • **50.** Sworn Statement James D. Henry, 28 Feb. 1970, p. 7, in NA, RG 319, AS, ODCS-PER, VWCWG, Box 5, Folder: Henry Allegation, CID Reports. • **51.** RAND Memorandum RM 5487-ISA/ARPA, Jul. 1968: The Viet Cong Style of Politics, in NA, RG 472, USFSEA, MACV, IG, ID, ROI, Box 57, Folder: ROK Marines, 4th Series and RG 319, AS, PI-AC, Box 29, Folder: Sensitive Material – My Lai – Folder # 5. This study is based on hundreds of interviews with former Viet Cong who also gave their views on the conduct of South Korean troops. Even American GIs constantly reiterated this criticism: 'The South Koreans, when they were there, hell, they didn't even have to get a shot. I mean, they didn't even have to get one round coming out of the village. If they suspected there was Viet-namese [*sic*] there they would kill everyone in that village. Everyone. And I have seen the villages they went through.' COHRO, Sanders Interview, p. 135. • **52.** Department of the Army, Office of the Chief of Staff, Memorandum Thru: Secretary of the Army, For: Assistant Secretary of Defense (Administration), Subject: Atrocity Allegations, 2 Feb. 1970, Incl. 1, p. 4, in NA, RG 319, AS, PI-AC, Box 33, Folder: Son My Chron. File # 6 (2 of 2). See also Hammer, *One Morning*, p. 91ff. • **53.** Jesse Frank Frosch, 'Anatomy of a Massacre', pp. 137–9, 184–92, here p. 185. Jesse Frank Frosch was interrogation officer in the US advisory team for Quang Ngai Province. Even in the Pentagon it was assumed that the South Korean after-action report of December 1967 pointed to a second massacre in the space of a few months in the My Lai (4) area: Memorandum, Office Chief of Staff Army, to: General Westmoreland, General Palmer, Subject: Magazine Article 'Anatomy of a Massacre', 13 Jun. 1970, in NA, RG 319, AS, PI-AC, Box 35, Folder: Son My Chron. File # 11 (1 of 2). • **54.** NA, RG 472, USFSEA, MACV, IG, ID, ROI, Box 57, Folder: Victory Dragon/Vol. 1A of Vol. 1 (Correction/Follow-Up Action). • **55.** L.D. Puckett, Province Senior Advisor, Quang Nam, to: Deputy for CORDS/III MAF/Danang, Subject: 2nd ROK Marine Brigade, 18 Mar. 1968, p. 2, in NA, RG 472, USFSEA, MACV, IG, ID, ROI, Box 57, Folder: Victory Dragon/Vol. 1A of Vol. 1 (Correction/Follow-Up Action). • **56.** Clarence W. Hannon, I CTZ Field Evaluator, Evaluation Report: Pacification in Hieu Nhon and Hoa Vang Districts, Quang Nam Province, 25 Mar. 1968, Confidential, in NA, RG 472, USFSEA, MACV, IG, ID, ROI, Box 57, Folder: Victory Dragon/Vol. 1A of Vol. 1 (Correction/Follow-Up Action). See ibid., Memorandum, James F. Mack, POLAD/Da Nang, to: Nicholas G.W. Thorne, POL/Saigon, Subject: Overview of 2nd ROK Marine Brigade Activities Jan. 1968–Apr. 1969 in Quang Nam Province, Secret, NOFORN, 25 Apr. 1969. • **57.** Colonel Louis Gelling,

Headquarter, 196th Light Infantry Brigade, Memorandum, Subject: Standards of Conduct, 9 Nov. 1967, p. 1, in NA, RG 319, AS, PI-OI, Box 13, Folder: Americal Division, Miscellaneous (1). • **58**. Creighton W. Abrams to Robert E. Cushman, Jr., Commanding General, III Marine Amphibious Force, Confidential, 15 Nov. 1967, in NA, RG 319, AS, PI-AC, Box 38, Folder: Son My Chron. File # 19 (1 of 2). • **59**. Samuel W. Koster, Memorandum, Subject: Acts of Discourtesy Towards Vietnamese People, 30 Jan. 1968, p. 2, in NA, RG 319, AS, PI-OI, Box 13, Folder: Americal Division, Miscellaneous (1). • **60**. NA, RG 472, USFSEA, MACV, IG, ID, ROI, Box 57, Folder: Victory Dragon/Vol. 1A of Vol. 1 (Correction/Follow-Up Action). • **61**. William Westmoreland to Lieutenant General Myung Shin Chae, 29 Apr. 1968, Confidential, p. 1, in NA, RG 472, USFSEA, MACV, IG, ID, ROI, Box 57, Folder: Victory Dragon/Vol. 1A of Vol. 1 (Correction/Follow-Up Action). The US Supreme Command even had photographic evidence of the massacre of Phong Nhi and Phong Nhut (2): see ibid., Memorandum, James F. Mack, POLAD/Da Nang, to: Nicholas G.W. Thorne, POL/Saigon, Subject: Overview of 2nd ROK Marine Brigade Activities Jan. 1968–Apr. 1969 in Quang Nam Province, Secret, NOFORN, 25 Apr. 1969. • **62**. NA, RG 472, USFSEA, MACV, IG, ID, ROI, Box 57, Folder: Victory Dragon/Vol. 1A of Vol. 1 (Correction/Follow-Up Action). • **63**. South Korean units committed at least two further massacres up to April 1969: on 22 October 1968 1st Platoon, 6th Company, 2nd Battalion of 2nd ROK Marine Corps Brigade murdered twenty-two villagers in Hoang Chau, Quang Nam Province (I Corps Tactical Zone), leaving sixteen seriously injured, and destroyed almost one hundred houses: MACV, IG, Memorandum, Subject: Alleged Atrocity Committed by ROK Marines on 22 Oct. 1968, Secret, 11 Jan. 1970, in NA, RG 472, USFSEA, MACV, IG, ID, ROI, Box 57, Folder: ROK Marines/Series 3. On 15 April 1969 3rd Platoon, 7th Company, 2nd ROK Marine Corps Brigade operated jointly with an American elite unit in the vicinity of Phuoc My, Quang Nam Province (I Corps Tactical Zone). Although the commander of the US Delta Team tried to stop them, the Koreans took revenge in their own way for the death of a colleague in a booby-trap. They stormed the place, randomly blew up houses, killed four civilians and wounded twelve: MACV, IG, Memorandum, Subject: Alleged Atrocity Committed by ROK Marines on 15 Apr. 1969, Secret, 10 Jan. 1970, in ibid., Folder: Alleged Atrocity Committed by ROK Marines on 15 Apr. 1969/Series 2. • **64**. William Westmoreland, circular letter to the Senior Advisors in all deployment areas in Vietnam and to the Commanding General of III Marine Amphibious Force, I Corps Tactical Zone, 10 Mar. 1968, Confidential, p. 4, in NA, RG 319, AS, PI-OI, Box 5, Folder: MACV Reports (6). • **65**. William Westmoreland, circular letter to the Senior Advisors in all deployment areas in Vietnam and to the Commanding General of III Marine Amphibious Force, I Corps Tactical Zone, 10.3.1968, Confidential, pp. 1, 2 and William Westmoreland, circular letter to all Commanding Generals of the US Armed Forces in Vietnam, Subject: Regaining Pacification Initiative, 2 Mar. 1968, Confidential, in NA, RG 319, AS, PI-OI, Box 5, Folder: MACV Reports (6). See also MACV, Combat Operations Center, Memorandum for Record, Subject: COMUSMACV Visit to I CTZ, 3 Mar. 1968, p. 2, in RG 319, AS, PI-AC, Box 6, Folder: Conduct of the War in Vietnam, Chron. File # 2 (2 of 2). • **66**. NA, RG 319, AS, PI-FR, Vol. I, Analyses, Box 1, Chapter 4: Organization, Operations, and Training of US Units, pp. 6, 7. See also 23rd Infantry Division (Americal) History, prepared by the 3rd Military History Detachment, Jan. 1971, in RG 319, AS, ODCS-PER, VWCWG, CaFi, Box 20, Folder: Hoag Allegation (Part 2 of 4), Case 232.1; Hammer, *One Morning*, p. 90 and Bilton and Sim, *Four Hours*, pp. 52, 64–5. In addition to Task Force Barker, a 'Task Force Miracle' was also formed about which, however, virtually nothing is known. • **67**. Deputy Chief of Staff for Personnel, Memorandum, Subject: Administrative Review of Son My Cases, 21 Sep. 1971, p. 4, in NA, RG 319, AS, ODCS-PER, VWCWG, MLM, Box 4, Folder: Administrative Review – Maj. Charles C. Calhoun (Part 1 of 2) and Bilton and Sim, *Four Hours*, pp. 67, 191ff. • **68**. Fact Sheets, To: Chief of Staff, United States Army, Subject: Company C, 1st Battalion, 20th Infantry, 21 Dec. 1969 and 12 Jan. 1970, in NA, RG 319, ODCS-PER, VWCWG, MLM, Box 1, Folder: My Lai Army Staff Monitor Summaries, Jan. 1970 and RG 319, AS, PI-FR, Vol. 1: Analyses, Box 1, Ch. 4: Organization, Operations, and Training of US Units, p. 9. • **69**. NA, RG 319, AS, PI-FR, Vol. II: Testimony, Box 51, Book 31, Lipscomb: APP T-213, p. 376. See also Box 3, Book 1, Balmer: SUM APP T-26, p. 2. • **70**. Tim O'Brien, 'Step Lightly', p. 138. See id., *Lake of the Woods*, pp. 4ff., 23, 26ff., 99–102, 123–6, 156. • **71**. Ernest Medina, witness statement in the case against William Calley, quoted in Sack, *Leutnant Calley berichtet*, p. 56. • **72**. NA, RG 319, AS, PI-FR, Vol. I: Analyses, Box 1, Ch. 4: Organization, Operations, and Training of US Units, pp. 7, 8; Ch. 8: Significant Factors which Contributed to the Son My Tragedy, p.4, and Bilton and Sim, *Four Hours*, pp. 70–2, 86, 93. A South Vietnamese unit had suffered fifty-five dead and injured in an operation in this area in mid January 1968, fifty-three of them from booby traps: Jesse Frank Frosch, 'Anatomy of a Massacre', p. 185. • **73**. Quoted in Bilton and Sim, *Four Hours*, p. 93. See O'Brien, *Lake of the Woods*, p. 298. • **74**. Sworn Statement Michael A. Bernhardt, 20 Nov. 1969, in NA, RG 319, PI-FR, Vol. IV: CID-Statements, Box 57, p. 127 and Sworn Statement Dennis Conti, 30 Oct. 1969, in ibid. p. 159. • **75**. NA, RG 319, PI-FR, Vol. II: Testimony, Box 33, Book 21, Carter: SUM APP T-173, p. 1; Thomas R. Partsch, diary entry 29 Feb. 1969, in ibid., Vol. III: Exhibits, Box 54, Book 4: Miscellaneous Documents, p. 301; Sworn Statement John H. Smail, 14 Dec. 1969, p. 2, in ibid., Vol. IV: CID-Statements, Box 57, p. 424; RG 319, AS, ODCS-PER, VWCWG, CaFi, Box 14, Folder: Plantz Allegation, Case 105; ibid., Box 11, Folder: Fox Allegation, Case 75; 'Mylai Unit Accused of New Crimes',

Washington Post, 3 Feb. 1970; Bilton and Sim, *Four Hours*, pp. 71, 76–9 and Hammer, *One Morning*, p. 104ff. • **76**. Sworn Statement Lones R. Warren, 5 Dec. 1969, p. 2, in NA, RG 319, I-FR, Vol. IV: CID-Statements, Box 57, p. 486; ibid., Vol. I: Analyses, Box 1, Ch. 4: Organization, Operations, and Training of US Units, p. 7 and ibid., Vol. II: Testimony, Box 23, Book 15, Calhoun: SUM APP T-6, p. 6. • **77**. William Calley, quoted in O'Brien, *Lake of the Woods*, p. 103. • **78**. 11th Light Infantry Brigade, Americal Division, together with the GIs who later joined Task Force Barker, were trained in Duc Pho by veterans of 3rd Brigade, 4th Infantry Division – former members of Task Force Oregon: NA, RG 319, PI-FR, Vol. II: Testimony, Box 5, Book 3, Kelley: SUM APP T-38, p. 1. For Task Force Oregon, see above pp. 152–68. • **79**. See above, pp. 137–42. • **80**. Ernest Medina, quoted in Hammer, *One Morning*, p. 92. • **81**. Sworn Statement Thomas W. Pfeifer, 9 Feb. 1970, pp. 2, 3 and Sworn Statement Michel F. Pagano, 8 Oct. 1970, in NA, RG 319, AS, ODCS-PER, VWCWG, CaFi, Box 11, Folder: Fox Allegation, Case 75. See also Jesse Frank Frosch, 'Anatomy of a Massacre', p. 187 and RG 319, AS, PI-FR, Vol. I: Analyses, Box 1, Chapter 8: Significant Factors which Contributed to the Son My Tragedy, p. 7. • **82**. NA, RG 319, AS, PI-FR, Vol. I: Analyses, Box 1, Ch. 8: Significant Factors which Contributed to the Son My Tragedy, p. 11. See also ibid., Chapter 12: Findings and Recommendations, p. 1. • **83**. NA, RG 319, AS, PI-FR, Vol. I: Analyses, Box 1, Chapter 8: Significant Factors which Contributed to the Son My Tragedy, p. 13; ibid., Ch. 9: Policy and Directives as to Rules of Engagement and Treatment of Noncombatants, p. 19; ibid., Ch. 4: Organization, Operations, and Training of US Units, p. 10 and ibid., Vol. II: Testimony, Box 37, Book 23, Medina: SUM APP T-5, p. 2. • **84**. An unnamed GI, C Company, Task Force Barker, quoted in Hammer, *One Morning*, p. 99. • **85**. Bilton and Sim, *Four Hours*, p. 79. • **86**. NA, RG 319, AS, ODCS-PER, VWCWG, CaFi, Box 11, Folder: Fox Allegation, Case 75. • **87**. Bilton and Sim, *Four Hours*, p. 75ff.; Hammer, *One Morning*, p. 99. • **88**. NA, RG 319, AS, PI-FR, Vol. I: Analyses, Box 1, Ch. 8: Significant Factors which Contributed to the Son My Tragedy, p. 10. • **89**. Sworn Statement Gregory Thomas Olsen, 30 Aug. 1969, p. 8, in NA, RG 319, AS, PI-FR, Vol. IV: CID-Statements, Box 57, p. 370. • **90**. Sworn Statement Leon J. Stevenson, 3 Nov. 1969, p. 2, in NA, RG 319, AS, PI-FR, Vol. IV: CID-Statements, Box 57, p. 440; see Sworn Statement John H. Smail, 14 Dec. 1969, p. 7, in ibid, p. 429. Similar verdicts were reached in internal army assessments: Fact Sheet, To: Chief of Staff United States Army, Subject: C Company, 1st Battalion, 20th Infantry, 21 Dec. 1969, p. 1, in RG 319, AS, PI-AC, Box 4, Folder: Army Staff Monitor Summary, Nov.–Dec. 1969. • **91**. NA, RG 319, PI-FR, Vol. II: Testimony, Box 37, Book 23, Alaux: SUM APP T-68, p. 7 and Bilton and Sim, *Four Hours*, p. 56. • **92**. Thomas Partsch, C Company, Task Force Barker, quoted in Conduct of the Men of Charlie Company, 1/20, during the Assault on My Lai 4 on 16 March 1968, p. 25, in NA, RG 319, AS,

ODCS-PER, VWCWG, MLM, Box 5, Folder: Administrative Review – SSG Kenneth L. Hodges (Part 3 of 4). • **93**. Frederick Widmer, C Company, Task Force Barker, quoted in Bilton and Sim, *Four Hours*, p. 77. • **94**. Sworn Statement Harry Stanley, 14 Oct. 1969, p. 6, in NA, RG 319, PI-FR, Vol. IV: CID-Statements, Box 57, p. 436. See also Talking Paper, Subject: Son My Cases, 6 Mar. 1971, p. 1, in RG 319, AS, ODCS-PER, VWCWG, MLM, Box 1, Folder: TJAG My Lai Talking Paper, Jan. 1970–Jun. 1971; Hammer, *One Morning*, p. 101 and Bilton and Sim, *Four Hours*, p. 79. • **95**. Gregory Olsen, C Company, Task Force Barker, quoted in Bilton and Sim, *Four Hours*, p. 79. • **96**. William Calley, quoted in Sack, *Own Story*, pp. 31, 45–6, 51, 57, 77–84, 99. • **97**. Since the term 'leadership breakdown' was used by the Peers Commission in its investigation report, this misleading concept has become established in the historiography of Task Force Barker. See Anderson (ed.), *Facing My Lai*, p. 130 and Bilton and Sim, *Four Hours*, p. 98. • **98**. See above, pp. 88–95. • **99**. CORDS, Evaluation Report: Pacification in Binh Son, Son Tinh, Tu Nghya and Nghia Hanh Districts, Quang Ngai Province, Confidential, 29 Apr. 1968, pp. 8–12, in NA, RG 319, AS, PI-OI, Box 6, Folder: MACV Reports (11). • **100**. CORDS, Evaluation Report: Pacification in Binh Son, Son Tinh, Tu Nghya and Nghia Hanh Districts, Quang Ngai Province, Confidential, 29 Apr. 1968, p. 1, in NA, RG 319, AS, PI-OI, Box 6, Folder: MACV Reports (11) and Office of the Province Senior Advisor, Quang Ngai Province, I CTZ, Memorandum, Subject: Province Monthly Report, 31 Mar. 1968, pp. 1–3, in RG 319, AS, PI-OI, Box 55, Folder: Exhibits: Reports (2). • **101**. Also called Thuan Yen by the inhabitants: 'The place where no trouble comes': Hammer, *One Morning*, pp. 4, 144. • **102**. Vietnamese place names were used in hardly any historiographical accounts. The village Dong De was known to the US troops only as My Lai (2) and Con Thieu as My Lai (3). My Lai (5) comprised the villages Phung Hoa and Binh Dong, and My Lai (6) stands for Thoung An. The correct name for My Khe (2) is My Xuan, for Co Lay (1) it is Xuan Duong, Co Lay (2) stands for Xuan Tung and Co Lay (3) for Xuan Cua. For the nomenclature see Hammer, *One Morning*, pp. 4ff., 26ff., 32ff. • **103**. Jesse Frank Frosch, 'Anatomy of a Massacre', p. 186. • **104**. NA, RG 319, PI-FR, Vol. I: Analyses, Box 1, Chapter 3: Background, p. 8. • **105**. Jesse Frank Frosch, 'Anatomy of a Massacre', p. 186. • **106**. Department of the Army, IG, Subject: Report of Investigation Concerning Alleged Atrocities Committed by Members of Co C, 1/20th Infantry, Task Force Barker, Americal Division, in the Republic of Vietnam, 19 Sep. 1969, p. 6, in NA, RG 319, AS, PI-AC, Box 12, Folder: IG Report – My Lai Task Force Copy; RG 319, AS, PI-FR, Vol. III: Exhibits, Box 55, Book 5: Miscellaneous Documents, Overlays, Sketches, Statements and Administrative, p. 541. For the estimates of the losses of 48th Local Force Battalion, see ibid., pp. 537–41; ibid., Box 54, Book 3: Reports, p. 254; Office of the Province Senior Advisor, Quang Ngai Province, I CTZ, Memorandum, Subject: Province Monthly Report, Confidential, 3 Mar. 1968, p. 4, in RG 319, AS, PI-OI, Box 9, Folder: I CTZ Reports and Statistical Highlights, Jan. 1968: Enemy Order of Battle, p. 103, in RG 127, USMC, HMC-HMD, BM-68, Box 5, Folder: FMF Repro Order of Battle Enemy and Folder: Enemy 13 Jan. 68. • **107.** Headquarters III Marine Amphibious Force, Memorandum, Subject: Project TAKEOFF Summary, Confidential, 22 Feb. 1968, p. 1, in NA, RG 319, AS, PI-OI, Box 4, Folder: MACV Reports (5). • **108.** Letter from the Commanding General of III MAF to William Westmoreland, dated 14 Jul. 1968, Confidential, p. 2, in NA, RG 319, AS, PI-OI, Box 4, Folder: MACV Reports (2). • **109.** Project TAKEOFF, CORDS – III Corps Tactical Zone, For Semi-Annual Period Ending 30 Jun. 1968, Appendix A, p. 3, in: NA, RG 319, AS, PI-OI, Box 4, Folder: MACV Reports (2). According to an internal estimate almost 800 civilian members of the Viet Cong had been 'eliminated' up to mid May 1968. More than half of them were probably executed immediately after capture: Bilton and Sim, *Four Hours*, p. 201. • **110.** See also Robert W. Komer, Deputy CORDS, to Lieutenant General Robert E. Cushman, Senior Advisor, I Corps Tactical Zone, 7 Apr. 1968, in NA, RG 319, AS, PI-OI, Box 3, Folder: MACV Directives (3). • **111.** Bilton and Sim, *Four Hours*, p. 200. See also CORDS, Evaluation Report: Pacification in Binh Son, Son Tinh, Tu Nghya and Nghia Hanh Districts, Quang Ngai Province, Confidential, 29 Apr. 1968, p. 1, in NA, RG 319, AS, PI-OI, Box 6, Folder: MACV Reports (11). In a letter to William Westmoreland dated 12 May 1968 Robert W. Komer, referring to the 'pacification', described Quang Ngai Province as 'our only priority province in the I CTZ', in RG 319, AS, PI-OI, Box 5, Folder: MACV Report (8). • **112.** Bilton and Sim, *Four Hours*, p. 90f. • **113.** Jesse Frank Frosch, 'Anatomy of a Massacre', p. 190. • **114.** Confidential Feature: Americal Against the Infra-structure, p. 23, in NA, RG 319, AS, PI-OI, Box 5, Folder: MACV Report (8) and CORDS, Evaluation Report: Pacification in Binh Son, Son Tinh, Tu Nghya and Nghia Hanh Districts, Quang Ngai Province, Confidential, 29 Apr. 1968, p. 12, in ibid., Box 6, Folder: MACV Reports (11). • **115.** See Deputy Chief of Staff for Personnel, Memorandum, Subject: Administrative Review of Son My Cases, 21 Sep. 1971, p. 4, in NA, RG 319, AS, ODCS-PER, VWCWG, MLM, Box 4, Folder: Administrative Review – Maj. Charles C. Calhoun (Part 1 of 2); Memorandum for the Record: Phonecon between LTC Stevens, OCINFO, and LTC Tucker, IO, Fort Benning, 23 Mar. 1970, in RG 319, AS, ODCS-PER, VWCWG, MLM, Box 1, Folder: My Lai Army Staff Monitor Summaries, Feb.–May 1970; Jack Taylor, 'Did CIA Plan '68 Massacre?', *Sunday Oklahoman*, 25 Mar. 1973; Bilton and Sim, *Four Hours*, pp. 88–92, and Valentine, *Phoenix Program*, p. 343ff. In the CID interrogations about My Lai (4) the subject of Phoenix was only mentioned once – with an equally unsatisfactory result: Sworn Statement Lones R. Warren, 5 Dec. 1969, p. 2, in RG 319, AS, PI-FR, Vol. IV: CID-Statements, Box 57, p. 486. • **116.** Lieutenant Colonel

Schopper, Talking Paper, 30 Oct. 1970, in NA, RG 319, AS, PI-AC, Box 36, Folder: Son My Chron. File # 4 (2 of 2). • **117**. NA, RG 319, AS, PI-FR, Vol. III: Exhibits, Box 55, Book 5: Miscellaneous Documents, Overlays, Sketches, Statements and Administrative, pp. 539–41; ibid., Vol. I: Analyses, Box 1, Chapter 2: Summary Report, p. 1 and Bilton and Sim, *Four Hours*, p. 90. • **118**. Evidence of the Senior Advisor for Son Tinh District, Lieutenant Colonel David C. Gavin, before the Peers Commission: NA, RG 319, AS, PI-FR, Vol. II: Testimony, Box 51, Book 31: Gavin: APP T-9, p. 78. Gavin referred here to the South Vietnamese Secret Services. As both the US Army and the CIA in Quang Ngai drew a large part of their information from South Vietnamese sources, his statement can also be applied to the American side. The Deputy Senior Advisor for Quang Ngai Province, Lieutenant Colonel William D. Guinn, spoke in similar terms: ibid. Guinn: APP T-24, p. 24. • **119**. Unattributed memorandum to Ambassador Ellsworth Bunker, Pacification, Secret, 17 Apr. 1968, p. 3, in NA, RG 319, AS, PI-OI, Box 65, Folder: Admin.-Secret (Open) # 2. The acting head of CORDS, Robert W. Komer, also made this argument in a letter dated 7 Apr. 1968 to Robert E. Cushman, Senior Advisor of I CTZ: RG 319, AS, PI-OI, Box 3, Folder: MACV Directives (3). • **120**. NA, RG 319, AS, PI-FR, Vol. I: Analyses, Box 1, Chapter 2: Summary Report, p. 1; ibid., Ch. 5: The Son My Operation, 16–19 Mar. 1968, p. 3; ibid., Ch. 8: Significant Factors which Contributed to the Son My Tragedy, p. 4; ibid,, Vol. II: Testimony, Box 4, Book 2, Gamble: SUM APP T-22, pp. 1–2; ibid., Vol. IV: CID-Statements, Box 57, pp. 476–7; Sworn Statement Charles C. Calhoun, 15 Jan. 1970, in RG 319, AS, ODCS-PER, VWCWG, MLM, Box 4, Folder: Administrative Review – Maj. Charles C. Calhoun (Part 1 of 2) and Bilton and Sim, *Four Hours*, pp. 87, 94. • **121**. Headquarters, 11th Infantry Brigade, 30 Jan. 1968, 11th Bde Regulation Number 525-1, § 6 (C), Paragraph c, in NA, RG 319, AS, PI-AC, Box 8, Folder: Conduct of the War, MACV Directives, RoE – Chron. File # 3. • **122**. Department of the Army, Office of the Deputy Chief of Staff for Military Operations, Memorandum for: Chief of Staff, United States Army, Confidential, 16 Dec. 1970, p. 1, in NA, RG 319, AS, PI-AC, Box 8, Folder: Conduct of the War, MACV Directives, RoE – Chron. File # 3. • **123**. Commanding General, III Marine Amphibious Force, Memorandum, Subject: Minimizing Noncombatant Battle Casualties, 13 Dec. 1966, p. 3 and III Marine Amphibious Force, Force Order PO 3121.5: Standing Operating Procedure for Ground and Air Operations (SOP), 10 Nov. 1967, Section IV, § 405, paragraph 2: Specified Strike Zone, in NA, RG 319, AS, PI-AC, Box 8, Folder: Conduct of the War, MACV Directives, RoE – Chron. File # 3. Colonel Oran Henderson's predecessor as Commander of 11th Light Infantry Brigade, Brigadier General Andy A. Lipscomb, confirmed the operational autonomy of Task Force Barker in his statement before the Peers Commission: RG 319, AS, PI-FR, Vol. II: Testimony, Box 51, Book 31, Lipscomb: APP T-213, p. 22;

see ibid., Box 4, Book 2, Granger: SUM APP T-367, p. 2. • **124**. NA, RG 319, AS, PI-FR, Vol. I: Analyses, Box 1, Ch. 5: The Son My Operation, 16–19 Mar. 1968, p. 5; ibid., Ch. 12: Findings and Recommendations, pp. 24, 28; ibid., Vol. II: Testimony, Box 25, Book 16, Stephens SUM APP T-74, p. 1 and Warren SUM APP T-192, p. 1. • **125**. Son My Village was also classified by the South Vietnamese as a Free Fire Zone and its inhabitants considered without exception to be enemy civilians: NA, RG 319, AS, PI-FR, Vol. I: Analyses, Box 1, Ch. 9, Policy and Directives as to Rules of Engagement and Treatment of Noncombatants, p. 26; ibid., Vol. II, Testimony, Box 51, Book 31, Ford APP T-204, pp. 18–19, Gavin APP T-9, pp. 21, 75–8 and Guinn APP T-24, p. 24. • **126**. Department of the Army, Office of the General Counsel, 3 Mar. 1972, Memorandum of Law (Maj. Calhoun), p. 3, in NA, RG 319, AS, ODCS-PER, VWCWG, MLM, Box 4, Folder: Administrative Review – Maj. Charles C. Calhoun (Part 1 of 2); RG 319, AS, PI-FR, Vol. I: Analyses, Ch. 10; Reports, Investigations, and Reviews, p. 20; ibid., Vol. II: Testimony, Box 51, Book 31, Calhoun SUM APP T-6A, p. 4. • **127**. Sworn Statement Charles C. Calhoun, 15 Jan. 1970, p. 5, in NA, RG 319, AS, ODCS-PER, VWCWG, MLM, Box 4, Folder: Administrative Review – Maj. Charles C. Calhoun (Part 1 of 2). An internal investigation confirmed this statement: MACV, IG, Memorandum, Subject: Report of Inquiry on Psychological Operations, Americal Division, 27 Jun. 1969, pp 2, 8, 9, in NA, RG 319, AS, PI-OI, Box 1, Folder: Psyops. See also RG 319, AS, PI-FR, Vol. I: Analyses, Ch. 5: The Son My Operation, 16–19 Mar. 1968, p. 5; ibid., Vol. II: Testimony, Keshel SUM APP T-177, pp. 1–5. • **128**. NA, RG 319, AS, PI-FR, Vol. I: Analyses, Ch. 5: The Son My Operation, 16–19 Mar. 1968, p. 2. • **129**. Sworn Statement Charles C. Calhoun, 15 Jan. 1970, p. 3, in NA, RG 319, AS, ODCS-PER, VWCWG, MLM, Box 4, Folder: Administrative Review – Maj. Charles C. Calhoun (Part 1 of 2). • **130**. NA, RG 319, AS, PI-FR, Vol. I: Analyses, Ch. 2: Summary Report, p. 1 and Department of the Army, Office of the General Counsel, 20 Jun. 1972, Memorandum of Law (Former CPT Medina), p. 2, in RG 319, AS, ODCS-PER, VWCWG, MLM, Box 4, Folder: Administrative Review – CPT Ernest L. Medina. • **131**. Lieutenant Colonel Robert B. Luper, Commander, 6th Battalion, 11th Artillery Regiment, Americal Division, quoted in NA, RG 319, AS, PI-FR, Vol. II: Testimony, Box 5, Book 3, Luper APP T-13, p. 46A. • **132**. Bilton and Sim, *Four Hours*, p. 94. • **133**. Department of the Army, IG, Subject: Report of Investigation Concerning Alleged Atrocities Committed by Members of Co C, 1/20th Infantry, Task Force Barker, Americal Division in the Republic of Vietnam, 19 Sep. 1969, p. 11, in NA RG 319, AS, PI-AC, Box 12, Folder: IG Report – My Lai Task Force Copy and RG 319, AS, PI-FR, Vol. II: Testimony, Box 23, Book 15, Beardslee SUM APP T292, p. 2. • **134**. NA, RG 319, AS, PI-FR, Vol. I: Analyses, Box 1, Ch. 5: The Son My Operation, 16–19 Mar. 1968, p. 4. • **135**. NA, RG 319, AS, PI-FR, Vol. I: Analyses, Box 1, Ch. 2:

Summary Report, p. 2 and ibid., Vol. II: Testimony, Box 25, Book 16, Kotouc SUM APP T-8, p.2. • **136**. Fact Sheet, to: Chief of Staff, United States Army, Subject: My Lai, 17 Dec. 1969, p. 2, in NA, RG 319, AS, PI-CI, Box 8, Folder: Admin. Fil. – Dec (1). • **137**. NA, RG 319, AS, PI-FR, Vol. I: Analyses, Box 1, Ch. 2: Summary Report, p. 2 and Ch. 5: The Son My Operation, 16–19 Mar. 1968, p. 8. • **138**. NA, RG 319, AS, PI-FR, Vol. I: Analyses, Box 1, Ch. 5: The Son My Operation, 16–19 Mar. 1968, p. 5. • **139**. This is how Captain Ernest Medina recalls a statement by Oran Henderson: NA, RG 319, AS, PI-FR, Vol. I: Analyses, Box 1, Ch. 5: The Son My Operation, 16–19 Mar. 1968, p. 4. • **140**. NA, RG 319, AS, PI-FR, Vol. I: Analyses, Box 1, Ch. 5: The Son My Operation, 16–19 Mar. 1968, p. 9 and Ch. 12: Findings and Recommendations, p. 20. • **141**. Fact Sheet, to: Chief of Staff, United States Army, Subject: Company C, 1st Battalion, 20th Infantry, 21 Dec. 1969, p. 1, in NA, RG 319, AS, PI-AC, Box 4, Folder: Army Staff Monitor Summary, Nov.–Dec. 69. • **142**. An unnamed GI from C Company, Task Force Barker, quoted in Hammer, *One Morning*, p. 99. • **143**. Sworn Statement, John H. Smail, C Company, Task Force Barker, 14 Dec. 1969, p. 1 in: NA, RG 319, AS, PI-FR, Vol. IV: CID Statements, Box 57, p. 423. • **144**. Abel Flores, C Company, Task Force Barker, quoted in NA, RG 319, PI-FR, Vol. II: Testimony, Box 51, Book 31, Flores APP T-60, p. 29; see ibid., Box 25, Book 16, Kotouc SUM APP T-8, p. 3; ibid, Box 37, Book 23, Alaux SUM APP T-68, p. 3; ibid, Box 40, Book 25, Bernhardt SUM APP T-46, p. 2; Vol. I: Analyses, Ch. 5: The Son My Operation, 16–19 Mar. 1968, p. 13; ibid., Ch. 8: Significant Factors which Contributed to the Son My Tragedy, p. 15; Vol. IV: CID Statements, Box 57, pp. 267, 364 and Testimony Michael B. Terry, 1 May 1969, p. 3, in RG 319, AS, PI-AC, Box 45, Folder: Son My – Biographical Data (Individuals Charged) (7 of 10). • **145**. Ernest Medina, quoted in Bilton and Sim, *Four Hours*, p. 98. • **146**. Frederick Widmer, C Company, Task Force Barker, quoted in Bilton and Sim, *Four Hours*, p. 101. See also NA, RG 319, AS, PI-FR, Vol I: Analyses, Box 1, Ch. 8: Significant Factors which Contributed to the Son My Tragedy, p. 14. • **147**. Sworn Statement Lones R. Warren, 5 Dec. 1969, p. 2, in NA, RG 319, AS, PI-FR, Vol. IV: CID Statements, Box 57, p. 486. • **148**. Diary entry of Private First Class Thomas Partsch, C Company, Task Force Barker, 15 Mar. 1968, in NA, RG 319, AS, PI-OI, Box 53, Folder: Exhibits: Miscellaneous (6). See also RG 319, PI-FR, Vol. I: Analyses, Ch. 5: The Son My Operation, 16–19 Mar. 1968, p. 12; Vol. II: Testimony, Box 37, Book 23, Alaux SUM APP T-68, pp. 2, 3; ibid., Medina SUM APP T-5, p. 3; ibid., Vol. IV: CID Statements, Box 57, p. 487; Sworn Statement Harry Stanley, 14 Oct. 1969, p. 1, in RG 319, AS, PI-AC, Box 45, Folder: Son My – Biographical Data (Individuals Charged) (5 of 10) and My Lai Incident, Weekly Update, 22–29 Dec. 1969, in RG, 319, AS, ODCS-PER, VWCWG, MLM, Box 1, Folder: My Lai Army Staff Monitor Summaries, Jan. 1970. • **149**. NA, RG 319, AS, PI-FR, Vol. II: Testimony, Box 41, Book 26,

Garza SUM APP T-70, p. 3; ibid., Box 43, Book 27, Smail SUM APP T-71, p. 2; ibid., Box 45, Book 28, Jolly SUM APP T-57, p. 2; ibid., Vol. IV: CID Statements, Box 57, pp. 121, 131, 145, 163, 209–10, 229, 327, 416, 431. See also Sack, *Leutnant Calley berichtet*, p. 77. • **150**. Sworn Statement John H. Smail, C Company, Task Force Barker, 14 Dec. 1969, p. 2, in NA, RG 319, AS, PI-FR, Vol. IV: CID Statements, Box 57, p. 424. Countless other GIs from C Company spoke in similar terms: ibid., Vol. II, Box 30, Book 19, Lias SUM APP T-144, p. 2; ibid., Box 37, Book 23, Murray SUM APP T-43, p. 2; ibid., Box 38, Book 24, Doines SUM APP T-72, p. 1; ibid., Box 40, Book 25, Kye SUM APP T-76, p. 1 and Lee SUM APP T-59, p.1; ibid., Box 41, Book 26, Garza SUM APP T-70, p. 2 and LaCroix SUM APP T-207, p. 2; ibid., Box 43, Book 27, Flores SUM APP T-60, p. 1 and Trevino SUM APP T-185, p. 2; ibid., Box 45, Book 28, Arcoren SUM APP T-69, p. 2; Fagan SUM APP T-67, p. 2 and Jolly SUM APP T-57, p. 2. • **151**. Testimony Michael B. Terry, 1 May 1969, p. 3, in NA, RG 319, AS, PI-AC, Box 45, Folder: Son My – Biographical Data (Individuals Charged) (7 of 10). • **152**. NA, RG 319, AS, PI-FR, Vol. II: Testimony, Box 45, Book 28, West SUM APP T-246, p. 2, and Bilton and Sim, *Four Hours*, p. 98. • **153**. NA, RG 319, AS, PI-FR, Vol. I: Analyses, Box 1, Ch. 8: Significant Factors which Contributed to the Son My Tragedy, p. 14, and ibid, Vol. IV: CID Statements, Box 57, pp. 431–2. • **154**. Ernest Medina, quoted in Bilton and Sim, *Four Hours*, p. 98 and NA, RG 319, AS, PI-FR, Vol. I: Analyses, Ch. 5: The Son My Operation, 16–19 Mar. 1968, p.13. • **155**. NA, RG 319, AS, PI-FR, Vol. I: Analyses, Box 1, Ch. 8: Significant Factors which Contributed to the Son My Tragedy, p. 14. • **156**. Lelyveld, 'Story of a Soldier', p. 110 and Bilton and Sim, *Four Hours*, p. 100. • **157**. See NA, RG 319, AS, PI-FR, Vol. IV: CID Statements, Box 57, pp. 139, 145, 280, 287, 335, 339, 345, 385, 393, 399, 409; Sworn Statement Harry Stanley, 14 Oct. 1969, p. 2, in RG 319, AS, PI-AC, Box 45, Folder: Son My – Biographical Data (Individuals Charged) (5 of 10); Sworn Statement Charles A. West, 6 Dec. 1969, pp. 1, 2, in ibid, Box 46, Folder: Son My – Biographical Data (Individuals Charged) (10 of 10) and Bilton and Sim, *Four Hours*, p. 99. • **158**. Sworn Statement Michael A. Bernhardt, 20 Nov. 1969, p. 1, in NA, RG 319, AS, PI-FR, Vol. IV: CID Statements, Box 57, p. 127. See ibid., pp. 117, 319, 327, 391, 416, 423, 431, 450. See also Vol. II: Testimony, Box 43, Book 27, SUM APP T-60, p. 1; ibid., Box 45, Book 28, West SUM APP T-246, p. 2; Testimony Michael B. Terry, 1 May 1969, p. 3, in NA, RG 319, AS, PI-AC, Box 45, Folder: Son My – Biographical Data (Individuals Charged) (7 of 10) and Talking Paper, Subject: My Lai 16 Jan. 1970, p. 2, in RG 319, AS, ODCS-PER, VWCWG, MLM, Box 1, Folder: CID My Lai Talking Papers and Fact Sheets Jan.–Jun. 1970. • **159**. Sworn Statement James J. Dursi, 29 Aug. 1969, p. 1, in NA, RG 319, AS, PI-FR, Vol. IV: CID Statements, Box 57, p. 181; see ibid., pp. 323, 385 and Vol. I: Analyses, Box 1, Ch. 5: The Son My Operation, 16–19 Mar. 1968, p. 13. • **160**. Talking Paper, Subject: Son My Cases, 6 Mar. 1971, p. 3, in NA, RG 319,

AS, ODCS-PER, MLM, Box 1, Folder: TJAG My Lai Talking Paper, Jan. 1970–Jun. 1971. • **161**. Michael A. Bernhardt, private first class from C Company, Task Force Barker, quoted in Bilton and Sim, *Four Hours*, p. 101. • **162**. NA, RG 319, AS, PI-FR, Vol. II: Testimony, Box 40, Book 25, Olsen SUM APP T-47, p. 2; ibid., Vol. IV: CID Statements, Box 57, p. 311 and Vol. I: Analyses, Box 1, Ch. 5: The Son My Operation, 16–19 Mar. 1968, p. 13. • **163**. Michael A. Bernhardt, private first class from C Company, Task Force Barker, quoted in Lelyveld, 'Story of a Soldier', p. 111. • **164**. Sworn Statement Thomas J. Kinch, C Company, Task Force Barker, 28 Nov. 1969, p. 2, in NA, RG 319, AS, PI-FR, Vol. IV: CID Statements, Box 57, p. 280. See ibid., p. 364; Sworn Statement James R. Bergthold, 3 Nov. 1969, p. 1, in RG 319, AS, PI-AC, Box 45, Folder: Son My – Biographical Data (Individuals Charged) (5 of 10); Testimony Michael B. Terry, 1 May 1969, p. 6, in NA, RG 319, AS, PI-AC, Box 45, Folder: Son My – Biographical Data (Individuals Charged) (7 of 10); Testimony Frederick J. Widmer, 15 Jul. 1969, in RG 319, AS, PI-AC, Box 46, Folder: Son My Suspects (3 of 3) and Conduct of the Men of Charlie Company, 1/20, during the Assault on My Lai 4 on 16 Mar. 1968, p. 31, in RG 319, AS, ODCS-PER, VWCWG, MLM, Box 5, Folder: Administrative Review SSG Kenneth L. Hodges (Part 3 of 4). • **165**. NA, RG 319, AS, PI-FR, Vol. I: Analyses, Box 1, Ch. 5: The Son My Operation, 16–19 Mar. 1968, pp. 9–10; ibid., Ch. 2: Summary Report, p. 2; ibid., Vol. II: Testimony, Box 27, Book 17, Boatman SUM APP T-184, p. 2; ibid., Box 28, Book 18, Congleton, SUM APP T-229, p. 1; ibid., Box 30, Book 19, Hall SUM APP T-240, p. 2; Fact Sheet, To: Chief of Staff, US Army, Subject: Son My, 18 Feb. 1970, pp. 3–4, in RG 319, AS, ODCS-PER, VWCWG, MLM, Box 1, Folder: My Lai Army Staff Monitor Summaries, Feb.–May 1970. • **166**. Fact Sheet, Subject: Son My, 4 Jun. 1970, p. 3, in NA, RG 319, AS, ODCS-PER, VWCWG, MLM, Box 1, Folder: CID My Lai Talking Papers and Fact Sheets, Jan.–Jun. 1970. See also RG 319, AS, PI-FR, Vol. II: Testimony, Box 28, Book 18, Dahner SUM APP T-152, p. 5, and ibid., Vol. I: Analyses, Box 1, Ch. 4: Organization, Operations, and Training of US Units, p. 10. • **167**. NA, RG 319, AS, PI-FR, Vol. I, Analyses, Box 1, Ch. 5: The Son My Operation, 16–19 Mar. 1968, p. 10; ibid., Ch. 8: Significant Factors which Contributed to the Son My Tragedy, pp. 13–14; ibid., Vol. II: Testimony, Box 28, Book 18, Congleton SUM APP T-229, p. 1; ibid., Box 30, Book 19, Hooton SUM APP T-376, p. 1; ibid., Box 35, Book 22, McCloud SUM APP T-353, pp. 1–2 and Fact Sheet, To: Chief of Staff, US Army, Subject: Son My, 18 Feb. 1970, p. 4, in RG 319, AS, ODCS-PER, VWCWG, MLM, Box 1, Folder: My Lai Army Staff Monitor Summaries, Feb.–May 1970. • **168**. Sworn Testimony Larry G. Holmes, 23 Jan. 1970, in NA, RG 319, AS, PI-FR, Vol. II: Testimony, Box 30, Book 19, Holmes SUM APP T-223, p. 2; see also ibid., Vol. I, Analyses, Box 1, Ch. 5: The Son My Operation, 16–19 Mar. 1968, p. 11. • **169**. Unsworn Statement Nguyen Dinh Phu, interpreter with C Company,

Task Force Barker, in NA, RG 319, AS, PI-FR, Vol. II: Testimony, Box 52, Book 32, Phu APP T-96, pp. 5–6. See also Bilton and Sim, *Four Hours*, p. 101. • **170**. Michael A. Bernhardt, private first class from C Company, Task Force Barker, quoted in Lelyveld, 'Story of a Soldier', p. 111. • **171**. NA, RG 319, AS, PI-FR, Vol. I: Analyses, Box 1, Ch. 5: The Son My Operation, 16–19 Mar. 1968, p. 16. • **172**. Headquarters 3rd Brigade, 1st Air Cavalry Division, Subject: Combat Operations After Action Report, Operation Masher, Operation Whitewing (Eagles Claw), 10 Mar. 1966, p. 11, in NA, RG 319, AS, ODCS-PER, VWCWG, CF, Box 4, Folder: Applegate Allegation, Case 22. Sheehan reports on the destruction in the wake of this operation in *Die Große Lüge*, p. 583. For the basic purpose of preparatory fire, see RG 319, AS, PI-FR, Vol. II: Testimony, Box 13, Book 8, Watke SUM APP T-10, p. 1. • **173**. Sworn Testimony, Lones R. Warren, C Company, Task Force Barker, 5 Dec. 1969, p. 3, in NA, RG 319, AS, PI-FR, Vol. IV: CID Statements, Box 57, p. 487; see ibid., p. 312. • **174**. NA, RG 319, AS, PI-FR, Vol. I, Analyses, Ch. 5: The Son My Operation, 16–19 Mar. 1968, p. 16 and Bilton and Sim, *Four Hours*, p. 105ff. • **175**. NA, RG 319, AS, PI-FR, Vol. II: Testimony, Box 13, Book 8, Boswell SUM APP T-66, p. 4. • **176**. William Calley, quoted in Sack, 'Own Story', p. 99. • **177**. NA, RG 319, AS, PI-FR, Vol. I: Analyses, Box 1, Ch. 5: The Son My Operation, 16–19 Mar. 1968, p. 16. • **178**. NA, RG 319, AS, PI-FR, Vol. I: Analyses, Box 1, Ch. 2: Summary Report, p. 3; ibid., Ch. 6: C Company, 1st Battalion, 20th Infantry: Actions on 16 and 17 Mar. 1968, pp. 19–21; Witness Statement Pham Lai, 5 Jan. 1970, in ibid., Vol. II: Testimony, Box 54, Book 32, Lai SUM APP T-114, p. 1; Conduct of the Men of Charlie Company, 1/20, during the Assault on My Lai (4) on 16 Mar. 1968, p. 2, in RG 319, AS, ODCS-PER, VWCWG, MLM, Box 5, Folder: Administrative Review – SSG Kenneth L. Hodges (Part 3 of 4) and Hammer, *One Morning*, p. 144. The figure given at one point of the Peers Report of 175–200 victims in My Lai (4) is based exclusively on statements from soldiers in C Company and is explicitly judged by the report's authors as being far too low: RG 319, AS, PI-FR, Vol. I: Analyses, Box 1, Ch. 6: Company C, 1st Battalion, 20th Infantry: Actions on 16 and 17 Mar. 1968, pp. 18–19. • **179**. NA, RG 319, AS, PI-FR, Vol. I: Analyses, Box 1, Ch. 7: Company B, 4th Battalion, 3rd Infantry: Actions on 16–19 Mar. 1968, pp. 3–7; ibid., Vol. II: Testimony, Box 28, Book 18, Congleton SUM APP T-229, p. 2; ibid., Box 33, Book 21, Duff SUM APP T-268, pp. 2–3 and Esterling SUM APP T-270, pp. 1–3 and Fact Sheet, To: Chief of Staff, US Army, Subject: Son My, 18 Feb. 1970, pp. 3–4, in RG 319, AS, ODCS-PER, VWCWG, MLM, Box 1, Folder: My Lai Army Staff Monitor Summaries, Feb.–May 1970. • **180**. Hammer, *One Morning*, pp. 5, 56, 60, 147. • **181**. Sworn Testimony Earl Rushin, 26 Jan. 1970, in NA, RG 319, AS, PI-FR, Vol. II: Testimony, Box 31, Book 20, Rushin SUM APP T-245, p. 3; see ibid., Box 30, Book 19, Holmes SUM APP T-223, p. 3; ibid., Box 33, Book 21, Mercer SUM APP T-349, p. 3; ibid., Vol. I: Analyses, Box 1, Ch.

2: Summary Report, p. 3; Ch. 7: Company B, 4th Battalion, 3rd Infantry: Actions on 16–19 Mar. 1968, pp. 7–9. • **182**. NA, RG 319, AS, PI-FR, Vol. I: Analyses, Box 1, Ch. 7: B Company, 4th Battalion, 3rd Infantry: Actions on 16–19 Mar. 1968, p. 6. See also ibid., Vol. II: Testimony, Box 30, Book 19, Hall SUM APP T-240, p. 3 and Jenkins SUM APP T-348, p. 2. • **183**. CID Report of Investigation, 70-CID011-00039, 20 Feb. 1970, p. 2, in NA, RG 319, AS, PI-AC, Box 47, Folder: Son My – Other Individuals (1 of 3). After interviewing 158 people the CID came to the following conclusion: 'There was insufficient evidence to substantiate or refute allegations that Mr Thomas Kent Willingham, formerly a platoon leader, ordered the killings': Talking Paper, Subject: The CID Investigation Concerning the Conduct of B/4/3rd Infantry and A/3/1st Infantry at Son My, 6 Jul. 1971, p. 1, in RG 319, AS, ODCS-PER, VWCWG, MLM, Box 7, Folder: Release of Peers Report to the Public, 13 Nov. 1974. • **184**. Witness Testimony James A. Braddock, 23 Jan. 1970, p. 7, in NA, RG 319, AS, PI-FR, Vol. II: Testimony, Box 33, Book 21. • **185**. NA, RG 319, AS, PI-FR, Vol. I: Analyses, Box 1, Ch. 7: B Company, 4th Battalion, 3rd Infantry: Actions on 16–19 Mar. 1968, p. 8. • **186**. NA, RG 319, AS, PI-FR, Vol. I: Analyses, Box 1, Ch. 2: Summary Report, p. 3; ibid., Ch. 7: B Company, 4th Battalion, 3rd Infantry: Actions on 16–19 Mar. 1968, p. 8; ibid., Vol. II: Testimony, Box 28, Book 18, Fernandez SUM APP T-309, p. 2; ibid., Box 30, Book 19, Hall SUM APP T-240, pp. 4–5, Hooton SUM APP T-376, p. 2 and Jenkins SUM APP T-348; ibid., Box 31, Book 20, Michener SUM APP T-209, p. 8 and Warner SUM APP T-336, p. 3; Andre C.R. Feher, Agent's Statement, 17 Dec. 1969, in RG 319, AS, PI-AC, Box 51, Folder: War Crimes Allegations – 9: Reid Allegation (Co Lay/Co Luy) and Fact Sheet, To: Chief of Staff, US Army, Subject: Son My, 25 Feb. 1970, p. 2, in RG 319, AS, ODCS-PER, VWCWG, MLM, Box 1, Folder: CID My Lai Talking Papers and Fact Sheets, Jan.–Jun. 1970. • **187**. NA, RG 319, AS, PI-FR, Vol. I: Analyses, Box 1, Ch. 2: Summary Report, p. 4 and Ch. 7: B Company, 4th Battalion, 3rd Infantry: Actions on 16–19 Mar. 1968, p. 2. • **188**. Testimony Thomas K. Willingham, 8 May 1969, p. 8, in NA, RG 319, AS, PI-AC, Box 47, Folder: Son My – Other Individuals (1 of 3). • **189**. Sworn Testimony Nguyen Thi Bay, 17 Dec. 1969, pp. 1–3, in NA, RG 319, AS, PI-AC, Box 51, Folder: War Crimes Allegations – 9: Reid Allegation (Co Lay/Co Luy). This file also contains the transcript of a statement from a second witness, Nguyen Thi Hien, recorded on 19 Dec. 1969. In contrast with Mrs Bay, Mrs Hien was only able to report from hearsay. • **190**. NA, RG 319, AS, PI-FR, Vol. I: Analyses, Box 1, Ch. 6: C Company, 1st Battalion, 20th Infantry: Actions on 16 and 17 Mar. 1968, p.19. • **191**. Ibid., p. 3; ibid., Vol. II: Testimony, Box 15, Book 9, McCrary SUM APP T-172, p. 3 and Sworn Statement Do Vien, 4 Jan. 1970, p. 2, in RG 319, AS, PI-AC, Box 46, Folder: Son My Suspects (1 of 3). • **192**. NA, RG 319, AS, PI-FR, Vol. I: Analyses, Box 1, Ch. 2: Summary Report, p. 4; ibid., Ch. 7: B Company, 4th Battalion, 3rd Infantry:

Actions on 16–19 Mar. 1968, pp. 2–9; ibid., Vol. II: Testimony, Box 28, Book 18, Fernandez SUM APP T-309, p. 2; ibid,, Box 35, Book 22, Myers SUM APP T-312, pp. 2–3; Department of the Army, Office of the Chief of Staff, Memorandum for Record, Subject: Follow-up Actions on the Peers Report, 8 Jul. 1971, in RG 319, AS, PI-AC, Box 38, Folder: Son My Chron. File # 19 (2 of 2) and Office Memorandum, Chief of Staff Army, Subject: Follow-up Actions on the Peers Report, 26 Jul. 1971, in ibid., Box 39, Folder: Son My Chron. File # 20 (2 of 2). See also Memorandum of Law (CPT Willingham), 22 Mar. 1971, p. 3, in RG 319, AS, ODCS-PER, VWCWG, MLM, Box 1, Folder: Administrative Review – My Lai Case (Part 1 of 4). • **193**. See above, pp. 8–10 • **194**. This refers to the CID's interviews with Ronald Haeberle on 25 Aug. 1969, James Dursi on 29 Aug. 1969, Gregory Olsen on 30 Aug. 1969, Charles Sledge on 1 Sep. 1969, Jay Roberts on 12 Sep. 1969, Paul Meadlo on 18 Sep. 1969, Dennis Conti on 30 Oct. 1969, Herbert Carter on 6 Nov. 1969, Dan Millians on 7 Nov. 1969, Varnado Simpson on 9 Nov. 1969 and Michael Bernhardt on 20 Nov. 1969. These interviews may be found in NA, RG 319, AS, PI-FR, Vol. IV: CID-Statements, Box 57, pp. 51–3. 85–94, 111–14, 127–9, 145–9, 153–60, 181–4, 335–57, 363–70, 409–12, 415–21. • **195**. Witness Testimony, Lawrence M. Colburn, B Company (Aeroscout), 123rd Aviation Battalion, 20 Dec. 1969, in NA, RG 319, AS, PI-FR, Vol. II: Testimony, Box 9, Book 5, Colburn APP T-31, p. 6. See also ibid., Vol. I: Analyses, Box 1, Ch. 5: The Son My Operation, 16–19 Mar. 1968, p. 17; ibid., Ch. 6: C Company, 1st Battalion, 20th Infantry: Actions on 16 and 17 Mar. 1968, pp. 5–6, and ibid., Ch. 10: Reports, Investigations, and Reviews, p. 20. • **196**. NA, RG 319, AS, PI-FR, Vol. II: Testimony, Box 15, Book 9, Messinger SUM APP T-147, p. 3. • **197**. Brian W. Livingston, B Company (Aeroscout), 123rd Aviation Battalion, to his wife dated 16 Mar. 1968, in NA, RG 319, AS, PI-FR, Vol. III: Exhibits, Box 54, Book 4: Miscellaneous Documents; see also ibid., Vol. II: Testimony, Box 10, Book 6, Livingston SUM APP T-132, p. 4. Livingston also confirmed the murder to the CID: see ibid., Vol. IV: CID Statements, Box 57, p. 41. • **198**. Witness Testimony Lanny J. McCrary, 17 Jan. 1970, in NA, RG 319, AS, PI-FR, Vol. II: Testimony, Box 15, Book 9, McCrary APP T-172, p. 42. • **199**. Sworn Statement Leon J. Stevenson, 3 Nov. 1969, p. 3, in NA, RG 319, AS, PI-FR, Vol. IV: CID Statements, Box 57, p. 441. See also ibid., p. 378 and Sworn Statement Charles A. West, 6 Dec. 1969, p. 2, in RG 319, AS, PI-AC, Box 46, Folder: Son My – Biographical Data (Individuals Charged) (10 of 10) and CID Report of Investigation, 69-CID011-00014, 25 Sep. 1970, p. 16, in RG 319, AS, ODCS-PER, VWCWG, MLM, Box 6, Folder: Case Folder – 1st Lt. William L. Calley, Jr. (Part 4 of 4). • **200**. William Calley, quoted in Sack, *Own Story*, p. 100. • **201**. Sworn Statement Dennis M. Bunning, C Company, Task Force Barker, 7 Dec. 1969, p. 1, in NA, RG 319, AS, PI-FR, Vol. IV: CID Statements, Box 57, p. 139. • **202**. Sworn Statement George A. Garza, C Company, Task Force Barker, 17 Sep. 1969,

p. 3, in NA, RG 319, AS, PI-FR, Vol. IV: CID Statements, Box 57, p. 211. See ibid., Vol. II, Testimony, Box 38, Book 24, Dursi SUM APP T-64. p. 2. • **203.** Sworn Statement Dennis I. Conti, C Company, Task Force Barker, 30 Oct. 1969, p. 3, in NA, RG 319, AS, PI-FR, Vol. IV: CID Statements, Box 57, p. 155; see ibid., p. 424. • **204.** Sworn Statement Harry Stanley, 14 Oct. 1969, p. 2, in NA, RG 319, AS, PI-FR, Vol. IV: CID Statements, Box 57, p. 432; see ibid., Vol. I: Analyses, Box 1, Ch. 6: C Company, 1st Battalion, 20th Infantry: Actions on 16 and 17 Mar. 1968, p. 4. • **205.** An unnamed GI, C Company, Task Force Barker, quoted in Hammer, *One Morning*, p. 121. • **206.** NA, RG 319, AS, PI-FR, Vol. I: Analyses, Box 1, Ch. 6: C Company, 1st Battalion, 20th Infantry: Actions on 16 and 17 Mar. 1968, pp. 3–7; ibid., Vol. II: Testimony, Box 38, Book 24, Carter SUM APP T-53, p. 2; ibid., Vol. IV: CID-Statements, Box 57, pp. 85–6, 139–41, 145, 432. See also Bilton and Sim, *Four Hours*, p. 109 and Hammer, *One Morning*, p. 122. • **207.** NA, RG 319, AS, PI-FR, Vol. II: Testimony, Box 38, Book 24, Bergthold SUM APP T-55, p. 2 and Cowan, SUM APP T-25, p. 2. See also Hammer, *One Morning*, p. 120 and Bilton and Sim, *Four Hours*, p. 110. • **208.** Captain Robert L. Hicks about a conversation with William Calley in July 1968, quoted in 'Witness Says Capt. Medina Didn't Know About Slaughter', *Evening Star*, 16 Sep. 1971. Robert L. Hicks's statement was confirmed by a survivor: CID Report of Investigation, 69-CID011-00014, 25 Sep. 1970, p. 26, in NA, RG 319, AS, ODCS-PER, MLM, Box 6, Folder: Case Folder – 1st Lt. William L. Calley, Jr. (Part 4 of 4). See also RG 319, AS, PI-FR, Vol. II: Testimony, Box 41, Book 26, Moss SUM APP T-63, p. 2 and Bilton and Sim, *Four Hours*, p. 154. • **209.** Witness Testimony Dennis M. Bunning, C Company, Task Force Barker, 16 Jan. 1970, in NA, RG 319, AS, PI-FR, Vol. II: Testimony, Box 41, Book 26, Bunning SUM APP T-168, p. 3 and ibid., Vol. IV: CID Statements, Box 57, p. 139. • **210.** See NA, RG 319, AS, PI-FR, Vol. II: Testimony, Box 22, Book 14, Roberts SUM APP T-23, p. 8; Statement Truong Ngu, 4 Jan. 1970, p. 3, in RG 319, AS, PI-AC, Box 46, Folder: Son My Suspects (1 of 3) and Hammer, *One Morning*, p. 123. • **211.** Sworn Statement Dennis M. Bunning, C Company, Task Force Barker, 7 Dec. 1969, p. 2, in NA, RG 319, AS, PI-FR, Vol. IV: CID Statements, Box 57, p. 139. See also Bilton and Sim, *Four Hours*, pp. 7, 128–30, 153 and Hammer, *One Morning*, p. 128. • **212.** NA, RG 319, AS, PI-FR, Vol. II: Testimony, Box 18, Book 11, Haeberle SUM APP T-174, p. 5 and ibid., Box 22, Book 14, Roberts SUM APP T-23, p. 9. • **213.** Two unnamed GIs, 3rd Platoon, C Company, Task Force Barker, quoted in Hammer, *One Morning*, pp. 130–1. Jay A. Roberts repeatedly confirmed what happened: see NA, RG 319, AS, PI-FR, Vol. II: Testimony, Box 22, Book 14, Roberts SUM APP T-23, p. 6 and ibid., Vol. IV: CID Statements, Box 57, p. 112. • **214.** Dialogue between unnamed GIs, C Company, Task Force Barker, in NA, RG 319, AS, PI-FR, Vol. II: Testimony, Box 22, Book 14, Roberts SUM APP T-23, p. 6; ibid., Box 45, Book 28, West SUM APP T-246, p. 3, and ibid, Vol. IV: CID Statements,

Box 57, p. 112. • **215**. NA, RG 319, AS, PI-FR, Vol. I: Analyses, Box 1, Ch. 2: Summary Report, p. 3; ibid., Ch. 6: C Company, 1st Battalion, 20th Infantry: Actions on 16 and 17 Mar. 1968, p. 13; ibid., Vol. IV: CID Statements, Box 57, pp. 87, 433; Memorandum of Law (Smith), undated, in RG 319, AS, ODCS-PER, VWCWG, MLM, Box 6, Folder: Administrative Review – My Lai Cases (Part 1 of 4) and Conduct of the Men of Charlie Company, 1/20, during the Assault on My Lai 4 on 16 Mar. 1968, pp. 14–21; in ibid., Box 5, Folder: Administrative Review – SSG Kenneth L. Hodges (Part 3 of 4). See also Hammer, *One Morning*, p. 131. • **216**. Ronald Haeberle, quoted in Bilton and Sim, *Four Hours*, p. 133. • **217**. An unnamed GI, C Company, Task Force Barker, quoted in Memorandum of Law (SGT Torres), undated, p. 2, in NA, RG 319, AS, ODCS-PER, VWCWG, MLM, Box 1, Folder: Administrative Review – My Lai Cases (Part 1 of 4). • **218**. Conduct of the Men of Charlie Company, 1/20, during the Assault on My Lai 4 on 16 Mar. 1968, p. 20, in NA, RG 319, AS, ODCS-PER, VWCWG, MLM, Box 5, Folder: Administrative Review – SSG Kenneth L. Hodges (Part 3 of 4); RG 319, AS, PI-FR, Vol. II: Testimony, Box 22, Book 14, Roberts SUM APP T-23, p. 7 and Hammer, *One Morning*, p. 133. • **219**. NA, RG 319, AS, PI-FR, Vol. II: Testimony, Box 40, Book 25, Stanley SUM APP T-231, p. 2; ibid., Vol. IV: CID Statements, Box 57, pp. 147, 268 and Testimony Frederick J. Widmer, 15 Jul. 1969, p. 23 (1002), in RG 319, AS, PI-AC, Box 46, Folder: Son My Suspects (3 of 3). • **220**. Sworn Statement Harry Stanley, C Company, Task Force Barker, 14 Oct. 1969, p. 6, in NA, RG 319, AS, PI-FR, Vol. IV: CID Statements, Box 57, p. 436 and Hammer, *One Morning*, p. 126. • **221**. William Calley, quoted in Sack, *Own Story*, pp. 108–10. See also Sworn Statement Charles W. Hall, 24 Oct. 1969, p. 2, in NA, RG 319, AS, PI-FR, Vol. IV: CID Statements, Box 57, p. 234 and Bilton and Sim, *Four Hours*, p. 372. • **222**. These words refer to Alf Lüdtke, 'Exterminating "Others"'. • **223**. Michael Bernhardt, C Company, Task Force Barker, quoted in Hammer, *One Morning*, p. 125. • **224**. NA, RG 319, AS, PI-FR, Vol. I: Analyses, Box 1, Ch. 2: Summary Report, p. 2; ibid., Ch. 6: C Company, 1st Battalion, 20th Infantry: Actions on 16 and 17 Mar. 1968, p. 8; ibid., Vol. II: Testimony, Box 18, Book 11, Haeberle SUM APP T-174, p. 1; ibid., Box 38, Book 24, Carter SUM APP T-53, p. 3; ibid., Box 40, Book 25, Stanley SUM APP T-231, p. 3; ibid., Vol. IV: CID Statements, Box 57, p. 147 and Conduct of the Men of Charlie Company, 1/20, during the Assault on My Lai (4) on 16 Mar. 1968, pp. 1, 10, in NA, RG 319, AS, ODCS-PER, VWCWG, MLM, Box 5, Folder: Administrative Review – SSG Kenneth L. Hodges (Part 3 of 4). • **225**. Witness Testimony Gregory T. Olsen, 30 Dec. 1969, in NA, RG 319, AS, PI-FR, Vol. II: Testimony, Box 40, Book 25, Olsen SUM APP T-47, p. 4. • **226**. Sworn Statement Dennis I. Conti, 30 Oct. 1969, p. 4, in NA, RG 319, AS, PI-FR, Vol. IV: CID Statements, Box 57, p. 156. • **227**. NA, RG 319, AS, PI-FR, Vol. I: Analyses, Box 1, Ch. 6, C Company, 1st Battalion, 20th Infantry: Actions on

16 and 17 Mar. 1968, p. 8. • **228**. NA, RG 319, AS, PI-FR, Vol. IV: CID Statements, Box 57, pp. 87, 113, 135, 147, 425. See also Bilton and Sim, *Four Hours*, p. 115ff. and Hammer, *One Morning*, pp. 124, 133. • **229**. NA, RG 319, AS, PI-FR, Vol. I: Analyses, Box 1, Ch. 6: C Company, 1st Battalion, 20th Infantry: Actions on 16 and 17 Mar. 1968, p. 7; Department of the Army, Office of the Inspector General, Report of Investigation Concerning Alleged Atrocities Committed by Members of C Co, 1/20th Infantry, Task Force Barker, Americal Division, in the Republic of Vietnam, 19 Sep. 1969, pp. 19–24. See also Hammer, *One Morning*, p. 136 and Bilton and Sim, *Four Hours*, p. 128. • **230**. Herbert Carter, C Company, Task Force Barker, quoted in Conduct of the Men of Charlie Company 1/20, during the Assault on My Lai 4 on 16 Mar. 1968, p. 9, in NA, RG 319, AS, ODCS-PER, VWCWG, MLM, Box 5, Folder: Administrative Review – SSG Kenneth L. Hodges (Part 3 of 4). • **231**. Bilton and Sim, *Four Hours*, p. 129. • **232**. For the spread of this attitude amongst American troops in Vietnam in general and in C Company in particular, see USCR, 6 Apr. 1971, p. E2883; CID Investigative Summary, 72-CID046027852, 10 Aug. 1974, p. 7, in NA, RG 319, AS, ODCS-PER, VWCWG, CaFi, Box 18, Folder: Coy Allegation (CID ROI 72 – CID 46 – 27852), Part 1 of 7, Case 221 and ibid., Folders, Part 2 of 7 and Part 3 of 7, Case 221. See also Richard Hammer, 'Interviews with My Lai Veterans', pp. 56–7 and Valentine, *Phoenix Program*, p. 63. • **233**. William Calley, quoted in Sack, *Own Story*, p. 10. • **234**. James H. Raynor, C Company, 1st Battalion, 20th Infantry Regiment, Americal Division, quoted in Conduct of the Men of Charlie Company, 1/20, during the Assault on My Lai (4) on 16 Mar. 1968, p. 35, in NA, RG 319, AS, ODCS-PER, VWCWG, MLM, Box 5, Folder: Administrative Review – SSG Kenneth L. Hodges (Part 3 of 4). Paul Meadlo spoke in similar terms during the trial of William Calley, pp. 153–4. • **235**. NA, RG 319, AS, PI-FR, Vol. II: Testimony, Box 38, Book 24, Konwinski SUM APP T-271, p. 2; ibid., Box 41, Book 26, Fields SUM APP T-156, p. 2; ibid., Box 43, Book 27, Raynor SUM APP T-339, p. 2; ibid, Vol. IV: CID Statements, Box 57, pp. 283–4, 287–8; Sworn Statement Stephen F. Rose, 27 Jan. 1970, pp. 3–4, in RG 319, AS, ODCS-PER, VWCWG, CF, Box 4, Folder: Rose Allegation, Case 24; Conduct of the Men of Charlie Company, 1/20, during the Assault on My Lai 4 on 16 Mar. 1968, pp. 31–3, in NA, RG 319, AS, ODCS-PER, VWCWG, MLM, Box 5, Folder: Administrative Review – SSG Kenneth L. Hodges (Part 3 of 4). See also Hammer, 'Interviews with My Lai Veterans', pp. 56–7 and Bilton and Sim, *Four Hours*, p. 182. • **236**. Lelyveld, 'Story of a Soldier', p. 110 and Hammer, *One Morning*, p. 125. • **237**. An unnamed GI, C Company, Task Force Barker, quoted in Hammer, *One Morning*, p. 128. • **238**. NA, RG 319, AS, PI-FR, Vol. I: Analyses, Box 1, Ch. 6: C Company, 1st Battalion, 20th Infantry: Actions on 16 and 17 Mar. 1968, p. 7; ibid., Vol. II: Testimony, Box 41, Book 26, Fields SUM APP T-156, p. 2; ibid., Vol. IV: CID Statements, Box 57, pp. 432–3, 470. See also Bilton and Sim, *Four Hours*, pp. 112–14, 123ff., 130, 153 and Hammer,

One Morning, p. 137. • **239**. Frederick J. Widmer, C Company, Task Force Barker, quoted in Sworn Statement Herbert L. Carter, 6 Nov. 1969, p. 3, in NA, RG 319, AS, PI-FR, Vol. IV: CID Statements, Box 57, p. 147; see ibid., p. 434 and Vol. II: Testimony, Box 40, Book 25, Stanley SUM APP T-231, p. 2. • **240**. Testimony Frederick J. Widmer, 15 Jul. 1969, p. 26 (1005), in RG 319, AS, PI-AC, Box 46, Folder: Son My Suspects (3 of 3). • **241**. NA, RG 319, AS, PI-FR, Vol. IV: CID Statements, Box 57, p. 373; Fact Sheet, To: Chief of Staff, US Army, 3 Apr. 1970, p. 3, in RG 319, AS, ODCS-PER, MLM, Box 1, Folder: CID My Lai Talking Papers and Fact Sheets, Jan.–Jun. 1970; Bilton and Sim, *Four Hours*, pp. 116, 298. • **242**. NA, RG 319, AS, PI-FR, Vol. II: Testimony, Box 41, Book 26, Moss SUM APP T-63, p. 2; ibid., Box 43, Book 27, Smail SUM APP T-71, p. 2; ibid., Vol. IV: CID Statements, Box 57, pp. 432–3; Conduct of the Men of Charlie Company, 1/20, during the Assault on My Lai (4) on 16 Mar. 1968, p. 6, in NA, RG 319, AS, ODCS-PER, VWCWG, MLM, Box 5, Folder: Administrative Review – SSG Kenneth L. Hodges (Part 3 of 4). • **243**. Hammer, *One Morning*, p. 137 and Bilton and Sim, *Four Hours*, p. 131. • **244**. NA, RG 319, AS, PI-FR, Vol. I: Analyses, Ch. 6: C Company, 1st Battalion, 20th Infantry: Actions on 16 and 17 Mar. 1968, p. 10; ibid., Vol. II: Testimony, Box 41, Book 26, Bunning SUM APP T-168, pp. 4–5; ibid., Vol. IV: CID Statements, Box 57, p. 140; and Conduct of the Men of Charlie Company, 1/20, during the Assault on My Lai 4 on 16 Mar. 1968, pp. 24–5, in: NA, RG 319, AS, ODCS-PER, VWCWG, MLM, Box 5, Folder: Administrative Review – SSG Kenneth L. Hodges (Part 3 of 4). • **245**. Sworn Statement Varnado Simpson, 9 Nov. 1969, p. 3, in NA, RG 319, AS, PI-FR, Vol. IV: CID Statements, Box 57, p. 411. • **246**. NA, RG 319, AS, PI-FR, Vol. I: Analyses, Ch. 6: C Company, 1st Battalion, 20th Infantry: Actions on 16 and 17 Mar. 1968, p. 10; ibid., Vol. II: Testimony, Box 41, Book 26, Bunning SUM APP T-168, p. 4 and Conduct of the Men of Charlie Company, 1/20, during the Assault on My Lai (4) on 16 Mar. 1968, pp. 7–8, in NA, RG 319, AS, ODCS-PER, VWCWG, MLM, Box 5, Folder: Administrative Review – SSG Kenneth L. Hodges (Part 3 of 4). • **247**. Bilton and Sim, *Four Hours*, pp. 129, 153. • **248**. Varnado Simpson, 3rd Platoon, C Company, Task Force Barker, quoted in ibid., p. 7. • **249**. NA, RG 319, AS, PI-FR, Vol. II: Testimony, Box 41, Book 26, Bunning SUM APP T-168, p. 2 and ibid., Vol. IV: CID Statements, Box 57, p. 140. For the varying reactions see ibid., Vol. IV: CID Statements, Box 57, pp 210–12, 287. • **250**. See above, pp. 124–42. • **251**. For this little-considered aspect of murderous violence, see Reemtsma, *Unzeitgemäßes über Krieg und Tod*, p. 12ff. • **252**. NA, RG 319, AS, PI-FR, Vol. I: Analyses, Ch. 2: Summary Report, p. 2, and H.V. Hammett, Department of the Army, Judge Advocate General Office: Memorandum of Conversation with Paul D. Meadlo, 26 Aug. 1969, in RG 319, AS, PI-AC, Box 31, Folder: Son My Chron. File # 1 (1 of 3). • **253**. CID Report of Investigation 69-CID011-00014, 25 Sep. 1970, pp. 8–20, in NA, RG 319, AS, ODCS-PER,

VWCWG, MLM, Box 6, Folder: Case Folder – 1st Lt. William L. Calley, Jr. (Part 4 of 4). • **254**. Conduct of the Men of Charlie Company, 1/20, during the Assault on My Lai (4) on 16 Mar. 1968, p. 15, in NA, RG 319, AS, ODCS-PER, VWCWG, MLM, Box 5, Folder: Administrative Review – SSG Kenneth L. Hodges (Part 3 of 4). See also Sworn Statement Paul D. Meadlo, 18 Sep. 1969, pp. 1–2, in NA, RG 319, AS, PI-FR, Vol. IV: CID-Statements, Box 57, pp. 335–6. • **255**. Witness Statement James J. Dursi, C Company, Task Force Barker, 5 Jan. 1970, in NA, RG 319, AS, PI-FR, Vol. II: Testimony, Box 38, Book 24, Dursi SUM APP T-64, p. 3 and ibid., Vol. IV: CID-Statements, Box 57, p. 182. • **256**. Dennis I. Conti, C Company, Task Force Barker, quoted in Conduct of the Men of Charlie Company, 1/20, during the Assault on My Lai (4) on 16 Mar. 1968, p. 15, in NA, RG 319, AS, ODCS-PER, VWCWG, MLM, Box 5, Folder: Administrative Review – SSG Kenneth L. Hodges (Part 3 of 4). • **257**. Sworn Statement Dennis I. Conti, 30 Oct. 1969, p. 4, in NA, RG 319, AS, PI-FR, Vol. IV: CID-Statements, Box 57, p. 156. • **258**. William Calley, quoted in Sack, *Own Story*, p. 107. • **259**. William Calley, quoted in ibid., p. 110. • **260**. Bilton and Sim, *Four Hours*, p. 119. • **261**. Conduct of the Men of Charlie Company, 1/20, during the Assault on My Lai (4) on 16 Mar. 1968, p. 15, in NA, RG 319, AS, ODCS-PER, VWCWG, MLM, Box 5, Folder: Administrative Review – SSG Kenneth L. Hodges (Part 3 of 4). See also Sworn Statement Paul D. Meadlo, 18 Sep. 1969, pp. 1–2, in NA, RG 319, AS, PI-FR, Vol. IV: CID Statements, Box 57, pp. 335–6. • **262**. Sworn Statement Dennis I. Conti, 30 Oct. 1969, p. 4, in NA, RG 319, AS, PI-FR, Vol. IV: CID Statements, Box 57, p. 156. • **263**. Sworn Statement Paul D. Meadlo, C Company, Task Force Barker, 18 Sep. 1969, p. 2, in RG 319, AS, PI-FR, Vol. IV: CID Statements, Box 57, p. 336. • **264**. Witness Testimony Dennis I. Conti, C Company, Task Force Barker, 2 Jan. 1970, in NA, RG 319, AS, PI-FR, Vol. II: Testimony, Box 38, Book 24, Conti SUM APP T-56, p. 2 and Conduct of the Men of Charlie Company, 1/20, during the Assault on My Lai (4) on 16 Mar. 1968, pp. 15–16, in NA, RG 319, AS, ODCS-PER, VWCWG, MLM, Box 5, Folder: Administrative Review – SSG Kenneth L. Hodges (Part 3 of 4). • **265**. CID Report of Investigation, 69-CID011-00014, 25 Sep. 1970, p. 40, in NA, RG 319, AS, ODCS-PER, VWCWG, MLM, Box 6, Folder: Case Folder – 1st Lt. William L. Calley, Jr. (Part 4 of 4). • **266**. The reference to Binh Dong comes from a survivor who was interviewed by Richard Hammer: Hammer, *One Morning*, p. 135. • **267**. Sworn Statement Paul D. Meadlo, C Company, Task Force Barker, 18 Sep. 1969, p. 2, in RG 319, AS, PI-FR, Vol. IV: CID Statements, Box 57, p. 336. • **268**. NA, RG 319, AS, PI-FR, Vol. IV: CID Statements, Box 57, pp. 182, 418–19, 434–5; Conduct of the Men of Charlie Company, 1/20, during the Assault on My Lai (4) on 16 Mar. 1968, p. 20, in NA, RG 319, AS, ODCS-PER, VWCWG, MLM, Box 5, Folder: Administrative Review – SSG Kenneth L. Hodges (Part 3 of 4) and CID Report of Investigation, 69-CID011-00014, 25 Sep. 1970, p. 11,

in NA, RG 319, AS, ODCS-PER, VWCWG, MLM, Box 6, Folder: Case Folder
– 1st Lt. William L. Calley, Jr. (Part 4 of 4). • **269**. NA, RG 319, AS, PI-FR,
Vol. IV: CID Statements, Box 57, pp. 312, 336–7. • **270**. CID Report of Inves-
tigation, 69-CIDO11-00014, 25 Sep. 1970, p. 40, in NA, RG 319, AS, ODCS-PER,
VWCWG, MLM, Box 6, Folder: Case Folder – 1st Lt. William L. Calley, Jr.
(Part 4 of 4). • **271**. NA, RG 319, AS, PI-FR, Vol. I: Analyses, Ch. 2: Summary
Report, p. 3; ibid., Ch. 6: C Company, 1st Battalion, 20th Infantry: Actions on
16 and 17 March 1968, p. 12; ibid., Vol. II: Testimony, Box 40, Book 25, Buchanon
SUM APP T-59, p. 3; ibid., Box 41, Book 26, Fields SUM APP T-156, p. 3 and
Bunning SUM APP T-168, p. 5; ibid., Box 43, Book 27, Trevino SUM APP T-
185, p. 3 and ibid, Vol. IV: CID Statements, Box 57, p. 140. There are indications
that also in My Hoi or My Khe (4) not all the inhabitants were murdered.
At the end of the operation there between twenty and thirty peasants were
allegedly sent back to their village; see ibid., Vol. II: Testimony, Box 30, Book
19, Hall SUM APP T-240 pp. 5–9; ibid., Hall, SUM APP T-240A, pp. 1–3; ibid.,
Holmes, SUM APP T-223, pp. 1–6; ibid., Hooton, SUM APP T-376, pp. 1–2. •
272. William Calley, quoted in Sack, *Own Story*, p. 116. • **273**. NA, RG 319, AS,
PI-FR, Vol. IV: CID-Statements, Box 57, pp. 320, 380 and Bilton and Sim, *Four
Hours*, p. 142. • **274**. William Calley, quoted in Sack, *Own Story*, p. 91. • **275**.
NA, RG 319, AS, PI-FR, Vol. II: Testimony, Box 40, Book 25, Olsen SUM APP
T-47, p. 3 and Hammer, *One Morning*, p. 136. • **276**. Hugh Thompson, quoted
in Anderson (ed.), *Facing My Lai*, p. 31. • **277**. William Calley, quoted in Sack,
Own Story, pp. 137–9. • **278**. CID Report of Investigation, 69-CIDO11–00014,
25 Sep. 1970, pp. 11, 40, in NA, RG 319, AS, ODCS-PER, VWCWG, MLM, Box
6, Folder: Case Folder – 1st Lt. William L. Calley, Jr. (Part 4 of 4); RG 319,
AS, PI-FR, Vol. II: Testimony, Box 40, Book 25, Stanley SUM APP T-231, p. 4;
ibid., Vol. IV: CID Statements, Box 57, p. 157. A survivor of the executions
in the irrigation ditch spoke of about five perpetrators: ibid., Vol. II: Testimony,
Box 52, Book 32, Dat APP T-93, p. 6. • **279**. See Sworn Statement Davey V.
Hoag, 5 May 1972, p. 2, in NA, RG 319, AS, ODCS-PER, VWCWG, CaFi, Box
20, Folder: Hoag Allegation (Part 2 of 4) and ibid., Box 12, Folders: Notley
Allegation. See also 'EX-GI's Atrocity Story Stirs Officials', *Evening Star*, 29
Apr. 1971. • **280**. Dennis I. Conti, C Company, Task Force Barker, quoted in
Bilton and Sim, *Four Hours*, p. 120. • **281**. NA, RG 319, AS, PI-FR, Vol. II: Testi-
mony, Box 40, Book 25, Stanley SUM APP T-231, p. 4; ibid., Vol. IV: CID
Statements, Box 57, p. 435; Conduct of the Men of Charlie Company, 1/20,
during the Assault on My Lai (4) on 16 Mar. 1968, p. 18, in NA, RG 319, AS,
ODCS-PER, VWCWG, MLM, Box 5, Folder: Administrative Review – SSG
Kenneth L. Hodges (Part 3 of 4). • **282**. Conduct of the Men of Charlie
Company, 1/20, during the Assault on My Lai (4) on 16 Mar. 1968, pp. 18–19,
in NA, RG 319, AS, ODCS-PER, VWCWG, MLM, Box 5, Folder: Administrative
Review – SSG Kenneth L. Hodges (Part 3 of 4). See also RG 319, AS, PI-FR,

Vol. IV: CID Statements, Box 57, pp. 182, 336 and Bilton and Sim, *Four Hours*, p. 123. • **283**. NA, RG 319, AS, PI-FR, Vol. IV: CID Statements, Box 57, pp. 182, 234 and ibid., Vol. I: Analyses, Ch. 6, C Company, 1st Battalion, 20th Infantry: Actions on 16 and 17 Mar. 1968, p. 16. • **284**. NA, RG 319, AS, PI-FR, Vol. IV: CID Statements, Box 57, pp. 287–8, 316. • **285**. NA, RG 319, AS, PI-FR, Vol. IV: CID Statements, Box 57, p. 419; ibid, Vol. II: Testimony, Box 40, Book 25, Sledge SUM APP T-81, p. 2 and William Calley, quoted in Sack, *Own Story*, p. 89. • **286**. William Calley, quoted William Styron, review of Richard Hammer (*The Court Martial of Lt. Calley*) and John Sack (*Lieutenant Calley*), *New York Times Book Review*, 12 Sep. 1971, p. 20. See also NA, RG 319, AS, PI-FR, Vol. IV: CID Statements, Box 57, p. 147. • **287**. James J. Dursi, C Company, Task Force Barker, quoted in Sworn Statement Joseph N. Konwinski, C Company, Task Force Barker, 26 Oct. 1969, p. 1, in NA, RG 319, AS, PI-FR, Vol. IV: CID Statements, Box 57, p. 287. Varnado Simpson, 3rd Platoon, C Company, Task Force Barker, claimed to have become a murderer in the same way as Meadlo: Hammer, 'Interviews' p. 23. • **288**. Paul Meadlo, C Company, Task Force Barker, quoted in Sworn Statement James J. Dursi, 29 Aug. 1969, p. 2, in NA, RG 319, AS, PI-FR, Vol. IV: CID Statements, Box 57, p. 182; see ibid., p. 156. • **289**. Paul Meadlo, C Company, Task Force Barker, quoted in Bilton and Sim, *Four Hours*, p. 120. • **290**. NA, RG 319, AS, PI-FR, Vol. I: Analyses, Ch. 6, C Company, 1st Battalion, 20th Infantry: Actions on 16 and 17 Mar. 1968, p. 11; ibid., Ch. 10: Reports, Investigations, and Reviews, p. 9 and ibid., Vol. II: Testimony, Box 9, Book 5, Colburn SUM APP T-31, pp. 2, 15. • **291**. NA, RG 319, AS, PI-FR, Vol. I: Analyses, Ch. 6, C Company, 1st Battalion, 20th Infantry: Actions on 16 and 17 Mar. 1968, p. 12 and ibid., Ch. 10: Reports, Investigations, and Reviews, p. 10. See also Sack, *Own Story*, p. 90. • **292**. Stephen Brooks, C Company, Task Force Barker, quoted in Sworn Statement Jerry R. Culverhouse, 12 Dec. 1969, p. 2, in NA, RG 319, AS, PI-FR, Vol. IV: CID Statements, Box 57, p. 30. Varnado Simpson confirmed that he and other soldiers from 2nd Platoon actually tried to murder these people: Sworn Statement Varnado Simpson, 9 Nov. 1969, p. 3, in ibid., p. 411. • **293**. NA, RG 319, AS, PI-FR, Vol. I: Analyses, Ch. 6, C Company, 1st Battalion, 20th Infantry: Actions on 16 and 17 Mar. 1968, p. 15; ibid., Ch. 10: Reports, Investigations, and Reviews, p. 11 and ibid., Vol. II: Testimony, Box 10, Book 6, Culverhouse SUM APP T-126, p. 2. • **294**. NA, RG 319, AS, PI-FR, Vol. I: Analyses, Ch. 6, C Company, 1st Battalion, 20th Infantry: Actions on 16 and 17 Mar. 1968, p. 15 and Brian W. Livingston, Warrant Officer, B Company (Aeroscout), 123rd Aviation Battalion, letter to his wife, 16 Mar. 1968, in NA, RG 319, AS, PI-FR, Vol. III: Exhibits, Book 4: Miscellaneous Documents. • **295**. Sworn Statement Dan R. Millians, B Company (Aeroscout), 123rd Aviation Battalion, 7 Nov. 1969, p. 2, in NA, RG 319, AS, PI-FR, Vol. IV: CID-Statements, Box 57, p. 52. For Thompson's description of the events in detail see Anderson (ed.), *Facing My Lai*, pp. 28ff, 50 and Angers, *Forgotten Hero*. • **296**. Bilton and

Sim, *Four Hours*, p. 161. • **297**. Ibid., p. 117 and Hammer, *One Morning*, p. 137. • **298**. Unsworn Statement Pham Thua, 5 Jan. 1970, in NA, RG 319, PI-FR, Vol. II: Testimony, Box 52, Book 32, Thua APP T-119, p. 5. • **299**. See NA, RG 319, AS, PI-FR, Vol. II: Testimony, Box 45, Book 28, West SUM APP T-246, p. 3. • **300**. There were said to have been about 150 survivors in Xom Lang, a further 50 from Binh Tay and possibly 20–30 villagers from My Hoi (My Khe (4)): NA, RG 319, AS, PI-FR, Vol. I: Analyses, Ch. 7: B Company, 4th Battalion, 3rd Infantry: Actions on 16–19 Mar. 1968, p. 11; ibid., Vol. II: Testimony, Box 30, Book 19, Hall SUM APP T-240, p. 5 and ibid., Hooton SUM APP T-376, p. 2; ibid., Box 52, Book 32, Lai SUM APP T-114, p. 1. • **301**. Michael Bernhardt, C Company, Task Force Barker, quoted in Lelyveld, 'Story of a Soldier', p 110. • **302**. Conduct of the Men of Charlie Company, 1/20, during the Assault on My Lai (4) on 16 Mar. 1968, p. 8, in NA, RG 319, AS, ODCS-PER, VWCWG, MLM, Box 5, Folder: Administrative Review – SSG Kenneth L. Hodges (Part 3 of 4). • **303**. Ibid., p. 10. • **304**. Gregory Olsen, C Company, Task Force Barker, quoted in Bilton and Sim, *Four Hours*, p. 82. • **305**. An unnamed GI, C Company, Task Force Barker, quoted in Hammer, *One Morning*, p. 129. • **306**. Lelyveld, 'Story of a Soldier', p. 110. • **307**. Bilton and Sim, *Four Hours*, p. 183. • **308**. Sworn Statement James D. Henry, 28 Feb. 1970, p. 9, in NA, RG 319, AS, ODCS-PER, VWCWG, CaFi, Box 5, Folder: Henry Allegation – CID Reports. • **309**. An unnamed GI, quoted in Baker, *Nam*, p. 190. • **310**. NA, RG 319, AS, PI-FR, Vol. I: Analyses, Ch. 5: The Son My Operation 16–19 Mar. 1968, p. 19; Ch. 6, C Company, 1st Battalion, 20th Infantry: Actions on 16 and 17 Mar. 1968, p. 18; ibid., Vol. II: Testimony, Box 15, Book 9, Lind SUM APP T-346, p. 64; ibid., Box 20, Book 12, Henderson SUM APP T-1, p. 2; ibid., Box 25, Book 16, Vasquez SUM APP T-32, p. 3 and Department of the Army, Judge Advocate, Memorandum of Law (Maj. McKnight), 18 Feb. 1971, in RG 319, AS, ODCS-PER, VWCWG, MLM, Box 2, Folder: Administrative Review – My Lai Cases (Part 3 of 4). • **311**. NA, RG 319, AS, PI-FR, Vol. I: Analyses, Ch. 10: Reports, Investigations, and Reviews, p. 19; see ibid., pp. 5, 18, 20; ibid., Ch. 5: The Son My Operation, 16–19 Mar. 1968, p. 17, and Ch. 6: C Company, 1st Battalion, 20th Infantry: Actions on 16 and 17 Mar. 1968, p. 15. • **312**. NA, RG 319, AS, PI-FR, Vol. I: Analyses, Ch. 5: The Son My Operation 16–19 March 1968, p. 19 and Ch. 11, Suppression and Withholding of Information, p. 4. • **313**. NA, RG 319, AS, PI-FR, Vol. I: Ch. 6: C Company, 1st Battalion, 20th Infantry: Actions on 16 and 17 Mar. 1968, p. 9. • **314**. NA, RG 319, AS, PI-FR, Vol. I: Analyses, Ch. 5: The Son My Operation 16–19 Mar. 1968, p. 18; ibid., Vol. II: Testimony, Box 10, Book 6, Czarnecki APP T-399, p. 17 and ibid., Box 12, Book 7, Newell APP T-381, pp. 22–23; for the remarkable gaps in Major General Koster's memory, see ibid., Box 5, Book 3, Koster SUM APP T-20, pp. 3–11. • **315**. NA, RG 319, AS, PI-FR, Vol. I: Analyses, Ch. 12: Findings and Recommendations, p. 15; see ibid., pp. 20, 24–5. • **316**. Ibid., Ch. 11: Suppression and Withholding of Information, p. 5. • **317**. Ibid., Ch. 10: Reports, Investigations, and Reviews, pp. 25–6. • **318**. Ibid., Ch. 6: C Company, 1st Battalion, 20th Infantry: Actions on 16 and 17 March 1968, p. 11. • **319**. Ibid., Ch. 12: Findings and Recommendations, p. 30. • **320**. Sworn Statement Herbert L. Carter, 6 Nov. 1969, p. 2, in NA, RG 319, AS, PI-FR, Vol. IV: CID-Statements, Box 57, p. 149. See also ibid., pp. 3, 4 and ibid., Vol. I: Analyses: Summary Report, Ch. 10: Reports, Investigations, and Reviews, p. 9; ibid., Vol. II, Testimony, Box 9, Book 5, Colburn SUM APP T-31, pp. 2, 15; ibid., Vol. IV: CID Statements, Box 57, p. 128. There was no question of the self-defence claimed by Medina. For the other accusations against Medina, see ibid., Vol. II: Testimony, Box 43, Book 27, Pendleton SUM APP T-221, p. 2. • **321**. 'Witness Testifies Medina Told Him of Losing Control', *Washington Post*, 10 Sep. 1971. See also NA, RG 319, AS, PI-FR, Vol. II: Testimony, Box 52, Book 32, Phu App T-96, p. 13; ibid., Box 40, Book 25, Stanley SUM APP T-231, pp. 2, 3. • **322**. NA, RG 319, AS, PI-FR, Vol. I: Analyses, Ch. 6: C Company, 1st Battalion, 20th Infantry: Actions on 16 and 17 Mar. 1968, p. 15 and ibid., Vol. IV: CID Statements, Box 57, pp. 87, 113, 379. • **323**. Witness Testimony Jay A. Roberts, 17 Dec. 1969, in NA, RG 319, AS, PI-FR, Vol. II: Testimony, Box 22, Book 14, Roberts SUM APP T-23, p. 8. Roberts had given evidence before the CID: 'Medina said that the old man had no military value and he didn't want him': Sworn Statement Jay A. Roberts, 12 Sep. 1969, p. 3, in ibid., Vol. IV: CID Statements, Box 57, p. 113. • **324**. Department of the Army, Judge Advocate, 21 Jun. 1972, Memorandum of Law (Former CPT. Medina), pp. 4–5. • **325**. Sworn Statement Jay A. Roberts, 12 Sep. 1969, p. 3, in NA, RG 319, AS, PI-FR, Vol. IV: CID Statements, Box 57, p. 113; see ibid., p. 148 and 'My Lai Pilot Aimed at GIs, Saved Viets', *Washington Star*, 11 Dec. 1969. • **326**. Witness Testimony Nguyen Dinh Phu, 1 Jan. 1970, in NA, RG 319, AS, PI-FR, Vol. II: Testimony, Box 52, Book 32, Phu APP T-96, p. 13. • **327**. NA, RG 319, AS, PI-FR, Vol. IV: CID Statements, Box 57, p. 88. • **328**. 'Viets Tell What They Saw at Mylai', *Washington Post*, 9 Aug. 1971. • **329**. NA, RG 319, AS, PI-FR, Vol. I: Analyses, Ch. 10, Reports, Investigations, and Reviews, p. 7; see ibid., Vol. II: Testimony, Box 21, Book 13, Kirkpatrick SUM APP T-281, p. 2. • **330**. Memorandum, Subject: Time Sequence of Radio Message Traffic, undated, p. 2, in NA, RG 319, AS, PI-CI, Box 4, Folder: Master Recall Folder. • **331**. Lieutenant Colonel Frank Barker, quoted in NA, RG 319, AS, PI-FR, Vol. II: Testimony, Box 45, Book 28, Kinch SUM APP T-202, p. 3 and ibid., Vol. IV: CID Statements, Box 57, p. 281. • **332**. Memorandum, Subject: Time Sequence of Radio Message Traffic, undated, p. 2, in NA, RG 319, AS, PI-CI, Box 4, Folder: Master Recall Folder. See also RG 319, AS, PI-FR, Vol. I: Analyses, Ch. 6: C Company, 1st Battalion, 20th Infantry: Actions on 16 and 17 Mar. 1968, p. 17; ibid., Ch. 10, Reports, Investigations, and Reviews, p. 7; ibid., Vol. II: Testimony, Box 23, Book 15, Calhoun SUM APP T-6, p. 3 and ibid., Vol. IV: CID Statements, Box 57, p. 477. • **333**. NA, RG 319, AS, PI-FR, Vol. I: Analyses, Ch. 2: Summary Report,

p. 3 and ibid., Ch. 6: C Company, 1st Battalion, 20th Infantry: Actions on 16 and 17 Mar. 1968, p. 12. • **334.** NA, RG 319, AS, PI-FR, Vol. II: Testimony, Box 45, Book 28, Kinch SUM APP T-202, p. 3 and ibid., Vol. I: Analyses, Ch. 6: C Company, 1st Battalion, 20th Infantry: Actions on 16 and 17 Mar. 1968, p. 16. • **335.** CID Report of Investigation, 69-CID011–00014, 25/9/1970, p. 14, in NA, RG 319, AS, ODCS-PER, VWCWG, MLM, Box 6, Folder: Case Folder – 1st Lt. William L. Calley, Jr. (Part 4 of 4). • **336.** Witness Testimony Harry Stanley, 24 Jan. 1970, in NA, RG 319, AS, PI-FR, Vol. II: Testimony, Box 40, Book 25, Stanley SUM APP T-231, p. 4. • **337.** NA, RG 319, AS, PI-FR, Vol. I: Analyses, Ch. 6: C Company, 1st Battalion, 20th Infantry: Actions on 16 and 17 Mar. 1968, p. 19. • **338.** Witness Testimony Nguyen Dinh Phu, 1 Jan. 1970, in NA, RG 319, AS, PI-FR, Vol. II: Testimony, Box 52, Book 32, Phu APP T-96, p. 24. • **339.** Witness Statement Joseph W. Konwinski, 29 Jan. 1970, in NA, RG 319, AS, PI-FR, Vol. II: Testimony, Box 38, Book 24, Konwinski SUM APP T-271, p. 3. • **340.** Dennis I. Conti, C Company, Task Force Barker, quoted in Bilton and Sim, *Four Hours*, p. 167. • **341.** NA, RG 319, AS, PI-FR, Vol. I: Analyses, Ch. 5: The Son My Operation 16–19 Mar. 1968, p. 23; ibid., Ch. 6: C Company, 1st Battalion, 20th Infantry: Actions on 16 and 17 Mar. 1968, pp. 19–20; ibid., Ch. 7, B Company, 4th Battalion, 3rd Infantry: Actions on 16–19 Mar. 1968, pp. 2–15; ibid., Vol. II: Testimony, Box 31, Book 20, Michener SUM APP T-209, pp. 1–11, 83–5; ibid., Box 51, Book 31, Boatman SUM APP T-184, pp. 4–5; ibid., Box 52, Book 32, Hien APP T-99, pp. 8–14 and Bilton and Sim, *Four Hours*, pp. 146–8, 166–77. • **342.** Witness Testimony Do Thanh Hien, 2 Jan. 1970, in NA, RG 319, AS, PI-FR, Vol. II: Testimony, Box 52, Book 32, Hien APP T-99, pp. 21–3. • **343.** Frey, *Geschichte des Vietnamkriegs*, pp. 169–73. • **344.** Pike, 'Vietcong Strategy', p. 45.

7 1968–1971 – War of Attrition in the Southern Provinces

1. Quoted in Berman, *No Peace*, p. 31. • **2.** Seymour M. Hersh, interview with *CBS Morning News*, 19 Jan. 1972, WTOP TV, Washington, DC, Transcript, p. 9, in NA, RG 319, AS, PI-AC, Box 39, Folder: Son My Chron. File # 22 (1 of 3). A similar question of Hugh Thompson's is also recorded: Robert N. Zara, Investigator's Statement, 18 Sep. 1970, p. 7, in NA, RG 319, AS, ODCS-PER, VWCWG, MLM, Box 6, Folder: Case Folder – 1st Lt. William L. Calley, Jr. (Part 4 of 4). See also Bilton and Sim, *Four Hours*, pp. 176–7. • **3.** NA, RG 319, AS, PI-FR, Vol. II: Testimony, Box 10, Book 6, Kubert SUM APP T-164, p. 3 and ibid., Vol. I: Analyses, Ch. 11: Suppression and Withholding of Information, p. 10. • **4.** NA, RG 319, AS, PI-FR, Vol. II: Testimony, Box 45, Book 28, Fagan SUM APP T-67, p. 4; ibid., Box 3, Book 1, Anistranski SUM APP T-135, pp. 2–4 and Bilton and Sim, *Four Hours*, pp. 172, 175–9. • **5.** Brian W.

Livingston, Warrant Officer B Company (Aeroscout), 123rd Aviation Battalion, letter to his wife, 16 Mar. 1968, in NA, RG 319, AS, PI-FR, Vol. III: Exhibits, Box 54, Book 4: Miscellaneous Documents (italics in the original). • **6**. Witness Statement Joseph Gualtier, 16 Jan. 1970, in NA, RG 319, AS, PI-FR, Vol. II: Testimony, Box 10, Book 6, Gualtier SUM APP T-169, p. 12. See also ibid., Vol. IV: CID Statements, Box 57, pp. 46–53; Fact Sheet, To: Chief of Staff, United States Army, Subject: My Lai, 14 Jan. 1970, p. 4, in RG 319, AS, ODCS-PER, VWCWG, MLM, Box 1, Folder: My Lai Army Staff Monitor Summaries, Jan. 1970 and Son My Army Staff Monitor Summary, 14 Mar. 1970, p. 3, in ibid., Folder: My Lai Army Staff Monitor Summaries, Feb.–May 1970. The mood amongst the pilots of 174th Aviation Company was similar: RG 319, AS, PI-FR, Vol. II: Testimony, Box 15, Book 9, McCrary APP T-172, p. 36. • **7**. Maurice E. Vorhies, quoted in Department of the Army, Office of the Judge Advocate General, Memorandum for: The Judge Advocate General, Subject: Report of Informal Investigation, 6 Jun. 1972, p. 5; see ibid., p. 3, in NA, RG 319, AS, PI-AC, Box 40, Folder: Son My Chron. File # 24, 3 May–21 Jun. 1972 (1 of 3). • **8**. NA, RG 319, AS, PI-FR, Vol. I: Analyses, Ch. 11: Suppression and Withholding of Information, p. 11. • **9**. John Ebinger, B Company, 4th Battalion, 3rd Infantry Regiment, 11th Light Infantry Brigade, Americal Division, letter to Lyndon B. Johnson, 30 Jul. 1968, in NA, RG 319, AS, PI-CI, Box 8, Folder: Admin. File – Dec (2). • **10**. Carroll E. Swain, Lieutenant Colonel, Inspector General, letter to Commanding General, United States Army Vietnam, 30 Aug. 1968, in NA, RG 319, AS, PI-FR, Vol. III: Exhibits, Box 54, Book 4: Miscellaneous Documents. • **11**. Tom Glen, A Company, 4th Battalion, 3rd Infantry Regiment, 11th Light Infantry Brigade, Americal Division, letter to General Creighton Abrams, 27 Nov. 1968, in NA, RG 319, AS, PI-CI, Box 8, Folder: Admin. File – Dec (2). See also Bilton and Sim, *Four Hours*, p. 175. • **12** Lieutenant Colonel Albert L. Russell, letter to Commanding General, Americal Division, 11 Dec. 1968, in NA, RG 319, AS, PI-CI, Box 8, Folder: Admin. File – Dec (2). • **13**. Headquarters Americal Division, Award of the Bronze Star Medal, 23 Apr. 1968, in NA, RG 319, AS, PI-FR, Vol. III: Exhibits, Box 54, Book 4: Miscellaneous Documents. Glenn Andreotta was fatally wounded immediately after the operation in My Lai (4) and was posthumously awarded the Bronze Star Medal with 'V' Device. Lawrence Colburn was awarded the same decoration on 14 May 1968. Hugh Thompson was awarded the Distinguished Flying Cross on 1 July 1968. • **14**. This is how Thompson describes the background to the awarding of the medals: Bilton and Sim, *Four Hours*, p. 204ff. Given the fact that documents were destroyed and perjury committed in the Americal Division Headquarters with a high degree of criminal energy, this assertion seems plausible. • **15**. Ronald Haeberle, quoted in ibid., p. 183. Other members of C Company, Task Force Barker, spoke in similar vein: see Sworn Statement Gregory Olsen, 30 Aug. 1969, p. 8, in NA, RG 319, AS, PI-

FR, Vol. IV: CID Statements, Box 57, p. 370. • **16**. Diary entry Thomas R. Partsch, C Company, Task Force Barker, 18 Mar. 1968, in NA, RG 319, AS, PI-FR, Vol. III: Exhibits, Box 54, Book 4: Miscellaneous Documents. • **17**. NA, RG 319, AS, PI-FR, Vol. I: Analyses, Ch. 2: Summary Report, p. 9 and ibid., Vol. II: Testimony, Box 37, Book 23, Medina SUM APP T-5, p. 6. See also Bilton and Sim, *Four Hours*, p. 180. • **18**. NA, RG 319, AS, PI-FR, Vol. I: Analyses, Ch. 11: Suppression and Withholding of Information, pp. 2, 10; ibid., Vol. IV: CID Statements, Box 57, p. 16 and Diary entry Thomas R. Partsch, C Company, Task Force Barker, 18 Mar. 1968, in NA, RG 319, AS, PI-FR, Vol. III: Exhibits, Box 54, Book 4: Miscellaneous Documents. • **19**. An unnamed GI from Task Force Barker, quoted in Bilton and Sim, *Four Hours*, p. 83. • **20**. Witness Statement Floyd D. Wright, C Company, Task Force Barker, 19 Jan. 1970, in NA, RG 319, AS, PI-FR, Vol. II: Testimony, Box 45, Book 28, Wright SUM APP T-180, p. 3. • **21**. Witness Statement Lawrence Colburn, B Company (Aeroscout), 123rd Aviation Battalion, 20 Dec. 1969, in NA, RG 319, AS, PI-FR, Vol. II: Testimony, Box 9, Book 5, Colburn APP T-31, p. 43. • **22**. Witness Statement Lawrence Colburn, B Company (Aeroscout), 123rd Aviation Battalion, 20 Dec. 1969, in NA, RG 319, AS, PI-FR, Vol. II: Testimony, Box 9, Book 5, Colburn APP T-31, p. 39. • **23**. Witness Statement Ernest Marck, 18 Feb. 1970, in NA, RG 319, AS, PI-FR, Vol. II: Testimony, Box 27, Book 17, Marck SUM APP T-379, p. 3. See ibid., Box 10, Book 6, Ezell APP T-208, pp. 13–14; ibid., Box 18, Book 11, Haeberle SUM APP T-174, p. 5; ibid., Box 18, Book 11, Dunn APP T-35, p. 3 and Ford SUM APP T-234, p. 2; ibid., Box 21, Book 13, Moody SUM APP T-211, p. 2; ibid., Box 38, Book 24, Konwinski SUM APP T-271, p. 5; ibid., Box 43, Book 27, Smith SUM APP T-48, p. 3; Testimony Michael D. Terry, C Company, Task Force Barker, 1 May 1969, p. 37, in NA RG 319, AS, PI-AC, Box 45, Folder: Son My – Biographical Data (Individuals Charged) (7 of 10). • **24**. Two unnamed GIs, quoted in Terry, *Bloods*, pp. 43, 128. See ibid., pp. 2ff., 7, 53, 58, 70, 82ff., 93, 166, 254; Baker, *Nam*, pp. 51ff., 55, 75ff., 78, 83–5, 99, 164, 174ff., 189, 199, 204ff., 212ff., 277; MacPherson, *Long Time Passing*, pp. 567–603; Caputo, *Rumor of War*, pp. 290–320; Sworn Statement Leland W. Carpenter, 18 Jan. 1973, p. 14, in NA, RG 319, AS, ODCS-PER, VWCWG, CaFi, Box 18, Folder: Coy Allegation (CID 72 – CID 46 – 27852, Exhibits 1–60), (Part 2 of 7), Case 221. • **25**. Joseph Neilson, Survey, undated, p. 7, in NA, RG 319, AS, PI-AC, Box 5, Folder: Background Info. The interviews were conducted by a member of the Vietnam Veterans Against the War in spring 1971 at San Francisco airport, where the soldiers were waiting for connecting flights home. The questionnaire had been drawn up in multiple-choice style. • **26**. Leaflet, National Liberation Front Committee, Quang Ngai Province, undated, The American Devils Divulge Their True Form, in NA, RG 319, AS, PI-FR, Vol. III: Exhibits, Box 54, Book 3: Reports, pp. 264–5. • **27**. Announcement, National Liberation Front Committee, Quang Ngai

Province, 28 Mar. 1968, p. 3, in NA, RG 319, AS, PI-FR, Vol. III: Exhibits, Box 54, Book 4: Miscellaneous Documents, pp. 145–8. • **28**. Sworn Statement Richard K. Blackledge, 17 Oct. 1969, p. 2, in NA, RG 319, AS, PI-FR, Vol. IV: CID Statements, Box 57, p. 82. • **29**. Memorandum William R. Peers, To: Col. Whalen, Peers Inquiry, MACV IG, Saigon 2 Feb. 1970, in NA, RG 319, PI-CI, Box 1, Folder: Vol. III – Chronology. • **30**. Document of the Committee to Denounce U.S. War Crimes in South Vietnam, published by the PRG Information Bureau in Paris, April 1971: Wholesale Massacres Perpetrated by U.S. Mercenary and Puppet Troops in South Vietnam in the Period between the Son My Case (3/68) and the End of 1970, in NA, RG 319, AS, ODCS-PER, VWCWG, CaFi, Box 1, Folder: Enemy Allegations. Henceforth referred to as PRG Information Bureau. • **31**. PRG Information Bureau, Case 9. The PRG memorandum refers to the provinces of Ben Tre and My Tho. Ben Tre was called Kien Hoa in the 1960s and My Tho was the capital in Dinh Tuong Province, later renamed Tien Giang. Henceforth all provinces are given the names in use at the time of the operations. • **32**. PRG Information Bureau, Case 10. The Chau Binh murders were brought to the attention of the international press by a survivor in December 1969. American media, including the *Baltimore Sun*, reported on them on 20 December 1969. The secret radio transmitter of the National Liberation Front (NLF) in South Vietnam reported on the mass murder of refugees in April 1969; see Unger, 'The Press'. • **33**. PRG Information Bureau, Case 11. • **34**. Ibid., Case 16. • **35**. Ibid., Case 25. • **36**. Sea Tiger was the second phase of Operation Sealords and was carried out as a 'pacification action' on the Cua Dai River and the regions along its banks between February and December 1969. This area situated to the south of Da Nang was a Viet Cong stronghold and the Cua Dai River itself was nicknamed 'Ambush Alley' by American soldiers. US Navy units conducted the 'pacification' to bring peace in conjunction with American and South Vietnamese ground troops. • **37**. Ibid., Case 26. The murder of 700 civilians in the course of this operation was announced by a female representative of the PRG on 20 January 1970 at a plenary session of the Paris ceasefire negotiations: Associated Press, 20 Jan. 1970. • **38**. PRG Information Bureau, Case 31. • **39**. Ibid., Case 28. • **40**. Ibid., Case 32. • **41**. Ibid., Case 33. • **42**. Ibid., Case 38. • **43**. Ibid., Case 39. • **44**. Ibid., Case 40. • **45**. Ibid., Case 42. • **46**. Ibid., Case 43. • **47**. Ibid., Case 45. • **48**. Ibid., Case 48. • **49**. Ibid., Case 49. • **50**. Ibid., Case 50. • **51**. Ibid., Case 52. • **52**. Ibid., Case 55. • **53**. Lyndon B. Johnson, handwritten letter to Creighton Abrams, end October 1968, quoted in Berman, *No Peace*, p. 31. • **54**. Announcement, National Liberation Front Committee, Quang Ngai Province, 28 Mar. 1968, p. 3, in NA, RG 319, AS, PI-FR, Vol. III: Exhibits, Box 54, Book 4: Miscellaneous Documents pp. 145–8. • **55**. See above, pp. 163–4. • **56**. Robert L. Keck, letter to Herman T. Schneebeli, 27 Nov. 1969, pp. 2–3, in NA, RG 319, AS, ODCS-PER, VWCWG, CaFi, Box 3, Folder: Keck Allegation – Re: Schneebeli Letter (Keck Letters

Incl.). • **57**. An unnamed GI quoted in Gross, 'Calley's Army', p. 200. • **58**. Diary entry Thomas R. Partsch, private first class, C Company, 1st Battalion, 20th Infantry Regiment, 11th Light Infantry Brigade, Americal Division, 3 May 1968, in NA, RG 319, AS, PI-FR, Vol. III: Exhibits, Box 54, Book 4: Miscellaneous Documents p. 301. See also Sworn Statement Thomas J. Kinch, 30 Nov. 1970, p. 2, in RG 319, AS, ODCS-PER, VWCWG, CaFi, Box 11, Folder: Fox Allegation, Case 75. • **59**. 23rd Infantry Division (Americal) History. Prepared by 3rd Military History Detachment, Jan. 1971, p. 9, in NA, RG 319, AS, ODCS-PER, VWCWG, CaFi, Box 20, Folder: Hoag Allegation (Part 2 of 4), Case 232.1. See also RG 319, AS, PI-FR, Vol. I: Analyses, Box 1, Ch. 4: Organization, Operations, And Training of US Units, p. 3; Tucker (ed.), *Encyclopedia*, p. 487. • **60**. Lewy, *America in Vietnam*, pp. 151–3. • **61**. After-action report on Operation Pipestone Canyon, quoted in ibid., p. 148. See ibid., p. 141. • **62**. On the US Army side two battalions of Americal Division took part in this operation: 4th Battalion, 3rd Infantry Regiment, 11th Light Infantry Brigade and 5th Battalion, 46th Infantry Regiment, 198th Light Infantry Brigade. • **63**. P/2 – P/3 Daily Staff Journal, 4th Battalion, 3rd Infantry Regiment, 11th Light Infantry Brigade, Americal Division, Situation Report, 13 Feb. 1969, quoted at http://sitrep69/archive, accessed 21 Sep. 2006. • **64**. 23rd Infantry Division (Americal) History. Prepared by 3rd Military History Detachment, Jan. 1971, p. 9, in NA, RG 319, AS, ODCS-PER, VWCWG, CaFi, Box 20, Folder: Hoag Allegation (Part 2 of 4), Case 232.1 and Department of the Army, United States Army CID Agency, Memorandum for: Deputy Secretary of the General Staff, Subject: Scanlan Article, 14 Jul. 1970, Incl. 1 and 2, in NA RG 319, AS, PI-AC, Box 29, Folder: Sensitive Material – My Lai – Folder # 6. • **65**. Fact Sheet, Subject: Son My Village, 29 Nov. 1969, p. 2, in NA, RG 319, AS, PI-OI, Box 5, Folder: MACV Report (7). See also Lewy, *America in Vietnam*, p. 141. • **66**. PRG Information Bureau, Case 10. • **67**. Vanderbilt University, Television News Archive: Vietnam/Viet Cong Charge, in http://openweb.tvnews.vandervilt.edu/1969-11/1969-11-28-CBS, accessed 21 Sep. 2006. • **68**. Unger, 'The Press'. • **69**. Memorandum for Secretary of the General Staff: Incident Report 28 Jan. 1970, in NA RG 319, AS, PI-AC, Box 33, Folder: Son My Chron. File # 6 (2 of 2); RG 319, AS, ODCS-PER, VWCWG, CaFi, Box 5, Folder: Blauveldt Allegation; Department of the Army, Memorandum for: Secretary of the General Staff, Subject: Incident Report, 28 Jan. 1970, in RG 319, AS, PI-AC, Box 33, Folder: Son My Chron. File # 6 (2 of 2) and Sworn Statement Michael A. Bernhardt, 24 Feb. 1970, pp. 1–2, in RG 319, AS, ODCS-PER, VWCWG, CaFi, Box 5, Folder: Blauveldt Allegation. Theodore Blauveldt served in 5th Battalion, 46th Infantry Regiment, 198th Light Infantry Brigade, Americal Division from March to June 1968 and in 4th Battalion, 21st Infantry

Regiment, 11th Light Infantry Brigade, Americal Division, from June 1968 to July 1969. The latter unit, the 4/21, was not involved in Russell Beach/Bold Mariner; however there are grounds for assuming that Blauveldt had been informed by a colleague in the 5/46 – his former unit which had participated in the aforementioned pacification action on the Batangan Peninsula after January 1969. • **70**. Miss Lien Allegation, as of 6 Jun. 1971, in NA, RG 319, AS, ODCS-PER, VWCWG, CaFi, Box 16, Folder: Miss Lien Allegation (Transferred to USMC), Case 164. • **71**. Department of the Army, United States Army CID Agency, Memorandum for: Deputy Secretary of the General Staff, Subject: Scanlan Article, 14 Jul. 1970, p. 2 and Incl. 2, § 1 e (emphasis in original), in NA RG 319, AS, PI-AC, Box 29, Folder: Sensitive Material – My Lai – Folder # 6. • **72**. See above, pp. 106–7. • **73**. Solis, *Son Thang*, pp. 20–30, 94–6, 145–55, 177. • **74**. Ibid, pp. 67–73. • **75**. Private First Class Danny S. Notley, E Company, 4th Battalion, 21st Infantry Regiment, 11th Light Infantry Brigade, Americal Division, ascribed this statement to Lieutenant Michael L. Bourgoine: 'Viet Women Say GIs Kill 60 Villagers', *Washington Post*, 10 May 1971. • **76**. NA, RG 319, AS, ODCS-PER, VWCWG, CaFi, Box 12, Folders: Notley Allegation (CCI), Part 1 of 2, Case 85 and Part 2 of 2, Case 85; ibid., Folder: Notley Allegation (Talking Papers), Case 85 and Folder: Notley Allegation (Press/Media), Case 85. See also Gross, 'Calley's Army', p. 154ff. • **77**. 'Viet Women Say GIs Kill 60 Villagers', *Washington Post*, 10 May 1971. • **78**. NA, RG 319, AS, ODCS-PER, VWCWG, CaFi, Box 11, Folder: Brenman-Beitzel Allegation (VVAW), Case 80. See also *Ramparts*, Feb. 1971. • **79**. NA, RG 319, AS, ODCS-PER, VWCWG, CaFi, Box 12, Folder: Notley Allegation (CCI), Part 1 of 2, Case 85. • **80**. Department of the Army, Office of the Secretary of the Army, Memorandum for the Record, Subject: Resume of Hearing, 29 Apr. 1971, Incl.: Substantiation, pp. 5–6, and Merlin S. Kuhlman, Investigator's Statement, 28 Jun. 1971, pp. 4–5, in NA, RG 319, AS, ODCS-PER, VWCWG, CaFi, Box 12, Folder: Notley Allegation (CCI), Part 1 of 2, Case 85. • **81**. Sworn Statement Larry M. Farmer, 29 Jun. 1972, p. 2, in NA, RG 319, AS, ODCS-PER, VWCWG, CaFi, Box 20, Folder: Hoag Allegation (Part 1 of 4), Case 232.1. • **82**. NA, RG 319, AS, ODCS-PER, VWCWG, CaFi, Box 20, Folder: Hoag Allegation (Part 1 of 4), Case 232.1 and ibid., Folder: Hoag Allegation (Part 2 of 4), Case 232.1. • **83**. Department of the Army, Judge Advocate General, Military Justice Division, Memorandum for Record, DAJA-MJ 1972/13221, Subject: Private First Class Julio Colon-Madera and Summary Fact Sheet, in NA, RG 319, AS, ODCS-PER, VWCWG, CaFi, Box 20, Folder: Hoag Allegation (Part 1 of 4). Case 232.1. In the following days the same platoon murdered two unarmed men and raped several women. • **84**. Department of the Army, United States Army Criminal Investigation Command, Memorandum for: Secretary of the Army, Subject: Hoag Allegation, 20 Oct. 1972, p. 4, in NA, RG 319, AS, ODCS-PER, VWCWG, CaFi, Box 20, Folder: Hoag

Allegation (Talking Papers), Case 232.2. • **85**. Sworn Statement Davey V. Hoag, 5 May 1972, p. 3, in NA, RG 319, AS, ODCS-PER, VWCWG, CaFi, Box 20, Folder: Hoag Allegation (Part 2 of 4), Case 232.1. • **86**. Headquarters, 198th Infantry Brigade, Americal Division, Subject: Report of Investigation, 9 Jul. 1969, Confidential, in NA, RG 319, AS, PI-AC, Box 20, Folder: Other Than Son My. Ky Trong Incident: Subject/ Suspects: Bell, Barnhart, Herron, Applegath. See also ibid., Box 38, Folder: Son My Chron. File # 19 (Part 2 of 2): Seymour Hersh Interview Report, 4 Jun.1971. The best journalistic research comes from Hersh, 'The Reprimand'. • **87**. Headquarters, 198th Infantry Brigade, Americal Division, Subject: Report of Investigation, 9 Jul. 1969, Confidential, pp. 7–9, in NA, RG 319, AS, PI-AC, Box 20, Folder: Other Than Son My. Ky Trong Incident: Subject/Suspects: Bell, Barnhart, Herron, Applegath. • **88**. Ibid., p. 8. • **89**. NA, RG 319, AS, ODCS-PER, VWCWG, CaFi, Box 6, Folder: Norris Allegation. One pilot reported in the *New York Times* on similar practices in Quang Ngai Province: 'Most Helicopter Pilots Are Eager for Duty in Vietnam', *New York Times*, 26 Apr. 1971. • **90**. Neal Incident, as of 26 Oct. 1973, in NA, RG 319, AS, ODCS-PER, VWCWG, CaFi, Box 21, Folder: Neal Allegation, Case 238. • **91**. Norris Allegation, as of 20 May 1970, in NA, RG 319, AS, ODCS-PER, VWCWG, CaFi, Box 6, Folder: Norris Allegation and ibid., Box 13, Folder: New York Times Allegation (Correspondence, Congressional Inquiries and Background Information), Case 92. • **92**. This refers to the Cases 9, 23, 31, 32, 40, 42, 45, 48, 49 and 50, set out in the above document. • **93**. The document provided by the PRG Information Bureau in April 1971 refers to Cases 3, 4, 20, 22, 23, 28, 29, 31, 32, 36, 37, 40, 41, 42, 45, 46 and 54. In six Cases (28, 31, 32, 40, 42 and 45) the operations were carried out in conjunction with US troops. • **94**. Headquarters, USAV, 16th MHD, Subject: Combat After Action Report of Operation SPEEDY EXPRESS, 14 Jun. 1969, Secret, p. 4, in NA, RG 472, USFSEA, USAV, CH, OSE-BF, Box 15, Folder: Speedy Express Report/16th MHD 14 Jun. 69. • **95**. Headquarters, 9th Infantry Division, Subject: LOI 7-69 (Kien Hoa Province Campaign, CY 69), 16 Jan. 1969, Confidential, Section 1, p. 1. • **96**. Department of the Army, Southeast Asia Analysis Report, Jul. 1969, Secret NOFORN, p. 20, in NA, RG 319, AS, PI-AC, Box 19, Folder: Operation SPEEDY EXPRESS (2 of 2), Chron. File # 1. • **97**. Melvin Gurtov, The RAND Corporation, Memorandum RM-5353-ISA ARPA, Sep. 1967, The War in the Delta: Views from Three Viet Cong Battalions, p. 5. See also Annex A (Intelligence) to OPLAN 1-68 (Dry Season Offensive), 22 Oct. 1968, Secret, p. 4, in NA, RG 472, USFSEA, USAV, CH, OSE-BF, Box 11, Folder: Update/OPLAN 1-68; Headquarters, 9th Infantry Division, Subject: Recommendation for Award of the Presidential Unit Citation, undated, pp. 1, 16, in NA, RG 472, USAV, MHD, 19th MHD, HBF, Box 7, Folder: Presidential Unit Citations, Recommended + Awarded 9th Inf Div 25 Jan.–26 Apr. 69; Spector, *After Tet*,

p. 145. • **98**. Central Intelligence Agency, Directorate of Intelligence, Intelligence Memorandum: Pacification in the Wake of the Tet Offensive in South Vietnam, 19 Mar. 1968, pp. 1, 34, in Texas Tech University, Vietnam Archive, Declassified Documents Reference System, No. 1990-003034. • **99**. Annex A (Intelligence) to OPLAN 1-68 (Dry Season Offensive), 22 Oct. 1968, Secret, p. 8, in NA, RG 472, USFSEA, USAV, CH, OSE-BF, Box 11, Folder: Update/OPLAN 1-68. See also ibid., pp. 9–11 and Headquarters, USA-AG, IV CTZ Advisory Team 96, Subject: Operation Plan, IV CTZ Dry Weather Offensive, 18 Oct. 1968, Secret, pp. 1–2, in RG 472, USFSEA, USAV, CH, OSE-BF, Box 11, Folder: Dry Weather Offensive/OPLAN 1-68/IV CTZ 18 Oct. 68; Headquarters, 9th Infantry Division, Subject: Recommendation for Award of the Presidential Unit Citation, undated, pp. 1, 16, in NA, RG 472, USAV, MHD, 19th MHD, HBF, Box 7, Folder: Presidential Unit Citations, Recommended + Awarded 9th Inf Div 25 Jan.–26 Apr. 69 and Department of the Army, 3rd Brigade, 9th Infantry Division, Subject: Quarterly Evaluation, 1 Oct. 1968, Confidential, pp. 1–3, in RG 472, USAV, MHD, 19th MHD, HBF, Box 5, Folder: Qtrly. Eval. Rpts/1st + 2nd Qtrs./9th Inf 68. • **100**. Department of the Army, Headquarters 1st Brigade, 9th Infantry Division, Subject: Intelligence After Action Report for Operation in AO Kudzu, 20 Nov.–17 Dec. 1968, Confidential, p. 2, in NA, RG 472, USFSEA, USAV, CH, OSE-BF, Box 15, Folder: AAR/9th Inf Div/Kudzu, 16 Feb. 69 and Senior Advisor, Headquarters, IV CTZX, Subject: IV Corps Outlook, December 1968, Confidential, p. 2, in ibid., Box 12, Folder: Documents/SA, IV CTZ 1–15 Dec. 68. See ibid., Box 12, Folder: Messages/SA IV CTZ Oct.–Dec. 68. • **101**. Major General George S. Eckhardt, Senior Advisor, US Army Advisory Group, Advisory Team 96, IV Corps Tactical Zone, letter to General Creighton Abrams, 3 Aug. 1968, in NA, RG 472, USFSEA, USAV, CH, OSE-BF, Box 11, Folder: Ltr./MG Eckhardt to Gen. Abrams/Proposed Dry Weather Campaign/3 Aug. 68. See also CORDS Field Overview, IV Corps Tactical Zone for the Period Ending 31 May 1968, undated, Confidential, p. 6, in RG 319, AS, PI-OI, Box 4, Folder: MACV Reports (3); Robert W. Komer, letter to James P. Grant, Agency for International Development, 18 Apr. 1968, in ibid., Box 5, Folder: MACV Reports (8); Interview with Major Caddigan, undated, p. 1, in RG 472, USFSEA, USAV, CH, OSE-BF, Box 11, Folder: AAR/Planning Documents/C-E/20th MHD Oct.–Dec. 68 and Headquarters, USAV, 16th MHD, Subject: Combat After Action Report of Operation SPEEDY EXPRESS, 14 Jun. 1969, Secret, p. 1, in ibid., Box 15, Folder: Speedy Express Report/16th MHD 14 Jun. 69. See also RG 472, USFSEA, USAV, CH, OSE-BF, Box 16, Folder: Interview/Maj. John T. Giambruno, S-3, 34th Engr. Group, 20th Eng Bde, 2 Dec. 68 and ibid., Box 12, Folder: Messages/SA IV CTZ Oct.–Dec. 68. • **102**. Headquarters, USAV, 16th MHD, Subject: Combat After Action Report of Operation SPEEDY EXPRESS, 14 Jun. 1969, Secret, p. 41: see ibid., Foreword and pp. 17, 34, 43, in NA, RG 472, USFSEA, USAV, CH, OSE-BF, Box 15, Folder: 'Speedy Express' Report/16th MHD 14 Jun. 69 and Headquarters, USA-AG, IV CTZ, Advisory Team 96, Subject: Operation Plan, IV CTZ Dry Weather Offensive, 18 Oct. 1968, Secret, p. 2, in RG 472, USFSEA, USAV, CH, OSE-BF, Box 11, Folder: Dry Weather Offensive/OPLAN 1-68/IV CTZ 18 Oct. 68. • 103. Headquarters, 9th Infantry Division, Subject: Recommendation for Award of the Presidential Unit Citation, undated, p. 92: Summary of Strength and Casualties, in NA, RG 472, USAV, MHD, 19th MHD, HBF, Box 7, Folder: Presidential Unit Citations, Recommended + Awarded 9th Inf Div 25 Jan.–26 Apr. 69. For the total strength of the Viet Cong in the IV CTZ, see also Annex A (Intelligence) to OPLAN 1-68 (Dry Season Offensive), 22 Oct. 1968, Secret, pp. 7–11, in NA, RG 472, USFSEA, USAV, CH, OSE-BF, Box 11, Folder: Update/OPLAN 1-68 and Headquarters, USA-AG, IV CTZ, Advisory Team 96, Subject: Operation Plan, IV CTZ Dry Weather Offensive, 18 Oct. 1968, Secret, p. 1, in RG 472, USFSEA, USAV, CH, OSE-BF, Box 11, Folder: Dry Weather Offensive/OPLAN 1-68/IV CTZ 18 Oct. 68. In 'Project Takeoff 1968' CORDS had set the target for the elimination of 12,000 Viet Cong political leaders for 1968: Project Takeoff 1968, CORDS, IV Corps Tactical Zone, May 1968, Appendix A, p. 2, in RG 319, AS, PI-OI, Box 4, Folder: MACV Reports (3). • 104. 9th Infantry Division, 9th Military Intelligence Detachment, Intelligence Bulletin # 3, Subject: Viet Cong Infrastructure, 4 Dec. 1968, Confidential, p. 3, in NA, RG 472, USAV, MHD, HBF, Box 4, Folder: OPORDS/Misc. OPNS Folder I '68. • 105. Headquarters, USA-AG, IV CTZ, Advisory Team 96, Subject: Operation Plan, IV CTZ Dry Weather Offensive, 18 Oct. 1968, Secret, p. 3, in RG 472, USFSEA, USAV, CH, OSE-BF, Box 11, Folder: Dry Weather Offensive/OPLAN 1-68/IV CTZ 18 Oct. 68 and Headquarters, USAV, 16th MHD, Subject: Combat After Action Report of Operation SPEEDY EXPRESS, 14 Jun. 1969, Secret, p. 3, in ibid., Box 15, Folder: 'Speedy Express' Report/16th MHD 14 Jun. 69. • 106. Headquarters 9th Infantry Division, Summary of the 9th Infantry Division Activities to Thwart the VC Winter–Spring Offensive, 1 Jan. 1969 to 31 May 1969, undated, p. 6, in NA, RG 472, USAV, 9th Infantry Division, Organizational History, Box 1, Folder: Unit Awards. • 107. Units from 1st Brigade were: 6th Battalion, 31st Infantry Regiment and 2nd, 3rd and 4th Battalions (all from 39th Infantry Regiment); they were mainly deployed in Dinh Tuong. 2nd Brigade deployed 3rd and 4th Battalions from 47th Infantry Regiment and 3rd Battalion from 60th Infantry Regiment; these units fought in Kien Hoa Province: Department of the Army, Southeast Asia Analysis Report, Jul. 1969, Secret, NOFORN, pp. 21–2, in NA, RG 319, AS, PI-AC, Box 19, Folder: Operation SPEEDY EXPRESS (2 of 2) Chron. File # 1. For the overall strength of the allied formations, see Headquarters, 9th Infantry Division, Subject: Recommendation for Award of the Presidential Unit Citation, undated, p. 92: Summary of Strength and

Casualties, in NA, RG 472, USAV, MHD, 19th MHD, HBF, Box 7, Folder: Presidential Unit Citations, Recommended + Awarded 9th Inf Div 25 Jan.–26 Apr. 69. • **108**. Troops taking part were: D Troop, 3rd Squadron, 5th Cavalry Regiment and B and D Troops from 3rd Squadron, 17th Cavalry Regiment: Pertinent Data Operation Speedy Express (1 Dec. 1968–31 May 1969), undated, Secret, p. 1, in NA, RG 319, AS, PI-AC, Box 19, Folder: Operation SPEEDY EXPRESS (1 of 2) Chron. File # 1. • **109**. Headquarters, USA-AG, IV CTZ, Advisory Team 96, Subject: Operation Plan, IV CTZ Dry Weather Offensive, 18 Oct. 1968, Secret, p. 4, in RG 472, USFSEA, USAV, CH, OSE-BF, Box 11, Folder: Dry Weather Offensive/OPLAN 1-68/IV CTZ 18 Oct. 68. • **110**. In the first quarter of 1969 about 3,300 ARVN soldiers deserted, almost double as many as the American military estimated that a force of this size could tolerate: Headquarters, USA-AG, IV CTZ, Advisory Team 96, Subject: First Quarter Review of Implementation of Combined Campaign Plan 1969, AB-144, 10 Apr. 1969, Secret, Section 15, pp. 1, 2, in NA, RG 472, USFSEA, USAV, CH, OSE-BF, Box 14, Folder: C.C.P. 69/1st Qtr. Review 1969. See also ibid., Box 12, Folder: Messages/SA IV CTZ Oct.–Dec. 68. • **111**. Julian J. Ewell to Senior Advisor, IV Corps, 4 Oct. 1968, Secret, p. 1, in NA, RG 472, USFSEA, USAV, CH, OSE-BF, Box 12, Folder: Recommended Tactics/CG 9th US Div to SA, IV CTZ, 15 + 20 Sep. 68. • **112**. Headquarters 9th Infantry Division, Subject: Quarterly Evaluation 2nd Quarter 1969, 10 Jul. 1969, Confidential, p. 7, in NA, RG 472, USAV, MHD, 19th MHD, HBF, Box 5, Folder: Qtrly. Eval. Rpts/1st + 2nd Qtrs./9th Inf. 68. See also Headquarters, 164th Aviation Group, Subject: Air Cavalry Operations in the Delta, 1 Nov. 1968, p. 2, in NA, RG 472, USFSEA, USAV, CH, OSE-BF, Box 11, Folder: Air Cav. OPNS in the Delta/1st Avn Bde, Nov. 68. • **113**. Headquarters, 9th Infantry Division, Subject: Recommendation for Award of the Presidential Unit Citation, undated, p. 1, in NA, RG 472, USAV, MHD, 19th MHD, HBF, Box 7, Folder: Presidential Unit Citations, Recommended + Awarded 9th Inf Div 25 Jan.–26 Apr. 69. • **114**. Headquarters, 9th Infantry Division, Subject: Recommendation for Award of the Presidential Unit Citation, undated, pp. 16–26: in NA, RG 472, USAV, MHD, 19th MHD, HBF, Box 7, Folder: Presidential Unit Citations, Recommended + Awarded 9th Inf Div 25 Jan.–26 Apr. 69; Headquarters, 9th Infantry Division, Subject: LOI 15-69, 6 Feb. 1969, Confidential, Incl. 1: Concept of Night Search Tactics, p. 1, in RG 472, USAV, MHD, 19th MHD, HBF, Box 6, Folder: OPORD/Toan Thang/9th Inf. Div. '68; Headquarters, USAV, 16th MHD, Subject: Combat After Action Report of Operation SPEEDY EXPRESS 14 Jun. 1969, Secret, p. 48, in ibid., Box 15, Folder: Speedy Express Report/16th MHD 14 Jun. 69; Department of the Army, 8th MHD, 1st Aviation Brigade, Snipers Operating with Gunships from B Troop, 3rd Squadron, 17th Air Cavalry, p. 1, in RG 472, USFSEA, USAV, CH, OSE-BF, Box 15, File: Gunship Snipers/9th US DIV/8th MHD, 1st Avn Bde, Apr. 69; Overview, Operation

Speedy Express, IV Corps Tactical Zone, 26 Jan. 1972, in RG 472, USFSEA, MACV, IG, ID, ROI, Box 143, Folder: Allegations by Newsweek re 9th Inf Div + The Delta (Part 1 of 2). • **115**. Headquarters, 9th Infantry Division, Subject: Recommendation for Award of the Presidential Unit Citation, undated, pp. 25–7, in NA, RG 472, USAV, MHD, 19th MHD, HBF, Box 7, Folder: Presidential Unit Citations, Recommended + Awarded 9th Inf Div 25 Jan.–6 Apr. 69. The sharpshooters were first deployed with B Troop, 3rd Squadron, 17th Air Cavalry Regiment in December 1968. Part of the time the snipers also accompanied ground patrols: Department of the Army, 8th MHD, 1st Aviation Brigade, Snipers Operating with Gunships from B Troop, 3rd Squadron, 17th Air Cavalry, p. 1, in RG 472, USFSEA, USAV, CH, OSE-BF, Box 15, File: Gunship Snipers / 9th US DIV / 8th MHD, 1st Avn Bde, Apr. 69 and Appendix 6 (Tactical Techniques Employed) to Annex K (9th US Div After Action Report) to Combat Operations After Action Report (Speedy Express), undated, Confidential, pp. 8–10, in RG 319, AS, PI-AC, Box 19, Folder: Operation SPEEDY EXPRESS (2 of 2) Chron. File # 1. • **116**. Headquarters, 9th Infantry Division, Subject: Recommendation for Award of the Presidential Unit Citation, undated, p. 18, in NA, RG 472, USAV, MHD, 19th MHD, HBF, Box 7, Folder: Presidential Unit Citations, Recommended + Awarded 9th Inf Div 25 Jan.–26 Apr. 69 (italics in the original). See also Headquarters, 9th Infantry Division, Subject: Quarterly Evaluation 3rd Quarter 68, 11 Oct. 1968, Confidential, p. 13, in RG 472, USAV, MHD, 19th MHD, HBF, Box 7, Folder: Quarterly Evaluation Oct. 68 and Appendix 6 (Tactical Techniques Employed) to Annex K (9th US Div After Action Report) to Combat Operations After Action Report (Speedy Express), undated, Confidential, pp. 1–2, in RG 319, AS, PI-AC, Box 19, Folder: Operation SPEEDY EXPRESS (2 of 2) Chron. File # 1. • **117**. Headquarters, 9th Infantry Division, Subject: Recommendation for Award of the Presidential Unit Citation, undated, p. 23, in NA, RG 472, USAV, MHD, 19 MHD, HBF, Box 7, Folder: Presidential Unit Citations, Recommended + Awarded 9th Inf Div 25 Jan.–26 Apr. 69. • **118**. Headquarters, 9th Infantry Division, Subject: Recommendation for Award of the Presidential Unit Citation, undated, pp. 20, 66–8, 90, in NA, RG 472, USAV, MHD, 19th MHD, HBF, Box 7, Folder: Presidential Unit Citations, Recommended + Awarded 9th Inf Div 25 Jan.–26 Apr. 69. • **119**. Captain Donald Price, Commanding Officer, A Company, 3rd Battalion, 39th Infantry Regiment, 1st Brigade, 9th Infantry Division, Combat After Action Interview 5-67, 17 Nov. 1967, p. 6, in NA, RG 472, USAV, MHD, 19th MHD, AAI, Box 9, Folder: Folder III AA-Interview (67); see ibid., Folder: Folder I AA Interview (68). 3rd Battalion, 39th Infantry Regiment was also involved in Speedy Express from December 1968. • **120**. Headquarters, 9th Infantry Division, Subject: Recommendation for Award of the Presidential Unit Citation, undated, p. 28, in NA, RG 472, USAV, MHD, 19th MHD, HBF, Box 7, Folder: Presidential Unit Citations,

Recommended + Awarded 9th Inf Div 25 Jan.–26 Apr. 69. • **121**. Department of the Army, 8th MHD, 1st Aviation Brigade, Snipers Operating with Gunships from B Troop, 3rd Squadron, 17th Air Cavalry, p. 4, in RG 472, USFSEA, USAV, CH, OSE-BF, Box 15, File: Gunship Snipers/9th US DIV/8th MHD, 1st Avn Bde, Apr. 69. See also Headquarters, 9th Infantry Division, Subject: Recommendation for Award of the Presidential Unit Citation, undated, p. 25, in NA, RG 472, USAV, MHD, 19th MHD, HBF, Box 7, Folder: Presidential Unit Citations, Recommended + Awarded 9th Inf Div 25 Jan.–6 Apr. 69. • **122**. Pertinent Data Operation Speedy Express (1 Dec. 1968–31 May 1969), undated, Secret, p. 3, in NA, RG 319, AS, PI-AC, Box 19, Folder: Operation SPEEDY EXPRESS (1 of 2) Chron. File # 1. • **123**. From mid December supervision lay with the Senior Advisor of the US Army Advisory Group, IV Corps Tactical Zone: Department of the Army, Office Chief of Staff Army, Office Memorandum to General Westmoreland, General Palmer, 12 Jun. 1972, Secret, p. 1, in NA, RG 319, AS, PI-AC, Box 19, Folder: Operation SPEEDY EXPRESS (1 of 2) Chron. File # 1. • **124**. Fact Sheet, Subject: Allegations Against LTG Julian J. Ewell, 13 May 1971, in NA, RG 319, AS, ODCS-PER, VWCWG, CaFi, Box 12, Folder: Haywood Allegation (Reported Separately), Case 84. Ewell is supposed to have described his command and control helicopter as a 'gook mobile': USCR, 7 Apr. 1971, p. E2923. Admiral Salzer spoke in retrospect about the body-count fever amongst senior commanders of 9th Infantry Division in the following words: 'He [a 9th Infantry Division brigadier] was a super fanatic on body count. He would talk about nothing else during an operation . . . You could almost see the saliva dripping out of the corners of his mouth. An awful lot of his bodies were civilians.' Quoted in Spector, *After Tet*, p. 221. • **125**. Fact Sheet, Subject: Allegations Against LTG Julian J. Ewell, 13 May 1971, in NA, RG 319, AS, ODCS-PER, VWCWG, CaFi, Box 12, Folder: Haywood Allegation (Reported Separately), Case 84. On CBS television Ewell said that he did not want to be drawn into mud-slinging but that he stood by 9th Infantry Division and the fact that they had done their job in Vietnam very well – namely, to kill as many of the enemy as possible. • **126**. Julian J. Ewell, Debriefing Report, quoted in Lewy, *America in Vietnam*, p. 143. • **127**. II Field Force had operational control over all allied forces in III Corps Tactical Zone. In this post too Ewell stood as out as a body-count fanatic, according to a communications officer employed in the headquarters of 25th Infantry Division: see Vietnam War Crimes Hearings, http://members.aol.com./warlibrary/vwch1.htm, accessed 31 Aug. 2004. • **128**. For Ewell's time with 9th Infantry Division, see also King, *Death of the Army* and Bunting, *Lionheads*. Bunting's book concerns the illiterate memoirs of a GI stationed in the Mekong Delta in 1968. His protagonist George Simpson Lemming is modeled on Julian J. Ewell. • **129**. 'Concerned Sgt.' to Major General William A. Enemark, 30 Jul. 1971, in NA, RG 319, AS, ODCS-PER, VWCWG, CaFi, Box

1, Folder: Concerned Sergeant Allegation. The letters to William West-moreland and Orwin C. Talbott are also in this folder. Strangely enough, Speedy Express played little part in the Winter Soldiers' hearings, one exception being the statement of Gregory R. Motoka, who gave evidence to the Citizens' Commission of Inquiry on US War Crimes in Vietnam (CCI) on 1 Dec. 1970: see RG 319, AS, ODCS-PER, VWCWG, CaFi, Box 11, Folder: Motoka Allegation, Case 72. • **130**. 'Concerned Sgt.' to General William C. Westmoreland, 25 May 1970, in NA, RG 319, AS, ODCS-PER, VWCWG, CaFi, Box 1, Folder: Concerned Sergeant Allegation. Unless otherwise marked, the following quotations are all taken from the letter to William A. Enemark dated 30 Jul. 1971. • **131**. David H. Hackworth describes his time in the Mekong Delta in a book he co-wrote with Eilhys England which appeared in 2002: *The Hopeless to Hardcore Transformation of 4th Battalion, 39th Infantry*. The title says it all: Hackworth declares himself proud of having transformed the 4/39 into a hardbitten fighting unit, and having executed Julian J. Ewell's command: 'It's a pussy battalion, Colonel. I want tigers, not pussies.' Ibid., p. 1. Hackworth wrote his triumphalistic war memoirs in a further book, *About Face*. • **132**. Air observers responsible for directing and coordinating fighter aircraft in their final approach. • **133**. Jeff Record, Richard Wilson, Paul Molineaux, letter to Province Senior Advisor, Bac Lieu, 7 Apr. 1969, p. 2, in NA, RG 319, AS, ODCS-PER, VWCWG, CaFi, Box 13, Folder: Record Allegation (Congressional Inquiries and Background Information), Case 90. See also Sworn Statement Jeffrey Record, 2 Sep. 1971, in ibid. • **134**. This observation of Record's was confirmed by a South Vietnamese major to the Criminal Investigation Division: Sworn Statement Le Van Sy, 7 Jun. 1972, in NA, RG 319, AS, ODCS-PER, VWCWG, CaFi, Box 13, Folder: Record Allegation, Case 90. • **135**. Record, 'Maximizing Cobra Utilization', pp. 9. 10, 12 (italics in the original). • **136**. Paul D. Molineaux, letter to the Editors, *Washington Monthly*, 13 May 1971, p. 1, in NA, RG 319, AS, ODCS-PER, VWCWG, CaFi, Box 13, Folder: Record Allegation, Case 90. • **137**. Vistica, 'One Awful Night'. See also id., *The Education of Lieutenant Kerrey*. • **138**. Robert Kerrey, quoted in Vistica, 'One Awful Night'. • **139**. Ibid. • **140**. US Army Radio Log, 27 Feb. 1969, quoted in ibid. • **141**. Colonel David H. Hackworth, quoted in Valentine, 'Fragging Bob'. • **142**. 'Concerned Sgt.' to Major General W.A. Enemark, 30 Jul. 1971, in NA, RG 319, AS, ODCS-PER, VWCWG, CaFi, Box 1, Folder: Concerned Sergeant Allegation. • **143**. PRG Information Bureau, Case 9. • **144**. NA, RG 472, USFSEA, MACV, IG, ID, ROI, Box 143, Folder: Allegations by Newsweek Re 9th Inf Div + The Delta (Part 1 of 2). • **145**. Buckley, 'Deadly Price', p. 43. • **146**. Maurice L. Clouser, Chief, Investigations Division, MACV, Operation Speedy Express – Allegations in Newsweek Article and Comments Concerning, 23 Jun. 1972, pp. 2, 3, 4, in NA, RG 472, USFSEA, MACV, IG, ID, ROI, Box 143, Folder: Allegations by Newsweek Re 9th Inf Div + The Delta (Part 1 of 2).

• **147**. Maurice L. Clouser, Chief, Investigations Division, MACV, Operation Speedy Express – Allegations in Newsweek Article and Comments Concerning, 23 Jun. 1972, pp. 2, 5, in NA, RG 472, USFSEA, MACV, IG, ID, ROI, Box 143, Folder: Allegations by Newsweek Re 9th Inf Div + The Delta (Part 1 of 2). See also ibid., Phillip H. Stevens, Chief of Information MACV, Memorandum to COMUSMACV, 29 Nov. 1971 and John T. Carley, Assistant Chief of Staff MACV, J 3, Memorandum to Chief of Staff MACV, 26 Jan. 1972, Confidential, Subject: Overview of Operations in the Delta, 1 Dec. 1968–31 May 1969, IV CTZ Overview – Incl. 2 (IV CTZ Results) and Overview, Operation Speedy Express, 9th US Division, p. 5. For the number of victims, see also Headquarters, USA-AG, IV CTZ, Advisory Team 96, Subject: First Quarter Review of Implementation of Combined Campaign Plan 1969, AB-144, 10 Apr. 1969, Secret, Section 11, p. 2, in NA, RG 472, USFSEA, USAV, CH, OSE-BF, Box 14, Folder: C.C.P. 69/1st Qtr. Review 1969. • **148**. Figures vary between 245 and 292: John T. Carley, Assistant Chief of Staff, MACV, J 3, Memorandum to Chief of Staff MACV, 26 Jan. 1972, Confidential, Subject: Overview of Operations in the Delta, 1 Dec. 1968–31 May 1969, Overview, Operation Speedy Express, 9th US Division – Incl. 4 (Casualties by Week), 5 (Composite Casualties), 6 (Weapons Captured), 7 (Comparative Data by Division), in NA, RG 472, USFSEA, MACV, IG, ID, ROI, Box 143, Folder: Allegations by Newsweek Re 9th Inf Div + The Delta (Part 1 of 2). • **149**. A ratio of even 1:54 is noted in the files for the second quarter of 1969: 9th Infantry Division in Vietnam, Dec. 1966–Jul. 1969, Statistics, p. 12: Enemy Losses/US KIA, in NA, RG 472, USAV, 9th Infantry Division, Organizational History, Box 1, Folder: Publications. • **150**. Harris W. Hollis to Commanding General, II Field Force Vietnam, undated, in NA, RG 472, USAV, MHD, 19th MHD, HBF, Box 7, Folder: Presidential Unit Citations, Recommended + Awarded 9th Inf Div 25 Jan.–26 Apr. 69. • **151**. 9th Infantry Division in Vietnam, Dec. 1966–Jul. 1969, Statistics, p. 2: Annual Results, in NA, RG 472, USAV, 9th Infantry Division, Organizational History, Box 1, Folder: Publications. • **152**. Operation Enterprise, in NA, RG 472, USAV, MHD, BHF, Box 4, Folder: OPORDS/Enterprise 1967–68. For Operation Enterprise, see ibid., Box 5, Folder: Operations in VN/9th Inf Div 1967–68 and Folder: Qtrly. Eval. Repts/1st + 2nd Qtrs./9th Inf 68. • **153**. John T. Carley, Assistant Chief of Staff, MACV, J 3, Memorandum to Chief of Staff MACV, 26 Jan. 1972, Confidential, Subject: Overview of Operations in the Delta, 1 Dec. 1968–31 May 1969, IV CTZ Overview – Incl. 2: IV CTZ Results, in NA, RG 472, USFSEA, MACV, IG, ID, ROI, Box 143, Folder: Allegations by Newsweek Re 9th Inf Div + The Delta (Part 1 of 2). • **154**. John T. Carley, Assistant Chief of Staff, MACV, J 3, Memorandum to Chief of Staff MACV, 26 Jan. 1972, Confidential, Subject: Overview of Operations in the Delta, 1 Dec. 1968–31 May 1969, Overview, Operation Speedy Express, 9th US Division, pp. 4–9, in ibid.; Headquarters, 9th Infantry Division, Subject: Recommendation for Award of the Presidential Unit Citation, undated, Summary, p. 2, in: NA, RG 472, USAV, MHD, 19th MHD, HBF, Box 7, Folder: Presidential Unit Citations, Recommended + Awarded 9th Inf Div 25 Jan.–26 Apr. 69. • **155**. Phillip H. Stevens, Chief of Information, MACV, to Kevin Buckley, 14 Dec. 1971, in NA, RG 472, USFSEA, MACV, IG, ID, ROI, Box 143, Folder: Allegations by Newsweek Re 9th Inf Div + The Delta (Part 1 of 2). The data about tactical air operations are contradictory. 3,381 'tactical air attacks' are mentioned elsewhere: Department of the Army, Office Chief of Staff Army, Office Memorandum to General Westmoreland, General Palmer, 12 Jun. 1972, Secret, p. 1, in NA, RG 319, AS, PI-AC, Box 19, Folder: Operation SPEEDY EXPRESS (1 of 2) Chron. File # 1 and John T. Carley, Assistant Chief of Staff, MACV, J 3, Memorandum to Chief of Staff MACV, 26 Jan. 1972, Confidential, Subject: Overview of Operations in the Delta, 1 Dec. 1968–31 May 1969, Overview, Operation Speedy Express, 9th US Division, Incl. 9: Air Operations, in NA, RG 472, USFSEA, MACV, IG, ID, ROI, Box 143, Folder: Allegations by Newsweek Re 9th Inf Div + The Delta (Part 1 of 2). The variations may be due to different methods of counting. Results differ according to whether only pre-planned strikes are counted or whether immediate requests are included. • **156**. John T. Carley, Assistant Chief of Staff, MACV, J 3, Memorandum to Chief of Staff MACV, 26 Jan. 1972, Confidential, Subject: Overview of Operations in the Delta, 1 Dec. 1968–31 May 1969, Overview, Operation Speedy Express, 9th US Division, Incl. 8: Artillery Support, in NA, RG 472, USFSEA, MACV, IG, ID, ROI, Box 143, Folder: Allegations by Newsweek Re 9th Inf Div + The Delta (Part 1 of 2). • **157**. Snipers allegedly killed 1,158 people from helicopters: 9th Infantry Division in Vietnam, Dec. 1966–Jul. 1969, Statistics, p. 9: 9th Div Sniper Kills, Nov. 1968–Jul. 1969, in NA, RG 472, USAV, 9th Infantry Division, Organizational History, Box 1, Folder: Publications and John T. Carley, Assistant Chief of Staff, MACV, J 3, Memorandum to Chief of Staff MACV, 26 Jan. 1972, Confidential, Subject: Overview of Operations in the Delta, 1 Dec. 1968–31 May 1969, Overview, Operation Speedy Express, 9th US Division, p. 4, in NA, RG 472, USFSEA, MACV, IG, ID, ROI, Box 143, Folder: Allegations by Newsweek Re 9th Inf Div + The Delta (Part 1 of 2). • **158**. 'Concerned Sgt.' to General William Westmoreland, 25 May 1970, in NA, RG 319, AS, ODCS-PER, VWCWG, CaFi, Box 1, Folder: Concerned Sergeant Allegation (emphasis in original). • **159**. There were said to have been 688 individual and 60 crew-served weapons – weapons generally handled by several people, for example heavy machine guns, mortars or trench mortars: John T. Carley, Assistant Chief of Staff, MACV, J 3, Memorandum to Chief of Staff MACV, 26 Jan. 1972, Confidential, Subject: Overview of Operations in the Delta, 1 Dec. 1968–31 May 1969, Overview, Operation Speedy Express, 9th US Division, Incl. 6: Weapons Captured, in NA, RG 472,

USFSEA, MACV, IG, ID, ROI, Box 143, Folder: Allegations by Newsweek Re 9th Inf Div + The Delta (Part 1 of 2). • **160**. NA, RG 319, AS, PI-FR, Vol. III: Exhibits, Box 54, Book 3, pp. 401–5: Task Force Barker, 11th Infantry Brigade, Combat Action Report, 28 May 1968. • **161**. 9th Infantry Division in Vietnam, Dec. 1966–Jul. 1969, Statistics, p. 2: Annual Results, in NA, RG 472, USAV, 9th Infantry Division, Organizational History, Box 1, Folder: Publications. See also RG 472, USAV, MHD, 19th MHD, HBF, Box 6, Folder: Commanders' Conference, 22 Jul. 68. • **162**. The average figure for III Corps Tactical Zone in 1969 was 1:4.1: Pertinent Data Operation Speedy Express (1 Dec. 1968–31 May 1969), undated, Secret, p. 3, in NA, RG 319, AS, PI-AC, Box 19, Folder: Operation SPEEDY EXPRESS (1 of 2) Chron. File # 1. See also Comparative Statistics, Enemy KIA vs. Individual Weapons Captured, undated, Confidential – Close Hold, in RG 319, AS, PI-AC, Box 19, Folder: Operation SPEEDY EXPRESS (2 of 2) Chron. File # 1 and Commanding General, II FFV, Circular, 30 Jan. 1969, p. 10, in RG 472, USAV, II FFV, G 3, Situation Reports, Box 3, Folder: G-3 SITREPS Jan. 1969. • **163**. Phillip H. Stevens, Chief of Information, MACV, to Kevin Buckley, 2 Dec. 1971, in NA, RG 472, USFSEA, MACV, IG, ID, ROI, Box 143, Folder: Allegations by Newsweek Re 9th Inf Div + The Delta (Part 1 of 2). For the after-action report of 9th Infantry Division, see ibid., Folder: Allegations by Newsweek Re 9th Inf Div + The Delta (Part 1 of 2): John T. Carley, Assistant Chief of Staff, MACV, J 3, Memorandum to Chief of Staff MACV, 26 Jan. 1972, Confidential, Subject: Overview of Operations in the Delta, 1 Dec. 1968–31 May 1969, Overview, Operation Speedy Express, 9th US Division, p. 5. • **164**. Assistant Secretary of Defense to Jacob K. Javits, 22 Sep. 1972, in NA, RG 319, AS, PI-AC, Box 19, Folder: Operation SPEEDY EXPRESS (1 of 2) Chron. File # 1. • **165**. Gary Wills, 'GI Outdrew Foe on a Giant Scale', *Washington Post*, 3 Jul. 1972. • **166**. ARVN units allegedly captured 7,485 weapons: John T. Carley, Assistant Chief of Staff, MACV, J 3, Memorandum to Chief of Staff MACV, 26 Jan. 1972, Confidential, Subject: Overview of Operations in the Delta, 1 Dec. 1968–31 May 1969, Overview, Operation Speedy Express, 9th US Division, Incl. 7: Comparative Data by Division, in NA, RG 472, USFSEA, MACV, IG, ID, ROI, Box 143, Folder: Allegations by Newsweek Re 9th Inf Div + The Delta (Part 1 of 2). • **167**. Summary of 9th Infantry Division Activities to Thwart the VC Winter–Spring Infantry Division, 1 Jan. 1969–31 May 1969, p. 4, in NA, RG 472, USAV, 9th Infantry Division, Organizational History, Box 1, Folder: Unit Awards. • **168**. These ratios have been taken from 9th Infantry Division battle statistics pre Speedy Express: 9th Infantry Division in Vietnam, Dec. 1966–Jul. 1969, Statistics, p. 2: Annual Results, in NA, RG 472, USAV, 9th Infantry Division, Organizational History, Box 1, Folder: Publications. See also Annex A (Intelligence) to OPLAN 1-68 (Dry Season Offensive), 22 Oct. 1968, Secret, p. 7, in RG 472, USFSEA, USAV, CH, OSE-BF, Box 11, Folder: Update / OPLAN 1-68. • **169**. John T. Carley,

Assistant Chief of Staff, MACV, J 3, Memorandum to Chief of Staff MACV, 26 Jan. 1972, Confidential, Subject: Overview of Operations in the Delta, 1 Dec. 1968–31 May 1969, IV CTZ Overview, p. 2, and Incl. 5: Enemy Strength, IV CTZ, in NA, RG 472, USFSEA, MACV, IG, ID, ROI, Box 143, Folder: Allegations by Newsweek Re 9th Inf Div + The Delta (Part 1 of 2); Maurice L. Clouser, Chief, Investigations Division, MACV, Operation Speedy Express – Allegations in Newsweek Article and Comments Concerning, 23 Jun. 1972, p. 2, in ibid.; Headquarters, USAV, 16th MHD, Subject: Combat After Action Report of Operation SPEEDY EXPRESS, 14 Jun. 1969, Secret, p. 10, in RG 472, USFSEA, USAV, CH, OSE-BF, Box 15, Folder: Speedy Express Report/16th MHD 14 Jun. 69 and Headquarters, 9th Infantry Division, Subject: Recommendation for Award of the Presidential Unit Citation, undated, p. 1, in NA, RG 472, USAV, MHD, 19th MHD, HBF, Box 7, Folder: Presidential Unit Citations, Recommended + Awarded 9th Inf Div 25 Jan.–26 Apr. 69. • **170.** Headquarters USA-AG, IV CTZ Advisory Team 96, Subject: First Quarter Review of Implementation of Combined Campaign Plan 1969, AB-144, 10 Apr. 1969, Section 8, p. 4, in NA, RG 472, USFSEA, USAV, CH, OSE-BF, Box 14, Folder: C.C.P. 69/1st Qtr. Review 1969. • **171.** Department of the Army, Office of the Chief of Staff, File note, 26 Jul. 1972 and 9 Aug. 1972, in NA, RG 319, AS, PI-AC, Box 19, Folder: Operation SPEEDY EXPRESS (1 of 2) Chron. File # 1. • **172.** Department of the Army, Office of the Chief of Staff, File note, 19 Jul. 1972, Subject: Speedy Express Letters to the Editor, in ibid. To the end of July *Newsweek* only published one reader's letter, by a former soldier from 9th Infantry Division. The writer complained of the total contempt for the laws of warfare in his unit. Stationed in Vietnam from 1965, he was not able to report on Speedy Express from first-hand knowledge: Donald A . Thompson, Letter to the Editor, *Newsweek*, 17 Jul. 1972. From 1965 to summer 1972 accusations were made against 9th Infantry Division by fourteen GIs, mostly at the end of January 1971 during the Winter Soldiers investigation. However, Speedy Express was not the subject: Department of the Army, Office of the Chief of Staff, Memorandum for Record, Subject: War Crime Allegations of Possible Relevance to Operation Speedy Express, 31 Jul. 1972, in NA, RG 319, AS, PI-AC, Box 19, Folder: Operation SPEEDY EXPRESS (1 of 2) Chron. File # 1. • **173.** Department of the Army, Memorandum for the Secretary of Defense, Subject: Operation Speedy Express, undated, Sensitive, p. 1, in ibid. • **174.** Department of the Army, Office of the Chief of Staff, Memorandum for record, Subject: Senator Javits 13 Nov. 1972 Letter to SECDEF Concerning Operation Speedy Express, 24 Nov. 1972, in ibid. See also ibid.: Assistant Secretary of Defense, letter to Jacob K. Javits, 22 Sep. 1972. The same arguments were used in the correspondence with Kevin P. Buckley: RG 472, USFSEA, MACV, IG, ID, ROI, Box 143, Folder: Allegations by Newsweek Re 9th Inf Div + The Delta (Part 1 of 2).

• **175**. Department of the Army, R. Kenly Webster, Acting General Counsel Memorandum for Secretary Resor, Subject: Letter to General Westmoreland from an Anonymous Enlisted Man Concerning 'Body Count' Pressures in Vietnam, 16 Jun. 1970, in NA, RG 319, AS, ODCS-PER, VWCWG, CaFi, Box 1, Folder: Concerned Sergeant Allegation. • **176**. 'Concerned Sgt.' To Major General William A. Enemark, 30 Jul. 1971 and to Major General Orwin C. Talbott, 30 Mar. 1971, in NA, RG 319, AS, ODCS-PER, VWCWG, CaFi, Box 1, Folder: Concerned Sergeant Allegation. • **177**. Department of the Army, IG, Telegram to MACV, IG, 22 Sep. 1971, in NA, RG 319, AS, ODCS-PER, VWCWG, CaFi, Box 1, Folder: Hackworth Allegations (Col. David H. Hackworth). • **178**. Maurice L. Clouser, Chief, Investigations Division, MACV, Letter to IG, MACV, Subject: Newsweek Article on Operation Speedy Express 'Pacifications's Deadly Price', 23 Jun. 1972, in NA, RG 472, USFSEA, MACV, IG, ID, ROI, Box 143, Folder: Allegations by Newsweek Re 9th Inf Div + The Delta (Part 1 of 2). After Kevin P. Buckley had first asked the Pentagon for information on Speedy Express staff worked on a public relations plan and on the terms of a denial: Department of the Army, Office of the Deputy Chief of Staff for Military Operations, Memorandum for: Chief of Staff, United States Army, Subject: Operation Speedy Express, 27 Jan. 1972, in NA, RG 319, AS, PI-AC, Box 19, Folder: Operation SPEEDY EXPRESS (1 of 2) Chron. File # 1. • **179**. Department of the Army, Memorandum for the Secretary of Defense, Subject: Operation Speedy Express, undated, Sensitive, p. 4, in ibid. • **180**. United States Army, Investigation Division / Criminal Investigation Division, Talking Paper, Subject: Colonel David H. Hackworth, 10 Sep. 1971, in NA, RG 319, AS, ODCS-PER, VWCWG, CaFi, Box 1, Folder: Hackworth Allegations (Col. David H. Hackworth). • **181**. Department of the Army, Lieutenant Colonel Johns, Memorandum, Subject: Colonel Hackworth, 10 Jul. 1972, in ibid. • **182**. David H. Hackworth, 'Commentary: A Soldier's Disgust', *Harper's*, Jul. 1972. See also id., 'Our Great Vietnam Goof', *Popular Mechanics*, Jun. 1972. • **183**. NA, RG 319, AS, ODCS-PER, VWCWG, CaFi, Box 13, Folder: Record Allegation (Congressional Inquiries and Background Information), Case 90. • **184**. Sworn Statement Jeffrey Record, 2 Sep. 1971, p. 2, in ibid. • **185**. NA, RG 319, AS, PI-FR, Vol. I: Analyses, Box 1, Annex B: Peripheral Issues, pp. 1, 2. See also Department of the Army, Office of the Adjutant General, Memorandum for: Secretary of General Staff, Subject: Lessons Learned from the Son My Incident, 31 May 1972, in NA, RG 319, AS, PI-AC, Box 14, Folder: Lessons Learned – My Lai (Input from Agencies and Col. Schopper's Compilation – 1972) (2 of 2). • **186**. NA, RG 319, AS, PI-AC, Box 6, Folder: Conduct of the War in Vietnam, Chron. File # 2 (2 of 2): Memorandum, An Analysis of the Evolution of MACV Rules of Engagement Pertaining to Ground Operations 1965–69, undated, pp. 8–9. • **187**. NA, RG 319, AS, PI-FR, Vol. I: Analyses, Box 1, Annex B: Peripheral Issues, p. 3. • **188**. Phillip H. Stevens, Chief of

Information, MACV, letter to Kevin Buckley, 14 Dec. 1971, in NA, RG 472, USFSEA, MACV, IG, ID, ROI, Box 143, Folder: Allegations by Newsweek Re 9th Inf Div + The Delta (Part 1 of 2). • **189**. Lieutenant Colonel Douglas A. Huff, Change to USARV Regulations Pertaining to Investigations of Friendly Fire Incidents, Memorandum, undated, in NA, RG 472, USAV, DCSO, PSOT, AOC, Accident Case Files, Box 2, Folder: Reports of Investigations (General) 1969. For internal criticism of this practice, see letter to the Commanding General of II Field Force, 20 Aug. 1966, in NA, RG 472, USAV, II FFV, S 3, Reports of Artillery Accidents and Incidents, Box 1, Folder: Vol. Aug. 1966; Lieutenant General Jonathan O. Seaman, Errors in Artillery and Mortar Fires, 21 Mar. 1967, in ibid., Box 2, Folder: Vol. IV, March 1967. See above, pp 70–1. • **190**. Briefing of Lt. General McCaffrey by Ollon D. McCool, 24 Apr. 1970, in NA, RG 319, AS, PI-AC, Box 21, Folder: Peers Report Fallout. • **191**. Amongst countless examples see 173rd Airborne Brigade (Separate), Operational Report Lessons Learned (1 Nov. 1968–31 Jan. 1969), in NA, RG 319, AS, ODCS-PER, VWCWG, CaFi, Box 7, Folder: Marhoun-Anderson Allegation (CCI) (Part 1 of 2), Case 56. • **192**. An unnamed major, quoted in Gibson, *Perfect War*, p. 152. • **193**. Wayne Novick, 1st Battalion, 26th Infantry Regiment, 1st Infantry Division, quoted in USCR, 7 Apr. 1971, p. E2924. • **194**. Gregory J. Hayward, letter to Major General Ellis W. Williamson, 2 May 1971, p. 3, in NA, RG 319, AS, ODCS-PER, VWCWG, CaFi, Box 12, Folder: Hayward Allegation (Case 84). • **195**. Fact Sheet, Allegations Against LTG Julian J. Ewell, 13 May 1971, in ibid. • **196**. USCR, 7 Apr. 1971, p. E2910. • **197**. Notley Allegation, as of 3 Dec. 1971, in NA, RG 319, AS, ODCS-PER, VWCWG, CaFi, Box 12, Folder: Notley Allegation (CCI) (Part 1 of 2), Case 85; 'Concerned Sgt.' letter to Major General William A. Enemark, 30 Jul. 1971, in ibid., Box 1, Folder: Concerned Sergeant Allegation. • **198**. Headquarters, 9th Infantry Division, Subject: Recommendation for Award of the Presidential Unit Citation, undated, p. 92: Summary of Strength and Casualties, in: NA, RG 472, USAV, MHD, 19th MHD, HBF, Box 7, Folder: Presidential Unit Citations, Recommended + Awarded 9th Inf Div 25 Jan.–26 Apr. 1969. • **199**. NA, RG 319, AS, PI-FR, Vol. I: Analyses, Box 1, Ch. 9: Policy and Directives as to Rules of Engagement and Treatment of Noncombatants, p. 24. See also RG 319, AS, ODCS-PER, VWCWG, CaFi, Box 4, Folder: Reporting and Investigating War Crimes Allegations – Procedures and Regulations: Memorandum, Procedures for Reporting War Crimes Involving US Army Personnel within HQ, DA, undated, p. 2; RG AS, PI-AC, Box 8, Folder: Conduct of the War, MACV Directives, ROE – Chron. File # 3: Memorandum, Policy and Directives as to Rules of Engagement and Treatment of Noncombatants, undated, pp. 9–24. • **200**. Lewy, *America in Vietnam*, p. 345. • **201**. Representative of numerous reports of this kind, see NA, RG 319, AS, ODCS-PER, VWCWG, CaFi, Box 12, Folder: Notley Allegation (CCI) (Part 1 of 2), Case 85 and Solis,

Son Thang, pp. 50–5, 63–5. • **202**. Sworn Statement Gerald E. Morse, 17 Mar. 1975, p. 5, and Sworn Statement Joseph A. Westbrook, 19 Jan. 1975, p. 4, in NA, RG 319, AS, ODCS-PER, VWCWG, CaFi, Box 19, Folder: Coy Allegation (CID ROI 72 – CID 46 – 27852, Exhibits 260–350) (Part 5 of 7), Case 221. • **203**. See Carl C. Turner, Provost Marshal General, letter to Karl W. Gustafson, Provost Marshal, USAV, 15 Jan. 1968, in NA, RG 319, AS, PI-AC, Box 5, Folder: Background Info. • **204**. Lewy, *America in Vietnam*, p. 344. Thereafter soldiers could turn directly to the Inspector General responsible for them, to the military police, military attorneys or military pastors. • **205**. Colonel Joseph N. Tenhet, Staff Judge Advocate General, undated, in NA, RG 319, AS, ODCS-PER, VWCWG, CF, Box 6, Folder: Background Information – War Crimes Reporting and Investigation. • **206**. NA, RG 319, AS, PI-FR, Vol. I: Analyses, Box 1, Ch. 2: Summary Report, p. 9, and ibid., Ch. 11: Suppression and Withholding of Information, pp. 1, 14. See also Hersh, *Cover-Up*, pp. 169, 205ff., 218–22 and Bilton and Sim, *Four Hours*, p. 300. • **207**. Task Force Barker, 11th Infantry Brigade, Americal Division, Combat Action Report, 28 Mar. 1968, p. 4, in NA, RG 319, AS, PI-FR, Vol. III: Exhibits, Box 54, Book 3: Reports, p. 404. See also RG 319, AS, PI-FR, Vol. I: Analyses, Box 1, Ch. 2: Summary Report, p. 10 and ibid, Ch. 11: Suppression and Withholding of Information, p. 7. • **208**. NA, RG 319, AS, PI-FR, Vol. III: Exhibits, Box 54, Book 3: Reports, pp. 15, 235–43. • **209**. NA, RG 319, AS, PI-FR, Vol. I: Analyses, Box 1, Ch. 10: Reports, Investigations, and Reviews, pp. 25–6. • **210**. NA, RG 319, AS, PI-FR, Vol. I: Analyses, Box 1, Ch. 6: C Company, 1st Battalion, 20th Infantry: Actions on 16 and 17 Mar. 1968, p. 17; Witness Testimony Hugh Thompson, 22 Dec. 1969, in RG 319, AS, PI-FR, Vol. II: Testimony, Box 13, Book 8: Thompson SUM APP T-3, p. 3. • **211**. NA, RG 319, AS, PI-FR, Vol. I: Analyses, Box 1, Ch. 2: Summary Report, p. 6; ibid., Ch. 10: Reports, Investigations, and Reviews, pp. 12–15; ibid., Vol. II: Testimony, Box 10, Book 6: Holladay SUM APP T-12, p. 5 and Box 23, Book 15: Calhoun SUM APP T-6, p. 3. See also ibid., Vol. IV: CID-Statements, Box 57, p. 478. • **212**. Brigadier General George M. Young, quoted in Investigator's Statement, 13 Dec. 1969, p. 3, in NA, RG 319, AS, PI-FR, Vol. IV: CID-Statements, Box 57, p. 25. • **213**. NA, RG 319, AS, PI-FR, Vol. I: Analyses, Box 1, Ch. 2: Summary Report, pp. 6, 11; ibid., Ch. 10: Reports, Investigations, and Reviews, p. 16 and ibid., Vol. II: Testimony, Box 10, Book 6: Holladay SUM APP T-12, p. 3. • **214**. Ibid., p. 4; ibid., Box 20, Book 12: Henderson APP T-1, p. 61; ibid., Vol. I: Analyses, Box 1, Ch. 12: Findings and Recommendations, p. 13. • **215**. NA, RG 319, AS, PI-FR, Vol. I: Analyses, Box 1, Ch. 2: Summary Report, p. 6; ibid., II, Testimony, Box 10, Book 6: Culverhouse SUM APP T-126, pp. 3–4; ibid., Box 13, Book 8: Thompson SUM APP T-3, p. 4; ibid., Box 20, Book 12, Henderson SUM APP T-1, p. 4. • **216**. NA, RG 319, AS, PI-FR, Vol. I: Analyses, Box 1, Ch. 10: Reports, Investigations, and Reviews, pp. 5, 32–4. Months later Medina admitted that he had deliberately lied to Henderson: Department of the Army, Judge Advocate, Memorandum of Law (Former CPT Medina), undated, p. 3, in NA, RG 319, AS, ODCS-PER, VWCWG, MLM, Box 4, Folder: Administrative Review – CPT Ernest L. Medina. • **217.** NA, RG 319, AS, PI-FR, Vol. I: Analyses, Box 1, Ch. 10: Reports, Investigations, and Reviews, pp. 34–5. • **218.** Witness Testimony Oran Henderson, 2 Dec. 1969, in NA, RG 319, AS, PI-FR, Vol. II: Testimony, Box 20, Book 12: Henderson SUM APP T-1, p. 9. • **219.** NA, RG 319, AS, PI-FR, Vol. I: Analyses, Box 1, Ch. 2: Summary Report, p. 7. Even in early December 1969 when journalistic reporting on My Lai (4) was at its height, Colonel Henderson was already strongly advocating a continued cover-up. In a letter to General Westmoreland dated 10 December 1969 he suggested that the Army should stop its investigations as soon as possible and that 'the responsibility without qualification be assigned solely to me.' Westmoreland rejected the request. Ibid, Vol. III: Exhibits, Box 54, Book 4: Miscellaneous Documents, p. 29. • **220.** Tran Ngoc Tan, District Chief, Son Tinh, letter to Lieutenant Colonel Khien, Province Chief, Quang Ngai, 11 Apr. 1968, in NA, RG 319, AS, PI-FR, Vol. III: Exhibits, Box 54, Book 4: Miscellaneous Documents, p. 127. See ibid., Book 3: Reports, p. 263; ibid., Book 4: Miscellaneous Documents, p. 231; RG 319, AS, PI-AC, Box 18, Folder: (OCLL) 5 Documents for Reddan. Tran Ngoc Tan's letter was immediately brought to the attention of the Americal Division leadership: RG 319, AS, PI-FR, Vol. I: Analyses, Box 1, Ch. 2: Summary Report, p. 7 and ibid., Ch. 10: Reports, Investigations, and Reviews, p. 61. • **221.** Oran K. Henderson, Report of Investigation, 24 Apr. 1968, in NA, RG 319, AS, PI-FR, Vol. I: Analyses, Box 1, Ch. 10: Reports, Investigations, and Reviews, pp. 57–78. 65. See also ibid., Vol. I: Analyses, Box 1, Ch. 2: Summary Report, p. 8. • **222.** Ibid., p. 9; ibid., Ch. 10: Reports, Investigations, and Reviews, pp. 40, 66. • **223.** Ibid., Ch. 2: Summary Report, p. 9. See also ibid., Ch. 11: Suppression and Withholding of Information, p. 14 and ibid., Ch. 12: Findings and Recommendations, pp. 9–12. • **224.** Sworn Statement James H. Raynor, C Company, 1st Battalion, 20th Infantry Regiment, Americal Division, 11 Dec. 1969, p. 2, in NA, RG 319, AS, PI-FR, Vol. IV: CID Statements, Box 57, p. 396. See also ibid., Vol. II: Testimony, Box 33, Book 21: Braddock SUM APP T-217, p. 7 and Box 37, Book 23, Hobscheid, SUM APP T-368, p. 4. See also Bilton and Sim, *Four Hours*, p. 164 and Sack, *Own Story*, pp. 99–100. • **225.** Sworn Statement James H. Raynor, C Company, 1st Battalion, 20th Infantry Regiment, Americal Division, 11 Dec. 1969, pp. 1–2, in NA, RG 319, AS, PI-FR, Vol. IV: CID Statements, Box 57, pp. 396–7. • **226.** Witness Testimony James H. Raynor, C Company, 1st Battalion, 20th Infantry Regiment, Americal Division, 7 Feb. 1970, in NA, RG 319, AS, PI-FR, Vol. II: Testimony, Box 43, Book 27: Raynor SUM APP T-339; Bilton and Sim, *Four Hours*, pp. 196–7. • **227.** Schwarzkopf, *Autobiography*, p. 155. See also ibid., pp. 151–4, 167; 'The Americal Goes Home', *Time*, 8 Nov. 1971; Headquarters Americal Division, Memorandum, Subject: Firing Incidents, 21 Apr. 1970, in NA, RG 319, AS, PI-AC, Box 18, Folder: (OCLL) Documents Seen by Hebert Special Subcommittee (Item AD). • **228**. Fire Support Base Mary Ann Incident Backup Papers: Background, p. 3, undated, in NA, RG 319, AS, PI-AC, Box 10, Folder: Fire Support Base Mary Ann File # 1 (4 Jul.–9 Feb. 72) (1 of 2). A Fire Support Base of A Company, 4th Battalion, 503rd Infantry Regiment, 173rd Airborne Brigade (Separate) had been stormed in similar fashion in early December 1968: Sworn Statement Anthony B. Herbert, 6 Nov. 1970, pp. 1–2, in RG 472, USFSEA, MACV, DRAC, IG, Preliminary Inquiry Re: Colonel Franklin, Box 2, Folder: Preliminary Investigation Re: Col. Franklin Vol. III (Pt. 3 of 4), 1971. • **229**. Headquarters, 196th Infantry Brigade, 23rd Infantry Division, Memorandum, Subject: Report of Investigation Concerning Alleged War Crime, 29 Mar. 1971, in LZ Mary Ann, 11 Aug. 1971, p. 6; see ibid., p. 4, in NA, RG 319, AS, ODCS-PER, VWCWG, CaFi, Box 19, Folder: Potter Incident (FSB Mary Ann Incident), Case 226 and Fire Support Base Mary Ann Incident Backup Papers; Assessment of Responsibility, p. 7, undated, in NA, RG 319, AS, PI-AC, Box 10, Folder: Fire Support Base Mary Ann File # 1 (4 Jul. 71–9 Feb. 72) (1 of 2). • **230**. Heinl, 'Collapse of the Armed Forces', p. 35. See Westmoreland, 'Facing Up to Challenges'. • **231**. Lewy, *America in Vietnam*, p. 154 and Spector, *After Tet*, p. 277. • **232**. 1971 General Officers' Symposium: Manpower Programs – The State of Marine Corps Manpower, pp. 28–9, in NA, RG 127, HMC-HDPT, TF, FRC Box 4, Folder: General Officers' Symposia, 1965–1971 – Extracts. • **233**. Lewy, *America in Vietnam*, p. 155; Gibson, *Perfect War*, p. 209ff.; Terry, *Bloods*, p. 252. See also NA, RG 127, HMC-HDPT, TF, FRC Box 4, Folder: Command Concerns: Drugs/Racial Strife/Fragging and Commanding General, III Marine Amphibious Force, circular, 31 Aug. 1969, in ibid., Folder: Federal Records Center. • **234**. Solis, *Son Thang*, pp. 211–12; Spector, *After Tet*, pp. 245, 249, 259; Moser, *New Winter Soldiers*, p. 74; Moskos, 'Dilemma in Uniform', pp. 94–116; NA, RG 127, HMC-HDPT, TF, FRC Box 4, Folder: Command Concerns: Drugs/Racial Strife/Fragging. • **235**. For the rebellion in Long Binh, see NA, RG 472, USFSEA, USAV, PM, AO-CGR, Box 5, Folder: Confinement Instruction File (Pt. 3 of 4), 1969. For the revolts in Camp Baxter, see RG 472, USFSEA, MACV, IG, ID, Miscellaneous Reports of Investigations, Box 8, Folder: ROI – Racial Incident at Camp Baxter, Da Nang (2 of 2) and RG 472, USFSEA, USAV, IG, ICD, ROI, CaFi, Box 39, Folder: Case # 71-48. Alleged Racial Disorder in 329th Trans Co. • **236**. Haynes Johnson/George C. Wilson, 'The U.S. Army: A Battle for Survival', in *Washington Post*, 12 Sep. 1972. See also Cortright, *Soldiers in Revolt*; Cincinnatus, *Self-Destruction*; Hauser, *Army in Crisis*. • **237** Seymour M. Hersh, quoted in interview with *CBS Morning News*, WTOP TV, Washington, DC, 19 Jan. 1972, Transcript, p. 5, in NA, RG 319, AS, PI-AC, Box

39, Folder: Son My Chron. File # 22 (1 of 3). See also RG 319, AS, PI-FR, Vol. II: Testimony, Box 37, Book 23: Alaux SUM APP T-68, p. 5; ibid., Box 45, Book 28: T'Souvas SUM APPT-293, p. 2; ibid., Vol. IV: CID Statements, Box 57, p. 454; Sworn Statement Victor Romero, C Company, 1st Battalion, 20th Infantry Regiment, Americal Division, 29 Oct. 1969, p. 1, in RG 319, AS, PI-AC, Box 46, Folder: Son My Biographical Data (Individuals Charged) (9 of 10) and Anderson (ed.), *Facing My Lai*, p. 39. • **238**. Department of the Army, Office of the Deputy Chief of Staff for Military Operations, Pertinent Data Operation Speedy Express (1 Dec. 1968–31 May 1969), undated, Secret, p. 2, in NA, RG 319, AS, PI-AC, Box 19, Folder; Operation SPEEDY EXPRESS (1 of 2) Chron. File # 1 and RG 472, USAV, MHD, HBF, Box 4, Folder: OPORD/Redeployment of 9th Inf. Div to Dong Tam/AAR May 68. • **239**. PRG Information Bureau: Cases 13–15, 17–20, 22–4, 26, 27, 29, 36, 37, 40, 41, 46–8, 50 and 54.

8 Judges

1. Richard Nixon, telephone conversation with Henry Kissinger on 17 March 1970, in NA, NPMP, NSC, Box 612, Folder: Israel Aid. • **2**. Henry Kissinger, undated memorandum to Gerald Ford, quoted in Berman, *No Peace*, p. 281. • **3**. ODCS-PER, Talking Paper, 3 Sep. 1971 and 1 Oct. 1971, in NA, RG 319, AS, ODCS-PER, VWCWG, CF, Box 1, Folder: War Crimes Allegations Talking Papers – Sep. 1971 and Folder: War Crimes Allegations Talking Papers – Oct. 1971; ibid., Box 3, Folder: War Crimes Allegations Index (for Allegations other than My Lai). See also Solis, *Son Thang*, p. 188. • **4**. Lewy, *America in Vietnam*, p. 456. • **5**. Department of the Army, Office of the Judge Advocate General, International Affairs Division, Memorandum for: The Judge Advocate General. Subject: Investigation and Prosecution of War Crimes and the Maintenance and Custody of Reports of Investigation and Other Records Pertaining to Such Crimes, 14 Jun. 1968, p. 3, in NA, RG 338, USA-AC, HD22-UR, Box 44, Folder: S11-02 Vietnam. Investigation and Prosecution of War Crimes (1968) and Department of the Army, Office of the Judge Advocate General, International Affairs Division, Fact Sheet, Subject: Possible or Suspected War Crimes, 9 Dec. 1969, in RG 319, AS, PI-AC, Box 32, Folder: Son My Chron. File # 3 (2 of 2). • **6**. This compound calculation uses as a basis the CID data given above and information from Guenter Lewy. See Lewy, *America in Vietnam*, pp. 324ff., 348, 352, 457–9. • **7**. NA, RG 319, AS, PI-FR, Vol. I: Analyses, Box 1, Ch. 9: Policy and Directives as to Rules of Engagement and Treatment of Noncombatants, p. 2; An Analysis of the Evolution of MACV Rules of Engagement Pertaining to Ground Operations 1965–69, undated, in RG 319, PI-AC, Box 6, Folder: Conduct of the War in Vietnam, Chron. File # 2 (2 of

2). See also Lewy, *America in Vietnam*, p. 343 and Solis, *Son Thang*, p. 187. • **8**. NA, RG 319, AS, PI-FR, Vol. I: Analyses, Box 1, Ch. 9: Policy and Directives as to Rules of Engagement and Treatment of Noncombatants, p. 3. • **9**. Quoted in Army Report – Southeast Asia Rules of Engagement, Law of War, Annex A, undated, p. 7, in NA, RG 319, AS, ODCS-PER, VWCWG, CF, Box 4, Folder: Army Report – Law of South Asia Rules of Engagement, Law of War (Undated). • **10**. Ibid., pp. 8–14; MACV Directive 20-4; Inspections and Investigations of War Crimes, in ibid., Folder: Reporting and Investigating War Crimes Allegations – Procedures and Regulations. • **11**. Army Report – Southeast Asia Rules of Engagement, Law of War, Annex A, undated, pp. 17–29, in NA, RG 319, AS, ODCS-PER, VWCWG, CF, Box 4, Folder: Army Report – Law of South Asia Rules of Engagement, Law of War (Undated) and A Commander's Responsibility for War Crimes Committed by Persons Subject to his Control, undated, in RG 319, PI-AC, Box 6, Folder: Conduct of the War in Vietnam, Chron. File # 2 (2 of 2). • **12**. Nuremberg Trials, Case 12: Supreme Command of the Wehrmacht, quoted in *Trials of War Criminals Before the Nuremberg Military Tribunals Under Control Law No. 10*, Washington, DC 1950, Vol. XI, pp. 543–4. (author's italics.) See also NA, RG 338, USA-AC, HD22-UR, Box 44, Folder: S11-02 Vietnam. War Crimes Allegations and Replies to Allegations (1971) (Folder 2 of 2). • **13**. In his case the existence of 'recognisable' information was only assumed to be plausible. Relevant documents were not available to the prosecution: Kenneth J. Hodson, Judge Advocate General, US Army, 'From Nuremberg to My Lai', *American Bar Association Journal*, 57 (1971) 3, p. 10. • **14**. Quoted in International Military Tribunal for the Far East, *International Japanese War Crimes Trial, Tokyo: US Navy, Office of the Judge Advocate General, 1946–1948*, Vol. 203, p. 49; see ibid., p. 809 (Author's italics). See also NA, RG 338, USA-AC, HD22-UR, Box 44, Folder: S11-02 Vietnam. War Crimes Allegations and Replies to Allegations (1971) (Folder 2 of 2). • **15**. See Belknap, *War on Trial* and Nill-Theobald, *'Defences' in War Crimes*. • **16**. Department of the Army, Field Manual 27-10: The Law of Land Warfare, Washington, DC, Department of the Army: 18 Jul. 1956, pp. 178–9: § 501. See also NA, RG 319, AS, ODCS-PER, VWCWG, CF, Box 4, Folder: Army Report – Law of South Asia Rules of Engagement, Law of War (Undated). • **17**. Eric J. Fygi, Military Justice Division, Judge Advocate General, Department of the Army, Memorandum 1969/8751, undated, pp. 2–4, in NA, RG 319, AS, PI-CI, Box 1, Folder: Vol. III: Chronology. The unlimited responsibility of subordinates is also stressed in the Manuals for Courts Martial, US Army, 1921 and 1928, § 415 and § 148a. • **18**. Department of the Army, Judge Advocate General, Military Justice Division, Fact Sheets 77317 (19 Jun. 1970) and 714187 (18 Jun. 1970), in NA, RG 319, AS, ODCS-PER, VWCWG, CF, Box 6, Folder: Background Information – History of War Crimes; Kenneth J. Hodson, Judge Advocate General, US Army, Presentation to the Minnesota

State Bar Association, 18 Jun. 1971, in USCR, Senate, 29 Jun. 1971, pp. S10209–11. • **19**. US War Department, Rules of Land Warfare, 1914, quoted in Solis, *Son Thang*, p. 269. (Author's italics.) For the acquittal of those accused of the multiple murder of Filipinos in 1902, see Department of the Army, Judge Advocate General, Military Justice Division, Fact Sheets 77317 (19 Jun. 1970) and 714187 (18 Jun. 1970), in NA, RG 319, AS, ODCS-PER, VWCWG, CF, Box 6, Folder: Background Information – History of War Crimes. • **20**. Kenneth J. Hodson, Judge Advocate General, US Army, 'From Nuremberg to My Lai', *American Bar Association Journal*, 57 (1971) 3, p. 10. • **21**. Solis, *Son Thang*, pp. 95, 144. • **22**. Piragoff, 'Article 30', pp. 732–40. • **23**. From a judge's jury instruction during the court martial of a GI accused of murder from D Company, 1st Battalion, 8th Cavalry Regiment, 1st Cavalry Division (Air-mobile), quoted in United States Army Judiciary, Office of the Judge Advocate General, Board of Review, 2 Jul. 1968, p. 3, in NA, RG 319, AS, ODCS-PER, VWCWG, CaFi, Box 14, Folder: Ogg Incident, Case 112. • **24**. Hillman, *Defending America*, p. 13ff. • **25**. Ibid., pp. 3, 17. • **26**. Ibid., pp. 14ff., 17. • **27**. Telford Taylor, 'The Course of Military Justice'. • **28**. Solis, *Son Thang*, p. 294. • **29**. See above, pp. 100–3. • **30**. See Lewy, *America in Vietnam*, p. 160 and Hillman, *Defending America*, pp. 15ff., 22. • **31**. Department of the Army, Office of the Chief of Staff, Memorandum for the Assistant Attorney General (Office of Legal Counsel), Subject: Trial of Discharged Servicemen for Violation of the Law of War, 2 Dec. 1969, pp. 2, 8, in NA, RG 319, PI-AC, Box 17, Folder: (OCLL) Miscellaneous Documents from Peers. See also Lewy, *America in Vietnam*, p. 365. • **32**. Department of the Army, Office of the Chief of Military History, Memorandum for: Secretary of the General Staff, Subject: Request by the Hebert Subcommittee for Information Regarding Charges Similar to Those of the Current Son My Charges Having Been Filed During a Period of Actual Combat, 2 Jul. 1970, in NA, RG 319, AS, ODCS-PER, VWCWG, CF, Box 6, Folder: Background Information – History of War Crimes. • **33**. US Supreme Court, Toth v. Quarles, 350 U.S. 11 (1955), Decided November 7, 1955, § 4, Paragraph g, quoted at http://caselaw.lp.findlaw.com. • **34**. Hugh LaFayette Black, quoted in Department of the Army, Office of the Chief of Staff, Memorandum for the Assistant Attorney General (Office of Legal Counsel), Subject: Trial of Discharged Servicemen for Violation of the Law of War, 2 Dec. 1969, p. 7, in NA, RG 319, PI-AC, Box 17, Folder: (OCLL) Miscellaneous Documents from Peers. Telford Taylor also interpreted Toth vs. Quarles in this sense: Telford Teylor, 'The Course of Military Justice'. • **35**. Department of the Army, Office of the Chief of Staff, Memorandum for the Assistant Attorney General (Office of Legal Counsel), Subject: Trial of Discharged Servicemen for Violation of the Law of War, 2 Dec. 1969, p. 8, in: NA, RG 319, PI-AC, Box 17, Folder: (OCLL) Miscellaneous Documents from Peers. • **36**. Grave Breaches Article in the Geneva Convention (1949), quoted in NA, RG 319,

AS, PI-FR, Vol. I: Analyses, Box 1, Ch. 9: Policy and Directives as to Rules of Engagement and Treatment of Noncombatants, p. 2. The drafting provides for no regulations governing exceptions among the category of suspected persons. See also US Supreme Court, Toth v. Quarles, 350 US 11 (1955), Decided November 7, 1955, § 4, Paragraph c, quoted at http://caselaw.lp.findlaw.com. • **37**. Sam J. Ervin, Jr., Chairman of the Committee on the Judiciary, United States Senate, letter to Secretary of Defense Melvin R. Laird, 1 Dec. 1969 and press announcement, Senate Subcommittee on Constitutional Rights: Ervin Introduces Bills to Permit Federal Court Trials of Former Servicemen, undated, in NA, RG 319, AS, ODCS-PER, VWCWG, MLM, Box 7, Folder: Congressional Correspondence My Lai: Hebert Subcommittee Investigation. See also Lewy, *America in Vietnam*, p. 365. • **38**. Department of the Army, Judge Advocate General, Military Justice Division, Memorandum: Status of Cases as of 23 May 1971, undated, in NA, RG 319, AS, ODCS-PER, VWCWG, MLM, Box 1, Folder: TJAG My Lai Talking Paper, Jan. 1970–Jun. 1971. • **39**. Department of the Army, CID, Army, Memorandum, Subject: Status of Investigations, 4 Sep. 1970, in NA, RG 319, AS, PI-AC, Box 36, Folder: Son My Chron. File # 13 (1 of 2). According to this, investigations up to the beginning of September 1970 had resulted in twenty-six cases of strong suspicion of misdeeds. See also ibid., Folders: Son My Chron. File # 13, 1 of 2 and 2 of 2; Son My Chron. File # 14, 1 of 2; ibid., Box 46, Folder: Son My Suspects (1 of 3); Department of the Army, Office of the Secretary of the Army, Memorandum, My Lai Investigation, undated, p. 1, in RG 319, AS, ODCS-PER, VWCWG, MLM, Box 7, Folder: Congressional Correspondence My Lai: Hebert Subcommittee Investigation. • **40**. Federal Law 18 USC, Sec. 2441 and 104th Congress, House Resolution 3680. • **41**. This behaviour hindered, *inter alia*, the investigations into Tiger Force. See NA, RG 319, AS, ODCS-PER, VWCWG, MLM, Box 18, Folders: Coy Allegation (Part 1 of 7). • **42**. See NA, RG 319, ODCS-PER, VWCWG, CF, Box 9, Folder: Halverson Allegation I (Part 1 of 2); ibid., Folder: Halverson Allegation II (Investigation Reports); ibid., Folder: Halverson Allegation II (Part 1 of 3); ibid., Folder: Halverson Allegation II (Messages, Correspondence, and Press). • **43**. This policy of obstruction by the South Vietnamese authorities would justify its own investigation. For relevant sources see NA, RG 319, AS, PI-FR, Vol. II: Testimony, Box 52, Book 32: Vien, Te APP T-102, and APP T-103, pp. 1–9; ibid., Vol. III: Exhibits, Book 3: Reports, pp. 487–92; RG 319, AS, PI-AC, Box 4, Folder: Army Staff Monitor Summary, Jan. 70; ibid., Box 14, Folder: Lessons Learned – My Lai (Input from Agencies and Col. Schopper's Compilation – 1972) (2 of 2); ibid., Box 18, Folder: (OCLL) 5 Documents for Reddan; RG 319, AS, PI-OI, Box 1, Folder: GVN Reports – Rogers Working Papers; ibid., Box 2, Folder: Department of State and RG 319, AS, PI-CI, Box 1, Folder: Volume II – Chronology. • **44**. Department of the Army, Army Criminal

Investigation Command, Memorandum: Lessons Learned from the Son My Incident (Revision 1), undated, pp. 34, 35, in NA, RG 319, AS, PI-AC, Box 14, Folder: Lessons Learned – My Lai (Input from Agencies and Col. Schopper's Compilation – 1972) (1 of 2). • **45**. Department of the Army, Army Criminal Investigation Command, Memorandum for: Chief of Staff, United States Army, Subject: Lessons Learned from the Son My Incident, 8 Jun. 1972, Section Q: Interview Techniques, in NA, RG 319, AS, PI-AC, Box 14: Folder: Lessons Learned – My Lai (Input from Agencies and Col. Schopper's Compilation – 1972) (2 of 2). • **46**. Solis, *Son Thang*, p. 136ff. • **47**. Department of the Army, Office of the Chief of Staff, Memorandum, Subject: Investigation of War Crimes Allegations, 10 Nov. 1971, p. 4, in NA, RG 319, AS, ODCS-PER, VWCWG, CF, Box 3, Folder: Procedures and Responsibilities for Monitoring War Crimes Allegations. Politically motivated refusals to make statements are documented *inter alia* in RG 319, NA, RG 319, AS, ODCS-PER, VWCWG, CaFi, Box 11, Case 71; ibid., Box 16, Cases 169, 170, 173, 174, 176, 177, 178, 179, 181, 182, 183; ibid., Box 17, Cases 184, 185, 186, 188, 189, 191, 200, 201, 203, 204, 206 and ibid., Box 18, Case 210 (2). • **48**. One of the moderators during the Winter Soldiers hearing in Detroit, 30 Jan. 1971, quoted in USCR, 7 Apr. 1971, p. E2923. • **49**. James D. Henry, 'The Men of B Company'. Henry had drawn attention to a massacre committed in February 1968: see above, pp. 188–9. • **50**. Elliott L. Meyrowitz, letter to General Creighton Abrams, 8 Nov. 1972, p. 2, in RG 319, NA, RG 319, AS, ODCS-PER, VWCWG, CaFi, Box 18, Folder: Meyrowitz Allegation (Correspondence and Messages), Case 210 (2). • **51**. COHRO, Camil Interview, p. 94. • **52**. Handwritten note to the Commanding General of 25th Infantry Division, 30 Oct. 1969. The signature is illegible. The paper used bore the letterhead, 'Office of the Assistant Division Commander': NA, RG 472, USFSEA, MACV, IG, ID, Miscellaneous Reports of Investigation, Box 5, Folder: ROI – Death of Vietnamese Civilian by Air Delivered Ord., 14 Oct. 69. • **53**. Commanding General, 25th Infantry Division, file note 31 Oct. 1969, in ibid. • **54**. Danh Allegation, as of 31 Mar. 72, in NA, RG 319, AS, PI-AC, Box 55, Folder: War Crimes Allegations – 224: Danh Allegation. • **55**. RSB Schuller Incident, as of 8 Jun. 1972, p. 1, in NA, RG 319, AS, ODCS-PER, VWCWG, CaFi, Box 20, Folder: RSB Schuller Incident, Case 235. • **56**. From a multitude of cases see NA, RG 472, USFSEA, MACV, IG, ID, ROI, Box 69, Folder: Alleged Rape and Folder: Alleged Rape/Vol. 1A of I; RG 319, AS, PI-AC, Box 42, Folder: Son My Chron. File SSG Kenneth L. Hodges (Part 2 of 4). Apart from the fact that only a few cases of rape were reported, the files provided are incomplete. It is noteworthy that countless documents have been locked away again since 2001 – parallel to the decision taken in The Hague to classify rape in future as a war crime. For this change in military jurisdiction see Mühlhäuser, 'Sexuelle Gewalt'. • **57**. NA, RG 472, USFSEA, MACV, IG, ICD, ROI, CaFi, Box 12, Folder:

Case # 69-16. Alleged Misconduct of US Military Personnel. In this case the division commander responsible, Major General Charles P. Stone from 4th Infantry Division, monitored the obstructive work of the CID. Whether his intervention had any effect is not clear from the files. • **58**. IG Investigation/Inquiry Summary, 29 Jun. 1970, in NA, RG 472, USFSEA, MACV, IG, ICD, ROI, CaFi, Box 25, Folder: Case # 70-50. Cpt. Fred L. Gleason Throwing Concussion Grenades at Children. The CID closed another incident of this type with almost identical words and, although no enemy soldiers were in the vicinity and there had been no gun battle, classified two children killed as 'combat related casualties': RG 319, AS-AC, Box 51, Folder: War Crimes Allegations – 10: Gray Allegation. • **59**. Department of the Army, Office of the Chief of Information, Memorandum for: Assistant Deputy Chief of Staff for Personnel, Subject: Administrative Review of Son My Cases, 14 Feb. 1972, in NA, RG 319, AS, ODCS-PER, VWCWG, MLM, Box 5, Folder: Administrative Review – SSG Kenneth L. Hodges (Part 2 of 4). • **60**. Morris Udall had been informed by an eye witness, George D. Chunko, about the Duffy case and the war crimes of C Company, 2nd Battalion, 47th Infantry Regiment, 3rd Brigade, 9th Infantry Division: NA, RG 472, USFSEA, USFSEA, MACV, IG, ID, Miscellaneous Reports of Investigations, Box 3, Folder: ROI – Shooting of an Alleged ARVN Soldier near Bin Phuoc, RVN (US ARV). For the background of the murder see RG 319, AS, ODCS-PER, VWCWG, CaFi, Box 3, Folders: Duffy – Lanasa Incident; Duffy – Lanasa Incident, Correspondence Udall (Chunko Letter) and Duffy – Lanasa Incident, Press Releases. See also *Scanlan's* 1 (1970) 2. Chunko was killed in an operation two days after writing his letter to Morris Udall. • **61**. For Ronald Dellums's initiatives, see Citizens Commission of Inquiry, *Dellums Committee Hearings* and Dellums, *Lying Down with Lions*. • **62**. Sworn Statement James D. Henry, 28 Feb. 1970, p. 3, in NA, RG 319, AS, ODCS-PER, VWCWG, CaFi, Box 5, Folder: Henry Allegation – CID Reports. • **63**. For the accusations see above, pp. 187–9. • **64**. Henry Allegation (CCI), as of 16 February 1973, in NA, RG 319, AS, PI-AC, Box 52, Folder: War Crimes Allegation – 32; Henry Allegation (Vol. I) and RG 319, AS, ODCS-PER, VWCWG, CaFi, Box 5, Folder: Henry Allegation (Part 1 of 3). • **65**. Agent's Statement 31 Dec. 1973, p. 8, in NA, RG 319, AS, ODCS-PER, VWCWG, CaFi, Box 5, Folder: Henry Allegation (Part 3 of 3). • **66**. Summary Fact Sheet, p. 2, undated, in NA, RG 319, AS, ODCS-PER, VWCWG, CaFi, Box 5, Folder: Henry Allegation (Part 1 of 3). • **67**. Department of the Army, Human Resources Development Division, Information Paper, To: Chief of Staff, Army, Subject: Allegations of War Crimes, 21 Feb. 1975, in NA, RG 319, AS, PI-AC, Box 56, Folder: Working File – Talker. • **68**. The essentially justified accusations made by Private First Class Richard Dell, who had accused Americal Division in early December of crimes which were not known about up to then, were similarly distorted in the concluding investigation report: NA, RG 319, AS, ODCS-PER, VWCWG, CaFi, Box 10, Folders: Dell Allegation, Parts 1-6. • **69**. See above, p. 254. • **70**. Notley Allegation, as of 16 Sep. 1971, p. 1, in NA, RG 319, AS, ODCS-PER, VWCWG, CaFi, Box 5, Folder: Notley Allegation (CCI) (Part 1 of 2), Case 85. • **71**. Testimony of Nguyen Thi Mam, 14 May 1971, Transcript, pp. 2, 11, 12, in: NA, RG 319, AS, ODCS-PER, VWCWG, CaFi, Box 5, Folder: Notley Allegation (CCI) (Part 2 of 2), Case 85. Even GIs report on similar interrogation methods: 'I had to threaten to go to the IG [Inspector General] and insisted that the statement be worded the way I wanted it to be': Sworn Statement Edwin B. Jackson, Jr., 4 May 1971, p. 2, in NA, RG 319, AS, ODCS-PER, VWCWG, CaFi, Box 13, Folder: Jackson Allegation, Case 91. • **72**. 'Ex-Sergeant Won't Testify on Atrocities', *Washington Post*, 8 May 1971. • **73**. Department of the Army, Deputy Chief of Information, Memorandum for: Secretary of the General Staff, Subject: Notley and Herbert Press Conference, 2 Jun. 1971, p. 1, in NA, RG 319, AS, ODCS-PER, VWCWG, CaFi, Box 12, Folder: Notley Allegation (Appearances of Danny S. Notley and LTC Anthony B. Herbert at a CCI News Conference, 2 Jun. 1971), Case 85. • **74**. See above, pp. 164–79. • **75**. Sallah and Weiss, *Tiger Force*, pp. 222–9. • **76**. There is similar striking negligence in the majority of the interrogation transcripts. See, amongst many other examples, the ignoring of the statement of David B. Johnson, a former sergeant with the Green Berets and later adviser to Tiger Force, who had returned to the USA after deserting for two years and had offered to identify other perpetrators to the CID: NA, RG 319, AS, ODCS-PER, VWCWG, CaFi, Box 21, Folder: Johnson Allegation, Case 246. • **77**. Robert DiMario, CID agent and an unnamed colleague, quoted in Sallah and Weiss, *Tiger Force*, pp. 268, 294. • **78**. NA, RG 319, AS, ODCS-PER, VWCWG, CaFi, Box 19, Folder: Coy Allegation (CID ROI 72 – CID 46 – 27852, Exhibits 260–350) (Part 5 of 7), Case 221 and Michael Sallah and Mitch Weiss, 'Day 2: Inquiry Ended without Justice', *Toledo Blade*, 22 Oct. 2003. • **79**. Anderson (ed.), *Facing My Lai*, pp. 34–5 and NA, RG 319, AS, PI-FR, Vol. II: Testimony, Box 22, Book 14: Ridenhour SUM APP T-266, p. 5. • **80**. Ronald Ridenhour, quoted in Bilton and Sim, *Four Hours*, p. 217 (author's italics). See ibid., pp. 215–16, 373. • **81**. Ibid., p. 218. • **82**. Ronald Ridenhour, letter dated 29 Mar. 1969, in NA, RG 319, AS, PI-FR, Vol. III: Exhibits, Book 4: Miscellaneous Documents, Box 54, pp. 289–93. • **83**. Letter from Ronald Ridenhour to leading politicians and military figures, 29 Mar. 1969, typed copy. This detailed description of the My Lai (4) massacre set the internal investigations in motion: NA, RG 319, AS, PI-FR, Vol. III, Book 4: Miscellaneous Documents. • **84**. The office managers of sixteen congressmen and senators claimed not to have received the letter. Only Congressman Morris K. Udall (Democrat from Arizona) remained in contact with Ridenhour and furthermore carried out his own investigations: *Congressional Quarterly*, National Report, 5 Dec.

1969, pp. 2464–5 and Chronology of Key Events and Congressional Notification Son My Incident, in NA, RG 319, AS, PI-AC, Box 36, Folder: Son My Chron. File # 14 (1 of 2). • **85**. In early July 1969 a statement by the MACV was still referring to heavy fighting on the morning of 16 March 1968. And: 'The residents of My Lai (4) village are Viet Cong, Viet Cong sympathisers or Viet Cong relations': Summary of Headquarters, MACV, Report of Inquiry to Obtain Information, Task Force Barker, 8 Jul. 1969, pp. 5, 6, in NA, RG 319, AS, PI-AC, Box 18, Folder: (OCLL) Summary of MACV Survey for Reddan (Item AB). • **86**. William V. Wilson, Report of Investigation Concerning Alleged Atrocities Committed by Members of C Co, 1/20th Infantry, Task Force Barker, Americal Division, in the Republic of Vietnam, 19 Sep. 1969, in NA, RG 319, AS, PI-AC, Box 12, Folder: IG Report – My Lai Task Force Copy. A transcript of Wilson's interview with Captain Thomas K. Willingham may be found in ibid., Box 47, Folder: Son My – Other Individuals (1 of 3). See also Belknap, *War on Trial*, pp. 105–10. • **87**. William Wilson, 'I had Prayed to God that this Thing was Fiction . . .', *American Heritage Magazine*, Vol. 41, No. 1, Feb. 1990, pp. 44–53; reprinted in Olson and Roberts, *History with Documents*, pp. 152–63. • **88**. William V. Wilson, Report of Investigation Concerning Alleged Atrocities Committed by Members of C Co, 1/20th Infantry, Task Force Barker, Americal Division in the Republic of Vietnam, 19 Sep. 1969, pp. 8, 9, in NA, RG 319, AS, PI-AC, Box 12, Folder: IG Report – My Lai Task Force Copy. For the bureaucratic continuation of this fabrication, see RG 319, AS, PI-CI, Box 8, Folder: Admin. Fil. – Dec (1) and ibid., Box 27, Folder: IG Report (Copy 1). • **89**. William V. Wilson, Report of Investigation Concerning Alleged Atrocities Committed by Members of C Co, 1/20th Infantry, Task Force Barker, Americal Division, in the Republic of Vietnam, 19 Sep. 1969, p. 16, in NA, RG 319, AS, PI-AC, Box 12, Folder: IG Report – My Lai Task Force Copy. • **90**. Bilton and Sim, *Four Hours*, pp. 239, 273. • **91**. Sworn Statement, Herbert L. Carter, 6 Nov. 1969, p. 1, in NA, RG 319, AS, PI-FR, Vol. IV: CID-Statements, Box 57, p. 145. • **92**. See NA, RG 319, AS, PI-FR, Vol. IV: CID-Statements, Box 57, pp. 263–8, 312, 345, 410. • **93**. Department of the Army, Army Criminal Investigation Command, Memorandum for: Chief of Staff, United States Army, Subject: Lessons Learned from the Son My Incident, 8 Jun. 1972, Section C: Language Skills for CID Investigators, in NA, RG 319, AS, PI-AC, Box 14, Folder: Lessons Learned – My Lai (Input from Agencies and Col. Schopper's Compilation – 1972) (2 of 2) and ibid., Folder: (1 of 2): Department of the Army, Army Criminal Investigation Command, Memorandum: Lessons Learned from the Son My Incident (Revision 1), undated, p. 26A; see also ibid., pp. 29, 30. • **94**. The most productive interviews were conducted with Ronald Haeberle (25 Aug. 1969), Paul Meadlo (18 Sep. 1969), Harry Stanley (14 Oct. 1969), Max Hutson (28 Oct. 1969), Herbert Carter (6 Nov. 1969), William Lloyd (10 Nov. 1969), Charles Hutto (17 Nov. 1969) and

Michael Bernhardt (20 Nov. 1969). See NA, RG 319, AS, PI-FR, Vol. IV: CID-Statements, Box 57, pp. 85–96, 127–31, 145–51, 261–6, 267–71, 311–15, 335–9, 431–9. • **95**. Sworn Statement Ronald L. Haeberle, 25 Aug. 1969, pp. 1, 5, in NA, RG 319, AS, PI-FR, Vol. IV: CID-Statements, Box 57, pp. 85, 89. • **96**. David Packard, Memorandum for the President, Subject: My Lai Atrocity, 4 Sep. 1969, p. 2, in NA, NPMP, NSC, AMH-SF, Box 1004, Folder: Possible My Lai Commission. • **97**. Belknap, *War on Trial*, p. 109. • **98**. Seymour M. Hersh, quoted in Anderson (ed.), *Facing My Lai*, p. 60. • **99**. Ronald Ridenhour, quoted in Bilton and Sim, *Four Hours*, p. 251. See also Anderson (ed.), *Facing My Lai*, p. 61ff. • **100**. See above, p. 6. • **101**. Bilton and Sim, *Four Hours*, pp. 289, 293–5. • **102**. Ibid., pp. 273, 287. • **103**. Sworn Statements Nguyen Thi Bay, 17 Dec. 1969 and Nguyen Thi Hien, 19 Dec. 1969, in NA, RG 319, AS, PI-AC, Box 51, Folder: War Crimes Allegations – 9; Reid Allegation (Co Lay/Co Luy). • **104**. Henry Kissinger, Memorandum for the Secretary of Defense, 8 Dec. 1969, Confidential, in NA, NPMP, NSC, AMH-SF, Box 1004, Folder: Possible My Lai Commission. The interview with Terrence Reid had appeared in the newspaper *The Paper* from Oshkosh, Wisconsin. In January 1970 Terrence Reid confirmed his accusations before the CID: Sworn Statement Terrence J. Reid, 21 Jan. 1970, in NA, RG 319, AS, PI-AC, Box 51, Folder: War Crimes Allegations – 9; Reid Allegation (Co Lay/Co Luy). • **105**. Alexander Haig, Memorandum for Henry A. Kissinger, Subject: Vietnam Atrocity Stories, 4 Dec. 1969, Confidential – Henry Kissinger's Handwritten Note, undated, in NA, NPMP, NSC, AMH-SF, Box 1004, Folder: Possible My Lai Commission. • **106**. Department of the Army, Office of the Secretary of the Army, Memorandum: Information for Members of Congress, 16 Oct. 1970, Incl.: Chronology of Key Events and Congressional Notification, Son My Incident, undated, p. 5, in NA, RG 319, AS, PI-AC, Box 36, Folder: Son My Chron. File # 14 (1 of 2). • **107**. The Department of the Army Review of the Preliminary Investigations into the My Lai Incident, in NA, RG 319, AS, PI-FR, Vols I–IV. • **108**. NA, RG 319, AS, PI-FR, Vol. I: Analyses, Box 1, Ch. 11: Suppression and Withholding of Information, p. 1. • **109**. The documentation refers in general to twenty-eight officers accused. This different figure includes three officers accused of murder and torture: William Calley, Ernest Medina and Eugene Kotouc. • **110**. Hillman, *Defending America*, p. 20. • **111**. Fact Sheet: Court Martial of First Lieutenant William Calley, undated, p. 1, in NA, RG 319, AS, ODCS-PER, VWCWG, MLM, Box 6, Folder: My Lai Lessons Learned Reports (Drafts and Working Papers). • **112**. NA, RG 319, AS, ODCS-PER, VWCWG, MLM, Box 1, Folder: Administrative Review – My Lai Cases (Part 2 of 4), and ibid, Box 5, Folder: Administrative Review, PVT Gerald A. Smith. • **113** Department of the Army, Provost Marshal General, Fact Sheet, to: Chief of Staff, United States Army, Subject: My Lai, 31 Dec. 1969, p. 2, in NA, RG 319, AS, ODCS-PER, VWCWG, MLM, Box 1, Folder: My Lai Army Staff Monitor Summaries,

Jan. 1970 and ibid., Box 4, Folder: Administrative Review – CPT Eugene M. Kotouc. • **114**. NA, RG 319, AS, ODCS-PER, VWCWG, MLM, Box 2, Folder: Administrative Review – My Lai Cases (Part 4 of 4); ibid., Box 2, Folder: Administrative Review – Col. Robert B. Luper (Part 1 of 2 and Part 2 of 2) and ibid., Box 4, Folder: Administrative Review – Maj. Charles C. Calhoun (Part 1 of 2). • **115**. NA, RG 319, AS, ODCS-PER, VWCWG, MLM, Box 2, Folder: Administrative Review – My Lai Cases (Part 3 of 4); ibid., Box 2, Folder: Administrative Review – BG George H. Young, Jr.; ibid., Box 3, Folder: Administrative Review – Col. Nels A. Parson, Jr. (Part 1 of 4 and Part 2 of 4); ibid., Box 3, Folder: Administrative Review – LTC William D. Guinn and ibid., Box 3, Folder: Administrative Review – LTC Frederick W. Watke. • **116**. NA, RG 319, AS, ODCS-PER, VWCWG, MLM, Box 1, Folder: TJAG My Lai Talking Papers, Jul. 1971–Jul. 1972 and ibid., Box 4, Folder: Administrative Review – Maj. Charles C. Calhoun (Part 1 of 2 and Part 2 of 2). • **117**. Ibid., Box 1, Folder: TJAG My Lai Talking Papers, Jul. 1971–Jul. 1972. In effect the Letter of Censure amounted to a guilty sentence for Samuel Koster, although he confirmed that the divisional commander definitely knew about the civilian victims of My Lai (4) and nevertheless gave the perpetrators his protection. Koster's military career was at an end because he was immediately demoted to brigadier general. • **118**. Ibid. • **119**. William Peers, quoted Lewy, *America in Vietnam*, p. 358. • **120**. For the six other murder suspects, see NA, RG 319, AS, ODCS-PER, VWCWG, MLM, Box 1, Folder: Administrative Review – My Lai Cases (Part 1 of 4); ibid., Box 5, Folder: Administrative Review – PVT Gerald A. Smith. For the twelve still incriminated officers, see ibid., Box 2, Folder: Administrative Review – My Lai Cases (Part 3 of 4 and Part 4 of 4); ibid., Box 2, Folder: Administrative Review – BG George H. Young, Jr.; ibid., Box 2, Folder: Administrative Review – Col. Robert B. Luper (Part 1 of 2 and Part 2 of 2); ibid., Box 3, Folder: Administrative Review – LTC William D. Guinn; ibid., Box 3, Folder: Administrative Review – Col. Nels A. Parson, Jr. (Part 1 of 4); ibid., Box 3, Folder: Administrative Review – LTC Frederick W. Watke and ibid., Box 4, Folder: Administrative Review – Maj. Charles C. Calhoun (Part 1 of 2 and Part 2 of 2). • **121**. Department of the Army, Judge Advocate General, Memorandum of Law (SSG Hodges), undated, p. 2, in NA, RG 319, AS, ODCS-PER, VWCWG, MLM, Box 5, Folder: Administrative Review – SSG Kenneth L. Hodges (Part 2 of 4). The played-down concept of 'sexual frolics' was used in Department of the Army, Judge Advocate General, Memorandum to: Secretary of the Army, Subject: Sergeant Kenneth L. Hodges, 12 Mar. 1973, in: NA, RG 319, AS, PI-AC, Box 42, Folder; Son My Chron. File # 28 (2 of 2). • **122**. Conduct of the Men of Charlie Company, 1/20, during the Assault on My Lai 4 on 16 Mar. 1968, undated, p. 26 in NA, RG 319, AS, ODCS-PER, VWCWG, MLM, Box 5, Folder: Administrative Review – SSG Kenneth L. Hodges (Part 3 of 4). • **123**. Anderson (ed.), *Facing*

My Lai, pp. 44, 49. For the discussion of this problem, see also Paust, 'Case for War Crime Jurisdiction' and Paulson and Banta, '"Grave Breaches" Under the Geneva Conventions'. • **124**. Department of Defense, The Secretary of Defense, Memorandum for the President, Subject: The My Lai Atrocity, Confidential, Draft, 3 Sep. 1969, in NA, RG 319, AS, PI-CI, Box 2, Folder: Related Chronology. • **125**. Department of the Army, Army Staff Monitor Section, My Lai Army Staff Monitor Summary, 10 Jan. 1970, p. 1, in NA, RG 319, AS, PI-AC, Box 4, Folder: Army Staff Monitor Summary, Jan. 1970. • **126**. Department of the Army, Office of the Deputy Chief of Staff for Military Operations, Memorandum, for: Secretary of the General Staff, Subject: Research Project: Conduct of the War in Vietnam, 29 Jan. 1971, Outline: Conduct of the War in Vietnam, p. 2, in NA, RG 319, AS, PI-AC, Box 7, Folder: Conduct of the War in Vietnam, Chron. File # 4 (2 of 2); Referral Slip CS 091 Vietnam, 13 Jan. 1971, p. 2, in ibid., Box 8, Folder: Conduct of the War, MACV Directives, RoE – Chron. File # 3. • **127**. Harry Robbins Haldeman, quoted in Bilton and Sim, *Four Hours*, p. 321. • **128**. Greiner, 'Nicht-Aufhören-Können', p. 381. • **129**. Richard Nixon in a discussion with his adviser Alexander Butterfield about My Lai (4), quoted in Bilton and Sim, *Four Hours*, p. 321. • **130**. Ibid., pp. 315–25. • **131**. Henry Kissinger, Memorandum for the President, Subject: My Lai Atrocities, 4 Dec. 1969, Secret/Sensitive, p. 2, in NA, NPMP, NSC, AMH-SF, Box 1004, Folder: My Lai Incident (2 of 2). • **132**. Hersh, *Cover Up*, pp. 248–50 and Bilton and Sim, *Four Hours*, pp. 306–10. • **133**. Department of the Army, Office of the Judge Advocate General, Memorandum, for: The Judge Advocate General, Subject: Review of Evidence Obtained by the Peers Inquiry, 11 Mar. 1970, Section: CPT (then 2LT) Thomas K. Willingham (1st Platoon Leader, B/4/3), in NA, RG 319, AS, PI-CI, Box 27, Folder: Col. H. Miller's report to TJAG on Offenses. For the witness statements by participants from B Company, Task Force Barker, see Department of the Army, Office of the Provost Marshal General, Memorandum, for: Deputy Secretary of the General Staff, Subject: Son My Investigation – B Company, 4th Battalion, 3rd Infantry, 11 Apr. 1970, in RG 319, AS, PI-AC, Box 46, Folder: Son My Suspects (2 of 3). • **134**. Department of the Army, United States Army CID Agency, Memorandum, Subject: Reorientation of My Lai (4) Investigation, 12 Feb. 1970, in NA, RG 319, AS, PI-AC, Box 33, Folder: Son My Chron. File # 7 (1 of 2). • **135**. Headquarters, United States Army Vietnam, Memorandum, to: Commanding Officer, United States Army Criminal Investigation Division Army, 17 Jan. 1970, in NA, RG 319, AS, PI-AC, Box 51, Folder: War Crimes Allegations – 9: Reid Allegation (Co Lay/Co Luy). • **136**. Department of the Army, Judge Advocate General, Military Justice Division, Memorandum of Law (CPT Willingham), 22 Mar. 1971, p. 4, in NA, RG 319, AS, ODCS-PER, VWCWG, MLM, Box 1, Folder: Administrative Review – My Lai Cases (Part 1 of 4). • **137**. Department of the Army, Military Justice Division, Talking

Paper, Subject: Son My Cases, 20 Mar. 1971, p. 11, in NA, RG 319, AS, ODCS-PER, VWCWG, CF Box 6, Folder: Background Information – History of War Crimes; Department of the Army, Judge Advocate General, Military Justice Division, Memorandum of Law (CPT Willingham), 22 Mar. 1971, p. 1, in NA, RG 319, AS, ODCS-PER, VWCWG, MLM, Box 1, Folder: Administrative Review – My Lai Cases (Part 1 of 4). • **138**. Department of the Army, Office of the Chief of Information, Memorandum, for: General Peers, Subject: 'One Morning in the War' by Richard Hammer, 10 Jun. 1970, in NA, RG 319, AS, PI-CI, Box 8, Folder: Admin. File – June. • **139**. Sworn Statement Terrence J. Reid, 21 Jan. 1970, in NA, RG 319, AS, PI-AC, Box 51, Folder: War Crimes Allegations – 9; Reid Allegation (Co Lay/Co Luy). Since November 1969 the publications of Seymour M. Hersh had been meticulously analysed from this point of view: Department of the Army, Executive Officer, Peers Inquiry, Memorandum, for: Lieutenant General Peers, Subject: Harper's Magazine Article, My Lai (4), 20 Apr. 1970, in RG 319, AS, PI-AC, Box 16, Folder: My Lai Allegations; Seymour M. Hersh, 'Comment: Uncovered', *New Yorker*, 10 Nov. 2003. Nevertheless it was not considered safe: 'I have known Cy Hersch [*sic*] for many years and he is totally unpredictable. The fact that he says he is going to do something means absolutely nothing. He is, however, an indefatigable worker and digger for information, and I have little doubt that he has uncovered some more information on the Son My case': Department of the Army, Office of the Chief of Information, Memorandum, for: Secretary of the General Staff, Subject: Follow-Up Actions on the Peers Report, 2 Aug. 1971, p. 2, in RG 319, AS, PI-AC, Box 39, Folder: Son My Chron. File # 20 (2 of 2). • **140**. Department of the Army, Charles J. Bauer, Executive Officer (Peers Inquiry), Memorandum for: Lieutenant General Peers, Subject: Harper's Magazine Article, 'My Lai (4)', 20 Apr. 1970, in NA, RG 319, AS, PI-AC, Box 16, Folder: My Lai Allegations. • **141**. Department of the Army, Office of the Chief of Staff, Memorandum for Record, Subject: Follow-up Actions on the Peers Report, 8 Jul. 1971, in NA, RG 319, AS, PI-AC, Box 38, Folder: Son My Chron. File • **142**. Seymour M. Hersh, interview with *CBS Morning News*, WTOP TV, Washington, DC, 19 Jan. 1972, Transcript, p. 4, in NA, RG 319, AS, PI-AC, Box 39, Folder: Son My Chron. File # 22 (1 of 3). • **143**. Seymour M. Hersh, 'The Army's Secret Inquiry Describes a 2nd Massacre, Involving 90 Civilians', *New York Times*, 5 Jun. 1972. • **144**. Department of the Army, Judge Advocate, Division for Military Justice, Talking Paper, Subject: 'Coverup', the Seymour Hersh Articles in *The New Yorker*, 29 Jan. 1972, p. 2, in NA, RG 319, AS, ODCS-PER, VWCWG, MLM, Box 1, Folder: TJAG My Lai Talking Papers, Jul. 1971–Jul. 1972 and Department of the Army, Judge Advocate General, Memorandum of Law (CPT Willingham), 22 Mar. 1971, p. 1, in NA, RG 319, AS, ODCS-PER, VWCWG, MLM, Box 1, Folder: Administrative Review – My Lai Cases (Part 1 of 4). • **145**. Belknap, *War on Trial*,

p. 200. • **146**. See Goldstein, Marshall and Schwartz, *Beyond the Reach of Law?*, pp. 1–20 and Knoll and McFadden (eds), *War Crimes and the American Conscience*, pp. 1–47, 104–82. • **147**. Robert Elliott, quoted in Bilton and Sim, *Four Hours*, p. 356. • **148**. Howard H. Callaway, Press Conference, 13 Nov. 1974, p. 5, in NA, RG 319, AS, ODCS-PER, VWCWG, MLM, Box 7, Folder: Release of Peers Report to the Public, 13 Nov. 1974. • **149**. Belknap, *War on Trial*, pp. 149–90, 217–33, 252, 256. • **150**. De John Incident, as of 6 Jul. 1971, in NA, RG 319, AS, PI-AC, Box 53, Folder: War Crimes Allegations – 124: De John Incident. See above, pp. 78–9. • **151**. See above, p. 250 and Hoag Allegation, as of 11 Mar. 1974, in NA, RG 319, AS, ODCS-PER, VWCWG, CaFi, Box 20, Folder: Hoag Allegation (Part 1 of 4), Case 232.1. • **152**. See above, pp. 104, 255 and NA, RG 319, AS, PI-AC, Box 20, Folder: Other than Son My – Ky Trong Incident: Subject/Suspects: Bell, Barnhart, Herron, Applegath. See also Brooks Incident as of 1 May 1972, in ibid., Box 54, Folder: War Crimes Allegations – 219: Brooks Incident; Helicopter Gunship Incident, as of 3 Jun. 1971, in RG 319, AS, ODCS-PER, VWCWG, CaFi, Box 8, Folder: Helicopter Gunship Incident, Case 57. • **153**. Haldeman Diary, pp. 86, 88, 90ff. • **154**. Green Beret Incident, as of 13 Jul. 1971, in NA, RG 319, AS, ODCS-PER, VWCWG, CaFi, Box 16, Folder: Green Beret Incident, Case 162 and Bilton and Sim, *Four Hours*, p. 235ff. • **155**. See above, pp. 164–79. • **156**. Ron Royhab, 'Massacre Story Needs to be Told', *Toledo Blade*, 20 Oct. 2003; Michael Sallah and Mitch Weiss, 'Day 2: Inquiry Ended without Justice. Army Substantiated Numerous Charges – Then Dropped Case of Vietnam War Crimes', *Toledo Blade*, 22 Oct. 2003; 'Vietnam Archive Casts a Shadow Across Decades', *New York Times*, 17 Nov. 2005; Sallah and Weiss, *Tiger Force*, pp. 262ff., 276–9, 300, 318ff. • **157**. Michael Sallah and Mitch Weiss, 'Day 2: Inquiry Ended without Justice. Army Substantiated Numerous Charges – Then Dropped Case of Vietnam War Crimes', *Toledo Blade*, 22 Oct. 2003. • **158**. As for example in the Article 32 investigation 'Hartmann, Lee, O'Connor', during which it was to be clarified whether a unit fired excessive ammunition at a village and deliberately killed or wounded several civilians: NA, RG 319, AS, Records Relating to the Courts Martial of 1st Lt. W. Calley, Capt. V. Hartman, 1 Lt. R. Lee and Capt. O. O'Connor, Box 23, Folder: 404-02 GCM Case – Lee, Robert G., Jr., 1 Lt-497-50-1779 (Folder 207) (1 of 2); ibid., Folder: CID Report of Investigation – Hartman and Lee (Folder 206) (3 of 3); ibid., Box 33, Folder: Charges and Allied Papers in Case of Captain Vincent N. Hartman – U.S. v. Capt Vincent N. Hartman (Folder 335) (1 of 2). • **159**. Major Carl Hensley, who was looking into the accusations of torture against 173rd Airborne Brigade (Separate), was advised by superior officers to consult a psychiatrist. If he rejected the advice he would have to be prepared for sanctions unknown. If he accepted it he would have to reckon on an entry in his personal files about alleged psychological instability. On 16 April 1971 Hensley chose to take his own life. See 'Colonel's Victory of

Sorts', *Evening Standard*, 13 Aug. 1971. This article also mentions massive attempts to intimidate Lieutenant Colonel Anthony B. Herbert. • **160**. Lewy, *America in Vietnam*, p. 352ff. This information related to 1967 to 1969 for Europe and between 1965 and 1970 for Vietnam. • **161**. Roy. E. Bumgarner, Sergeant with 1st Cavalry Division and later with 173rd Airborne Brigade (Separate), had murdered three peasants at the end of February 1969, mutilated their corpses with hand grenades and tried to give the impression that the dead were Viet Cong by later planting weapons: NA, RG 319, AS, ODCS-PER, VWCWG, CaFi, Box 15, Folder: Bumgarner Incident, Case 147; Department of the Army, Office of the Deputy Chief of Staff for Personnel, letter to Congressman Peter H.B. Frelinghuysen, 2 Apr. 1972, in NA, RG 319, AS, ODCS-PER, VWCWG, CF, Box 5, Folder: Congressional Correspondence – War Crimes Allegations, 1971–1972. • **162**. See NA, RG 319, AS, ODCS-PER, VWCWG, CaFi, Box 3, Folder: Duffy – Lanasa Incident; ibid., Folder: Duffy – Lanasa Incident – Correspondence – Udall (Chunko Letter); ibid, Folder: Duffy – Lanasa Incident – Press Release; ibid., Box 6, Folder: Parker Allegation; ibid., Box 14, Folder: Ogg Incident, Case 112 and Folder: Esquire Allegation, Case 113; ibid., Box 14, Folder: CBS News Allegation, Case 119; ibid., Box 15, Folders: Jones Allegation, Case 122; Zupho Incident, Case 127; Pilago Incident; Gilbert Incident, Case 135; Ulysses Williams Incident, Case 136; Son Tinh Incident, Case 139; Kapranopoulous Incident, Case 142; Swain Allegation, Case 143; Somers Incident, Case 144; Trotta Incident, Case 145; Kneer Incident, Case 148; Lawhon Incident, Case 149; Garcia, Incident, Case 150; ibid., Box 16, Folders: Ambrose Incident, Case 157; Alvarado Incident, Case 159; Albert Anderson Incident, Case 160; Torres Allegation, Case 161; Green Beret Incident, Case 162; Greer Incident, Case 163 and ibid, Box 20, Folder: Hoag Allegation (Part 1 of 4), Case 232.1. • **163**. See above, p. 159. Appeal judges released those convicted after a few years: Lang, *Die Meldung*, pp. 23, 35, 39, 42, 64 and NA, RG 319, AS, ODCS-PER, VWCWG, CaFi, Box 15, Folder: Garcia Incident, Case 150. • **164**. See above, pp. 159–60, 175–7. The Marine given a life sentence was still serving in prison in August 1969, his fifty-year sentence reduced to ten years. All the others convicted were released within three years: 'An American Atrocity', *Esquire*, Aug. 1969. • **165**. See above, pp. 128–9, 246. The life sentence for Michael A. Schwarz was reduced to five years by the Commanding General of 1st Marine Division and Samuel G. Green was released after nine months: Solis, *Son Thang*, pp. 276, 282ff. • **166**. Lewy, *America in Vietnam*, p.370ff. This information comes from extrapolations based on well-documented individual cases. • **167**. Solis, *Son Thang*, p. 267 and Lewy, *America in Vietnam*, p. 370ff. • **168**. Solis, *Son Thang*, p. 215. • **169**. Brigadier General William Tiernan quoted in ibid., p. 297. See also ibid., p. 250ff. • **170**. Ibid., p. 216. See also ibid, pp. 213ff., 294. • **171**. Randell Dean Herrod, Michael A. Schwarz, Thomas R. Boyd and Samuel

G. Green were in the dock. A fifth suspected murderer, Michael S. Krichten, was granted immunity from prosecution as a state witness. • **172**. For example, the prosecutors had not brought to the attention of their state witnesses the fact that once a description of a crime had been given, it could not be added to or corrected in any other way in subsequent cross-examination: ibid., p. 295. Both of those convicted, Michael A. Schwarz and Samuel G. Green, were defended by inexperienced military attorneys. • **173**. Ibid., pp. 217-26, 251-4. • **174**. Brgadier General Edwin H. Simmons, United States Marine Corps, quoted in ibid., p. 266. • **175**. An unnamed juror, quoted in ibid., p. 103. • **176**. Ibid., p. 210. • **177**. Geneva Convention, 1949, Article 17: Treatment of Prisoners of War, quoted in Department of the Army, Memorandum of Law (CPT Kotouc), undated, p. 10, in NA, RG 319, AS, ODCS-PER, VWCWG, MLM, Box 4, Folder: Administrative Review – CPT Eugene Kotouc. • **178**. This Field Manual was brought in by high-ranking soldiers to justify torture practices. The Inspector General of I Field Force Vietnam rejected as being legally invalid the accusations of electric torture made against 2nd Lieutenant Warren Ambrose as follows: 'Since no apparent harm or permanent injury was inflicted, it appears to be relatively low level': Headquarters I Field Force Vietnam, IG, Memorandum, Subject: Report of Investigation Concerning Allegations Made Against 2LT Warren Ambrose, 561-60-8722, for Possible War Crimes, 14 Jan. 1971, p. 13, in NA, RG 319, AS, ODCS-PER, VWCWG, CaFi, Box 16, Folder: Ambrose Incident, Case 157. • **179**. Department of the Army, Memorandum of Law (CPT Kotouc), undated, pp. 9, 10, in NA, RG 319, AS, ODCS-PER, VWCWG, MLM, Box 4, Folder: Administrative Review – CPT Eugene Kotouc. • **180**. Department of the Army, Field Manual 27-10: The Law of Land Warfare, Washington, DC, Department of the Army: 18 Jul. 1956, pp. 178-9: § 501. • **181**. Kenneth A. Howard, quoted in Belknap, *War on Trial*, p. 232. • **182**. Homer Bigart, 'Medina May Get a Lesser Charge. Jury to Weigh the Option of Misdemeanor Conviction', *New York Times*, 22 Sep. 1971. • **183**. Telford Taylor, 'The Course of Military Justice'. • **184**. Ibid. See also Lewy, *America in Vietnam*, p. 360ff. • **185**. Belknap, *War on Trial*, p. 230ff., and Kathryn Johnson, 'Acquitted Medina – Not Bitter but Leaving', *Evening Star*, 22 Sep. 1971. • **186**. Lewy, *America in Vietnam*, p 361. The atmosphere in the courtroom is vividly described in McCarthy, *Medina*. • **187**. Bilton and Sim, *Four Hours*, p. 349. • **188**. Solis, *Son Thang*, p. 106. • **189**. For the soundness of the Taylor's criticism, see Lewy, *America in Vietnam*, pp. 238-42. • **190**. Captain Frank P. Jevne, quoted in Solis, *Son Thang*, p. 173. See ibid, pp. 144, 157. • **191**. Ibid., p. 179. • **192**. William Calley, quoted in Department of the Army, Military Justice Division, Status of Cases as of 14 Mar. 1971, p. 4, in NA, RG 319, AS, ODCS-PER, VWCWG, CF, Box 6, Folder: Background Information – History of War Crimes (author's italics). • **193**. Belknap, *War on Trial*, pp. 168-85. For details of the procedures of the Calley case, see NA, RG 153,

Records of the Judge Advocate General (Army), U.S. Army Judiciary, Office of the Clerk of Court Records of the Calley General Court Martial, 1969–1974, Box 1-30. • **194**. Sworn Statement Charles E. Hutto, 17 Nov. 1969, p. 2, in NA, RG 319, AS, PI-FR, Vol. IV: CID-Statements, Box 57, p. 268. • **195**. Department of the Army, Judge Advocate General, Memorandum of Law (Hutto), undated, p. 2, in NA, RG 319, AS, ODCS-PER, VWCWG, MLM, Box 1, Folder: Administrative Review – My Lai Cases (Part 1 of 4). See ibid., Box 5, Folder: Administrative Review – SGT Charles E. Hutto. • **196**. An unnamed colonel, quoted in USCR, 6 Apr. 1971, p. E2876. • **197**. William Eckhardt, quoted in Belknap, *War on Trial*, p. 226. • **198**. NA, RG 319, AS, ODCS-PER, VWCWG, MLM, Box 5, Folder: Administrative Review – My Lai Cases (Part 1 of 4); ibid., Box 5, Folder: Administrative Review – SP 4 Kenneth F. Doherty and RG 319, AS, PI-AC, Box 37, Folder: Son My Chron. File # 15 (2 of 2). • **199**. Belknap, *War on Trial*, p. 224 and Bilton and Sim, *Four Hours*, p. 329. • **200**. Seymour M. Hersh, interview in the TV programme 'Firing Line', WETA-TV, 7 Jul. 1971, Washington, DC, transcript, p. 38, in NA, RG 319, AS, PI-AC, Box 38, Folder: Son My Chron. File # 20 (1 of 2). • **201**. McCarthy, *Medina*, p. 44.

Conclusion

1. From a reader's letter to the *Toledo Blade*, after the newspaper had published the first article in a four-part series about the Tiger Force murders in October 2003. Quoted in Sallah and Weiss, *Tiger Force*, p. 320. • **2**. Mendel Rivers, quoted in 'Mylai Trials' End Sought', *Washington Post*, 12 Apr. 1970. The trial of several Green Berets who had to answer for the murder of a South Vietnamese double agent was surprisingly brought to a halt in autumn 1969 – allegedly, according to Secretary of the Army Resor, because the CIA refused to summon important witnesses for reasons of 'national security': press statement by Stanley Resor, 29 Sep. 1969, p. 1, in NA, RG 319, AS, PI-AC, Box 11, Folder: Green Beret Case – Accused of Murder. • **3**. Mendel Rivers, quoted in 'Rivers Urges "Win" Policy in Asia, Decries Latest Mylai Charges', *Washington Post*, 20 May 1970. See also Department of the Army, Office of the Secretary of the Army, Memorandum, for: Chief of Staff, Subject: Status Report as to the Hebert Special Subcommittee on Son My, 10 Apr. 1970, in NA, RG 319, AS, PI-AC, Box 11, Folder: Hebert Subcommittee Hearings, 15–24 Apr. 70. • **4**. Mendel Rivers, quoted in UPI Special Wire Service News, 19 Mar. 1970, in NA, RG 319, AS, PI-AC, Box 5, Folder: Army Staff Monitor Summary and Backup Material. • **5**. Mendel Rivers, quoted in 'My Lai Pilot Aimed at GIs, Saved Viets', *Washington Star*, 11 Dec. 1969. • **6**. 'Army Gets Rivers to Close My Lai "Massacre" Hearing', *Washington Star*, 13 Dec. 1969. Even William Peers accused Rivers of wanting to block the pending trials:

Department of the Army, Office Memorandum, Office Chief of Staff Army, Memorandum, to: General Westmoreland, General Palmer, Subject: Brief Analysis of Hebert Subcommittee Report, Confidential, 22 Jul. 1970, p. 2, in NA, RG 319, AS, PI-AC, Box 35, Folder: Son My Chron. File # 12 (1 of 2). See also Anderson (ed.), *Facing My Lai*, p. 46. • **7**. Mendel Rivers, quoted in House of Representatives, Stenographic Transcript of Hearings before the Committee on Armed Services, Secret, 5 Mar. 1970, pp. 18–19, in NA, RG 319, AS, PI-AC, Box 48, Folder: Untitled – 22 Sep. 72 (2 of 2). • **8**. Department of the Army, Office of the Secretary of the Army, Memorandum, for: Chief of Staff, Subject: Status Report as to the Hebert Special Subcommittee on Son My, 10 Apr. 1970, in NA, RG 319, AS, PI-AC, Box 11, Folder: Hebert Subcommittee Hearings, 15–24 Apr. 70. See also Department of the Army, Office of the Secretary of the Army, Memorandum: Information for Members of Congress: Son My, Chronology of Key Events and Congressional Notification Son My Incident, p. 16, in ibid., Box 36, Folder: Son My Chron. File # 14 (1 of 2); Stanley R. Resor, Secretary of the Army, letter to F. Edward Hebert, 14 Apr. 1970, in RG 319, AS, ODCS-PER, VWCWG, MLM, Box 7, Folder: Congressional Correspondence My Lai: Hebert Subcommittee Investigation. • **9**. Bilton and Sim, *Four Hours*, p. 348. • **10**. F. Edward Hebert, quoted in Transcript of Hebert Subcommittee News Conference in Rayburn House Office Building, 15 Jul. 1970, p. 10, in NA, RG 319, AS, PI-AC, Box 35, Folder: Son My Chron. File # 12 (1 of 2). • **11**. F. Edward Hebert, quoted in ibid., p. 15. By now the authenticity of the photographs had been verified long since: Department of the Army, Office of the Secretary of the Army, Memorandum: Information for Members of Congress: Son My, Chronology of Key Events and Congressional Notification Son My Incident, p. 9, in ibid., Box 36, Folder: Son My Chron. File # 14 (1 of 2). • **12**. F. Edward Hebert, quoted in ibid., p. 6. See also Department of the Army, Office of the Secretary of the Army, Memorandum for the Record, Subject: Resume of Congressional Hearings, 9 Dec. 1969, p. 2, in NA, RG 319, AS, PI-AC, Box 18, Folder: OCLL MFRs. • **13**. F. Edward Hebert, quoted in Transcript of Hebert Subcommittee News Conference in Rayburn House Office Building, 15 Jul. 1970, p. 16, in NA, RG 319, AS, PI-AC, Box 35, Folder: Son My Chron. File # 12 (1 of 2); see ibid., p. 4. • **14**. F. Edward Hebert, letter to Stanley R. Resor, 27 Apr. 1970, in NA, RG 319, AS, PI-AC, Box 17, Folder: (OCLL) Item B-H Folder. Hebert also held to this position before the press: see Department of the Army, Office of the Secretary of the Army, Memorandum for the Record, Subject: 15 Jul. 1970, Press Conference by Chairman Hebert Concerning Subcommittee Report 'Investigation of the My Lai Incident', in NA, RG 319, AS, PI-AC, Box 35, Folder: Son My Chron. File # 12 (1 of 2). • **15**. Tuchman, *Torheit*, p. 418. Senator J. William Fulbright, who emerged at this time as a critic of the Vietnam policies, kept a low profile on the subject of war crimes. Senator

Edward Kennedy on the other hand joined in parts of the criticism of the Winter Soldiers. In the preceding years Kennedy had already strongly criticised the strategy of attrition and the excesses of violence in Vietnam through the Subcommittee on Refugees of the Senate Committee on the Judiciary: see Edward M. Kennedy, letter to Secretary of Defense Melvin R. Laird, 10 May 1971, in NA, RG 319, AS, PI-AC, Box 6, Folder: Conduct of the War in Vietnam, Chron. File # 2 (1 of 2). • **16**. F. Edward Hebert, Press Release, 4 Dec. 1970, in NA, RG 319, AS, PI-AC, Box 36, Folder: Son My Chron. File # 14 (2 of 2). • **17**. NA, RG 319, AS, PI-AC, Box 36, Folder: Son My Chron. File # 14 (1 of 2). See also Bilton and Sim, *Four Hours*, p. 329, and Belknap, *War on Trial*, p. 224. • **18**. Roy H. Steele, Investigations Division Office, Office of the Secretary of the Army, Department of the Army, letter to John T.M. Reddan, Special Subcommittee – My Lai, Committee on Armed Services, House of Representatives, 24 Nov. 1970, in NA, RG 319, AS, ODCS-PER, VWCWG, MLM, Box 7, Folder: Congressional Correspondence My Lai: Hebert Subcommittee Investigation. • **19**. Congressman Stratton (New York), quoted in USCR, House, 8 Feb. 1972, p. H895. For the criticism of the Hebert Committee see also Anderson (ed.), *Facing My Lai*, p. 28ff. • **20**. Report of the Armed Services Investigating Subcommittee of the Committee on Armed Services, House of Representatives, 91st Congress, Second Session, 15 Jul. 1970: Department of the Army, Memorandum: Discussion of Recommendations Contained in the Report of the My Lai Incident Subcommittee of the House Armed Services Committee, undated, p. 2, in NA, RG 319, AS, ODCS-PER, VWCWG, MLM, Box 7, Folder: Congressional Correspondence My Lai: Hebert Subcommittee Investigation; Department of the Army, Information Division, Fact Sheet, Subject: Press Coverage of the Hebert Subcommittee News Conference, undated, in NA, RG 319, AS, PI-AC, Box 35, Folder: Son My Chron. File # 12 (1 of 2); 'Mylai Probers Would Allow Insanity Plea on War Crimes', *Washington Post*, 16 Jul. 1970. The demands of Rivers and Hebert also found a clear echo outside Washington: see Lewy, *America in Vietnam*, p. 356. • **21**. Engelhardt, *Victory Culture*, pp. 231–5, 244; Chatfield, *Peace Movement*, pp. 137–46 and Lewy, *America in Vietnam*, p. 357. • **22**. *Time*, 12 Jan. 1970, p. 11. • **23**. 'The Clamor over Calley', *Time*, 12 Apr. 1971, p. 14. • **24**. See Steinfels, 'Calley and the Public Conscience'; Lesher, 'The Calley Case Re-Examined'; Greiner, '"You'll Never Walk Alone"'. • **25**. *Minneapolis Tribune*, 21 Dec. 1969, p. 4B. • **26**. 'The Clamor over Calley', *Time*, 12 Apr. 1971, p. 18. See also *Time*, 12 Jan. 1970, pp. 8, 10–11 and Oliver, *History and Memory*, pp. 89, 106, 116. • **27**. 'Assessing Songmy. Doves Recoil but Hawks Tend to See "Massacre" as Just a Part of War', *Wall Street Journal*, 1 Dec. 1969. • **28**. Schell, *Observing the Nixon Years*, pp. 17, 19. • **29**. *Time*, 12 Dec. 1969, pp. 70–1. This text was part of a series of advertisements called 'The Power of Print', run in *Time* from May 1969. Under this title *Time* had invited advertising agencies throughout the country to present any subject they chose in four columns and with their own choice of means. Commercial products aside, any idea could be promoted. 'We gave them four columns of free space in which we hoped to see much inventive use of the printed page,' as the publisher explained ('To our Readers: A Letter from the Publisher', *Time*, 1 Jun. 1970). Of over 200 suggestions sent in, 34 were published free of charge from May 1969, including texts on racism, pollution, child abuse, patriotism – and even Vietnam. The advertisement of 12 December 1969 was undoubtedly a comment on the discussion about the My Lai (4) massacre which had been going on since mid November. • **30**. A supporter of Randell Dean Herrod, quoted in Solis, *Son Thang*, p. 220. • **31**. Ibid., p. 217ff. • **32**. Department of the Army, Office of the Secretary of the Army, Memorandum, Information for Members of Congress: Son My, Chronology of Key Events and Congressional Notification Son My Incident, p. 23, in NA, RG 319, AS, PI-AC, Box 36, Folder: Son My Chron. File # 14 (1 of 2). • **33**. 'The Battle Hymn of Lieutenant Calley', quoted in 'Sales of Calley Record Soar, but Battle Stirs on Air Waves', *Miami Herald*, 6 Apr. 1971. • **34**. Shelby Singleton, quoted in ibid. • **35**. ABC TV Reports, The Calley Case: A Nation's Agony, 23 May 1971, Transcript, p. 1, in NA, RG 319, AS, PI-AC, Box 38, Folder: Son My Chron. File # 18 (1 of 2). • **36**. The American Legion had at that time 700,000 members, the Veterans of Foreign Wars 500,000 and the Disabled American Veterans 196,000. Approximately 350,000 Vietnam veterans had joined these three associations; they comprised about a quarter of their membership: Fact Sheet, undated, in NA, RG 127, HMC-HDPT, TR, FRC Box 4, Folder: Command Concerns: Drugs/Racial Strife/Fragging. In December 1969 a symbolic meeting between the President and the leaders of the veterans' organisations was considered: NPMP, NSC, AMH-CF, Box 960, Folder: Haig Chron 17–20 Dec. 1969 (2 of 2). • **37**. Reverend Michael Lord, quoted in Bilton and Sim, *Four Hours*, p. 340. • **38**. Jimmy Carter, quoted in ibid., p. 340. • **39**. A representative of the American Legion, quoted in Oliver, *History and Memory*, p. 158. • **40**. Ibid., p. 90. See ibid., p. 108 and Bilton and Sim, *Four Hours*, p. 341. • **41**. Bilton and Sim, *Four Hours*, pp. 338–400. • **42**. Halberstam, *Powers*, p. 567. He was referring to the article by Neil Sheehan, 'War Crimes Trials?' In his review of thirty-three books about the Vietnam War Sheehan argued decisively in favour of trials for all suspects, be they GIs or officers. • **43**. Bilton and Sim, *Four Hours*, pp. 341, 345. • **44**. *Look*, 2 Jun. 1970. • **45**. Trent Angers, quoted in 'My Lai Hero Hugh Thompson Jr. Dies at 62', Associated Press, 7 Jan. 2006. On the thirtieth anniversary of the massacre, 16 March 1998, Thompson and his gunners Lawrence Colburn and Glenn Andreotta (posthumously) received the Soldier's Medal, one of the highest decorations awarded by the US Army. They were commended for 'heroism in the absence of the enemy'. • **46**. Hugh Thompson, quoted in Richard Goldstein, 'Hugh Thompson, 62, Who Saved

Civilians at My Lai, Dies', *New York Times*, 7 Jan. 2006. • **47**. John F. Kerry
during a rally in New York City in April 1971, quoted in Oliver, *History and
Memory*, p. 110. • **48**. John F. Kerry on 22 April 1971 before the Senate Committee
on Foreign Relations, quoted in 'The Voice of the Winter Soldier', *Playboy*,
Aug. 1971. For comparable comments by other Winter Soldiers and related
organizations, see USCR, 6 Apr. 1971, pp. E2825–65 and 'Ex-GI Tells Atrocities
Panel He Saw Another U.S. Massacre Near My Lai', *Washington Post*, 29 Apr.
1971. In order for their sacrifices to be recognised the Winter Soldiers placed
a free, whole-page advertisement in *Playboy* in February 1971, which allegedly
brought them an influx of 10,000 new members. • **49**. ABC TV Reports,
The Calley Case: A Nation's Agony, 23 May 1971, Transcript, p. 23, in NA, RG
319, AS, PI-AC, Box 38, Folder: Son My Chron. File # 18 (2 of 2). The aforementioned Frank Reel was the attorney who had defended the Japanese
General Yamashita, accused of war crimes, in the 1945 Tokyo trial. In both
newspapers and magazines which had taken different lines on My Lai (4) up
to this point, the assumption of legal responsibility by soldiers was described
as 'gross oversimplification' and rejected. In the case of Vietnam, according
to *Newsweek*, court judgments were not an expression of law but rather of
'vengeance': 'Who Else is Guilty?', *Newsweek*, 12 Apr. 1971, p. 32. See also
'Alleged My Lai Photograph Shows Armed Boys, Women', *Columbus Inquirer*,
18 Dec. 1969 and 'Footnote on My Lai', *Chicago Tribune*, 8 Apr. 1970. • **50**. Bilton
and Sim, *Four Hours*, p. 341 and NA, RG 319, AS, PI-AC, Box 42, Folder: Son
My Chron. File # 29 (1 of 2). • **51**. State of Florida, House of Representatives,
Resolution No. 5265, p. 1, in NA, RG 319, AS, ODCS-PER, VWCWG, MLM,
Box 7, Folder: Congressional Correspondence My Lai: Hebert Subcommittee
Investigation. • **52**. Oklahoma State Senate, Senate Concurrent Resolution
No. 51, 29 Jan. 1970, p. 1, in NA, RG 319, AS, PI-AC, Box 33, Folder: Son My
Chron. File # 7 (1 of 2). • **53**. Richard Nixon, quoted in diary entry of Harry
Robbins Haldeman, dictated onto tape, in Oliver, *History and Memory*, p. 162.
• **54**. 'Interview with Prominent Psychiatrist: Why Civilians are War Victims',
US News & World Report, 15 Dec. 1969, pp. 25–8 and Kelman, 'Social Context
of Torture', in Crelinsten and Schmidt (eds), *Politics of Pain*. • **55**. Stephen
Ambrose, quoted in Anderson (ed.), *Facing My Lai*, pp. 115–16. • **56**. John F.
Kerry, quoted in ABC TV Reports, The Calley Case: A Nation's Agony, 23
May 1971, Transcript, p. 25, in NA, RG 319, AS, PI-AC, Box 38, Folder: Son
My Chron. File # 18 (2 of 2). • **57**. Engelhardt, *Victory Culture*, pp. 4ff., 9–15,
24–8, 41–6; Kolko, *Century of War*, pp. 373–485. See also Gibson, *Warrior Dreams*,
p. 23; Lewis, *The Tainted War*; Greiner, '"First to Go, Last to Know"'. •
58. Department of the Army, Office of the Chief of Staff, Memorandum,
Subject: Response to Calley Verdict, 1 Apr. 1971, in NA, RG 319, AS, PI-AC,
Box 37, Folder: Son My Chron. File # 17 (1 of 2). • **59**. Department of the
Army, Office Memorandum, Office Chief of Staff Army, to: General West-

moreland, Subject: Five Representative 'Calley' Letters, 12 Apr. 1971, p. 2, in ibid. • **60**. Oliver, *History and Memory*, p. 231, and Belknap, *War on Trial*, p. 195. • **61**. The 'Calley Correspondence' fills thirty archive boxes, deposited in NA, RG 319, referred to in the following as CC. Up to and including Box 12 the first folder out of each odd-numbered box and the last folder out of each even-numbered box were evaluated; from Box 13 on the selection was made in reverse order. Other letters to Calley, albeit a significantly smaller number, are to be found in NA, RG 319, AS, Records Relating to the Courts Martial of 1st Lt. W. Calley, Capt. V. Hartman, 1st Lt. R. Lee, and Capt. O. O'Connor, Box 15, Folder: Freedom Mail; ibid., Box 24, Folder: Incoming Unsolicited Letters Concerning Trial Counsel; Folder: Incoming Unsolicited Letters Concerning the Trial of 1st Lt. Calley; Folder: 401-34 GCM Case File – Calley – Incoming Unsolicited Letters; RG 319, AS, PI-AC, Box 37, Folder: Son My Chron. File # 16 (3 of 3); ibid., Folder Son My Chron. File # 17 (2 of 2); ibid., Box 38, Folder: Son My Chron. File # 18 (1 of 2); ibid., Box 41, Folder: Son My Chron. File # 25 (2 of 2) and Folder: Son My Chron. File # 26 (1 of 3); ibid., Box 42, Folder: Son My Chron. File # 27 (1 of 3) and ibid., Folder: Son My Chron. File # 28 (2 of 2); ibid., Box 43, Folder: Son My Chron. File # 29 (2 of 2); ibid., Folder: Son My Chron. File # 30 (2 of 2) and ibid., Folder: Son My Chron. File # 31 (1 of 2); RG 319, AS, ODCS-PER, VWCWG, MLM, Box 7, Folder: Public Correspondence – My Lai, Part 1 and Part 2 and ibid., Folder: Congressional Correspondence – My Lai: Constituent Letters. • **62**. 'Loyal American Citizens', letter to Richard Nixon, 30 Mar. 1971, in CC, Box 16, first Folder. • **63**. This observation also applies to other collections of letters. See NA, RG 319, AS, PI-AC, Box 37, Folder: Son My Chron. File # 16 (3 of 3). • **64**. See Elizabeth Cummings, letter to US Army Headquarters, 30 Mar. 1971, in: CC, Box 16, first Folder; Richard Brown, undated letter, in: CC, Box 1, first Folder; employees of the Business Supplies Corporation, Marietta, Georgia, letter to Melvin R. Laird, 30 Mar. 1971, in CC, Box 4, last Folder. • **65**. Fred Johnson, letter 'To whom it may concern', undated, in CC, Box 7, first Folder. • **66**. A.E.Tilton, letter to the Joint Chiefs of Staff, 31 Mar. 1971, in CC, Box 1, first Folder. • **67**. Mary A. Carr, letter, 'Dear Sirs', 31 Mar. 1971, in CC, Box 1, first Folder. • **68**. Mrs C. Leo Detunler, letter 'Sirs', 6 Apr. 1971, in CC, Box 16, first Folder. • **69**. Laurence Saleeby, letter to the Joint Chiefs of Staff, 29 Mar. 1971, in CC, Box 1, first Folder. • **70**. See 'Concerned in Columbus, Georgia', letter to Richard Nixon, 31 Mar. 1971, in CC, Box 1, first Folder; Mrs and Mr H.G. Kuehn, letter to the Joint Chiefs of Staff, 3 Apr. 1971, in CC, Box 1, first Folder; Cogil Medical Electronics Corp., letter to General William Westmoreland, 30 Mar. 1971, in CC, Box 9, first Folder; Kathy R. Riley, letter 'Sir', undated, in CC, Box 16, first Folder; Mrs Jack Tinsley, letter to Richard Nixon, 1 Apr. 1971, in CC, Box 21, last Folder; Mrs Fred W. Schraelge, letter to Richard Nixon, 30 Mar. 1971, in CC, Box 21, last Folder;

James T. Mann, letter to Richard Nixon, 1 Apr. 1971, in CC, Box 23, last Folder.
• **71**. Keith and Peggy Schulz, letter 'Gentlemen', 31 Mar. 1971, in CC, Box 1,
first Folder. • **72**. See Benjamin R. Day, letter to the Joint Chiefs of Staff, 31
Mar. 1971, in CC, Box 1, first Folder; A. Lynch, letter to Stanley Resor, 4 Apr.
1971, in CC, Box 7, first Folder; William L. Hinkson, letter to US Army Chief
of Staff, undated, in CC, Box 9, first Folder; Jim Newsome, letter to General
William Westmoreland, 30 Mar. 1971, in CC, Box 9, first Folder; 'Concerned
Citizens' of Los Angeles, California & Livonia, Michigan, letter to Richard
Nixon, 30 Mar. 1971, in CC, Box 16, first Folder. • **73**. 'A Group of not-so-
proud citizens of America', letter to Stanley Resor, 31 Mar. 1971, in CC, Box
11, first Folder. • **74**. See Everette S. McDonald, letter to Judge Advocate
General, 1 Apr. 1971, in CC, Box 14, first Folder. • **75**. The brother of one of
the accused, quoted in Jack Shepherd, 'Incident at Van Duong', *Look*, 17 Aug.
1969, p. 22. This referred to a soldier from A Co, 1st Battalion, 27th Regiment,
1st Marine Division, who together with several colleagues had murdered prisoners to the east of Huê, Thua Thien Province (I Corps Tactical Zone) in
early May 1968. • **76**. Arthur G. Trudeau, letter to Major General Benjamin
F. Evans, Jr., Third US Army, 29 Sep. 1970, in NA, RG 319, AS, PI-AC, Box 37,
Folder: Son My Chron. File # 16 (3 of 3). • **77**. Mary Beth Willey, letter to
Richard Nixon, 5 Apr. 1971, in CC, Box 20, first Folder. In fact the magazine
National Review headed a four-page article in its 20 April 1971 issue 'Calley
for President?' See Mitchell N. Daroff, letter to Adjutant General, Department
of the Army, 12 Apr. 1971, in CC, Box 16, first Folder; Pat Krumenauer, letter
to the Joint Chiefs of Staff, 7 Apr. 1971, in CC, Box 1, first Folder; Lyn Baker,
letter to Richard Nixon, 3 Apr. 1971, in CC, Box 18, first Folder; Donna Penn,
letter to Richard Nixon, 2 Apr. 1971, in CC, Box 23, last Folder; joint letter to
William Westmoreland, 1 Apr. 1971, in CC, Box 11, first Folder. • **78**. See Chris-
tianne M. Hearn, letter to Melvin Laird, 31 Mar. 1971, in CC, Box 2, last Folder;
Eddie Huckabee, letter to Melvin Laird, 31 Mar. 1971, in CC, Box 5, first
Folder; Ronald C. Peterson, letter to Melvin Laird, 30 Mar. 1971, in CC, Box
5, first Folder; Mr and Mrs James C. Davis, letter 'Dear Sir', undated, in CC,
Box 6, last Folder; James and Sharon Strohl, letter to Stanley Resor, 31 Mar.
1971, in CC, Box 6, last Folder; Glenda Grooms Davis, letter 'To Whom It
May Concern', 30 Mar. 1971, in CC, Box 9, first Folder; Lyle O. Grenchef,
letter to Chief of Staff – Armed Forces, 12 Apr. 1971, in CC, Box 10, last
Folder; Richard A. Wuenker, letter to Commanding General – Department
of the Army, 5 Apr. 1971, in CC, Box 11, first Folder; E.A. Baker, letter to
Department of the Army, 30 Mar. 1971, in CC, Box 15, last Folder; Don R.
Pearson, letter to Senator Howard H. Baker, 1 Apr. 1971, in CC, Box 17, last
Folder; Mrs Lois S. Dunn, letter to Representative Wilmer Mizell, 31 Mar.
1971, in CC, Box 17, last Folder; Edward J. Callahan, letter to Richard Nixon,
4 Apr. 1971, in CC, Box 23, last Folder. • **79**. A. Lynch, letter to Stanley Resor,

4 Apr. 1971, in CC, Box 7, first Folder. • **80**. Jerry E. Stanford, letter to Stanley Resor, 31 Mar. 1971, p. 2, in CC, Box 5, last Folder. • **81**. Jerry E. Stanford, letter to Stanley Resor, 31 Mar. 1971, p. 2, in CC, Box 6, last Folder. See Carolyn S. Thomas, letter to Melvin Laird, 31 Mar. 1971, in CC, Box 2, last Folder; Pearl Reed, letter to Melvin Laird, 3 Apr. 1971, in CC, Box 2, last Folder; Pete Thompson, letter to Melvin Laird, April 1971, in CC, Box 4, last Folder; Bob Green, letter to Stanley Resor, undated, in CC, Box 9, first Folder; Joseph A. Shelley, letter to Richard Nixon, 1 Apr. 1971, in CC, Box 19, last Folder; Mary Beth Willey, letter to Richard Nixon, 5 Apr. 1971, in CC, Box 20, first Folder; Pearl Williams, letter to Richard Nixon, 31 Mar. 1971, in CC, Box 21, last Folder; Donna Penn, letter to Richard Nixon, 2 Apr. 1971, in CC, Box 23, last Folder. • **82**. G.M. Davis, letter to Melvin Laird, 31 Mar. 1971, in CC, Box 6, last Folder. • **83**. Edward J. Callahan, letter to Richard Nixon, 4 Apr. 1971, in CC, Box 23, last Folder. • **84**. Martin C. Sandor, letter to Richard Nixon together with enclosure from the *Detroit Free Press*, 1 Apr. 1971, in CC, Box 16, first Folder. • **85**. See Donald J. Tobkin, letter to Stanley Resor, 4 Apr. 1971, in CC, Box 7, first Folder; Gertrud J. Thompson, letter to General William Westmoreland, 30 Mar. 1971, in CC, Box 10, last Folder; Dan Alpton, letter to General William Westmoreland, 31 Mar. 1971, in CC, Box 11, first Folder; Mrs John Sisko, letter to Richard Nixon, 31 Mar. 1971, in CC, Box 15, last Folder; Stanley McCaffrey, letter, no addressee, April 1971, in CC, Box 15, last Folder: Shirley V. Sinclair, undated letter, no addressee, in CC, Box 17, last Folder; James B. Kostelnik, letter to Richard Nixon, 2 Apr. 1971, in CC, Box 21, last Folder: J.E. Clare, letter to Richard Nixon, 31 Mar. 1971, in CC, Box 21, last Folder; Charles L. Patterson, Jr., letter to Richard Nixon, 31 Mar. 1971, in CC, Box 22, first Folder. • **86**. 'A Disgusted Veteran', letter to Stanley Resor, 31 Mar. 1971, in CC, Box 6, last Folder. • **87**. Earl F. Higgins, undated letter, together with photo, no addressee, in CC, Box 15, last Folder. • **88**. See Betty Pittman, letter 'Dear Sir', 31 Mar. 1971, in CC, Box 6, last Folder; Donald J. Tobkin, letter to Stanley Resor, 4 Apr. 1971, in CC, Box 7, first Folder; Madeleine V. Woodland et al., Resolution to Richard Nixon, 31 Mar. 1971, in CC, Box 18, first Folder; Mr and Mrs Gerald F. Mahsem, Sr., letter to Richard Nixon, 31 Mar. 1971, p. 1, in CC, Box 20, first Folder. • **89**. Kelman and Hamilton, *Crimes of Obedience*, pp. 168ff., 173ff., 181, 212, 233, 236ff., 241ff. See also Kelman and Lawrence, 'Assignment of Responsibility' and Lawrence and Kelman, 'Reactions to the Calley Trial'. • **90**. Myrtle Meadlo, quoted in Bilton and Sim, *Four Hours*, p. 263. • **91**. Lieutenant Stengo during instruction on the international laws of warfare in Fort Benning, quoted in William Greider, 'Teaching of War Law Revitalized by Army', *Washington Post*, 14 Feb. 1971. • **92**. Kelman and Hamilton, *Crimes of Obedience*, pp. 262–77, 292–7, 318–24, 348ff. and Kelman and Lawrence, 'Assignment of Responsibility', pp. 188, 199. • **93**. 'Our Country, Right or Wrong', *Philadelphia Inquirer*, 19 May 1972. • **94**. A.E.Tilton, letter to the Joint

Chiefs of Staff, 31 Mar. 1971, in CC, Box 1, first Folder. • **95**. For the relevant opinion polls, see Oliver, *History and Memory*, pp. 154, 162ff., 273. • **96**. Countless opinion polls from the late 1960s and early 1970s cover this subject: the majority criticised not the war as such but the allegedly indecisive way in which it was conducted. It is no contradiction that in spring 1968 Lyndon B. Johnson lost in primaries against the 'peace candidate' Eugene McCarthy: the majority of the McCarthy voters were not casting a vote for peace. They were voting much more against Johnson and in favour of a harder line in Vietnam: Braestrup, *Big Story*, pp. 500, 506; Spector, *After Tet*, p. 315; Belknap, *War on Trial*, p. 133. • **97**. Taylor, *Nuremberg and Vietnam*, p. 207.

Sources

National Archives, College Park (Maryland)
Record Group 127:
Records of the United States Marine Corps, Headquarters United States Marine Corps, Historian's Department:
- Trial by Fire 1968–1969, NA, 127-94-0012

Record Group 127:
Records of the United States Marine Corps, Headquarters United States Marine Corps, History and Museum Division:
- Background and Draft Materials for US Marines in Vietnam: 'The Defining Year 1968'

Record Group 153:
Records of the Judge Advocate General (Army), United States Army Judiciary:
- Office of the Clerk of Court: Records of the Calley General Court Martial, 1969–1974

Record Group 273:
Records of the National Security Council:
- National Security Action Memoranda (NSAM)

Record Group 319:
Records of the Army Staff, Office of the Deputy Chief of Staff for Personnel, Vietnam War Crimes Working Group:
- War Crimes Allegations Case Files
- Central File
- Records Pertaining to the My Lai Massacre, 1969–1974

Record Group 319:
Records of the Army Staff, Records of the Peers Inquiry, Final Report, Edited Version, 1970–1975 (Report of the Department of the Army Review of the Preliminary Investigations into the My Lai Incident):
- Vol. I: Analyses, Findings, Conclusions and Recommendations
- Vol. II: Testimony Developed by the Peers Inquiry
- Vol. III: Exhibits
- Vol. IV: Testimony Developed by the Criminal Investigation Division

Record Group 319:

Records of the Army Staff, Records of the Peers Inquiry:
- Records Created after the Completion of the Peers Inquiry, 1969–1975
- Administrative and Background Materials Files – Closed Inventory, 1967–1970
- Administrative and Background Materials Files – Open Inventory, 1967–1970

Record Group 319:

Records of the Army Staff, Calley Correspondence:
- Unanswered Letters, 1971

Record Group 319:

Records of the Army Staff, Office of the Chief of Military History:
- Records Relating to the Courts Martial of 1st Lt. W. Calley, Capt. V. Hartman, 1st Lt. R. Lee, and Capt. O. O'Connor

Record Group 319:

Records of the Army Staff, Assistant Chief of Staff for Operations (G 3) Plans Division:
- Security Classified General Records

Record Group 334:

Records of Interservice Agencies, MACV, DRAC:
- Staff Judge Advocate: General Records

Record Group 338:

Records of United States Army Commands Headquarters, Headquarters Detachment:
- 22 United States Army, Prisoner of War/Civilian Internee Information Center: Confidential Records
- 22 United States Army, Prisoner of War/Civilian Internee Information Center: Secret Records
- 22 United States Army, Prisoner of War/Civilian Internee Information Center: Unclassified Records

Record Group 472:

Records of the United States Forces in Southeast Asia, Headquarters United States Army Vietnam:
- Command Historian: Operation Speedy Express Background Files

Record Group 472:

Records of the United States Forces in Southeast Asia, Military Assistance Command Vietnam:
- Inspector General, Investigations Division: Reports of Investigations
- Inspector General, Investigations Division: Miscellaneous Reports of Investigations

Record Group 472:

Records of the United States Forces in Southeast Asia, Headquarters United

States Army Vietnam:
- Inspector General Section, Investigation and Complaint Division: Reports of Investigation Case Files
- Provost Marshal Section, Administrative Office: Security Classified General Records

Record Group 472:

Records of the United States Forces in Southeast Asia, Military Assistance Command Vietnam, Delta Regional Assistance Command:
- Inspector General: Preliminary Inquiry Re: Colonel Franklin
- Assistant Chief of Staff for Intelligence (G 2) Advisor: Security Classified General Records
- Staff Judge Advocate: General Records

Record Group 472:

Records of the United States Forces in Southeast Asia, Military Assistance Command Vietnam, Third Regional Assistance Command:
- Staff Judge Advocate: Reports of Investigations

Record Group 472:

Records of the United States Army Vietnam, Headquarters United States Army Vietnam:
- Deputy Chief of Staff for Operations, Plans and Security Operations and Training Division, Army Operations Center: Accident Case Files

Record Group 472:

Records of the United States Army Vietnam, II Field Force Vietnam:
- Assistant Chief of Staff for Operations (G 3), Plans Division: Security Classified General Records
- Assistant Chief of Staff for Operations (G 3): Situation Reports
- Assistant Chief of Staff for Operations (G 3): Daily Journal
- Assistant Chief of Staff for Operations (G 3): Operational Reports – Lessons Learned
- Assistant Chief of Staff for Operations (G 3): VC/NVA Base Area Neutralization Reports
- Assistant Chief of Staff for Operations (S 3): Reports of Artillery Accidents and Incidents
- Staff Judge Advocate: Reports of Investigations

Record Group 472:

Records of the United States Army Vietnam, 9th Infantry Division:
- Organizational History
- Assistant Chief of Staff (G 5): Command Reports

Record Group 472:

Records of the United States Army Vietnam, 16th Military History Detachment:
- Operation Speedy Express Background Files

Records of the United States Army Vietnam, 19th Military History Detachment:
- Historian's Background Files
- After Action Interviews

Nixon Presidential Materials Project:
National Security Council Files:
- Name Files
- Alexander M. Haig Special File
- Alexander M. Haig Chronological File
- Presidential/HAK MemCons
- Staff Files: Lake Chron. Series

Nixon Presidential Materials Project:
White House Special Files:
- Charles W. Colson

Columbia University, New York City
Butler Library, Oral History Research Office:
- Interviews conducted for the Oral History Research Office by Professor Clark Smith

Texas Tech University:
Vietnam Archive, Declassified Documents Reference System

Bibliography

Anderson, David L. (ed.), *Facing My Lai: Moving Beyond the Massacre*, Lawrence, Kan., 1998.

Andrade, Dale, *Ashes to Ashes: The Phoenix Program and the Vietnam War*, Lexington, Mass., 1990.

Angers, Trent, *The Forgotten Hero of My Lai: The Hugh Thompson Story*, Lafayette, La., 1999.

Appy, Christian G., *Patriots: The Vietnam War Remembered From All Sides*, New York, 2003.

—— *Working-Class War: American Combat Soldiers and Vietnam*, Chapel Hill, 1993.

Arreguin-Toft, Ivan, *How the Weak Win Wars: A Theory of Asymmetric Conflict*, Cambridge and New York, 2005.

Bacevich, Andrew J., *The New American Militarism: How Americans are Seduced by War*, Oxford, 2005.

Bailey, Brian, *Massacres: An Account of Crimes Against Humanity*, London, 1994.

Baker, Michael, *Nam: The Vietnam War in the Words of the Men and Women Who Fought There*, New York, 2001.

Ball, George, *The Past Has Another Pattern: Memoirs*, New York, 1982.

Baritz, Loren, *Backfire: A History of How American Culture Led Us into Vietnam and Made Us Fight the Way We Did*, Baltimore, 1985 (1998).

Barrett, Frank J., 'Die Konstruktion hegemonialer Männlichkeit in Organisationen: Das Beispiel der US-Marine', in Christine Eifler and Ruth Seifert (eds), *Soziale Konstruktionen – Militär und Geschlechterverhältnis*, Münster, 1999.

Baskir, Lawrence M. and Strauss, William A., *Chance and Circumstance: The Draft, the War and the Vietnam Generation*, New York, 1978.

Bates, Milton J., *The Wars We Took to Vietnam: Cultural Conflict and Storytelling*, Berkeley, 1996.

Beckett, Ian F. W., *Modern Insurgencies and Counter-Insurgencies: Guerrillas and their Opponents since 1750*, London, 2001.

Belknap, Michael R., *The Vietnam War on Trial: The My Lai Massacre and the Court-Martial of Lieutenant Calley*, Lawrence, Kan., 2002.

Bergerud, Eric M., *Red Thunder, Tropic Lightning: The World of a Combat Division in Vietnam*, New York, 1994.

Berman, Larry, *Lyndon Johnson's War: The Road to Stalemate in Vietnam*, New York, 1989.

—— *No Peace, No Honor: Nixon, Kissinger, and Betrayal in Vietnam*, New York, 2001.

—— *Planning a Tragedy: The Americanization of the War in Vietnam*, New York, 1982.

Best, Geoffrey, *Humanity in Warfare: The Modern History of the International Law of Armed Conflicts*, London, 1980.

Bilton, Michael and Sim, Kevin, *Four Hours in My Lai*, New York, 1992.

Blaufarb, Douglas S., *The Counter-Insurgency Era: U.S. Doctrine and Performance 1950 to the Present*, New York, 1977.

Boulanger, Ghislane and Kadushin, Charles (eds), *The Vietnam Veteran Redefined: Fact and Fiction*, London, 1986.

Bourke, Joanna, *An Intimate History of Killing: Face-to-Face Killing in Twentieth-Century Warfare*, London, 1999.

Bourne, Peter G., *Men, Stress, and Vietnam*, Boston, 1970.

Braestrup, Peter, *Big Story: How the American Press and Television Reported and Interpreted the Crisis of Tet 1968 in Vietnam and Washington*, Garden City, 1978.

Browne, Malcolm W., *Das neue Gesicht des Krieges*, Frauenfeld, 1966 (orig. *The New Face of War: A Report on a Communist Guerrilla Campaign*, London, 1965).

Brownmiller, Susan, *Gegen unseren Willen. Vergewaltigung und Männerherrschaft*, Frankfurt am Main, 1978 (orig. *Against Our Will: Men, Women and Rape*, London, 1975).

Buckley, Kevin P., 'Pacification's Deadly Price', *Newsweek*, 19 Jun. 1972.

Burr, William and Kimball, Jeffrey, 'Nixon's Nuclear Ploy', *Bulletin of the Atomic Scientists*, Jan./Feb. 2003.

Buzzanco, Robert, *Masters of War: Military Dissent and Politics in the Vietnam Era*, New York, 1996.

Cable, Larry E., *Conflict of Myths: The Development of American Counterinsurgency Doctrine and the Vietnam War*, New York, 1986.

Camp, Norman M., Stortch, Robert H. and Marshall, William C. (eds), *Stress, Strain and Vietnam: Bibliography of Two Decades of Psychiatric and Social Science Literature*, Westport, Conn., 1988.

Caputo, Philip, *A Rumor of War*, New York, 1977.

Carlton, Eric, *Massacres: An Historical Perspective*, Aldershot, 1994.

Casella, Alexander, 'The Politics of Prisoners of War', *New York Times Magazine*, 28 May 1972.

Chanoff, David and Van Toai, Doan, *'Vietnam': A Portrait of its People at War*, London and New York, 1996.

Chatfield, Charles, *The American Peace Movement: Ideals and Activism*, New York, 1992.

Chickering, Roger, Förster, Stig and Greiner, Bernd (eds), *A World at Total War: Global Conflict and the Politics of Destruction, 1937–1945*, Cambridge, 2005.

Cincinnatus, *Self-Destruction: The Disintegration and Decay of the United States Army During the Vietnam Era*, New York. 1981.

Citizens Commission of Inquiry (ed.), *The Dellums Committee Hearings on War Crimes in Vietnam: An Inquiry into Command Responsibility in Southeast Asia*, New York, 1972.

Clergy and Laymen Concerned About Vietnam, *In the Name of America: The Conduct of the War in Vietnam by the Armed Forces of the United States as Shown by Published Reports*, New York, 1968.

Colby, William, *Lost Victory: A Firsthand Account of America's Sixteen-Year Involvement in Vietnam*, Chicago, 1989.

Cook, John L., *The Advisor*, Philadelphia, 1973.

Cooling, B. F. (ed.), *Close Air Support*, Washington, DC, 1990.

Cortright, David, *Soldiers in Revolt: The American Military Today*, New York, 1975.

Cuordileone, K. A., *Manhood and American Political Culture in the Cold War*, New York and London, 2005.

Daase, Christopher, *Kleine Kriege – Große Wirkung. Wie unkonventionelle Kriegführung die internationale Politik verändert*, Baden-Baden, 1999.

Daum, Andreas, Gardner, Lloyd C. and Mausbach, Wilfried (eds), *America, the Vietnam War, and the World*, Cambridge, 2003.

Davidson, Phillip, *Vietnam at War*, New York, 1988.

Dean, Jr., Eric T., *Shook Over Hell: Post-Traumatic Stress, Vietnam, and the Civil War*, Cambridge, Mass. and London, 1997.

Dellums, Ronald V. (with H. Lee Halterman), *Lying Down with the Lions: A Public Life from the Streets of Oakland to the Halls of Power*, Boston, 2000.

Diem, Bui (with David Chanoff), *In the Jaws of History*, New York, 1987.

Di Leo, David L. and Ball, George, *Vietnam, and the Rethinking of Containment*, Chapel Hill, 1991.

Dower, John, *War Without Mercy: Race and Power in the Pacific War*, New York, 1986.

Draper, Theodore, *Abuse of Power*, New York, 1967.

Duiker, William J., *The Communist Road to Power in Vietnam*, Boulder, Col., 1981.

—— *Ho Chi Minh: A Life*, New York, 2000.

Duncan, Donald, *The New Legions*, New York, 1967.

Dunn, Peter W., *Armed Forces and Modern Counterinsurgency*, New York, 1985.

Dunnigan, James F. and Nofi, Albert A., *Dirty Little Secrets of the Vietnam War*, New York, 1999.

Eckhardt, William G., 'Command Criminal Responsibility: A Plea for a Workable Standard', *Military Law Review*, 97 (1982) 1.

Edelmann, Bernard (ed.), *Dear America: Letters Home from Vietnam*, New York, 1986.

Ellsberg, Daniel, *Secrets: A Memoir of Vietnam and the Pentagon Papers*, New York, 2002.

Engelhardt, Tom, *The End of Victory Culture: Cold War America and the Disillusioning of a Generation*, New York, 1995.

Eszterhas, Joe, 'The Toughest Reporter in America', interview with Seymour Hersh, pt 1, *Rolling Stone*, 10 Apr. 1975.

Falk, Richard A., Kolko, Gabriel and Lifton, Robert Jay (eds), *Crimes of War: A Legal, Political-Documentary, and Psychological Inquiry into the Responsibility of Leaders, Citizens, and Soldiers for Criminal Acts in Wars*, New York, 1970.

Falk, Richard A. (ed.), *The Vietnam War and International Law*, 4 vols, Princeton, 1976.

—— 'Nuremberg and Vietnam: An American Tragedy, by Telford Taylor', *New York Times Book Review*, 27 Dec. 1970.

Fall, Bernard B., *Street Without Joy*, Harrisburg, 1961.

—— 'This Isn't Munich, It's Spain', *Ramparts*, Dec. 1965.

—— *Hell in a Very Small Place: The Siege of Dien Bien Phu*, Philadelphia and New York, 1967.

FitzGerald, Frances, *Fire in the Lake: The Vietnamese and the Americans in Vietnam*, Boston and Toronto, 1972.

Flynn, George Q., *The Draft, 1940–1973*, Lawrence, Kan., 1993.

Foley, Michael S. (ed.), *Dear Dr. Spock: Letters about the Vietnam War to America's Favorite Baby Doctor*, New York, 2005.

French, Peter A. (ed.), *Individual and Collective Responsibility: Massacre at My Lai*, Cambridge, Mass., 1972.

Frey, Marc, *Geschichte des Vietnamkriegs. Die Tragödie in Asien und das Ende des amerikanischen Traums*, Munich, 1998.

Frey-Wouters, Ellen and Laufer, Robert S., *Legacy of a War: The American Soldier in Vietnam*, New York, 1986.

Friedman, Leon (ed.), *The Law of War: A Documentary History*, vol. 1, New York, 1972.

Frosch, Jesse Frank, 'Anatomy of a Massacre', *Playboy*, Jul. 1970.

Fursenko, Alexander and Naftali, Timothy, *One Hell of a Gamble: Khrushchev, Castro, and Kennedy, 1958–1964*, New York, 1997.

Gabriel, Richard A. and Savage, Paul L., *Crisis in Command: Mismanagement in the Army*, New York, 1987.

Gaiduk, Ilya V., *The Soviet Union and the Vietnam War*, Chicago, 1996.

Gardner, Lloyd C., *Pay Any Price: Lyndon Johnson and the Wars for Vietnam*, Chicago, 1995.

Gardner, Lloyd and Gittinger, Ted (eds), *International Perspectives on Vietnam*, College Station, Tex., 2000.

Garfinkle, Adam, *Telltale Hearts: The Origins and Impact of the Vietnam Antiwar Movement*, New York, 1995.

Gelb, Leslie H., 'Vietnam: Nobody Wrote the Last Act', *Washington Post*, 20 Jun. 1971.

—— and Richard K. Betts, *The Irony of Vietnam: The System Worked*, Washington, DC, 1979.

Gellhorn, Martha, *The Face of War*, London, 1993.

Gettleman, Marvin E., Franklin, Jane, Young, Marilyn B. and Franklin, H. Bruce, *Vietnam and America: A Documented History*, New York, 1995.

Giap, Vo Nguyen, *People's War, People's Army: The Viet Cong Insurrection Manual for Underdeveloped Countries*, London, 1979.

Gibson, James William, *The Perfect War: The War We Couldn't Lose and How We Did*, New York, 1988.

—— *Warrior Dreams: Violence and Manhood in Post-Vietnam America*, New York, 1994.

Gilbert, Marc Jason, *Why the North Won the Vietnam War*, New York, 2002.

Gilkes, Madeleine, 'Missing from History: The Other Prisoner of War', *Trouble & Strife*, 41, 2000.

—— '"There Was No One Who Could Escape This Horrible Situation". Gender-Based Violence in the American–Vietnam War, 1954–1975', PhD dissertation, York, 2000.

Gleichmann, Peter and Kühne, Thomas (eds), *Massenhaftes Töten: Kriege und Genozide im 20. Jahrhundert*, Essen, 2004.

Goldstein, Joseph, Marshall, Burke and Schwartz, Jack, *The My Lai Massacre and Its Cover-Up: Beyond the Reach of Law. The Peers Commission Report with a Supplement and Introductory Essay on the Limits of Law*, New York and London, 1976.

Goodwin, Richard N., *Remembering America: A Voice from the Sixties*, Boston, 1988.

Gottlieb, Sherry Gershon, *Hell No, We Won't Go! Resisting the Draft During the Vietnam War*, New York, 1991.

Greider, William, 'Teaching of War Law Revitalized by Army', *Washington Post*, 14 Feb. 1971.

Greiner, Bernd, '"A Licence to Kill": Annäherungen an die Kriegsverbrechen von My Lai', *Mittelweg 36*, 6, 1998.

—— '"First To Go, Last to Know": Der Dschungelkrieger in Vietnam', *Geschichte und Gesellschaft*, 29, 2003.

—— '"Mad Man" zu Weihnachten: Das Pariser Friedensabkommen vom 27. Januar 1973', *Damals*, 1, 2003.

—— '"The silent majority is beginning to speak and we beg the officials to listen": Die amerikanische Debatte um Kriegsverbrechen in Vietnam', *Amerikastudien/American Studies*, 3, 2004.

—— '"Violence Hits Home": Kriegsverbrechen in Vietnam und die amerikanische Debatte über die Ursachen von Gewalt und Destruktivität', in Andreas Ranft and Markus Meumann (eds), *Traditionen – Visionen: Berichtsband zum 44. Deutschen Historikertag in Halle an der Saale 2002*, Munich, 2003.

—— '"Die Beschäftigung mit der fernen Vergangenheit ist nutzlos": Der "Totale Krieg" im Spiegel amerikanischer Militärzeitschriften', in Stig Förster (ed.), *An der Schwelle zum Totalen Krieg: Die militärische Debatte über den Krieg der Zukunft 1919–1939*, Paderborn and Munich, 2002.

—— '"You'll Never Walk Alone": Amerikanische Reaktionen auf Kriegsverbrechen in Vietnam', *Mittelweg 36*, 5, 2000.

—— 'Das alltägliche Verbrechen: Sexuelle Gewalt im Vietnamkrieg', in Peter Gleichmann and Thomas Kühne (eds), *Massenhaftes Töten: Kriege und Genozide im 20. Jahrhundert*, Essen, 2004.

—— 'Der "Alice in Wonderland"-Präsident', *Damals*, 11, 2003.

—— 'Der kurze Sommer der Anarchie: Zur Rolle der amerikanischen Presse während des Vietnamkriegs', *Mittelweg 36*, 3, 2001.

—— 'Die amerikanische Guerilla: Zur Wiederentdeckung der Special Forces', *Blätter für deutsche und internationale Politik*, 7, 2003.

—— 'Die Blutpumpe: Zur Strategie und Praxis des Abnutzungskrieges in Vietnam, 1965–1973', in Bernd Greiner, Christian Th. Müller and Dierk Walter (eds), *Heiße Kriege im Kalten Krieg*, Hamburg, 2006.

—— 'Gesellschafts-Bilder: Philip Jones Griffiths' Fotoreportage über den Vietnamkrieg', *Fotogeschichte*, 85/86, 2002.

—— 'Spurensuche: Akten über amerikanische Kriegsverbrechen in Vietnam', in Wolfram Wette and Gerd R. Ueberschär (eds), *Kriegsverbrechen im 20. Jahrhundert*, Darmstadt, 2001.

—— 'Vietnam und die Falle des Nicht-aufhören-Könnens: Richard Nixon (1913–1994)', in Stig Förster, Markus Pöhlmann and Dierk Walter (eds), *Kriegsherren der Weltgeschichte: 22 historische Porträts*, Munich, 2006.

—— 'Zwischen "Totalem Krieg" und "Kleinen Kriegen": Überlegungen zum historischen Ort des Kalten Krieges', *Mittelweg 36*, 2, 2003.

Grimsley, Mark and Rogers, Clifford J., *Civilians in the Path of War*, Lincoln, Nebr., 2002.

Gross, Robert A., 'Lieutenant Calley's Army', *Esquire*, Oct. 1971.

Grossman, Dave, *On Killing: The Psychological Cost of Learning to Kill in War and Society*, Boston, 1995.

Hackworth, David H. (with Julie Sherman), *About Face: The Odyssey of an American Warrior*, New York, 1998 (1989).

—— 'A Soldier's Disgust', *Harper's Magazine*, Jul. 1972.

—— 'The War Was Winnable. Army Leadership Is Ineffective', *Washington Post*, 29 Jun. 1971.

—— 'Our Great Vietnam Goof', *Popular Mechanics*, Jun. 1972.

—— *Steel My Soldiers' Hearts: The Hopeless to Hardcore Transformation of 4th Battalion, 39th Infantry, United States Army, Vietnam*, New York, 2002.

Halberstam, David, *The Powers That Be*, London, 1979.

—— *The Best and the Brightest*, New York, 1969.

Haldeman, Harry Robbins, *The Ends of Power*, New York, 1978.

Hallin, Daniel C., *'The Uncensored War': The Media and Vietnam*, Berkeley, 1989 (1986).

Hammer, Richard, 'Interviews with My Lai Veterans', *Evergreen*, n.d.

—— *One Morning in the War: The Tragedy at Son My (Pinkville)*, London, 1970.

—— *The Court-Martial of Lt. Calley*, New York, 1971.

Hammond, William, *Public Affairs: The Military and the Media, 1968–1973*, Washington, DC, 1996.

Hauser, William L., *America's Army in Crisis: A Study in Civil-Military Relations*, Baltimore and London, 1973.

Head, Steven, 'The Other War: Counterinsurgency in Vietnam', in James S. Olson, *The Vietnam War: Handbook of the Literature and Research*, London, 1993.

Heinemann, Larry, *Paco's Story*, New York, 1986.

Heinl, Jr., Robert D., 'The Collapse of the Armed Forces', *The Armed Forces Journal*, 108 (19) 1971.

Henry, James D. (as told to Donald Duncan), 'The Men of "B" Company', *Scanlan's*, 1 (1970) 3.

Herbert, Anthony B., 'Confessions of the Winter Soldiers', interview, *Life*, 9 Jul. 1971.

—— *Soldier*, New York and Chicago, 1973.

Herde, Robert, *Command Responsibility: Die Verfolgung der 'Zweiten Garde' deutscher und japanischer Generäle im alliierten Prozeßprogramm nach dem Zweiten Weltkrieg*, Baden-Baden, 2001.

Herr, Michael, *Dispatches*, New York, 1968.

Herring, George C., *America's Longest War: The United States and Vietnam, 1950–1975*, New York, 1996.

Herrington, Stuart A., *Silence was a Weapon: The Vietnam War in the Villages*, Novato, Calif., 1982.

Hersh, Seymour M., *Cover-Up: The Army's Secret Investigation of the Massacre at My Lai 4*, New York, 1972.

—— *My Lai 4: A Report on the Massacre and its Aftermath*, New York, 1970.

—— 'The Army's Secret Inquiry Describes a 2nd Massacre, Involving 90 Civilians', *New York Times*, 5 Jun. 1972.

—— 'The Reprimand', *New Yorker*, 9 Oct. 1971.

—— 'The Story Everyone Ignored', *Columbia Journalism Review*, Winter 1969/1970.

—— *The Price of Power: Kissinger in the Nixon White House*, New York, 1983.

Herzog, Tobey C., *Vietnam War Stories: Innocence Lost*, London, 1992.

Hillman, Elizabeth Lutes, *Defending America: Military Culture and the Cold War Court-Martial*, Princeton and Oxford, 2005.

Hoffmann, Michael, 'Das Massaker von My Lai am 16. März 1968 und die (späte) Würdigung der Leistungen der Soldaten Thompson, Colburn und Andreotta', *Humanitäres Völkerrecht*, 11 (1998) 2.

Hoopes, Townsend, 'The Nuremberg Suggestion', *Washington Monthly*, Jan. 1970.

Hosmer, Stephen T., *Viet Cong Repression and Its Implications for the Future*, Santa Monica, 1970.

Huan, Any Cheng, *The Vietnam War from the Other Side: The Vietnamese Communists' Perspective*, New York, 2002.

Isaac, Arnold R., *Without Honor: Defeat in Vietnam and Cambodia*, Baltimore, 1983.

James, Lawrence, *The Savage Wars: British Campaigns in Africa, 1870–1920*, New York, 1985.

Jamieson, Neil L., *Understanding Vietnam*, Berkeley, Calif., 1995.

Janowitz, Morris, *The Professional Soldier: A Social and Political Portrait*, Chicago, 1985 (1954).

—— and Little, Roger William, *Sociology and the Military Establishment*, Chicago, 1974.

Jeffords, Susan, *The Remasculinization of America: Gender and the Vietnam War*, Bloomington, 1989.

Jeffreys-Jones, Rhodri, *Peace Now! American Society and the Ending of the Vietnam War*, New Haven and London, 1999.

Joes, Anthony James, *America and Guerilla Warfare*, Lexington, Kt., 2000.

Johnson, Haynes and Wilson, George C., 'The U.S. Army: A Battle for Survival', *Washington Post*, 12 Sep. 1972.

Jones, Adams (ed.), *Genocide, War Crimes and the West: History and Complicity*, New York, 2004.

Jones, Howard, *Death of a Generation: How the Assassinations of Diem and JFK Prolonged the Vietnam War*, Oxford, 2003.

Joseph, Paul, *Cracks in the Empire: State Politics in the Vietnam War*, New York, 1987.

Kahin, George McT., and Lewis, John W., *The United States in Vietnam*, New York, 1969.

Kaiser, David, *American Tragedy: Kennedy, Johnson, and the Origins of the Vietnam War*, Cambridge, Mass., 2000.

Karlin, Wayne, *Rumors and Stones: A Journey*, Willimantic, Conn., 1996.

Karnow, Stanley, *Vietnam: A History*, New York, 1984 (1983).

Karsten, Peter, *Law, Soldiers and Combat*, Westport, Conn., 1978.

Kelman, Herbert C., 'The Social Context of Torture', in Ronald D. Crelinsten and Alex P. Schmidt (eds), *The Politics of Pain: Torturers and Their Masters*, Boulder, Col., 1995.

— and Lawrence, Lee H., 'Assignment of Responsibilty in the Case of Lt. Calley: Preliminary Report on a National Survey', *Journal of Social Issues*, 28 (1972) 1.

— and Hamilton, V. Lee, *Crimes of Obedience: Toward a Social Psychology of Authority and Responsibility*, New Haven, 1989.

Kimball, Jeffrey, *Nixon's Vietnam War*, Lawrence, Kan., 1998.

— *The Vietnam War Files: Uncovering the Secret History of Nixon-Era Strategy*, Lawrence, Kan., 2004.

Kindsvatter, Peter S., *American Soldiers: Ground Combat in the World Wars, Korea, and Vietnam*, Lawrence, Kan., 2003.

King, Edward L., 'Making It in the U.S. Army', *New Republic*, 30 May 1970.

— *The Death of the Army: A Pre-Mortem*, New York, 1972.

Kinnard, Douglas, *The War Managers: American Generals Reflect on Vietnam*, New York, 1991 (1977).

Kissinger, Henry, *Nuclear Weapons and Foreign Policy*, New York, 1957.

Kitfield, James, *Prodigal Soldiers: How the Generation of Officers Born of Vietnam Revolutionized the American Style of War*, New York, 1995.

Klein, Thoralf and Schumacher, Frank (eds), *Kolonialkriege: Militärische Gewalt im Zeichen des Imperialismus*, Hamburg, 2006.

Knoll, Edwin and McFadden, Judith Nies (eds), *War Crimes and the American Conscience*, New York, 1970.

Kolko, Gabriel, *Anatomy of a War: Vietnam, the United States, and the Modern Historical Experience*, New York, 1985.

— *Century of War: Politics, Conflict, and History since 1914*, New York, 1994.

Kovic, Ron, *Born on the Fourth of July*, New York, 1976.

Kramer, Paul A., 'Race-Making and Colonial Violence in the U.S. Empire: The Philippine-American War as Race War', *Diplomatic History*, 30 (2006) 2.

Krepinevich, Jr., Andrew F., *The Army and Vietnam*, Baltimore, 1986.

Lane, Mark, *Conversations with Americans: Testimony from 32 Vietnam Veterans*, New York, 1970.

Lang, Daniel, *Die Meldung: 18. November 1966, Vietnam*, Hamburg, 1970 (orig. *Casualties of War*, New York, 1969).

Langguth, A. J., *Our Vietnam: The War 1954–1975*, New York, 2000.

Lanning, Michael Lee and Craig, Dan, *Inside the VC and NVA: The Real Story of North Vietnam's Armed Forces*, New York, 1992.

Lawrence, Lee H. and Kelman, Herbert C., 'Reactions to the Calley Trial: Class and Political Authority', *Worldview*, 16 (1973) 6.

Leepson, Marc (ed.), *Webster's New World Dictionary of the Vietnam War*, New York, 1999.

Lehrack, Otto J., *No Shining Armor: The Marines at War in Vietnam. An Oral History*, Lawrence, Kan., 1992.

Lelyveld, Joseph S., 'Most Helicopter Pilots are Eager for Duty in Vietnam', *New York Times*, 26 Apr. 1971.

—— 'The Story of a Soldier Who Refused to Fire at Songmy', *New York Times Magazine*, 14 Dec. 1969.

Lesher, Stephan, 'The Calley Case Re-Examined', *New York Times Magazine*, 11 Jul. 1971.

Levene, Mark and Roberts, Penny, *The Massacre in History*, New York and Oxford, 1999.

Levy, David W., *The Debate over Vietnam*, Baltimore and London, 1995 (1991).

Lewis, Lloyd B., *The Tainted War: Culture and Identity in Vietnam War Narratives*, Westport, 1985.

Lewy, Guenter, *America in Vietnam*, Oxford, 1978.

—— 'The Punishment of War Crimes: Have We Learned the Lessons of Vietnam?', *Parameters*, 9 (1979) 4.

Lifton, Robert Jay, *Home From The War. Vietnam Veterans: Neither Victims nor Executioners*, New York, 1973.

Logevall, Fredrik, *Choosing War: The Lost Chance for Peace and the Escalation of War in Vietnam*, Berkeley, 1999.

Lüdtke, Alf, 'The Appeal of Exterminating "Others": German Workers and the Limits of Resistance', *Journal of Modern History*, 64, Supplement, Dec. 1992.

—— and Weisbrod, Bernd (eds), *No Man's Land of Violence: Extreme Wars in the Twentieth Century*, Göttingen, 2006.

Lurie, Jonathan, *Pursuing Military Justice. Vol. 2: The History of the United States Court of Appeals for the Armed Forces, 1951–1980*, Princeton, 1998.

Lutz, Catherine, *Homefront: A Military City and the American Twentieth Century*, Boston, 2001.

Lynn, John A., *Battle: A History of Combat and Culture*, Boulder, Col., 2003.

Mack, Andrew, 'Why Big Nations Lose Small Wars: The Politics of Asymmetric Conflict', *World Politics*, 2, 1975.

MacPherson, Myra, *Long Time Passing: Vietnam and the Haunted Generation*, New York, 1984.

Maguire, Peter, *Law and War: An American Story*, New York, 2000.

Manning, Frederick J., 'Morale, Cohesion, and Esprit de Corps', in David Mangelsdorff et al. (eds), *Handbook of Military Psychology*, New York, 1991.

Marquis, Susan L., *Unconventional Warfare: Rebuilding U.S. Special Operations Forces*, Washington, DC, 1997

Marshall, S. L. A., *Battles in the Monsoon: Campaigning in the Central Highlands, South Vietnam*, Nashville, Tenn., 1967.

Maurer, Harry, *Strange Ground: An Oral History of Americans in Vietnam, 1945–1975*, New York, 1998.

McCarthy, Mary, *Medina: Die My Lai-Prozesse*, Zurich, 1973 (orig. *Medina*, London, 1973).

McMahon, Robert J., *Major Problems in the History of the Vietnam War*, Boston and New York, 2003.

—— (ed.), *Major Problems in the History of the Vietnam War: Documents and Essays*, Boston and New York, 2003.

—— 'Contested Memory: The Vietnam War and American Society, 1975–2001', *Diplomatic History*, 26 (2002) 2.

McNamara, Robert S., Blight, James G. and Brigham, Robert K., *Argument Without End: In Search of Answers to the Vietnam Tragedy*, New York, 1999.

Military History Institute of Vietnam, *Victory in Vietnam: The Official History of the People's Army of Vietnam, 1954–1975*, Lawrence, Kan., 2002.

Moise, Edwin, *Land Reform in China and Vietnam*, Chapel Hill, 1983.

Morgan, Joseph G., *The Vietnam Lobby: The American Friends of Vietnam 1955–1975*, Chapel Hill, 1997.

Moser, Richard R., *The New Winter Soldiers: GI and Veteran Dissent During the Vietnam Era*, New Brunswick, 1996.

Moskos, Jr., Charles C., 'The American Dilemma in Uniform: Race in the Armed Forces', *Annals of the American Academy of Political and Social Science*, 406, 1973.

—— *The American Enlisted Man: The Rank and File in Today's Military*, New York, 1970.

Moyar, Mark, *Phoenix and the Birds of Prey: The CIA's Secret Campaign to Destroy the Viet Cong*, Annapolis, 1997.

Mühlhäuser, Regina, 'Sexuelle Gewalt als Kriegsverbrechen: Eine Herausforderung für die Internationale Strafgerichtsbarkeit', *Mittelweg 36*, 13 (2004) 2.

Münkler, Herfried, *Der Wandel des Krieges: Von der Symmetrie zur Asymmetrie*, Weilerswist, 2006.

—— 'Guerillakrieg und Terrorismus', *Neue Politische Literatur*, 25, 1980.

Murphy, Audie, *To Hell and Back: The Epic Combat Journal of World War II's Most Decorated G.I.*, New York, 1977 (1949).

Myers, Thomas, *Walking Point: American Narratives of Vietnam*, New York, 1988.

Neier, Aryeh, *War Crimes: Brutality, Genocide, Terror, and the Struggle for Justice*, New York, 1998.

Neill, Kevin Gerard, 'Duty, Honor, Rape: Sexual Assault Against Women During War', *Journal of International Women's Studies*, 2, 2000.

Nelson, Deborah and Turse, Nick, 'A Tortured Past', *Los Angeles Times*, 20 Aug. 2006.

Newman, John M., *JFK and Vietnam: Deception, Intrigue, and the Struggle for Power*, New York, 1992.

Nicosia, Gerald, *Home to War: A History of the Vietnam Veterans' Movement*, New York, 2001.

Nill-Theobald, Christiane, *'Defences' bei Kriegsverbrechen am Beispiel Deutschlands und der USA. Zugleich ein Beitrag zu einem allgemeinen Teil des Völkerstrafrechts*, Freiburg i. Br., 1998.

Oates, Joyce Carol, *Man Crazy*, New York, 1997.

O'Brien, Tim, *If I Die in a Combat Zone*, New York, 1999 (1975).

—— *In the Lake of the Woods*, New York, 1994.

—— *The Things They Carried*, New York, 1998 (1990).

—— *Going after Cacciato*, New York, 1978.

—— 'Step Lightly', *Playboy*, Jul. 1970.

Oliver, Kendrick, *The My Lai Massacre in American History and Memory*, Manchester and New York, 2006.

Olson, James S., *The Vietnam War: Handbook of the Literature and Research*, London, 1993.

—— and Roberts, Randy, *My Lai: A Brief History with Documents*, Boston and New York, 1998.

Palmer, Jr., Bruce, *The 25-Year War: America's Military Role in Vietnam*, Lexington, Ky., 1984.

Paulson, Stanley L. and Banta, John S., 'The Killings at My Lai: "Grave Breaches" under the Geneva Conventions and the Question of Military Jurisdiction', *Harvard International Law Journal*, 12 (1971) 2.

Paust, Jordan J., 'After My Lai: The Case for War Crime Jurisdiction over Civilians in Federal District Courts', *Texas Law Review*, 50 (1971) 1.

—— 'My Lai and Vietnam: Norms, Myths and Leader Responsibility', *Military Law Review*, 57 (1972) 2.

Pearson, Willard, *Vietnam Studies: The War in the Northern Provinces, 1966–1968*, Washington, DC, 1975.

Peers, William R., *The My Lai Inquiry*, New York, 1979.

Peterson, Michael E., *The Combined Action Platoons: The U.S. Marines' Other War in Vietnam*, Westport, Conn., 1989.

Pike, Douglas, *A History of Vietnamese Communism, 1925–1978*, Stanford, 1978.

—— 'The Viet-Cong Strategy of Terror', Saigon, Feb. 1970.

—— *PAVN: People's Army of Vietnam*, Novato, Calif., 1986.

Piragoff, Donald K., 'Article 30: Mental Element', in Triffterer, Otto (ed.), *Commentary on the Rome Statute of the International Criminal Court. Oberservers' Notes, Article by Article*, Baden-Baden, 1999.

Poirier, Normand, 'An American Atrocity', *Esquire*, Aug. 1969.

Prados, John, *The Blood Road: The Ho Chi Minh Trail and the Vietnam War*, New York, 1999.

Preston, Andrew, *The War Council: McGeorge Bundy, the NSC, and Vietnam*, Cambridge, Mass., 2006.

Prochnau, William, *Once Upon a Distant War: David Halberstam, Neil Sheehan, Peter Arnett – Young War Correspondents and Their Early Vietnam Battles*, New York, 1995.

Record, Jeffrey, 'Maximizing Cobra Utilization', *Washington Monthly*, 3 (1971) 2.

—— *The Wrong War: Why We Lost in Vietnam*, Annapolis, 1998.

Reemtsma, Jan Philipp, *Warum Hagen Jung-Ortlieb erschlug: Unzeitgemäßes über Krieg und Tod*, Munich, 2004.

Resic, Sanimir, *American Warriors in Vietnam: Warrior Values and the Myth of the War Experience during the Vietnam War, 1965–1973*, Malmö, 1999.

Reston, James, 'Who Is to Blame for Song [*sic*] My?', *International Herald Tribune*, 27 Nov. 1969.

Robertson, Geoffrey, *Crimes Against Humanity: The Struggle for Global Justice*, New York, 2000.

Rogers, Clifford J., 'By Fire and Sword: Bellum Hostile and "Civilians" in the Hundred Years' War', in Mark Grimsley and Clifford J. Rogers (eds), *Civilians in the Path of War*, Lincoln, Nebr., 2003.

Rorty, Richard, *Achieving Our Country: Leftist Thought in Twentieth-Century America*, Cambridge, Mass. and London, 1998.

Rose, Kenneth D., *One Nation Underground: The Fallout Shelter in American Culture*, New York, 2001.

Rosenberg, Douglas, 'Arms and the American Way', in Bruce M. Russett and Alfred Stepan, *Military Force and American Society*, New York, 1973.

Rowe, Terry E., 'Nevada Reacts to My Lai', *Nevada Historical Society Quarterly*, 17 (1974) 2.

Russell, Kent A., 'My Lai Massacre: The Need for an International Investigation', *California Law Review*, 58 (1970) 3.

Sack, John, *Lieutenant Calley: His Own Story*, New York, 1971.

Sagan, Scott D. and Suri, Jeremi, 'The Madman Nuclear Alert: Secrecy, Signaling, and Safety in October 1969', *International Security*, 27 (2003) 4.

Sallah, Michael and Weiss, Mitch, *Tiger Force*, London, 2006.

Santoli, Al (ed.), *Everything We Had: An Oral History of the Vietnam War*, New York, 1981.

Schell, Jonathan, *Observing the Nixon Years. 'Notes and Comment' from* The New Yorker *on the Vietnam War and the Watergate Crisis, 1969–1975*, New York, 1989.

—— 'Quang Ngai and Quang Tin', *New Yorker*, 9 and 16 Mar. 1968.

—— *The Real War: The Classic Reporting on the Vietnam War*, New York, 1987.

Schell, Orville, 'Cage for the Innocents', *The Atlantic*, Jan. 1968.

Schlesinger, Jr., Arthur M., *A Thousand Days: John F. Kennedy in the White House*, Boston, 1965.

—— *The Imperial Presidency*, Boston, 1973.

Schulzinger, Robert D., *A Time for War: The United States and Vietnam, 1941–1975*, New York, 1997.

Schwarzkopf, H. Norman, *It Doesn't Take a Hero: The Autobiography*, London and New York, 1992.

Segal, David, *Recruiting for Uncle Sam: Citizenship and Military Manpower Policy*, Lawrence, Kan., 1989.

Seifert, Ruth, 'Der weibliche Körper als Symbol und Zeichen: Geschlechtsspezifische Gewalt und die kulturelle Konstruktion des Krieges', in Andreas Gestrich (ed.), *Gewalt im Krieg: Ausübung, Erfahrung und Verweigerung von Gewalt in Kriegen des 20. Jahrhunderts*, Münster, 1995.

—— 'Krieg und Vergewaltigung: Ansätze zu einer Analyse', in Alexandra Stiglmayer (ed.), *Massenvergewaltigung: Krieg gegen die Frauen*, Freiburg i. Br., 1993.

Semelin, Jacques, *Säubern und Vernichten: Die politische Dimension von Massakern und Völkermorden*, Hamburg, 2007.

Shaw, Martin, *War and Genocide: Organized Killing in Modern Society*, Oxford, 2003.

Shay, Jonathan, *Achill in Vietnam: Kampftrauma und Persönlichkeitsverlust*, Hamburg, 1998 (orig. *Achilles in Vietnam: Combat Trauma and the Undoing of Character*, New York, 1995).

—— *Odysseus in America: Combat Trauma and the Trials of Homecoming*, New York, 2002.

Sheehan, Neil, *Die Große Lüge: John Paul Vann und Amerika in Vietnam*, Wien and Zurich, 1992 (orig. *A Bright Shining Lie: John Paul Vann and America in Vietnam*, New York, 1988).

—— 'Five Officers Say They Seek Formal War Crimes Inquiries', *New York Times*, 13 Jan. 1971.

—— 'Should We Have War Crime Trials?', *New York Times Book Review*, 28 Mar. 1971.

—— 'Westmoreland Predicted Big 1968 Gains in Vietnam', *New York Times*, 21 Mar. 1968.

—— 'Not a Dove, But No Longer a Hawk', *New York Times Magazine*, 9 Oct. 1966.

Sheehan, Susan, *Ten Vietnamese*, New York, 1967.

Shephard, Ben, *A War of Nerves: Soldiers and Psychiatrists in the Twentieth Century*, Cambridge, Mass., 2001.

Shepherd, Jack, 'Incident at Van Duong', *Look*, 17 May 1969.

Shils, Edward A., *The Torment of Secrecy: The Background and Consequences of American Security Policies*, Chicago, 1996 (1956).

Showalter, Dennis, 'The War That Was Never Fought: The U.S. Army, the Bundeswehr, and the NATO Central Front', unpublished manuscript, 2004.

Shultz, Jr., Richard H., *The Secret War Against Hanoi: Kennedy's and Johnson's Use of Spies, Saboteurs, and Covert Warriors in North Vietnam*, New York, 1999.

Slotkin, Richard, *Gunfighter Nation: The Myth of the Frontier in Twentieth-Century America*, New York, 1992.

Small, Melvin and Hoover, William D., *Give Peace a Chance: Exploring the Vietnam Antiwar Movement*, Syracuse, NY, 1992.

Solis, Gary D., *Marines and Military Law in Vietnam: Trial by Fire*, Washington, DC, 1989.

—— *Son Thang: An American War Crime*, Annapolis, 1997.

Spector, Ronald H., *After Tet: The Bloodiest Year in Vietnam*, New York, 1993.

Stacewicz, Richard, *Winter Soldiers: An Oral History of the Vietnam Veterans Against the War*, New York, 1997.

Steinfels, Peter, 'Calley and the Public Conscience', *Commonweal*, 94, 16 Apr. 1971.

Steinman, Ron, *Women in Vietnam: The Oral History*, New York, 2000.

Stuhldreher, Karen, 'State Rape: Representations of Rape in Viet Nam', in *Nobody Gets Off the Bus: The Viet Nam Generation Big Book*, 5 (1994) 1–4.

Suid, Lawrence H., *Guts and Glory: The Making of the American Military Image in Film*, Lawrence, Kan., 2002.

Summers, Harry G., *On Strategy: A Critical Analysis of the Vietnam War*, New York, 1984 (1982).

Tang, Truong Nhu, *A Viet Cong Memoir*, New York, 1985.

Taylor, Maxwell, *The Uncertain Trumpet*, New York, 1960.

Taylor, Sandra C., *Vietnamese Women at War:. Fighting for Ho Chi Minh and the Revolution*, Lawrence, Kan., 1999.

Taylor, Telford, *Nürnberg und Vietnam: Eine amerikanische Tragödie*, Munich, 1971 (orig. *Nuremberg and Vietnam: An American Tragedy*, Chicago, 1970).

—— 'Nuremberg and Son My', *New York Times*, 21 Nov. 1970.

—— 'The Course of Military Justice', *New York Times*, 2 Feb. 1972.

Terry, Wallace, *Bloods: An Oral History of the Vietnam War by Black Veterans*, New York, 1985.

Thompson, Kenrick S., Clarke, Alfred C. and Dinitz, Simon, 'Reactions to My-Lai: A Visual-Verbal Comparison', *Sociology and Social Research*, 8 (1974) 2.

Triffterer, Otto (ed.), *Commentary on the Rome Statute of the International Criminal Court. Oberservers' Notes, Article by Article*, Baden-Baden, 1999.

Trullinger, James W., *Village at War: An Account of Conflict in Vietnam*, Stanford, 1994.

Truscott, Colonel Lucian K. 3rd, 'Duty, Honor (and Self)', *New York Times*, 4 Feb. 1972.

Tuchman, Barbara, *Die Torheit der Regierenden: Von Troja bis Vietnam*, Frankfurt an Main, 1989 (orig. *The March of Folly: From Troy to Vietnam*, London, 1984).

Tucker, Spencer C. (ed.), *The Encyclopedia of the Vietnam War: A Political, Social and Military History*, Oxford, 1998.

Turner, Karen Gottschang, *Even the Women Must Fight: Memories of War from North Vietnam*, New York, 1998.

Unger, Jon, 'The Press: The NLF Radio Scooped the American Press By a Year and a Half on Son My. That Makes It News', *Scanlan's*, 1 (1970), 3.

Valentine, Douglas, *The Phoenix Program*, New York, 1990.

—— 'Fragging Bob: Bob Kerrey, CIA War Crimes, and the Need for a War Crimes Trial', *CounterPunch*, 17 May 2001.

Valentino, Benjamin A., *Final Solutions: Mass Killing and Genocide in the Twentieth Century*, Ithaca and London, 2004.

van den Haag, Ernest, 'When is a Crime a War Crime?', *National Review*, 5 Nov. 1971.

Vandervort, Bruce, *Wars of Imperial Conquest in Africa 1830–1914*, Bloomington, Ind., 1998.

Vietnam Veterans Against the War, *The Winter Soldier Investigation: An Inquiry into American War Crimes*, Boston, 1972.

Vistica, Gregory L., 'One Awful Night in Thanh Phong', *New York Times Magazine*, 25 Apr. 2001.

—— *The Education of Lieutenant Kerrey*, New York, 2003.

Wakin, Malham M. (ed.), *War, Morality, and the Military Profession*, Boulder, Col. and London, 1986.

Walter, Dierk, 'Symmetry and Asymmetry in Colonial Warfare c. 1500–2000: The Uses of a Concept', Norwegian Institute for Defence Studies (IFS), Info 3/05, Oslo, 2005.

Weigley, Russell F., *The American Way of War: A History of United States Military Strategy and Policy*, New York, 1973.

Westmoreland, William C., *A Soldier Reports*, New York, 1976.

—— 'Facing Up to the External and Internal Challenges', *Armed Forces Journal*, 108 (1971) 9.

Wills, Gary, *John Wayne's America: The Politics of Celebrity*, New York, 1997.

Wilson, William, '"I had Prayed to God that this Thing was Fiction ..."', *American Heritage Magazine*, 41 (1990) 1. Reprinted in James S. Olson and Randy Roberts, *My Lai: A Brief History with Documents*, Boston and New York, 1998.

Wyatt, Clarence R., *Paper Soldiers: The American Press and the Vietnam War*, Chicago and London, 1995.

Young, Marilyn B., *The Vietnam Wars 1945–1990*, New York, 1991.

—— and Buzzanco, Robert (eds), *A Companion to the Vietnam War*, Oxford, 2006 (2002).

Zaffiri, Samuel, *Hamburger Hill*, New York, 1988.

Zhai, Quing, *China and the Vietnam Wars*, London, 2000.

Zipfel, Gaby, '"Blood, Sperm and Tears": Sexuelle Gewalt in Kriegen', *Mittelweg 36*, 5, 2001.

Index of Military Units

General Index